Virgil's Experience

Virgil's Experience

Nature and History: Times, Names, and Places

RICHARD JENKYNS

CLARENDON PRESS · OXFORD

1998

Oxford University Press, Great Clarendon Street, Oxford OX2 6DP
Oxford New York
Athens Auckland Bangkok Bogota Bombay Buenos Aires
Calcutta Cape Town Dar es Salaam Delhi Florence Hong Kong Istanbul
Karachi Kuala Lumpur Madras Madrid Melbourne Mexico City
Nairobi Paris Singapore Taipei Tokyo Toronto Warsaw
and associated companies in
Berlin Ibadan

Oxford is a registered trade mark of Oxford University Press

Published in the United States
by Oxford University Press Inc., New York

British Library Cataloguing in Publication Data
Data available

Library of Congress Cataloging-in-Publication Data
Virgil's experience : nature and history, times, names,
and places / Richard Jenkyns.
Includes bibliographical references and index.
1. Virgil—Knowledge—Natural history.   2. Literature and history—
Rome.   3. Virgil—Knowledge—History.   4. Virgil—Contemporary
Rome.   5. Landscape in literature.   6. Nature in literature.
7. Names in literature.   8. Time in literature.   9. Rome—In
literature.   10. Rome—Civilization.   I. Title.
PA6825.J46   1998   873'.01—dc21   98–12862
ISBN 0–19–814033–9

1 3 5 7 9 10 8 6 4 2

Typeset by Graphicraft Limited, Hong Kong
Printed in Great Britain on acid-free paper by
Biddles Ltd., Guildford and King's Lynn

To Olivia Jones

Preface

This is both more and less than a book about Virgil: less, in that it treats a part of his art, not the whole; more, because it also examines the literary, cultural, and social influences which acted upon him, and the effect which he had upon others. At the heart of the book is an investigation into his attitude to nature and landscape; his feeling for Rome, Italy, and small-scale locality; his sense of history, process, and the passing of time; his capacity to crystallize moments of experience and things seen; and the relationship within his imagination between these several areas of mental life. One of my primary purposes is to illuminate the meaning of the verse through a close study of the text, an enquiry into the details of language and sense (a good deal that is written about Latin poetry would apply equally if the words were prose) but also into the larger form; for no one understood better than Virgil how structure could express meaning.

It has also been my purpose to look at its central figure, or one element in him, from various angles: not only to get inside his verse, but to walk round him, to look at what lies before and behind him, to see the world that he saw, to show him in the current of his time while bringing out his uniqueness. In terms of method, I have sought to apply different kinds of thought or argument to the issue at hand: close reading, literary history, cultural history, politics and political thought, philosophy. Partly this is for the sake of Virgil himself: few poets reward a close analysis better, and yet, even more than most writers, he needs also to be seen in relation to the circumstances in which he found himself if he is to be fully appreciated. He is both a child of his time and an exceptionally original mind; here literary tradition, popular ideas, and conventional attitudes meet an acutely personal vision, and the interplay between tradition and the individual talent is as fascinating in him as anywhere in literary history. Accordingly, both the treatment of nature in Greek poetry and the culture of Italy form part of my enquiry, and are handled in the second and third chapters. His distinctiveness can be brought out too by setting him beside other poets, including those whom he immediately affected, and I have therefore included an account of his influence on Augustan poetry. I have also given a large amount of space to Lucretius, since it is part of my argument that he and Virgil between them effect a transformation in the poetic perception of nature.

Though my discussions of Greek poetry, Lucretius, and so on find a place here because of their significance to Virgil, I hope that they are of value in their own right. They are also designed to contribute to another of my aims: to present a general interpretation of the cultural milieu of the first century BC. There is a further theme too which permeates the whole of this book, woven across and through it, and this criss-crossing is part of its design. One story that I tell is about Virgil, and here my aim has been to penetrate deep into him; but another story is about the development of attitudes to nature, a linear history which begins with Homer, argues for Lucretius and Virgil as the promoters of a revolution in sensibility, takes the tale on to Virgil's younger contemporaries, and offers a few glimpses further forward still. The transformation which I describe is part of the history of European thought and feeling, and has been permanent in its effect; and thus I hope too that the enquiry may tell us something about ourselves. In terms of method again, I have tried to combine a diachronic history with an intense focus on one spot. I have written in this way because it is what the subject seemed to demand as I thought it through (when I first proposed to myself a book on Virgil, I had in mind a slim volume less than the usual length), but I think that in any case there may be a worth in bringing together different kinds of approach, trying to exemplify for readers of poetry the use of history and for historians the significance that may lie for them in the shape or rhythm of a sentence, in metre, diction, or tone. I have also written in the belief that great literature invites us to an adventure of the imagination and that it is, in the deepest sense of a plain word, useful; and so while there is plenty of literary detail in this book, it also deals, sometimes explicitly, more often by implication, with politics and religion, with man as a social and a spiritual being. A book about poetry ought to be a book about life.

There is a place for controversial, even polemical books, but this is not meant to be one of them; my aim has been, as far as possible, to engage directly with Virgil and the ancient world, and to search

out new territory. But where the ground is disputed, it is impossible not to engage in controversy from time to time. I have not usually mentioned views that seem to me obviously wrong; it should
be clear, I trust, that where I have expressed my divergences from
other scholars, it is in token of respect, because their interpretations
are influential or powerfully argued; in particular, I have spelled out
my disagreement with one or two views which I once accepted myself,
being well aware of their charms. I have also made the experiment
of occasionally indicating disagreement obliquely, so that those who
know the issue will understand the reasons for my own position,
while others need not be distracted.

All students of the past know that they owe a vast amount to those
who have gone before, the best of whom easily become invisible,
because their insights or discoveries have come to be taken for granted.
I feel myself an especial gratitude to the commentators, who have
so often revealed to me a difficulty, shown a solution, or pointed to
unguessed possibilities. I am conscious that the names of some eminent Virgilians appear seldom in my footnotes, and some not at all;
this is not because I am incapable of learning from them, but usually because their work has not been on the immediate concerns of
this book. But I should also explain that though I hope that I have
acknowledged my debts, I have attempted, without complete consistency, to be sparing in the citation of modern scholarship. Some
books seem to me too cluttered with secondary references; it is not
the function of monographs to provide running bibliographies, nor
do I see much value in trying to list all those who have previously
expressed common or widely accepted opinions. My translations,
like the footnotes, are meant to be useful to the reader: they aim
to be literal rather than elegant, and I have tolerated one or two
stilted expressions where they kept close to the pattern of the original or preserved an ambiguity. In the text I have allowed myself
the well-established solecism 'first', 'second Georgic', etc., and for the
same reasons of convenience and euphony have spoken also of the
'first Aeneid', etc. This makes 'first Eclogue' (self-standing poem or
part of a larger whole?) equivocal in a way that is itself expressive.
Some portions of the text have appeared, in different form, in the
Journal of Roman Studies in 1985 and 1989, and a version of the appendix
was published in *Classical Quarterly* in 1993; one or two sentences
have found their way into my little book *Classical Epic: Homer and
Virgil* (1992).

This book has been written, suitably perhaps, in four countries on three continents. I was lucky to be offered five months in the calm setting and lively community of the Humanities Research Centre of the Australian National University. Returning after many years to the country and the town where I had spent part of my childhood, I shared Aeneas' experience of leaving my native land for a place which was very distant and yet obscurely, deeply part of my past. Later, the Rockefeller Foundation gave me a month in the incomparable Villa Serbelloni at Bellagio, where even staring out of the window might be reckoned a study of Virgil's experience (though I regretfully conclude from the vagueness of *Geo.* 2. 159 that he probably never saw Lake Como). I am very grateful to both these institutions. Ann Schofield in Kansas and Richard and Voula McKirahan at Galaxidi in Greece gave me places where I could work peacefully on the book's later stages. Warm thanks to them; thanks also to Voula Tsouna McKirahan for reading and commenting on a part of my manuscript, to Elaine Matthews for consultations of the database of the *Lexicon of Greek Personal Names*, and to Hilary O'Shea and her assistants at the Press for their help and support.

Some benefits are hard to pin down. I know that I have learnt a great deal from lectures, classes, and conversations over the years, from teaching and being taught. I have been most fortunate in my teachers, among whom at school were the late Richard Martineau, David Simpson, John Roberts, Charles Willink (from whom I first heard the name of Fraenkel) and Peter Needham (from whom I first heard the name of Syme). As an undergraduate my luck continued: I studied classical literature with the late Robert Ogilvie and with Jasper Griffin, from whose teaching and writing I have learnt so much, even on those matters concerning which I have found myself carried to a different conclusion. I was taught the history of the late republic by Peter Cuff, of the early empire by Oswyn Murray, and that stimulus too has gone into the making of this book. My greatest debt is to Virgil, and after him to Lucretius; it will be best repaid if the book helps others to enjoy them.

R.H.A.J.

Contents

Abbreviations

Abbreviations follow the conventions of standard reference works (*L'Année Philologique*, *OLD*, etc.) or else are readily recognizable from the context. Texts and commentaries are usually referred to by the scholar's surname alone, and one or two others works are similarly treated, as follows:

R. G. Austin, *P. Vergili Maronis Aeneidos Liber Secundus* (Oxford, 1964).

—— *P. Vergili Maronis Aeneidos Liber Sextus* (Oxford, 1977).

C. Bailey, *Titi Lucreti Cari De Rerum Natura Libri Sex*, 3 vols., corrected edition (Oxford, 1949).

W. A. Camps, *Propertius Elegies Book IV* (Cambridge, 1965).

W. Clausen, *A Commentary on Virgil Eclogues* (Oxford, 1994).

R. Coleman, *Vergil Eclogues* (Cambridge, 1977).

J. Conington and H. Nettleship (eds.), *P. Vergili Opera*, 3 vols. (London, 1858–63).

P. T. Eden, *A Commentary on Virgil, Aeneid VIII* (Leiden, 1975).

C. J. Fordyce, *P. Vergili Maronis Aeneidos Libri VII–VIII* (Oxford, 1977).

M. Geymonat (ed.), *P. Vergili Maronis Opera* (Turin, 1973).

A. S. F. Gow, *Theocritus*, 2 vols., 2nd edition (Cambridge, 1952).

K. W. Gransden (ed.), *Virgil Aeneid Book VIII* (Cambridge, 1976).

P. Hardie, *Virgil Aeneid Book IX* (Cambridge, 1994).

S. J. Harrison (ed.), *Oxford Readings in Vergil's Aeneid* (Oxford, 1990).

R. Heinze, *Virgils epische Technik*, 3rd edition (Leipzig and Berlin, 1915).

H. Huxley, *Virgil: Georgics I and IV* (London, 1963).

F. Klingner, *Virgil: Bucolica, Georgica, Aeneis* (Zürich, 1967).

R. A. B. Mynors (ed.), *P. Vergili Maronis Opera*, corrected edition (Oxford, 1972).

—— *Virgil Georgics* (Oxford, 1990).

H. A. J. Munro, *T. Lucreti Cari De Rerum Natura Libri Sex*, 2 vols., 4th edition (London, 1886).

T. E. Page, *The Aeneid of Virgil*, 2 vols. (London, 1894–1900).

—— *P. Vergili Maronis Bucolica et Georgica* (London, 1898).

W. Richter, *Vergil Georgica* (Munich, 1957).

D. Ross, *Virgil's Elements: Physics and Poetry in the Georgics* (Princeton, 1987).

R. Thomas, *Virgil Georgics*, 2 vols. (Cambridge, 1988).

R. D. Williams, *Virgil The Eclogues and Georgics* (London, 1979).

—— *The Aeneid of Virgil*, 2 vols. (London, 1972–3).

PART ONE

Before Virgil

CHAPTER I

Introduction

Every man is an island, entire of himself; an island, however, which is part of an immense archipelago encompassing innumerable specks of land, each with its own shape and pattern, its distinct configuration of rock and inlet, yet all ruffled by the same breezes, fretted by the same unceasing seas. The historian is a species of surveyor or cartographer; his task is to map these territories. The interpreter of a recent period may hope to work on both the large and the small scale, to learn something of the character of individual men and women, and thus to balance the general with the particular. The historian of a remote era is not commonly so fortunate: the distance between himself and the countless islands of humanity that he studies is so great that they are usually reduced to indistinguishable dots or blurred into an undifferentiated mass. Where writers have survived, though, the case is somewhat altered. A poem, play, speech or treatise is the product of an individual mind (so much is a truism), and sometimes at least we may be tempted to think that its author, perhaps by design, perhaps willy-nilly, has revealed something of himself.

This book is concerned with ideas of nature, time, history, and nation; as such, it is a story about thoughts and feelings. It examines these conceptions in the work of a great poet; as such it is in some sense a study of Virgil's mind. It measures his originality by investigating how his mentality may be related to his literary, cultural, social, and political experience; as such, it is a historical study, and one that aims to combine detail with a broader view. It is not at all a quest for the historical Virgil, but it might be said to consider his *Bildung* to the extent that it enquires into the likely forces acting upon the imagination of a man with literary talent born in his time and place. We shall find that he is indeed the child of his age, yet unique in his response to that age and in his interpretation of it, one who experiences the *zeitgeist* but also helps to make it. The uniqueness of his work will not be in doubt; but the question may remain whether we shall not, by the way, have seen something of the uniqueness of the man.

We need not make ourselves the prisoners of critical or philosophical dogma about the unknowability of an author's mind; the issue is an empirical one, and the answer will vary from author to author. It may even vary in the case of a single author: we may be confident enough what a poet felt about some matters, unclear about others. The man who read through *Paradise Lost* and doubted whether its author were a sincere Christian would not be a wise sceptic but a fool; Shakespeare, on the other hand, is extraordinarily opaque (those who claim to discern his political or religious beliefs, or lack of them, have usually misunderstood this opacity). Virgil might seem to stand somewhere in between, less forthright than Dante or Milton, less hidden than Shakespeare. It would be perverse, for example, to deny that he felt deeply about the landscape and antiquity of Italy. On the other hand, we cannot surmise what he felt on some very large issues: there is no guessing to what extent or in what sense, if any, he believed in the gods. All we can say is that within the universe of the *Aeneid* we must regard Jupiter and the Olympian pantheon as veritably existing; but we would say the same about Wotan and the Germanic pantheon within the universe of the *Ring*, and no one supposes Wagner to have believed in them. There ought to be no question of setting what Virgil 'really' believed against his poem. In this area at least, the poem is all we have.

There is a further consideration: we may know a great deal about a writer's opinions and yet very little about his character. Lucretius is perhaps a case in point. His beliefs and the passion with which he maintained them are not in doubt, but his poetry, in itself, does not offer a basis on which either to support or confute the theory that he was neurotic or manic depressive; the claim to be made in this book that he has a broad and healthy appetite for the world is a statement about his poetic personality, offering no judgement about the historical Lucretius at all. There is surely some relationship between the personality expressed in a work and the personality of its creator, but that relationship, direct in some cases, may in others be so complex and oblique that little can be founded on it. In more recent cases we may expect to have some knowledge of the artist independent of his work, and new temptations arise in consequence. Thus it is a commonplace that Bruckner's simple-mindedness is reflected in his music; perhaps there is a kind of truth in this, yet if we had been told that he was cultured and well educated, critics would be pointing to his harmonic and constructional originality, his intertextual relationships to Beethoven and Wagner, as evidence of his sophistication. Wolf's music gives no hint of his disturbed mind; on the other hand, the Douanier Rousseau's paintings could only be the work of a *naïf*, though one of genius. Sometimes a balance must be struck. Mozart's letters reveal certain oddities that one would never have guessed from the music; yet one can be sure that he was not the kind of imbecile portrayed in Shaffer's *Amadeus*, for it required a kind of moral imagination to write *Figaro* and *Così*; which is to say not that the composer must have been a good man but that he must at least have been able to have a conception of spiritual capaciousness which would be necessarily foreign to the crass idiot in Shaffer's play.

As it happens, we do seem to have some information about Virgil independent of his verse. Most of the biographical material about poets collected in antiquity was either fabricated or deduced, not always intelligently, from their own works,[1] but Donatus' life of Virgil, though it includes some obvious nonsense, also contains facts that have the air of authenticity; besides, it appears to be largely a transcription of Suetonius' life of the poet, with additions, and Suetonius' sources for the Augustan period were good. However, part of Donatus' (or Suetonius') story is that Virgil was a shy and retiring man; if we choose to credit this, we may suppose that he guarded his privacy.[2] In one respect we can indeed detect him baffling the world's curiosity. He published nothing until he was in his thirties, and then only ten poems, of expert accomplishment; we must suppose a dozen years or so of work that he suppressed.[3] But his early fame meant that the cultivated soon wanted these juvenilia. The world abhors a gap in its knowledge, and in Martial's time the *Culex* is already being read as a prentice piece by the master; in due

[1] This is shown, for Greece, by M. Lefkowitz, *The Lives of the Greek Poets* (London, 1981). [2] *Vita Verg.* 11.

[3] Of course, we do not usually expect to read the juvenilia of classical authors, but in Virgil's century Cicero thought his youthful version of Aratus worth extensive quotation in later life, and some of the poems in Ovid's *Amores* may have been written when he was very young (the fact that he reduced the work from five books to three for a second edition suggests that he had not shared Virgil's reluctance to expose his work too soon). Horace may have imitated his older friend's reticence; Maecenas' patience was exemplary.

course the list of Virgil's early works becomes extensive.[4] In almost every case it is transparently clear that these verses cannot be his, as scholars now agree, though a few still want to attribute to him one or two poems from the *Catalepton*.

Their hope is vain. No one denies that most items in this miscellany of short pieces are plainly not by Virgil, but the authenticity of the fifth, eighth, and tenth poems is occasionally upheld. Each contains references which might seem to link it to Virgil: the fifth and eighth name Siro, his master in philosophy, the latter if genuine providing the fascinating information that he acquired or inherited Siro's villa and moved his father there. The eighth and tenth both refer to Mantua, Virgil's home town, and nearby Cremona, prominently commemorated in the ninth Eclogue. But suppose, by analogy, that we were offered a collection of poems as the work of the young Shakespeare. Suppose, further, that most of them were obviously not his, while each of the remainder discussed Stratford or Anne Hathaway, or offered some new titbit of biography. Would not the assiduity with which these pieces advertised themselves as Shakespeare's add to our suspicions? The same doubts must fall upon the *Catalepton*. Besides, it is a poor methodology that having ruled out most of the poems on one ground or another, preserves one or two merely because they are quite attractive or because there is no decisive internal reason for ejecting them. How are we to imagine that these few morsels, and no others, were transmitted? The moral must be that the world's lust for the great man's juvenilia was frustrated; pastiche and credulity then did the rest. Concerning Virgil's genesis as a poet we know nothing, as Virgil intended.

The inquisitiveness of antiquity extended into his personal life, and here moderns have often been willing to follow: it is commonly maintained that his poetry reveals enough of his character for us to recognize that he was homosexual.[5] If it is indeed true that his poetry

---

[4] Mart. 8. 55. 20 represents the *Culex* as an early work of Virgil's; in the *Vita Verg.* (17) it is among six works that he composed at the age of 16; he may also have written the *Aetna* (ibid. 19).

[5] Perhaps a British obsession; some examples: Conington regrets the difficulty of supposing that the second Eclogue is wholly imaginary (commentary, ad loc.). Robert Graves describes Virgil's 'notorious passion for beautiful boys' and the 'gilded bedrooms where sleep kissed the eyelids' of his favourites; Lucan (Graves fancies) probably decried the great man 'as an effeminate old toady' (Lucan, *Pharsalia*, tr. Graves (Harmondsworth, 1956), 11). D. Wishart states simply, 'He was almost certainly homosexual' (*I Virgil* (London, 1995), 3). Coleman thinks it 'conceivable that some youthful disappointment' in a homosexual

is suffused with a homosexual sensibility, that is important for our appreciation of it; so the matter deserves investigation. The starting point for the enquiry must be Donatus' life, in which the relevant sentences are these:[6]

cibi vinique minimi, libidinis in pueros pronior, quorum maxime dilexit Cebetem et Alexandrum, quem secunda Bucolicorum ecloga Alexim appellat, donatum sibi ab Asinio Pollione, utrumque non ineruditum, Cebetem vero et poetam. vulgatum est consuesse eum et cum Plotia Hieria. sed Asconius Pedianus adfirmat ipsam postea narrare solitam invitatum quidem a Vario ad communionem sui, verum pertinacissime recusasse. cetera sane vita et ore et animo tam probum constat ut Neapoli Parthenias vulgo appellatus sit, ac si quando Romae, quo rarissime commeabat, viseretur in publico, sectantes demonstrantesque se subterfugeret in proximum tectum.

He ate and drank very little. He was inclined to passions for boys, of whom he was fondest of Cebes and Alexander. The latter, whom in the second poem of his *Bucolics* he calls Alexis, was given to him by Asinius Pollio; neither of them was without education, and Cebes was actually a poet. It is widely said that he also had a relationship with Plotia Hieria. But Asconius Pedianus states that she herself used later to say that although Virgil was invited by Varius to have a relationship with her, he persistently refused. Anyway, it is agreed that in the other aspects of his life he was so pure in speech and thought that at Naples he was commonly nicknamed Parthenias, and if he ever went about in public in Rome, to which he very seldom came, he would hide in the nearest house to take refuge from people following him and pointing him out.

Under examination, this emerges as little more than a statement of ignorance; Virgil had kept his private life private. Later generations might speculate about it: there was a pederastic version and a heterosexual version, but no one knew. The latter version has some

love may lie behind the second Eclogue, and speculates that Virgil may have been in love with Gallus (*Eclogues*, ed. Coleman (Cambridge, 1977), 109, 297). 'Virgil . . . may have had homosexual inclinations,' K. W. Gransden observes, citing the story of Nisus and Euryalus in support (*Virgil: The Aeneid* (Cambridge, 1990), 8). Most deliberate is J. Griffin: 'The scandal which ancient gossip had to tell about Virgil was of a homosexual sort, and the sensibility of the *Aeneid*, as we shall see, does not, to say the least, contradict that implication'; 'It is tempting to see in all this'—the treatment of women in the *Aeneid*—'the expression of a sensibility to which heterosexual love made comparatively little appeal'; 'essentially homosexual sensibility . . .' (*Virgil* (Oxford, 1986), 26, 84, 94).

   These claims presuppose that in Roman society, as in ours, there were people who were physically drawn mainly or wholly to others of their own sex. That supposition, though it has recently come under challenge, seems fair, but as it happens, the view of Virgil that will be put forward here does not depend upon it.

   [6] *Vita Verg.* 9–11.

appearance of solidity—Plotia Hieria looks like a real name—but
the Life is unable to vouch for it. What should be clear is that the
pederastic version has no basis. Most of it is transparently fabricated
out of the second Eclogue, not only the name Alexander but also
the claim that the boy was given to the poet by Pollio, reflecting
the poem's description of Alexis as 'delicias domini', the master's pet.[7]
We cannot be sure how Cebes, a refugee from the dialogues of Plato,
got into the story, but where fabrication is complete, guesswork has
little point.[8] We can be confident of this: that the inventor of the
story about Alexander had no more evidence to go on than we have;
he has made his fiction out of an ineptly biographical reading of the
eclogue. In the circumstances, the chances of the claim about Cebes
being any more solidly based are negligible.

The other 'evidence' for Virgil's pederasty can be briskly dismissed.
Servius' commentary tells us that Virgil was said to have loved three
people, Alexis, Pollio's gift, and Cebes and Leria (presumably a corruption of Ieria), who were said to have been gifts from Maecenas;
this is merely the account given in the Life, repeated with minor
variations and (to Servius' credit) with some caution. Martial in a
poem which is obviously presented as a fantasy has Maecenas offering his slave Alexis to Virgil. The historicity of this may be judged
from the fact that Martial has Maecenas as Virgil's patron many
years before the event. Apuleius states that Corydon in the second
Eclogue represents Virgil, Alexis a slave of Pollio's—again a guess,
and a bad guess at that. At least Apuleius does not claim, as the other
sources do, that Pollio gave the boy to Virgil, which makes nonsense of Corydon's frustrated passion in the poem and the master
Iollas' intransigence.[9]

The conclusion should be plain. The ancient testimonia are worthless here, and we are thrown back on Virgil's own words. Now it
was common enough for Roman poets to treat homoerotic themes
alongside the love of women: Catullus, Horace, and Tibullus all do
so. The fact that homosexual love appears in Virgil is in itself entirely
unsurprising; even Ovid, unequivocally heterosexual in his personal
poetry, includes some stories of homosexual love in his narratives.

---

[7] Ecl. 2. 1.
[8] Possibly the fact that an Alexis is addressed in an epigram attributed to Plato (Anth.
Pal. 7. 100) may have something to do with it.
[9] Serv. ad Buc. 2. 15; Mart. 8. 56. 11 ff.; Apul. Apol. 10. Hieria also appears in the Schol.
Bern. on Ecl. 6. 17.

If we take Virgil as a whole, we find that the love between men and women is a large and prominent theme in all three of his works; homosexual love is directly treated in hardly more than two places, the second Eclogue and the story of Nisus and Euryalus in the ninth Aeneid. But perhaps these passages are especially personal? We shall see.

The second Eclogue is modelled on Theocritus' eleventh Idyll, most of which consists of Polyphemus' song to Galatea, the serenade of a male to a female. There could be various reasons why Virgil chose to make the love homosexual in his reworking. He may have been interested in conflating two aspects of Theocritus. The love theme in Theocritus' bucolic idylls is almost always heterosexual, but the non-bucolic idylls 29 and 30 are pederastic. The second Eclogue can be seen as a *contaminatio* of the structure and *mise-en-scène* of the eleventh Idyll with the anguished pederastic emotions of the twenty-ninth. Perhaps Virgil felt that the homoeroticism gave a Grecian, literary colour to what is in part a consciously artificial poem. Perhaps he simply wanted a variation, from his model or from the other poems that he planned. We do not know; what we can say is that the homosexual theme is not of itself distinctive. It would perhaps be more remarkable if a collection of poems deeply influenced by Greek precedent and treating a variety of love stories nowhere found a place for a homosexual version.

There is another consideration, subjective but crucial. The second Eclogue, dazzling in parts, is an imperfect poem, and its flaw is that Virgil has failed to realize imaginatively Corydon's love for Alexis. It is hard to believe in Alexis; we never doubt the strength of Polyphemus' passion for Galatea, but it is tempting to feel that the person whom Corydon most loves is himself.[10] By contrast, everyone feels in the eighth Eclogue that the scene of the boy and the girl in the orchard engages Virgil's highest imaginative powers.[11] This too is made out of Theocritus, yet the picture of lost childhood idyll and the *coup de foudre* of first love is intensely felt. Again, the absent Lycoris, lamented by Gallus in the tenth Eclogue, is realized, whereas the absent Alexis in the second is simply a datum: mingled with a

[10] W. R. Johnson ingeniously defends Virgil by supposing him to be portraying Corydon as 'a pompous hayseed with a yen for the trendy artsy world . . . an amusingly boring clown . . . hopelessly neurotic'—a misguided interpretation which has none the less felt the poem's flaw (*The Idea of Lyric* (Berkeley and Los Angeles, 1982), 166).

[11] *Ecl.* 8. 37–41.

certain self-indulgence, there are both affection and sexiness in Gallus' language.[12] There is plenty more on the love between men and women in the *Eclogues*, but it should be enough to say just this: only pre-judgement can take the *Eclogues* as a whole to be the expression of a naturally homosexual imagination.

The deaths of Nisus and Euryalus stir Virgil to this exclamation:[13]

> fortunati ambo! si quid mea carmina possunt,
> nulla dies umquam memori vos eximet aevo,
> dum domus Aeneae Capitoli immobile saxum
> accolet imperiumque pater Romanus habebit.

Happy pair! If my songs have any power, no day shall ever blot you out of time's memory, as long as the house of Aeneas shall dwell on the Capitol's immovable rock and the Roman father maintain his sway.

Nowhere else in the *Aeneid* does Virgil intrude himself so openly, and it is from these lines that the most immediately plausible case for his homosexuality can be made. But here too we should hesit-ate. In the first place, what Virgil celebrates is devotion and loyalty; it is the fact of love itself that moves him, not the fact that this par-ticular love is homosexual in character. Given the nature of his story in this part of his poem, it could hardly have been otherwise. The *Aeneid* as a whole places a very high value on love, while showing what disaster it can bring in its train; in this respect, Nisus' ruin in the poem's second half corresponds to Dido's ruin in the first. If we forget this, it is because his story is so far inferior to hers.

This brings us back to subjective considerations, which have their proper place. There will be enough praise of Virgil to follow, and so let us venture an uncomfortable judgement now: the episode of Nisus and Euryalus is weaker than we expect from him. We even meet an uncharacteristically clumsy attempt to jack up the pathos: we had thought that the Trojan women had all stayed behind in Sicily, but we now learn that Euryalus' mother alone had come on to Italy in order to be with her son.[14] In the books of warfare Virgil has some difficulty in maintaining variety of narrative and force of feeling: we detect signs of strain from time to time. His 'fortunati ambo' may be an attempt to add emotional weight to an episode which is in danger of lacking it. Let us imagine for a moment that

---

[12] *Ecl.* 10. 46–9, discussed below. This note of languorous eroticism is heard again in the sensuous verses of Propertius; see Ch. 14.

[13] *Aen.* 9. 446–9.   [14] *Aen.* 9. 216–18.

he had broken off from Dido's story to tell us how impressive it was: how painfully superfluous we should have found that. We are bound to agree that Dido's story has engaged Virgil's deepest imagination as Nisus' has not: across two thousand years how many readers can have dissented from that judgement?

As evidence of his homosexuality it has been claimed that Virgil feared and disliked women, whom the *Aeneid* accordingly depicts as violent or alarming.[15] But even if it were true that Virgil was a misogynist, this would not make him homosexual; indeed, many homosexual men, far from disliking women, enjoy easy friendships with them, free from the complications of friendships with other males. Happily, though, it is not true. Indeed, to examine his women is not only to weaken the case for his being homosexual but to reveal a poet susceptible to feminine charm. We have already seen this in the *Eclogues*. Though the *Georgics* is for most of its length a poem without people in it, the ending is dominated by the story of Orpheus and Eurydice, a tale of love between man and woman, and even that rare thing in literature, a tale of passion burning within marriage. No one doubts that it exhibits Virgil's pathos at its highest; and what is more, he has chosen to include it in a poem from which its ethos might seem very remote.

To do justice to the women of the *Aeneid* would be to fill a volume. Nobody (one might have thought) could doubt the sympathy that Virgil has for Dido. We are shown different aspects of her personal being as with no other character in the poem, Aeneas included. When we first see her, the comparison with Diana—and by implication, through the allusion to the *Odyssey*, with Homer's Nausicaa—presents her as young and innocent. When she fondles Ascanius, and when her first great denunciation collapses into a tender, plaintive domesticity, we see her maternal aspect. We see the great queen and the madness of passion.[16] Virgil yields to his feeling for Dido in spite of the problems that it makes for him. The sense of many readers that Aeneas is a stuffed shirt, which runs counter to what the poet tries to tell us, is surely due to the way in which his experience is hidden from us in the course of his love affair, when we most need to know about it. And Dido, we may think, unbalances the poem as a whole: no one later can match her, not Turnus

---

[15] Examples offered are Juno, Dido in her last phase, Amata's madness, the shrieks of Andromache in the third book and Euryalus' mother in the ninth, the hysteria of the Trojan women in the fifth.   [16] *Aen.* 1. 498 ff., 717 ff.; 4. 327 ff., 653 ff., 465 ff.

or Latinus, let alone poor Nisus. Virgil tolerates these consequences,
as do we, for the sake of the warmth with which Dido is portrayed.

Virgil is interested in a range of female types: naturally he depicts
unpleasant as well as pleasant ones. He does the same with men too:
there is no one in the *Iliad* as repellent as Mezentius, tyrant and tor-
turer. And in fact most of Virgil's unpleasant females belong to the
supernatural order: without the goddess Juno, the Fury Allecto, and
the Harpy Celaeno, the case for a misogynist Virgil amounts to not
much more than saying that his women tend to shriek when they
are unhappy (as they do, of course, in Homer). Perhaps no one in
the *Aeneid* is more lovingly treated than Creusa (unless it be Dido in
the sixth book). As we shall see, the scene of her farewell deserves
to rank with the *Odyssey* and the story of Orpheus and Eurydice
in the *Georgics*; they are classical literature's three highest tributes to
married love.

Especially intriguing for our present enquiry are those places where
Virgil brings a sexual feeling into his depiction of women. The present book is concerned with nature, but his feeling for this is bound
up with his feeling for humanity, and we shall have opportunity to
observe his use of erotic colouring. The embraces of Venus and Vulcan
are lushly and voluptuously described; Montaigne was startled to meet
such passion in a married woman, opining that even a naked, living, breathing Venus would not be as lovely as Virgil's.[17] No Latin
poet can match him for the evocation of an impalpable, evanescent
femininity. Venus in the first book is one such instance, and we shall
see how masculine is his way of presenting her.[18] Camilla is another
case: there is no female warrior in the *Iliad*; and he departs widely
from the Homeric ethos in giving so much space to her story. Here
too we shall find sexual feeling in the charm and romance that surround her.

A general point may be made about homosexuality in the ancient
world. Modern experience shows that there are different kinds of
homosexuality. One kind may be called inversion: where a man is
attracted to other men more or less as a woman is attracted to men.
Another kind is *paiderasteia*. Pederasty in modern usage is a term usually applied to desire for young boys, but to the Greeks *paiderasteia*
meant desire for youths or adolescents—that is, for males at the age

---

[17] *Aen.* 8. 387–93; Montaigne, 'Sur des vers de Virgile'.
[18] See the beginning of Ch. 9.

when they are physically most like young women. It is well known that many adolescents themselves pass through such a phase, and that it can be prolonged or created in institutions from which women are excluded, or in societies with a strong sense of male superiority. The ancients themselves seem commonly to have regarded *paiderasteia* not as an abnormality but as an overflow of normal sexuality. The homoerotic elements in Catullus, Horace, and Tibullus may or may not be wholly fictitious (each case must be judged individually), but such at least is the social reality behind them. And this is the society from which Virgil came. It does seem right to find a lightly erotic colouring in the similes describing the dying Euryalus and the dead Pallas, even though the first of these is modelled on Homer and the second also owes something to Catullus.[19] Such slight nuances are perhaps the best evidence there is for homoeroticism in Virgil.

The ancient testimonia have a terrible power, even over those who think that they have discounted them. The old search for signs of unbalanced mind in the text of Lucretius (now indeed out of fashion) is a case in point. The worthless references to Virgil's pederasty have interacted with an idea of his poetry as soft, melancholy, and perhaps a little limp to produce a received opinion. Of course, this area of enquiry is one where few hard certainties are to be had. It is possible that he had a homosexual streak, possible even that the streak was a strong one—there are no means of disproving such claims. But these propositions are probable. First, the only evidence that we have is the text. Second, the text, in all three of Virgil's works, reveals a man who had known physical desire for women. Third, such desire was predominant in his sexuality, contributing to some of his greatest imaginative achievements, as homosexual themes did not.

Several morals may be drawn from this enquiry. A first is that claims to have found the author's personality in his work may easily be misguided; a second, however, that it has proved possible after all to say something about the poet's character with a pretty fair degree of confidence, negatively in rejecting a common belief about him, but to some extent positively too. We may perhaps entertain another thought: that while those who suppose themselves to have learnt Virgil's personality from reading him may have drawn false conclusions, they may be right at least in this, that the poetry does offer itself as the expression of a distinctive sensibility—it is marked by

[19] *Aen.* 9. 435 ff.; 11. 68 ff.

an impress of individuality, though veiled. In the *Aeneid* this effect seems to be designed. Though the *Iliad* and *Odyssey* never indicate that the poet is a Greek, Virgil begins the second half of his poem by referring to 'our shores': we are Italians.[20] And later, at the cost of historical anachronism and geographical implausibility, he has warriors from Mantua travelling a vast distance from home to join a small war in central Italy:[21]

> ille etiam patriis agmen ciet Ocnus ab oris,
> fatidicae Mantus et Tusci filius amnis,
> qui muros matrisque dedit tibi, Mantua, nomen,
> Mantua, dives avis . . .

Ocnus too summons a troop from his ancestral lands, the son of Manto the prophetess and the Tuscan river, who gave you walls, Mantua, and his mother's name, Mantua, rich in ancestors . . .

'Mantus . . . Mantua . . . Mantua'—the repetition forces the name on our attention; and as the poet continues to linger over this theme, describing the city's polity and situation, any reader is likely to wonder why. Of course, most readers will know the answer—while remaining formally impersonal, Virgil is pressing his own *sphragis* or seal upon his poem—but even those ignorant of his origins might suspect some private concern. He could indeed, as in the ninth book, have chosen to allow the explicit intrusion of self ('my city, my ancestors'), but reticence was the better choice. His personal experience suffuses the poem by subterranean currents; his presence, with rare exceptions, is not overt but obscurely felt.

The river Mincius, which flows around Mantua, is the key. Here in the *Aeneid*, as before in the *Eclogues* and *Georgics*, he proceeds to describe it briefly, indicating its distinctive characteristics. It is indeed a *sphragis*, an individualized mark of origin, used in each of his works. Though he modelled the first Georgic on Hesiod, he does not follow him in talking about his life and family; for a long while it appears that the poem will be as reticent in this respect as Lucretius. But Mantua and the Mincius get into the third book, and the fourth includes a personal reminiscence of an acquaintanceship at Tarentum.[22] Finally the work ends with a *sphragis* more individual than had been written before: Virgil gives his name, states when and where the poem was written, identifies himself as previously the author of the

---

[20] *Aen.* 7. 1.   [21] *Aen.* 10. 198–201.   [22] See below, pp. 147 f., 302.

Eclogues, indicates that he is past his youth, and offers just a hint of his character as he implies that he is devoted to the private pursuits of the leisured life and in some sense is less venturesome than he used to be.[23] This *envoi* seems to have been an inspiration for the conclusion which Horace gave to his first book of *Epistles*, where he tells us that he is the son of a freedman, short, strikingly white-headed, dark-complexioned, quick tempered but easily pacified, and born in December, 65 BC.[24] But the differences between Horace and Virgil are as significant as the likenesses. Horace, uniquely among ancient writers, is so specific that we ought to be able to pick him out at an identity parade. Earlier, he had decided that the great merit of Lucilius was that in his verse one could see the whole of the old man's life as though written up on a votive tablet;[25] now he goes further, and offers a photograph. But Virgil offers a sort of impersonal individuality: while pressing his own stamp on his work, he still guards most of his privacy; as when hearing a voice of marked character on the radio, we may have a sense of distinctive personality which we are nevertheless unable to pin down. The difference between Horace and Juvenal as satirists is partly analogous. Whereas Horace presents a persona, Juvenal presents none: the voice has a very distinctive timbre, but the character that we find in the verse is that of the voice itself not of the man behind it. However, Juvenal is an arguer, a declaimer; the barrister in court hopes to exploit such charm or strength of character as he may possess, but he does not expect to reveal himself. Virgil's poetry, on the other hand, has a distinctive vision of the world—of nature, history, and nation, among other things. To that extent, his verse is bound to be the expression of an individual mind.

The occasional idiosyncrasy will peep through by chance; thus the way that Virgil treats (or avoids) the topic of slavery. The slave's fear of a beating is a staple of Roman comedy, and the supposedly humane Ovid thinks it funny to tell Corinna that he is not carrying on an affair with her maidservant because he would not want to have to do with a girl whose back is scarred.[26] But though the management of slaves was a standard topic in agricultural writers, Virgil keeps it out of the *Georgics*, and that seems a sign of sensitivity rather than complacency; Juvenal may wax nostalgic over the

---

[23] *Geo.* 4. 559–66.   [24] *Epist.* 1. 20.   [25] *Serm.* 2. 1. 32–4.
[26] *Am.* 2. 7. 22—one of the most chilling lines in Latin literature, not by intention.

happily shared lives of masters and servants in the countryside of old, but such prettiness is no more for Virgil than is the brisk callousness of an agriculturalist like Columella.[27] The word 'servus' does not occur anywhere in his work, and in contrast to the *Iliad* and *Odyssey* the *Aeneid* has no role for a slave. At times the *Aeneid* briefly but tellingly depicts the miseries of slavery; most remarkably, his first Eclogue, standing at the head of his first poetry book, includes an outpouring of joy from an old slave over his freedom, late achieved.[28] That is a distinctive note: we would not expect it from another Augustan poet—not indeed from Horace, though he was a freedman's son.

And there may be broader, more nebulous areas in which idiosyncrasy comes through, in a fashion which may seem neither intended nor unintended—where an individual cast of mind or temper has drawn forth a particular outlook or a particular quality of experience. Loneliness, or at least aloneness, is much present in Virgil's verse. The *Eclogues* provided easy opportunities to depict friendship; they are not taken. The solitary Corydon in the second poem and the isolated Gallus in the tenth seem the classic figures in Virgil's pastoral landscape. Tityrus and Meliboeus in the first Eclogue seem absorbed each in his private world of happiness or sorrow, hardly engaging with one another; even the amoebaean pieces convey little sense of a community of affection. The *Georgics* is effectively empty of individual human beings until the last book, where we meet the self-sufficient gardener of Tarentum and the bereaved, solitary Orpheus; Aristaeus, for that matter, is seen in isolation, without wife, neighbours or companions, and severed, in normal circumstances, from his divine mother, as Aeneas will be.

There is a sense in which the *Iliad* may be said to portray the ultimate loneliness of the hero more darkly than anything in Virgil. But an intense friendship—between Achilles and Patroclus—is of course at the centre of the *Iliad*'s plot, and the twenty-third book shows Achilles restored to the companionship of his peers in an extended scene of brilliant social comedy. The hero of the *Odyssey* is essentially a social animal, and his story tells of his escape from isolation on Calypso's island and restoration to his proper place in his society. Jason in Apollonius' *Argonautica* is accompanied by

---

[27] Juv. 14. 166 ff. Columella assumes that part of the estate's workforce will be kept in chains (1. 8. 16); Varro advocates kindness, as more efficient, but the whip may be necessary (*Rust.* 1. 17. 5).   [28] *Aen.* 2. 766 f., 785 f.; 3. 325 ff.; *Ecl.* 1. 27 ff.

heroes who match his calibre, and what is more, the poem turns into a story of love and its consummation. To all of this the *Aeneid* stands in contrast. The only time that we see Aeneas in his domestic setting is when he and his family must abandon it for ever.[29] He and Dido may be lovers, but they are not friends. He has indeed had one intimate friendship, it is implied, and that was with Creusa; but we see only its loss. As for friendship with another man, that is not to be thought of: the faithful Achates is notoriously a mere cipher. There is aloneness even among the gods. Jupiter and Juno, unlike Zeus and Hera in the *Iliad*, are mysteriously apart, and in fact not seen in the same place at all until the tenth book. Zeus and Hera, despite their differences, despite their divinity, do feel like a human husband and wife, as Jupiter and Juno do not. This sense of solitariness does not, in most places, seem like Virgil's conscious design; but he followed his star, and this is where it led him. His seeking for salvation through community and institutions—into which we shall see him binding his ideas of history, earth, and landscape—may be a response to his sense of the loneliness that threatens human beings. Looking in these terms, we may perhaps better understand how it is that he can blend melancholy and hope.

He displays some idiosyncrasy in his response to landscape itself: he is impassioned by rivers, and little attracted by the sea. The sea is the most evocative natural element in the *Iliad*'s landscape: Achilles weeps by the edge of the grey sea, gazing upon the boundless deep, heralds and ambassadors pass along the shore of the sounding sea, the sea sunders the hero from his father and his home.[30] The sea in this poem is not symbolic but archetypal; possessed of an intrinsic emotional force, it can be left simply to be itself, and we shall find that it is recurrently described, not in the language familiar from more recent literature which guides the reader through metaphor and personification, but in strictly factual terms.[31] The poem mentions other elements of the Trojan scene—the fig tree, the rivers Simois and Scamander—because they are features of the battlefield, and not because they are interesting in themselves, but the sea is something more.

'The sea washes off all the ills of mankind,' Euripides wrote; Prometheus cries to the 'innumerable laughter of ocean's waves'; and the shout of Xenophon's Ten Thousand, '*Thalatta, thalatta*', has echoed

---

[29] *Aen.* 2. 634 ff.   [30] *Il.* 1. 349 f., 327; 9. 182.   [31] See below, pp. 22 f.

down the centuries.[32] But surprisingly, there is no echo of these notes
in Virgil. We first meet Aeneas in mid-ocean, in a storm, the sea
his enemy; and the first landscape in the poem is a harbour which
offers safety from the waves. The poem's plot requires the Trojans
to plough vast tracts of ocean, but unlike his model, the *Odyssey*,
Virgil does not at all exploit the romance of the sea, neither its mystery nor its perennity nor even its salt indifference. We might say
that the Homeric epics were children of the Aegean, Virgil the child
of an inland plain, but the matter seems to be more one of individual temper: immense and undifferentiated, the sea was not readily
suggestive to a sensibility that cherished variety and particularity in
nature, and growth, accretion, and quiddity in human institutions.
Catullus, another son of the Po basin, put into his longest poem
the most delectable descriptions of the sea in Latin literature; and
as minor a figure as Valerius Flaccus could beautifully evoke the
shadows lengthening over the rippling water as evening falls: 'magnae
pelago tremit umbra Sinopes.'[33] Virgil declines such opportunities;
but rivers . . .

Rivers are individuals to Virgil: Tiber, Mincius, and Eridanus have
each his own character, and the brief description of Mincius in the
seventh Eclogue is his first attempt to represent a real, particularized scene. Rivers might also be taken as emblematic of what we
shall find to be one of his recurrent themes, the blend of change
and continuity, for they are immemorially ancient and yet 'you cannot step into the same river twice'. They are part of the land and yet
not part of the land. On the one hand, a Roman might worship
Tiber among the guardians of the state or city, as he might worship
Romulus, Vesta, or the Indigites. As he names and describes Italian
rivers, Virgil makes them part of his imaginative, humanized landscape, inspirers of patriotic sentiment and sense of place. He relates
them to the works of man: Vesta preserves 'Tuscan Tiber and the
Roman Palatine'; Tiber himself tells Aeneas that he waters lofty cities;
the glory of Italy is its towns built on steep rocks and rivers flowing
under ancient walls.[34] But in this harmony of man and nature there
is an implicit contrast, for the significance of the harmony lies in
the very fact that human effort and natural forces are things distinct.
If Virgil associates rivers with culture and civility, he associates them

---

[32] Eur. *Iph. Taur.* 1193; Aesch. *Prom.* 89 f.; Xen. *Anab.* 4. 7. 24.
[33] Cat. 64. 12–18, 269–75; Val. Fl. 5. 108 ('the shadow of great Sinope trembles on
the ocean').   [34] *Geo.* 1. 499; *Aen.* 8. 65; *Geo.* 2. 156 f.

also with terrifying violence. In the middle of the first Georgic he describes the storms of autumn: ditches fill, the rivers swell and roar.[35] The theme returns, louder and more furious, near the end of the book, as Eridanus king of rivers bursts his banks and washes away forests, sweeping cattle and cattle-sheds across the plains.[36] The beautiful picture in the second Georgic gains a further significance from the contrast with these dreadful scenes. Similarly, in the *Aeneid*, when the Trojans first catch sight of the Tiber, it is a swirling, silty stream, bursting out into the sea from amid the enveloping forest; and when Tiber in the following book welcomes Aeneas to Latium and transforms his waters into the stillness of a lake to speed the Trojans on their journey to the site of Rome, that earlier vision might remind us that the river, friend to the new arrivals and spokesman for the Italian earth, is also a formidable power.[37] In another place Aeneas himself compares his prospect of the fall of Troy to a torrent in spate flattening crops and fields and tearing forests headlong.[38]

Virgil is ready to show us all this, the destruction as well as the charm, because he is fascinated by rivers as they are. We shall discover that this is the spirit in which he treats nature altogether, not flattening it into a symbol—of peace, say, or beneficence—but finding it to be lovable in itself, for its own sake, and therefore depicting it complete, in both its good and bad aspects. At the same time he surrounds it with ideas and associations, interfusing it with the music of humanity and the historical consciousness; in his handling of Tiber and Mincius he stands at the head of a process which, combining the cult of nature with a secular mythologizing, will one day turn the Rhine into the supreme river of the European imagination. Indeed, this is one way in which he stands among the makers of the European sensibility; we shall meet others. The fascination with the thing itself and the abstract play with associations may sound like divergent impulses, but Virgil's is the most digestive of imaginations: just as whatever Miss T eats turns into Miss T, so all that he read, saw, thought, and felt turned into Virgil. Life and literature are not wholly apart in the experience of any writer, but in him the fusion is exceptionally complete. His integrative power can be seen in the *Aeneid*. The lament for Marcellus in the sixth book must be an afterthought, since the young man did not die until 23 BC, but it becomes a pivot

---

[35] *Geo.* 1. 311 ff. [36] *Geo.* 1. 481–3.
[37] *Aen.* 7. 30–2; 8. 36 ff., 86 ff. [38] *Aen.* 2. 305–8.

in the poem's development, chastening the loud patriotism that has preceded it and foreshadowing the young deaths of the last four books. The Battle of Actium should have been an embarrassment, expected by Caesar Augustus from his poets, but out of place in a mythological epic; yet Virgil can make it the culmination of his keenly personal vision of the Italian experience. The *Georgics* was written partly when civil conflict seemed endless, partly after peace was secure, and both times are reflected in it; he must have begun it without knowing what vision of the nation he would be able to present, and yet this is the most perfectly constructed of all longer poems. The final result appears so inevitable, so effortless, that we can easily fail to see how extraordinary an achievement this was. His ideas of nature, time, and history are likewise a digestion of complex influences, a coalescence of many materials. The next two chapters will therefore study the forces acting upon his time and place, examining first the development of landscape in Greek poetry, and then the social and cultural circumstances of Italy and Rome.

CHAPTER 2

A Reader's Experience:
Landscape in Greek Poetry

Betrachtet, forscht, die Einzelheiten sammelt,
Naturgeheimnis werde nachgestammelt.

(Goethe)

From his own verse we know that Virgil read very widely and
with an extraordinarily retentive memory.[1] The breadth of his literary
experience was unusual in a world where books were uncommon
and expensive, and though Latin poets often advertise their knowledge of Greek precedent, Virgil should be considered exceptional.[2]
But it is not the purpose of this chapter either to assert or to deny
that he had read all the works discussed in it. Our concern is with
the broad picture of the Greeks' perception of landscape, and with
the question of how far it influenced Virgil, how far he was new.
In a short compass it is of course impossible to survey the whole
area in detail;[3] instead we shall pick out a few pinnacles and leap
like the chamois from crag to crag. Even so, we should be able to
see in the development of Greek ideas of landscape the gathering

---

[1] G. N. Knauer has demonstrated how intimately Virgil knew Homer (*Die Aeneis und
Homer* (Göttingen, 1964)). Most telling of all is the way in which time and again *new* discoveries have illuminated Virgil's text. The unearthing of Bacchylides late last century showed
that Virgil was not the first to compare dead spirits to leaves; the discovery of an Orphic
papyrus first published in 1951 shed fresh light on Virgil's underworld, the discovery of
Callimachus' *Victoria Berenices* on the opening of *Geo.* 3.

[2] Modern scholarship easily argues in ways which entail the assumption that all Latin
poets were equally well read in Greek (and even that all were scholars). Of course, they
varied. Propertius makes plenty of noise about Callimachus and Philetas in his third book,
but scepticism is in order (it is already suspicious that he tends to produce them as a pair,
undifferentiated). In Book 3 he seems not to know very much of Callimachus, and to
exploit him little after the third poem. See the salutary cautions of J. Griffin, 'Propertius
and Antony', *JRS* 67 (1977), 17–26, at 19 (= *Latin Poets and Roman Life* (London, 1985),
36); R. O. A. M. Lyne, *The Latin Love Poets* (Oxford, 1980), 147.

[3] A thorough and judicious study is W. Elliger, *Die Darstellung der Landschaft in griechischer
Dichtung* (Berlin, 1975).

of a momentum which will ultimately sweep across into Latin poetry. And besides, however widely Virgil read, he did not read as a scholar or historian: for him too the great masters, the salient strokes of imagination, will have mattered most.

Ruskin's *Modern Painters* is still a useful starting-point for a discussion of Greek landscape.[4] It was here that he coined the term 'pathetic fallacy', by which he meant the practice of attributing feeling (in Greek, *pathos*) to inanimate nature. As an example he took Kingsley's *Sands of Dee*: 'They rowed her in across the rolling foam— | The cruel, crawling foam . . .' The foam is not cruel, he observed, neither does it crawl; the poet 'fallaciously' invests the sea with sentience, as though it were an animal or human being. Another of his instances was drawn from Keats, who describes a wave breaking out at sea,[5]

> Down whose green back the short-lived foam, all hoar,
> Bursts gradual, with a wayward indolence.

Again, salt water is incapable of indolence or waywardness; it has no mind, no moods.

Ruskin held that the pathetic fallacy was 'eminently characteristic of the modern mind', and he was surely right. Although in Keats's case even the casual reader will probably notice the spirit of fancy that animates the inanimate, we constantly use the pathetic fallacy without realizing what we are doing at all: we are always talking about storms raging, savage seas, wild mountains, threatening skies, gloomy shadows, gentle hills, quite unaware that these are 'fallacious' fashions of speaking. To try and do without the pathetic fallacy would be like that game in which one is forbidden to say 'yes' or 'no': we should stumble constantly. A way of talking about nature which did not include the pathetic fallacy would be strikingly different from our own.

And indeed Ruskin used the pathetic fallacy as a touchstone by which to judge the contrast between 'modern landscape' and 'classical landscape'; by the latter he meant the Greek attitude, and principally Homer. Homer, on Ruskin's account, does not use the pathetic fallacy: he could never have called a wave wayward or indolent, because 'he could not by any possibility have lost sight of the great fact that the wave . . . , do what it might, was still nothing else than salt water'.

---

[4] *Modern Painters*, iii (= part 4), Chs. 12, 13, 16.   [5] *Endymion* 2. 350.

He calls the sea 'unharvested', 'full of fish', 'wine-dark'; but 'every one of these epithets is descriptive of pure physical nature'. Now as a matter of strict fact, Ruskin is not entirely correct: the attribution of *pathos* to inanimate things is found occasionally in Homer, as when spears eagerly strike a man's chest or long to enjoy flesh.[6] But such instances are comparatively rare, especially in the case of natural objects. They tend anyway to be deliberately striking in a way that makes them different in effect from the instinctive habit of thought that characterizes the modern use of the pathetic fallacy. And as we shall discover, the finest animation of the inanimate within the *Iliad* is of such a kind that the term 'pathetic fallacy' no longer seems appropriate. Rather, it presupposes a way of thinking and speaking in which the pathetic fallacy plays a negligible part.

Ruskin distinguished a second great difference between Homer and ourselves: when he describes landscapes which he means us to regard as pleasant, they are mild and gentle scenes: cultivated ground, tilth, and vineyard; or a mixture of spring, meadow, and shady grove (not an exact scholar, Ruskin may here be conflating the *Odyssey* with other Greek poetry, but again his claim is in broad terms reasonable). The landscapes in which the modern sensibility most delights— wilderness and mountains, savagery and solitude—are not celebrated. When rocks appear in a pleasant scene, it is in the form of caves, which provide shade or shelter. For the landscapes that please Homer are those suited to man's convenience, whereas we incline to admire above all others those parts of the natural world which we have not subdued to our own purposes.

Accepting Ruskin's distinction, at least in general terms, we should not find it hard to imagine the cause. In an age when people must struggle to scratch a living from the soil, with little defence against the violence of the elements, an admiration for infertile and inhospitable landscapes is a luxury to which they are little likely to be attracted. The way in which the ancient world thought about gardens is revealing. Whereas the landscape garden, which most Englishmen and even some others believe to be the highest form of garden art yet devised, affects to mimic the spontaneity and asymmetry of uncultivated nature, the ancient garden tames and regularizes it. Typically it is symmetrical and enclosed; and it is useful, growing fruits and vegetables. Alcinous' garden in the *Odyssey* is a case in point: with its fence or

---

[6] *Il.* 15. 542, 11. 573 f., 15. 316 f., 21. 70, 21. 168.

wall along the boundaries, its orchard-trees and vines, its neat beds, and its pair of springs it exemplifies order, balance, enclosure, and usefulness.[7] Now the land of the Phaeacians is half a fairyland, and this is a fairytale garden, but that makes it all the more revealing, for it is the *ne plus ultra* of what a garden might be in paradise. Fruits grow there all the year round: the poet gives it magical qualities to make it not more romantic, but more serviceable. The word *paradeisos* itself, derived from the Persian, was to enter the Greek language meaning a park or pleasure ground. It was then adopted by the Septuagint for Adam and Eve's home in Eden; for they too begin in a garden, not in a place where nature is left to itself.

In later antiquity the land was to be better under control than when Homer sang, but of course even the Romans never succeeded in domesticating nature to anything like the extent that has been possible since the industrial revolution. Floods were a perennial hazard in Italy, as Virgil reminds us,[8] and would remain so for many more centuries;[9] storms could destroy a homestead. In the first century BC bandits could still be a menace in the Italian countryside and marauders had descended from the Alps only a few years before. We might expect to find that a taste for nature's wilder aspects had grown to some degree in the many centuries since Homer, but still had its limits. Rich men had their villas at Baiae, or Tivoli; but the highest and coldest mountains do not attract much praise. Rome was noisy, crowded, and much larger than any city had been before; it was also full of spongers and pretentious persons, vivid in Horace's verse. These things would seem likely to make the countryside at least, and perhaps the wilds also, appear more of a refreshment to the spirit. On the other hand, there was nothing in antiquity quite like the nineteenth-century industrial city or the twentieth-century megalopolis. From ancient urbanism, therefore, one would expect, again, some change in attitude towards nature, but still a limited change in comparison with what has come in the last two hundred years. We shall see how far these expectations are met.

The reason why the pathetic fallacy should be uncommon in early Greek literature but ubiquitous today is less obvious. Ruskin

---

[7] *Od.* 7. 112–32.   [8] *Geo.* 1. 311 ff. (and cf. the simile at *Aen.* 2. 304–8).

[9] Cf. F. Braudel, *The Mediterranean and the Mediterranean World in the Age of Philip II*, tr. S. Reynolds, vol. i (London, 1972), 62 f., 247 f.; Gibbon, *Decline and Fall*, ch. 71. In his ch. 30 also, Gibbon notes the 'capricious and irregular abundance of waters' in Italy, sometimes bringing disaster to unsuspecting invaders from the north. The Florentine flood of 1966 showed that Italian weather can still be perilous.

supposed the growth of the pathetic fallacy to be connected with a loss of belief in gods or spirits of nature. For Homer, he argues, the tree and the tree-nymph, the sea and the sea-god were sharply separate; he could thus fill his landscape with spiritual presences and still depict nature itself exactly as it is, without recourse to fantasy. Modern man desires to invest nature with a large and deep significance, but cannot believe in the nymph or the god; he is thus driven to the fancy of attributing sentience to the trees and waters themselves.

There is indeed good reason to suppose that for the early Greeks a more than usually keen apprehension of nature, and especially of uncultivated nature, was intimately linked to their apprehension of the divine. Consider Poseidon's journey in the thirteenth book of the *Iliad*: 'He climbed on to his chariot, and went his way driving over the waves. And the beasts, gathering from their lairs on every side, frolicked at his presence, and they failed not to recognize their lord; and in jubilation (*gethosune*) the sea divided.'[10] The last phrase is splendidly dramatic: *gethosune* is a strong word, and emphatically placed at the beginning of a line. The point is that the god fills nature; the sea-beasts know him and finally even the insentient sea becomes sentient and joins in the jubilation. Now nature is not normally described by Homer like this; nor, for that matter, are the gods. The scheme of the *Iliad* requires gods to pass among men and even to meet them openly upon the battlefield. This required the poet to play down the supernatural, awesome, or numinous aspect of these deities. In exceptional circumstances it is even possible for a hero to get the better of a god: Diomedes wounds Aphrodite and Ares.[11] When Diomedes and later Patroclus meet Apollo, it is as though they were confronting another hero, albeit one very much stronger than themselves.[12] In each case Apollo warns the hero to withdraw and in each case the hero obeys; but so likewise might a hero have obeyed had Achilles confronted him and allowed him the opportunity of retreat. What we do not find in such passages is the feeling that to be in the presence of a god is to enter into an order of experience quite different in quality from the usual. They do not express what we should call a sense of the numinous. We might suppose that Homer lacked this sense, as we understand it, but for one or two passages. One such passage is the encounter, by night, of Priam and the disguised god Hermes.[13] That has something uncanny, dreamlike

[10] *Il.* 13. 26–9.   [11] *Il.* 5. 334 ff., 855 ff.
[12] *Il.* 5. 436 ff.; 16. 702 ff.   [13] *Il.* 24. 349 ff.

about it. Why does Priam seem so little puzzled by the presence of a youth wandering without reason between the Greek and Trojan lines? Why the strange sympathy that seems to pass between him and this unknown person? Why does he speak as though he knows and yet does not know that the youth is really a god? Commonly we feel Homer's gods, though immortal and very powerful, to be still part of a natural order; here we feel the presence of the supernatural, a change in the quality of experience.

And so with Poseidon's epiphany. The drama of the scene is that nature is not normally like this; the salt water comes alive and rejoices, vivified by the divine numen. To call this 'pathetic fallacy' is to mistake its meaning, for Homer means strongly what he says. Indeed, his conception derives its force from the absence of the pathetic fallacy. In a modern poet a joyful sea might not seem much: in its Homeric context it is spectacular, for it signifies that supernature here informs nature, and the sea is thrilled through by the god.

This sense of numen reappears at least once more in the *Iliad*, and in a surprising place. Hera beguiles Zeus and they join in sexual union:[14]

Beneath them the holy earth put forth fresh blossoming grass and dewy clover and crocus and hyacinth thick and soft, which held them up from the ground. On this they lay, and wrapped themselves in a cloud, fair and golden; and glittering dewdrops fell.

To see this episode as quaint and comic, light relief from the grim monotony of the slaughter, is at best a half truth; for here superbly, and as nowhere else in the poem, what might be called the poetic and cultic aspects of the gods fuse. On one level the deception of Zeus is a move in the social politics of Olympus, part of the story of feasts and squabbles, laughter and occasional buffoonery that makes up the bulk of the gods' life as Homer depicts it. But at the same time it is a glorious, wholesome and sacred act. For this is the *hieros gamos*, the sacred marriage of the sky and the earth. At Eleusis, in later centuries, the worshippers would look up at the heaven and cry *hue*, 'rain', then down at the ground and cry *kue*, 'conceive'.[15]

---

[14] *Il.* 14. 347–51.

[15] Proclus *in Tim.* 40e (iii. 176 Diehl); cf. W. K. C. Guthrie, *The Greeks and their Gods* (London, 1950), 54. The theme receives its most intense expression in Aeschylus' *Danaids* (fr. 44; Aphrodite is speaking): 'The pure sky lusts to pierce the earth, and lust grips the earth to attain marriage. Rain fallen from her lover the sky makes the earth pregnant; she brings forth for mortals the pasture of flocks and the life that is Demeter's, and from that moist marriage the trees' due season is accomplished. Of these things I am a cause.' This passage was to be imitated by Euripides (fr. 898. 7 ff.) and to influence Lucretius (see below, pp. 245 f.).

The Sky is the male principle, the Earth the female, and the rain is the life-giving semen which impregnates the ground that it may bring forth crops and flowers. Fertility cults are excluded from the Homeric epics; Demeter, the earth mother, never appears in them, though she is occasionally mentioned. But there are many things in Homer which are either kept in the background, to be felt occasionally as a dim presence, or else admitted into the poems very rarely, for special and dramatic effect: monsters, ecstatic cults, chthonic cult, hero cult, ritual pollution, ghosts, second sight, even adultery; as we have seen, the idea of the god as a numen informing and vivifying the natural world is one such thing. So too with fertility religion: the springing up of the flowers at the coupling of Zeus and Hera, who here takes on the role of the Earth, has the magnificence of its uniqueness. The effect is thus extremely different from the comic amours of Ovid's gods. The Latin poet is nearer to Offenbach than to Homer; his gods become figures of fun, because we do not seriously believe in them any more, whereas in the *Iliad* the gods' frivolity and irresponsibility is part of their divine glory; it is what lifts them so high above the wretched mortals who fight and die upon the Trojan plain. It is because the gods are so much stronger than men that Hera can afford to deceive Zeus and Zeus afford to be deceived; it is their blessedness that they can make love while men make war; and when Zeus lists to his wife the women with whom he has slept, concluding with the observation that none of them filled him with such desire as she does now, it is not a catalogue of lechery, like Leporello's recital in *Don Giovanni*,[16] but a paean to the splendour of sexuality. And so of course the flowers spring up around them as they unite; how should they not?

Now certainly physical nature has only a subordinate part to play in this scene. But the distinctive glory of the Homeric idea is that everything described here simply *is*; nothing is metaphor, parable, or allegory. Zeus and Hera are not symbols, but two people making love; immortal people, but people none the less. The flowers are not symbolical either, nor are they poetic decoration, embroidered on to the scene like the background of a *mille fleurs* tapestry. They are real flowers, because real flowers will naturally bloom around the sky god when he mates with his wife. We shall find flowers prettily scattered across the verse in (say) Moschus;[17] but that is not Homer's

---

[16] *Il.* 14. 315 ff.   [17] Mosch. 2. 63 ff.

way. In Lucretius and Virgil we shall meet the *hieros gamos* again,[18] but though Lucretius is a materialist and Virgil presents himself as a conventional worshipper of the gods, for both of them alike the idea has necessarily become secularized. Nature itself is now the primary theme, and the divine marriage has become a partially or wholly figurative way of conveying nature's emotional effect upon us. But for Homer neither do the gods represent the force of nature, nor does nature ornament the gods. Both gods and plants are part of the created order, and flowers burgeon as simply and inevitably upon this occasion as they do under the influence of sun and showers. To be sure, blooms do not normally open out in a moment of time— that is where the divine numen comes into play—but this scene is none the less not so much a breach of the natural order as a heightening of nature's proper processes. The scene is unlike Poseidon's epiphany in that no sentience is attributed to insentient nature; it is like in that nature's ordinary being is intensified by the presence of deity.

In the *Odyssey* we occasionally seem to find landscape used, as it is not used in the *Iliad*, to enhance mood or express temperament. Now of course a man may by his own will make his surroundings fit his way of life and behaviour. Alcinous' garden is orderly and symmetrical because he is the rich king of an orderly society, much as Eumaeus' piggery is symmetrical and well organized because he is a good pigman.[19] But sometimes Homer gives a character a background or a landscape setting which seems to fit him in a way that cannot entirely be explained in literal terms. The idea enters the *Odyssey* that the natural world is somehow responsive to human vice and virtue: in the land of a good king the black earth bears wheat and barley, the trees are heavy with fruit, flocks bring forth young in abundance, the sea offers fish in plenty, and the people prosper.[20] Appropriately, therefore, a character's setting may have an expressive or moral function. Even with Alcinous and Eumaeus, the settings are perhaps not purely the result of their own virtue or volition: Alcinous is a good king, but his garden is magical, beyond the power of mere human devising; Eumaeus is a good swineherd, but surely his homestead is grand and regular in an improbable degree, and this is because it has a moral significance which goes beyond simple realism: it exemplifies good order in contrast to the disorder of Odysseus' palace, infested by the suitors. That the monster

---

[18] See below, pp. 245 f., 332 f.   [19] *Od.* 14. 5 ff.   [20] *Od.* 19. 109–14.

Polyphemus does not inhabit the well-watered meadows down by the shore of his island, ideal soil (so Odysseus tells us) for vines and corn,[21] is partly his choice: he lives in solitude and lawlessness,[22] and presumably by his own desire. But Homer also gives him an imaginative or poetic unity with his landscape. He lives in a high cave, with lofty pines and oaks about it; and he is himself of monstrous size, like a wooded peak among high mountains, which stands out solitary, apart from the other hills.[23]

The first half of the *Odyssey* relates the hero's encounter with three women. Each is distinctive: the passionate Calypso is in contrast to the cool Circe, a sort of divinized *demi-mondaine*, and the maidenly simplicity of Nausicaa. And each is found in a setting appropriate to her. When Odysseus first catches sight of Nausicaa, she has gone with her handmaids to wash clothes by the fair stream of the river, where the lovely water wells up in abundance, pure and never-failing; the washing done, they bathe and eat on the bank, where the grass grows lush and 'honey-sweet'.[24] It would be a pity to say that this setting symbolized Nausicaa's freshness and purity; rather, it is the kind of place in which a young princess like this, leading the kind of life that she does, will rightly and naturally be found. It is natural, equally, that the shaggy shipwrecked Odysseus should watch the scene from the tangles of thick brushwood, and come forth 'like a mountain-bred lion'.[25] He is naked and briny, they are fair-tressed maidens;[26] he is in the brush, they beside the fair flowing stream. Yet to point out these equivalences is almost to make too much of them. Of course a dirty and unclad stranger will hide himself in a thicket; the relation of the man and the women to their landscapes is not made ponderous with figurative significations; it just happens, unforcedly, with a kind of inevitable fitness.

Circe's island is covered in forest and thick brushwood; her palace, built of polished stone, lies *en besseissi*, in a wooded glen.[27] It would be possible, again, to say that these things represent Circe's uncivilized spirit, her concealments and deceptions, her stylish woman-of-the-world behaviour; but once more it is unnecessary. This is the sort of place that Circe will naturally inhabit, being the sort of person that she is.

[21] *Od.* 9. 132–5. [22] *Od.* 9. 189. [23] *Od.* 9. 182–6, 190–2.
[24] *Od.* 6. 85–98. [25] *Od.* 6. 127–30. [26] *Od.* 6. 135–7.
[27] *Od.* 10. 150, 197 (both times the distinctive phrase *dia druma pukna kai hulen*, 'through the dense thickets and woodland'), 210 f., 252, 274, 308.

Homer comes nearest to depicting what we might call an affective landscape—that is, a landscape which reflects the mood or emotions of its occupant—when he describes Calypso's island of Ogygia. The usual features of the conventionally pleasant scene are there—cave, trees, and fountains—but the detail adds a good deal more. The scene-setting is unusually lavish in its mere length—between fifteen and twenty lines of continuous landscape description—and that lavish-ness of verse matches the lushness of what is portrayed. Three senses are appealed to, sound and scent as well as sight. Within a great cave is a fire, fragrant with burning cedar and juniper, melodious with the song of the goddess at her loom. Around the cave is a wood, not thicket as on Circe's isle, but a mixture of alder, poplar and sweet-smelling cypress; a richer blend, we may observe, than one would expect to find in a natural Mediterranean landscape. Birds roost in the branches, owls, falcons, and seacrows, the last described as *tanu-glossoi*, 'of lengthy speech'. A flourishing vine runs round the cave, rich with clusters. Four springs flow with clear water; around are soft meadows, blooming with parsley and violet.[28]

Now Calypso is shown by her name to be the Concealer; she who hides, *kaluptei*. Ogygia itself 'lies afar', in a distant ocean.[29] And within the island she is concealed: her singing and the fragrance of the burning wood come from inside the cave and are perceived from without (one of the distinctive features of the whole description is that it is seen through an individual pair of eyes, those of the god Hermes who observes and admires). The vines about the mouth of the cave, the grove before it all push the nymph deeper into an unseen interior, away from the immediate field of vision. Her name, her function and her landscape form a unity. The strength of her desire for Odysseus is evoked by the scene about her; this setting, dark and yet luxuriant, thick with leaves and flowers, heavy with fruit-age, is surely the landscape of passion. Indeed, if one's fancy is for allegory or symbolism, the wooded cave-mouth suggests an anatomical significance. At all events, the cave seems to be the most essential feature of Calypso's environment, as Odysseus implies in his very brief summary to Alcinous: 'There Calypso . . . kept me, in her hol-low caves, longing that I should be her husband.'[30] In a world where men and even goddesses live in houses or palaces, it is significant that she does not: her cave suggests her remoteness, and in some

[28] *Od.* 5. 55–74.　　　[29] *Od.* 5. 55.　　　[30] *Od.* 9. 29 f.

sense a wildness about her. We observe too, in Odysseus' words, the close association of the cave with her sexual passion. Yet the scene as a whole is not allegorical: it would be vain to ask of each item in the description, 'What does this mean?' The harmony of Calypso's nature with her surrounding is suggestive rather than exact. Virgil was to pick up the suggestion: when he put Circe into the *Aeneid*, he made her animals howl and moan, unlike the wolves and lions in Homer's version, which are tame and fawning.[31] Virgil's picture suggests the frustrations of passion, the torments of our animal appetite; accordingly he gives to Circe's setting features taken from Homer's Ogygia, Calypso's isle.

In this description can be seen the ancestor of both the symbolic landscape and the affective landscape. Yet to a large extent it remains within the ordinary Homeric scheme of things. The pathetic fallacy is completely absent; whatever association there may be between Calypso and her landscape is achieved without bending nature into an anthropomorphic shape. Even the rich shadowy depths which seem so important a part of the scene are evoked entirely by implication; there is no word for 'dark' or 'shade' anywhere in the passage, simply a succession of natural features, listed one by one, with a perfect lucidity. None the less, though Homer's famous clarity and objectivity remain, the scene is felt to be exceptional within the poem itself: 'Even an immortal who came there would marvel on seeing it and delight in his heart. There the messenger, the slayer of Argus, stood and gazed.'[32] And only an immortal, perhaps, could hope to possess a setting of such mingled aptness and beauty. Ithaca, certainly, is not so comfortable, 'rough, but a good nurse of young men', as Odysseus describes it.[33] That phrase was to be quoted, centuries later, by a successful Roman, in sentimental memory of an Apennine boyhood: Cicero slips it into one of his letters to Atticus.[34] But there is a subtle difference between Odysseus' spirit and Cicero's. Odysseus, to be sure, speaks of his home with affection, for he continues, in words which Cicero too quotes, 'For my part, I can see no sight sweeter than my own land';[35] but the implication is, 'a poor thing but mine own'. He could have stayed with Calypso, more beautiful than his wife Penelope, in a landscape lovelier than Ithaca's; he chooses not to, but he does not pretend that Ithaca would be

---

[31] *Aen.* 7. 15 ff.; *Od.* 10. 212–19.   [32] *Od.* 5. 73–5.
[33] *Od.* 9. 27.   [34] *Att.* 2. 11. 2.   [35] *Od.* 9. 27 f.

especially desirable, were it not his. When the Roman statesman retires
to what he elsewhere, quoting an unknown poet, perhaps Ennius,
calls, 'my native mountains, the cradle of my being',[36] he goes for
the sake of rest and refreshment from a city of a size that an Odysseus
could not even conceive. (The context of this latter quotation makes
that very clear: better the company of country people ('rustici'), he
says than that of the 'perurbani', the 'excessively citified'.) The roughness and simplicity (one may suspect) are beginning to become a
pleasure in themselves. Even so, Cicero quotes Odysseus in order
to amplify the observation that Arpinum is a place to which he can
hardly invite his friend.

A Roman grandee did not have to scrape his living from those
rough hillsides. Odysseus, had be been a real person, would not have
been so fortunate; and Hesiod, who is real enough, was harshly frank
about his home: Ascra, he said, was 'nasty in winter, oppressive in
summer, never good'.[37] (When Virgil takes Hesiod as the nominal
model for the *Georgics*, he will transform this, drawing a severe satisfaction from the recalcitrance of nature and the hardness of the farmer's
life.) Archilochus was scarcely more flattering than Hesiod when he
came to speak of his home, the island of Thasos, 'like an ass's back,
crowned with wild woodland'.[38] Now Homer describes a particular
geography in and around Ithaca: Odysseus tells his host that Ithaca
is 'clear-seen', with a mountain upon it named Neriton, leafy and
conspicuous from afar; about it lie many other islands close to one
another, Dulichium, Same, and wooded Zacynthus. These other islands
lie apart and towards the east; Ithaca itself is in a different position
(it is uncertain what, for the meaning at this point is disputed).[39]
The passage has been a battleground for those who have sought to
reconcile it with the actual geography of the Ionian isles or who
have wanted to know whether Odysseus' home is to be identified
with the modern Ithaca. These may perhaps be reasonable objects
of enquiry (though the simplest response is to suggest that the poet
had never been anywhere near); but for our purposes it does not
matter whether he meant to describe the real facts about the area
or was describing a pattern of islands which is real only within the
universe of his poem, just as it does not matter in the *Iliad* whether
the rivers Simois and Scamander, the fig-tree, the springs and washing

---

[36] *Att.* 2. 15. 3.   [37] *Works and Days* 640.
[38] Archil. 21 W.   [39] *Od.* 9. 21–6.

troughs, and even Troy, ever existed in the real world: it is sufficient that they be solid and credible within the poem itself. At this moment in the *Odyssey* the hero is identifying himself. 'Who are you?' Alcinous has asked, and his guest replies that he is Odysseus son of Laertes, known among men for wiles of every kind, a man whose fame reaches to heaven. Having thus given his name, parentage, and reputation, he then gives his homeland. In the context, therefore, his account of the islands, insofar as it is individually distinctive, is distinctive as part of his *sphragis* or seal; like the pattern on the gemstone, the pattern of the isles identifies and authenticates the man who describes them. It is, to shift to modern metaphor, his signature or fingerprint. Once the co-ordinates have placed Odysseus, Homer no longer seems much further interested in a distinctive geography; true, not every island known to the Greeks had a wooded hill, but the brief depiction of Ithaca fits recognizably into the mould of the Homeric generalized description. The mount is conspicuous and seen from afar; what mountain is not? It is 'waving-leaved'; but all leaves wave. There is thus something in Archilochus' picture of Thasos which we do not find in Homer; so far as we know, this is the first attempt to take a particular landscape in the real world, known and named, and convey its individual character. The comparison to a donkey's back implies a particular shape and at the same time suggests a visual awareness of the landscape's texture—not defined, but surely vivid: we may imagine rock, scrub, and thicket. Moreover, we have here, as never in Homer, the landscape's quality evoked by an odd, quirky comparison; we feel that the poet has seen the island keenly, and responded personally to what he has seen. And there seems to be a touch of the pathetic fallacy, by implication at least: the 'wild' woodland answers to the intransigent character of the ass.

The pathetic fallacy appears spectacularly in a fragment of Alcman:[40]

The crests and gullies of the mountains are asleep, the headlands and torrents, the forest and all the animals that the black earth nurtures, the mountain beasts, the race of bees and the monsters in the depths of the dark sea, and the tribes of long-winged birds are asleep.

Despite our ignorance of the context, we can detect a vigorous 'feeling for nature' of some kind here. But this feeling is still far from

---

[40] Alcman fr. 89 P. In one other place this poet appears dramatically out of time: a look of melting love, 'softer than sleep or death' (3. 61 f.), as though Tristan had called in at archaic Sparta.

particularity or exactness of perception; Alcman gives an account of nature as a whole, not of a single scene or aspect; and he offers statement rather than depiction. Upon a casual reading some people have been unsure whether the scene is set at noon or night;[41] though the answer is surely the latter, it is revealing that doubt can creep in at all. As for the pathetic fallacy, it is so conspicuously used that in one sense it is hardly 'fallacious' at all: the sleep of cliffs and gullies seems to be a dramatically irrational idea to which the poet calls attention rather than an instinctive habit of thought.

Among the fragments of Sappho is a very beautiful piece of landscape:[42]

Come hither, pray, from Crete to this holy shrine, where is your pleasant grove of apple-trees, and altars fuming with frankincense. Here cold water babbles through apple-trees, all the place is shadowed with roses, and from the flickering leaves slumber comes down. Here a meadow, pasture for horses, blooms with spring flowers, the breezes blow graciously . . . Here, Cyprian, take garlands and pour gracefully in golden cups nectar mingled with our festivities.

There is no name here, as in Homer or Archilochus, and yet it is here that we must look for the first appearance of the sentiment of place; that is, the combination of personal emotion or experience with the description or evocation of the individual character of a scene. This poem contains both a mood and a picture, both subjectivity and objectivity, as Sappho conveys how she feels, being in a particular place at a particular time.

She bids Aphrodite come from a specific place, Crete,[43] to her shrine, presumably on Lesbos, but at any rate to another specific place which need not be named, as it is the known spot where Sappho and her fellow worshippers are situated, at this present moment. The place has a degree of particularity, first because it is a known place, chosen out and sanctified to the goddess, but also because the description has some individuality about it. A grove of apple-trees with roses mingled among them, running water and a meadow beyond—that

[41] Iris Murdoch, *The Unicorn* (London, 1963), ch. 13: 'Max . . . had just retired to rest after quoting to Effingham a poem of Alcman about sleep, which Effingham had always imagined referred to the night. He murmured it now, seeing it as the account of a sinister enchanted siesta.'

[42] Sappho fr. 2. A longer analysis: Jenkyns, *Three Classical Poets* (London, 1982), 22 ff.

[43] The text, at this point known only from a scrawl on a sherd, is unsure, but 'from Crete' is probable.

is not an enormously distinctive scene, but it is distinctive enough. The season can be fairly closely defined: it is early summer, the time when the roses bloom. The description is ample enough to appeal to three senses, including the smell of frankincense and the babble of water besides the visual elements. The *aithussomenon . . . phullon*, the shimmering and rustling leaves, express sight and sound with a single epithet.

There is something else new in this poem: a blurriness, to which the mingling of several sense perceptions contributes. The place is 'shadowed with roses', a strange phrase, suggestive of an opulent dimness; the water babbles not along the ground but through the apple boughs; sleep comes down from the shimmer of the leaves. We are a long way from the clarity with which Homer described even Calypso's bower. Sappho is concerned to convey an experience of drowsiness: the shadows and the shimmer are mesmeric; to a sleepy half-consciousness the boughs and the sound of water seem to merge, so that the babbling comes through the branches. Paradoxically, the blurriness is very precisely imagined. The pattern of sounds, which is extraordinarily careful and restrained, enhances the slumberous mood.

As an evocation of a human mood within a natural setting the poem is very refined, and it can seem in some ways remarkably modern; there is indeed nothing else in archaic poetry quite like it. But it remains within the early Greek's conventional idea of what makes an agreeable spot: grove, meadow, shade, and running water are still the scene's basic elements; the character of the place has been formed by human hand; there is no interest in nature as something autonomous, to be studied closely or for its own sake. Yet the subjectivity with which these elements are presented is highly original. If we find in Sappho's poem a response to nature which we can recognize and share, that is a sign of the authenticity of imagination, for in important respects her experience and her assumptions are very different from ours. The sleepy beauty of the scene makes sense to us with our secular attitude to landscape, but for her it is inseparable from the expected coming of Aphrodite. The word for slumber, *koma*, means a magical or enchanted sleep; we enter a numinous sphere, so that when the goddess comes and pours a divine drink in person, we no longer sense in what order of experience or on what level of reality we are.

Once more, then, we find an enhanced feeling for nature coming in association with the presence of the divine. The grove contains an altar sacred to Aphrodite; and there are other things which have a connection with her. Apples and horses are both found, sometimes at least, in association with her cult. There are no apples in this poem, as the season is spring or early summer, only apple-trees; 'pasture for horses' leaves it unclear whether there are horses in the field now; but it is reasonable to suppose that these things would be in the place at certain times and seasons because they are appropriate to the goddess. This is not symbolism, however, as the absence of the apples and Sappho's insouciance about the presence of the horses help to show. Aphrodite exists and the grove exists, as in the fourteenth book of the *Iliad* Zeus and Hera exist and the flowers exist. Apple-trees are here because apple-trees naturally belong in the sort of place where Aphrodite might naturally be found, rather as Nausicaa was naturally found in a place of fair water and sweet grass.

For nature as symbol we can turn to Ibycus:[44]

In spring the Cydonian quinces bloom, watered from flowing rivers, where is the inviolate garden of the Maidens, and the vine flowers bloom, growing beneath the shady vine sprays; but for me love sleeps at no season. Like the Thracian North Wind, flaming with lightning, shooting from the Love Goddess, with parching frenzy, dark, shameless, it mightily shakes my heart at its foundations.

The purpose of the nymphs' garden is to contrast with the parching wind in the fragment's second half; by an elegant variation the wind is in a formal simile and the garden is not, but essentially they are upon the same level and correspond to one another. The description is thus neither an autonomous scene, valued for itself, nor a setting for a person or action, but a term of comparison; and the elements of the description are chosen not primarily because they are what one would expect to find in a real garden or what one would hope to find in an especially beautiful place, but for a symbolic end. This is not to say that Ibycus' garden is unrealistic, merely that the evocation of a landscape is not his first concern. For his attention is fixed not on a place but a person, and the elements of the description are selected to symbolize various aspects of his beloved. Garden, maidens, water, blossoms, vines 'swelling to strength'—these things are variously representative of protection, virginity, innocence, youth, ripening to manhood, and so on.

[44] Ibycus fr. 286.

It is interesting to observe a similarity between Ibycus' garden and some lines written by Euripides a century later. The virgin hero Hippolytus prays to his patroness, the virgin Artemis:[45]

To you, my lady, I bring this plaited garland which I have fashioned from an inviolate meadow, where neither the shepherd presumes to pasture his beasts nor has iron yet come, but the bee in spring passes through the inviolate meadow and Shamefastness tends it with river waters, for those who have nothing which comes by teaching but in whose nature virtue in all things always has its destined place—for them to pluck, whereas for the base it is not permitted.

Within Euripides' fiction this meadow is a real place. Clearly it is also symbolic—of restraint, reverence, chastity and so on—but it has become so because real men have chosen to create the symbols: they have decided to keep out the animals and leave the grass unmown. Nor is the link between the actuality of the innocent field and its figurative significance arbitrary: Hippolytus' open-air existence, spent hunting and occasionally gathering garlands, and his religious dedication to sexual abstinence are both parts of a single way of life; both aspects are summed up in the divine person of Artemis, virgin and huntress. Ovid can be revealingly compared and contrasted with Euripides when he gives Narcissus a setting which in some ways resembles, and probably echoes consciously, Hippolytus' speech; once again, the details are designed to figure purity and virginity.[46] The later writer is willing to allow impossibilities: no animal comes near Narcissus' pool, no bee gathers honey, no branch falls from a tree. The landscape has become fully literary or paradisal; the poet is not interested to investigate what a landscape might actually look like; far from letting nature itself guide him, he will put into the scene only what he might wish to find there. Euripides is a long way from Ovid; yet one may feel that he has taken the first steps along the path which will eventually lead to him. The similarity to Ibycus is perhaps revealing; though there is nothing unrealistic in Euripides' meadow, everything described exemplifies the figurative theme; the poet is not interested in anything else that might be there. Sappho's grove is subtly but vitally different: she simply sets about saying what there is in it and evoking the mood that it inspires in her, and this will lead us to Aphrodite with a beautiful inevitability. Euripides' approach is also just a touch more secular than Sappho's. He inherits

[45] *Hipp.* 73–81.   [46] *Met.* 3. 407–12; see below, pp. 623 ff.

the archaic pattern in that he has taken an especial interest in nature at this moment because it has come into connection with the divine, but the connection now seems to be something that has been willed and imposed by men. We are brought back to the issue of choice; it has been a human decision that the meadow should be kept from the flocks and the scythe. In Sappho's grove, though it is true that men must have consecrated it and built the altar, we feel differently: the presence of Aphrodite in the place is simply a fact about it; merely describe the trees, flowers and water in it and we shall know it to be numinous.

If we regard Homer as the fountainhead, we can see that one direction in which the poetic description of nature could develop away from him was towards the symbolic landscape. A cousin of the symbolic landscape is what might be called the golden landscape. This ideal is elegantly explained by Sir Philip Sidney: 'Nature never set forth the earth in so rich tapestry as divers poets have done, neither with pleasant rivers, fruitful trees, sweet smelling flowers, nor whatsoever else may make the too much loved earth more lovely. Her world is brazen, the poets only deliver a golden.'[47] Sidney's idea is that if we describe nature exactly as it is we shall have to see it, like everything else in this sublunary world, with warts and all. Literature has the advantage that it can remove the warts and it should exploit the advantage. This is the reverse of the idea that one should study and submit to nature; an idea which leads ultimately to Blake's advice that one should stare at the knot in a tree for an hour. In that conception, which was to suffuse the prose of Ruskin and the poetry of Hopkins, the wartiness of nature—its detail, particularity, quiddity— has become an interest or pleasure in its own right. Ancient poets were in the end to travel a certain distance along that road: we shall find in Roman literature both the celebration of the ordinary, the sense of particularity and the seizing of detail.

The symbolic and golden landscapes were one possible development out of Homer; but there was another. In Euripides' *Bacchae* the note first sounded in Homer's epiphany of Poseidon is heard again, and more strongly. A messenger comes from the mountainside, where he has been watching the maenads: 'The entire mountain and the wild beasts joined in their Bacchic ecstasy, and nothing was unstirred by their motion.'[48] The general absence of the pathetic

[47] *An Apology for Poetry.*   [48] *Ba.* 726 f.

fallacy makes this powerfully dramatic, for it is not just a literary or fanciful manner of speaking. With the coming of Dionysus, the whole of nature becomes instinct with him; the wild animals know his ecstasy, even brute stone is alive and stirred by the revel. A later messenger describes the space of terrible silence between the cry of Dionysus to his maenads and the rout in which they tear Pentheus apart: 'The air fell silent, and the wooded glen held its leaves in silence; you could not have heard the cry of any beast.'[49] Once more, much of the impressiveness comes from the context. At a rite, the priest calls on the congregation to be silent; and in the silence the god comes. The hush here is the hush of worship; inanimate nature becomes sentient, and knows the being of the god. Is this the pathetic fallacy or is the messenger describing the reality of Dionysus' vivifying power? We have reached a point at which we can scarcely tell.

The play is filled with a passion for liberation, for escape. Bound up with this is a communion with nature wild and in the raw— literally, for the climax of the Bacchic ecstasy is the *omophagia*, the rending and devouring of a young animal. The Maenads are out upon the hillsides, away from their menfolk, away from restraints and conventions; the language of the play is full of woods and glens and mountains. The women of the chorus yearn to be once again in the Bacchic revel, tossing their necks up to the dewy air 'like a fawn gambolling in the green delight of a field';[50] the transference of the epithet, strangely anticipatory of Marvell's 'green thought in a green shade',[51] momentarily merges human or creaturely pleasure with nature. Euripides is both like and unlike Homer. The impassioned engagement, the feeling for the wild, the sense of communion with nature may all seem new, and more like modern or perhaps romantic sentiment than anything we have met hitherto; on the other hand, it is not ordinary nature that we see in the *Bacchae* but nature in an abnormal and heightened state. Dionysus' transforming power is miraculous in the strongest sense: honey drips from the thyrsus, milk and wine spurt up from the earth.[52] Without the god the enthusiasm for nature, the *enthousiasmos* within nature would not be there.

In the closing years of the fifth century, when the aged Euripides wrote the *Bacchae*, the aged Sophocles put into his last play a choral ode praising the beauties of Colonus.[53] It is exceptionally long

---

[49] *Ba.* 1084 f.   [50] *Ba.* 864–7.
[51] As E. R. Dodds observed in his commentary, ad loc.
[52] *Ba.* 704–11; cf. 143.   [53] *Oed. Col.* 668–719.

and continuously sustained for a description of landscape in Greek poetry; what is more, it is a description of a specific, named landscape which exists in the real world and was presumably known to Sophocles and his audience, since Colonus was a place of cult lying only a few miles outside Athens.

Once more, this is a consecrated place, and the presence of the divine is part of its significance. No mortal treads in it, but Dionysus ever walks there in company with the nymphs who nursed him; Aphrodite and the Muses favour the place. The narcissus grows there, because it is the coronal of the Great Goddesses, Demeter and Persephone; so too does the golden crocus, the colour of which we find elsewhere associated, like the goddesses themselves, with death.[54] But in this case religious is combined with patriotic sentiment. Oedipus will be buried here and become the object of a hero-cult; it is vital that his bones should lie in Attica, not in his native soil of Thebes, that they may give strength to the land. The chorus begin by telling Oedipus that Colonus is the fairest spot in their territory; they turn later to praising the olive for growing in Attica with a strength and spontaneity unknown in Asia or the Peloponnese; it nurtures children, and Athena watches over it.

How strong is the sentiment of place in this ode? The name of Colonus matters, both for its beauty and its cult. The unsleeping springs of Cephisus water it and do not diminish; Sophocles has seized upon something that distinguishes it from the other rivers of Attica, such as Ilissus, which often dries up completely. Colonus is called 'white' (*arges*), and the soil is said to be indeed light in colour. But beyond this he does not seem to have looked for features distinctive to this one spot. Grove, shade and running water are, as ever, the basis of the description. Sophocles adds other elements, nightingales, green glades, ivy, crocus, and narcissus, but some of these things are what one might hope to find in any pleasant place, and others seem to be put in mainly for their association with one or another god (the ivy was associated with Dionysus). He has not sought to observe even Cephisus at all closely: it may be true that it never fails, but one may doubt that it never decreases. By contrast, when Virgil looks at his local river, the Mincius, he not only notices its unusually regular flow but has seen the effect of this upon the current, the

---

[54] N. J. Richardson (ed.), *The Homeric Hymn to Demeter* (Oxford, 1974), notes on lines 6 and 19.

shape of the stream and the vegetation on the banks.[55] Nor has Sophocles conceived that fusion of religious and patriotic sentiment with perception of the natural scene which Virgil will achieve. He has described a beautiful place and he has described a place of national cult, but the two things do not really come together. Despite the divine presences, the chorus's pride in the beauty of Colonus seems largely secular in quality; but we are still far from Virgil's binding of the abstract to the concrete, his realization that a person may feel history, identity, the divine through a lively perception of the outward and visible scene.

Thus far we have been surveying descriptions of landscape, and pursuing this theme, we shall next pick up the thread in the third century. But there is one more figure in the fifth century who should not be left out of the story. In Aeschylus' case we are not concerned with the direct depiction of landscape but with an original vision of nature and man's relation to it, including kinds of perception which Virgil will rediscover, travelling by a quite different route. Here we are dealing not, it would appear, with the influence of one poet on a successor but with the discovery by one genius of a mode of thought and feeling that will be separately explored by another much later.

The *Eumenides*, the last play of the *Oresteia* trilogy, begins with the priestess of Delphi gazing back into an immensely ancient, chthonic, female past. First was primeval Earth (called by Aeschylus both Gaia and Chthon); her daughter was Themis, 'Right'. Another child of Earth was the Titan Phoebe, who was to be mother of Apollo.[56] So behind the Olympians lie earlier generations of obscure nature deities. Not until Virgil will poetry again express such a sense of the dark immensity of the past, plunging down through the generations as through geological strata; the depth and blackness from which the Furies are awakened is imagistically linked to their immeasurable antiquity. Aeschylus' conception also unifies nature and culture (to borrow the anthropologists' terms): Themis, the binding power of morality, is born of Earth herself.[57]

---

[55] *Geo.* 3. 13–15.   [56] *Eum.* 1–8.

[57] There seems to be a similar concept in *Prometheus Bound* (though we must now suppose the author not to be Aeschylus). Prometheus' character as a nature deity is stressed: his first words and his last are an appeal to the elements, earth, air, fire, and water (88–91, 1091–3); he is one of the Titans, children of Ouranos and Gaia, Sky and Earth (205). But he is also built up as a culture hero, with a role going far beyond his traditional function as the one who brought fire to men: he taught them astronomy, mathematics, writing, horsemanship, sailing, and shipbuilding (454–72). His mother too unites nature and culture,

After the earlier plays of the trilogy, the public drama of *Agamemnon* and the domestic drama of *Choephoroe*, the *Eumenides* surprises by turning to vast cosmic issues: much of the action concerns the relation between the Olympian gods and older deities, most of the characters are divine, and no mortals appear in the last quarter of the play at all except as onlookers. Yet at the same time it refers to the modern issues buzzing in the Athenian politics of the poet's own day with an openness that has no parallel in surviving Greek tragedy.[58] It is a cardinal error to play down these allusions: the *Eumenides* is very deliberate in combining cosmic immensity with a uniquely tight particularity. Meanwhile, the Furies too combine what might appear extremely divergent functions. As the play draws to its end their character as nature deities is newly stressed; having threatened to blight and poison the land, they now become fertility goddesses, whose life beneath the soil will bring increase. At the same time, they evolve into culture goddesses also, whose subterranean presence will undergird the Areopagus, their ancient role as the avengers of homicide transmuted into that of guarantors of a human and civilized institution, the law court. In Athena's words, they will honour both the earth and the city, and they will become lovers of the land, a phrase of extraordinary boldness and passion, pallid in English translation.[59]

Out of these elements comes a vision of totality, of a unity to which the largest and the smallest things alike belong. The temporary and immediate concerns of one city's politics exist in a continuum which extends outwards to the fundamental order of the

for she is one shape having many names, and is both Chthon and Themis (209 f.). The action of *Prometheus Bound* concerns a cosmic dislocation, a quarrel between different kinds of deities, which was presumably resolved in the sequel into a new harmony. There is a likeness to the action of the *Eumenides*, where both a divine quarrel is healed and a fusion of nature and culture achieved.

[58] The most explicit allusions are to Athens' alliance with Argos (287 ff., 762 ff.), opposed by those who leaned towards Sparta, and more broadly to the function of the Areopagus, especially the issue of whether it should be limited to acting as a homicide court (681 ff.). The sense of modern immediacy is enhanced by Aeschylus' extraordinary dramaturgy, which comes close to dissolving the boundaries between actors and audience. Uniquely in Greek tragedy Athens in this play does not have a king, and when she calls, 'People of Attica' (681), the spectators in the Theatre of Dionysus may have the sense that they too are being addressed. At the end of the drama the Furies prepare to descend beneath the rock of the Acropolis, under the very ground where the audience is now sitting, and the torch-lit procession which escorts them is not only the last action of the trilogy but can be felt as a part of Athens' own festival celebrations.

[59] *Eum.* 993 f., 851 f. (*ges tesd' erasthessesthe*, a metaphor drawn from sexual love).

universe itself. Within this wholeness nature and culture, earth and state are parts of a universal harmony, disrupted at the beginning of the *Eumenides* but now restored and enlarged. This sense of the land— of city and soil—is to be apprehended with a strength that can be likened to sexual love, and to be seen, besides, in relation to historical process, to the immense operations of time.[60] This rich, complex, and original vision—not well represented in bald summary—was to be without sequel; it grows from Aeschylus' uniquely powerful imagination. For a comparable fusion of nature, state and history we shall have wait for the very different mind of Virgil, more than four centuries later.

The *Argonautica* of Apollonius of Rhodes is the longest poem to survive from the great age of Hellenistic verse—an epic, but one which seeks to adapt a traditional form to a modern sensibility. Its central theme is not war but love—the story of Jason and Medea—and within the love narrative, the woman is the more closely studied than the man. Other signs of 'modernism' have been found or suspected in Apollonius: an attention to the poetry of Callimachus, and—in this the great period of Greek science and scholarship—an interest in applying medical terminology to mental states, in the geography of remote lands, and in the origins of cults and customs. Not surprisingly, he uses nature and landscape in a variety of ways, some new.

He has an eye for the curious or distinctive scene. One simile likens Lynceus, who thinks he has spotted Heracles a vast distance away, to a man who sees or thinks he sees the new moon through cloud; another compares the throb of Medea's anxious heart to a sunbeam darting about a wall, reflected from the water that has just been poured into a pail.[61] Each of these similes of his was to be annexed and adapted by Virgil.[62] He imagines a god's aerial view of the earth as he sweeps down from Olympus: cities and rivers, mountains and ocean. (Ovid was to treat the flight of Icarus rather similarly, but that would be more than two centuries later.)[63] He tells of a strange plant whose colour is like the Corycian crocus, but whose root in

---

[60] Time in the *Oresteia* is a large and complex theme, and one which awaits a full analysis. Late in *Eum.* we may note the phrase, applied to the Athenian people, *sophronountes en khronoi*, 'learning good sense through time' (1000). Against the *Oresteia*'s feeling for extent of time should be set the theme, important in the middle of *Agamemnon*, of *kairos*, the long-prepared, ripe or focal moment.   [61] Ap. Rh. 4. 1477–80; 3. 755–60.
[62] *Aen.* 8. 22–5; 6. 453 f.   [63] Ap. Rh. 3. 161–6; Ov. *Met.* 8. 220–2.

the earth is like newly cut flesh.[64] He can enjoy a scene of brilliant light and colour: as the Argo speeds over the sea, the heroes' arms shine in the sun like flame; their long wake is white, like a path across a green field.[65] In all of this he shows a keen feeling for the visible world; not so much for ordinary things, however, as for those things that are bright, decorative, remarkable or strange.

The *Odyssey* has one recurrent phrase for the coming of a new day—'As soon as early rosy-fingered dawn shone forth'—unforgettable, but more evocative than precise. Apollonius prefers to vary his phrases, and to pick out some aspect of the dawn's appearance. He observes how the early light first catches the hills, or how the paths stand out gleaming and the dewy plains shine in that slanting light; or he sets an incident precisely at the moment of half light between night and day.[66] In his use of the pathetic fallacy he moves a certain distance from the 'Greek' to the 'modern' attitude (to keep to Ruskin's terms). When it appears, it does not have the startling quality that the attribution of *pathos* to nature tends to have in early Greek poetry; but it still does not occur very often, and it usually seems marked and deliberate rather than instinctive. In a simile bees hum around lilies, 'and the dewy meadow rejoices'; dawn looses the night, and the shores and the dewy paths laugh.[67] Perhaps Apollonius' most effective use of the pathetic fallacy comes when he describes night putting to bed the works of men and soothing the whole earth to quiet; but to Medea in her distress sleep brought no rest.[68] Her isolation is the more complete, the more touched with poignancy, in that not only is the remainder of the expedition asleep, but nature herself enjoys a repose in which she cannot share. The development of the pathetic fallacy in the later European tradition leads eventually to a sense of the possible union between man and nature; but at the same time it leads also to the opposite feeling, a sense of nature's indifference to man's doings. That indifference is the more keenly apprehended if it is felt to be wilful, and not merely caused by the plain fact that land, sea and weather lack all power of sensation. Apollonius has begun to see how the pathetic fallacy can make a man seem the more utterly alone.

In the relations of gods to nature, the poem again shows Apollonius at a distance from early poetry and yet developing from that

---

[64] Ap. Rh. 3. 854–7.   [65] Ap. Rh. 1. 544–6.
[66] Ap. Rh. 2. 164; 1. 1280–2; 2. 669–71.
[67] Ap. Rh. 1. 879 ff.; 4. 1170–3.   [68] Ap. Rh. 4. 1058–61.

older tradition. The Great Mother rewards the pious sacrifices of the Argonauts by granting favourable signs: the trees drop quantities of fruit, and the earth puts forth flowers, among other marvels.[69] We recall the deception of Zeus in the *Iliad*; but what was there the very essence of deity has here become a purely decorative miracle. When the dread goddess Hecate arises from the underworld, amid the writhings of serpents and the howling of her hounds, the nymphs shriek 'and all the meadows trembled at her step'.[70] But this is not quite like the animation of nature at the epiphanies of Poseidon in the *Iliad* or Dionysus in the *Bacchae*; it is part of a predictable apparatus of horror, used vigorously but without much religious feeling. We have moved some way towards the sensationalism of Lucan. The act or presence of a divine being is necessary in both these cases, but the sense of the numinous has dwindled close to vanishing point.

It has perhaps vanished altogether in the scene that adorns the union of the two lovers: 'The nymphs gathered flowers of divers colours, which they brought to them held to their white bosoms, and a gleam as of fire surrounded them all, such was the light that shone from the golden tufts of wool.'[71] Hera, we shall learn, has sent these nymphs to do honour to Jason,[72] but we feel their divinity scarcely or not at all. Like their coloured flowers and white bosoms, their presence itself is part of a decor appropriate to Jason and Medea; appropriate because they are the protagonists of a heroic myth, not because they walk through a god-filled landscape. Virgil, as it happens, will never use the nymphs in so purely decorative a fashion. The uncanny nymphs who shriek at the union of Aeneas and Dido; the nymphs who dwell near the fiord where the Trojans make landfall in north Africa; even the nymphs who shall bear flowers to Corydon's beloved Alexis; all, in one way or another, modify the landscape or the atmosphere into which they enter.[73]

Apollonius has a nice understanding of where a decorative use of nature is apt. The love-god Eros is found tossing golden dice with Ganymede—two boys together—in a 'flourishing' or 'fruitful' orchard.[74] This setting is obviously a symbolic landscape, in the manner of Ibycus' garden of the Nymphs; at the same time, the expensive prettiness well conveys the spirit of divine frivolity, glittering, desirable, and irresponsible. When Medea falls in love with Jason,

[69] Ap. Rh. 1. 1142 f.   [70] Ap. Rh. 4. 218.
[71] Ap. Rh. 4. 1143–6.   [72] Ap. Rh. 4. 1151 f.
[73] *Aen.* 4. 168; 1. 168; *Ed.* 2. 46.   [74] Ap. Rh. 3. 144 ff., 158.

her heart warms within her, melting as the dew melts away around roses when it is warmed by the light of morning.[75] The refinement and prettiness of this simile, delicate almost to excess, are just right for the context in which Apollonius has put it. We should consider the seduction of Hylas in similar terms. It is night; the time when the nymphs who haunt the lovely headland ever sing their songs to Artemis. The water-nymph, rising from her fountain, sees the fair boy rosy with beauty and sweet graces, for the full moon sheds its beams upon him. Her spirit is faint within her, but then the water rings out as it splashes into the bronze pot that Hylas has brought for collecting it; at once she lays one arm upon his neck, longing to kiss his tender mouth, while with the other she draws him down into the eddying water.[76] The somewhat etiolated beauty of this scene is part of a landscape of affect, lovely, uncanny, slithery. The half light is both beautiful and sinister; the boy's rosiness blends with the pale moonlight upon his face; the nymph's faintness of spirit matches the dimness of the illumination. The sudden ring of water upon metal is a fine contrasting touch; a moment of clarity—of masculinity, one might almost say—before a languishing dimness overspreads the scene again and Hylas merges, literally, into the nymph-haunted landscape.

There has always been a temptation to see the history of Greece, whether cultural or political, in terms of a pattern of rise and fall, with the fifth and fourth centuries at the apex and the Hellenistic age as a period of decline. In that account the accomplished decadence of Apollonius' Hylas scene may seem a kind of poetry appropriate to its time. But history is never so simple in its patterns; and the old idea of an almost symmetrical rise and fall conceals the fact that the Hellenistic age was when Greece spread its power, culture, and influence most widely; this was also its greatest period of science and scholarship. The third century is a time of invention and vitality, and part of Apollonius' concern with landscape is caught up with this new and enquiring spirit. On their return from Colchis he sends the Argonauts on an immense voyage, not, like Odysseus' through fairyland, but through distant parts of the known and half-known world, up into great lakes in the heart of central western Europe, down to the coasts of Africa, and so forth. This is a poetry which belongs to an age of geographical enquiry. The scientific spirit,

---

[75] Ap. Rh. 3. 1019–21.   [76] Ap. Rh. 1. 1222–39.

curious both to map and explain the physical geography of countries, lies also behind Apollonius' digression on the River Thermodon:[77]

There is no river like it, and none divides itself into so many streams as it advances across the land. If a man were to count them all, he would fall four short of a hundred, but the true source is only one. It descends to the plain from high mountains, which they say are called Amazonian. From there it scatters through the hillier land that faces it, and so the channels are winding. Each one twists on its own course, wherever it may best find low ground, some going far from the main channel, others keeping close; many streams drain away into the earth and have no name, but the river itself, mingling with a few branches, in full view discharges itself into the inhospitable Pontus below a curving headland.

A passage such as this shows how a scientific or scholarly interest in the world naturally encourages or reinforces a concern with the particularity of landscape; for it is the unique character of the Thermodon which makes it worth describing. At one point Apollonius gives a long account of a landscape simply, it would seem, for its own sake:[78]

The wind dropped during the darkness, and at dawn they gladly reached the harbour of the Acherusian headland. It rises up with steep cliffs, overlooking the Bithynian sea; the rocks beneath it are set firm, smooth and beaten by the sea; around them the rolling waves thunder loudly, while above spreading plane-trees grow on the summit. Down from it a hollow glen slopes away towards the interior, and here there is a cave of Hades, overarched by trees and rocks, from which an icy vapour, continually breathing forth from the chilly depth, ever forms a glistening white rime, which melts in the midday sun. Silence never holds this dread headland, but there is heard the groaning of the sounding sea and the leaves rustling in the draught from the cavern.

This is a picture in words; not primarily the evocation of a mood or atmosphere nor the selection of one or two significant features, but an account of a complex landscape full enough to have the air of completeness. The sounds as well as the sights of the place are included, and all these details work towards the creation of a distinctive, individual landscape. The scene is of course imaginary, but in principle one could go along a shoreline confident that one would recognize the place when one came to it, simply by reference to the poet's account. Truth to tell, it is not entirely satisfactory: it sprawls,

[77] Ap. Rh. 2. 972–84.   [78] Ap. Rh. 2. 727–45.

it is too little selective, too much the 'photograph'. Nor is it well
fitted into the poem: there is not sufficient reason why this landfall, rather than another, should be singled out for such treatment.
But the imperfection of the passage makes it the more revealing: the
landscape enters not because it is required by plot or tone, but because,
for Apollonius, such a description has an interest of its own. To us
the passage is also interesting for comparison and contrast with Virgil.
The Trojans' first landfall in the *Aeneid* will be the occasion for a
masterpiece of poetic landscape.[79] Virgil's appreciation of landscape
will be no less than Apollonius', but he will be much briefer and
less detailed, and he will see small need to itemize the separate elements of the scene, one after the other. And superb though the passage will be in itself, it will also be perfectly fitted to its place in
the poem. The kind of secularized interest in landscape for its own
sake shown in Apollonius' passage prepares the way for Virgil, but
the later poet will realize that detail and quantity of information in
themselves do not take one far. He will take us beyond landscape
as picture to landscape—still no less vivid to the mind's eye of a
sympathetic reader—as mood, atmosphere, emotion.

Apollonius himself, though not capable of Virgil's degree of evocative compression, knew how to link a landscape to the emotions
of those beholding it. His description of Syrtis is a remarkable picture
of desolation: the shoals and the seaweed and the light foam washing
across them; the dim expanse of sand, the absence of every beast
and bird; the mist and an immensity of land like mist, stretching
unbroken into the distance; no trace of human presence, but everything held—phrase of sinister gentleness—in an 'easy calm'.[80] The
passage is unusual in several ways. Most of the landscapes of ancient
literature, even in those writers most concerned to observe the natural scene, fall into a few, basically conventional patterns, representing
the beautiful, the grand or the terrible. Among the Augustan poets,
only Horace is interested in the atmosphere of such less obvious places
as the everyday urban scene or the marshlands south of Rome, and
he does not so much describe appearance as evoke character.[81] But
Apollonius has escaped from the conventional path. Through a sometimes bold use of language he has created a picture of dimness and
flatness; and it is essentially a real landscape, in the sense that it is a

    [79] *Aen.* I. 159–68.   [80] Ap. Rh. 4. 1237–49.
    [81] Hor. *Serm.* I. 6. III ff., *Epist.* I. 7. 49 ff., *Serm.* I. 5. 14 ff.

kind of scenery that does exist in the world, whether or not there is a place exactly like it on the African coast. (Only in the absence of living creatures does Apollonius improve upon reality for the sake of conventional emotional effect; for surely such a spot would be haunted by gulls and waders.) Yet at the same time this real landscape, vividly imagined in itself, holds up a mirror to the minds of the Argonauts: it is also a landscape of affect. It fills them with despair. Would that they had perished between the clashing rocks, one says;[82] anything seems better than this limitless emptiness. And we feel such a response to be natural: this is indeed the appropriate landscape of despair, more sinister than some more obviously terrible scene.

In a quite simple sense, the landscape matters more in the bucolics of Theocritus than it has in poetry hitherto. His herdsmen live and sing in the midst of nature, and they make their living from the land. It has been observed that far more plants and trees are named in the Idylls than in the whole of Homer, and that Theocritus displays an accurate knowledge of their character and habitat.[83] This alone suggests an enlarged interest in the natural scene.

The first Idyll begins at once with the landscape:[84]

Thyrsis: Sweet is the whispered music of that pine-tree by the springs, and sweetly do you too pipe; you will take the second prize to Pan . . .
Goatherd: Sweeter, shepherd, is your song than that water that pours down plashing from the rock . . .
Thyrsis: By the nymphs, goatherd, would you like to sit down here and pipe, where there is this sloping hillock, and the tamarisks? I will tend the goats meanwhile.
Goatherd: . . . Come let us sit under the elm, opposite Priapus and the springs, where that shepherds' seat and the oaks are.

It is significant that the setting is developed in four short, separate passages, interspersed with snatches of conversation, not quoted here, about sheep, goats, and singing, which set the 'plot', such as it is, in motion. The story is enmeshed in the landscape, which is in turn part of the story, for figures-in-a-landscape are the poet's theme. Compared, say, to Apollonius' Syrtis this may seem rather a conventional piece of scenery, 'idyllic' in the later sense of the word;

---

[82] Ap. Rh. 4. 1253 f.
[83] A. Lindsell, 'Was Theocritus a Botanist?', *GR* 6 (1937), 78–93.
[84] Theoc. I. 1–3, 7 f., 12–14, 21–3.

and to be sure, Theocritus limits his interest to the more charming aspects of landscape, but the Sicilian scene is indeed beautiful, the picture he creates is perfectly credible, and it is set out with an economy of which Apollonius seldom seems capable. In a modest degree even so 'conventional' a pretty spot as this has its individuality; from a few words we have quite a full picture of spring and waterfall, rocks and pine tree, with a foreground made from a clump of tamarisks beside a comfortable slope. At the same time the scene is full of sound (enhanced by delicate onomatopoeia and the extreme melodiousness of the verse): the soughing of the pine, the babble of the water, and, again and again, the melody of the pipe, so that in sound as well as setting, man and nature blend in harmony. All Theocritus has done, from one point of view, is to list a few elements of his imagined scene, but the effect is quite different from that of the far fuller description in Apollonius' second book. Both poets share a type of interest in landscape for its own sake which seems to be comparatively new in Greek sensibility, but whereas Apollonius merely attaches one item to the next without cumulative effect, Theocritus makes the various aspects of his scene mutually reinforcing: he chooses particularly those objects which suggest sight and sound at the same time—the stream, the pine—and lets everything work towards a single mood of comfort, relaxation and cool amid the heat. He manages to feel both for nature itself and for man within nature, and neither thing seems to detract from the other.

By far the finest of his natural descriptions comes at the end of the seventh Idyll:[85]

He bent his way to the left and took the road to Pyxa, while I and Eucritus and fair Amyntas turned to Phrasidamus' farm and lay down delighted on deep couches of sweet rush and newly cut vineleaves. Many poplars and elms rustled above our heads, and nearby the sacred water from the cave of the Nymphs fell babbling down (*kateibomenon kelaruze*). On shady boughs dusky cicadas toiled away with their chattering, and at a distance the tree-frog croaked in the thick, thorny brambles (*ha d'ololugon telothen en pukinaisi baton truzesken akanthais*). Larks and finches were singing, the dove moaned (*estene trugon*), bees flew buzzing around the springs. Everything smelt of the full fatness of summer, smelt of the fruit time (*pant'osden thereos mala pionos, osde d'oporas*). Pears at our feet, apples at our sides rolled abundantly, and branches hung to the ground weighed down with sloes. The four-year-old seal was released from the necks of the wine-jars.

[85] Theoc. 7. 130–57.

Nymphs of Castalia, who dwell on the heights of Parnassus, was it such a bowl that old Chiron set before Heracles in Pholus' rocky cave? Was it such a nectar that persuaded the herdsman by the Anapus, mighty Polyphemus who used to pelt ships with mountains, to dance among the sheepfolds?—such a drink, Nymphs, as you then mixed for us to drink by the altar of Demeter of the Threshing-Floor. On her heap may I again plant the big winnowing-fan, and may she smile, holding sheaves and poppies in her two hands.

Here particularity of mood and particularity of time and place are carried further than ever before. The lines describe a real place (or what purports to be a real place) on the indubitably real island of Cos; its name and location are carefully specified: the farm of Phrasidamus, a little to the right off the road to Pyxa. Further, Theocritus depicts a particular time of day and a particular season of the year. It is the hottest part of the day: we could infer that from the character of the description itself, but in fact we have been told as much earlier in the poem.[86] Simichidas, the narrator, and his friends are on the way to the festival of Thalysia, or harvest home, and equally, the description explores this precise season of the year. *pant'osden thereos mala pionos, osde d'oporas*—the repetition, the pressing forward from the more general word *theros*, summer, to the more limited *opora*, late summer, the season for gathering the fruits, shows the poet searching for exactness. And indeed the whole description explores this time of day and year. As in Sappho's poem, the figures in the landscape drift towards slumber; that does not mean that Theocritus is unobservant, but that he understands sleepiness to be, as much as alertness, a state of mind and body which may be fully studied.

The description is full of the sights and sounds and even the scents of high summer. Through these different senses and elements Theocritus accumulates a feeling of heaviness and sappiness: the heavy fragrance of reeds, the juiciness of newly cut vine leaves, fruits so abundant that they may seem, in a momentary extravagance of expression, to be rolling at our feet; and the whole summed up in the line just quoted, where the three long *o*'s superbly convey the slow rich ooziness of late summer. *osden . . . osde*—in that repetition we can feel the fragrant fatness of the year being gradually squeezed out. The long *o*'s pick up earlier long *o*'s which, together with long *u*'s,

---

[86] Theoc. 7. 21 f.

characterize some of the sounds of the place: the noise of the tree frog (*ololugon . . . truzesken*), the coo of the dove (*estene trugon*).[87] The sounds are complemented by the sense: words suggestive of weariness, transferred from man to nature and thus sinking humanity into the landscape, enhance the heavy, sleepy atmosphere. The cicadas toil, the dove moans, the branches are weighed down by the mass of the fruits upon them. Other sounds, however, are soothing: the soughing of the trees, the trickling water (*kateibomenon kelaruze*— a delectably onomatopoeic phrase borrowed from Homer),[88] the song of lark and finch; Simichidas does not tell us that the bees he mentions are humming, but surely he has no need to: we add that detail for ourselves. As with Sappho, wine is drunk, and no ordinary wine, but a drink of special quality; as with Sappho, there is deity in the place; but the balance of importance between these things has changed. In the archaic poem the presence of Aphrodite is all-important; she comes first, and then the nectar is poured. In the Idyll, the wine is significant, first and foremost, in a naturalistic way; it completes the hot, wearying atmosphere, the sprawl of the companions upon their leaves and rushes—one need only drink wine through a Mediterranean afternoon to appreciate that much. Yet though the experience described in this passage has been largely secularized, it has not been entirely so; the Nymphs and their cave and the 'sacred water' do make a difference. That *nektar* which they mix for the travellers (and it is interesting that Theocritus has Sappho's word)—is it just a fantasy brought on by warmth and liquor, or does it indicate some kind of supernatural presence? Perhaps the question is not precisely answerable (after all, it is an imprecise state of consciousness that is being evoked); but to complain that the Nymphs are irrelevant or ornamental is to miss the point. We have not understood Theocritus until we see that this passage, for all its sympathetic naturalism, still describes a special kind of experience; it is not quite—though it is nearly—something that might be accessible to anyone on any summer day.

In a straightforward sense, the passage is particularized in that it contains a large number of particulars: several kinds of trees, a various collection of fauna, a cave, and a spring. But quantity of detail does not in itself make for quality of descriptive force. These

---

[87] The meaning of *ololugon* is not certain: it is probably a tree frog, but may be a kind of dove (see Gow's exhaustive note ad loc.). [88] *Il.* 21. 261.

lines tell because the details accumulate, so that the total impression makes an effect that could not have been achieved by just one or two of the items individually. Though much is explicit, much too is implied; there are things that the reader will hardly fail to add for himself. When the babbling stream is mentioned, our sense of the day's heat is enhanced; for that is why the mention is so attractive. The combination of soothing and laborious sounds suggests sleepiness; nothing need be stated. The noises of all those birds and insects remind us that the bees must be humming as they flit about the waters; the poet need not spell it out. It would indeed be impossible to map the local topography, as we are almost invited to do with the set piece in Apollonius' second book, but that goes to show Theocritus' wisdom. As Jane Austen shrewdly observed, readers are distracted by 'too many particulars of right hand and left'.[89] Though we talk in dead or half-dead metaphors of 'scenes', 'depictions' and 'pictures' when we talk about literature, it is a great mistake to suppose that literary description should try to mimic the possibilities of pictorial art. When we look at a painting, we know immediately what is the relation of the hill to the stream, of the stream to the cottage, and so on; we can multiply these facts indefinitely—such is the nature of eyesight. Poetry does not work like that; and the reader may choose to respond by imagining the niceties of topography for himself, if indeed he supposes them to be in the least serviceable. It is in reality an enhanced feeling for nature that enables Theocritus to do without such mechanical details. And that feeling is both for nature itself and for the mood of the people within it; the two things work together. Much of his description is literal, but it is wrong to regard the other parts of it as unreal or 'literary', or as a 'poetic fantasy' showing an unconcern with nature as it actually is. The touches of the pathetic fallacy, explicit or implied—that weariness which seems to exude from plants and creatures—increase the vividness with which the scene is imagined; it is the poet's strength of feeling for his scene, not weakness of feeling, which requires the attribution of emotion to nature in order to do itself full justice. Equally, it is prosaic to object that it is unreal for apples and pears to be rolling at the companions' feet; for what words could better express the sense of sprawl, or superabundance and—can it be?—a hint of the supernatural as well. This is not a flight from fact, but

[89] Letter of 9 Sep. 1814.

a concentration upon the fact, for the fact itself cannot be fully appreciated without going beyond the merely literal.[90]

Theocritus can be seen within the broad sweep of a developing tradition: the likeness and unlikeness to Sappho's orchard are revealing. But at the same time the brilliance of the seventh Idyll is a personal achievement; we should not expect to find such quality in the *petits maîtres* of the Hellenistic age. And indeed the poetry that survives from the next centuries does suggest the limitations of the newer sensibility in the absence of a poetic talent of the highest order.

Moschus' *Europa*, written at about the middle of the second century, is characteristic of later Greek poetry in the amount of space it gives to natural description, but such description, by intention, is now floridly decorative. The archaic charm of Nausicaa and her maidens has now been elaborated into a glossy prettiness:[91]

With these words she jumped up and sought her dear companions, who were the very same age as herself, her heart's delight and of noble family, with whom she always played, when there were preparations for dancing or they were to wash their bodies in the streams of river water or gather scented lilies from the meadow. They were quickly in her sight, each had in her hand a basket for flowers, and they went to the meadows by the shore, where they always used to collect together, delighting in the growing roses and the sound of the waves.

This passage is followed by more than two dozen lines describing the golden basket which Europa carries. Next comes a flower catalogue: the damsels reach the blossomy meadows and gather narcissus, hyacinth, violet, all the blooms of the springtime (in fact Moschus mixes some flowers that grow at different seasons, little caring for nature as it is).[92] Europa alone plucks the rose, and for a symbolic reason:[93]

---

[90] G. Williams, in his important and influential *Tradition and Originality in Roman Poetry* (Oxford, 1968), sets up this passage of Theocritus as an example, in contrast to some Latin poetry, of ornamental effect being preferred to precise and accurate observation (647–9). The above paragraph is meant partly as an answer to this unsympathetic account. One detail: Williams objects (648), 'The epithet *skiarais* ["shadowy"] is inaccurate of boughs on which cicadas chatter.' Is it? The interior parts of a bough lie generally in shadow, and one may stare long and hard at a tree which is almost deafening with the noise of cicadas without being able to determine where they are. By setting the 'dusky' insect amid the 'shadowy' branches, Theocritus conveys the way in which the cicada conceals itself. Meanwhile the *ololugon* makes its own noise at a distance. The way in which the sounds come out of the landscape, from a source not clearly seen, is both imaginative and realistic.

[91] *Europa* 28–36.   [92] *Europa* 63–71.   [93] *Europa* 72–6.

But she was not long to delight her heart with the flowers, nor indeed to keep her maiden girdle undefiled, for as soon as the son of Cronos noticed her, he was disturbed in heart, subdued by the unexpected shafts of Aphrodite, who alone can subdue even Zeus . . .

—and so on. But even the obvious symbolism—of virginity and defloration—is merely ornamental and upon the surface. Realism is cast to the winds: the other maidens have no cause to refrain from picking the roses; it is as though they knew in advance that Zeus was about to pounce. When the god, now in the form of a bull, swims across the sea, we recognize a motif that goes back ultimately to Poseidon in the *Iliad*:[94]

The sea grew calm at Zeus' coming and the sea-beasts sported before his feet, and joyfully the dolphin came up from the deep and tumbled above the swell; the Nereids rose out of the brine and formed a row, all riding on the backs of sea-beasts. The deep-roaring sea-god, the Earthshaker himself, made straight the waves and guided the way over the brine for his brother; the Tritons gathered about him, those deep-sounding bassoonists of the ocean, proclaiming the marriage song with their long conches.

But in the context it is clear that the archaic idea of the god inspiring or vivifying nature has been quite lost: Zeus has shed his awesomeness and become part of a harmless rococo display.

Such a spirit only becomes possible once the old feeling that the natural world is full, actually or potentially, of divine presences, has begun to fade. But it also serves to show, yet again, that the development of Greek nature poetry from the Homeric fountainhead was not a linear movement in one clear direction. Nature, in the *Europa*, is not, as in Theocritus' seventh Idyll, something to be explored, but a counter in a fantastical game. Lucretius and Virgil would not be able to carry further the investigation of nature simply by latching on to a plainly visible Hellenistic tradition: they would have to search within Greek poetry and select if they were to find what was germane to their purposes.

One last piece of later Hellenistic poetry needs a brief mention: the anonymous *Epitaphium Bionis*, or *Lament for Bion*, composed around 100 BC, a work which drew Virgil's attention. Here is elaborated the idea that nature sympathizes with the dead man. For example:[95]

---

[94] *Europa* 115–24.   [95] *Ep. Bion.* 81–5.

At your death the trees have shed their fruit and the flowers are all withered. The goodly milk has not flowed from the flocks nor honey from the hives, but it has died in the comb through grief; for it is no longer to be gathered now that your honey is dead.

This motif, which reappears in Virgil's *Eclogues*, is commonly labelled 'pathetic fallacy', but the term is really a misnomer here, for the poet's idea is almost the opposite of what Ruskin wanted to describe. This is blatantly a literary fantasy: far from the poet being swept along by a current of instinctive feeling, the idea derives its effect precisely from our sure knowledge that in reality nature does not behave in this way. It is significant that his model is Thyrsis' song from Theocritus' first Idyll, in which wolves, lions, and cattle lament the death of Daphnis (though he goes considerably further, making even insensate nature wither in sympathy with a human death): here Theocritus does not speak in his own person, but Thyrsis takes us away from reality into a world of poetic imagination, mysterious, fantastical, unreal. The sober truth about nature's relation to mankind emerges later in the *Epitaphium Bionis*:[96]

Alas, the mallows, when they perish in the garden, and the green parsley and the flourishing crinkly dill live again after and grow another year; but we clever men, so big and strong, as soon as we die, unhearing in the hollow earth slumber through a very long, unending, unwaking sleep.

Here the contrast is made explicitly, for perhaps the first time in European poetry, between the finality of human mortality and inanimate nature's endless power of renewal. It is the opposite of the fantasy indulged earlier in the poem, that flowers and trees might wither at the withering of a human life. Little is made of this idea again in ancient poetry, but many centuries later it was to haunt the romantic sensibility, appearing in such diverse works as Matthew Arnold's *Thyrsis*, in which the classical pastoral tradition is consciously evoked, and Mahler's *Song of the Earth*, where man's perishing is contrasted with the eternal burgeoning of the springtime and the heavens, blue eternally.[97]

---

[96] *Ep. Bion.* 99–104.

[97] Curiously, this modest poem is also the forerunner of another tradition, distinctively English, which establishes itself a millennium and a half later: the pastoral lament for a dead poet. It begins with Spenser's *Astrophel*, and continues with Milton's *Lycidas*, Shelley's *Adonais* and Arnold's *Thyrsis*. Without the *Epitaphium Bionis* this noble sequence might not have begun.

The development of Greek poetry across the centuries suggests a growing secularization in the attitude towards nature. But it is of the first importance for Latin poetry that this secularizing process was never quite completed: Lucretius and Virgil will find ways of using the vestiges of religious feeling in the appreciation of landscape as a means of creating new effects of jubilation, engagement, poignancy, or charm. In simplified terms, one might find in the changing depiction of nature two main tendencies: a growing interest in nature for its own sake; and a consciously artificial treatment of nature, symbolic or mannerist or ornamental. Virgil was to treat nature in both these very different ways, the latter in the *Eclogues*, the former in all three of his works.

In the third century the current of literary interest in exploring nature begins to join the current of scholarly or scientific enquiry. That tendency can be detected at moments in Apollonius of Rhodes; perhaps also in the *Phaenomena*, Aratus' didactic poem on astronomy and weather signs. In a way this work shows the divorce of poetry from science: whereas in the fifth century philosophers such as Parmenides and Empedocles might genuinely pursue cosmological enquiry through the medium of verse, in the third the didactic purpose has become a pretence, and the claim to inform and instruct a literary game. But Aratus and the works of the other didactic poets (or 'metaphrasts')—for example, Nicander's *Georgica*, *Theriaca*, and *Alexipharmaca*—do suggest that the imaginations of literary men were being stirred by the business of examining and committing to record all that could be discovered about the world. It is a mistake to separate too far the 'bookishness' which some people complain of finding in the Hellenistic world from their energy and invention in such fields as medicine, astronomy, hydraulics, and mathematics. The desire to list the origins of cults, unearth obscure myths, or describe the oddities of distant lands and peoples is part of a great impulse of curiosity to learn all that can be known, an impulse which finds another outlet in attempts to measure the diameter of the earth or explain the movements of the heavens. Consider the metaphrasts again: some write of medicines, some of astronomy, some record the foundations of cities, gather myths about birds, or list stories of metamorphosis. Together their works suggest how all these various activities form part of a collective spirit. Virgil will draw upon literary sources and scientific treatises alike—both Aratus and Theophrastus—to get matter for his *Georgics*; for him there are facts to be found in poetry, and stimulus in prose. That might be seen as recognizing, in effect, a kind of unity in the Hellenistic intellectual project.

No doubt the merit of Hellenistic research varied, and some of their scholarship may have been trivial or silly. The Hellenistic age exhibits both genius and pedantry, and though these two qualities may be incompatible, there are individuals at this time in whom near genius and near pedantry seem close allied. It may be that not many people looked hard, or looked in an original spirit; but there is no case for the allegation, sometimes made, that the period witnesses a decline in liveliness or accuracy of observation. It is true that classical authorities, throughout antiquity, make claims which could have been disproved by experiment, but instead of judging them by the measure of a scientific age, we should do better to be impressed that they achieved so much, attaining standards that were not to be matched again in the west for nearly two thousand years. Nor should the savants of antiquity be censured for declining powers of observation if they seem willing to believe improbabilities. Why should it be so foolish for Varro to believe that a shrew had nested in a hole in the flesh of a very fat pig? or the elder Pliny to suppose that lightning never strikes laurel-bushes and does not penetrate more than five feet into the ground?[98] We have many means of testing stories and hypotheses which the ancients did not have. Besides, even if we do find ourselves thinking that they trusted tall stories too easily, we should reflect that there is no great virtue in being incredulous rather than credulous. Told of the giraffe, Dr Johnson would not permit himself to be gulled by so obvious a fiction; and most Greeks or Romans, informed that there was a continent beneath their feet in which large animals hopped about carrying their young in pockets, would have seen through such nonsense at once. Today we have lost the sense of *terra incognita*; but the ancient world was full of amazing and inexplicable facts in a way that ours is not. Augustine was astonished by the magnet; he lists marvellous facts, beyond explanation, among them the behaviour of the grafted olive (he had of course read the second Georgic). It was, in fact, an advantage to Virgil that he could combine explanation of the natural world with a sense of wonder at a world so much of which could not be explained. His imagination could work upon the Hellenistic experience; a sense of

---

[98] These examples are cited by Williams (*Tradition and Originality*, 635) to support his case for a decline of observation in the Hellenistic period and after.

curiosity and a sense of the limits of knowledge could combine, enabling him, as we shall see, to present a world that was both ordinary and mysterious.

In any case, credulity about things that had not been seen or tested (insofar as it existed), is quite different from an inability to observe what lies before the eyes. We do not suppose Shakespeare unobservant because he may have believed in anthropophagi whose heads do grow beneath their shoulders. And turning to the Hellenistic poets, we do not find the best of them inferior to their predecessors in the power of observing nature; if anything, the reverse. It would be left to Lucretius to turn natural science into the material of great poetry, to Virgil to inspire the metaphrastic tradition with emotion and moral depth, but imaginatively as well as formally they owed something to the Hellenistic poets who went before them. As far as the evocation and interpretation of the natural world was concerned, we can say both that their originality was very great and that they were able to benefit from a broad current which was flowing their way.

Virgil's Haven

It is not down in any map; true places never are.
(Melville, *Moby-Dick*)

To go from Greek poetry, even Hellenistic poetry, to the *Aeneid* is to make a long leap. Two centuries and more separate Virgil from Theocritus and Apollonius; and as important as the distance in time is the extent of the imaginative adventure in between. By the coming of the Augustan age two works have transformed the place of nature in poetry: *De Rerum Natura* and the *Georgics*. None the less, it will be worth while to glance ahead now, and to set the first of Virgil's epic landscapes against the landscapes of Greek verse:[99]

> defessi Aeneadae quae proxima litora cursu
> contendunt petere, et Libyae vertuntur ad oras.
> est in secessu longo locus: insula portum
> efficit obiectu laterum, quibus omnis ab alto   160

---

[99] *Aen.* I. 157–73.

frangitur inque sinus scindit sese unda reductos.
hinc atque hinc vastae rupes geminique minantur
in caelum scopuli, quorum sub vertice late
aequora tuta silent; tum silvis scaena coruscis
desuper, horrentique atrum nemus imminet umbra.   165
fronte sub adversa scopulis pendentibus antrum;
intus aquae dulces vivoque sedilia saxo,
Nympharum domus. hic fessas non vincula navis
ulla tenent, unco non alligat ancora morsu.
huc septem Aeneas collectis navibus omni   170
ex numero subit, ac magno telluris amore
egressi optata potiuntur Troes harena
et sale tabentis artus in litore ponunt.

Aeneas' exhausted company strive to direct their course to the nearest shore, and turn towards the coast of Libya. There is a place set in a long inlet: an island makes a harbour with the barrier of its flanks, on which every wave coming from the deep breaks, dividing into the deep inlets. On this side and that vast crags and two cliff-faces loom upward toward the sky, while beneath their peaks a wide expanse of safe water lies silent; there is a backdrop of shimmering forest above, and the woodland looms with shuddering shade. Under the brow of the cliff face is a cave with hanging crags; within are sweet waters and seats of living rock, the home of the Nymphs. Here no ropes secure the tired ships, nor anchor fastens them with curved bite. Here Aeneas arrives with seven ships gathered from the full complement, and with great love for the land the disembarking Trojans possess the longed-for sands and lay their salt-caked limbs down on the shore.

In the *Aeneid* the landscape is more deeply embedded in the poem than it has ever been in narrative verse before. Among the poem's themes is man's need to fix himself, to be rooted, to be based solidly on some particular portion of the earth. Right at the beginning we learn that Aeneas is a man whose destiny was to endure many things until he should found a city, 'dum conderet urbem'.[100] 'Condo' means 'bury' as well as 'found'; the sense of fixity, of depth to the foundations is stronger than English translation can show. The city, a work of man—that is one aspect of man's desire for a firm basis upon the earth. But he is also drawn to the earth itself. The strength of his attachment to his native land—in an abstract sense certainly, but also physically—a feeling for the ground, the very soil—these are things which the poem will explore across its twelve books.

[100] *Aen.* 1. 5.

We first see Aeneas in mid-ocean, buffeted by a terrifying storm. He and his men are 'all at sea'; the English phrase is hackneyed, but its very triteness may suggest the deep, archetypal emotion to which Virgil appeals. Just how significant it is that in this of all poems the hero should be introduced lost and floating and without any bottom of stability is something that we shall only fully understand as the great design unfolds; but already the themes of land, history, nation start to appear. The hero's first words are filled with misery: would that he had perished at Troy, where Hector and great Sarpedon lie, where the river Simois has grasped so many valiant bodies and rolled them beneath its waters. Why could Diomedes, bravest of the Greek race, not have killed him? Thrice and four times blessed are those who died at Ilium.[101] Distress breeds exaggeration, and in part this extremity of despair represents Aeneas' confused and irrational state of mind; but beyond the immediate despondency we hear also a theme of longer duration. The dead heroes are blessed because they fell in the sight of the elders of the city.[102] 'ante ora patrum'— literally, 'before the faces of the fathers'—that last word reaches back towards the ancestry of the race. The dead are blessed also because they fell beneath the high walls of Troy, and because they lie in Trojan ground, 'Iliacis . . . campis' (on the fields of Ilium).[103] Parentage, city, soil—tossed on the fluid, shapeless element, with no dry land in sight, Aeneas instinctively directs his envy towards those who are grounded upon the history of their people and embedded in the earth on which they have lived. Simois conveys the same impression. As we have already seen, and shall see again, rivers for Virgil express essentially a man's sense of belonging to his home and territory. To be whelmed beneath the waves of Simois, like lying below the fields of Ilium, is to be taken to the bosom of one's native land.

Virgil is composing on a very large scale, and there are elements in Aeneas' first short speech that look right forward to the second half of the poem. His loss of Simois sets up a dissonance that will not be resolved until Tiberinus offers himself as a new national and ancestral river in the eighth book;[104] the allusion to Diomedes, while looking back to Aeneas' escape from death at his hands in the *Iliad*, also looks forward to a time when he will no longer seem so formidable but in chastened mood will be urging peace and reconciliation

[101] *Aen.* 1. 94–101.   [102] *Aen.* 1. 95.
[103] *Aen.* 1. 95, 97.   [104] *Aen.* 8. 36 ff.

with the Trojans.[105] But Aeneas cannot, any more than the reader, see so far at this stage; what the Trojans need now is dry land, any land. When they have come ashore, their leader recovers his spirits, encourages them and recalls the certainty of a future home in Latium; and here too the choice of words has a particular significance, both immediately and in the longer term:[106]

> per varios casus, per tot discrimina rerum
> tendimus in Latium, sedes ubi fata quietas
> ostendunt; illic fas regna resurgere Troiae.

Through diverse adventures, through so many moments of peril, we make for Latium, where destiny reveals to us an abode of peace; there it is appointed for Troy's realm to rise again.

'Sedes' is the exactly fitting word at this time, rather than 'domus' or 'patria'; the Trojans seek a place to rest, settle, abide.

For several reasons, therefore, the first landfall in the poem is an essential moment. We expect Aeneas' men to be full of gladness, and sure enough they possess the beach 'magno telluris amore'.[107] That is one of those simple Virgilian phrases that seem pregnant with a deeper significance. Its immediate sense is that the Trojans are over-joyed to be on dry land again, but behind this we hear once more that larger theme: a man's 'great love of the earth' is a fundamental part of his humanity, and goes beyond simple relief at escaping from a watery grave.[108] We might equally expect the description of the beautiful harbour to suggest welcome and security; that idea is indeed present but there seem also to be other notes of a different tone. How are we to understand them?

The bare bones of Virgil's description are derived from three passages of the *Odyssey*; describing the harbours of the Cyclopes, of the Laestrygonians, and of Phorcys in Ithaca.[109] Putting these passages together, we find in them the cliffs, the trees, the narrow entrance to the haven and the calm within, the spring, the cave and the presence of the nymphs—almost all the individual elements of Virgil's account, in fact, except for the island at the harbour's mouth, and that too may have been suggested to him by Homer, for at the land of the Cyclopes there is an isle offshore where Odysseus puts in before

---

[105] *Il.* 5. 297 ff.; *Aen.* 11. 252 ff.   [106] *Aen.* 1. 204–6.

[107] *Aen.* 1. 171.   [108] Compare *Aen.* 3. 509, discussed on p. 437.

[109] *Od.* 9. 136 ff., 10. 87 ff., 13. 96 ff. The passages are conveniently collected, together with translations, in Williams, *Tradition and Originality*, 638 ff.

venturing on to the mainland.[110] With so much being formally derivative, the more striking is the transformation of mood and spirit that Virgil effects.

Part of that transformation is the use of curious and original language in place of the simplicity in Homer's descriptions. By an odd mischance Virgil's two most dramatic phrases look deceptively like clichés of modern English usage (though indeed it is not pure chance: his imagination attracted imitators, and his innovations lost the force of their strangeness). So some care is needed to recover his meaning. Milton picked the phrase 'sylvan scene' out of this passage and used it in *Paradise Lost*;[111] from there it grew into a banality of eighteenth-century usage and 'scene' came to acquire the sense that it bears today. But when Virgil used the word 'scaena', he was taking a metaphor from the theatre (as Milton well understood): he means the painted backdrop behind a stage. The primary implications of the phrase, presumably, are the steepness of the hanging wood and perhaps the spectacular rocky wildness, like that depicted in the fantasy landscapes painted on the walls of Pompeii and Herculaneum. 'Scaena' makes the landscape fantastic, theatrical, immense.

Equally striking, in its context, is the expression 'vivo . . . saxo'. It seems to be Virgil's own invention; it appealed to Ovid, and we find it also in Tacitus.[112] In some of these later instances it appears to mean little or no more than 'living rock' in the conventional English sense, that is, unquarried rock, still fixed in its original position. But in at least one place Ovid suggests that rock is 'alive' in a stronger sense, likening it to organic nature: 'saxo quod adhuc vivum radice tenetur' (rock which is still held living by its root).[113] And surely Ovid is drawing upon what he has found in Virgil, for the phrase, on its first appearance in Latin literature, is distinctive enough to be taken strongly; and besides, it occurs in a passage steeped in the pathetic fallacy. Virgil has made the rock within the cave instinct in some mysterious way with life.

The use of the pathetic fallacy is another change that Virgil has wrought upon his Homeric models. The rocks tower towards the sky: 'minantur'. The word means 'loom' or 'project'; so Servius explains it, and we can compare a later phrase 'minaeque murorum ingentes' (the mighty looming of the walls).[114] Its root is picked up by 'imminent' three lines later, and that repetition has the effect, on one level, of pressing the word's strictly factual meaning upon our attention. But 'minor' also, and very commonly, means 'to threaten', and we shall catch this further implication, with its pathetic fallacy, looming, likes the rocks themselves, behind the word's literal signification. For the context almost compels it. The cliffs are 'vastae'—an adjective of size, but one from which connotations of desolation or emptiness are seldom altogether absent. Add to that the sound of the line, with its cold bare long vowels and its assonance of nasal consonants, those sounds with which Lucretius so often evoked the wonder of immensity—and the whole effect is icily awesome. The awe is felt again three lines later, and the pathetic fallacy along with it: 'horrenti'—the shadow shudders. 'Horror' is the emotion inspired by an awareness of the numinous, a sense of divine presence; and so Lucretius has written, likening the contemplation of Epicurus' philosophy to religious experience, 'his ibi me rebus quaedam divina voluptas | percipit atque horror' (at this a kind of divine pleasure and shudder grips me).[115] The reverberance of *m* and *n* returns; and while 'imminet' on one level reinforces the literal sense of 'minantur', it also, by keeping the word echoing in our consciousness, reminds us, especially amid the darkness and shuddering with which it is surrounded, of the more sombre overtone. In 'vivus' the pathetic fallacy is unconcealed, as is the weariness transferred from the men to their ships. The 'feeling' attributed to the ships casts its effect back on to the natural description: the fleet gratefully responds, as it were, to the sensations that seem present in the land. In such a context we shall surely sense the pathetic fallacy once more when we learn that the waters are silent (or 'keep silence'): like the silence of the forest in the *Bacchae* before Dionysus' irruption, this seems like the watchful silence of a living thing.

The scene is beautiful; the harbourage is genuinely safe; why then the undercurrent, however faint, of threat? To some the answer seems plain. The landscape, they say, symbolizes the situation of Aeneas and his people: Carthage and its queen are about to provide welcome, rest and security, but trouble lies ahead. Likewise the harbour provides repose and safety, but in the background the landscape shudders and quivers, portentous of future woe. Now possibly this is indeed part of the harbour's significance, and certainly it is important to see the passage in relation to the narrative around it, not just

---

[115] Lucr. 3. 28 f.

as a splendid set piece; but some doubt may be felt. In the first place, there is very little in the passage to suggest disagreeable emotion. 'Horror' is in itself a word that can suggest pleasing mysteries and enchantments: the strange trembling delight of religious contemplation, as in Lucretius, or the awesome wonder of Latinus' palace in the seventh Aeneid, 'horrendum silvis et religione parentum'.[116] Take away 'minantur', and it would be hard to argue for even a hint of unease. Now Virgil is a subtle and exact writer, and a single word can make a difference; the reader should indeed catch some kind of overtone here sounding above the literal sense; but equally we should not take it out of proportion. If there is any suggestion at all of misfortune coming, it is, as it should be, very light.

Besides, if the scene is in some degree symbolic of future events, the symbolism is of a rather muddy kind. It would be apt if Dido were, like Circe, a deceitful woman whose words of welcome disguised a darker purpose, or if the splendours of the young city were the mask of luxury and corruption.[117] But these things are not so: Dido's welcome is sincere, Carthage is authentically fine and dignified. And the essential goodness of the city and its queen is vital to Virgil's scheme; and much of the bleakness of Aeneas' position, much of Dido's tragedy resides in the fact that there seems to be no evident reason why he should not settle contentedly in Carthage and found the new nation there beyond the stark datum that inexplicable providence wills otherwise. In a straightforward sense there is nothing to threaten the Trojans in Africa. Using the word in a transferred sense perhaps more characteristic of English than Latin idiom, we might say that there will be a threat to the determinations of the divine will or to the outcome which Italian patriotism desires; but it is not obvious that such ideas are well represented by the mysterious emotions breathed out of this romantic foreign landscape. If the scene is at all prophetic of what is to come, it would be better to say merely that the scene is tremulous with expectancy or obscure foreboding, and to seek no more precise omen of the future.

---

[116] *Aen.* 7. 172 (shuddersome with woods and the awe of the ancestors).

[117] A gloomy puritanism grumbles misguidedly about the splendour of Dido's palace. Aeneas is also censured for his fine clothes and jewelled scabbard (at 4. 261 f.). That is to miss the point. Aeneas is not idle in this passage but at work directing the building of the city. He is all that a prince should be, splendid, active, happy. The poignancy lies in our being shown this good glory at the moment when Mercury's message is about to shatter it. The nobility of Carthage is felt especially at 1. 421 ff., where it is implicitly likened to Rome (see below, p. 547).

At all events, symbolism or prophecy is not Virgil's sole or central purpose here; and indeed it is a part of his skill that a passage so shaped to its context is also so effective in itself as an evocation of landscape. We have seen that the shuddering shade, the hushed waters, the animate rock press towards a sense of the numinous; that pressure reaches its goal at the very end of the description, with the appearance of the Nymphs. This again both continues and transforms the Homeric idea. For the poets of early Greece, the Nymphs were perhaps almost as much part of the furniture of the natural world as trees, rocks, or waters, and certainly within the fictional universe of the *Odyssey* the Nymphs simply exist: Homer may record their presence in a landscape without especial excitement or surprise. Odysseus describes himself drawing near to a cave where the Nymphs held their fair dances and meetings.[118] That is all: he merely states the fact and moves on. Homer lingers longer over the Nymphs when describing the harbour of Phorcys:[119]

Nearby is a cave, beauteous and dimly lit, sacred to the nymphs who are called Naiads. Within are bowls and jars of stone, and the bees store up honey there. Long looms of stone are within, where the nymphs weave robes of sea-purple, a wonder to behold, and there are waters that never fail. The cave has two entrances, one to the north by which men may descend, while that to the south is for the gods: men do not enter by it, but it is the way for the immortals.

But here too the description is solidly factual. The Nymphs are present in their cave not mysteriously but palpably: they have ways in and out, bowls and jars and fabrics to weave; they seem as down-to-earth as Nausicaa directing the household laundry. And therein lies the charm. If there is a sense of the numinous in this, it is not the numinous as we or Virgil might understand it, something strange, special and apart; rather, the whole of the world is, as a matter of course, filled with gods. Nor is this like the *Georgics'* self-conscious discovery of wonder and even sanctity in the ordinary, everyday world. That poem, like Lucretius before it, seeks to transfigure common things; it presents a discovery for those who have eyes to see. In the *Odyssey* the divine simply *is* present in the ordinary world; saying that has no revelatory force, it is something to be taken for granted and told without emphasis or animation.

---

[118] *Od.* 12. 318.   [119] *Od.* 13. 103–12.

Now plainly Virgil does not feel that the Nymphs are a normal part of the landscape, but this does not mean that 'Nympharum domus' here is a piece of epic convention or that the phrase is the equivalent of an ornamental adjective.[120] On the contrary: the Nymphs come at the very end of the description, as a climax, a fulfilment of that suggestion of the numinous that has been trembling on the verge of explicitness; and the phrase receives still further emphasis from the sudden stop at the end of the second foot. The beauty of this moment is that the Nymphs come as a culmination and yet are strangely fugitive, like that farthest, highest peak which fades into the summer sky. The instant they appear the scene-painting ceases; the monosyllable 'hic' presses in immediately before the caesura; no sooner have the Nymphs been glimpsed, so to speak, than they are gone again, and the narrative turns away from the landscape to the ships and their crews. The form here is expressive of the content, for it is the essence of these Nymphs, in contrast to their Homeric predecessors, that we cannot picture them clearly. In what sense is the cave their home? Are they accessible to human sight? Are they within the cave now or is it rather a place of possible epiphany? Not only are no answers offered to such questions, but it may even be that no answers could be given, and that the Nymphs, like the Italian deities to be evoked later in the poem, are beings resistant to clear definition.

Virgil's harbour can be described as an imaginary landscape; but that description is in itself ambiguous, and needs investigation. First of all, the scene is imaginary in the simple sense that it does not describe an actual inlet to be found somewhere on the Tunisian coast. Further, Virgil may have supposed it to be more perfectly spectacular than any harbour existing in the real world. But this does not mean that the description is in an important sense 'unreal'. It is a landscape that may remind the modern reader of Claude, or of Turner in mythological mood; and though such comparisons can be a distraction, the analogy may briefly be of service. A painting by Claude may be more exactly picturesque, in the strict and original meaning of that word, than any existing landscape, but it is still a landscape of which the elements are perceived to be real, and which is indeed distinctive enough to be recognizably Italian. It may be an improved or simplified version of reality, rather as the men and women

---

[120] As suggested by Williams, *Tradition and Originality*, 641.

of heroic poetry are improved or simplified versions of ordinary
humanity; but if the landscape or the epic hero were wholly unreal,
they would have failed of their purpose. So it is with Virgil's harbour: for the poet himself it was undecidable whether such a place
could be found somewhere on the surface of the globe, and it is in
any case unimportant.[121] Probably he was aware both that the coast
around Carthage is flattish and that the climate would not allow the
richness of vegetation that he has depicted, but if he has created a
landscape that might possibly exist, it would be prosaic to object that
he has put it in the wrong place. What matters, as with the painting
by Claude, is that it is a distinctive landscape of a kind that might
exist. We should also remember that Virgil does not purport to be
describing an ordinary scene; this place is meant to be exceptionally
beautiful, dramatic, peaceful, and strange. And that too is real: the world
does contain rare places of exceptional and haunting loveliness.

Virgil's lines do not contain a great amount in the way of precise visual description, and though there is less vagueness in regard
to detail here than in some of his evocations of landscape, his method
is obviously rather different from the accumulative description of individual elements in a scene that we find in Homer, or for that matter in the homestead of Theocritus' seventh Idyll. But as before, it
would be wrong to deduce from this that the poet lacked powers
of observation or imagination in this area, or that he had no strong
feeling for nature, and this for several reasons. In the first place, we
shall learn from Lucretius that a powerful sense of nature can be
expressed without any description of specific features at all; and Virgil's
great evocation of Italy in the second Georgic will devote hardly
more than two of its lines to the strict business of depiction. But in
any case, there is, for what it may be worth, a certain amount of
'itemization' in Virgil's account of the harbour; also one piece of

---

[121] We may be teased by experience unavailable to Virgil. The fiords of New Zealand
realize his harbour perfectly and on a larger scale than he will have imagined. Fiords are
formed by glacial action and are thus no part of the Mediterranean scene, but it still seems
a strength in Virgil's imagination that he could invent a landscape best realized far from
any place he could have known and created by a type of geology that he could not have
seen. Robert Louis Stevenson 'found' Virgil's harbour in Samoa: 'I had Virgil's bay all
morning to myself, and feasted on solitude, and overhanging woods, and the retiring sea
. . . I would stroll out, and see the rocks and woods, and the arcs of beaches . . . and huge
ancient trees, jutting high overhead out of the hanging forest, and feel the place at least
belonged to the age of fable, and awaited Aeneas and his battered fleets' (diary of 1891,
quoted in G. Balfour, *The Life of Robert Louis Stevenson* (London, 1901), ii. 100 f.).

dramatically original observation—observation meaning not purely literal reporting but a realization of things seen through imaginative interpretation—in the vision of the woods as 'scaena'. But most importantly, the passage is observant because what Virgil perceives is not straightforwardly the pictorial character of the landscape but its mood.

Part of his creation of mood comes from the feelings attributed to the scenery itself. Now the pathetic fallacy is not an alternative to observation, but may even spring from an intensity of observation. And what is impressive about it here is that it seems to grow almost inevitably out of the facts presented to the eye; it does not feel as if it were imposed upon the landscape by the will of the poet or spectator. In the phrase 'silvis scaena coruscis' not only is the idea of a stage backdrop striking in itself, but at the very moment that it is introduced it is seen to be, in a sense, inappropriate. For the woods are quivering, and no backdrop can do that. It may shake or buckle, if flimsily made, but it cannot break up, as the woods do, into innumerable tiny movements. So what we see in Virgil's superbly compressed phrase is a backcloth, flat, pictorial, static; and yet that flat canvas is suddenly perceived to be a multitude of small activities—one is tempted to say, it comes to life. And that is just what happens in the next line, as 'coruscis' modulates into 'horrenti', the quiver becomes a shudder, the movement becomes animation.

Thus the pathetic fallacy comes to seem both apt and inevitable, to be part of the very nature of the scene. But that is not all; for Virgil does not just rest in the pathetic fallacy: the impulse towards animation continues. As Ruskin saw, the pathetic fallacy can be simply a habit of mind, virtually or entirely unnoticed by those who use it. That is not how Virgil handles it here. Though it seems to come about so naturally, he is alert to the seriousness, to the excitement of attributing emotion to landscape. The famous fallacy is not here a cliché of thought or language; it will not rest in metaphor or symbol but presses beyond these things into actuality. If shade may shudder, then rocks may become organic, and deities infuse the scene. And so out of what the eye beholds there grows by a seemingly irresistible process a feeling for the quality of the landscape which goes beyond the perceptions of the senses and can include even the Nymphs. And this is not the product of an eye that fails to see but of an eye that sees in union with the mind, so that the literal vision, available as it were to any spectator of the scene, is taken into an imaginative vision distinctive to this poet.

The pathetic fallacy is also especially significant here because of the place of the description within the narrative. Beautiful as the passage is in isolation, it gains greatly from its context. As we have seen, this is not just a fine piece of scenery for the reader to enjoy as a sort of romantic tourist; for the Aeneadae it represents safety and refreshment, a fact impressed upon us the more forcefully for this being the first landfall in the poem. The emotions attributed to the landscape respond to the emotion in the sailors; they are like an echo struck off the rocks. The magic of the atmosphere is that the air of heightened expectancy seems to suffuse everything, blurring and merging men, ships, and woodland alike into a unity of mood and feeling.

As so often in the *Aeneid*, Virgil's method here is subjective, and here his description not only sets the scene but suggests the emotions of the actors in his drama. We might notice that the Trojans' emotion is one of pure relief and pleasure. Line 171 makes their delight explicit, but if we have caught Virgil's tone, we might have assumed as much anyway from their weariness, their escape from the storm and the entrancement with which the scene is evoked. If there is a disturbing note in this landscape, it is one of which they are unaware; the troubling overtones, if there are any, are put there by the poet for us, not for the Aeneadae to hear.

What then are our own instinctive feelings? Modern sensibility finds the scene idyllic, and the looming cliffs and trembling woods no detraction from the idyll but a further enhancement of delight. Eighteenth-century writers, in the crepuscular beginnings of romanticism, spoke of mountain scenery as exciting a 'pleasing terror'; 'terror' is too strong a word for anything in this passage, and for that matter the modern spirit does not pretend to such an excess of agitation at the grander works of nature; but we are the heirs of romantic sensibility to this extent, that we find the more formidable places of the earth peculiarly soothing. We seek out rocks and mountains, cliffs and crashing seas with the clear purpose of repose; and the language of the pathetic fallacy—'wild', 'savage', 'fierce', 'roaring' —seems to us the appropriate medium through which to express our enjoyment. Awe is for us, so far as landscape is concerned, a vehicle of pleasure, and not only of pleasure but of refreshment and release. Is it an anachronism to read this kind of sentiment back into Virgil?

Surely it is not. Everything points in the same direction: the instinctive modern response, the obvious intention to depict a beautiful place, the emotions of the exhausted Trojans, the sense of the numinous. Virgil has discovered that the kind of landscape which inspires awe also inspires peace; and the discovery is a landmark in the history of western sensibility. It is not something to be rationally explained, but to be described in the language of paradox, analogously to religious experience, where, as Lucretius knew, both 'horror' and 'voluptas' are felt, for reasons beyond analysis. Virgil is conscious of the analogy, for, as we have seen, he presses onward from the pathetic fallacy into making the place a home of deities. Now an epic landscape is not necessarily the same as a landscape in the actual world, just as the heroes of epic do not live under exactly the same conditions as ordinary humanity; Aeneas is directed upon his course by gods and visions, which is not people's common experience in the world as we know it; and just as Venus and Mercury and Tiberinus are 'real' within the fictional universe created by the epic, so are the Nymphs 'real' within the epic landscape. It is a confusion to suppose that because Virgil does not put the Nymphs in the same way into the ordinary Italian landscapes of the *Georgics*, their appearance here is a matter of ornament or literary convention. Consciously and perceptively he creates a heightening of ordinary landscape, and this heightening is of two kinds. First, in straightforwardly visual terms this is an unusually dramatic scene; second, it is a landscape that divinities have taken for their dwelling.

And yet outside the world of epic also Virgil has found a secular equivalent to religious experience. Beautifully fitted though the passage is to its place in the poem, we can yet detach it from its context and find an appreciation of nature for its own sake; it illuminates our own experience as well as the Trojans'. Beautifully fitted though the Nymphs are to provide the culmination of the scene, we can remove them too without making a large difference to the overall tone and atmosphere. Virgil takes the fictive personification of inanimate natural objects and pushes at it until the fiction becomes (within the universe of the poem) reality; but we feel that in its origins the pathetic fallacy here is just that—a fallacy. The verse develops from saying that the shade shudders to saying that the rock is live, and from saying that the rock is live to revealing the dwelling places of the Nymphs. This epic scene achieves its special quality

by growing away from its starting-point, but that starting-point itself
is Virgil's response to landscape in the world that he knew.

The Nymphs' presence is a brilliant touch, beautiful in its evanescence, but it is not essential. We could not have said that about
the *Bacchae*. When Euripides says that the whole mountain joined
in the Bacchic revel or that the glen held its leaves in silence, Dionysus'
immanence is of the essence; when Sappho describes an orchard and
a meadow, it is the very nature of the place that it should be holy,
a place where the epiphany of Aphrodite can be expected; Sophocles'
depiction of Colonus would lose its meaning were it not a place
where gods and goddesses walked. With Virgil it is different. One
might compare Ruskin's description of Monsal Dale: 'There was a
rocky valley between Buxton and Bakewell, once upon a time, divine
as the Vale of Tempe; you might have seen the Gods there morning
and evening—Apollo and all the sweet Muses of the light—walking
in fair procession on the lawns of it, and to and fro among the
pinnacles of its crags.'[122] The attraction of this way of speaking lies
precisely in the fact that Victorian Derbyshire is not where you expect
to find Apollo and the Nymphs; the appeal of the game lies in the
way that they have become an enhancement of an essentially secular
appreciation of nature. And in that respect he seems not far from
Virgil. Of course there are important differences. Ruskin is describing a real and specific landscape, Virgil one of his own invention;
Ruskin as a child of the Christian centuries cannot believe in the
gods of antiquity, and there is something mannered, shading towards
the whimsical, in his putting the pagan gods into a Christian, northern, modern scene—which is unlike any part of Virgil's effect.[123] But
where Virgil anticipates the later centuries is in a proto-romantic
feeling about nature which is willing to use the gods but does not
need them. One of the strange charms of his harbour is that it both
belongs to the wonderful realm of heroic myth and speaks to a feeling for nature that we can share; it is both alien to our experience
and something that we know.

[122] *Fors Clavigera* 5.
[123] Ruskin himself later muddied the waters by claiming that he had meant what he
said about Apollo and his companions literally—the self-deception of a mind near to collapse. But this at least suggests that he was trying to do more than give a pretty scene
some whimsical ornamentation.

CHAPTER 3

A Transpadane's Experience

> To be attached to the subdivision, to love the little platoon we
> belong to in society, is the first principle (the germ as it were)
> of public affections. It is the first link in the series by which
> we proceed towards a love to our country, and to mankind.
>
> (Burke)

The last chapter looked for Virgil's imaginative ancestry in terms
of literary history; this chapter turns from Greece to Italy, and from
literary to political, cultural, and social history. Greek poetry influences his ideas of nature and landscape, though we have already found
that even when constructing scenery from the raw materials offered
him by the *Odyssey*, he begins to bring it into connection with conceptions of home and city. From Italian history we should expect to
find an influence principally upon his sense of 'patria' and ancestry,
though we shall discover that even before Virgil these things cannot
be wholly separated from the use of landscape as an imaginative resource.

Let us begin with a few very broad and simple statements. For
centuries much of Italian history was the history of the relations
between Rome and the other communities of the peninsula. Conflict and war within Italy continued for hundreds of years. Rome was
an Italian power before it became a Mediterranean power, and before
it became an Italian power it was a city-state. That spectacular expansion was achieved by force of arms. In its early years Rome fought
with little local cities like Veii and with the hill peoples of the Apennines,
Sabines and Samnites. It fought Etruria. Later it warred with the
prosperous cities of the south, such as Hellenized Capua and Greek
Tarentum. In the greatest crisis of Rome, Hannibal's invasion, the
issue upon which everything depended was whether Rome's alliances
within Italy would hold. They did hold; and Rome was able to survive and eventually defeat the enemy. But Italy was still far from being
comfortably reconciled to the Roman order. Grievances continued

to fester, and in 90 BC, only twenty years before Virgil was born, the allies rose against Rome and fought the *Bellum Italicum* or Social War. There were forces within Italy making both for unity and for division, and the pull between these forces shaped much of the peninsula's history.

Among the forces for unity was Rome's openness to men and influences from outside. The legend of the expulsion of the Tarquins conceals the fact that in its infancy Rome was for a time under Etruscan control. Early Rome was ethnically mixed. Many of the leading families were Etruscan; others were Sabine or Alban in origin, or of other Italian stock unknown to us. Pompey the Great was the most powerful man in Rome when Virgil was a boy; his father had crushed the Italian insurgents in the Social War. But the family was not of Latin stock; probably they came from Picenum, where they had an enormous clientage.[1] The Romans' readiness to absorb outsiders distinguishes them from the Greek cities, and the Greeks themselves remarked the difference. Philip V of Macedon observed, as a fact worthy of note, how willing the Romans were to extend the citizenship: even slaves, he said, might acquire it.[2]

Every municipal Italian, Cicero said, has two *patriae*: Rome and his home town.[3] In the generation before he wrote, there was more than one route by which men might arrive at a dual loyalty. Italian cities received the Roman citizenship; conversely Rome planted *coloniae*, settlements of veterans, in Italy. The growth of the Roman empire might help to give a sense of common identity or interest with Rome both to the Italian upper classes and to the peasantry. Italian businessmen were able to go out and exploit the Greek east, and when they did so, they found that the natives did not make nice distinctions: to them Italians were all *Rhomaioi*. Economic advantage, political prestige, and that other impalpable force, so potent in shaping a sense of national identity—the simple consciousness of being different from the others—were starting to push the prosperous Italians of the municipia towards feeling themselves to be Roman. As for their humbler compatriots: Rome conquered half the Mediterranean world with a peasant army. Armies are powerful agents of national unification, as European statesmen of the eighteenth and nineteenth centuries were to be well aware. When Italy had been unified in

[1] R. Syme, *The Roman Revolution* (Oxford, 1939), 28.
[2] *SIG* 543.   [3] *Leg.* 2. 5.

the Risorgimento, conscription came to have more than a military purpose: it gave young men from the south, who had not previously felt themselves to be Italian, a sense of national consciousness. Ukrainians who joined the Tsar's army were taught Russian. Earlier, in revolutionary France, the Jacobins had seen the army as a centralizing force, which would assist them to eliminate the local patois and with them, local particularisms; perhaps Roman militarism hastened the decline of Oscan. Horace expresses horror at the thought that Marsian and Apulian soldiers, Italians of the high country or from the far side of the Apennines, should so far forget Vesta and the *ancilia*, the shields which were talismans of the Roman state, as to kowtow to an oriental king.[4] The poet came from Apulia himself; and he had stood in the line of battle. Perhaps he was disingenuous or self-deceived in expecting such distinctively Roman sentiment from these country peoples; but it is expressive that he can speak in such terms at all.

The self-importance of the municipia plays a part in this story. Consider Cicero's speech in defence of Caelius: it is a powerful testimony to the young man's innocence (the orator maintains) that his fellow townsmen regard him so highly; the jury could assuredly not approve him 'si . . . municipio tam illustri ac tam gravi displiceret' (if he had offended so distinguished and important a town).[5] We cannot confidently identify this glorious municipality; its name is obscure enough to have been corrupted in the manuscripts beyond the power of certain healing. The modern reader's first instinct may be to suppose that Cicero is making fun of the place; but he is not. In his defence of Aulus Cluentius of Larinum he is willing to spread the butter very thick. Let the jury consider the deputations that have come to speak in the defendant's favour: gentlemen of the utmost nobility from Ferentum, families of the Marrucini alike in dignity; 'homines amplissimi nobilissimique' from Bovianum and all the Samnite land; and from Larinum itself 'honesti homines et summo splendore praediti'.[6] It is a catalogue of backwaters; and some of Cicero's own speeches reveal eloquently enough how narrow, brutal, and obscure life in the towns of Italy could be. But the Roman knights who sat in judgement upon these defendants were evidently

---

[4] *Carm.* 3. 5. 9–12.   [5] *Cael.* 5.

[6] *Clu.* 197 ('men of the greatest affluence and nobility', 'honourable men of the highest illustriousness').

insatiable of self-esteem, and Cicero was confident that he could manage them; in the case of Cluentius at least he happily boasted afterwards that he had flooded the jury with darkness.[7] These knights
were *domi nobiles*, aristocrats in their home towns; regarded with condescension by the consular families of Rome, they might none the
less claim descent from monarchs and heroes. A complex snobbery
lies behind the terms in which Horace addresses Maecenas, the unassuming knight, the scion of ancient kings.[8]

The towns themselves conducted their affairs with a solemn
sense of their own significance. We find that at Pompeii there was
lively competition for the post of *duovir*.[9] In the imperial period
the municipia would increasingly ape the metropolitan style, with
statuary and ceremonies, baths, temples, and inscriptions modelled
upon Rome itself. In part this behaviour reflects Italy's place in the
Hellenistic world, which she entered when Rome began to conquer the Greek cities of the south. Greek city-states retained a high
view of their own distinction long after they had lost their independence. Inscriptions reveal the little cities of Asia Minor, vassals
of Alexander and his successors, continuing to make pompous pro-
clamation of their liberty and eminence, conferring freedoms upon
visiting notabilities and dispatching honorific embassies to their
neighbours; a few scholars have been tempted to argue from such
evidence that the towns of the Aegean seaboard preserved a genuine independence in the age of the Hellenistic monarchies. That is
to confuse style with substance; the self-important noise of decrees
that echoes across the waters is mere bombination, reverberant and
hollow, like the sound of a small boy trying out his voice in an
empty hall.[10]

The miniature dignities of the municipia were partly an imitation
of the great Hellenistic world; but partly too they breathe a spirit
which is natively Italian, a complacent provincialism untroubled by
self-awareness. The difficult terrain of the Apennines, which kept small
communities isolated and separate, must have helped to sustain local
idiosyncrasies. Even now the sentimental traveller in Italy, observing the proud communal life of the Apennine towns, so different

---

[7] Quint. 2. 17. 21.   [8] e.g. *Carm.* 1. 1. 1 f., 1. 20. 5, 3. 29. 1.

[9] C. Wells, *The Roman Empire* (London, 1984), 208.

[10] On the relations of Hellenistic kings to Greek cities see A. H. M. Jones, *The Greek
City from Alexander to Justinian* (Oxford, 1940), Ch. 5 (95–112), and G. E. M. de Ste. Croix,
The Class Struggle in the Ancient Greek World (London, 1981), 302 ff.

from (say) the deep slumber of provincial France, and contemplating their innocently pompous monuments, may wonder if the nature of the land or its people has not preserved something of the ancient municipal character to this day.[11]

Sometimes Cicero looks complaisantly upon his municipal origins; sometimes, and usually with more appearance of conviction, he displays an urban disdain for the life of the backwoods. Insofar as he is not being disingenuous (and often he is) these are two separate parts of his being, and it makes little sense to try to reconcile them. He is too early—a generation too early—to feel fully the charm of small-town life. Above all, he had known real power: to a man who had governed Rome influence and eminence in Arpinum would be for ever uninteresting. Some said that he was descended from Attus Tullius, king of the Volscians, but the orator himself, a man not careless of social distinction, makes nothing of it. Even in the next generation it was Virgil alone who made an emotional unity out of the mixed fashion with which sophisticated people regarded the local *patriae* of Italy. Mark Antony (it was alleged) took his name from Anton, son of Hercules; the Aemilii numbered Pythagoras (or Numa) among their forebears; the Aelii Lamiae descended from the Laestrygonians of the *Odyssey*; and in the municipia the pattern is repeated: the Vitellii of Nuceria traced their line from the god Faunus and the goddess Vitellia, and there seem to have been other similar claims.[12] From such genealogical absurdities Virgil created the blend of Greek, Trojan, and Italic which in the *Aeneid* goes to the formation of the new people. The Italians in the poem have deities among their ancestors, but this does not lead Virgil to give them an exaggerated dignity; instead, from the combination of divinity and modesty he creates a new and peculiar charm. It was his achievement to see through municipal self-importance and yet to accept and enjoy it; we shall find him, as he commemorates the towns of old Italy,

[11] The town of Pisa set up an inscription commemorating the deaths of Gaius and Lucius Caesar, Augustus' grandsons, at excessive length. (*ILS* 139 f.) The present writer happened to be in Italy when Mao Tse-Tung died. Within a few days a poster had appeared in Urbino, close to the Risorgimento monument, reproducing the extensive epistle of advice and condolence dispatched by the town council to Chairman Hua Guo-Feng.

[12] Plut. *Ant.* 4 (cf. the coin depicting Anton illustrated by P. Zanker, *Augustus und die Macht der Bilder* (Munich, 1987), 53); Plut. *Aem. Paul.* 1 and *Numa* 8; Hor. *Carm.* 3. 17. 1 ff.; Suet. *Vitell.* 1. Varro's *De Familiis Troianis* found the ancestors of various aristocratic houses among Aeneas' companions. Such is the raw material transmuted by Virgil in *Aen.* 5 (Sergestus, Cloanthus, and Atys the ancestors of the Sergii, Cluentii, and Atii).

Tibur and Atina, Bola, Gabii, and Fidenae, allowing irony to infuse affection.[13] Perhaps in no earlier generation could this mixture of admiration and condescension have been brought off; but even in his own time it was Virgil alone who achieved it.

We have been considering the forces that drew the municipia towards Rome or repelled them from her. But in this another question is left out: what forces were there to give the municipia a fellow feeling with each other? When Cicero says that all municipals have two *patriae*, Rome and their home town, he says nothing of Italy. We can easily fail to appreciate how hard it was for the peoples of ancient Italy to think of themselves emotionally as Italian. Yet we do not have to look very far back into the past to find a sense of identity different from the modern one: among the common people at least, the idea of the nation state as the primary object of loyalty has been a comparatively recent development in much of Europe. It was no simple task to teach nineteenth-century Italians that they were a single people, and even in parts of France the sense of nation might be frail: it was discovered in a village school in Lozère that none of the children knew themselves to be French; asked if they were English or Russian, they were unable to say.[14] In antiquity a sense of Italian nationhood must have been far harder still to come by. The Greeks were unusual among ancient peoples in that despite their tribal, political, and geographical divisions, they had an indestructible sense of their own unity: whether you lived in Marseilles or Turkestan, if you were a Hellene, you knew that you were a Hellene. The chief bond was language: it would not be very far wrong to say that if you spoke Greek, you were one of the elect; the rest were *barbaroi*.[15] But the peoples of Italy were not united by race, language, or culture; nor had they shared elements of common polity unless by connection with the Roman state, whether through the Roman franchise, Latin rights, or some other form of alliance. Metternich's scornful remark was in antiquity the plain truth: Italy was a geographical expression, and the people who lived between the Po and the Straits of Messina had scarcely more than this in common, that they inhabited the same peninsula. But in the ancient world, and in a mountainous country, physical contiguity was not

---

[13] See below, pp. 400 f.

[14] T. Zeldin, *France 1848–1945: Intellect and Pride* (Oxford, 1980), 3.

[15] Of course there were uncertainties at the margins: for example, Macedonians and *mixobarbaroi*.

the unifying force that we might think it. A city was close to you if you could reach it readily by water, and not because of belonging to the same land mass;[16] newsprint and broadcasting did not exist, instruments by which modern states have most powerfully propagated the national idea; and this was also a world where maps were rare, and commonly fanciful.[17] Maps have been effective in strengthening and symbolizing the identities of modern states, giving their citizens an instinctive sense of the extent and coherence of their country.[18] In ancient Italy, where visible symbols were far fewer, the Samnite, the Ligurian and the Tarentine might each be proud of his Roman citizenship; but why should they have fellow feeling one with another? Simply imagining Italy must have been harder then than we readily conceive.

Italy first became a political idea and a focus for emotional attachment as late as 90 BC, with the Social War; and even then the insurrection left much of the peninsula unaffected. The allies issued coins showing a bull, symbol of Italy, trampling the Roman wolf.[19] It is a profound irony that the new kind of national feeling which was to flower most brilliantly in the poetry of Roman Virgil was born from hatred of Rome.

The rebellion was harshly suppressed, in the Roman fashion. Crucial to the happiness of Italy in the future would be the question whether defeat would deepen resentment or permit reconciliation between Rome and the disaffected. The story is long and partly obscure; but two things may be said. First, it was certain that reconciliation

[16] Columella advises that an estate should have access to running water, so that goods may be brought in and out (1. 2. 3). An ox team could be expected to cover hardly more than 10 miles a day, and hauling materials 25 miles would add about 15 per cent to the cost of an olive mill (T. Frank, *An Economic Survey of Ancient Rome*, i (Baltimore, 1933), 201). The cost of land transport remained very high in many parts of the world at least until the coming of the railways. Thus in early 19th-cent. Australia farms near the Tasmanian estuaries could ship their wheat to Sydney, 700 miles away, almost as cheaply as farmers could carry it who lived near trunk roads only 30–40 miles from the city; the cost of carrying goods for gold-diggers was less from Britain to Australia than from the nearest Australian seaport to the goldfields (G. Blainey, *The Tyranny of Distance* (rev. edn., Melbourne, 1983), 121, 141).

[17] Ancient writers seem unaware that Italy is shaped like a boot; contrast the modern journalistic trope, 'la stivale' (or in France, 'l'hexagone'). The Elder Pliny believed that Italy was shaped like an oak-leaf (3. 43).

[18] India and Eire used to put maps on their commonest postage stamps, to enforce the feeling that their irredentist claims were inevitably just. Modern states have of course multiplied symbols: flags, national anthems, etc.

[19] M. Crawford, *The Roman Republic* (London, 1978), pl. 7c.

would not be easy. Bitterness continued to fester, erupting in 77 when Etruria rose for Lepidus; unhappiness in the countryside provided Catiline with some of his support in 63; and after the death of Julius Caesar Italy rose once more. The separateness of Rome and Italy was still a living memory in the time of Virgil's maturity, not just a matter of sentimental or antiquarian reflection. Despite the kind attentions of Maecenas, Propertius remembered the Perusine War.[20]

Yet the fact is that by design or accident, Rome brought off the trick. By the time that Imperator Caesar became Caesar Augustus, it was clear that Italy would not be a problem to tax Roman statecraft again. And if we turn our attention to the Italian upper classes, we may detect some of the reasons why. The municipia had this difference from the Greek *poleis*, that they had not been centres of urban life which engaged in trade and diplomacy with a multitude of other cities. A place like Priene (say) might be small and far from powerful, but it looked out across the wine-dark sea at a brilliant and sophisticated world; and even in the time of its vassalage it preserved, on however modest a scale, an urban manner and the style of autonomy. The municipia, locked within their mountains, innocent of high culture, were, in the modern sense of the term, profoundly provincial, *tiefste Provinz*; compared with the Greek cities, their self-importance could more readily be absorbed into a larger patriotism and indeed be better expressed through it. Julius Caesar's alleged saying, that he would sooner be the first man in an Alpine village than the second at Rome, had the character of paradox; it was remembered because it was so evidently implausible.[21] Cicero's speeches show Rome becoming a focus for the enhancement of local and particular loyalties. How happy Murena seemed, he declares, when he thought himself the first to bring the consulship to his old-established family, to his most venerable municipality.[22] Is this Roman or Italian sentiment? It is no longer possible to make the distinction.

Cicero's defence of Plancius is especially interesting in this respect. The prosecutor, Laterensis, had belittled the accused's origins. Cicero does not reply with a charge of snobbery; the municipals—it is revealing to see—defer to the eminence of the great Roman families. Instead, the orator concedes that Laterensis is of superior birth to the defendant, since he hails from 'the most ancient municipality of Tusculum', the origin of so many consular houses, whereas Plancius

---

[20] Prop. 2. 1. 29; cf. Prop. 1. 21 and 22.   [21] Plut. *Caes.* 11. 2.   [22] *Mur.* 86.

comes from the prefecture of Atina, which is 'not so old, not so distinguished and not so close to the city'.[23] However, the further an Italian town is from Rome, Cicero suggests, the greater its pride in success there. Atina was greatly stirred when Saturninus became the first of her sons to be elected aedile, then praetor, but the Tusculans are more blasé: they do not talk about Cato, Coruncanius, or the Fulvii. In Arpinum, Cicero continues, there is by contrast frequent talk about her great men; perhaps about himself—a token gesture of modesty here—certainly about Marius. The municipia are strongly influenced 'coniunctione . . . vicinitatis', by fellow feeling for the neighbouring towns. Cicero knows this from his own experience: Arpinum is near Atina, and there was no one there, no one from Soranum, Casinum, or Aquinum who did not favour Plancius. Laterensis could not count on backing of this kind: the people of Labicum, Gabii, and Bovillae do not feel that they must support their own. Cicero's argument suggests that local feeling could become Roman feeling: it was cashed out in the Roman elections. The particularist sympathies of the municipia, their regional patriotisms, thus turn into a binding force.

The facts of geography and demography meant two things, in antiquity as again in the eighteenth and nineteenth centuries: that Italy would be late in coming to unity; and that unity must come in the end. Though modern forms of propaganda and mass communication were lacking, there were other forces making for uniformity, some of a kind absent in modern times. Once again we can look at this matter under two aspects: we can regard Roman culture as a sub-species of Hellenic culture; and we can examine the distinctive characteristics of Italy. The style of urban life was astonishingly uniform across the whole of the Greek world, a fact graphically demonstrated by the discovery at Ai Khanum of a purely Hellenic city only a few miles from the banks of the Oxus. When the Roman world came under Hellenic influence, it was inevitable that the principal towns would acquire inscriptions and market-places, rectangular street plans and public buildings all much like one another, whatever the variations of scale or sophistication, and all, despite some Roman characteristics, founded originally upon Greek models. The time will finally come when the respectable classes of the Roman empire live in villas of the same style and enjoy the same pattern of life from

[23] *Planc.* 19–23.

the Atlantic to the Euphrates, amid the damps of Northumberland
and on the fringes of the Sahara. Ultimately the dividing line will
be one not of locality, nor purely of class: it will be between those
who share the life of the Graeco-Roman towns and those outside,
the bumpkins in the country; the towns of Asia, Africa, and Gaul
will have more in common with one another than with the shaggy
denizens of their hinterlands.

But in the first century BC that result was still distant. And the
very fact that the process of standardization or cultural unification
was incomplete helped, paradoxically, to bind the *domi nobiles* to Rome.
The gentlemen of Italy, if they got to the great city, had the chance
of entering a glamorous and sophisticated society. Consider the poets:
Catullus, from far Verona, acquires a mistress from the patrician nobility; the young Propertius, from Asisium, writes on terms of equality to coevals of consular family;[24] Ovid, from Sulmo, mixes with
the aristocratic Messallae. And there must have been much that
they were glad to leave behind them. Several of Cicero's speeches
and some of Catullus' poems uncover the narrowness of life in the
municipia, with its casual violence, shabby secrets, and prurient gossip.[25] This was a society in which the possessing classes all over Italy
had more in common with one another than they had with the poor
of their own towns. We may contrast nineteenth-century Europe,
where the abler young men of the provinces, including sons of the
more prosperous peasantry, got to the big cities, qualified as doctors, lawyers, and suchlike, and returned to their home towns with
metropolitan notions about politics, culture, and society, which thus
spread to new places and classes. This process, with its tendency to
lessen cultural differences across a nation and across classes within
each part of a nation, did not occur in ancient Italy, where the pro-
fessions, insofar as they existed, were in the hands of Greeks and
freedmen. The villas of the cultured rich—who knew Rome and
the people that counted—were sealed and secluded worlds of their
own, islands of pure Hellenism in an Italian sea, spreading no influence around them.[26]

---

[24] Tullus and Gallus (on their families: R. Syme, *History in Ovid* (Oxford, 1978), 103).
[25] Cic. *Caec.*, *Rosc. Am.*, *Clu.*; Cat. 17 and 67. Cicero's *Planc.* 30 f. is expressive. Plancius
was alleged to have abducted (or raped?) a ballet girl. So what? This was regular and traditional at Atina, and Plancius was entitled to his fun. Only as a second line of defence does
Cicero add that the charge is false.   [26] Zanker, *Augustus und die Macht der Bilder*, 35–41.

Birth and property count for much, cutting across the divisions of political geography. Perhaps that is true of all societies; but in first-century Italy there was another consideration also. Cicero's *Pro Roscio Amerino* reveals that in a single municipal family one member might be often in Rome conversing with grandees like the Metelli and Scipiones, while another stayed at home as an obscure squireen, ignorant of the world. In such circumstances education and urbanity might count for as much as wealth and family; and education and urbanity virtually entailed loyalty to Rome. In more recent European history the danger of a divisive regionalism has been closely related to the behaviour of the upper classes. Particularism was strong in Catalonia because the upper classes rejected Spain and chose to speak the Catalan language; in Provence, where the higher ranks preferred the metropolitan model, the problem did not arise. In the ancient Mediterranean world the cultured or would-be cultured classes were drawn by centripetal forces of a peculiarly strong kind. There was no Oscan or Italic high culture; indeed, with the partial exception of Etruria, itself deferential to Greek example, there was only one high culture, the Hellenic, out of which Latin literature and Roman architecture had sprung as a sort of provincial offshoot. Except in the Greek south, where Hellenism was to be had pure and undiluted, the pleasures of sophistication were available to the gentlemen of Italy through one channel only, Hellenized Rome. Our sources may give us a one-sided picture. Every writer, and especially every poet, has already made his decision before he picks up his pen: he will write in the Roman language, using Greek forms, Greek myths, and Greek metres; and if he needs a patron, a Roman aristocrat with Hellenic sympathies is his one hope. Not all municipals will have been so cultivated: some will have been more like Squire Allworthy than the glittering figures who take the light in our sources, and others more like Squire Western than Squire Allworthy. But even those who preferred importance in their own localities to life at Rome had the advantage if they had spent time in the great city and made friendships there; advantage in style, in splendour, and in the secure enjoyment of their substance. It was because Sextus Roscius was ignorant of Rome that he got into such difficulty.[27]

---

[27] This truth applies even if Roscius was not innocent. It does not depend on trusting Cicero, not a safe proceeding.

Moreover, the invention of printing has changed the social function of the written word. The ancient world was predominantly illiterate, chiefly of course because most people had no chance to learn, but also because there was little incentive to acquire more than an elementary knowledge: for what then would they have to read?[28] Books were few and expensive: Cicero's letters to Atticus show that even he had difficulty in getting hold of some Greek philosophical texts; Quintilian reflects that learned men have perhaps suffered from too long an immersion in too few books. Since the invention of printing popular reading matter—books, pamphlets, newspapers—has been peddled in vast quantities. The broadsheet ballad was a genuine people's art; books and papers in regional languages or dialects have kept alive local idiosyncrasies. Even so, history suggests that mass literacy and the mass production of print tend to spread uniformity in the long run. Before printing the social function of the book as a unifier was horizontal only: it linked the local ruling classes to each other by offering them a shared cultural inheritance unavailable to most of those whom they ruled. There could not be a Dickens at Rome, read by noble and workman alike. Moreover, since there were so many fewer books, the discovery of specialized literary interests was not easily made: genres such as the detective novel, science fiction, and children's literature have been powerful unifiers across the lines of class in our own time. There was no equivalent to these in the ancient world: even the Greek romance is far from being a genuinely popular form. Apuleius pretends that his novel is a 'Milesian story' such as might be heard or bought at a street corner, but it is of course nothing of the sort.[29] There were, no doubt,

[28] Literacy in the ancient world is a vast and complex subject. W. Harris, *Ancient Literacy* (Cambridge, Mass., 1989), makes a strong case for a low estimate. The importance of distinguishing different degrees of literacy is obvious: the ability to read and write simple sentences is a far cry from coping with Virgil and Cicero. Literary scholars have sometimes been too sanguine. E. Fraenkel (*Horace* (Oxford, 1957), 311) apparently supposed Horace's *Epist.* 1. 14 to be an authentic letter to his bailiff, to which G. Williams (*Tradition and Originality in Roman Poetry* (Oxford, 1968), 12) rightly retorts that it is 'difficult to see the most literate bailiff telling the foot of *Epistles* i. 14 from its head'. Varro advises that a bailiff should be able to read and write (*Rust.* 1. 17. 4), but that surely implies basic literacy only. Such a person would never see written poetry or literary prose; how then should he learn to understand them?

[29] *Met.* 1. 1. In the 20th cent. new and immensely powerful agents of vertical unification bring about a new phenomenon: the pseudo-self-proletarianization of the élite. A Chairman of the Arts Council is pleased to confess his addiction to *Dallas*. That purports to be self-deprecation, though really it is nothing of the kind. Ancient culture does not tempt the élite to stoop.

oral cultures in ancient Italy, which may at some time have worked as vertical unifiers between different classes within particular tribal, regional, or political groupings; but they are lost and beyond our power of recovery. We can, however, say this: if those anthropologists are right who hold that oral and literate cultures are fundamentally distinct, we should expect there to have been two kinds of culture in most parts of the ancient world where a literary tradition had developed. Oral traditions might in principle be regional, but there was never a prospect of a regional literature in Italy; a Hebel or a MacDiarmid would have been an impossibility. Whereas in modern circumstances the lines of force emanating from a literary culture can, in principle at least, run vertically as well as horizontally, in ancient times they ran along one axis only. Against the sense of locality that made Sabines Sabines and Transpadanes Transpadanes was the pull that made literate Sabines and Transpadanes members of Hellenized Latin culture. There was an educated class which could be told, 'We Marrucines, Campanians, and Transpadanes are all Italians'; there was not a reading public to be told, 'We landowners, slaves, peasants, women, farmers are all Transpadanes (or Campanians or Marrucines).' If Augustus seized the commanding heights of literature, he would thereby seize what was within Italy a naturally unifying force. In the event genius intervened unpredictably: it could not have been foretold that Virgil would so intimately mesh the Augustan spirit with the sense of being Italian and find in the dual patriotism of the Romanized Italians so deep a significance. But it was part of that genius to work with the grain of literary culture in his time: even without him, poetry would probably have developed along similar lines. This does not mean that local loyalties diminish; rather the reverse. Consider Ovid's affectionate reminiscence of the streams and pastures of his native Sulmo. Far from being a counterpoise to his urbanity, that is the metropolitan voice itself, speaking with the confidence which comes from possessing a choice.[30] We may contrast Hesiod: he lived in Ascra; he had to live in Ascra; he hated Ascra.[31]

---

[30] However, one might question the depth of Ovid's feeling for Sulmo. Unlike Virgil, Horace, Propertius, and Martial he does not give us any local proper names. His chief descriptions of Sulmo (in *Am.* 2. 16) are used as a foil: what pleasure can there be in the place, since the beloved is not there? And they are scarcely individualized, apart from the stress on a well-watered fertility: it is rich in corn and olives and pasturage alike (how different the particularizations of the *Georgics*). Is the picture truthfully observed? In later life Ovid will be insouciantly mendacious about the Romanian riviera.   [31] Hes. *Op.* 640.

We have seen that a municipal Italian might think of himself as a Roman—through possession of the citizenship or incorporation of his town into the Roman state—or he might feel a local patriotism; he did not so naturally feel an emotional tie binding him to the peninsula as a whole. From the city of Rome itself the view looked rather different. The Italians, seen collectively, presented a problem. Tiberius Gracchus, in Appian's account, asserts the Italians' kinship with the Romans and praises their courage in war;[32] for the next century Italy would be an issue in Roman politics, and the ironic workings of history were such that Rome was to do as much as Italy itself to create the Italian idea. From the time of the Gracchi there would be at least one faction that looked to Italy for support, and eventually all parties would be keeping an anxious or eager eye upon the municipia and the countryside. Cicero persuaded himself that all Italy rejoiced at his return from exile and would secure his authority. In the civil war between Pompey and Julius Caesar it was crucial that Caesar could reckon upon much disaffection in Italy, that Pompey could not count even upon Picenum to fight for him. Naturally there were various and conflicting interests within Italy itself, and different factions might gather support from different groups or places, but whatever their outlook, all were coming to see that Italy counted. Sentiment was happily conformable to realpolitik. Cicero looks to the solid citizens of the coloniae and municipia, 'florem totius Italiae ac robur', to defeat Catiline; in a later speech it is the Sabines' turn: 'florem Italiae ac robur rei publicae'.[33] 'Flos' and 'robur' are unambitious metaphors of organic growth to which Virgil will give depth, raw material which he will blend into his amalgam of landscape, history, and manly patriotism.

The efflorescence of a nostalgic patriotism directed towards Italy was made easier by the Romans' traditional belief that their national virtues were above all thrift, simplicity, and hardihood. It was some time since these qualities had been conspicuous in the city, but among the peasantry, it might be hoped, 'prisci mores' still survived, and perhaps among the gentlemen of Italy also. It is common for a high aristocracy to be more careless of traditional manners than a petty aristocracy; thus in the England of the late nineteenth and early twentieth centuries the small gentry can be observed preserving pure

---

[32] App. *Bell. Civ.* I. I. 9.

[33] *Cat.* 2. 24 'the flower and strength of all Italy'; *Lig.* 32 'the flower of Italy and sinew of the state'. The vestigial metaphor in 'robur' (strength, timber) is hard to retain in translation.

upper-class values at a time when some of the nobility were grown loud, vulgar, or reckless. The local aristocracies of the Italian towns, those 'Roman knights' in whose praise Cicero is so fervent and from whom he himself sprang, will upon the whole have been less contaminated by Greek influences and the temptations of luxury than the *nobiles*. And the further from Rome, the stronger perhaps the attachment to old ways. The Sabines were a byword for prudery; later their role will be taken over by distant Patavium, a city of that Transpadane Italy where Virgil was born. He describes Italian places, in a strikingly anomalous phrase, as 'Roman towns'; a century later Juvenal will sourly dismiss Rome as a 'Greek city'.[34] Italy was becoming more Roman than Rome.

Augustus declared in his political testament, 'All Italy swore allegiance to me of its own will.'[35] 'Tota Italia', 'all Italy'—it is tempting to wrench these words out of context and treat them as a catchphrase adopted by the new order. That may be a mistake. In 32 Caesar solemnly declared war on Cleopatra, reviving archaic ritual for the purpose; it was expedient to degrade the importance of Antony and present a civil conflict as war against an external foe. He does not seem to have represented himself as the champion of Italy before that date, and even now, though the emphasis was upon the alien threat, there is no clear evidence that he issued pan-Italian propaganda. The legend 'tota Italia' is not found on the coinage; and Horace, writing soon after Cleopatra's death, sees her rather as menacing the Capitol, the symbolic heart of Rome.[36] Nor is Italy mentioned in his ninth Epode, which does by contrast describe Sextus Pompey 'threatening the City'—Rome again—'with chains'.[37] Many things had happened between the Battle of Actium and the time that Augustus composed his *Res Gestae*, but not the least of them was the writing of the *Aeneid*, where for the first time in our sources Actium is portrayed as a struggle of Italy against the barbarian. We tend to think of the poets responding (or not) to the men in power; in this case it may have been the poet who inspired the ruler of the world.

Cicero's practice is instructive. Phrases meaning 'all Italy', using the adjectives 'totus', 'cunctus', 'omnis', and 'universus' occur many times in his works. They are comparatively infrequent in the early

---

[34] *Geo.* 2. 176; Juv. 3. 61.   [35] *Res Gest.* 25.
[36] *Carm.* 1. 37. 6–8.   [37] *Epod.* 9. 7–10.

speeches; the general pattern is that they become steadily more common in the later speeches, except that they are especially numerous in those delivered immediately after his return from exile, a time when he had convinced himself that he was everybody's darling. These expressions do not seem to be catchphrases; rather, with both the passage of time and the deepening of the national crisis the words 'all Italy', by a kind of natural process, came the more often to the lips. When Cicero says that Catiline's followers have crept forth from every corner throughout the 'whole of Italy' (totius Italiae), the phrase clearly has no special resonance; it just happens.[38] When he defended Flaccus against charges of corruption, he had frequent occasion to refer to the province which his friend had governed, and the phrase 'tota Asia' recurs often, once in contrast with 'tota Italia'.[39] Passages such as this suggest that the phrase 'tota Italia' arises naturally and almost inevitably from the oratorical habit of emphasis and exaggeration; the force of rhetoric carries it into the general currency as a river carries silt to its mouth. Warming to his theme in the speech *De Domo Sua*, Cicero declares again and again that all Italy had rejoiced in his restoration.[40] How could he say less? 'Many Italians' or 'several towns' would not have had the same ring. Augustus himself can speak of 'all Italy' without any particular emphasis; when he says that a vast crowd came 'cuncta ex Italia' to attend his election as pontifex maximus, the adjective carries no special weight: 'Italia' would seem bald without an epithet to support it, and 'cunctus' is ready to hand. However, the spread of such phrases does indeed suggest that the time was at hand for someone to envision the whole of Italy from the Alps to the Greek south and make that totality the object of patriotic emotion. It was not Augustus who did so; that honour belongs to the poet of the *Georgics*.

The municipal aristocrat of equestrian rank was a 'novus homo' or 'new man' if he stood for office at Rome. He might be the object of disdain from the high aristocracy. Sallust, a new man from the Sabine country, wrote no doubt with his own later experience in mind when he depicted the nobility earlier in the century regarding the consulship as polluted if a new man attained it.[41] He represents Catiline as deriding Cicero for being 'civis inquilinus urbis Romae' (a citizen who is just a lodger in the city of Rome);[42] from

---

[38] *Cat.* 2. 8.   [39] e.g. *Flacc.* 37, 92, *frag. Med.* 'tota ex Italia . . . tota Asia . . .'.
[40] *Dom.* 5, 26, 30, 57, 75, 82, 90, 132, 147.   [41] *Cat.* 23. 6.   [42] *Cat.* 31. 7.

Rome Arpinum is not much above seventy miles. Clodius accused Cicero of spending time in Baiae, adding the gibe, 'What has a fellow from Arpinum to do with hot waters?'[43]

Such petty frictions helped to keep the sense of difference between Rome and Italy alive; but they are also a sign of the centripetal tendencies that were pulling Rome and Italy together, for they are the frustrated noises of a group that cannot entirely preserve its exclusiveness. Cicero destroyed Catiline and lived to see one of his associates murder Clodius. It suits him, on occasion, to depict himself as one who had 'broken down the bars' that the nobility had erected between a new man and the consulship, and he was pleased to tell a jury that a noble had abused him as a despot and interloper, 'peregrinus rex'.[44] Such things suggest the importance of the municipals as a constituency, but they do not indicate anti-Roman feeling. Exclusivity seldom breeds contempt in those excluded; rather a desire to cross the forbidden threshold. Respectable families from north of the Po might be caricatured as Gauls or wearers of trousers; it is no surprise that among poets of the republican period it is one from this region who most assiduously advertises his metropolitan style. Catullus is the man from a distance who has got inside: for him 'urbanus' is a favourite term of praise; and he mocks Arrius, the man who puts aspirates in the wrong places, thinking himself very *comme il faut*.[45] It has been noted that under the empire it is the sons of knights who are most scornful of equestrian upstarts; the new man Tacitus derides Sejanus as a bourgeois fornicator, 'municipalis adulter'.[46]

Cicero again makes an interesting study. There was snobbish feeling about him occupying a house which had once belonged to Catulus. He must have felt the sting: in a private letter, far from asserting the claims of merit above rank, he merely answers weakly that people forget that the insignificant Vettius had lived in it before him.[47] In his public utterance too a disdain for the municipia sometimes peeps through even in passages which purport to praise them. Has Torquatus called him 'peregrinus' because he comes from a municipium? Let him know that Cicero is proud of the fact, and understand that such

---

[43] Cic. *Att.* 1. 16. 10. In *Clod. et Cur.* (fr. 19 Crawford) Cicero makes the nature of the insult more explicit: '"What," he said, "would a man from Arpinum, a country bumpkin (agresti et rustico) have to do with Baiae?"'

[44] *Mur.* 17; *Sulla* 22 'peregrinum regem'.   [45] *Cat.* 84.

[46] *Ann.* 4. 3 'municipali adultero'.   [47] *Att.* 4. 5. 2.

insult applies to most of his fellow citizens. These seem proud words; but then Cicero makes a curious change of tack. Why, Torquatus himself is of municipal extraction on his mother's side; from a most honourable and distinguished family, 'sed tamen Asculani' (from Asculum all the same). Let him show that the people of Picenum alone (the region in which Asculum was situated) are not 'peregrini', or else 'let him be grateful that I do not rank my family above his'.[48] In a way this shows the strength of the snobbish argument. Cicero himself, with suitable caution, tries to use it so far as he is able, and presumably he does so without offending those municipals who were on the jury. In another way his words show up the weakness of this snobbery: too many high-born Romans had municipals among their ancestry. But this fact in itself made Romans conscious of their Italian side, Italians concerned with Rome.

'Sed tamen Asculani'—the phrase suggests how hard it still was for a municipal to feel an emotional attachment to the fact of being an Italian. Local pride and loyalty asserted themselves through a con-sciousness of superiority to other towns; and that superiority was perceived in terms of the relationship to Rome. Asculum ranks below Arpinum because it is so much further from Rome, because it is more loosely and recently attached to the historic core of the Roman state. The celebration of patriotic feeling about Italy as a whole would come most naturally from an Italian who was born too far away from the centre of things to have an interest in competing in the game of comparative distance; best of all, perhaps, from a man born north of the Po, in that region which officially was not even part of Italy until the triumviral period.

Cicero damns Vatinius as a man who has climbed out of the gut-ter. But in the same speech he attacks from another angle: Vatinius has been branded with dishonour by the Sabines, a people of admir-able morality, and by those most valiant men, the Marsi and Paeligni, his fellow tribesmen.[49] The game could be played either way: Cicero treats the peoples of the Apennines, whence Vatinius took his origin, with sentimentality or disdain, as suits his convenience. He abuses the consular Piso for his Gaulish or Insubrian ancestry. Presumably this is a fiction, concocted out of the antecedents of his mother's family in Placentia, a municipium on the banks of the Po. Of course Cicero denies that he has anything against that town: he proceeds

[48] *Sulla* 22–5.   [49] *Vat.* 36.

with care, expressing himself aware of its distinction; but sometimes the mask slips. Consider this phrase: 'o familiae non dicam Calpurniae sed Calventiae, neque huius urbis sed Placentini municipi, neque paterni generis sed bracatae cognationis dedecus' (Oh you disgrace—I will say not on the Calpurnian family but the Calventian, not on this city but on the municipality of Placentia, not on your father's family but on your trousered kinsmen).[50] Placentia belongs with the Calventii (that is, with Piso's allegedly Gaulish taint) and the men in trousers as objects of an urbane contempt. Piso's grandfather was 'an auctioneer from Mediolanium';[51] his Transpadane origin is as much a part of the sneer as the humbleness of his occupation.

Cicero's language suggests a tension between two attitudes: a disdain for the backwoods, and a pride of locality which mingles with an affection for the rustic, rugged life of the mountains and the countryside. The first of these sentiments seems to be the stronger: he is always carefully explicit when he talks about his love for Arpinum or his admiration for municipal distinction; it is the condescension that slips out half unawares. Other evidence confirms. Though so fascinated by the history of Roman ceremonies and institutions, he betrays no interest in the local customs and antiquities of Arpinum. It is at Arpinum that he bestows on his son the toga that marks his coming of age, but only because he cannot be at Rome and it pleases the locals.[52] His more personal correspondence, from which calculation and premeditation are largely absent, is especially revealing. From Cilicia he wrote to Atticus, 'lucem, forum, urbem, domum, vos desidero' (It is the world, the forum, the city, my home, and you that I long for).[53] That is a cry from the heart; and he does not think to mention Arpinum. To Caelius he wrote again and again of his longing for Rome: 'mirum me desiderium tenet Urbis', 'miroque desiderio me Urbs afficit', 'Urbem, Urbem, mi Rufe, cole, et in ista luce vive.'[54] In his more leisured and self-conscious writings he remembers to speak of his fondness for his native hills, but under stress Arpinum is forgotten. When Caesar crossed the Rubicon, Cicero was appalled that Pompey abandoned Rome. In his letters to Atticus at the time he repeatedly uses the word 'patria' in the narrow sense of the city itself. Sometimes he even advertises the narrowness: Pompey

---

[50] *Pis.* 53.   [51] *Pis.* 62.   [52] *Att.* 9. 19. 1.   [53] *Att.* 5. 15. 1.
[54] 'I am gripped by an incredible longing for the City', 'The City fills me with incredible longing', 'Stick to the City, the City, Rufus, my friend, and live in that bright world' (*Fam.* 2. 11. 1; 2. 13. 4; 2. 12. 2).

is condemned as one 'qui urbem reliquit, id est patriam' (who has abandoned the city, that is, our *patria*); as for himself, 'urbem, id est patriam, amamus' (I love the city, that is, my *patria*).[55] Once he even distinguishes Italy from his 'patria' in so many words, when he brands Pompey as the man 'qui nostra tradidit, qui patriam reliquit, Italiam relinquit' (who has betrayed our cause, who has abandoned the *patria* and is abandoning Italy).[56] Virgil could never have spoken so; nor anyone else, once Virgil had written.

It is not that Cicero was insincere about his feelings for his native patch; but most people believe that they feel some things more than they really feel them, and he was no exception. And like most people, his feelings allowed place for some inconsistency, as well as for changes of mood or emphasis from time to time. What he says in *De Legibus* deserves a closer look, both for its intrinsic interest and because we find there in simple form themes that Virgil was to take up and turn into great art. The treatise takes the form of a dialogue set in Arpinum. It begins with Cicero's friend Atticus and his brother Quintus conversing about the beauties of the landscape in this place. In the second book the theme is briefly picked up again, and Cicero goes on to explain that this charming spot is really his and Quintus' 'germana patria', in which they are rooted from great antiquity: 'hic enim orti stirpe antiquissima sumus' (We spring from a very old stock here). Atticus expresses surprise: how is it possible to have two 'patriae'? Surely Cicero would not claim that the great Cato's 'patria' was Tusculum rather than Rome? The statesman replies that he considers all municipals to have two 'patriae', 'unam naturae, alteram civitatis, ut ille Cato . . . habuit alteram loci patriam, alteram iuris' (one by nature, the other by citizenship, just as the great Cato . . . had one homeland of place and another by law). But he goes on to insist that of these two 'patriae' the one which bears the name of 'res publica' and which signifies the common citizenship of all—in other words, Rome—must of course have first place in one's affections.[57]

It is a common failing of those who write dialogues to represent their interlocutors as duller than they are likely to have been; and we may doubt whether the astute Atticus would really have been so puzzled by his eminent friend, whose enormous talents, after all, did not include strong originality of mind. We may indeed conclude that Atticus in some ways understood the changing temper

⁵⁵ *Att.* 8. 2. 2; 9. 6. 2.   ⁵⁶ *Att.* 8. 7. 2.   ⁵⁷ *Leg.* 2. 3–5.

of the times better than did Cicero: not only did he survive, but he married his daughter to Agrippa, and died peacefully of old age, with Balbus and his son-in-law at his bedside, long after the famous friend had sacrificed his life to his heroic misunderstanding of political fact.[58] But once we have made allowance for the distortions of the dialogue form, the very conventionality of Cicero's outlook makes the passage revealing. The significance of what he says lies in the fact that he thinks it worth saying. The sense of a dual loyalty genuinely exists in him, but it is a comparatively new kind of feeling: it needs to be declared. And the fact that the Roman loyalty is on his account so much the dominant one also conveys an impression of newness, in two ways: partly because, as we have seen, Cicero did indeed feel much more strongly about Rome than he did about his native town, and partly because he is so evidently anxious not to be misunderstood. When Virgil wrote, he no longer felt the need to be so cautious or defensive: Mantua or Italy could be loudly celebrated without careful indication that this was no diminution from loyalty to Rome.

We may notice too that Cicero's account of the two 'patriae' is enmeshed both with the visible world and with more private considerations of pride in family and locality. The beauty of nature, the sense of antiquity and rootedness in a particular spot of earth—all these things will become parts of the Virgilian amalgam. We shall find in Virgil a personal and original vision, but that originality will consist in large part in his ability to transform the ordinary sentiments of his age. We may detect also a certain equivocation or complexity in the way that Cicero talks about nature here. The second book of *De Legibus* is set in a remarkable place: on an island where the river Fibrenus briefly divides just before plunging down to join the larger river Liris. Cicero's full description of this spot is clearly meant to show us how striking it is: he is proud of the fact that his native patch should include such an unusually fine piece of landscape, rather as a Roman might be especially proud of his state's military glory or an Athenian of his city's achievement in art and philosophy. But mingling with this sentiment are three other slightly different ideas. First, Atticus is made to observe that just as Cicero in discussing law and justice has traced everything back to nature, so nature is supreme in everything which people seek in order to

[58] Nepos, *Att.* 21. 4.

refresh and delight their spirits. 'Nature' is a notoriously slippery word, and Atticus is here shifting its meaning from 'what permanently exists' to a meaning that roughly approximates to 'landscape' or 'the countryside'. This shift—a very natural shift, if one may say so—ought to carry with it a further implication: that hills, trees, rocks, and waters—in other words, all the elements of the landscape which we see and hear about us whenever we go into the countryside—can always best soothe and restore us. If nature can best refresh people simply because it is 'natural', then it should follow that it can best refresh them anywhere and everywhere, and not only in an especially spectacular place like the island in the Fibrenus. Into his praise of an exceptional landscape, Cicero slips what is in effect praise of ordinary landscape—or all landscape, wherever it may be. He was probably unaware himself of this ambiguity or imprecision in his argument, but that is all the more revealing: in celebrating the everyday and universal operations of nature Lucretius and Virgil, in their different ways, created a new way of imagining and enjoying the world; yet they built upon what was becoming the common cultivated sensibility of their time.

Atticus has already added another similar and yet slightly different idea: 'equidem, qui nunc huc potissimum huc venerim, satiari non queo magnificasque villas et pavimenta marmorea et laqueata tecta contemno; ductus vero aquarum, quos isti Nilos et Euripos vocant, quis non, cum haec videat, inriserit?' (I cannot have enough of this place, especially as I have come here at this season, and I scorn those grandiose villas, marble pavements, and coffered ceilings; as for the watercourses which those fellows call Niles and Euripuses, who would not laugh at them, if he could see what we have here).[59] Even in this simple statement there appear to be two notions: first the superiority of simple nature to man-made splendours; second, the idea that the charms of nature cannot be faked. Part of Atticus' idea is presumably that the grandest of artificial waterways will look pretty insignificant in comparison with a good example of the real thing; a judgement with which no doubt we should agree. But the run of his argument suggests that he has also another idea: that these artificial waters may indeed be very grand (like those coffered ceilings) but they fail to please for a different reason. The 'naturalness' of nature is among the secrets of its charm, and the artificialities of landscape

[59] *Leg.* 2. 2.

gardening cannot give a comparable pleasure. In this area the interpreter of Cicero should tread cautiously; as should the interpreter of Virgil, for that matter. It is evident from other places that neither Cicero nor Atticus was generally scornful of urban magnificence or high style: the feeling of satiety with the pompositics of wealth and artifice is only the ghost of a feeling, sensed faintly and occasionally. In Virgil this feeling will emerge once or twice, and a little more strongly, but here too it will be wise to walk warily, and not to imagine a fixed antipathy to wealth or the city or the splendours of architecture. The idea that the beauty or value of nature lies in its authenticity, that it is distasteful to try to improve upon nature or simulate its loveliness, is perhaps even fainter in Cicero's dialogue. It comes and goes in Roman sensibility: Ovid lacks it altogether, as evidently did the grandees who commissioned those mimic Niles, and it is perhaps most strongly expressed, rather surprisingly, by Juvenal.[60] But even if it is never much developed, it is an interesting symptom, however slight, of an incipient feeling that nature is valuable in itself, simply by virtue of being nature, even if it is neither spectacular nor serviceable to man.

Cicero's third idea concerns the associative quality of places. Here, he says, many traces of his ancestors remain: 'hic maiorum multa vestigia.' And he continues,

sed hoc ipso in loco, cum avus viveret et antiquo more parva esset villa . . . me scito esse natum. quare inest nescio quid et latet in animo ac sensu meo, quo me plus hic locus fortasse delectet, siquidem etiam ille sapientissimus vir, Ithacam ut videret, immortalitatem scribitur repudiasse.

I would have you know that I was born in this very place, when my grandfather was still alive and the villa was small in the old-fashioned style . . . And so some feeling is seated and lies deep in my heart and mind, thanks to which this place perhaps gives me a greater delight, much as the wisest of men is recorded to have refused immortality for the sake of seeing Ithaca again.

Atticus agrees: 'movemur enim nescio quo pacto locis ipsis, in quibus eorum, quos diligimus aut admiramur, adsunt vestigia' (For we are moved in some strange way by the actual places in which traces are present of those whom we love or admire).[61] These may look very commonplace notions, but they deserve a slightly closer look. There are in fact two sentiments brought together here: a man's

---

[60] Juv. 3. 17–20.   [61] *Leg.* 2. 3 f.

feeling for his own home ground, and (in Atticus' reply) the spirit of pilgrimage with which those places are approached where great men have lived and died. The very act of associating these two sentiments creates the idea that a man may make his own modest homeland into his personal Athens, as it were; in imagination he can become a pilgrim to the site of his own origins. The very ordinariness or even humbleness of the place in question seems to become part of the effect; Cicero does not forget to mention how small was the house in his grandfather's day. The allusion to the *Odyssey* points in the same direction, for the drama of Odysseus' choice, as we have noticed already, was not just that he gave up immortality but that he gave up a goddess for a mortal woman, less beautiful, and preferred to return to an island that was nothing special as territory, 'rough but a good nurse of men'. Yet Cicero seems to be trying to reach vaguely beyond the idea of 'a poor thing but mine own'. The phrases that he uses—'nescio quid', 'nescio quo pacto'—hint that there is something mysterious about this kind of emotion, something not readily put into words. Twice he speaks of 'vestigia', traces or footprints. That is a metaphor, of course, but it is the kind of metaphor that seems to be straining towards a more literal signification. To borrow the language of a much later writer, there is something interfused in the landscape, some rumour of humanity perceptible through the natural objects which the eye beholds.[62] A little later Cicero offers a comparison which is both amusing and suggestive; speaking of the Fibrenus, he says, 'It plunges promptly into the Liris and, as though entering a patrician family, it loses its rather obscure name . . .'[63] In his defence of Caelius he had spoken of his municipal origins as the source from which he had flowed forth into celebrity among men; now the metaphor is reversed, and it is the actual Apennine river which is like one of municipal birth attaining a grand Roman status. These things are only straws in the wind, but straws have their significance: the interplay of metaphor suggests a current of feeling in which man's emotions are starting to blend with his landscape in a newly intimate way, in which the abstract and the concrete are beginning to merge. It is Virgil who will best realize the possibilities: he will use the word 'vestigia' to marvellous effect, as a metaphor and yet more than a metaphor.[64]

---

[62] Wordsworth, *Lines composed a few miles above Tintern Abbey*, discussed in Ch. 8.
[63] *Leg.* 2. 6.   [64] See below, pp. 205 f.

And he will evoke Clitumnus in terms that suggest the flow of its waters out of Umbria and down (mingled with the Tiber) to the city of Rome—both an actuality and the expression of an Italian's complex national identity.[65] He was not echoing Cicero, to be sure; rather bringing to an unsuspected maturity those germs of feeling that had been broadcast by the spirit of the age.

Our evidence, then, suggests that in Virgil's generation the time was ripe for his blend of Roman and Italian patriotism: fifty years before would have been too early. Equally, he could hardly have written as he did if he had lived very much later. We have seen two forces at work: the standardizing effect of Graeco-Roman culture; and the tendency of the circle of power to expand from its original nucleus in the city of Rome to embrace the wealthy of an ever wider area. In the first century BC these forces were increasing the importance of Italy in the affairs of Rome, but in the longer run they would reduce it again to insignificance. The portents were there in Virgil's own lifetime, ambiguous as portents are supposed to be. In 40 Balbus became consul, the first man from outside Italy to achieve this office; though of Italian stock, he came from Gades in distant Spain, and only sixteen years earlier his very entitlement to the citizenship had been challenged in court. One of the next men from outside the historic borders of Italy to attain high position—and the first perhaps to win significantly independent power—was Gallus, also a poet and a friend of Virgil, appointed first prefect of Egypt by Caesar Octavian in 30. He came from either Cisalpine or Narbonese Gaul; if the former, then from that Transpadane region which produced Catullus, Cinna, and Virgil; if the latter, from a similarly prosperous, semi-provincial background.[66] But the symptoms of the success of Transpadane Italy and Narbonese Gaul are also the omens of Italy's eventual decline. The rise of the municipal Italians had been bound

---

[65] Geo. 2. 146–8.

[66] Gallus came from Forum Iulii, which might be either modern Fréjus or modern Cividale da Friuli. Even this much is not quite certain. No Forum Iulii yet existed when Gallus was born (but the anachronism seems in itself easy enough—cf. 'Rubens was born in Belgium', 'when Pushkin was here in Leningrad'). On the basis of an inscription recording Gallus' construction of a 'Forum Iulii' in Egypt, it has lately been suggested that the information about his birthplace might be garbled (E. Courtney, The Fragmentary Latin Poets (Oxford, 1993), 259 f.); but there is no strong reason to reject the evidence of our sources. The Forum Iulii in Narbonese Gaul (Fréjus) is first met with in 43 BC, and was far better known than its Transpadane namesake; the natural presumption is that it was Gallus' birthplace (so R. Syme, 'The Origin of Cornelius Gallus', CQ 32 (1938), 39–44, reprinted in his Roman Papers, i (Oxford, 1979), 47–54).

to lead on to the rise of ambitious Italians born outside the peninsula; and the process could not stop there: the great provincial mag-
nates of whatever race—above all, the Greeks—would in due course
claim their share of Roman influence and prestige. The rich and
educated, from whatever corner of the empire, would be more suavely
Romanized and speak better Latin than small-town Italians. In the
middle of the second century AD men from Africa and the eastern
empire are predominant in the senate; in the same century we find
Transpadane Italy, Virgil's homeland, governed by an imperial legate,
as though it were a province.[67] That made permanent a degradation which had been inflicted, on occasion, very much earlier; a
Transpadane orator, Albucius Silo of Novaria, writing a few years
after Virgil's death, laments that his homeland has been reduced to a
province again.[68] Once emperor, Tiberius never left Italy, nor Augustus
in his later years; a century later emperors might be proclaimed outside Italy and not visit it for years at a time.

The Roman empire of Virgil's time was also, in a sense, an Italian
empire; Rome was not yet, as it would eventually be, the symbol of
a power whose true capital or capitals lay elsewhere. Thus it may seem
that in celebrating the whole of Italy from the Alps southward—
that is, an area comprising both the peninsula and the former Cisalpine Gaul—what he chose to celebrate was the space where power
resided in his own day; effectively, the boundaries of the governing
state. But this is not the whole truth, for Italy itself had reached the
limits of its own expansion in Virgil's lifetime, and the area which
he celebrates is the area which in its totality still seems to us, two
thousand years later, rightly called Italy. Consider the speech of
Claudius (as Tacitus reports it) in which the emperor defends the
admission of Gauls from beyond the Alps into the senate. He argues
that the growth of Rome's power in the time of the republic was
accompanied by the incorporation of new peoples: men from Lucania,
Etruria, and finally from all Italy were brought into the senate. Now
we cross the Po: 'postremo ipsam ad Alpis promotam ut non modo
singuli viritim sed terrae gentes in nomen nostrum coalescerent' (Later
Italy itself was extended to the Alps so that not only particular individuals but lands and peoples should come together, sharing our
name).[69] The argument is that the zone of power has steadily been

---

[67] *ILS* 1040; R. Syme, *Tacitus* (Oxford, 1958), 224.

[68] Suet. *Rhet.* 6; for the date and circumstances, R. Syme, *The Augustan Aristocracy* (Oxford, 1986), 331 f.   [69] Tac. *Ann.* 11. 24. 2.

widened, but in the middle of it Claudius is forced to change tack. Hitherto he has been talking about the extension of power within Italy; 'Italy' itself can be extended beyond the Po; but once it has reached the Alps it can go no further. Transalpine Gauls can be made Roman citizens, even senators, but the master of the world himself cannot make them men of Italy. Like style, the geographical expression abides, outlasting dynasties. And what Virgil saw as the completion of Italy and what Tacitus saw and what we still see, so many centuries later, as the completion of Italy was fresh when the *Georgics* were composed. The matter can be looked at in either of two ways. Perhaps Virgil was lucky: Italy was in his time at once a political fact and a geographical fact and an emotional fact to a degree that it has seldom been for most of the past two and a half thousand years; and what is more, the political fact was new. Or we might praise him for helping to create the emotional fact; for he is distinct from all his contemporaries in the strength and complexity of his sense of Italy. In the last analysis it may be best to say that there is no antithesis, and acknowledge that genius is the capacity to see where one's luck lies and make use of it.

Virgil, then, was born at the right time; and he was born in the right place: in the Transpadane country, Italy-north-of-the-Po.[70] In the first century this was a conspicuously prosperous area, its wealth based upon the fertile alluvial plain of the Po, good soil for vines and corn. The Via Emilia gave it easy communications with Rome and the rest of the peninsula; also important in an age when bulk transport by land was impossibly expensive over more than short distances was the easy access to the Adriatic Sea. It was therefore richer and more cultivated than most of the mountain country to the south of it, although the Apennine lands were closer to Rome and were legally part of Italy as in Virgil's boyhood the Transpadana was not. Catullus, from Verona, even ventured a humorous rebuke to Asinius, brother of the great Pollio, for lack of *savoir faire*, with a teasing glance at his origins among the Marrucini, from the rough heartland of the high central Apennines.[71] But something more than simple economic advantage is needed to account for the prominence of Transpadana in the first century, for the towns north of the Po seem to have been more vigorous, inventive and successful than those cities which lay

---

[70] G. Chilver, *Cisalpine Gaul* (Oxford, 1941) is an essential resource; among more recent studies of the area are R. Chevallier, *La Romanisation de la Celtique du Pô* (Rome, 1983), D. Foraboschi, *Lineamenti di storia della Cisalpina Romana* (Rome, 1992).   [71] Cat. 12.

south of them along the Via Emilia itself: Parma, Mutina, and
Placentia, for example, also cities of the plain but apparently lacking some of the dynamism of the places to the north of them.
Archaeological evidence represents them as towns of less wealth and
civic ambition; and the witness of our written sources confirms the
picture. Patavium, modern Padua, at one time had more citizens with
a knight's census than any city save Rome itself.[72] No great men seem
to come from the southern cities of the plain in the last generations
of the republic, a period in which Transpadana gave birth to the
historian Nepos, the philosopher Catius, the critic Valerius Cato,
and the poets Cinna, Catullus, Furius Bibaculus, Cassius Parmensis,
Volusius, and Virgil—a good mixture of genius, talent, and the vigorously second-rate.[73]

Where did this energy come from? Some of the towns had been
sacked and the countryside despoiled by the Gaulish invaders of the
late second century. And settlers from various parts of Italy had been
moving into the area both before and after the invasions. The experiences of Germany after the Second World War and of America in
the nineteenth century suggest that the need to rebuild after destruction and the settlement in new territory can alike act as a stimulus
to stir up social energies. More imponderable is the question of race.[74]
The evidence of nomenclature suggests that the Italians who settled
in the Transpadana were themselves of mixed origins: Oscans, Latins,
Etruscans. And they came to a region which was already home to
a variety of peoples. Celts, Raetians, Venetians, and Illyrians had all
established towns in Cisalpine Gaul, and it is possible that non-Italians
continued to be a majority. Patavium was a Venetic foundation, Mantua
was supposedly Etruscan (Virgil indulged the fancy that Etruscans
had settled it long before even Aeneas came to Italy);[75] Mediolanium
was originally the home of the Insubres, a Gallic tribe; Cremona was
a Latin colony. The name Vergilius may well be Etruscan; the name
of the poet's mother, Magia, is most probably Oscan.[76] The mixture
of races may have fizzed together to produce a peculiar vitality. Equally,
though, we should be aware of our ignorance: we cannot tell what
story of murder, racial bitterness, or conflict between new possessors

[72] Strabo 3. 5. 3 (= C 169).
[73] For other literary gentlemen and scholars certainly or probably from Transpadana see
E. Rawson, *Intellectual Life in the Late Roman Republic* (London, 1985), 35 n.
[74] Chilver, *Cisalpine Gaul*, 80–6.   [75] *Aen.* 10. 198 ff.
[76] The name Vergilius is widely found, but most often in Etruria.

and the dispossessed lies behind the smooth picture of Transpadane prosperity presented by our sources.

This much, however, can be said: the diversity of the Transpadanes' origins is not visible in those among them who became prominent in Roman life or literature. Out of that variety there had grown a unity, at least within the upper class. Time rubs away nice distinctions, it is true; but we may detect a certain community of outlook in the coming men from the north. Perhaps it is not merely fanciful to think that Virgil, Livy, Pliny, even Catullus maybe—people of very different temperament—have something in common: a certain old-fashionedness of attitude combined with an ability to get on in the modern world, a sense of locality mixed in with their self-conscious urbanity and sophistication. But one could not guess by their manners or opinions from which of the Transpadane towns any of these men came, nor what were their ultimate origins. The 'Patavinitas', 'Paduan-ness', that Pollio superciliously detected in Livy was surely to be found as readily in Mantua and Verona and the other cities of the plain.[77] A century after Virgil the Plinii at least (from Comum, a Roman colony) thought of Transpadane Italy as a whole: the elder Pliny calls Catullus 'conterraneum meum', and his nephew speaks of a family from Brixia as being 'ex illa nostra Italia'.[78] And that feeling of solidarity presumably existed much earlier: it is no accident that we find Catullus in close connection with his fellow Transpadanes, dedicating a volume to Nepos and commending 'my dear Cinna' for his verse.[79]

Yet for all their social and literary dash, a successful municipal from closer to the City might still detect in the Transpadanes a trace of provincialism: Cicero warns Brutus that when he becomes governor of Cisalpine Gaul he will meet words unfamiliar in Rome; these can be unlearnt. And Brutus will notice that Roman orators speak with a tone and accent that is somehow 'urbanius', more metropolitan.[80] We may now look with a touch of irony on Catullus' mockery of Arrius' pronunciation, his dig at Asinius' Marrucine extraction, his adoption of 'urbanus' as a term of praise, and wonder how much unlearning the young poet had to do when he came to Rome.

---

[77] Quint. 1. 5. 56 and 8. 1. 3. Quintilian himself supposed 'Patavinitas' to refer to Livy's style or language; Syme, The Roman Revolution, 485 f., argues that it referred to outlook.

[78] Nat. Hist. praef. 1 'my fellow countryman'; Ep. 1. 14. 4 'from that Italy of ours . . .'.

[79] Cat. 1 and 95.   [80] Brut. 171.

His touches of cliquishness should not surprise us: it is commonly the last man to gallop across the drawbridge who is most eager to bang the portcullis down. However, during the long principate of Augustus no *novus homo* from north of the Po was to attain the consulship;[81] despite affluence and cultivation the Transpadanes still did not move with perfect ease, it seems, in the very highest ranks of the state. The younger Pliny relates that Tacitus was once asked, 'Are you an Italian or a provincial?' Getting an ambiguous reply, the questioner continued, 'Are you Tacitus or Pliny?'[82] The story has an equivocal moral. It suggests that there was indeed felt to be a difference between Italy and even the most Romanized province, but that the difference could be hard to detect. It implies, also, that a man might pick up a trace of something provincial in even so cosmopolitan a Transpadane as Pliny, who had houses in Rome and elsewhere in peninsular Italy in addition to his estates on Lake Como.[83] The elder Pliny called Narbonese Gaul 'more truly Italy than a province', but by the same token Transpadana was as much provincial as Italian.[84] Gallus and Catullus—poets, lovers, and contemporaries—come from the same background and belong to the same class and milieu; it matters little which side of the Alps the former was born. The Transpadanes were Italian, to be sure, but they were Italians with a distinctive timbre.

The combination of a half-provincial position, local energy and increasing contact with a larger metropolitan society can prove a sharp spur to creativity. One might compare eighteenth-century Edinburgh or Edwardian Dublin. In one respect such a high-provincial culture even has the edge over the metropolis: it may be readier to look further afield. Edinburgh was particularly receptive to the ideas of the Enlightenment; the Transpadane poets advertised their exceptional interest in Alexandria.[85] Political power and autonomy do not seem to be the catalysts in such cases, or at least not in an obvious way. Edinburgh's great period began after it had ceased to be a national capital; and since becoming a national capital Dublin has seemed

---

[81] Syme, *Tacitus*, 589.   [82] *Ep.* 9. 23. 2 f.

[83] If Tacitus was from Gallia Narbonensis, as some think, it is especially interesting that the Narbonese and Transpadane flavours were so hard to tell apart. Syme, *Tacitus*, 614–24, discusses his origins.   [84] *Nat. Hist.* 3. 31.

[85] Consider esp. Cat. 63, 64, 65, 66, Cinna's *Zmyrna* (on which see Cat. 95), Virgil's *Eclogues*; and perhaps Gallus, if not an actual Transpadane, may be reckoned an honorary one. Of course, all Roman poets wrote under the shadow of Greece, and few escaped some touch of Alexandrian influence; but the elaborate and sometimes precious homage of these Transpadane poets to the Alexandrians is distinctive.

less brilliant, more self-absorbed. In either case one may suspect a relationship of cause and effect: the best conditions for regional creativity seem to be where there is a balance between contact with the metropolitan culture and a certain separateness; where pride of locality is strong but at the same time sufficiently confident to look outwards to a wider world. In the eighteenth century Scotsmen could feel themselves for the first time to be Scots and North Britons and Europeans, while conversely Ireland's cultural retreat seems related to or at least deepened by an ideology which has cried 'Ourselves Alone' and refused to contemplate the proposition that Irish culture is a regional form of a British culture whose metropolis is bound to remain in England. Returning to the Roman empire, we observe with interest that in the first century AD the Transpadana, now firmly classed as part of Italy, is no longer so productive of literary talent, whereas a disproportionate number of writers now come from Spain: Lucan, the two Senecas, Martial, Quintilian. And indeed Spain had reached a position similar to that which Transpadane Italy had occupied in the century before. It was well separated from Rome, but had connections with metropolitan culture and power (for a few years Seneca was one of a pair who virtually ruled the world); the inhabitants were a mixture of Italian settlers and native peoples (it has been surmised that Martial and Quintilian, both from the Ebro basin, had Celtiberian blood);[86] and those Italians, though 'colonial', were richer and more sophisticated than many of their race and class who had remained in the aboriginal homeland. The balance of closeness and apartness was right, it seems, for Spain in this period as it had been earlier for the northern plain.[87]

But one difference at least would always remain between Spain and the Transpadane country, as we can see from the case of Martial. When he writes with affection about the natural beauties of his native Bilbilis, he has inherited a sensibility of which Virgil was a principal creator; we can compare Virgil's descriptions of the river Mincius, Propertius on Umbria, Ovid on the well-watered meadows of Sulmo. But as a poet and a lover of his homeland, Martial faced a dilemma: either he could remain in the urbane, cultivated sphere of Rome and middle Italy, or he could return to Bilbilis. He chose Bilbilis;

[86] Syme, *Tacitus*, 618.
[87] When thinking about closeness, we should distinguish between trade in commodities and trade in ideas. Of course commerce is often an engine for the transmission of culture, but we need to remember that the traffic in ideas can be rapid in times and places where the traffic in goods is not.

and he lived to regret the choice.[88] A Transpadane was not so painfully placed: we can watch Catullus (for example) moving between Rome and Verona, at home both in the urbanity of the metropolis and amid the natural charms of Sirmio. He could be a Roman and an Italian and a visitor upon occasion to his local *patria*; and even if he had never crossed the Po again after his first journey south, he would still have been able to feel himself an Italian in Italy as a man in Martial's position could not. A Transpadane created the sensibility of the *Georgics*; a poet from Spain, even though he had been Italian by blood and Roman by citizenship, could not have done so.

We commonly observe those on the edge of a group or community feeling the pride of belonging most keenly, and patriotism is often strongest among those who in one sense or another are at the margins of their country. Of course, the Transpadanes had straightforwardly practical reasons for wanting to assert their Italian identity. They were at the margin of Italy in a literal sense; and though other Italians were as far from Rome, they alone were on a frontier, with barbarous and as yet unsubdued tribes perilously close in the mountains above; the Cimbri had threatened catastrophe within thirty years of Catullus' birth.[89] It was expedient for Cisalpine Gaul that Rome should regard its people as her people and their country as her country. But there were considerations of sentiment also. The margins, literal or figurative, tend to be more conservative than the centre. We have seen that the more Rome became Hellenized and corrupted by moral rot, real or imagined, the more the small towns of the Apennines became the repositories of traditional Roman values; we have also seen the north associated with an old-fashioned severity of manners which had once been proverbially associated with Apennine countryfolk, like Sabines and Marsians. It is revealing that in his dedicatory poem Catullus praises Nepos as the one Italian ('unus Italorum') who has dared to unfold the whole of history:[90] no one would have troubled to honour Pompey or Cicero in quite those terms. In the next generation it will be another Transpadane who

[88] Mart. 12, *praef.*

[89] Verona today is dotted with plaques recording 19th-cent. Austrian atrocities; at Lovere a memorial to the partisans of the 1940s blames 'il furore Teutonico'. Until recently at least the Veronese and their neighbours have wanted to keep alive a sense of dangerous foreigners close at hand. (For that matter, 'Deutschland, Deutschland über alles' contains a verse envisaging the extension of Germany to the Adige, on which river Verona stands.) The proximity of one of the richest parts of Italy to the Alps, and hence to other peoples felt as alien and hostile, has been a persistently important fact in European history.

[90] Cat. 1. 5 f.

presents the Battle of Actium as an Italian victory, in the eighth book of the *Aeneid*.[91] Presumably Catullus includes among the 'Itali' all those who live between the Alps and the Straits of Messina; yet perhaps one may detect the beginnings of a process that leads, it seems, to a quirk of nomenclature. By a dynamic similar to that by which southern Italy became 'Magna Graecia' (Great Greece), Italia itself becomes, in the mouth of some Transpadanes, the name of their own region. So speaks Albucius Silo, the orator from Novaria;[92] and we have already heard Pliny describing a Transpadane family as 'ex illa nostra Italia'.[93] Transpadana was in the process of becoming more Italian than the Italians.

Sentiment, as well as anxiety, enlarges the patriotism of frontier zones. Indeed, national heroes have quite often come from the edges, or from beyond the edges, of the countries they have inspired. Napoleon was Italian; Garibaldi, a Savoyard born in Nice, was almost French; De Valera was born in New York, the son of a Spaniard, and escaped execution after the Easter Rising because he was American. Churchill had an American mother, as did Parnell; Lloyd George, the Welsh wizard, was born plain George in Manchester; Dufour, Switzerland's national hero, was born in Germany; Joan of Arc and De Gaulle (that poet of 'la France profonde') were the children of border lands. The two monsters of European nationalism also fit the pattern: the Austrian Hitler and the Georgian Stalin. A similar moral may sometimes be drawn from literature, high and low. Possibly the most eloquent expressions of Englishry in the last century and in this were produced by Americans: Henry James and T. S. Eliot. Conversely, the author of 'God bless America' was a native of Siberia. As for Ireland, it is the Anglo-Saxons who have drifted entranced through the Celtic twilight, while the native Irishry have kept their hard, satiric eye. These phenomena are not deeply surprising: the national feeling is likely to be especially strong among those in whom it is an achieved thing, not mere instinct; who have pondered it, chosen it, perhaps striven for it.

Under Augustus it is gentlemen from middle Italy who write love elegy and appear less impressed by the patriotic zeal of the new order. The Ovidii were one of the two leading families of Sulmo; Ovid has no need of a patron, declines the public career that lay open to

---

[91] *Aen.* 8. 678, 715.

[92] Suet. *Rhet.* 6: defending a client at Mediolanum, Albucius lamented that Italy was being reduced again to a province. See above, p. 98.

[93] *Ep.* 1. 14. 4, i.e. 'from our part of Italy which . . .'.

him, and numbers high aristocrats among his acquaintances. Albius
Tibullus presents himself as a *déclassé* gentleman, with most of his
property lost but still clinging on to a modest amount of land. We
do well to be suspicious of anything that he says about himself,[94]
but this account at least is probably not far from reality. He did need
the patronage of Messalla, but if he is the Albius addressed by Horace,
he enjoyed a tolerable prosperity.[95] Propertius comes from a good
family in Asisium, at the heart of Umbria; in the first book he is
independent of any patron and writes to friends of consular family
on equal terms. These poets celebrated irresponsibility, the life of
love; contrast the dutiful Livy, on the margins, in distant Patavium.
Unlike Livy, Virgil did not continue to live in his native Transpadana,
but it is perhaps significant that he is said to have spent most of his
adult life in Campania, at some distance from the centre of events,
in Italy but not in Rome. Horace's origins were in remote Venusia,
on the borders of Apulia and Lucania, and he was marginal in another
sense also: his father had once been a slave, and the taint could never
be forgotten. With that parentage, there must be a good chance that
he was not of Italian race.[96]

Social background influences habit of mind: we are not surprised
to find one tendency in the gentlemen of the Apennines, another in
the men of the margins. Social class is not identical with economic
class, but there is an obvious interdependence. One of the causes
that drew Virgil, Horace, and others into Maecenas' circle will

[94] Few will imagine that there is much historicity in Marathus or Nemesis; perhaps there
is not much more in Delia; but 1. 3 has an autobiographical air. Yet it can hardly be, as
it purports, the work of a man gravely ill, possibly near death.
[95] Hor. *Carm.* 1. 33; *Epist.* 1. 4 (line 7 indicates that he is well-to-do). The identity is
usually assumed; there seems to be no evidence beyond the fact that this Albius writes
elegies (*Carm.* 1. 33. 3). Tibullus' early death earned him an elegy from Ovid (*Am.* 3. 9);
Horace is silent.
[96] The self-portrait of *Epist.* 1. 20 notes his dark complexion; the whiteness of his hair
was striking. Speculation can hardly go further. One or two snub-nosed portrait sculp-
tures have sometimes been identified as Horace—not, it seems, on any defensible basis.
G. Williams ('*Libertino Patre Natus*: True or False?', in S. J. Harrison (ed.), *Homage to
Horace* (Oxford, 1995)) suggests that Horace was the son of an Italian rebel in the Social
War, captured at the fall of Venusia, sold into slavery, and later freed. His ingenious case
is much weakened if he is right (as he probably is) to concede that such a person would
not naturally be described as a freedman. He must therefore maintain that each time Horace
calls himself a freedman's son the words represent not his own description of himself but
the derisive view of others. That claim, correct at *Serm.* 1. 6. 45 and 46, is doubtful at
Serm. 1. 6. 6 and very improbable at *Epist.* 1. 20. 20. The case is necessarily speculative
but Williams's positive arguments for it are thin.

have been crudely economic: the need for money. We need not be excessively cynical: the interplay between advantage and emotion is a subtle one. Is the man who rejoices at the return of stability and secure possession patriotic or concerned for himself? Looking back from the reign of Tiberius, Velleius Paterculus sums up the blessings of Augustus' settlement: 'rediit cultus agris, sacris honos, securitas hominibus, certa cuique rerum suarum possessio' (Tillage returned to the land, respect to religion, security to people, and to everyone the assured possession of his own property).[97] Much of this recalls the Virgilian amalgam, as we meet it in the *Georgics*: a vision that blends the land and its life, peace, and the continuance of traditional religious observance. But there is also, avowedly, the note of personal advantage: the possessing classes can hold on to what they have got with confidence. Patriotism, tradition, and comfort are indivisibly mixed together. To the question whether the man who writes thus is sincerely loyal or a time-server the answer must be that the complexity of human nature does not allow so neat an unravelling; people weave a mesh of idea and sentiment into their own self-interest.

Maecenas acquired Virgil, Varius, and Horace early; Propertius is a more complicated case. At the start of his second book we find him addressing Maecenas, but with patches of asperity. It would seem to be Maecenas who has been making the advances; the poet can afford the odd gesture of recalcitrance. Hence a paradox, which goes unobserved. The sharper his touches of acerbity towards Caesar are, the more freely chosen does his accommodation with the regime appear, for these sharpnesses are signs that he does not absolutely need Maecenas and can choose his degree of distance. In his third book he can still, in effect, decline the invitation to write in praise of the great man.[98] In his last book he declares a desire to serve his 'patria',[99] and turns to the early legends of Rome; he even celebrates Caesar's victory at Actium, albeit with dashes of acidity.[100]

---

[97] Vell. 2. 89.

[98] Prop. 3. 9. 47 ff.: the poet is prepared to contemplate large mythological themes, and even the triumphs of Caesar—'te duce' (with you to guide me). This ambiguous phrase can be interpreted as an offer to write about Caesar 'when you do'—that is, never.

[99] Prop. 4. 1. 60.

[100] Prop. 4. 6. The remark at line 65 f.—how paltry a triumphal procession with Cleopatra in it would have seemed to a city which had seen Jugurtha—can hardly fail to be an impertinence, and 'bella satis cecini' (I have sung enough of war), line 69, is insouciantly dégagé. But we should also remember that Propertius is writing under Virgil's shadow and will have been anxious to vary his presentation of the battle for reasons of purely aesthetic

Thereafter, unless he died young, he exercised another freedom: the choice of silence. We cannot know what circumstances lie behind all this: a softening with the years? the placidity of incipient middle age? a recognition of the blessings of peace? Maecenas' tact? a style of life that ran beyond the poet's income?—most likely some interplay between several of these things. And there will also have been the spell of the *Aeneid*. The eighth book had opened up a new imaginative field which drew all three elegists;[101] Propertius even bases two of his five aetiological poems upon it, one on Actium and the other on Hercules' slaughter of Cacus.[102] But there remains this difference, that when he talks of his 'patria', Propertius is thinking of Umbria and of Rome. The name of Italy does not occur in any of these aetiological pieces.[103]

A Transpadane was well placed to apprehend a sense of national unity-in-diversity. Looking inward, at his own region, he could see that it combined racial variety with the sentiment of local solidarity; looking outward, beyond its borders, he would wish to see it as unambiguously a part of Italy, adding a distinctive element to the larger whole. In the second half of the *Aeneid* we find both things: a diversity within Italy itself and a people from outside its borders, the Trojans, aspiring to be added to it. The *Aeneid* is a Roman and an Italian and a Transpadane poem; proleptic of future history, the Mantuans come to fight on the Trojan side.[104] And there were other reasons why a Transpadane might well feel an all-Italian loyalty more easily than (let us say) an Umbrian. His region had not been caught up with the revolt of the Apennine highlanders in the Social War; later, under the triumvirs, Transpadane Italy suffered from the confiscations, like the peninsula, but its troubles did not match the horror of Perusia. A sophisticated Transpadane might be able to view Italy both from without and within; the mixture of engagement

ambition. (The poem is taken in a subversive sense by K. Galinsky, 'The Triumph Theme in Augustan Elegy', *WS* 82 (1969), 75–107, at 86 f.; W. R. Johnson, 'The Emotions of Patriotism: Propertius 4. 6', *CSCA* 6 (1973), 151–80; and J. P. Sullivan, *Propertius* (Cambridge, 1976), 145–7; whereas W. Richter, 'Divus Julius, Octavianus und Kleopatra bei Aktion', *WS* NS 79 (1966), 451–65, at 463, believes that Propertius is trying to outdo Horace in patriotic fervour; J. Griffin, in F. Millar and C. Segal (eds.), *Caesar Augustus: Seven Aspects* (Oxford, 1984), 189–221, at 208 f., strikes a judicious balance.)

[101] See below, pp. 604 ff.   [102] Prop. 4. 6; 4. 9.

[103] In 3. 22, his homage to Virgil's *laus Italiae*, he calls Italy 'Romana terra'; see below, p. 605.   [104] *Aen.* 10. 198 ff.

and detachment in the *Georgics* was indeed a personal and original achievement of Virgil's, but it may none the less owe something to his standing-ground.

The fall of the republic must have affected both winners and losers, not only materially but in moral tone. For men of the margins, with less stake in the old oligarchy than the traditional governing class, the new order will often have been easy enough to accept: to those content with private life it offered peace and stability, while those with public ambitions might find new opportunities in a disturbed time. We have already noted Balbus and Gallus; and Caesar's vital military commanders in the later 30s BC were Agrippa and Tarius Rufus, both men of undistinguished birth and geographically remote ancestry.[105] Such people, from conviction or policy, would quickly absorb the moral and patriotic resonances of the Augustan settlement. The effects on those who lost or appeared to have lost from the years of upheaval make a subtler study. We should not assume them to have been flatly resistant to the Augustan tone, for it is human nature to make the best of a bad job, and by an adjustment of sentiment to tap new sources of emotional satisfaction once circumstances have irrevocably changed. Sentiment is soft by nature; gripped in the fist of necessity, it proves readily malleable. Sentiment mollifies misfortune and imparts dignity to humiliation. We can catch glimpses of a complex process of emotional adjustment in the period of revolution, and after.

Quietism flourishes at a time of political disturbance, and especially among a ruling group or class which is losing power and influence. It has been estimated, for example, that in the 24 years of Charles I's reign more poems were written about the happiness of a retired life in the country than in the 67 years of Elizabeth I and James I put together.[106] In the 1650s, above all, the royalist gentry made a virtue of necessity by praising the delights of rural existence; *The Compleat Angler* was a favourite book. Similarly, when Cicero in his later letters extols the pleasures of a philosophical withdrawal, his feeling is prompted, without insincerity, by the fact that withdrawal from political leadership had been forced on him. He exemplifies a tendency which in due course comes also to affect those, like Virgil, who would never have aspired to political prominence in any case.

[105] Syme, *The Augustan Aristocracy*, 44, 55.
[106] M.-S. Røstvig, *The Happy Man* (Oslo, 1954), 174.

It is interesting to compare two glimpses of landscape from the writings of Cicero's later years. One is from *De Natura Deorum*; the words are put into the mouth of Lucilius Balbus, the spokesman for Stoicism in the dialogue, whose views may not be entirely the author's own. That does not matter for our purpose; indeed, the passage is valuable not for offering a personal outlook but as an official, representative expression of an influential world-view. The divine providence is exhibited in the beauty and utility of the world:[107]

ac principio terra universa cernatur, locata in media sede mundi, solida et globosa et undique ipsa in sese nutibus suis conglobata, vestita floribus herbis arboribus frugibus, quorum omnium incredibilis multitudo insatiabili varietate distinguitur. adde huc fontium gelidas perennitates, liquores perlucidos amnium, riparum vestitus viridissimos, speluncarum concavas altitudines, saxorum asperitates, inpendentium montium altitudines immensitatesque camporum; adde etiam reconditas auri argentique venas infinitamque vim marmoris. quae vero et quam varia genera bestiarum vel cicurum vel ferarum! qui volucrium lapsus atque cantus! qui pecudum pastus! quae vita silvestrium! quid iam de hominum genere dicam? qui quasi cultores terrae constituti non patiuntur eam nec inmanitate beluarum efferari nec stirpium asperitate vastari, quorumque operibus agri, insulae litoraque collucent distincta tectis et urbibus.

First let us look at the whole earth, stationed in the middle of the universe, solid, rounded, formed into a sphere by its own gravitational force on every side, clothed with flowers, grass, trees, and crops, an amazing multitude of plants diversified by an inexhaustible variety. Consider further the cool springs that never fail, the pellucid flow of rivers, the bright green garb of their banks, the hollow heights of caves, the roughness of rocks, the heights of looming mountains, and the vastness of plains; consider too the hidden veins of gold and silver and the limitless mass of marble. How many and various are the kinds of animals, both tame and wild! Those birds flying and singing! The cattle at pasture! The life of the woodland creatures! What need I say of the race of men? Appointed as it were tillers of the earth, they do not allow it to become wild with savage beasts or to become a waste tangle of scrub; by their industry fields, islands and coasts sparkle, picked out with houses and cities.

And the speaker goes on to expatiate on the beauties of sea and air. At the root of this is still the old Homeric view, that nature is delightful when it is commodious—when its roughness has been tamed by man to his own profit and convenience. Cities (or towns) are seen

107 *Nat. D.* 2. 98 f.

as purely pleasing. But grafted on to this is a more romantic idea: caves, rough rocks, and overhanging mountains are attractive in themselves, part of the evidence for divine providence and the good planning of the world. Here we catch the sensibility that Virgil was to deepen and enrich when he created the harbour of the first Aeneid; we may also fancy a likeness to the landscapes that were being painted on the walls of rich men's homes at this period. In this passage we feel Cicero (or Stoicism) to fit a large pattern of cultural history and to be comfortably in the flow of an old but evolving tradition: as he moves from wild to cultivated nature, he seems closer to the second Georgic than to Homer. Houses and towns take their modest place in a broadly expansive prospect that embraces shores and islands as well as agricultural land; nature is valued first and foremost for its beauty and only secondarily for its practical use.

This vision of nature is still centred upon man, and indeed is offered as a demonstration of the divine forethought for humankind; even the caves and cliffs are put into the world, as on to the walls of those villas, to gratify our eyes. It is a formal picture; informally Cicero could experience nature in a less complacently tidy way. In 45 BC, distressed and anxious, he retreated to Astura, on the coast south of Rome, from where he wrote to Atticus: 'In this lonely place I do not speak to a soul. In the morning I hide myself away in a thick, tangled wood, and I do not emerge from it until evening. After you I have no better friend than solitude.'[108] Here the feeling for uncultivated nature is significantly different from that in Lucilius Balbus' speech. The wildness is no longer an agreeable decoration, fitted harmoniously into a larger whole: Cicero submits to it, plunges into it, surrounds himself with it. And the very thickness, roughness, loneliness are themselves soothing and consoling. Cicero is still a fair distance from a settled delight in wilderness for its own sake: plainly it is a disturbed state of mind that wrings out of him this new response to his natural surroundings, so different from that educated taste for the picturesque which he brings to the island in the Fibrenus. But this fact has its own significance: it is political upheaval that drives him, literally as well as metaphorically, into the wilderness. The retreat into the thickets of Astura is emblematic both of changes in Cicero's life and of change in the sensibility of the age. However, his taste even for the picturesque was still limited: on a later occasion he

[108] *Att.* 12. 15.

confessed that he could soon have enough of scenic charm: 'I can tell you, this place is lovely, secluded certainly, and free from over-lookers, if you want to do some writing. But somehow, "there's no place like home".'[109]

We may easily enough infer that a taste for retreat to the country or to the small towns grew in the years of civil war; but it is also true that there was a strong streak of quietism among the upper classes before ever Julius Caesar fought Pompey. Once again, Cicero is a telling witness, partly because he is sometimes an unconscious or a reluctant witness. In his speech for Cluentius he is loud in praise of those Roman knights who could have reached high office, who saw what splendour and distinction there would be in such a career but none the less preferred the life of calm and peace away from envy's storms: 'vitam illam tranquillam et quietam remotam a procellis invidiarum'. Such men are brave spirits, the strength and heart of the Roman people ('o viros fortes . . . illa robora populi Romani').[110] The reader of the *Aeneid* recognizes the tone. But in the crisis of the republic the optimates found to their dismay that the peaceableness of these gentlemen was often passivity; writing to Atticus (who himself kept his head down, and survived), Cicero complains bitterly that the men of the small towns and the country ('municipales homines et rusticani') care for nothing but their land, their paltry houses and their paltry cash.[111] Fifteen or twenty years on we hear the truth of this indifference curiously echoed, but in a quite different spirit, as Virgil extols the blessings of country life. Happy the man who has known the rural gods; he is not turned from his course by public office, royal purple or military anxieties, by the affairs of Rome and kingdoms that shall pass away. He who gathers the produce that the country gladly affords sees nothing of the brawling forum; while others rush to arms and exile themselves from the charms of home life, the farmer goes on ploughing.[112]

When the equestrian Ovid rejected a senatorial career, he was doing nothing new: it was only the flamboyant and defiant manner in which he advertised that rejection which set him apart from the respectable. The most eloquent expression of quietism after the civil wars comes not from any of the elegists but from the new regime's greatest ornament, in the *Georgics*: 'flumina amem silvasque

---

[109] *Att.* 15. 16A (it is probable but not certain that this was written from Astura).
[110] *Clu.* 153.   [111] *Att.* 8. 13. 2.   [112] *Geo.* 2. 493–513.

inglorius', 'studiis florentem ignobilis oti'.[113] With his unique power of fusion, assimilation and irony, Virgil is able to combine political assertiveness with political quietism. When he speaks of the country-man giving no thought to the affairs of Rome, he is not strik-ing an un-Augustan note.[114] Augustus' greatest success, perhaps, was to give Italy what she had always wanted, the freedom to be left alone. It was a loyal citizen who, having survived the proscriptions, set up an inscription of gratitude to the new order with the words, 'pacato orbe terrarum, res[titut]a re publica, quieta deinde n[obis et felicia] tempora contigerunt' (With the world pacified and the con-stitution restored, we enjoyed calm and prosperous times).[115] More than a century later, Tacitus, no friend to monarchy, admitted where the strength and popularity of Augustus' achievement lay: 'cunctos dulcedine otii pellexit' (He seduced everyone with the charms of peace).[116] What fools these rich men are, Cicero had told Atticus, to suppose that the state can be lost and their fishpools still be safe.[117] But Augustus would in the end justify their complacency.

The Roman concern with *dignitas* might encourage a man to with-stand the new order—or to accept it. *Dignitas* could be an ideal of fierce independence, such as Homer's Achilles would have under-stood: both Catiline and Julius Caesar appealed to it as a cause for their taking up arms.[118] But *dignitas* could be a much poorer thing: when Metellus Celer snubbed Cicero by referring to the *dignitas* of his own family, this was hardly more than social snobbery.[119] The question was whether *dignitas* was a matter of inner pride or out-ward distinction of rank. Brutus told Atticus that he thought Cicero himself would put up with slavery, provided it were honorific, and his appetite for praise were kept fed.[120] That seems a hard judgement —we know from Cicero's private letters that he felt deeply humili-ated at a time when outwardly he was putting on a good face—yet it is not altogether false. Servius Sulpicius Rufus told Cicero that they had lost everything: country, honour, *dignitas*.[121] But Cicero had written to Sulpicius in somewhat different terms. He had resolved

---

[113] *Geo.* 2. 486 (may I love the rivers and woods, in obscurity); 4. 564 (blossoming in the pursuits of inglorious ease).   [114] *Geo.* 2. 498.

[115] *ILS* 8393.   [116] *Ann.* 1. 2.   [117] *Att.* 1. 18. 6.

[118] Sall. *Cat.* 35, quoting what may well be an authentic letter of Catiline's: see R. Syme, *Sallust* (Berkeley and Los Angeles, 1964), 71 f. Caesar's *dignitas*: Cic. *Att.* 7. 11. 1; Caes. *BC* 1. 9. 2 etc.   [119] Cic. *Fam.* 5. 1. 1.

[120] Cic. *ad M. Brut.* 1. 17. 4.   [121] *Fam.* 4. 5. 2.

(he said) never to speak in the senate again, since he felt the loss of his old *dignitas*, but when Marcellus fell at Caesar's feet and the whole body approached the dictator in supplication, he seemed to imagine the republic reviving, and moved by Caesar's magnanimity and the senate's duteousness, he thanked the great man at length.[122] Cicero's strange interpretation of this inglorious episode curiously anticipates a coin, issued some twenty years later, that shows Augustus restoring liberty to the republic, which is depicted allegorically as a figure who kneels before him.[123] That is frank about the reality of power; but it is not exactly cynical.

If the orator himself could equivocate, how much the more would others consent to the new order; and consent always comes easier when one knows that the state of affairs is anyway unalterable. 'The king has been killed,' Cicero told Atticus after Julius Caesar's death, 'but we are not free.'[124] As early as 50 BC, he could at moments see the truth: 'ex victoria cum multa mala tum certe tyrannus exsistet' (Out of victory a despot will certainly emerge, along with many other ills).[125] Augustus' achievement was to provide the despotism without many of the ills that might have been expected. And in appearance, at least, the old forms of public life were preserved. Again, the issue would be whether one cared about form or substance. Those with real influence, like Virgil's patron, might disdain the traditional kinds of self-assertion: Maecenas held no public office, and did not even trouble to become a senator. But while Augustus' house stood above the Roman Forum on the Palatine to the south, Maecenas' palazzo, with its huge gardens, rose on the Esquiline to the northeast. If visible demonstration of greatness were wanted, that would suffice. To praise him, Horace looks not to the Roman state but to old Italy: he is an Etruscan of royal ancestry, the scion of primeval kings.[126]

Others could not so readily make clear what they were not boasting about. But they might still hope to broaden the stripes on their togas, or compete for status, 'contendere nobilitate', in Lucretius' phrase.[127] Monarchy might even have its advantages for players of the status game. Cicero had once confessed, in a bitter moment, that he did not mind one man possessing all the power: at least it choked those who were jealous of his own success.[128] Here was a

[122] *Fam.* 4. 4. 3 f.   [123] Zanker, *Augustus und die Macht der Bilder*, 96.
[124] *Att.* 14. 11. 1.   [125] *Att.* 7. 5. 4.   [126] *Carm.* 1. 1. 1; 3. 29. 1.
[127] Lucr. 2. 11.   [128] *Att.* 4. 18. 2.

spirit that Augustus could exploit: if one man ruled the roost, at least no one else could crow over you. And in any case, the old game could now be played without the old dangers. Cicero set out his idea of 'otium cum dignitate' in his speech for Sestius; the son of that Sestius, after supporting the tyrannicides and surviving proscription, was to get most advantage from the years of peace; after a period of philosophic withdrawal, he became suffect consul and proconsul in Syria, and received the honour of an ode from Horace.[129] The orator's own son gained as much distinction as his talents could reasonably earn, becoming suffect consul in the year after Actium and proconsul, also in Syria;[130] and unlike his father, he could live on in tranquillity. Once the Augustan settlement was firm, we should expect to find the names of old families returning to the *fasti*. Modern historiography confirms, in ample detail and sardonic tone. Lesser gentlemen could hope for genuine power on a smaller scale: an ancient oligarchy, rulers of the world, might collapse in ruin, but back home, one could still be *duovir*. This too would tend to draw people's interests back to the old Italy, to their local *patriae*.

Sentiment plays a part as well as selfishness, for adversity has its own bleak consolations. One might compare the tone of the Vichy government in France. Humiliation and catastrophe had brought it into being, yet it was welcome to many. With its slogan, 'Work Family Country'—'Travail Famille Patrie'—it captured the mood of censorious penitence; it claimed that a lack of moral solidity had brought about the fall of France; and it backed the call for a return to the land. Without labouring parallels or underestimating differences, one can see similarities with the mood in the years around Actium. It is with a kind of black relish that Livy and Horace stress the depravity of modern Rome, the stern hard task of redemption required of the state's saviour (a mood which we do not, however, catch in Virgil).[131] This attitude of mind was encouraged by the Roman tendency both to idealize the past—a tendency, again, from which we shall find Virgil himself largely free—and to look for moral explanations of political and social misfortune. The moralism of Roman writers receives easy censure today, but it should not greatly surprise us. They lived in a world without experts—there were no

[129] *Carm.* 1. 4; his years of Epicurean quietude are the supposition of Syme, *The Augustan Aristocracy*, 383 f., 393. [130] App. *Bell. Civ.* 4. (51.) 221.
[131] e.g. Livy, *praef.* 9, 11 f.; Hor. *Carm.* 3. 6; 3. 24.

economists, psychologists, sociologists, statisticians—and many of the ways by which we explain historical change were not available to them. It may be that some of our own modes of explanation are themselves at root moral, but moralism embarrasses us and our style is different; Roman writings, by contrast, are commonly coloured by ethical tone and a reverence for *mos maiorum*. This makes Virgil's willingness to see advance and development among the complex processes of history the more striking; but he will not have been wholly unaffected by the national tone.

There was strong and genuine feeling, therefore, behind the call for moral regeneration and the religious renovation. What was to be done? One influential voice answers: 'revocanda fides, comprimendae libidines, propaganda suboles' (Honesty must be restored, lust repressed, the birthrate fostered). This sounds like a loyalist of the Augustan age, but it is Cicero, in the 40s:[132] history's irony would show that his traditionalist programme could only be carried through by the autocrat who overthrew the old order for which he gave his life. We might risk another analogy from more recent times and suggest that Augustus invented Bonapartism. Guizot attributed the strength of Bonapartism to the diversity of its appeal: it stabilized the gains of the revolution, but also reasserted order and authority, and emblazoned the nation's glory. Later, under Napoleon III a revived Bonapartism could be seen as fundamentally conservative, a bulwark against radical malcontents; or as patriotic, the cause of glory and national renewal; or as liberal, destroying inherited power and opening the way to new men (the ennoblement of parvenus was a conveniently ambiguous procedure, which could be interpreted as sustaining the aristocratic principle or as subverting it). Was Augustus conservative or revolutionary? The advantage of him was that the question could be burked. Stolypin's 'Russian Bonapartism', as socialists called it, under Tsar Nicholas II fortified that element of clericalism which Napoleon III's reign had added to the original Bonapartist mixture: along with land reform and nationalist causes went the effort to renovate religion and use it as a political force. More than 5,000 churches were built and some 100,000 new priests appointed;[133] which makes Augustus' reformation of priestly colleges and restoration of eighty temples in Rome seem small beer.

---

[132] *Marc.* 23.   [133] N. Stone, *Europe Transformed* (London, 1983), 228.

But distinctive to the Romans was their relationship to their past. As it happens, antiquarian enquiry flourished in the late republic.[134] In itself this probably owed less to nostalgia than to the earnest spirit of research that entered the intellectual life of the time, in provincial imitation of Greek scholarship, but it could easily come to enhance longing for a lost past. Varro's treatise 'On the Life of the Roman People' lamented the depopulation of Italy's towns;[135] and one may wonder about the tone in which Messalla Rufus, a former consul, wrote during the triumviral period about old families and religious practices.[136]

But the Romans' love affair with antiquity was deep rooted, and one of the salient differences between them and the Greeks. 'O Solon, Solon,' says the Egyptian priest in Plato's *Timaeus*, 'you Greeks are always children, and there is no Greek who is an old man . . . You are all young in your souls, and you have in them no ancient belief handed down by old tradition nor any knowledge that is hoary with age.'[137] This is a significant story because it is a Greek story: the Greeks felt themselves to be new in comparison with the immemorial depths of Egyptian civilization.

With the Romans it was otherwise. 'Antiquus' was a word of warm, native resonance. 'Moribus antiquis res stat Romana virisque,' Ennius had written (The Roman state rests upon traditional manners and men).[138] Balance demands that the adjective be taken with both nouns, 'moribus' and 'viris': 'antiquus' can be applied favourably to people, even indeed when alive and vigorous—the young Cicero knows to speak approvingly of 'homines antiqui', men of the good old stamp.[139] Late in life, he will assert that antiquity comes closest to the gods,[140] and that for this reason the rites of family and ancestors must be preserved. The past was present to the Roman gentleman every time that he looked at the *imagines* on his walls; the vocabulary of ancestry, by its extensiveness—'proavus', 'abavus', 'atavus'—presses backward through time.[141] Attacking Verres, Cicero recurs to the antiquity of

---

[134] Rawson, *Intellectual Life*, 93 provides a substantial list of upper-class antiquarians; matters of religious expertise were a favourite topic.

[135] *Vit. Pop. Rom.* fr. 115 Riposati.

[136] Pliny, *Nat. Hist.* 7. 143, 34. 137, 35. 8; Gell. 13. 14 ff.

[137] *Tim.* 22b.   [138] *Ann.* 156 Sk.   [139] *Rosc. Am.* 26.

[140] 'antiquitas proxume accedit ad deos', *Leg.* 2. 27.

[141] Literally 'great-', 'great-great-', and 'great-great-great-grandfather'. 'Tritavus', one generation earlier still, is occasionally found.

the temples he had despoiled and the cities he had persecuted, as an especial cause of offence.[142] When the task is to defend a governor against charges of corruption, that appeal can be suavely inverted: many things plead for Fonteius' acquittal, and firstly the antiquity of his family, recorded on the monuments of Tusculum, that most distinguished municipality.[143]

This association of antiquity with local pride and loyalty is to be met again in Propertius, writing no doubt under Virgil's shadow also, who mourns the 'eversosque focos antiquae gentis Etruscae' (the razing of the homes of the ancient Etruscan people).[144] Private grief sharpens the pain in this case, but Livy too sees the expulsion of the people of Alba from their city in like terms: the fact that the home they are losing has been theirs for four hundred years is an especial source of pathos.[145] It is Virgil, characteristically, who can both feel this sentiment most keenly and stand at a certain distance from it, giving it a distinctive twist: the ploughman clears the woodland, 'antiquasque domos avium cum stirpibus imis | eruit' (in tearing out the deep roots tears down the birds' ancient homes).[146] 'Antiquus' gives a tiny stab of poignancy, and by delicate implication, compares the birds to mankind: driven from homes which have been theirs for so long they are like, say, the Albans. The subtlest touch is the bringing of the adjective into association with the noun 'stirps'. Virgil is talking of roots in a literal sense, but the word is so often applied to family trees that it gives a touch of further pressure to the implied likening of birds to men. At the same time it enhances the sense of what it is to be human: to desire a rootedness in home and time and landscape.

Livy confessed that when he wrote about olden times his mind itself somehow became antique.[147] The theme could grow tiresome. Horace shows Augustus his annoyance with the prevalent reverence for anything that is old and done with, a habit vexing to the modern poet.[148] It was a short step from antiquarianism to triviality: Seneca complains of the pedantry with which people gather scraps of useless knowledge about the remote past or discuss the origin of cognomina:

---

[142] *Verr.* 2. 1. 47, 50; 2. 2. 2; 2. 4. 7, 72, 74, 107–9, 111; 2. 5. 125.   [143] *Font.* 41.

[144] Prop. 2. 1. 29. Antiquity is not a theme in the laments for Etruria in Propertius' first book; it is tempting to surmise that the influence of the *Georgics* has introduced this new note. He will again associate 'antiquus' with his homeland at 4. 1. 121.

[145] Livy 1. 29. 6.   [146] *Geo.* 2. 209 f.

[147] Livy 43. 13. 2.   [148] *Epist.* 2. 1. 18 ff., 34 ff.

why a Claudius was called Caudex, how the name Messalla arose.[149] Perhaps the topic was fresher in Virgil's day, but still it was not obvious that when he introduced some (fictitious) origins of Roman nomenclature into the fifth book of the *Aeneid* he would be able to make the theme come alive. He brings the word 'antiquus' to a climactic moment of his *laus Italiae* in the *Georgics*. The adjective is commonplace in itself; it is in transforming the language of common sentiment that the genius lies. But this awaits our later scrutiny.[150]

Sometimes the Romans' sense of the past allowed them to conceive of their state in organic terms, or to see its history as a process of long evolution. The organic metaphor is in Varro's striking title, 'On the Life of the Roman People'. Cicero suggests that four hundred years are not long in the life of a city or nation, indeed scarce time enough for it to become completely grown.[151] His treatise on the state, he tells us, will describe its birth and adolescence and its arrival at the full strength of adulthood.[152] Yet more often the note is one not of Burkean conservatism but of conservatism absolute. Cicero knows that the Roman constitution was formed over many generations,[153] but can somehow combine this with the confidence that the oldest institutions are the best. The biological metaphor is adjusted to exempt the state from the common laws of nature: it is immortal, or should be, provided it lives by ancestral *mores* and institutions.[154] That sense of the many layers of the past which becomes so strong in Virgil is vestigially present in Cicero: he can speak, for instance, of the form of government 'which our fathers received from their ancestors and duly passed on to us'.[155] But this is flow without flux: there is no sense of change or adaptation in the course of history. Augustus too sees himself in the flow of time, a mediator between past and future: 'legibus novis me auctore latis multa exempla maiorum exolescentia iam ex nostro saeculo reduxi et ipse multarum rerum exempla imitanda posteris tradidi' (By new laws passed on my initiative I restored many exemplary practices of our ancestors which were growing out of use in our time and myself handed down many exemplary practices for posterity to imitate).[156] The biological metaphor seems to lurk in 'exolescentia'—and Virgil had used 'inolescere' marvellously to evoke the irremediable effects

---

[149] *De Brev. Vit.* 13. 3 ff.   [150] *Geo.* 2. 157, discussed below, pp. 363 f.
[151] *Rep.* 1. 58.   [152] *Rep.* 2. 3.   [153] *Rep.* 2. 2.   [154] *Rep.* 3. 41.
[155] '[res publica] quam patres nostri nobis acceptam iam inde a maioribus reliquerunt', *Rep.* 1. 70.   [156] *Res Gest.* 8.

of time and process in ordinary human experience[157]—but that one word apart, there is no sense here of historical development as an organic process: if ancestral practices are growing out of use, they can simply be re-established.

'O wad some Pow'r the giftie gie us | To see oursels as others see us!' The Romans, understandably, were liable to see their state at the centre of the world and its history; self-awareness—the ability to view one's time and nation from the outside—came to them most readily when they were philosophizing, and thus drawing on Greek rather than native patterns of thought. So in *De Republica* Cicero reflects upon how small the earth is within the total sum of the universe, and how small is Rome within the earth, unknown to many peoples.[158] In his story of Scipio's dream he imagines the great man drawn up into heaven and perceiving the tininess of the Roman empire, the littleness of glory.[159] The world is divided into several zones, and only a lesser part even of the northern zone, Scipio learns, belongs to the Romans, who are the possessors merely of a small island surrounded by Ocean. From a perspective which embraces Caucasus and Ganges, the Roman empire seems a narrow territory; and how long will it last? Floods and conflagrations destroy all things, from time to time.[160] Cicero's self-consciousness here is both geographical and historical: a man's fame is limited in area, and in time also, for oblivion will ultimately blot it out.[161] Fine words; but one wonders how to connect them with that more familiar Cicero who talks of the eternity of the Roman state and is scarcely indifferent to the claims of glory.

The finest expression of self-consciousness in any Roman before Virgil, to whose imagination it becomes essential, is in the famous letter of consolation which Sulpicius Rufus sent to Cicero on the death of his daughter. The writer recalls sailing on the Aegean, passing cities once glorious, now defeated and decayed. And to think that we little men—'nos homunculi'—should wax indignant if one among us has died before his time.[162] Here the grand commonplaces of consolation mingle with a distinctively Roman experience. More vividly than the Greeks in their prime, the Romans had the complete rise and decline of a civilization close before their eyes; that, and the habit of reflecting upon antiquity and very long tracts of time,

---

[157] *Aen.* 6. 738, discussed below, p. 207. [158] *Rep.* 1. 26. [159] *Rep.* 6. 16, 20.
[160] *Rep.* 6. 21 f. [161] *Rep.* 6. 25. [162] Cic. *Fam.* 4. 5. 4.

could be the basis for a new style of historical self-consciousness, such as we meet at the end of the first book of the *Georgics*. But Virgil goes deeper, reaching beyond the easy self-disparagement of Sulpicius' 'nos homunculi' to a vision that sees the Romans of his own age, from the far perspective of a remote future, as both small and splendid at the same time.[163] In Cicero the thinker and the public man, the philosophic voice and the clamorous demand for fame, are separate; we shall see that Virgil achieves a fusion of man's littleness and his glory.

The idea of progress—indeed, the idea of any kind of process—was difficult to fit with the habit of idealizing the past and the *mos maiorum*. Celebrants of the Augustan principate tend to clamp a glorious restoration, inorganically, on to a conventional view of steady decline—or alternatively, of immutable tradition. Virgil, perhaps alone, finds a way of combining affection for the past with a sense of progress. He shows us that some things are lost with the passage of time (and a sense of loss is as keen in Virgil as in any Latin writer), but other things are gained; we shall discover that compared to most Roman pictures of the distant past Virgil's is less rosy. In one area only do his self-awareness and sense of process give way. In the *Aeneid* Jupiter pronounces that the Roman empire will be limitless in extent and duration; Anchises reveals that Augustus will bring back the golden age—and history, so far as one can see, comes to an end.[164] In these places the demands of patronage and panegyric have overridden the historical sense; there is a loss in this, and we feel it the more because Virgil's sense of process is usually so keen.

More characteristically, Virgil brings the idea of development even to 'mos', that word redolent of changelessness. The Roman's imperial task, as Anchises unfolds it, shall include 'pacique imponere morem'.[165] 'impono' is used as a word for grafting in the *Georgics*,[166] and what Virgil envisions, through Anchises' words, is process; perhaps he even has the organic metaphor in mind. A little earlier, describing the purgatorial sufferings of the dead, he has told us that habitual sinfulness can only gradually be cleansed from the human spirit;[167] now he suggests that good habits too need to be built up, with peace

---

[163] *Geo.* 1. 493 ff., discussed below, pp. 381 ff.   [164] *Aen.* 1. 278 f.; 6. 792 ff.

[165] *Aen.* 6. 852.   [166] *Geo.* 2. 73.

[167] *Aen.* 6. 735 ff. One may note the subtle force of the *in-* compound: 'inolescere' at 738, 'imponere' at 852.

as their foundation.[168] Most Romans, surely, would not have associated 'mos' with this progressive note, and indeed there might seem
to be a conservative bias embedded in the very language. It is telling
that 'mos', the Latin word for custom, should cover both civilization, in the political and social sense—civilization in the aesthetic
sense is 'cultus'—and tradition. To be civilized was to abide in the
old ways. (Virgil's means of saying that the aboriginal people of Italy
were uncivilized is to say that they had neither 'mos' nor 'cultus':
no tradition, no grace.)[169]

The Greeks' language, by contrast, offered them a ready opening, should they choose to take it, towards moral relativism and philosophical debate. Custom for them was *nomos* or *ta nomima*. The root
meaning of *nomos* is law, and the Greeks habitually used the word
in a way which brought out that law is a system of conventions,
and adaptable. *nomos* was commonly contrasted with *phusis*, nature.
It stands for moral or cultural relativism in Herodotus' story of Darius
consulting Greeks and Indians on their funeral customs. For how
much money, he asked the Greeks, would they be willing to eat
their dead fathers; the Greeks replied that they would not do it at
any price. Darius then asked the Indians, who did eat their parents,
for what price they would burn them instead; the Indians were shocked
at the thought. This shows (says the historian) how right Pindar
was to declare that *nomos* is the king of everything.[170] For Creon, in
Sophocles' *Antigone*, *nomoi* are simply whatever he, the new ruler of
the city, decides.[171] Antigone defies his *nomoi*, appealing instead to
the unwritten and sure *nomima* of the gods. These are not of today
or yesterday but live always, and no one knows their origin.[172] Even
here, where we do meet a sense of perennity and deep past, the
divine command is still seen as something decreed, imposed, even if
at an unknowably early time. 'Mos', however, simply *is*—established,
integrated into the experience of man as a social animal.

Since the Romans were constantly examining themselves in relation to Greece, these differences in conceptual language become significant. When Ennius said that 'antiqui mores' sustained the Roman
state, he surely meant more than that they were the basis of any
strong polity: the Romans' especial attachment to old *mores* was

---

[168] The phrase is a classic example of the difference a single letter can make: take the
inferior reading 'pacisque imponere morem', 'to impose the habit of peace', and the sense
of accretion is lost at once.   [169] *Aen.* 8. 316.
        [170] Hdt. 3. 38.   [171] *Ant.* 177, 191; cf. 738.   [172] *Ant.* 454 ff.

distinctive to themselves. Traditionalism was all the more enforced because *mos* came to seem peculiarly Italian, national as well as virtuous. It was difficult, in any case, for Romans to change or develop their morality because in their society religion and public action, the conventional ascent up the *cursus honorum* and the conventional acquisition of priesthoods, formed a unity, an organic whole. To break with established patterns of behaviour was, it seemed, to break with morality. No counter-culture had become articulate, and there was no obvious alternative system of values at hand to replace the old. True, the philosophical systems imported from Greece taught how one should lead the good life, sometimes in terms which were at sharp variance with Roman habit, but the philosophical pursuit of virtue was usually kept apart, in the private sphere, seldom impinging on public life or a man's dealings with with his fellows, as is illustrated by the careers of the Epicurean Cassius, the Academic Brutus, the eclectic Cicero, and even the Stoic Cato, whose passionate adherence to the old order was in breach of that remote indifference which was the Stoic's proper goal.

A man like Clodius had no moral soil in which to root himself. Rebels in Rome lacked the vocabulary and conceptual framework for attacking old values and asserting new ones. The adversaries of Catiline and Clodius said plainly that they were bad men. One may ask—although, since their enemies wrote the history books, one cannot confidently answer the question—whether they did not themselves, in some sense, agree. And as Thucydides had understood long before, there is an interdependence between how one speaks and how one acts: if Clodius acted destructively and without clear purpose (as is probably the case), one part of the cause may have been that he lacked the words and concepts to give his attack upon conservative values coherence and aim. For the military autocrats who actually overthrew the old order the alternatives were a self-conscious hedonism which set aside moral values—the attitude which his enemies attributed to Mark Antony, probably with justice—or Augustus' method: the claim to be restoring the traditional order after all.

In some poetry this conceptual weakness of the Roman language could produce fascinating effects. The love poets sometimes seem to be trying to say, 'Your values are wrong, ours are better', but without the equipment to say it. Hence an emotional tension enters their language, as they toy with such pejorative terms as 'nequitia', 'furta', 'desidia', half eagerly, half ashamed. In Propertius especially, there is an oscillation between defiance and self-laceration. There is a precedent for such emotional ambiguity, ironically, in Virgil, who in the *Georgics* moves the word 'durus' across a spectrum, sometimes seeming a term of praise, sometimes of harshness.[173] Yet there remains a difference: with Virgil, however complex his emotional texture may be, we feel that he knows where he is standing; Propertius' feelings sometimes seem to be beyond his own comprehension. When he laments (or revels in) his slavish dependence on Cynthia, when he compares himself to the glamorous and self-destructive Antony, is he defying Augustus' opinion on the consequences of sexual licence, or agreeing with it? Perhaps he does not know himself, and therein lies the fascination.[174] But such moral bewilderment, which could be made an asset in the poetry of private experience, was of scant help to poetry with a public dimension, wrestling with ideas and values.

The traditionalist temper appears to have bred among the Romans, in paradoxical combination with their arrogant self-assertiveness, a certain failure of nerve, or of imagination. They seem reluctant to admire or enjoy some of their most striking achievements. Augustus' public works in Rome were a very remarkable phenomenon, social and cultural, but the poets give them rather little attention. Horace expresses mild distaste at grandiose building schemes; Virgil, who had disparaged the bronze and tortoiseshell of cities in the *Georgics*, observes that Roman sculpture will never match the best Greek work.[175] In the eighth book of the *Aeneid* he does allow that the Capitol is now golden,[176] but without the enthusiasm which he brings to the splendour of Dido's palace. Horace is loud in praise of events which are not going to happen—the imminent conquest of Britain and Persia; his gaze is over all the world, except those places where things are actually going on: the Spanish cordillera subjugated, the city of Rome transformed. Such recoils from modern reality suggest how

---

[173] See below, pp. 333 f.

[174] It is simple-minded to suppose that if Propertius implicitly compares himself to Antony, he is standing out against Augustus; the 'political' allusions in 2. 14, 2. 15, and 2. 16 are particularly liable to misinterpretation. They should be read in the light of 3. 8, where the outrage (and mischief) are most plainly to the fore: the poet implicitly likens himself to Paris, who gets an extra frisson from making love to Helen just after quitting the battlefield, while that awful Hector ('barbarus Hector') continues to risk his life for his country (3. 8. 27–32). This is self-consciously wicked.

[175] Hor. *Carm.* 3. 1. 33 f., 3. 24. 1 ff.; Virg. *Aen.* 6. 847 f. (cf. *Geo.* 2. 461 ff.).

[176] *Aen.* 8. 347; some think that Virgil is equivocal about the grandeur of modern Rome even here, but that is probably a mistake.

thin was some of the material with which Virgil had to work. What he did in the sixth *Aeneid* was to bring the sense of underachievement out into the open, to articulate it, to make it the very stuff of poetry, indeed of patriotism itself. To be a self-aware Roman, in his eyes, was to hold together a sense of the limitlessness of Rome's power and the limits of its culture. Commonly we think of Virgil as bestriding one of the summits of world civilization, and indeed we do so upon the authority of the poet himself; yet one element in the complex texture of the *Aeneid* is the shoring up of the Roman spirit against the sense of an inferiority.

Virgil creates an amalgam of sentiment which is a fusion of the past and the countryside and Italy, the name and experience of his nation. Despite his influence on contemporary poets, this particular amalgam remains distinctive to himself, a fact which may surprise us, who are likely to find it natural and familiar. For it resembles such forms of modern sentiment as, for example, the Englishry developed in the later nineteenth and early twentieth centuries. 'To me,' said Stanley Baldwin, 'England is the country and the country is England . . . The country represents the eternal values and the eternal traditions from which we must never allow ourselves to be separated.'[177] Nation, countryside, a perennity rooted in the past, and *mos* (the blend of values and traditions)—all are there. Tennyson wrote of an English home as 'A haunt of ancient Peace'.[178] Alfred Austin, who succeeded him as poet laureate, borrowed the phrase to describe England itself. 'Haunt'—the word suggests abidingness, together with a vague sense of semi-numinous presence. Through the mouth of an imaginary female friend who is evidently meant to seem amusing and sympathetic, Austin evokes a yearning for '*Old* England' (note the emphasis), for 'the Past' (note the capital letter), 'for feminine serviceableness, washing days, home-made jams, lavender bags, recitation of Gray's *Elegy*, and morning and evening prayers'.[179] This is very poor stuff; yet in its mixture of the past, the simplicity of country

[177] Baldwin, *This Torch of Freedom* (London, 1935), 125, 120. Baldwin is not the last Prime Minister to strike this note. John Major, echoing George Orwell's brilliant essay 'England Your England', recently told a party conference that his nation would continue to be the land of warm beer and old maids biking to early communion through the mist. But this statesman's ignorance of his own country may be exceptional. (Orwell himself, who gives a mordant twist to the sentimental-patriotic theme and yet is hopelessly in love with his *patria*, displays, as Virgil does in a different form, a combination of detachment and engagement.)   [178] *The Palace of Art*, lines 85–8.
[179] *Haunts of Ancient Peace* (London, 1902), 168, 18 f.

life, tradition, and undemanding forms of worship which permit one to enjoy religion without getting inside it we may recognize the vulgarization of something which Virgil first discovered. 'One is offered, in place of them,' Austin's lady continues, 'ungraceful hurry and worry, perpetual postmen's knocks, an intermittent shower of telegrams.' Again, to compare the laureate of Edwardian England with the laureate of Augustan Rome is to move from the ridiculous to the sublime; and yet there is an echo of Horace in the townsman's patronage of the country at weekends, in loose complaint about the bustle of metropolitan life which covertly advertises the importance of the complainer (in Horace's case with a self-mocking irony, in the case of Austin and his Egeria probably not).

We may wonder whether these similarities reflect any similarity of historical experience. One difference is plain: it is partly in response to the physical changes wrought by industrialization that traditional Englishry is developed, elmy pastures and hedgerows, squire and parson and rosy cheeks in the milking parlour, the invocation of talismanic names drawn from the hills and villages of Sussex and Gloucestershire. The idyll is evoked at a time when, insofar as it had ever existed, it is under threat; it will be an urban nation that is urged to fight by the declaration that 'There'll always be an England, Where there's a country lane . . .' The very shrinkage of the peasantry makes nostalgia easier: in countries where the agricultural population is large enough to form a distinct political class, clamouring for subsidy or sporadically violent, idealization is harder. Clearly, this idyllic vision of the country and the past is blind to many pains and hardships; less obviously, it is geographically restricted. The north of England is left out of these effusions, which linger round a few especially evocative names and places: the Cotswolds, the Malverns, the Sussex Downs, not the grandest scenery but hills of moderate size, domesticated mountains. Even the splendours of the past are set aside in favour of humbler charms: the talk is of thatch rather than brick or ashlar, the quaint place of rustic worship rather than the big wool churches of East Anglia or the west. It is not the greatness of the past that is sought but its ordinariness. We are to say 'This is workaday', and yet to find it romantic and lovely.

The function of all this in the national psychology is understandable enough. The industrial revolution altered more than the landscape: it brought about huge social and economic changes, and ultimately a political transformation from oligarchy to mass democracy. Remarkably, this was achieved in Britain without violence; and one may speculate that the possessing classes were helped to accept a vast if gradual adjustment by a sense that the real England was still there, rural and unchanging, amid the changes and chances of politics and society. Comparably, Virgil's amalgam, however distinctive to himself, grows out of a world in which the higher classes are looking to the past or to the country for comfort in an age of turmoil. Here too a few names are picked out for ready emotional response: Sabines, for instance, and Marsians. Here too quaint or simple things are preferred to the grander parts of the Italian heritage: the hill peoples of the Apennines are often brought into play, Etruria more seldom, rarely the Greek south or the northern plain. Those idylls of the English earth commonly like to set the homely beauties of the familiar scene against the larger splendours of other, exotic landscapes. But this style of patriotic sentiment too had been discovered by Virgil. The landscape of the Apennines—often to be used by English writers as a glamorous contrast to their native scene—is set by him against the marvels of the east: familiar Italy is, in a way, modest compared to these wonders, and yet it is also, somehow, the best country of all. Virgil can see Italy, in the way that later Englishmen will see England, as ordinary and romantic at once.

It is Virgil's achievement to have discovered a nexus of emotions which now seems a permanent possession of the European sensibility; in consequence, we may miss his originality. But this emotional complex does risk vulgarization: Edwardian poetry lapsed all too easily into a babble of Amberley and Chipping Campden. Anyone can use names; it will be necessary to show that Virgil uses them tellingly. Talk of the good old Italy, in Roman writers themselves, can already seem tiresome, hackneyed and self-deceiving; it will be important to see that Virgil does not merely borrow stock responses but makes of them something both new and profound.

PART TWO

The *Eclogues*

CHAPTER 4

The Neoteric Experience

Sweet especial rural scene.
(Hopkins)

However proud they might be of their power, their ancestry, and their *mores*, the Romans were constantly aware of an inferiority. Wherever the Greeks' rule or influence had spread, they had over-whelmed the native culture; even the Jews were only a partial exception. The first Roman gentlemen with literary ambitions, men like Fabius Pictor and Cincius Alimentus, naturally chose to write in the civilized language, Greek. Latin literature was reckoned to begin with Livius Andronicus, a Greek prisoner of war, who translated Homer, making a Greek masterpiece more accessible to his rude conquerors. The first great figure in their literature, so later Romans thought, was Ennius, an Italian from the Hellenized far south of Italy, who spoke Latin, Greek, and Oscan alike; he could have addressed the great world in the world language. Instead, he chose Latin; it was a momentous choice.

Even in the first century a deference remained; Rome's proudest acknowledged it. Pompey the Great visited the great Posidonius on Rhodes and dipped his fasces at the philosopher's door, the homage of power to wisdom.[1] Cicero admits that he is defending the poet Archias in the hope of extracting from him a panegyric upon his own consulship: writing in Greek, Archias will be able to extend the fame of the Romans and their consul as far as the bounds of their empire, whereas the Latin language is confined within narrow limits.[2] The period of the late republic, a time of political decay, can be seen as a time of cultural and intellectual vigour; yet such a view is a partial one. Much of this vigour still had a provincial flavour. Varro was celebrated as Rome's great polymath, active in many fields;

[1] Plin. *Nat. Hist.* 7. 112 (cf. Posidonius, testimonia 35–9 EK).   [2] *Arch.* 23.

but in none of them, perhaps, was his contribution first-rate. The critic Valerius Cato was extravagantly praised by M. Furius Bibaculus as an exceptional teacher, scholar, and poet, by an anonymous versifier as 'the Latin Siren, who alone chooses and makes poets'; it would surprise us if he were a giant mind.[3] Cicero, indeed, saw the Romans as steadily colonizing one field of intellectual endeavour after another, but the very self-confidence of his outlook displays this sophisticated figure at his least urbane. To anthologize the Greek philosophies and adjudicate between them, however elegantly the job may be done, falls short of original thought. Lucretius is superior to Cicero simply as a philosopher; but Cicero, who admired him as a poet, had not the wit to see it. In his attitude to history also, Cicero is too simple-minded. He represents his friends as urging him to take up history so that in this area too the Romans may match the Greeks.[4] It is true that many of the best historians in antiquity, starting with Thucydides, had been men of action, but the idea that serious history could be the easy product of a statesman's leisure hours betrays a failure to understand what the Greek historians had achieved. Subtler spirits will not have been so complacent; indeed Virgil puts at the centre of his epic the assertion that the Romans will forever be inferior to the Greeks in some of the noblest arts and sciences, including that oratory in which Cicero took such pride.[5]

In poetry above all, the Greek achievement loomed over the Romans like an upas tree, threatening to blight everything upon which its shadow fell. 'All [other] subjects are now hackneyed,' says Virgil: 'omnia iam vulgata.' Ironically, he was voicing a sentiment which had already been uttered by Choerilus of Samos, as early as the fourth century. He continues,[6]

> quis aut Eurysthea durum
> aut inlaudati nescit Busiridis aras?
> cui non dictus Hylas puer . . . ?

Who does not know of harsh Eurystheus or the altars of unadmired Busiris? Who has not told of the boy Hylas?

More ironies: he had told of Hylas himself, in the sixth Eclogue.[7] The stories at which he chafes are those elegant, and sometimes out-of-the-way, myths which had been the material for Callimachus and

---

[3] Suet. *Gramm.* 11.   [4] *Leg.* 1. 5.   [5] *Aen.* 6. 847 ff.
[6] *Geo.* 3. 4–6.   [7] *Ecl.* 6. 43 ff.

other Hellenistic poets, yet he echoes Callimachus in this very para-graph (though he will have remembered, as modern scholars often forget, that Callimachus was a praise poet—the context is panegyrical).[8]

The Roman poets' assertions of originality sometimes take a curi-ously subdued and deferential form, when they boast of being the first man to follow some Greek predecessor in Latin. Virgil says that he is the first to have written in the manner of Theocritus, Horace that he was the first to have brought Archilochus and Alcaeus to Rome.[9] Such claims are to be taken seriously in some cases, while in others they may be a kind of game: Virgil pretends to be singing 'Ascraean song' when he has left Hesiod far behind, and we may suspect that Horace's debt to Alcaeus was less than he implied, so that even where a poet adopts the disciple's posture, he may be essen-tially new and independent.[10] At all events, it is often when they find fresh fields, undiscovered by the Greeks, that Roman poets are most successful. But where were they to be found? A third of the way through the first century the prospects for Latin poetry may not have looked very bright. A series of Greek genres—comedy, tragedy, epic—had been tried, and failed, it might seem, to have taken firm root. Perhaps a mannered preciosity was all that was left; such at least was what Cicero found in the more prominent poets of his time.

In the event two men of genius, Lucretius and Catullus, sent Roman poetry in directions which could not have been foretold. Genius can never be predicted; but in these cases we must also take into account the sheer accidents of temper and circumstance—odd chances which were to have momentous consequences. As we shall see, it was a very particular philosophical outlook which led Lucretius to find a way of beating the Greeks at their own game by developing a kind of didactic poetry larger in scale, range, and depth than had ever been imagined

[8] On the allusion to Callimachus here see R. Thomas, 'Callimachus, the *Victoria Berenices*, and Roman Poetry', *CQ* NS 33 (1983), 92–113, at 92–101.

[9] Virg. *Ecl.* 6. 1 f.; Hor. *Epist.* 1. 19. 23 ff., 32 f. (cf. *Carm.* 3. 30. 13 f.).

[10] Virg. *Geo.* 2. 176. The alcaic was Horace's favourite lyric metre because he had found a way of transforming it, giving greater weight to the first and second lines of the stanza, and even more to the third line; the contrast between the massiveness of the third line and the rippling movement of the fourth makes Horace's alcaic stanza particularly shapely. The grandeur of his remodelled alcaic form made it a possible vehicle for public verse in a Pindaric vein (for example in *Carm.* 3. 1–6, esp. 3. 4). In other words, he valued Alcaeus for a metre which he could change for his own purposes; Sappho was less imitated because more inimitable.

before. That showed Virgil, by first instinct a miniaturizer—the *Eclogues* compress Theocritus, the *Aeneid* shadows both the *Iliad* and the *Odyssey*, though less than the length of either—how he could write a didactic work of his own, which is indeed longer than any Greek didactic poem which has come down to us; and the experience of the *Georgics* taught him that he could compose on a scale grand enough for epic. Without Lucretius, there would probably have been no *Aeneid*.

Lucretius' revolution and its effects upon Virgil are so large and important a topic that they will be postponed to the next part of this book. With Catullus too we may suspect that mere chance transformed Latin literature. If he had not met Clodia, if Clodia had not been so promiscuous, the history of Roman elegy might have been very different. For his obsession with Lesbia may well have struck his contemporaries more oddly than it does us. We have been brought up on the story of Romeo and Juliet; we have revelled in the *égoisme à deux* of Antony and Cleopatra; and we have perhaps learnt that Tristan and Isolde's absorption into each other makes the heroine's final self-willed extinction not a tragedy but a dissolution into bliss. The Romans of the republic had none of this literary tradition behind them; the most original and powerful love poet known to them, Sappho, regards falling in love not as a unique event but as something that has befallen her many times; and though she does not ask to be cured of her capacity for passion, she does consider it to be in some ways like an unpleasant disease. Life, as well as literature, may have made the educated Roman's attitude rather different from ours. The pangs of misprized love must have been known to Roman men as to us, but they had means of soothing them to hand: sexual relations, more or less lasting, more or less gratifying, could be bought from *scorta* or cultivated courtesans, or compelled from slaves. In such a world Catullus' continued dependence upon Lesbia may have seemed odder, unhealthier even, than it does to us; indeed the intended shock of his poetry, obvious in some aspects, is a thing that here we need to take care to recover.

Roman love elegy flourishes because it is strikingly new; it is a mistake to suppose that there were important Greek models for it, now lost, in the fourth century or the Hellenistic age.[11] It is implausible that such persons as Antimachus and Hermesianax—something

---

[11] The case, here rejected, for supposing a large Hellenistic influence on Latin love elegy is argued with much learning by F. Cairns, *Tibullus: A Hellenistic Poet at Rome* (Cambridge, 1979), ch. 9.

less than towering geniuses anyway, from what we can ascertain—
mattered much to the Latin elegists. In the first place, these Roman
poets hardly ever refer to them, and, when we reflect how common was the game of taking a Greek poet and claiming to be his
Latin counterpart, that silence is eloquent. Equally revealing is to
observe which poets are spoken of. Propertius talks of Callimachus
and Philetas, but he begins to do so at the point where he is turning
away from a concentration upon the poetry of love: he contrasts verse
in their manner with his accustomed sphere, poems about his girl.[12]
If he requires the name of a Greek to stand for love elegy, it is the
archaic poet Mimnermus; that in itself is striking enough, but even
he is mentioned only once.[13]

Further, where Hellenistic models are most clearly to be detected,
they are not extended elegy but epigram (and Philodemus was in
Rome in the middle of the first century). The few morsels of Latin
love elegiacs earlier than Catullus' generation that we possess—the
little pieces by Porcius Licinus, Valerius Aedituus, and Q. Lutatius
Catulus—are simply traditional Greek epigrams done in Latin; Catulus'
piece is actually an adaptation of Callimachus. There is no evidence
that there was ever anything more substantial at this date. We catch
the Augustan elegists using epigram material from time to time. The
survey of Corinna's body in Ovid's *Aestus erat* can be paralleled in
an epigram by Philodemus.[14] In Propertius' *Qualis Thesea* the moonlight through the window falling on the woman is a motif from Greek
epigram, again found in Philodemus, and the poet's impulse to take
his girl while she is still asleep is found also in Paul the Silentiary.[15]
Paul is centuries later than Propertius, but it is likely that they both
draw, directly or indirectly, upon a common Hellenistic source. However, these examples only demonstrate the essential newness of Latin
love elegy, for these little Hellenistic motifs are merely raw material, tiny pieces to be incorporated into a poetry which is substantially different in scale, scope and spirit. It is not only a question of
length, important though that is; the whole cast of mind is changed.
Philodemus produces a bald catalogue; Ovid is more elusive and sophisticated. He plays the part of the practised seducer (not, surely, without
casting an ironic and humorous glance upon his own assumption of
savoir faire); instead of a list of parts of the body which stands on its

[12] Prop. 3. 1. 1 ff. with 3. 2. 1 ff. (cf. 3. 9. 43 f.); 4. 1. 59 ff. with 4. 1. 135 ff.
[13] Prop. 1. 9. 11.   [14] Ov. *Am*. 1. 5. 19 ff.; *Anth. Pal*. (Philod.) 5. 132.
[15] Prop. 1. 3. 13 ff. and 31 ff.; *Anth. Pal*. 5. 275 (Paul); 5. 123 (Philodemus).

own as virtually a complete poem, Ovid's assessment of the naked Corinna, coldly lustful though it is, marks one stage in the unfolding of a story which begins with him awaiting the girl's arrival and ends with his desire accomplished. Instead of the cool brutality of Paul's piece—in effect an account of rape—Propertius refines: he contemplates taking Cynthia asleep, but then refrains. And herein lies the greatest difference between the Hellenistic epigram and the Roman elegy: the girls count. The Nico or Menecratis of the Greek poems does not matter at all; these are mere names, interchangeable with one another. But central to Latin elegy is the individual being of the beloved: it is her resistances and her pliabilities, her cruelty or her kindness that shape the poet's experience, and his verse. And despite the occasional infidelity, no other woman will do in place of Lesbia or Cynthia, or even Delia and Nemesis; it is she and she alone who is the cynosure of desire.

Everything about Catullus suggests an essential novelty. As we have seen, there is no sign of anything even faintly comparable in an earlier generation. His polymetric poems are an extraordinary conception —writing of love in hendecasyllables, hitherto the metre of skits and lampoons—so extraordinary that no one at all follows him along this path, for all his prestige. And his way of writing about love is new: the obsession with one woman, the ordinary intimacy, the sense of experience unmediated by recollection, the lover's puzzlement at his own emotions: is this love or hatred? (Scholars should not speak of Catullus 'analysing' his emotions, still less blame him for attempting analysis in a medium unsuited for the purpose; rather he dramatizes the impossibility of analysis.) Strangest of all, perhaps is the feeling sometimes offered to us that we are present at the talk of lovers. Almost all love poetry, when it is not about the lover himself, is a narrative or reflection about the beloved, even when it is nominally addressed to her; and of course some of Catullus' poetry falls into this familiar pattern. But it is remarkable that he never describes any part of Lesbia's person, except just once, where he briefly describes her foot, not bare but shod, in a poem unlike any other that he wrote.[16] The staples of so much love poetry—the radiant eyes, rosy lips, alabaster skin, and the rest—are absent from the poems about Lesbia. And there is no description of any love-making that goes beyond a kiss (we may contrast Propertius or Ovid; we may

---

[16] Cat. 68. 70 ff.

contrast Catullus himself when he addresses Juventius or Ipsitilla, describes the mythical Peleus and Thetis, or rhapsodizes over the nakedness of the sea nymphs).[17] And why? Catullus suggests that he is not telling us about his experience but that his poems are the working out of that experience itself. And sometimes we feel that we are actually in the room with Catullus and Lesbia. When he tells every Venus and Cupid to mourn for the death of Lesbia's sparrow and rebukes the bird itself for passing away, they are not the real addressees.[18] The humour, the baby talk, the half serious lamentation are all tactics for restoring Lesbia's spirits, by sympathy and a touch of absurdity; it is as though he has his arm around her as he speaks. Another poem begins, 'Quaeris quot mihi basiationes . . .' (You ask, Lesbia, how many kissings of you are enough and more for me). Why should Lesbia so ask?—the answer must surely be that we are in mid-embrace. 'Really, isn't that enough?' she says; Catullus leaps in with his reply, and we call it Poem 7.

We should expect his poems in elegiac couplets to be hardly less original, and we are not disappointed. Epigram is again the starting-point; most of these poems can be given this label, though their theme and tone are new. But some of them seem to be struggling to break out of the case that wants to enclose them. *Multas per gentes*, on his brother's death, though only ten lines long, has the amplitude and melodiousness of a threnody, and the full flow of personal sorrow replaces the reticence and impersonality traditional to the epitaph.[19] *Siqua recordanti* has gone far beyond the bounds of epigram, expanding to 26 lines; yet we appreciate it best if we see it in context as a would-be epigram which under the pressure of strong and difficult emotion has erupted out of the crust which epigram would seek to impose upon it.[20] From another point of view, however, looking back from the Augustan age, we seem to see the protoplasm evolving before our eyes. Out of Catullus' messy life, his genius as a poet and his experiments in style, form and genre comes, more or less by accident, what will later be recognized as the beginnings of Roman love elegy. True, *Siqua recordanti* is not quite like Augustan elegy; Catullus' poem is simply reflective, a meditation upon a single point, while the later elegists usually tell a story. But the evolution has started none the less.

---

[17] Cat. 48; 32; 64. 330 ff. and 12 ff.   [18] Cat. 3.
[19] Cat. 101.   [20] Cat. 76.

In a different way his sixty-eighth poem is also a forerunner of the developed Latin love elegy: for the first time we have an episode, a story involving the lover and the unique beloved. This time the poem is far longer than any later love elegy will be, but again we see Catullus, by a kind of accident, making a discovery from which his successors will be able to learn. For see what has happened. The long poems of Catullus, experimental, decorated with literary reference, sometimes bizarre, are—by design—dramatically different from his shorter works.[21] One of the strangest such experiments is a poem in which he connects the mannerism and the multiplicity of his longer pieces with the personal immediacy—Lesbia, his dead brother—that we find in the short poems. It is thus by a weird neoteric preciosity that Lesbia finds herself placed in a poem of some extensiveness, made part of a narrative, and compared to a story taken from Greek myth. All these things were to become typical features of Roman elegy; yet nothing could have been further from Catullus' mind than the forming of a convention when he wrote the piece.

Everything, then, that we can glean from a study of the surviving poetry suggests that Latin love elegy was essentially new, without Greek precedent. Of course, if we ask whether anyone had written love poetry in the first person before Catullus, the answer is yes; but the distinctive and unifying characteristics of Roman elegy amount to more than that. To define its peculiar character would not be easy. It is an amalgam: not all the elements of the amalgam may be present in one poem, or even one poet, but it is the sharing of a number of these elements, sometimes in greater quantity, sometime in less, which gives Latin elegy its individual quality. (It is vital to recognize the elusiveness of definition. To take an analogy: we can all see that gothic architecture is different from romanesque, and separate them one from another, but since there are romanesque buildings with pointed arches and gothic buildings with round-headed arches, the obvious quick definition will not in fact work. If the new and individual quality of Latin love elegy were easily definable, it would not be very interesting. Whether the Greeks had written any 'subjective love elegy' is not greatly important; whether they had written anything like Roman love elegy is.)

Turning from the texts and looking to Roman life and society, we find the same conclusion suggesting itself. What is the necessary

---

[21] Which is not to say that there are no points of contact at all.

condition for a developed tradition of love poetry? Surely that the beloved is able to say no. That is what makes the affair complicated, uncertain, and various enough to supply matter for the poet. (Hence the rarity of works about married love—love that is secure and assured of acceptance—even in those societies which have most prized it. Significantly, two of the works which explore this most profoundly, the *Odyssey* and *The Magic Flute*—perhaps the only two fully successful celebrations of conjugal love in three thousand years of the European tradition—do so not directly, but through myth and symbol.) In Greece the necessary uncertainty did not exist so far as relations between the sexes were concerned: men met two classes of women whom they might desire, their wives, who did as they were told, and hetaerae, whom they paid. It is no accident that the best Greek love poetry is homoerotic: the boy could choose whether to accept or no. It is said that the best love poetry of Persia and Arabia is addressed to males; surely for the same reason. Nor is it strange that the finest of Greek love poets should be both homosexual and a woman. Sappho is doubly vulnerable: not only may her girls refuse her, but she may soon lose them in any case, for they will marry and leave her for another life. Many of the surviving fragments are about parting or absence.

In Rome the situation was otherwise, at least for a few. Nominally the woman was wholly under the authority of the paterfamilias, her father or husband; in the high society of the first century BC this was in practice not so. Powerful and independent women emerged: Servilia, the mother of Brutus, who could silence Cicero in five words, succeeding where strong men had failed;[22] Sempronia, cast as a glamorous villainness in Sallust's *Catiline*; and the notorious Clodia Metelli, who plays the same part in Cicero's defence of Caelius. She is probably Catullus' Lesbia; if not, we can be pretty confident that Lesbia is one of her sisters, so that we can at least identify the family and society from which she comes. Had Catullus not entered this aristocratically rakish milieu, Latin love poetry might have been rather different. The years of civil war bring a new class of women into the picture: young widows, wives whose husbands have been long away, daughters of decent Italian families left orphaned or destitute.[23] Late in his third book Propertius depicts himself picking up a woman

---

[22] The incident is reported by Cicero himself, *Att.* 15. 11. 2.
[23] As argued by R. Syme, *History in Ovid* (Oxford, 1978), 202 f.

of respectable origin but ambiguous status:[24] she is educated, and
has had a distinguished grandfather, but she has lost her protector,
and is thus easy game for the predatory poet. Cynthia seems to be
a similar type, as perhaps are others of the elegiac women also.

A mixture of social and literary circumstances also brought about
love elegy's decline—or perhaps we should say its abrupt ending,
for though others continued in the same vein after Ovid, they seem
never to have been thought of much significance. As the years passed,
the women stranded by the civil wars must have slipped gradually
from the scene, through death or marriage, or by sinking into a deeper
degradation as time took away their charms. Eventually, Augustus'
last years ushered in a grimmer mood: Ovid's poetry became a charge
against him, and whether it were a pretext for his exile or a genuine cause, the fact that such a charge could be made at all is startling
and novel enough. But there were literary causes also. There was a
limit to the variations that the elegist could play upon his theme:
certain motifs—the military rival, the crone who corrupts the girl
—start to recur too often. The growing habit of public recitation
may have encouraged a kind of verse that relied more on wit and
point than intimacy, a quality not well suited to the lecture room.
In any case, there was the effect of Ovid, who created a poetry poised
between literary joking—that is, good-natured fun at the expense
of the elaborated agonies of Propertius and his like—and the advo-
cacy of a new attitude to life: the idea that the life of love should
be alert, vivid, and inventive, not revelling in its own torpor.[25] Such
is the message of *Militat omnis amans*, in which the exuberant context hides the sting of what is really quite a sharp pricking not only
of official values but of Ovid's fellow elegist Propertius.[26] After this,
it became harder to go on languishing beautifully.

To examine the history of Latin love elegy is to learn that in this
field too Roman poetry flourishes because it has stumbled upon something radically new, partly by a fitting response to changed circumstances, partly through the accidents of individual genius. Again we
see how difficult it was to write good poetry in the first century:

---

[24] Prop. 3. 20. She is probably not meant to be Cynthia herself. The sketching in of
her background suggests the invention of a new character, and if the poem were meant
to relate the first love-making with Cynthia, it would be hard to account for so momentous an event being so unemphatically placed within the third book as a whole. The idea
that the last six poems of the book are a cycle depicting the entire affair is a fantasy.

[25] Ov. *Am.* 1. 9, esp. 31 f., 41–6.   [26] e.g. Prop. 1. 1. 6, 17; 1. 6. 27 f.; 3. 7. 72.

the task was not a matter of capturing the Greek achievement by a programme of colonisation which could have been mapped out in advance. Virgil had his own part to play in the development of Latin love poetry, as we shall see later;[27] the influence of the earlier love poets upon him can be only imperfectly assessed. We are handicapped by the loss of Gallus; and whereas Lucretius' influence on Virgil is easy to see, the effect of Catullus is to be found more in the catching of mood and tone than in direct imitation or allusion.

One such effect, perhaps, is a sense of particularity. Much of Catullus' Poem 68 is leisurely and discursive. Its first part takes the form of a letter to a friend, unemphatic for the most part, but with two sharp pieces of private pain breaking into the conversational texture: the death of Catullus' brother and the fact of Lesbia's promiscuity.[28] The second part of the poem expresses gratitude to Allius, probably but not certainly the same person as the friend addressed earlier; it is even more discursive than the first part, with space for Greek mythology and even a digression on the drainage system in Thessaly. The unhurried flow and apparently disjointed construction make the reappearance of Lesbia and the brother's death stand out the more keenly. Allius is thanked for providing a house where Lesbia and Catullus could meet:[29]

> quo mea se molli candida diva pede
> intulit et trito fulgentem in limine plantam
> innixa arguta constituit solea . . .

There my bright goddess came with soft tread and set her gleaming foot on the worn threshold with the pressure of her tapping sandal . . .

Lesbia has come; and we expect Catullus to press on with a description of his love's fulfilment. But instead he deviates for some sixty lines into the myth of Protesilaus and Laodamia, and we are kept in pleased suspense until at last, at lines 131 ff., the poem blazes out in celebration of love consummated. The effect finally is like a delayed resolution in music: the long postponement adds force to the mood of triumphant happiness, when nothing else seems to matter and Catullus can declare that he is able to put up with Lesbia's infidelities, even comparing himself and his lover to Juno and Jupiter, before remembering abashedly that 'it is not right to liken men to gods'.[30]

---

[27] See below, pp. 601–4.   [28] Cat. 68. 19 ff., 27 ff.
[29] Cat. 68. 70–2.   [30] Cat. 68. 141.

The effect immediately is to heighten Lesbia's moment on the threshold by isolating it.

These lines seize one brief, small moment of remembered experience. Catullus could have chosen some dramatic or ecstatic memory; instead, he focuses on something oddly ordinary. Maybe he has needed Lesbia to open his eyes to small things, but once he has fixed his gaze upon this little patch of reality, he seems to enjoy the detail of the external world for its own sake. For he gives us a contrast of textures, the gleaming sandal seen against the worn threshold, while the tap of the foot, adding sound to sight, crystallizes the particular instant, sharply, precisely.

But this ordinary moment is elevated, for Catullus has called Lesbia a goddess, thus evoking the traditional motif of the theoxeny. In one version of theoxeny mortals entertain divine beings unawares. The story of Abraham, Sarah, and the angels is an example from the Old Testament; the tale of Philemon and Baucis giving hospitality to Jupiter and Mercury, related by Ovid, is a classical equivalent.[31] A variant on this motif is provided by stories of heroes or demigods welcomed into humble homes. Theseus was taken in by Hecale, Heracles by Molorchus; Evander tells Aeneas, in Virgil's eighth book, how Hercules deigned to enter his modest dwelling, and Aeneas takes upon himself the same role as he stoops to enter the house; the anecdotes about Julius Caesar courteously accepting an unappetizing meal and bivouacking in a peasant's hut depict a historical personage in the same style.[32]

Essential to these stories is the contrast between the god or hero and the ordinariness of the abode to which he condescends. In a sense Catullus fits this pattern: Lesbia, the goddess, crosses the simple, well-worn threshold. But in another sense he inverts the pattern. When the god in a story of theoxeny is disguised, the fascination lies in the fact that a scene that is in truth strange and wonderful appears to the hosts to be everyday; they have no sense of the numinous, and yet a divinity is among them. The visitor is Jupiter, but Philemon does not know it; Lesbia, by contrast, is not a goddess, yet seems so to her lover. In a theoxeny a rare event appears plain; Catullus takes a plain event and irradiates it. The scene is not

---

[31] Genesis 18; Ov. *Met.* 8. 618 ff.

[32] Callimachus' *Hecale* told her story; the third book of his *Aetia* included the tale of Molorchus. Virg. *Aen.* 8. 362 ff.; Plut. *Caes.* 17. 5 f.

picturesquely rustic, like the flitches of pork hanging from Philemon and Baucis' ceiling in Ovid's account, or quaintly inept like the ill-dressed meal that Caesar consented to get down; it is simply ordinary, a still life in words.

There has not, perhaps, been anything quite like this in poetry before. Theocritus' seventh Idyll lovingly recreates the external world, but even this is a strange, slightly mysterious occasion, when the nymphs themselves minister to the friends. Here perhaps the divine presence is already half metaphor, but it is left to Catullus to make it fully so. We can think of Lesbia at the door in two ways: Catullus captures and preserves a small moment of experience, and he looks at two objects, a foot and a doorstep, in relation to one another. Each of these styles of seeing and feeling will be found again in the *Eclogues*.

The eighth Eclogue includes a very brief memory of two children meeting in an orchard. Like the memory of Lesbia at the door, the scene is islanded within verse of a different and indeed varied character. The *mise en scène* is that two shepherds, Damon and Alphesiboeus, are holding a singing competition. Damon goes first; his song, told in the first person, describes a blighted and despairing love, ending with the speaker's declaration that he will take his life by casting himself from a high rock into the sea. This extravagance reveals that Damon is not singing about himself: we are not to suppose that, racked by such torments, he has the heart to turn them into the matter of a competition, or that he politely waits to hear Alphesiboeus' song of response before carrying out his plan of suicide. That is confirmed when Alphesiboeus takes up the challenge, for he takes the role of a woman. The songs of the two shepherds parallel one another, and just as Alphesiboeus assumes a part, so too does Damon. Thus the story that each of the herdsmen tells is set at a distance; there is a consciousness of the poem as exquisite artefact, a careful avoidance of the tragic note.

And yet the meeting in the orchard is both vivid and affecting:[33]

> saepibus in nostris parvam te roscida mala
> (dux ego vester eram) vidi cum matre legentem.
> alter ab undecimo tum me iam acceperat annus,
> iam fragilis poteram a terra contingere ramos:
> ut vidi, ut perii, ut me malus abstulit error!

[33] *Ecl.* 8. 37–41.

I saw you in our enclosure as a little girl (I was your guide) gathering dewy apples with your mother. At that time I had just reached my twelfth year, I could just reach the brittle branches from the ground. When I saw, how I died, how wretched delusion carried me away!

In this picture all is so small, all so tender. The girl is little ('parvam'), and she is found in an enclosure ('saepibus in nostris'). This is a telling change from the lines of Theocritus taken by Virgil as his model here, in which the girl came 'wanting to pick hyacinths from the hill';[34] the whole little scene is delicately enclosed by the landscape just as the brief passage itself is enclosed by the rather different poetry around it. The image is the more tender in that the enclosed garden was a common symbol in antiquity for a girl's virginity. 'A garden inclosed is my sister, my spouse,' says The Song of Songs; 'a spring shut up, a fountain sealed.'[35] Closest to Virgil is an image of the bride in one of Catullus' wedding poems:[36]

> ut flos in saeptis secretus nascitur hortis,
> ignotus pecori, nullo convolsus aratro,
> quem mulcent aurae, firmat sol, educat imber;
> multi illum pueri, multae optavere puellae . . .
> sic virgo, dum intacta manet, dum cara suis est . . .

As a flower is born secretly in an enclosed garden, unknown to the cattle, wrenched up by no plough, a flower which the breezes caress, the sun strengthens, the showers rear; many boys have desired it, many girls . . . Even so a maiden, while she remains untouched, is dear to her people . . .

This simile enlarges the image of the enclosed garden to suggest also the parents' protecting care, and Virgil picks up the suggestion. For whereas in Theocritus' scene the mother was the man's, here she is the girl's.[37] There is a sort of shy urgency in the way in which 'dux ego vester eram' is put into parenthesis;[38] and there is delicate exactness in the lines that follow. The language focuses upon the detail of time and scale: we see this in the repetition 'iam . . . iam', the word strengthened the first time by an accompanying 'tum'.[39]

---

[34] Theoc. 11. 26 f.

[35] Song 4. 12. Cf. Ibycus 286 and Eur. *Hipp.* 73 ff., discussed in Ch. 2.

[36] Cat. 62. 39–42, 45. The passage receives detailed analysis in Jenkyns, *Three Classical Poets* (London, 1982), 50–3.

[37] This is sure, despite the uncertainty voiced by Servius, because of the plurally possessive adjective 'vester' ('I was guide to both of you').

[38] There is some likeness to the technique at the start of *Aen.* 7, discussed at the beginning of Ch. 11.   [39] For Virgil's use of 'iam' and 'iam tum' cf. pp. 200–2, 472, 551.

The boy is *just* 11 years old.[40] Now it is true that the adjective 'duodecimus' (twelfth) cannot be fitted into a hexameter; still, the periphrasis in 'alter ab undecimo' helps the focusing effect: one year past the eleventh—we feel the searching for precision. And as this line focuses on the boy's age, so the next focuses on his height: *now* he could reach the boughs of the tree. The whole scene is on tiptoe, so to speak. 'Fragilis' is the perfect epithet for those branches, since the whole scene seems delicate, vulnerable, easily broken. And broken it shall be in the very next line, as the boy is swept away into disaster. These few lines have extraordinary intensity and clarity, and yet how far from immediacy they are. Virgil introduces the poem in his own person (as he does not in his four other pastoral dialogues); he then invents the shepherd Damon; Damon then invents an imaginary lover; the imaginary lover then recalls an event long ago in his past. It is like looking through a telescope the wrong way round: we see the scene in the orchard with extreme precision, but far away and very small.

This is a strange aesthetic, and again we may come nearest to it in Catullus. His Poem 65 is a letter to a friend accompanying his translation of Callimachus' *Lock of Berenice*, and explaining that he is sending it although grief for his dead brother has kept him away from the Muses. The whole poem, twenty-four lines long, is essentially a single sentence, with a long parenthesis of ten lines in the middle. The brother's death comes in this parenthesis, which can be read in either of two ways. We might say that the pain of it is keen enough to force its way into the elegant expansiveness of the main sentence. Or we might say that the poet has set his bereavement at a certain distance: it is merely a parenthesis, no more. In melodious language, subtly assonant, he dissolves his sorrow into a perpetual music and then wraps it in a soothing blanket of Greek mythology, likening his mourning song to the Daulian bird, the nightingale, embowered in woodland, bewailing the loss of her Itylus:[41]

> at certe semper amabo,
> semper maesta tua carmina morte canam,
> qualia sub densis ramorum concinit umbris
> Daulias, absumpti fata gemens Ityli . . .

---

[40] This seems the natural interpretation. Servius, however, maintains that 'alter ab unde-cimo . . . annus' means that the boy is *two* years past his eleventh year; in other words that he is, as we should say, 12 years old.   [41] Cat. 65. 11–14.

But assuredly I shall always love you, always sing sorrowful songs because of your death, such as the Daulian bird sings deep in the shade of the boughs, lamenting the fate of her lost Itylus . . .

The brother's own presence is curiously oblique: even within the parenthesis, he enters as a genitive case, governed by the accusative 'pedem' (foot)—an odd likeness to Lesbia on the threshold here—in a clause whose subject, seemingly, is the flow of water, charmingly described:[42]

> namque mei nuper Lethaeo gurgite fratris
>   pallidulum manans alluit unda pedem . . .

For the flowing stream has lately washed my brother's pale foot in Lethe's flood . . .

The pattern of sounds in the second line is very refined, an elegance that matches its decorative content; the diminutive 'pallidulus' is prettily sentimental. Are these the pangs of irremediable loss?

Certainly Catullus is shunning the tragic tone, like Virgil in the eighth Eclogue; the reason, however, is not that he feels too little but that he feels too much. The indirection has its own poignancy: we feel that the elaborated form and ornamental content are bandages over a wound that would otherwise be too raw. Catullus implies that he has been translating Callimachus because a more personal form of poetic expression would be too painful. One might compare Dean Inge's touching poem on his daughter's death, written in Latin elegiacs so that discipline and artifice might set a necessary space between the pain and its expression.

Virgil's scene in the orchard shows his capacity to crystallize a moment of experience; to which may be added an almost indefinable quality, an evocation of childhood that blends the senses of innocence and loss.[43] That is perhaps without near parallel, but the feeling for particularity recurs in the *Eclogues*. The seventh poem begins with a herdsman encountering three of his fellows. All have Greek names and two are identified as Arcadians; the tone seems literary and detached. But suddenly we find that we are not in Arcadia or even in Greece but in north Italy, on Virgil's own native patch:[44]

---

[42] Cat. 65. 5 f.

[43] Macaulay held these lines to be the finest in the Latin language (T. Pinney (ed.), *The Letters of Thomas Babington Macaulay*, iii (Cambridge, 1976), 62); E. J. Kenney ventures to risk anachronism by comparing their feeling for the lost paradise of childhood with *Le Grand Meaulnes* (*ICS* 8 (1983), 44–59, at 53).   [44] *Ecl.* 7. 12 f.

>   hic viridis tenera praetexit harundine ripas
>   Mincius.

Here Mincius fringes his green banks with tender reed.

Virgil was evidently pleased with this description, for he reworked and expanded it in the *Georgics*:[45]

>   et viridi in campo templum de marmore ponam
>   propter aquam, tardis ingens ubi flexibus errat
>   Mincius et tenera praetexit harundine ripas.

And I shall build a marble temple in a green expanse, by the waterside, where broad Mincius wanders with sluggish windings and fringes his banks with tender reed.

In the first passage the descriptive elements are the green bank and the fringe of reeds; in the second passage the greenness (now applied to the surrounding fields) and the reed fringe remain, but some new details are added: the width of the river, the meandering course, the slow current.

The significance of these descriptions lies in the way that they capture the individual character of one particular stream. Most Italian rivers, small or large, are really mountain torrents: in dry season their streams run shrunken through boulders or gravel; after rain, or when the snows melt, they are turbid and swollen. The Tiber is conventionally 'flavus', yellow, because it is thick with the soil that it has scoured from its banks in its rapid descent from the Umbrian plateau; in the seventh book of the *Aeneid* Virgil will describe its mouth, the river bursting forth from among thick forest, its yellow eddies spreading out into the clear sea-water.[46] The rivers of the northern plain, including the Po itself, mostly do not differ much from other Italian rivers in this respect, since they are fed either from the Apennines or the Alps. Mincius, however, is something of an exception. Its headwaters are collected in the enormous basin of the Lake of Garda, which in any case lies unusually low for a mountain lake, its southern end lapping the Italian plain.[47] The lake supplies a relatively steady flow of water throughout the seasons, and the modest declivity between the lake and the river's confluence with the Po makes the current

---

[45] *Geo.* 3. 13–15.   [46] *Aen.* 7. 30–2.
[47] It is only 65 m. above sea level; compare Maggiore (193 m.), Como (199 m.), Lugano (270 m.). (The more northerly Alpine lakes—Geneva, Lucerne, Constance, etc.—lie much higher still.)

slow; today, in fact, wide marshy lakes have formed around Mantua, apparently since Virgil's lifetime; reed beds remain a distinctive feature of its course. He seems to have recognized the link between the Lake of Garda (Benacus) and the distinctive character of his local river, for when he returns to it in the *Aeneid*, he describes it as 'patre Benaco velatus harundine glauca Mincius' ('veiled in grey reed by father Benacus' or 'coming from father Benacus, veiled in grey reed').[48] Here he is terser than in the *Georgics*; he retains a colour adjective but changes it and transfers it to the reeds, leaving out the grassy banks altogether: grey sedge replaces green grass. The more sombre note suits the gravity of epic, as does the grand and emotional 'patre Benaco', but this is recognizably the same distinctive river. Mincius is still Virgil's *sphragis*; the seal stone is unchanged but now impressed upon a slightly different material.

A few words in the seventh Eclogue, then, set before us a particular landscape; the second Eclogue offers particularity on a smaller scale. Corydon lists the gifts that he will bring his beloved:[49]

> ipse ego cana legam tenera lanugine mala
> castaneasque nuces, mea quas Amaryllis amabat;
> addam cerea pruna (honos erit huic quoque pomo),
> et vos, o lauri, carpam et te, proxima myrte,
> sic positae quoniam suavis miscetis odores.

I myself will gather quinces, hoary with a delicate down, and chestnuts, which my Amaryllis used to love; I will add waxy plums (this fruit too shall have its honour), and you too, laurels, I will pick, and you, myrtle close by, since placed thus you mingle your fragrances.

The description of the fruits must be heard for its full effect to be appreciated. Sound enhances content: the long *a*'s and the predominance of liquid and nasal consonants in 'cana legam tenera lanugine mala' evoke the soft downy bloom on the quince or peach; the snappy sounds of 'castaneasque nuces' are apt for the crispness of the nuts; the long vowels in 'cerea pruna', one before a liquid, the other before a nasal, convey the shiny smoothness of the plums. This is something new in poetry: ordinary natural objects solidly apprehended, with the individual essence of each caught in a very few words. What is more, the three sets of objects, the mattness of the peach, the waxy plums, the chestnuts, are seen in relation to each other, compared,

---

[48] *Aen.* 10. 205 f.   [49] *Ecl.* 2. 51–5.

contrasted: this is a still life in verse. In Catullus' poem the foot on the threshold was an ordinary action but a special occasion; here the objects are simply ordinary, nothing more.

We meet here a style of sensibility which seems to be a discovery of Virgil's century. We have glimpsed it in Catullus, and we shall find that it is vital to Lucretius' re-creation of the philosophy of Epicurus. It is in part the sense, to borrow Pater's misquotation of Gautier, that the visible world exists. If we look at a still life by (say) Chardin, we do not suppose that the jug, the bowl, and the loaf are anything other than an ordinary jug and bowl and loaf, but the painter's art is to make these commonplace things seem endlessly interesting. In the case of the second Eclogue, however, to call the description a still life is to tell only part of the story, for it is also important that Corydon's gifts are, quite simply, good to eat. The poetry of good eating is a subject somewhat neglected by critics (admirers of Juvenal's vehemence and obscenity forget to praise him as a poet of food), and perhaps by poets themselves: drink has often been celebrated by writers who shun the low business of mastication. But Keats, for one, knew what could be done:[50]

> And still she slept an azure-lidded sleep,
> In blanched linen, smooth, and lavender'd,
> While he from forth the closet brought a heap
> Of candied apple, quince, and plum, and gourd;
> With jellies soother than the creamy curd,
> And lucent syrops, tinct with cinnamon;
> Manna and dates, in argosy transferr'd
> From Fez; and spiced dainties, every one,
> From silken Samarcand to cedar'd Lebanon.

Leigh Hunt noted the 'epicurean nicety' of the sixth line, and the manner in which we are made to 'read the line delicately, and at the tip-end, as it were, of one's tongue'.[51] The effect is realized through the dainty *i* sounds, the fancy diction of 'lucent' and 'tinct', and, as in Virgil, by contrast with a different texture, in this case the creamy jellies of the line before. Flecker manages a comparable 'nicety' in *The Golden Journey to Samarkand*, partly through exotic words but mostly by the adverb 'meticulously', neatly, indeed meticulously, placed:

[50] *The Eve of St Agnes*, st. 30.
[51] *Imagination and Fancy*, 'Keats', commentary ad loc.

We have rose-candy, we have spikenard,
    Mastic and terebinth and oil and spice,
And such sweet jams meticulously jarred
    As God's own Prophet eats in Paradise.

Yet the techniques of these later poets help to define a difference. While both Keats and Flecker call upon the romance of the orient to make the saliva flow, Virgil's fruits are merely the fruits that all his readers know. Yet the context in which they appear is, in its own way, exotic:[52]

> huc ades, o formose puer: tibi lilia plenis
> ecce ferunt Nymphae calathis; tibi candida Nais,
> pallentis violas et summa papavera carpens,
> narcissum et florem iungit bene olentis anethi;
> tum casia atque aliis intexens suavibus herbis
> mollia luteola pingit vaccinia calta.
> ipse ego . . .

Come hither, lovely boy: see, for you the Nymphs bring lilies in full baskets; for you the fair Naiad, picking pale violets and the heads of poppies, mingles narcissus and the flower of fragrant dill; then twining them with casia and other scented herbs, she paints the contrast of soft hyacinths with yellow marigold. I myself . . .

Whereas Mincius appeared suddenly, an unexpected item of Italian actuality in an apparently Grecian context, here Virgil effects a gradual transition. He begins with exquisite fantasy, with Nymphs and lilies, in a world where goddesses minister to a shepherd's whim. Then he begins to descend gracefully to more ordinary flowers, while still preserving, for a moment, an extreme delicacy and refinement: *pale* pansies, just the *tops* of the poppies. Then scents begin to waft from the baskets and some colour is 'painted' into the scene. The transition takes us from flowers to herbs and from herbs to fruits; it is a passage—effortless, as it seems—through three senses, sight, smell, and taste. This series of movements, from fantasy to reality, from divine to human, from decorative blooms to a more solid, immediately apprehensible, indeed edible nature is elegant in itself; it also enhances, by the force of subtly controlled distinctions, the taste and perfume of Corydon's own offerings. 'Ipse ego' marks a light contrast: the catalogue will continue to be lovely but it will become, in a small degree, more robust.

[52] *Ecl.* 2. 45–51.

The whole poem, indeed, is full of changes and contrasts, which may be stronger and more sudden than the slight and delicate transition that we have been tracing. Some of these are psychological: the shepherd's mood lurches abruptly from pride to humility, from hope to despair, and back again. So much is naturalistic; but complementing these changes, the degree of reality in the poem fluctuates also. Corydon talks about the rough countryside and its lowly cottages, but he also quotes what seems to be a snatch of Greek poetry: 'Amphion Dircaeus in Actaeo Aracyntho' (Dirce's Amphion on Attic Aracynthus).[53] This bizarre line draws attention to its oddity in that it has in terms of Virgil's usual practice no less than three irregularities of scansion: a weak caesura in the third foot without a strong caesura in the fourth to follow, a hiatus between the last two words, and a tetrasyllabic ending. But it can be virtually transliterated into Greek, with *epi* in place of 'in', whereupon it becomes regular according to the prosody of that language: *Amphion Dirkaios ep'Aktaioi Aracynthoi*. Virgil is either quoting a piece of Hellenistic poetry or pretending to do so, and he has chosen a line which by its metrical character will advertise its Greekness. Some have asked why the mountain Amphion is here wrongly placed in Attica (is this a sign of Corydon's rustic ignorance?), but to ask the question is to mistake the poem's aesthetic, and to expect a steady psychological realism which it declines to provide. Its model is Theocritus' eleventh Idyll, the song of the Cyclops Polyphemus. When Corydon declares that he has a thousand lambs roaming the Sicilian hills and that he has lately seen his reflection, when the sea was calm, he talks in the terms of Theocritus' mythological giant, though they make little or no sense in his own case.[54] But is it Virgil who is echoing the Greek poet, or Corydon? That is not the kind of question we ask when meeting allusions to earlier poetry in (let us say) the words of Dido. It is the peculiar quality of this particular poem—the very oddity and apparent inappropriateness of the Grecian intrusions— which tease the reader, leaving an uncertainty about how far from naturalism Virgil has been prepared to go.

The effect is perhaps not wholly pleasing. The veerings of mood are handled a little stiffly; the artificiality and the emotion are not fused, as they will be, for example, in the tenth Eclogue, but somewhat awkwardly juxtaposed. We may feel that here is a

---

[53] *Ecl.* 2. 24.   [54] *Ecl.* 2. 21, 25 f.; cf. Theoc. 11.

case, extremely rare in this poet, where his ambition has outrun his technique. Much happier is the fluctuation between fancy and a down-to-earth rusticity. Nymphs may come with lilies, but we also encounter the hard labour of the harvest field:[55]

> nunc etiam pecudes umbras et frigora captant,
> nunc viridis etiam occultant spineta lacertos,
> Thestylis et rapido fessis messoribus aestu
> alia serpyllumque herbas contundit olentis.

Now the cattle too seek out the cool shade, now the thorn brakes hide even the lizards, and Thestylis is pounding garlic and thyme, scented herbs, for the reapers exhausted by the tearing heat.

Arable farming was commonly excluded from later pastoral as too toilsome and commonplace for the poetic swain; this is an example of how Virgil for all his delicacy was more robust than his later followers. Before the coming of the combine harvester reaping was backbreaking work even in climates less warm than the Italian: in the last century the field ration of cider in Somerset for farm labourers was raised from two to ten pints during the harvest season. And in Virgil's picture the weather is brutally hot: 'rapido . . . aestu'. (The derivation of 'rapidus' from 'rapio', 'snatch', is seldom altogether lost in Latin; in the first Eclogue Meliboeus speaks of the river Oaxes 'rapidum cretae', scouring the chalk along its banks, and Lucretius had used 'rapidus' of rivers in a context of eager violence.)[56] Virgil's first readers would have known at once how exhausting was the work momentarily shown to them. However, like so much in the *Eclogues* it is set at a distance: Corydon is idle while the reapers toil; he is buried in the cool of beech woods, while the workers are yonder, out in the open.[57] Still, for its concision this is a strikingly vivid and vigorous little scene, depicted in smells as well as in visible things: garlic and sweat. Briefly we are in that world of the everyday picturesque which was to be more expansively treated by Ovid in his story of Philemon and Baucis or by the anonymous author of the *Moretum*.[58] It may be felt that such comfortable enjoyment of a quaint if energetic rusticity is some way from true realism, but it is certainly different from the elegance that we find elsewhere in the *Eclogues* and in this very poem. And indeed Virgil's little vignette does seem

---

[55] *Ecl.* 2. 8–11.   [56] *Ecl.* 1. 65; Lucr. 1. 15.   [57] Shady beeches: *Ecl.* 2. 3.
[58] Ov. *Met.* 8. 618–724, esp. 630, 641 ff., 660 ff., 684 ff.; [Virg.] *Moretum*, esp. 90 ff. (crushing garlic for a rustic meal).

to be free of condescension or sentimentality: with its picture of the reapers and their greasy Joan, its evocation of heat and pounded herbs, it is straightforward and economical.

In the catalogue of flowers and fruits we watched Virgil moving from the divine to the human, and towards a greater apprehensibility; a passage in the tenth Eclogue shows a movement in the opposite direction. It is fairly closely modelled on part of Theocritus' first Idyll, but Virgil imposes a shape not present in the Greek poem by beginning on a humble plane and only lifting himself to the gods' level by stages:[59]

> stant et oves circum; nostri nec paenitet illas,
> nec te paeniteat pecoris, divine poeta:
> et formosus ovis ad flumina pavit Adonis.
> venit et upilio, tardi venere subulci,
> uvidus hiberna venit de glande Menalcas.
> omnes 'unde amor iste' rogant 'tibi?' venit Apollo:
> 'Galle, quid insanis?' inquit . . .

The sheep too stand around; they are not ashamed of us, and you should not be ashamed of them, god-filled poet: even the fair Adonis fed sheep by the riverside. The shepherd too came, the slow swineherds came, Menalcas came, damp from the winter's acorns. All of them ask, 'Whence comes this love of yours?' Apollo came; 'Gallus, why this madness?' he said . . .

Virgil begins with mere sheep standing about, and indeed apologizes for their lowliness. The first visitors are a shepherd, mysteriously unnamed, and swineherds. In the bucolic writings of the Renaissance pigs and their keepers are almost always excluded as too coarse and homely for the gracious world of pastoral; some editors of the time emended 'subulci' to 'bubulci', 'neatherds', to save the poet from grossness. But he was not so squeamish: he starts at the bottom. The next line forms a transition: there comes another countryman, no idyllic figure, but damp from the mast of acorns in the winter. But when we reach the last word of the line we discover that this is no ordinary rustic after all: for surely, we tell ourselves, this Menalcas is the same as the enigmatic poet Menalcas, much spoken of but never seen, in the ninth poem, and apparently a figure for the poet himself. We do not know that it is the same Menalcas—that is part of the enigma—but we suspect it. In a way the picture given by this line is 'realistic', in a way it carries us to a region more remote and literary than we were in before; the ground is prepared for a yet further degree of fantasy with the entry of the first deity in the next line. From pigmen to Apollo in three lines—the transition is rapid, and not perhaps especially subtle, but characteristic of the way in which Virgil works.

Just as there are changes in tone or degree of reality within each Eclogue, so there are on a broader scale from one poem to another. Even between poems which seem to form a pair there may be light distinctions: the first and ninth Eclogues both treat the land confiscations in Italy, but the strange allusions to Menalcas, and the quotations of his versions of Theocritus, give the latter piece a significantly different tone. But whereas both the first and ninth Eclogues allude to contemporary politics, the seventh is set in a timeless world. We can hardly imagine a god or goddess wandering on to the scene in the first or ninth poem, but Corydon in the second can expect the Nymphs. Even so there remains a down-to-earth element in Corydon, his situation, and his landscape that makes him closer to reality than the divine shepherd Daphnis in the fifth Eclogue, or than Damon and Alphesiboeus in the eighth, who can astound the animals by their song and stop the rivers in their courses. Different again is the riddling, literary-fantastical world of the sixth Eclogue, in which Silenus sings about Gallus (surely, we say, it should be the other way round?), and the tenth poem, in which Gallus, who in sober reality was vigorously advancing a brilliant public career, is seen perishing in a far, lonely landscape.

While some of the Eclogues differ from each other in the extent to which they follow precedents in Theocritus' poetry, a few have difficulty in remaining pastoral at all. This was already noted by Servius, who remarks that seven of the Eclogues are 'merae rusticae', purely on country matters, but that in three Virgil departs from bucolic song.[60] Two of these he identifies as Eclogues 4 and 6; the third is presumably Eclogue 10. It is part of the teasing, paradoxical nature of the book that Virgil should assert his dependence on Theocritus most plainly at the start of those poems which owe the least to him. 'Sicelides Musae' (Muses of Sicily), he begins the fourth Eclogue, and speaks of his 'Syracusan verse' in the first line of the sixth. (The tenth poem is a less clear case. By invoking Arethusa, the fountain

---

[60] *Buc. prooem.* (Thilo–Hagen, iii. 3) 'sane sciendum, VII. eclogas esse meras rusticas . . .'.

of Syracuse, it again takes us, a touch more indirectly, to Theocritus' homeland. It is hardly at all pastoral, though it does echo a mythological passage from the first Idyll.)

The *Eclogues* shun consistency, eluding our attempts to pin them down—even in the matter of names. The Tityrus of the first poem, an elderly freedman, is different from the Tityrus of the sixth, a *nom de guerre* by which Apollo addresses the poet,[61] and neither is the same as the Tityrus mentioned in Eclogue 8; the Corydon of the second Eclogue is not the Corydon of the seventh; the Daphnis of the seventh seems to be a different sort of figure from the divinized Daphnis of the fifth. And yet the poet is not even consistent in his inconsistency: Menalcas does seem to be in part a figure for Virgil himself in both Eclogues 5 and 9, presented in the first of these poems as the creator of Eclogues 2 and 3,[62] in the other as a singer whose material moves between imitations of Theocritus and laments over the distresses of contemporary Italy.

It is thus a mistake to suppose that Virgil created in these poems a personal, self-consistent imaginary universe like Tolkien's Middle Earth or, more loosely, the 'Dickens world'. There is no pastoral world of the *Eclogues* but a number of worlds, which may or may not overlap one another, which may or may not be stable in themselves. That may seem surprising when we consider how closely woven the poems are together. There is really no parallel for this in ancient poetry: Horace's Odes are very carefully arranged, but with one or two exceptions they are single independent poems, gathered into books, whereas we feel unsure whether to think of the *Eclogues* as a collection or as one composition. Much has been written on the structure and patterning of the book and correspondences within it between poems. Not all of this has been persuasive, but it is inescapable that, for example, the poems, unlike their models in Theocritus, do not vary much in length, and that eight of them are arranged concentrically in pairs around Eclogue 5: 4 and 6 are the two non-pastoral poems, 3 and 7 the two singing competitions, 2 and 8 the love laments, 1 and 9 the treatments of the land confiscations. But the ten Eclogues are so tightly bound together not because they are uniform in tone and atmosphere but for the opposite reason: that otherwise they would risk falling apart. Virgil needs a firm framework that he may have a greater freedom of movement inside it;

[61] *Ecl.* 1. 27 ff., 6. 4.   [62] *Ecl.* 5. 86 f.

the delicate discriminations within the apparently rigid structure are a part of the fascination.

This account of the *Eclogues*, stressing their fluidity, elusiveness, and inconsistency, has to compete with another, which sees them as inventing or adhering to a number of clear and fixed conventions. There is a view of pastoral literature and Virgil's place within it which goes something like this. Pastoral arises, it is said, as a reaction to loss of contact with the land. It is no accident that it comes into being in Alexandria, the first really large city of the Greek world, or that it appears in Latin literature when Rome had grown into the greatest city of the Mediterranean. Pastoral is distinct from other writings about the country in being essentially an urban literature, expressing the longing of city sophisticates for vanished simplicities. It depicts the happy lives of nymphs and swains and sometimes satyrs, whom Virgil put into Arcadia, a realm of poetry and love, a natural idyll, his symbol for a land of lost content.

This theory has several attractions: it is clear and plausible and it pleasingly ties developments in literature to social and economic changes. But as a theory it has one fault: that it is very largely wrong.

We need not stand in awe of received opinions. The *Eclogues* form probably the most influential group of short poems ever written: though they take Theocritus as a model, they were to become the fountainhead from which the vast and diverse tradition of pastoral in many European literatures was to spring. To use them as a model was in itself to distort their character: it is one of the greatest ironies of literary history that these fugitive, various, eccentric poems should have become the pattern for hundreds of later writers. Moreover, the growth of the later pastoral tradition meant that many things were attributed to Virgil which are not in Virgil. Sometimes they were derived from interpretations which were put upon Virgil in late antiquity but which we now believe to be mistaken; sometimes they are misinterpretations of a much later date; sometimes they originated from new developments in pastoral literature which their inventors had not meant to seem Virgilian, but which in the course of time got foisted back on to Virgil nevertheless. It is hard, therefore, to approach the *Eclogues* openly and without preconceptions about what they contain, and even scholars who have devoted much time and learning to them have sometimes continued to hold views about them for which there are upon a dispassionate observation no good grounds at all. No poems perhaps have become so encrusted by the barnacles of later tradition and interpretation as these, and we need to scrape these away if we are to see them in their true shape. This may be seen as a process of restoration rather than destruction; a *via negativa* can lead us to find what is in the *Eclogues* as well as what is not.

We may begin with perhaps the most deeply rooted of all these misconceptions. A classic essay describes Virgil's Arcadia as 'the discovery of a spiritual landscape'.[63] 'Arcadia,' it begins, 'was discovered in the year 42 or 41 BC'—not of course the actual geographical region of Arcadia, an austere, mountainous area of the Peloponnese, but Arcadia as an imaginative creation: 'The Arcadia which the name suggests to the minds of most of us today is a different one; it is the land of shepherds and shepherdesses, the land of poetry and love. And its discoverer is Virgil.' This summarizes a belief that has in essence been held for centuries, and scholars have continued to maintain it.[64]

Nevertheless, these claims about Virgil's use of Arcadia are simply wrong.[65] Instead of 'in the year 42 or 41 BC' we should read 'around

[63] Bruno Snell, *The Discovery of the Mind*, tr. T. G. Rosenmeyer (Oxford, 1953), ch. 13, 'Arcadia: the discovery of a spiritual landscape'. 'Spiritual' translates the German 'geistig', which includes the connotations 'mental', 'imaginative'. The German title of the book is *Die Entdeckung des Geistes*.

[64] Some examples. G. Highet: 'Vergil was the discoverer of Arcadia, the idealized land of country life, where youth is eternal, love is the sweetest of all things even though cruel, music comes to the lips of every herdsman, and the kind spirits of the country-side bless even the unhappiest lover with their sympathy' (*The Classical Tradition* (Oxford, 1949), 163). J. Perret: Virgil's Arcadia is 'the ideal land of leisure and pastoral song, of nature at its loveliest and of the most exquisite refinement' (*Virgile: l'homme et l'œuvre* (Paris, 1952), 32). F. Klingner: Arcadia was for Virgil a dream landscape, the soul's homeland, an enchanted realm of higher existence in the midst of a brutal and destructive reality (*Virgil* (1967), 14). T. G. Rosenmeyer: Virgil 'replaced Theocritus' Sicily and Cos with Arcadia' (*The Green Cabinet: Theocritus and the European Pastoral Lyric* (Berkeley and Los Angeles, 1969), 232). In more recent authorities a note of discomfort can sometimes be detected. R. Coleman believes that 'Vergil saw in the myth of Arcady . . . an embodiment of certain moral ideals that he could himself identify closely with the real countryside: a simple way of life, contentment with little, delight in natural beauty, homely piety, friendship and hospitality, devotion to poetry and to peace'; and he claims that the seventh Eclogue is set in this mythical Arcady. But he allows that 'The definitive presentment of this Arcady occurs only in the last pastoral that he wrote, *Ecl.* 10', and concedes that the poet's 'references to [Arcady] are infrequent' (*Virgil: Eclogues* (Cambridge, 1977), 32, 22, 209). W. Clausen comes closest to the truth when he remarks, in parenthesis, that 'pastoral Arcadia is mainly the invention of Sannazaro and Sir Philip Sidney', but he continues to hold that 'la pastorale Arcadia' is 'the ideal, harmonious landscape Virgil discovered as a young poet' (*Virgil's Aeneid and the Tradition of Hellenistic Poetry* (Berkeley and Los Angeles, 1987), 66).

[65] The simplicity of this claim should perhaps be stressed. Because the *Eclogues* are pre-eminently poetry for which some fashionable words—'ambiguous', 'multivalent', 'polysemous'—work so well, it is easy to slip into supposing that nothing can be said of them which is plainly right or plainly wrong; but this is not so. Cf. G. B. Conte, *The Rhetoric*

AD 1500', and for Virgil we should read the name of Jacopo Sannazaro. We shall come back to Sannazaro; for the moment a few words about his most famous work, *Arcadia*, will suffice. It is a romance, a mixture of prose narrative and verse eclogues, in which Silvio, a gentleman suffering from the woes of love, retires into an idyllic countryside populated by shepherds and shepherdesses; to this countryside Sannazaro gives the name Arcadia. The book was a success all over Europe, and spawned many imitators, notably Montemayor's *Diana* (now chiefly remembered for its effect upon Don Quixote) and, finest of all, Sir Philip Sidney's *Arcadia*, which again enjoyed an international esteem. It was one of the most popular works of fiction in England for a hundred and fifty years, and was still widely read up to the end of the eighteenth century; Richardson called his novel *Pamela* after one of Sidney's two heroines. Out of the enormous popularity of such pastoral romances (which inspired, among other things, two of Shakespeare's plays) grew a vast literature of pastoral prose and poetry; the setting was often though not always Arcadia, and the place became so familiar that it was commonly Anglicized as Arcady. A mood of idyllic beauty combined with a kind of melancholy was summed up in the phrase 'et in Arcadia ego'. This motto was invented in the seventeenth century, in the course of which it changed meaning.[66] Originally it was death who spoke: 'Even in Arcadia, there am I.' Soon the words were transferred to the dead shepherd, who declares, more evocatively but with inferior Latinity, 'I too was once in Arcadia';[67] bitterness is softened into wistful charm. The history of these famous words is a remarkable instance of an apparently classical tradition growing and changing since the Renaissance; it may warn us to look at Virgil's Arcadia too with a sceptical eye.

We should note, first of all, that there is no sign of anyone in the ancient world realizing that Virgil had discovered a spiritual Arcadia symbolic of pastoral. The writers of pastoral subsequent to Virgil— Calpurnius Siculus, Nemesianus and the author of the Einsiedeln eclogues—are unaware of what Virgil is supposed to have done (one

---

of Imitation (Ithaca, 1986), 103 (in an essay on *Ecl.* 10): 'We need a method that is internally coherent and also devises a critical discourse that is consistent with the text, not an undisciplined surrender to arbitrary inferences sanctioned by supposed ambiguity.'

[66] This was shown by E. Panofsky in R. Klibansky and H. J. Paton (eds.), *Philosophy and History: Essays Presented to Ernest Cassirer* (Oxford, 1936), 223–54; the article is reprinted in Panofsky, *Meaning and the Visual Arts* (New York, 1955), 295–320.

[67] For which the Latin would naturally be 'et ego in Arcadia' or 'in Arcadia et ego'.

might add that Mantuan, writing Latin eclogues imitative of Virgil in the fifteenth century, is equally innocent of such awareness).[68] Servius has no knowledge of such an Arcadia either. He knows that 'silvae' are one of Virgil's symbols for the pastoral world; he knows that allusions to Sicily are allusions to pastoral; but he does not say this of Arcadia. The observation is a simple one, but it should be stressed; it would be extraordinary, if Virgil had really created the myth of Arcadia, that no ancient writer known to us should have noticed the fact.

Let us then look at the references to Arcadia in Virgil's own text. The process is like melting snow in a bucket: there is surprisingly little water left at the end, and what there is looks rather muddy. To start with, there is in more than half of the eclogues, six out of ten, no reference or allusion to Arcadia whatsoever: these eclogues are 1, 2, 3, 5, 6, and 9. Suppose that treating the *Eclogues* as a single work we simply read through them, in succession. We shall not find any mention of Arcadia until near the end of the fourth Eclogue:[69]

> Pan etiam, Arcadia mecum si iudice certet,
> Pan etiam Arcadia dicat se iudice victum.

Pan too, if he were to compete with me with Arcadia as judge, Pan, even with Arcadia as judge, would confess himself beaten.

Once we rid ourselves of preconceptions, it becomes clear that this is just a passing reference: Arcadia is mentioned because it is the region traditionally associated with Pan. If Virgil had been speaking of some beautiful woman and said, 'She is more lovely than Venus, as even Cyprus would admit', no one would suppose that the scene was set in Cyprus. The phrase 'Pan deus Arcadiae', 'Pan the god of Arcadia', comes not only in the tenth Eclogue but also in the third book of the *Georgics*, and in the latter case at least it is surely plain that Arcadia carries no distinctly private or symbolic meaning for the poet.[70] In any case, this poem is not in a straightforward sense pastoral at all. The fourth and sixth Eclogues differ from the others in that they have no landscape background; all the rest are set in

---

[68] 'Henceforth Arcady became *the* pastoral setting' (Coleman on *Ecl.* 7. 4); this, the conventional view, ignores later classical poetry and the pastorals of the Carolingian period, the Middle Ages and the early Renaissance. On this extensive literature see e.g. H. Cooper, *Pastoral: Mediaeval into Renaissance* (Ipswich, 1977), E. Lambert, *Placing Sorrow: A Study of the Pastoral Elegy Convention from Theocritus to Milton* (Chapel Hill, 1976).
[69] *Ecl.* 4. 58 f.   [70] *Geo.* 3. 392.

some kind of landscape, elusive and imaginary though it may be. The fourth poem is not set in Arcadia for the simple reason that it is not set anywhere at all; it is just not that sort of poem. It is an address to a patron, a panegyric, a *genethliacon*; it is not dramatic or descriptive of locality. The point need not be further laboured; one has only to read the poem to see why it cannot be 'placed' in a geographical area.

Let us look onwards. As there is no trace of Arcadia in the fifth or sixth Eclogues, we can read through more than half of the poems without any indication that Arcadia is the symbol of Virgil's 'spiritual landscape'. Of the four eclogues that remain, the ninth again has nothing of Arcadia in it; the other three will require a longer scrutiny.

The eighth Eclogue does not name Arcadia as such; however, three lines of Damon's song describe the mountain Maenalus, which is in Arcadia:[71]

> Maenalus argutumque nemus pinusque loquentis
> semper habet, semper pastorum ille audit amores
> Panaque, qui primus calamos non passus inertis.

Maenalus ever keeps its sounding woods and whispering pines, it ever hears the loves of shepherds; it hears too Pan, who first forbade the reeds to remain idle.

Moreover, the refrain of Damon's song is 'incipe Maenalios mecum, mea tibia, versus' (My flute, begin with me my Maenalian songs).[72] The reason for Maenalus' appearance here seems tolerably clear: it is associated with Pan, as Delphi and Delos were associated with Apollo, or Cyprus with Aphrodite; Maenalian songs are songs accompanied by the Pan pipes.

So there is an undoubted reference to Arcadia in the eighth Eclogue; are there any grounds for thinking that the poem is itself set in Arcadia? The answer is no, because, as we have already seen, Damon is not singing *in propria persona* but adopting a role that is not his own. Might one, though, make a more limited claim: that Damon has placed the invented hero of his song in Arcadia? No, even this is not the case. The imagined singer says something of Maenalus, but he does not in fact say that he is on Maenalus; the name gives us

---

[71] *Ecl.* 8. 22–4.

[72] First at *Ecl.* 8. 21 and repeated eight times before its final appearance, in altered form, at line 61.

no indication of setting one way or the other. More significant is that a few lines later he does provide another and different geographical indication: 'sparge, marite, nuces: tibi deserit Hesperus Oetam' (Scatter nuts, bridegroom; for you the Evening Star is leaving Mount Oeta).[73] Oeta is of course in Thessaly. This name is like the brief appearance of 'Sicilian hills' in the second Eclogue:[74] one might say either that the imagined scene is set in Thessaly, or in a fantasy world that momentarily becomes Thessaly, or that this morsel of geography is a brief, romantic flourish which is not to be further pressed; perhaps the third of these formulations is the best, but Virgil's use of proper names in the *Eclogues* is often anti-naturalistic, encouraging us to doubt whether he is himself much concerned to choose between the alternatives.[75] There is, in theory, one more geographical indicator at lines 59–60: the blighted lover will cast himself from a mountain into the sea. Are we to search for some coastal region of Greece with cliffs along the shore? Surely not. Here is another poetical flourish, derived, no doubt, from the story of Sappho and Phaon; another artificial, operatic gesture. One thing, at least, can be firmly stated: there are no grounds for saying that the imaginary persona which Damon assumes (a role so sketchy that he does not have a name) is an Arcadian or that he is living in Arcadia; the former claim would have to be based on a misunderstanding of lines 21–4, the latter is ruled out by line 30.

We have now passed eight out of the ten eclogues in review, and already it should be clear that the traditional belief in Virgil's Arcadia is untenable; but let us press on with our quest. In the seventh Eclogue the herdsman Meliboeus describes two other herdsmen, Thyrsis and Corydon, as 'Arcades ambo', 'both Arcadian', in line 4; in line 26 Thyrsis apostrophizes Arcadian shepherds. There are no other references of any sort to Arcadia in the poem. What are we to make of this?

At line 12 f. we are not in Arcadia, or even in Greece, for the simple reason that we are in north Italy, by the Mincius. We have

---

[73] *Ecl.* 8. 30.   [74] *Ecl.* 2. 21.

[75] Catullus at 62. 7 associates Oeta with the rising of the Evening Star, to be followed by Virgil, Statius and the author of the *Culex* (R. Ellis, *A Commentary on Catullus* (2nd edn., Oxford, 1889), ad loc.); Servius alleges a cult of Hesperus on Oeta. Whether Virgil simply echoes Catullus or alludes to some older convention is unclear. Coleman on *Ecl.* 8. 30 ('So this could be a clue to the notional setting of the singing contest') wrongly conflates the world of the singer with the world of his song.

already seen that Virgil's brief description of this stream is particularized, setting a rather distinctive kind of Italian landscape sharply and immediately before our eyes. And this is a landscape extremely unlike that of Arcadia, which is fiercely mountainous, not flat and green.

It might be disputed whether the seventh Eclogue is in north Italy throughout or in an imaginary world which for a moment becomes north Italy, though one may indeed feel as before that an insouciance about such matters is part of these poems' aesthetic. In any case, the issue does not affect our immediate argument. What can be firmly said, once again, is that there are no grounds at all for supposing that Virgil intended to place the herdsmen of this poem in an Arcadia either literal or metaphorical. We can go further: there is in fact a decisive reason, even apart from the appearance of Mincius, why the setting cannot be Arcadia, and it lies in the words 'Arcades ambo' themselves. If some character in a book says 'I have just met two Englishmen', we can be virtually certain that the scene is not laid in England. The words would be natural in Paris, but not in Surrey. When Meliboeus tells us that his friends are both Arcadians, the poet has indicated to us that we are somewhere other than Arcadia; probably this would never have been doubted, had we not been brought up to believe in a Virgilian Arcadia for which there is no good evidence.

So a new question arises: what are these Arcadians doing away from their native soil? For reasons which will appear shortly it seems likely that a complete answer is not available to us, but we may hope for partial answers which will give us a reasonably good understanding of what Virgil was trying to do. First, we should keep in mind that the *Eclogues* are playfully elusive poems; some modern interpreters lose sight of this and impose upon them a consistency and purposefulness—a degree of 'message'—alien to their character. 'Arcades ambo' is perhaps one of Virgil's teases. The alert reader will realize at this point that we are not in Arcadia, but even he may presume that we are somewhere in Greece (the herdsmen all of course have Greek names) and be brought up short when a north Italian scene is set before him with an especial clarity and precision. This would be similar to the technique which Virgil employs in the first poem. As his first readers we open the book of *Eclogues* (we do not yet have two thousand years of scholarship to lead us astray), and we find a Greek shepherd piping melodiously: we suppose, naturally, that we are in some part of the Greek world; perhaps, if we know Theocritus, in Sicily. Soon we hear of things that are likely to make us think of recent events in Italy, but possibly only by way of allusion or parallel; eventually, with the massive spondees of line 19, great Rome is placed monumentally before us: 'urbem quam dicunt Romam . . .', 'The city which they call Rome'. And Virgil celebrates his piece of mischief by following the resonant name of Rome immediately with the repetition of one of those Greek names: 'urbem quam dicunt Romam, Meliboee . . .' There is a piquancy in this.

Another reason why Thyrsis and Corydon in the seventh Eclogue are Arcadians is apparently because of an association of Arcadia with rustic song. This seems clear enough at lines 4 f.: the two Arcadians are well-matched singers, ready to answer each other's verses. There is presumably the same implication in the words of Thyrsis' song at 25 f.:

> Pastores, hedera crescentem ornate poetam,
> Arcades, invidia rumpantur ut ilia Codro.

Shepherds, Arcadians, garland with ivy your rising poet, so that Codrus may burst his guts with envy.

We might look ahead to the tenth Eclogue, where we hear 'soli cantare periti | Arcades' (Arcadians alone are skilled at singing).[76] The association of Arcadia with country singing is again probably due to Pan, god of Arcadia, and his pipes; but it is now time to bring another piece of evidence into play.

Among the epigrams of the *Palatine Anthology* is one attributed to a poet whose name is given as Ἐρύκιος (in conventional Latinized form Erycius); however, it is clear that this is a transliteration of the Roman name Erucius.[77] In this poem there are two oxherds described as *Arkades amphoteroi*, both Arcadians.[78] Erucius is probably to be dated to the second half of the first century BC.[79] There are three possibilities (other than pure coincidence, which can be ruled out); first, that Erucius is echoing Virgil; second, that Virgil is echoing Erucius; third, that both poets are echoing a common original, either directly or at a remove. Let us consider these possibilities in turn.

---

[76] *Ecl.* 10. 32 f.

[77] The data held on computer by the *Lexicon of Greek Personal Names* (which do not yet comprise the whole Greek world) indicate no other Ἐρύκιος or Ἐρούκιος except in places where Roman nomenclature is being used.   [78] *Anth. Pal.* 6. 96. 2.

[79] A. S. F. Gow and D. L. Page (eds.), *The Greek Anthology: The Garland of Philip and some Contemporary Epigrams* (Cambridge, 1968), ii. 279.

Is Erucius echoing Virgil? Notoriously it is rare for any Greek poet to display the influence of even the finest Roman verse; an echo of Latin literature in a Greek epigram would be a surprise.[80] Moreover, if he were following in Virgil's footsteps, we cannot explain why he should have made his two herdsmen Glaucon and Corydon, rather than Thyrsis and Corydon as in the Eclogue.[81] Since Erucius bears a Roman nomen, we may surmise that the poet was a Greek who had acquired Roman citizenship and taken his patron's name.[82] So it might possibly (though not plausibly) be argued that he could have been untypically subject to the influence of Latin poetry. If this were so, Erucius would not shed any light on the seventh Eclogue.

Is Virgil echoing Erucius? One is perhaps reluctant to think that he would bother to echo anything so insignificant, but there is a more substantial reason for doubt, which is that he is echoing— or if not echoing, pretending to echo—someone else. For like Corydon's line about Amphion in the second Eclogue,[83] his phrase is virtually a fragment of Greek, but not of Erucius' Greek. The ordinary Latin for Arcadians is 'Arcadii', but instead Virgil uses a poeticism of Greek derivation, and the Greek flavour is manifest, because 'Arcades' has to belong to the Greek declension in order that the last syllable may be scanned short. In fact, 'Arcades ambo' is almost an exact transliteration of the Greek *Arkades ampho*. Virgil is again either quoting or pretending to quote the end of a Greek hexameter, probably the former. He is not quoting Erucius, who used the word *amphoteroi* for 'both'. Virgil and Erucius therefore seem to descend from a common original; whether Erucius' descent is through Virgil (in which case the first and third possibilities mentioned earlier would both be true) or independent of him is a matter of no importance to us.[84]

[80] Though not impossible; G. Williams, *Change and Decline* (Berkeley and Los Angeles, 1978), 124–36, argues (not altogether convincingly) for echoes of Augustan poetry in some Greek epigrams. On p. 126 he suggests that Erycius imitated Virgil, 'since it was Virgil who first set pastoral in Arcadia (that fact rules out both the possibility of the opposite [that Virgil imitated Erycius] and of a common source)'. On the contrary: the likelihood of a common source is an argument against the belief that Virgil 'set pastoral in Arcadia'.

[81] Gow–Page, loc. cit.

[82] Fourteen epigrams are attributed to him; in one place the *Palatine Anthology* describes him as being from Cyzicus, in another as Thessalian. It is not even certain whether we are dealing with one man or two. (Gow–Page, 278).   [83] *Ecl.* 2. 24.

[84] A common original was already the conclusion of R. Reitzenstein, *Epigramm und Skolion* (Giessen, 1893), 132 n. E. L. Bowie, 'Theocritus' Seventh *Idyll*, Philetas and Longus', *CQ* NS 35 (1985), 67–91, at 82 f. suggests Philetas as the ultimate source both for the name

So Virgil is making an allusion to Greek poetry here; and it seems to be almost certain that he is quoting a specific Greek text. Now in other parts of the *Eclogues* where we know Virgil to be quoting or alluding (for example the quotation of 'a, virgo infelix' from Calvus' *Io* at Eclogue 6. 47 and 52; the reference to the prologue of Callimachus' *Aetia* earlier in the same poem; the many echoes of Theocritus throughout the book) we commonly find that some knowledge of the context is necessary to a full understanding of his meaning. We cannot expect fully to understand the allusion in the seventh Eclogue, because we have lost the key. Pan probably had a part to play here; but if we reflect upon the subtlety and wit of Virgil's allusive technique in other places, we shall realize that it is vain to seek for an accuracy of appreciation which we have not the power to attain. What should be clear is that an allusion to a Greek poet is a very different thing from the construction of a new 'spiritual landscape' to which the name of Arcadia is to be given.

We can now turn to the tenth Eclogue. Now this poem is indeed set in Arcadia, and of course we want to know why. It is as well to realize right away that our curiosity must remain in part at least unsatisfied. We have already seen reason to believe that there was something about Arcadia in some Greek poet now lost to us. Gallus is the hero of this poem; it is beyond reasonable doubt that Gallus' verse would be essential for a full understanding of it. We should not therefore be downcast if we cannot explain everything in the poem; on the contrary, we can be confident at least of one thing: that an account of the poem which does explain everything in it is sure to be wrong.

However, we can still understand enough to demonstrate that the poem is incompatible with the traditional belief in Virgil's Arcadia; we have not found this traditional Arcadia in nine out of the ten eclogues; we shall not find it in the tenth either. Let us look a little closer.

We may start by returning to one of Virgil's paradoxes: that he proclaims his adherence to Theocritus at the beginning of those poems in which he moves most away from him. Now there is indeed a

Corydon (also found in Theocritus) and for the Arcadian setting. The links in his avowedly speculative chain of argument are made the more tenuous by two assumptions which should be rejected: that Corydon in *Ed.* 2 is to be identified with Corydon in *Ed.* 7; and that Virgil 'relocated' pastoral in Arcadia. Of course, the identity of any common original does not affect the present argument.

difference between the fourth and sixth Eclogues on the one hand and the tenth Eclogue on the other. The fourth and sixth poems are not pastoral at all, or if pastoral only in the most vestigial sense. The tenth Eclogue, by contrast, in a passage of more than ten lines conspicuously echoes the scene of the dying Daphnis in Theocritus' first Idyll. (It might perhaps be noted, though, that this echo is of the song of Thyrsis; in other words, it is an allusion to the remote, fantastic, artificial world conjured up in the song of one of Theocritus' herdsmen, a world quite unlike that inhabited by those herdsmen themselves.)

The tenth Eclogue has some pastoral content, but it is not straightforwardly pastoral, because it seems to express a dissatisfaction with the pastoral mode, a desire to escape from its limits. The poem begins by announcing that it is to be the last of these pastoral pieces: 'extremum' is the very first word. It would be strange indeed if Virgil were to be creating in Arcadia a new symbol for pastoral at the very moment that he is affirming his intention to abandon it henceforth. A note of satiety enters the poem towards the end: the sphere of pastoral poetry, so Virgil implies, is no longer enough; it is time for him to move on.[85] This differs from his other pastoral eclogues partly because much of the treatment of Gallus is not pastoral in any ordinary sense, partly because its pastoral allusions contain within themselves a resistance to pastoral, an urge to get beyond it. No poem could be less suited to be normative; it is a grand irony that it should be the main basis for the Arcadia created by Sannazaro and handed down from him to the later pastoral tradition.

We have found no cause to regard the Arcadia of the tenth Eclogue as standing for the pastoral world; and once again we can go further: there is good cause not to. The Arcadia of this poem is much unlike the rolling, verdant landscape of the Renaissance Arcadia, populated by sociable shepherds and studded with purling brooks and enamelled meads. It is unlike Virgil's pastoral landscapes also, which contain woods and bushes, mossy springs and shade and greenery by flowing streams, beeches and elms, myrtle and tamarisk; these are well-populated landscapes, with not only flocks and herds, but also viticulture and arable farming, and small towns at no great distance. All of which is a far cry from the Arcadia of the tenth Eclogue, which is romantic and beautiful indeed, but cold, strange, lonely and remote. Virgil creates his atmosphere through a mixture

---

[85] See below, p. 184.

of diction, sound and content. In the phrase 'Aonie Aganippe' we hear an exotic name with bare long vowels and Grecian metre (again a hiatus and a tetrasyllabic ending).[86] There follow such phrases as 'sola sub rupe' (beneath a *lonely* rock), 'gelidi . . . saxa Lycaei' (the rocks of *chill* Lycaeus), 'in silvis inter spelaea ferarum' (in the woods among *the caverns of the wild beasts*), and 'non me ulla vetabunt | frigora Parthenios canibus circumdare saltus' (No *cold* will prevent me from circling the glens of Parthenius with my hounds).[87] One has only to read line 14 or line 52 aloud to hear their lovely cold romantic sounds. This is a world of rocks and resonance, as Virgil says in another line bleakly beautiful to the ear: 'iam mihi per rupes videor lucosque sonantis | ire' (Already I seem to myself to pass through rocks and echoing woods).[88] Thus Virgil makes for us a mysterious world at once austere and entrancing; it is all very strange and riddling, and— here is the point of vital aesthetic significance—we miss the special tone and quality of this poem if we assimilate it to the Arcady of later tradition or to an Arcadia falsely supposed to exist in other eclogues. In the last poem of the collection there sounds a new note, not heard before, and if we are not alert to this novelty, we fail to do justice to Virgil's originality and command of subtle variety.

The Arcadia invented by Sannazaro probably owed something to the *Aeneid* as well as the *Eclogues*, but the epic poem can offer us one more demonstration that Virgil did not mean by Arcadia what he has usually been taken to mean, for he has pastoral allusion in one place and Arcadians in another, and he makes no connection between the two. His portrait of Italy in the *Aeneid* is concerned to bring out the variety of the country and its peoples. As part of this picture of diversity he gives a pastoral colouring to Tyrrhus' family and their neighbours, Latinus' rustic subjects. The Arcadian city of Pallanteum and its king Evander introduce us to a quite different style of society: a sort of modest country-gentlemanliness, blending heroic dignity with simplicity of life. The pastoral tone is distinct- ive to Tyrrhus and his society; we should not expect to meet it again in the quite different milieu of Pallanteum.

Nor do we. There is no puzzle about why Evander and his folk are Arcadians; this was simply the tradition that Virgil had inherited.[89]

---

[86] *Ecl.* 10. 12.   [87] *Ecl.* 10. 14, 15, 56 f.   [88] *Ecl.* 10. 58.

[89] The belief in Arcadians on the site of Rome can be traced back at least to Fabius Pictor (Dion. Hal. *Ant. Rom.* 1. 79. 4 and 8 = Fabius fr. 5b Peter). For the literary and antiquarian tradition see C. J. Fordyce's commentary on *Aen.* 7 and 8 at 8. 51, and for the background to the idea J. Poucet, *Les Origines de Rome* (Brussels, 1985), 74 ff., 128 ff., 200, 210.

We might pause to note that the only reference to the land of Arcadia itself in the book refers to its 'chilly regions', 'Arcadiae gelidos . . . finis'.[90] This may recall the tenth Eclogue; we should lay to heart the simple and telling fact that Virgil associates Arcadia especially with cold, while his pastoral settings are warm, and sometimes fiercely hot. The shivering shepherd was never a feature of the ancient pastoral myth. The literary antecedents of Evander and his people are, in fact, very far from pastoral poetry, since they are out of the *Odyssey*; the allusions that go into their creation are heroic, not bucolic, and it would be a grievous distraction to intrude here a pastoral reference. It would also flatten out Virgil's delicate sense of diversity.

It is easy for us to be misled here because distressed gentlefolk are indeed a feature of Renaissance pastoral. The theme of the gentleman concealed among shepherds was taken over from Sannazaro by Sidney and is most familiar to us from Shakespeare's *As You Like It* and *A Winter's Tale*, in which noblemen find themselves living modestly, in pastoral disguise, among country people. But this is a new kind of pastoral developed in the Renaissance, partly out of Longus, who by putting pastoral motifs into the novel was to make himself one of the most influential of all Greek writers: his Daphnis and Chloe, a shepherd and a shepherdess, turn out in the end to be the children of gentlefolk, exposed as infants. Mixing verse and prose together, Sannazaro blended Longus and Virgil;[91] his Arcadia was inspired, presumably, by the tenth Eclogue, the scattered references to Arcadia in Eclogues 4, 7, and 8, and perhaps some admixture of influence from the eighth book of the *Aeneid*. The development of the 'gentleman in the country' out of Virgilian pastoral was no doubt encouraged by the fact that in some (partial) sense Menalcas in the fifth and ninth Eclogues represents the poet; to which should be added the idea, foisted on to posterity by Servius, that Tityrus in the first Eclogue is an allegorical cloak behind which Virgil himself is hidden. Whether Sannazaro consciously used Virgil as a springboard for his own invention or simply misread him must be

---

[90] *Aen.* 8. 159.

[91] *Daphnis and Chloe* first became widely known through Amyot's French translation, published in 1559, englished by Angel Day in 1587, and thus early enough to have been able to influence Lodge's *Rosalynde* (1590) and Greene's *Pandosto* (1588), the sources for *As You Like It* and *The Winter's Tale* respectively. Presumably Sannazaro at least knew what was in *Daphnis and Chloe*; if his decision to write a pastoral tale in prose was wholly independent of Longus, the present argument is not affected, but it seems very unlikely.

uncertain; if he misunderstood, it was a misunderstanding with a touch of genius in it. But though we may be grateful to him for being midwife to the birth of a new myth, we should not allow him to throw our own appreciation of Virgil into confusion.

Arcadia, as commonly understood, is not the only misconception to have become deep rooted over the centuries. Servius' influence both direct and, more insidiously, indirect has imposed the idea that Virgil had a farm confiscated and returned to him through the agency of Octavian and that this event is reflected in the first Eclogue, where Tityrus is a figure of the poet. The last of these claims may be briskly dismissed. If we forget for a while what tradition has taught us and read through the first Eclogue without preconceptions, we shall find in the poem itself not a line, not a word, to indicate that Tityrus stands for Virgil. On the contrary, there are good reasons why Tityrus should not be Virgil. Virgil was young and free born; Tityrus is elderly and a former slave. In any case, another name in the *Eclogues* stands for the poet: Menalcas.[92] It is clear enough what happened: someone, looking for allegory and autobiography, has noticed that Apollo addresses Virgil as Tityrus in the sixth Eclogue, and mistaking the method of these poems, has deduced that Tityrus in the first Eclogue is Virgil also.[93]

A good deal of Servius' information about Virgil's early life has evidently been invented in the same way. The delicate stuff of the *Eclogues* was roughly handled as covert autobiography—an attempt to make sows' ears out of silk purses. The story of the poet's infatuation for his slave Alexander is fabricated out of Eclogue 2.[94] We are told that Virgil began to write 'res Romanae', presumably an epic on Roman history, but finding the subject intractable, turned to the *Eclogues*; this is obviously based on his playful pretence in the sixth poem that he was trying to write about kings and battles when Apollo tweaked his ear and turned him to more slender themes.[95] Servius' credulity can sometimes lift the eyebrows: he assures us that when Virgil was on his way to Rome, he was almost killed by the centurion Arrius, and only escaped by jumping into the Mincius; hence the words in the third Eclogue: 'ipse aries etiam nunc vellera

---

[92] Servius' influence has curious effects on the later tradition. In *The Shepheardes Calender* Spenser puts himself twice into the poems, as Colin Clout and as Cuddie. The latter is an old man, although Spenser was in his twenties at the time.

[93] It must be conceded that no strong reason for Apollo's use of the name is apparent.

[94] As we saw in Ch. 1.   [95] *Vita Verg.* 19; cf. *Ecl.* 6. 3–5.

siccat' (the ram himself is even now drying his fleece).[96] That is indeed inept: the ram in the Eclogue has thoughtlessly strayed too near the bank, whereas in the putative allegory the poet's quick thinking has saved him from death. (If, as one fears, there is meant to be a play on the words Arrius and 'aries' (ram), the allegory is yet more massively incompetent, since it should be the poet not the centurion who has fallen into the water.)[97]

The claim that Pollio, Gallus, and Varus were members of a commission handling the land confiscations in the later 40s had doubtless been cobbled together by some grammarian out of names found in the *Eclogues*.[98] In fact, it is pretty plain that the entire story of Virgil losing and then recovering his farm was drawn from the poems themselves and had no independent basis. Someone presumed that Tityrus as well as Menalcas represented the poet. In the ninth Eclogue there is talk of land being lost through confiscation and Menalcas trying to save it by his verses. In the first Eclogue Tityrus is able to stay on the land thanks to the beneficence of a young man in Rome, unlike Meliboeus, whose property has been seized. How are we to fit these pieces of evidence together? The scholiast has the answer: Virgil must have lost his farm and then recovered it through the agency of Octavian.

It is not a good answer. As a matter of fact, Tityrus does not say that he has got back the farm he had lost but something different: that he was freed from slavery and that he and others were told by their young benefactor in Rome to carry on with their work as before. As a matter of fact, Menalcas in the ninth poem seems to be pleading for other people's land. As a matter of common sense, if the first Eclogue is meant as an expression of thanks to Caesar for restoring Virgil's land, it is, with at least half the weight of emotion upon the luckless Meliboeus, one of the oddest poems of gratitude ever penned. Scholars have come to see that the traditional story of Virgil's farm can hardly be true as it stands, but there seems to linger a hope that some part of it can be salvaged.[99] That is poor method. The

---

[96] *Ecl.* 3. 95; Serv. *in Verg. Buc. prooem.*

[97] Modern scholarship is sometimes no better: witness the claims that the sparrow in Catullus represents the poet's penis, although he regrets that his girl can play with it while he cannot (2. 9). Persistent efforts to allegorize the bees in the *Georgics* ignore difficulties of the same order.

[98] This is persuasively argued by G. Bowersock, 'A Date in the *Eighth Eclogue*', *HSCP* 75 (1971), 73–80.

[99] Treatment of the *Catalepton* is similar. Most of these poems cannot be Virgil's, but the wistful hope remains that one or two may yet be assigned to him.

first step is to be clear that the testimonia are worthless. The second is to ask if the poems themselves, our only basis for a decision, offer any grounds for believing that Virgil is alluding to his own loss and gain. The answer is that they do not. Certainly he is concerned for the distresses of his fellow countrymen, the Mantuans—so much is explicit—and to that extent personal experience enters into his allusions to the confiscations; and of course it remains possible that he himself lost some land, possible even that Caesar restored it, or compensated him in some other way. But that is pure speculation, nothing more; Virgil does not suggest this to us, either directly or by implication. This is not merely a matter of antiquarian interest: to understand the *Eclogues* as literature we need to see that they are not poems *à clef*, whose meaning is to be unlocked by finding correspondences with Virgil's life. It would be truer to say that they resist such enquiry. Tityrus appears to be both a newly freed slave and a possessor whose security has been freshly confirmed. Maybe there could be an explanation of the discrepancy, but Virgil is not troubled to give it; that is part of the poems' evanescence.[100]

We have been dealing with cases of simple misinterpretation or falsification, but there are other areas of more shaded judgement where some common opinions should be challenged. Among these is the notion that pastoral poetry is essentially anti-urban, or at least that it expresses the city-dweller's envy of the countryman and his life. This is indeed true of much pastoral writing from the sixteenth century onwards, but it should not be read back into the ancient world. Theocritus was born in Sicily and came to Alexandria; we do not know when most of his work was written, and we cannot say at what stage of his career he started composing bucolic poems. To say that they were a reaction to life in Alexandria would be, at the very best, an assumption. But in any case it is hard to find any dislike of the city in him. In the fifteenth Idyll, the *Adoniazusae*, the bustle of the big city is treated with liveliness and enjoyment. In the eleventh Polyphemus the unrequited lover is treated with elegant condescension as a gawky bumpkin, half pathetic, half humorous. The poem begins and ends with Theocritus speaking to his friend, the physician Nicias, in his own person and in a tone of graceful banter; this address makes a frame for Polyphemus' song, so that we look

---

[100] R. Coleman tries to reconstruct the story of Tityrus ('Tityrus and Meliboeus', *GR* 2nd ser. 13 (1966), 79–97). Against this approach see the remarks of J. Griffin in his review of Coleman's commentary (*CR* NS 28 (1978), 245–7 at 246) and his conclusion: 'The Vergilian mystification in all this is under-rated.'

down, from our cultivated viewpoint, on his clumsy wooing of the nymph Galatea. Somewhat different is the twentieth Idyll, not by Theocritus: a countryman complains that Eunice laughed when he tried to kiss her and retorted, 'Get away from me. Do you who herd cows want to kiss me, you wretch? I haven't learnt to love in rustic style (*agroikos*) but to press city lips (*astika kheilea*).' Still, the herdsman protests, he is a fine fellow really.[101] Here are the first beginnings of the theme of tension between town and country, and that is a theme from which anti-urban feeling could eventually grow. But in this Idyll, as in the eleventh, we are still enlisted on the side of the city: the tone is *faux-naïf*, and we observe the poor rustic from a great height, with a lightly contemptuous pity.

Virgil's Tityrus is in awe of Rome. In his folly he had supposed it to be like his local town, only bigger, but now he knows that it towers above all other places as the cypress above the wayfaring tree.[102] Corydon, in the second Eclogue, is aware of an inferiority. 'Rusticus es,' he tells himself, 'You are a bumpkin', and he speaks of the 'sordida rura', the shabby countryside, and its lowly cottages, 'humilis . . . casas'.[103] 'Habitarunt di quoque silvas,' he declares later, in words much quoted in the Renaissance to suggest the higher joys of country life; 'Gods too have dwelt in the woods.' But the context shows that his tone is different, and defensive:[104]

> quem fugis, a! demens? habitarunt di quoque silvas
> Dardaniusque Paris. Pallas quas condidit arces
> ipsa colat; nobis placeant ante omnia silvae.

From whom are you fleeing, ah madman? Gods have lived in the woods too, and so did the Trojan, Paris. Let Pallas dwell herself in the citadels that she has established; but let us delight in the woods above all things.

Corydon is trying to scrape together any arguments for life in the country that he can find. There is no doubt that the city has its gods, like Pallas. There are stories of gods stooping to live in the woods—yes, and Paris too; the addition of this equivocal figure suggests that Corydon is struggling for ideas. The subjunctive mood of 'placeant' is plaintive rather than confident. A goddess—Virgil's Muse—does deign to inhabit the woods at the start of the sixth Eclogue, but with much condescension:

---

[101] *Id.* 20. 1–4, 18 f.   [102] *Ecl.* 1. 19–25.   [103] *Ecl.* 2. 56, 28, 29.
[104] *Ecl.* 2. 60–2. Compare Babrius' fable (2. 6–8): 'People suppose that those gods who live in the country are simpletons, whereas those living within city walls are unerring and see everything.'

Prima Syracosio *dignata* est ludere versu
nostra neque *erubuit* silvas habitare Thalea.

My Thalea is the first who has deigned to sport in Syracusan verse, and
not blushed to live in the woods.

Alphesiboeus' song in the eighth Eclogue, in which a girl casts
spells to get her lover back, is modelled on Theocritus' second Idyll,
the song of Simoetha. Virgil shifts the setting, urban in the Greek
poem, to the country. His girl's refrain is, 'ducite *ab urbe* domum,
mea carmina, ducite Daphnim' (Bring Daphnis home from the town,
my song, bring him home).[105] This does hint—though lightly—at a
tension between the town and the country. But again it suggests
the power and glamour of the town (how can the girl defeat the
temptations that have drawn Daphnis there?), not that it is drab or
unappealing. In any case, what does Virgil mean by 'urbs' in these
poems? He tells us in the *Georgics* that Italy has many splendid cities
('tot egregias urbes').[106] Evidently 'urbs' need signify no more than a
country town, and that is surely the meaning when Tityrus describes
his old life:[107]

> quamvis multa meis exiret victima saeptis
> pinguis et ingratae premeretur caseus urbi,
> non umquam gravis aere domum mihi dextra redibat.

Though many a victim went forth from my folds and fat cheese was pressed
for the ungrateful town, my hand never came home heavy with coin.

Here is another of those unexpectedly solid and ordinary pictures
that find their way into the *Eclogues*. 'Ingratae' is the accurate touch;
herdsmen carry their produce to the market towns and haggle
over the price, and whatever they get, they reckon it to be not
enough.[108] The tension lightly but realistically sketched here is not
between countryfolk on the one hand and big business or a vast
urban proletariat on the other, but between people living essentially within the same community: the small producers who do the
selling and the small shopkeepers or consumers to whom they sell.
It is not unlike the tension between the cowboys and the arable
farmers sarcastically expressed in *Oklahoma*:

---

[105] First at *Ecl.* 8. 68.   [106] *Geo.* 2. 155.   [107] *Ecl.* 1. 33–5.
[108] The context shows that Tityrus, like many makers of excuses, is finding fault wherever he can. He is blaming both the ungrateful town and the fecklessness of his woman,
Galatea.

Oh the farmer and the cowman should be friends,
Oh the farmer and the cowman should be friends.
The cowman ropes a cow with ease,
The farmer steals her butter and cheese,
But that's no reason why they cain't be friends.

The theme goes back to Cain and Abel, and it turns up in a modern musical not because Oscar Hammerstein II had been reading Virgil or the Book of Genesis but because it is drawn from life. We should not, indeed, think of Virgil as a townsman: the *Georgics* demonstrates, even if the *Eclogues* in themselves might not, that he knew and understood the life of the country from his own observation.

In any case, we have grown up with the idea of town and country as two separate spheres, whose economies and ways of life are sharply distinct. That is an anachronistic model for almost all the ancient world, and indeed for almost all societies before the Industrial Revolution. Plenty of industry and manufacturing went on in the small country towns of the ancient world and outside them: the making of clothes, the processing of food, building, milling, tanning, fulling, smithying.[109] In the course of the nineteenth century mass production and the railway train concentrated manufacturing in larger centres and drew the non-agricultural population away from the country. The number of nailsmiths in Upper Austria dropped from two hundred and ninety-nine to sixty-seven between 1870 and 1890; a village in the Dauphiné which had some thirty-five craftsmen or artisans in 1851 had no more than five by 1896 (a cobbler, a wheelwright, a dressmaker, a carpenter and a mason), and after 1914 only two.[110] Virgil will have grown up in a world where the division between those who lived off the soil and those who drew their income from a city economy was much less marked than the one to which we are used. We often hear today about the divergent interests of town and country; Virgil will have been more aware of conflicting

---

[109] F. Millar, 'The World of the *Golden Ass*', *JRS* 71 (1981), 63–75, at 72 f.: 'What is more striking in Apuleius is the level and nature of economic activity outside the towns, first in villages . . . , and secondly in the countryside itself', 72. Of course, Apuleius' novel reflects a world two centuries later than Virgil's, but it will not in these respects have been very different. (For comparison with a more recent period, a study of towns in the Var in the nineteenth century with a population between 1,500 and 5,000 noted a considerable number of small industries like tanneries, paper-mills, silk-weaving, cork, and oil manufacture (T. Zeldin, *France 1848–1945: Politics and Anger* (Oxford, 1979), 113).)

[110] N. Stone, *Europe Transformed 1878–1919* (London, 1983), 25 (nailsmiths); Zeldin, *France 1848–1945: Ambition and Love* (1979), 179.

interests within the country itself, between farmers and artisans, say, or between shepherds and consumers, and just in passing the *Eclogues* reflect these realities. Virgil's pastoral worlds may be very modest in scale. Iollas, Alexis' master, keeps the boy away from rustic Corydon; but all three must belong to the same small sphere if the situation is to make any sense at all. We should imagine Iollas as belonging to, at most, one of the petty aristocracies that ran the towns of the Roman world, not as residing in the splendours of some far metropolis.[111]

In the matter of anti-urbanism in Latin literature we should tread delicately. Distrust or dislike of the great city is a feeling of which we detect perhaps the first stirrings in Virgil's lifetime; he himself lets a hint of it into the *Georgics*.[112] Horace likes to complain of the stress and bustle of city life, contrasting it with the delights of his Sabine estate; he calls himself a lover of the country when he writes to tease his friend Aristius Fuscus, a lover of the town.[113] But no other Latin poet writes with such vividness and affection about the ordinary life of the capital[114] His complaints about the city are accompanied by a smile of knowing self-complacency: he lets us know that the importunities he suffers there are due to his gratifying intercourse with the great.[115] And as he tells us himself, he is a fickle fellow: at Rome he loves Tivoli, at Tivoli Rome.[116] We may be reminded of Cicero, who is loud in praise of the peace and beauty of his Sabine home but eager to return to Rome in due course. There is some difference in emphasis between the two men, but a good deal of that can be attributed to Cicero's zest for the political battle, an ambition that Horace could not hope to share.

Virgil did feel rather differently, it seems; we are told that he came rarely to Rome.[117] And in the imperial age city life is indeed regarded sometimes with a hostile spirit. We meet it in Juvenal (though in him it is partly the anger of a frustrated love: Rome ought not to be like this). Very striking is the rhapsodical speech of Seneca's Hippolytus

[111] As often in the *Eclogues*, the situation is not fully clear, and a close likeness to real life is not to be looked for. Alexis is 'delicias domini', the master's pet (line 2); the presumption that Corydon is also a slave is challenged by R. Mayer, 'The Civil Status of Corydon', *CQ* ns 33 (1983), 298–300.

[112] *Geo.* 2. 461 ff. The passage is subtle and equivocal; see below, pp. 372 ff.

[113] *Epist.* 1. 10. 1 f.   [114] Notably *Serm.* 1. 6. 111–28; *Epist.* 1. 7. 49–51.

[115] e.g. *Serm.* 2. 6. 32 ff. Fraenkel well observed that 'Rome is to Horace by no means all unpleasantness and worry. While he is sighing so movingly, his face is all the time lit up by a faint yet unmistakable smile' (*Horace*, 142).

[116] *Epist.* 1. 8. 12.   [117] *Vita Verg.* 11.

in praise of the charm, peace, and romance of the countryside.[118] Seneca's hero is an urban neurotic, with an anxious, passionate long- ing for escape, a far cry from the eager, athletic Hippolytus of Euripides. The speech of Seneca's Hippolytus draws a good deal on Virgil, but his desperate spirit is not Virgil's at all. Virgil's idea could be developed into an exaltation of the country at the expense of a more sophisticated life, but that is a step that the *Eclogues* themselves do not take.

In the sixth Eclogue the boys Chromis and Mnasyllos, joined by the Naiad Aegle, capture Silenus.[119] Servius started the mistaken notion that the two youths were satyrs,[120] and the difference of this poem from the other Eclogues was ignored; hence the frequent appear- ance of nymphs and satyrs in the pastorals of the sixteenth and sev- enteenth centuries. At this date, too, shepherds and shepherdesses are often seen side by side, and this also is a divergence from Virgil. The women in the *Eclogues* remain off stage, or are seen only in the background. No woman speaks in these poems; that is a part of their enclosed, restricted character. The one exception proves to be no exception at all, for it is Alphesiboeus in the eighth Eclogue taking on the role of a woman—a curious device which draws attention to the absence of women from the poems' foreground. And the women in the *Eclogues* do not gracefully tend their flocks among the male shepherds as in Renaissance pastoral; the poetic shepherdess descends instead from the heroine of Longus' *Daphnis and Chloe*. Virgil's women, where they are not divine, are usually more down to earth: Thestylis pounds garlic for lunch, the Amaryllis of the second Eclogue scolds and fusses, the Amaryllis of the first is thrifty with money, while Galatea squanders it.[121]

The Arcadias of a later age tended to confine themselves to shepherds and neatherds, but the *Eclogues* give a wider picture of country life. As we have seen, towns are part of the background; slavery, effectively kept out of the *Georgics*, gets into the first two poems, and pigs, also absent from the *Georgics*, receive a fleeting mention in the last. Nature is not wholly friendly. Tityrus may be a fortunate man, but his land has patches of rock and marsh.[122] 'Nunc formossimus annus,' says Palaemon in the third poem, 'Now is the

---

[118] Sen. *Hipp.* 483–564.   [119] *Ecl.* 6. 13 ff.

[120] Serv. on *Ecl.* 6. 13. But they are shepherds, as is clear from 6. 85, where they gather their flocks.

[121] *Ecl.* 2. 10 f., 14 f.; 1. 30 ff.   [122] *Ecl.* 1. 47 f.

loveliest time of the year';[123] that is the foreground, but we are reminded that there are less comfortable seasons. Rain may threaten travellers, or damage the ripened crops; winds may torment the trees.[124] The herdsmen are in the open air, resting from the warmth in the cool shade; but Thyrsis' song takes us into a sooty winter interior, while the north wind rages outside.[125] Menalcas in the fifth poem looks forward to rustic feasts, in the shade if it is harvest time, by the hearth if it is cold; and Alphesiboeus will do his obscenely comic dance—another of those momentary glances at a coarser realism.[126] So brief are these touches that to dwell upon them risks unbalancing our idea of the poems, but they are none the less important to the effect of the *Eclogues* as a whole: as we linger among the mossy springs and yielding grass, we are made aware that the poet is selecting one small part of a wider world which may be much less comfortable.

Work also has a place in the *Eclogues*. Toil is one of those things —like women, like war, like winter—which are not in the foreground of the poems but are seen or heard of at a distance. It may also be said that the herdsmen's leisure, so prominent in several Eclogues, has a kind of reality behind it. A shepherd would take his flock out to pasture in the morning and would have nothing more to do until he brought it home at the day's end. (Virgil was to give an idyllic picture of the shepherd's day in the third book of the *Georgics*.)[127] The transhumant shepherds of the high Apennines lived a harsh life, with fierce dogs to protect them and their flocks from wild animals and banditry,[128] but such rough figures do not find a place in the *Eclogues*: Virgil's herdsmen live near arable land. Moeris and Lycidas in the ninth poem see farmers cutting back foliage; Meliboeus in the first has grown corn, vines, and fruit-trees; Corydon in the second also tends some vines, and makes baskets too.[129] These are the tasks to which he must bend himself, but—this is characteristic of the *Eclogues*—his work will begin just after the poem has ended:

---

[123] *Ecl.* 3. 57.   [124] *Ecl.* 9. 63; 3. 80, 81.
[125] *Ecl.* 7. 49–52.   [126] *Ecl.* 5. 69–73.
[127] *Geo.* 3. 322–38. More generally, some modern scholars seem to assume that the lives of all but the well-to-do in the ancient world were toilsome. But anyone who has lived in the third world knows how many people do very little. *Paupertas* should not be confused with *labor*; indeed, one reason why people are poor is that there is not enough gainful work for them.
[128] This life is discussed by N. Tarleton, 'From Pasture to Page: Aspects of Realism in the Representation of Herdsmen in Latin and Greek Literature', unpublished Oxford D. Phil. thesis, 1989.   [129] *Ecl.* 9. 60 f.; 1. 69–74 (cf. 9. 48–50); 2. 70–2.

the poem itself represents his inertia while in the grip of frustrated passion. Moeris ends the ninth Eclogue by telling Lycidas to stop singing: they have pressing business to which they must give their attention.[130] The Meliboeus of the seventh Eclogue has a job on hand, looking for a stray goat, but he is urged by a friend ('If you can leave off for a while') to listen to a singing contest between a couple of other herdsmen, and though he did not have Alcippe or Phyllis—two more of those off-stage women—to fold the lambs for him, he yielded; 'posthabui tamen illorum mea seria ludo' (Still, I put aside my business for their sport).[131] If a single line were to stand as an epigraph for the *Eclogues* as a whole, that might be it. The poetry itself is 'ludus', sport; the serious business of life is not quite forgotten, but it is put off or subordinated for a while. Listening to poetry—and poetry that is competitive, striving for display—is what distracts Meliboeus from his proper business, but the poetry cannot do away with that business. After the singing contest is over, after Virgil's Eclogue is over, just beyond the range of our vision, he will have to get back to finding that goat and folding those lambs.

Though Virgil is the father of the vast pastoral literature written in the Renaissance and after, we have been finding that some of the themes and conventions that have come to seem to us most classically pastoral are not in his *Eclogues*. The time has come for a more sweeping claim. In a significant sense it is misleading to talk about pastoral at all in relation to ancient literature. Of course, the term (or its variant, 'bucolic') cannot in practice be avoided without tiresome circumlocution, and it has been used often in this chapter, but it is none the less liable to mislead. For pastoral, as we have come to understand the term, is not just writing about the country, but a particular way of writing: it requires the use of certain literary conventions. Few pastoral works, if any, have used every single one of the conventions which we recognize as pastoral, but some use of conventions, or at the least some echo of an earlier pastoral, is necessary if the work is to fall into the pastoral category at all. So essential is the idea of convention, indeed, that a pastoral work, in the developed tradition, need not be about the country at all; Milton's *Lycidas* is a case in point. If we lack the right equipment—if we have no knowledge of pastoral convention and tradition—we shall fail to see that *Lycidas* is a pastoral poem; and failing to see this,

---

[130] *Ed.* 9. 66 f.   [131] *Ed.* 7. 6–17 (quotations from lines 10 and 17).

we shall not understand it. Without some literary knowledge we would be unable to imagine why a lately deceased Cambridge fellow should be addressed by the Greek name Lycidas, though his actual name was Edward King, or why nymphs and shepherds should be supposed to care a whit about his fate. Pastoral literature is necessarily self-conscious; it latches on to a tradition.[132]

And yet classical pastoral hardly fits this description. Theocritus, of course, did not know that he was inventing a tradition or set of conventions that would last for centuries. Perhaps he would have been surprised at the division between bucolic and non-bucolic idylls that a later scholarship has imposed upon his work.[133] Into which category does the eleventh Idyll fall? Maybe even we should have hesitated to class it as bucolic if it had not become the model for the second Eclogue. Writing in the great age of Alexandrian poetry, Theocritus was surely seeking to produce works that were varied, distinctive, and individual, sometimes strange and puzzling; all of which is a long way from trying to establish norms, patterns, or conventions for others to follow. Nor does it seem right to think of a bucolic tradition evolving in later Greek poetry: those few poems which we today class as pastoral are best seen as imitations or developments of Theocritus himself, not as adhering to a set of generic conventions. We do not shuffle poems after Callimachus away into a separate generic package; only historical accident has made us treat poems after Theocritus otherwise.

Roman literature affords much the same story. Virgil tells us himself that he was the first to follow Theocritus.[134] Since the Romans had been imitating Greek literature so widely for two centuries, that is a striking fact. They had tried their hand at most Greek genres, and if the pastoral genre had escaped their attention, the best explanation is that there was no pastoral genre. And as in Greece, none seems to evolve. The Eclogues of Calpurnius Siculus and Nemesianus and the two anonymous Eclogues from Einsiedeln should be treated not as examples of a determinate genre but as pastiche of Virgil—in part of the *Georgics* also.[135] The literary critics of antiquity confirm this

---

[132] For a fuller account of the evolution of the pastoral tradition and the significance of pastoral as a literary term see Jenkyns, 'Pastoral', in R. Jenkyns (ed.), *The Legacy of Rome* (Oxford, 1992), 151–75, esp. 151–3.

[133] The point is made by G. O. Hutchinson, *Hellenistic Poetry* (Oxford, 1988), 143 ff.

[134] *Ecl.* 6. 1 f.

[135] Calp. Sic. 2 self-consciously puts 'georgic' material into an eclogue frame.

picture. At least until the fourth century, none of them shows any awareness of pastoral or bucolic as a literary type, not even Quintilian, when he surveys Greek and Latin literature, dividing each up according to genre.[136] In the fourth century we find a change, with Donatus' notion that Virgil followed the natural order of a poet's life, working his way up from the lowly style of the *Eclogues* to the middle style of the *Georgics* and thence to the grandeur of epic.[137] The Renaissance developed this into the theory that pastoral stands at the lowest point of a hierarchy of genres, and the idea of pastoral as an independent genre, comparable to epic, didactic, lyric or satire, has been with us ever since. But it is, upon reflection, a pretty odd idea. Most of these genres seem to belong to the nature of things—we cannot readily imagine a developed literary culture that could do without heroic story, lament, or lyric or satiric utterance—but there is no compelling reason for the congeries of conventions that we call pastoral at all. Pastoral is, in fact, an odd accident of the European literary tradition. It is necessarily self-conscious, and that self-consciousness has been felt from at least the fifteenth century, and perhaps from much earlier, but we would be wrong to project it back on to Virgil.

Once rid of the idea that the *Eclogues* are normative, we may be ready to find in them instead a kind of instability. These poems seem to be conspicuously well made and controlled, yet with a pressure against their careful frameworks; both formally and emotionally they suggest a poised but precarious equilibrium. We feel such tensions at the end of several of the Eclogues. The second concludes, 'invenies alium, si te hic fastidit, Alexin' (You will find another Alexis, if this one disdains you).[138] Four of the Eclogues finish with evening at hand. On the surface such endings seem tidy and serene: the herdsmen live according to nature's rhythms; the day closes, and the poem closes with it. The second Eclogue conforms to this pattern: Corydon's lament begins in the heat of the day, and lasts until he tells us that the shadows are lengthening and the oxen plodding home.[139] Once we hear this, we know that the poem is about to cease, and right on cue, as it were, Corydon rebukes himself for his folly, resolves to neglect his work no more, and declares that he will find a new boy to love if Alexis scorns him. The poem is over and

---

[136] Quint. 10. 1.   [137] Serv. *Buc. prooem.*
[138] *Ecl.* 2. 73.   [139] *Ecl.* 2. 8 ff., 66 f.

the passion is over (so Corydon says) at one and the same moment, and the neatness of the conclusion is enhanced by an echo of the beginning: the last word of the first line and the last word of the whole poem are the same, 'Alexin'.

And yet we are forced to disbelieve in that neatness. We have heard at the start of the poem that Corydon's lamentations were a constant habit;[140] so we know that the apparent common sense at the end is a vain defiance. And Virgil, by a psychological irony, has made him betray himself, for he says not 'I will find another boy'— the intention he means to convey—but 'I will find another Alexis.' Alexis is replaceable—only by himself. And thus even the echo of the opening line, which formally works to bring the poem to a rounded conclusion, works emotionally in an opposite sense. Alexis' name sounds at the start and the end of the poem, and in Corydon's very first words too,[141] because he is the lover's recurrent and inescapable obsession.

Corydon is not quite the first poetic lover to display his emotions rapidly backing and veering. In the last two and a half stanzas of *Furi et Aureli* Catullus shows his mood lurching from apparent calm to abusive anger and then to a blend of defiance and tender regret.[142] He begins *Miser Catulle* by telling himself to face the fact that his love affair is over; in the middle of the poem he announces that his resolution is taken and he will hold firm; but then he gradually drifts away through a mixture of ambivalent moods into a kind of tender passion, from which he pulls himself back in the last line, commanding himself to stand by the decision he has made. But despite this apparent forthrightness the ambivalence lingers. On the one hand the poet has asserted his resolve again, echoing the firmness in the middle part of the poem, with the concluding words, 'at tu, Catulle, destinatus obdura' (But you, Catullus, be resolute and hold fast).[143] On the other hand that very echo works also in an opposite sense, for the earlier words were,[144]

> sed obstinata mente perfer, obdura.
> vale, puella. iam Catullus obdurat . . .

But with a stubborn will endure, hold fast. Goodbye, girl. Catullus now holds fast . . .

---

[140] *Ecl.* 2. 2–5. The verbs in the first five lines are all imperfects.
[141] *Ecl.* 2. 6: 'O crudelis Alexi' (O cruel Alexis).   [142] Cat. 11. 15 ff.
[143] Cat. 8. 19.   [144] Cat. 8. 11 f.

'Obdura . . . obdurat . . .'—the imperative mood gives way to a seemingly confident indicative. But at the end the imperative returns, and once more Catullus has to exhort himself to toughness. That firm resolve no longer looks so secure; the last line rounds off the poem neatly, creating a piece that seems balanced in structure and proportion, and yet it tells us at the same time that the tidy ending is not really tidy after all. It 'satisfies' and 'dissatisfies' simultaneously.

The pangs of love readily lead poets to the study of the divided mind and to endings in which the perplexities of feeling remain unresolved, but in the *Eclogues* the resolution that is no resolution extends beyond the theme of love to become almost an aesthetic principle. The last lines of the ninth poem are flooded with the sounds of singing:[145]

> L.   hic, ubi densas
> agricolae stringunt frondes, hic, Moeri, *canamus*;
> hic haedos depone, tamen veniemus in urbem.
> aut si nox pluviam ne colligat ante veremur
> *cantantes* licet usque (minus via laedet) eamus;
> *cantantes* ut eamus, ego hoc te fasce levabo.
> M. Desine plura, puer, et quod nunc instat agamus;
> *carmina* tum melius, cum venerit ipse, *canemus*.

Lycidas: Here where the husbandmen are stripping the thick leafage, here, Moeris, let us sing; here set down the kids—we shall reach the town all the same. Or if we fear that night may first bring on rain, we may go straight on, singing—it makes the road less wearisome. That we may go our way singing, I shall relieve you of this bundle.

Moeris: Enough, my boy: let us give our mind to the task on hand. We shall sing songs better when the man himself comes.

The words for singing become ever more frequent, and yet what they tell about is an end to song. In one sense, this is another formally tidy conclusion: Moeris stops the singing, and Virgil ceases also. Yet a dissonance lingers, because we seem at once to hear more singing, and less.

In the last line of the first Eclogue the lengthening shadows make a typical and satisfying closing motif. It rounds off a picture of rural peace, with smoke rising from the farmsteads in the distance and Tityrus preparing to take Meliboeus home to a meal of mellow fruits, nuts, and curded milk and offering him a night's rest on a couch of

[145] *Ecl.* 9. 60–7.

green leaves. And yet we know that for Meliboeus this comfort and
good cheer are to be brief: very soon he must become an exile from
the land that was once his. The final balance of feeling is precarious;
it trembles upon the fulcrum. The sounds of distant war still rumble
at the edge of the pastoral range of perception.

An unstable equilibrium is to be found at the end of the eighth
poem too. On the formal level the last line conveys a sense of finality by changing the refrain from 'ducite ab urbe domum, mea carmina,
ducite Daphnim' (Bring Daphnis, my song, bring him home from
the town) to a new variation, 'parcite, ab urbe venit, iam parcite
carmina, Daphnis' (Cease, my song, cease, Daphnis is coming from
the town).[146] Formally again, Alphesiboeus' song in the second half
of the Eclogue balances Damon's song in the first: in the first song
a man speaks, in the second song a woman; in the first song a
lost love is lost forever, in the second song it is restored. And yet
Alphesiboeus finishes before his story is complete: Daphnis has yet
to step on to the stage. Virgil has chosen to stop at a point which
of its nature is very transitory—the instant between a sudden surge
of expectancy and its fulfilment. A moment between—that, paradoxically, is the moment with which we end. The very speed of
the ending, too, denies the reader a sense of completion; after all
the tension and passion a single rapid line is not enough to allow
us the sense of a settled consonance. Indeed, the syntax is agitated,
with 'parcite, iam parcite carmina' fretfully interlocked with 'ab urbe
venit Daphnis'.

And surely our doubts may go still further, aroused by the lines
immediately before:[147]

> aspice: corripuit tremulis altaria flammis
> sponte sua, dum ferre moror, cinis ipse. bonum sit!
> nescio quid certe est, et Hylax in limine latrat.
> credimus? an, qui amant, ipsi sibi somnia fingunt?

Look: while I was delaying its removal, the ash itself, of its own accord,
has caught the altar offerings with flickering flames. May the omen be
good! Something is certainly up, and Hylax is barking at the door. Can I
believe it? or do lovers fashion their own dreams?

Do lovers wishfully imagine things? Can one hurried line be enough
to dispose of that doubt? It is not that we know the woman to be

---

[146] *Ecl.* 8. 68 ff., 109.   [147] *Ecl.* 8. 105–8.

self-deceived, rather that we do not know the answer one way or the other.[148] We cannot be certain that it is indeed Daphnis who is approaching, or if he is, what his arrival portends. It may be that the woman is about to live happily ever after, but if so, we shall never be assured of it.

The tenth Eclogue has perhaps the most complex and enigmatic of these ambivalent endings:[149]

> haec sat erit, divae, vestrum cecinisse poetam,
> dum sedet et gracili fiscellam texit hibisco,
> Pierides . . .
> surgamus: solet esse gravis cantantibus umbra,
> iuniperi gravis umbra; nocent et frugibus umbrae.
> ite domum saturae, venit Hesperus, ite capellae.

Goddesses, Muses of Pieria, this will suffice for your poet to have sung while sitting and twining a little basket of slender mallow . . . Let us arise: the shade can often be heavy upon singers, heavy the shade of the juniper; and the shade harms the crops too. Go home full fed, my goats, for the Evening Star comes, go home.

On the surface here is another neat, calm conclusion, fitting comfortably into a pattern: the beasts are well fed, the day closes, and the poem closes with it. Yet there is a new, perhaps even a slightly sinister note. Hitherto cool shade has been one of the charms of the herdsman's life (in the very first line of the book Tityrus is seen at ease beneath the cover of a spreading beech); now it is seen as a threat. The very repetition in 'umbra . . . umbra . . . umbrae . . .' seems to darken the colour. There is a note of weary restlessness in 'haec *sat* erit, divae . . .' That faintly troubled tone casts its own shadow over the very last line, when the idea of satiety returns: 'ite domum *saturae* . . . ite capellae.' The goats are full fed; does this symbolize the poet's sense that his pastoral work has been amply satisfying, or does it seem, like the last line of the eighth Eclogue, a 'happy ending' too quickly added at the close? 'Surgamus' implies an uncertainty: are we to arise that we may continue within the herdsman's daily round, or are we to escape from the pastoral world altogether? Milton was to catch this ambiguity exactly at the end of *Lycidas*:

---

[148] 'The happy outcome . . .' (Coleman, *Vergil: Eclogues*, ad loc.); 'A similar lack of imagination seems required to suppose that Eclogue 8 ends happily with the coming of Daphnis' (G. Williams, *Tradition and Originality in Roman Poetry* (Oxford, 1968), 304). Imagination should prevent confidence in either view.   [149] *Ecl.* 10. 70–2, 75–7.

> At last he rose, and twitched his mantle blue:
> Tomorrow to fresh woods and pastures new.

The poet appears to be bidding his farewell to the pastoral and preparing to enter new regions of literary endeavour, and yet those woods and pastures seem to keep us still within the pastoral realm; as a further subtlety, the rhythm puts the stress upon 'woods' in the first phrase, upon 'new' in the second.[150] We are left uncertain whether the pastoral framework still holds firm or is splitting open.

Of all the *Eclogues* the last is the one in which the dying fall is most assiduously worked, a taste for languorous and plangent lamentation most exquisitely gratified. 'Gallus was dying of love'—but we know that Gallus is a real man, who is doing no such thing; indeed his energetic public career is unique among the major Roman poets. His recumbent posture, his melodious complaints, in a remote and lovely landscape, seem to be a kind of self-indulgence—whether by Gallus or by Virgil we should be hard put to it to say. Like Propertius and Trimalchio after him, he enjoys the half-childish fantasy of imagining himself dead and listening, as it were, to the sounds of mourning:[151]

> tristis at ille, 'tamen cantabitis, Arcades,' inquit
> 'montibus haec vestris; soli cantare periti
> Arcades. o mihi tum quam molliter ossa quiescant,
> vestra meos olim si fistula dicat amores!'

But he sadly said, 'Yet you, Arcadians, will sing of this to your mountains; Arcadians alone know how to sing. Oh how softly would my bones repose, if your pipe might some day tell of my love!'

Unlike Propertius and Trimalchio, he hears not just words but music; being dead has become one more aesthetic treat.

The wilting poet purports to care still for his faithless lover's comfort:[152]

> tu procul a patria (nec sit mihi credere tantum)
> Alpinas, a! dura nives et frigora Rheni
> me sine sola vides. a, te ne frigora laedant!
> a, tibi ne teneras glacies secet aspera plantas!

---

[150] Milton has also echoed *Ecl.* 10 in drawing back in the last eight lines of the poem (exactly as in Virgil), presenting all that has come before as the song of the poet-shepherd, with a kind of distancing or framing effect: 'Thus sang the uncouth swain to th'oaks and rills, While the still morn went out with sandals gray' (*Lycidas* 186 f.; cf. *Ecl.* 10. 70 f.).

[151] *Ecl.* 10. 31–4. Cf. Prop. 1. 7. 21 ff.; Petron. *Sat.* 78.   [152] *Ecl.* 10. 46–9.

You, though, far from your homeland (though may it not be mine to believe such a thing) are looking—ah hard creature!—upon the Alpine snows and the chill of the Rhine. Ah, may the chill not harm you! Ah, may the jagged ice not cut your tender feet!

Yet somehow we cannot quite believe in this tender concern. The ice cutting into those delicate feet is too keenly, too lovingly felt; the place names are too extravagantly exotic; the polyptoton of 'tu . . . te . . . tibi' is too flawlessly controlled; the repeated 'a', an exclamation which will be excluded from the more serious and severe world of the *Aeneid*, is too melodiously operatic. (It may have been a neoteric mannerism: Virgil's evocation of the neoteric epyllion in the sixth Eclogue, an anthology of themes for the modern poet, quotes 'a, virgo infelix' from Calvus' *Io*, and repeats it five lines later.)[153] Gallus seems to be enjoying himself; pain is dissolved into an exquisite egoism, turned in upon itself, cocooned within a finely spun verbal beauty. After all, as sophisticated poets like Virgil and later Propertius must have known, normal people do not want to die, and the death-wish game is almost bound to imply some kind of insincerity.[154]

From one point of view Gallus' lament, placed within a poem which is Virgil's farewell to a certain style of verse, may be seen as almost the last expression of that kind of voluptuous, sensuous artificiality which had been most superbly realized in Catullus' *Peleus and Thetis*. (Gallus is romantically posed, lying 'sola sub rupe', beneath a lonely rock; that phrase, as it happens, is drawn from Ariadne's lament in Catullus' poem.)[155] We do not catch this tone in surviving Hellenistic verse; perhaps it was recurrent in the showpieces of the neoteric generation, such as Cinna's *Zmyrna* and Calvus' *Io*, but it may have been a distinctive product of Catullus' genius, not easily imitable, yet to which one side of Virgil's technique and temperament readily responded. Virgil will in fact return to the tone of *Peleus and Thetis* once more, with the story of Aristaeus at the end of the *Georgics*, and here his engagement does seem to be with that single work of Catullus rather than with a whole school of poetry. He plays several of the games which Catullus had played. In each

---

[153] *Ecl.* 6. 47, 52; Calvus, fr. 9 Courtney (known from Servius auctus ad loc.).

[154] An exception is Wolf's song, 'Sterb' ich, so hüllt in Blumen meine Glieder'. Is there another? We cannot quite believe Isolde, for all the greatness of her music—or if we believe her, it is because we suppose that she is saying something else.

[155] *Ecl.* 10. 14; Cat. 64. 154.

case there is a story within a story, the inner story, though formally subsidiary, being disproportionate in length and even more in emotional weight. In each case two wholly separate myths are brought together by means of an obviously thin and casual link. In each case there is a dislocation between speaker and utterance: Ariadne's speech, in Catullus, supposedly gulped out with sobs, expands gracefully over eighty lines; Proteus' speech in Virgil, supposedly uttered with rolling eyes and grinding teeth, proves to be the *ne plus ultra* of melodious poignancy. It is unlikely that all these features, or even most of them, had occurred in poem after poem; more probably *Peleus and Thetis* was as quirky and experimental as Catullus' other longer works, and Virgil in the fourth Georgic engaged specifically with this distinctive and singular poem, as he did elsewhere with the *Iliad*, the *Odyssey*, *Works and Days*, and so on.

Gallus' lament has the sensuous musicality of *Peleus and Thetis*, but it also contains an element which is not in that poem or in the fourth Georgic, a tone of enervated self-contemplation which will be heard again in love elegy, especially in Propertius. This is the first time that we find it; was it Virgil's creation, or was he echoing the first of the big four elegists, Cornelius Gallus himself? The Eclogue must contain allusions to Gallus' work, as Servius indeed assures us;[156] the point at issue is rather whether its distinctive tone is Virgil's own contribution. No certain answer can be given, but recalling Quintilian's judgement that Gallus was 'durior', harder, than the other elegists, we may suspect that this man of action was less likely to have affected languor than the poet who wrote 'studiis florentem ignobilis oti'.[157] If Virgil is indeed the originator of this mood, he has an important part in the story of how the elegiac sensibility developed, but we may also notice that he affects the languishing tone most extravagantly at the moment when he also expresses a dissatisfaction with it. The conflict between two opposing impulses is intended.

The lingering, languorous, soft and melancholy side of Virgil has been much dwelt upon at some periods. It should not be denied or

---

[156] Servius on 10. 46: 'All these verses are Gallus', carried across from his very own poems.' The truth behind this exaggeration is presumably that the passage was allusive.

[157] If we could, with safety, indulge the pleasing supposition that the elegiacs found at Qasr Ibrim were the work of Gallus himself, in a contemporary manuscript, our belief in Virgil's originality would be increased, for it is hard to credit that the author of those empty and clumsy lines was capable of subtle refinement in mood and expression at any time.

wished away, but it ought to be set in a context. Virgil makes it part of his apprehension of the world, not the whole of it, and this may be seen even in his bucolic poetry. The *Eclogues* as a totality represent a pause from the sterner, or at least the more down-to-earth, side of life: as we have seen, there is work to be done, once the singing is over, and a pitiless soldiery prowls around the edges of the pastoral world. This poetry is not ignorant of hard realities, therefore, but even so, perhaps its elegant indirections are not enough. Right at the end of his book, Virgil suggests to us the insufficiency of the pastoral manner. The poet plaiting his pretty basket—does it not begin to sound a little too pretty? 'Nocent et frugibus umbrae'—that is an odd conclusion at first glance, for crops take us into the realm of the arable farmer, and the speakers in the *Eclogues* are all herdsmen. But in this respect too Virgil has produced one of those endings that rounds off and yet does not complete, that frames and yet strains against the frame, for we may surmise that he is already looking on to his next work, which immediately catches up the theme of crops from the dying words of the Eclogue: 'Quid faciat laetas segetes . . .' (What makes the crops flourish . . .). Arable farming is shown throughout the first book of the *Georgics* as toil, and in this tougher world 'umbra' will no longer represent the herdsmen's ease but will be a real and practical nuisance: it does indeed hurt the crops, as Virgil tells us in a famous passage.[158]

But just as the *Eclogues* are not all ease, so the *Georgics*, conversely, is not all severity. Sometimes it describes leisure and relaxation without reproach or anxiety. That is not the mood, however, in the passage where the enchantments of lingering are perhaps most eloquently evoked:[159]

> sed fugit interea, fugit inreparabile tempus,
> singula dum capti circumvectamur amore.

But meanwhile time is flying, flying irrecoverably, while we, gripped by love of our theme, perambulate each detail.

At once a sternly practical voice cuts in, deliberately brisk and prosaic: 'hoc satis armentis: superat pars altera curae, . . .' ('Enough of cattle; the job's other aspect remains, . . .'). The lingering is delightful, but a temptation that must be resisted. And here we may get a glimpse of the poet's imaginative process. As it happens, 'inreparabilis'

---

[158] *Geo.* 1. 121 (the very words 'umbra nocet'), 156 f.   [159] *Geo.* 3. 284 f.

is not found before Virgil, and twice only in him, each time with
the same noun. The other occasion is in the *Aeneid*, when Hercules
weeps at his inability to help Pallas, and Jupiter responds to his tears
with a bleak consolation:[160]

> 'stat sua cuique dies, breve et inreparabile tempus
> omnibus est vitae; sed famam extendere factis,
> hoc virtutis opus.'

'Each man's appointed day stands firm, and the span of life is short and
irrecoverable for all; but to spread one's fame by one's deeds—that is
valour's task.'

The context is very different from that in the *Georgics*, but Virgil's
instinct is to recreate the same emotional shape. The melodiously
threnodic cadence of 'breve et inreparabile tempus' is answered by
a sterner, harder note. The details are telling: in each case a line
begins with 'hoc', with a heavy stop at the caesura immediately
following. In the earlier poem a charming light melancholy, in the
later a majestic austerity—it is because the two passages are so different (and Virgil probably does not mean us to recall the first of
them when we read the second) that the persistence of a pattern is
revealing. And it is not, we should observe, a pattern that ends on
a dying fall: the plangency comes first, then the resumption of a
new energy. However, the sense of sorrow is not the less because
it is enclosed within a larger whole.

A passing phrase in the *Aeneid* puts the temptation to linger and
the temptation to weep together:[161]

> et fors omne datum traherent per talia tempus,
> sed comes admonuit *breviter*que adfata Sibylla est:
> 'nox ruit, Aenea; *nos flendo ducimus horas.*
> *hic* locus est, partis ubi se via findit in ambas:
> dextera quae Ditis magni sub moenia tendit,
> *hac* iter Elysium nobis; at laeva malorum
> exercet poenas et ad impia Tartara mittit.'
> Deiphobus contra: 'ne saevi, magna sacerdos;
> discedam, . . .'

And perhaps they might have drawn out all the allotted time in such things,
but his companion the Sibyl warned him in brief words: 'Night is coming on apace, Aeneas; we squander the hours in weeping. This is the place
where the path splits into two: the right-hand path, which runs below the

---

[160] *Aen.* 10. 467–9.   [161] *Aen.* 6. 537–45.

walls of great Dis, is our way to Elysium; but the left one provides punishments for the wicked and sends them to unholy Tartarus.' Deiphobus
answered, 'Do not be wrathful, great priestess; I shall go, . . .'

The Sibyl's is a harsh rebuke, as Deiphobus recognizes by his apologetic intervention. We notice too the briskness of her words, sig-
nalled even before she speaks by the adverb 'breviter', and the pressing
note maintained by the deictics 'hic' and 'hac'. In the middle comes
the slow drawn phrase, 'nos flendo ducimus horas'. To weep, to
linger—these are the temptations for Aeneas now, but the words seem
also to have a significance wider than their immediate context. They
might almost serve as a motto for the poem as a whole, provided
that we hear the note of rebuke in them. On the one hand stands
the impulse—humane and natural—to linger compassionately over
man's suffering; but there is also the urge, no less natural and proper
to humanity, to advance with vigour towards new achievement. Perhaps
the temptation is as much for the poet as for his hero. How agreeable it would be if the poem could occupy itself always in dropping
leisurely tears over the past. There are places in the *Aeneid*, no doubt,
where the pleasures of a soothing lamentation are indulged, but at
other times Virgil indicates that sorrow may not always be softened
into the material of a refined and instructed art. In a way that makes
the poem, at moments, grimmer: a means of consolation is denied
us. But in another way it makes new hope possible: there is the
prospect of something happier than shedding tears over past woes.
That moral too can be drawn from the Sibyl's few words. For why
does she urge Aeneas to press on?—because, as she reminds him,
he is on the road to Elysium; and there a vision of glory will be
unfolded.

The splendours and austerities of an imperial destiny may seem
to have taken us a long way from the *Eclogues*, and yet we meet
here one of those odd continuities that run through Virgil's diverse
career. The tenth Eclogue luxuriates in languor; the restlessness at
its end seems to be in part the expression a desire to get beyond
this mood, however subtle and beautiful it may be, but it is also a
chafing against the small scale of the poem: the basket is little ('fiscella',
a diminutive), and the mallow from which it is woven is 'gracilis',
slender. Three times earlier in the book Virgil has claimed to have
felt the urge to grander themes, martial or panegyric. In the fourth
Eclogue he prays to live long enough to sing of the new child's

glorious deeds; then he may hope for such inspiration that not even Orpheus and Linus shall surpass him, and even Pan shall confess himself outdone. In the sixth poem Virgil pretends that he was trying to sing of kings and battles when Apollo drew him back. In the eighth, addressing an unnamed patron, he longs for the time when he may tell of this great man's achievements and spread them across the world.[162] Taken together, these passages cannot all be explained away as due to the exigencies of patronage; in the fourth Eclogue especially Virgil is emphatic in his enthusiasm for singing the praises of a boy who is as yet not even born. In a sense he is playing a game—he does not try to deceive us or indeed his patrons into believing that he seriously plans thousands of lines of eulogy—but the game has an aesthetic meaning and a structural purpose: repeatedly we are to feel the pressure of a burgeoning ambition straining against the delicate framework of these poems.

It is part of their elusiveness that where they most advertise their debt to Theocritus, they also wriggle to get out of his grip. The fourth, sixth, and tenth Eclogues begin by invoking Sicily, Theocritus' birthplace, but the first two of these owe hardly anything to him, a fact already noticed by Servius. Does the fourth Eclogue belong to the pastoral sphere or does it not?—its opening fluctuates and tantalizes:

> Sicelides Musae, paulo maiora canamus.
> non omnis arbusta iuvant humilesque myricae;
> si canimus silvas, silvae sint consule dignae.

Sicilian Muses, let us sing a slightly higher strain. Copses and lowly tamarisks do not please everyone; if we sing of woods, let the woods be worthy of a consul.

'Sicelides' takes us straight to Theocritus, but 'maiora' suggests something grander than bucolic verse. Yet 'paulo' modifies 'maiora', keeping the scale small. The use of this simple adverb (praised by Servius) has a focusing power: it concentrates our attention upon the nicety, the exactness of Virgil's effect; he is lifting the tone, but only by so little. Then the second line implies, apparently, a rejection of the pastoral sphere, represented metaphorically by the copses and shrubs of modest growth. But then the third line seems to correct that implication: the song is about woods, so that we are still

---

[162] *Ecl.* 4. 53–9; 6. 4–6; 8. 7–10.

in the pastoral realm—and yet 'si' insinuates a doubt. Finally, the poem proposes a generic paradox: consular bucolic. 'Let the woods be worthy of a consul'—woods stand in the *Eclogues* for the pastoral world, so the conclusion must be that the bounds of pastoral decorum are stretched but not broken. The gear lever keeps threatening to slip but never quite does so.

In the sixth Eclogue the game is still more elaborate:[163]

> Prima Syracosio dignata est ludere versu
> nostra neque erubuit silvas habitare Thalea.
> cum canerem reges et proelia, Cynthius aurem
> vellit et admonuit; 'pastorem, Tityre, pinguis
> pascere oportet ovis, deductum dicere carmen.'
> nunc ego (namque super tibi erunt qui dicere laudes,
> Vare, tuas cupiant et tristia condere bella)
> agrestem tenui meditabor harundine Musam:
> non iniussa cano.

My Thalea is the first who has deigned to sport in Syracusan verse, and not blushed to live in the woods.[164] When I sought to sing of kings and battles, Apollo tugged at my ear and warned me: 'Tityrus, a shepherd should feed fat sheep, but sing a fine-spun song.' Now, since there will be plenty of people eager to tell your praise and relate grim warfare, I shall contemplate a rustic Muse upon a slender reed: not unbidden is my song.

[163] *Ecl.* 6. 1–9.

[164] Two understandings of the first sentence are possible. 1. 'My Muse first deigned to sport . . .'—in other words, 'I began by writing Theocritean verse' (presumably before trying something grander). 2. 'My Muse is the first who has deigned to sport . . .'—that is, 'I was the first Latin poet to follow Theocritus.' Most commentators—Conington (with the qualification that Virgil may have intended both meanings), Page, Williams, Coleman—favour the first interpretation; Clausen does not discuss the issue, but evidently favours the second. The first interpretation can hardly be right. The sentence fits the familiar pattern in which a poet either asserts that he is the first ever in his field (Lucr. 1. 926 ff., following Call. *Aet.* fr. 1. 25–8; Virg. *Geo.* 3. 40 f.; Manil. 3. 1 ff.) or that he is the first in Latin to follow a particular Greek poet or poetic type (Hor. *Carm.* 3. 30. 12–14 ('Aeolian song'); *Epist.* 1. 19. 23–5 (Archilochus: 'Parios ego *primus* iambos | ostendi Latio'), 32 f. (Alcaeus); Prop. 3. 1. 1–4 (Callimachus). Most of these examples are later than the *Eclogues*; some at least are influenced by this very passage. This second interpretation also makes much better sense of Virgil's emphatic 'prima', the first word in the poem ('My Muse was *the very first* . . .'), which with the first interpretation seems inept. Followers of the first interpretation presumably understand the force of the second sentence to be adversative: '*But* when I sought to sing of kings and battles . . .'. That in itself is strained. The sentence is explanatory: '*For* when I sought to sing . . . , Apollo checked me . . .' (The first interpretation may have been encouraged unconsciously by Donatus' idea, so influential upon later poets, that Virgil followed the 'naturalis ordo' of a poet's life, *beginning* with the low style (pastoral) before advancing to the middle style with the *Georgics* and the high style of epic.)

Lines 3 to 5 echo the prologue of Callimachus' *Aetia*, in which the poet haughtily sweeps aside the carpings of his critics. That allusion in itself suggests that we shall find in the eclogue a tone of pride, an expectation met by the very first word, for 'prima' asserts the poet's originality. Yet at once some notes of diffidence are also heard. Virgil's claim to originality is of a limited and deferential sort, for it is merely that he is the first Latin poet to model himself upon a particular Greek, while 'dignata est' and 'nec erubuit' add touches of humility. Callimachus had simply declared that Apollo gave him his charge and told him (through metaphor) to write with novelty and refinement;[165] that is in its way as proud as Ennius' claim to have received his staff from Homer. Virgil adds a humorous twist of self-deprecation: he had wanted to handle an epic subject ('kings and battles'), but had been checked. This witty variation on a theme takes us some distance from Callimachus—no suggestion there of a misjudgement or an ambition to which the poet had proved unequal.[166] Yet despite Virgil's adaptation, the pride that was in his Greek model remains: he is divinely guided, as he tells us not only in lines 3 to 5 but again in line 9 with the lapidary boast 'non iniussa cano'. Between these two assertions comes his claim that he will contemplate a rustic Muse ('agrestem . . . Musam') on a slender reed ('tenui . . . harundine'). The tone of this is ambivalent. 'Tenuis' might be modest, but because it recalls Callimachus' language,[167] we may be rather inclined to take it as self-confident: the poet declares his elegance and refinement. 'Agrestis', however, does seem modest: this

---

[165] Call. *Aet.* fr. 1. 21 ff.

[166] A. Cameron, *Callimachus and his Critics* (Princeton, 1995), demonstrates that the deep-rooted idea that the *Aetia* rejects epic poetry is mistaken, and that the poem is not concerned with epic at all. It is written in elegiac couplets, and the poet taken as an example in the prologue is the elegist Mimnermus. The sparkle of Virgil's performance lies in giving Callimachus a new twist: he takes a motif from the most famous praise poet of the Hellenistic age and uses it to explain why he will *not* compose a poem in praise of Varus. Callimachus tells us in his opening lines that his critics have complained that he has not written about 'kings . . . in many thousands of lines . . . or heroes . . .' (*Aet.* fr. 1. 3–5; the papyrus is damaged here). 'Kings and heroes' need not exclude epic, but it could equally well point to writers of mythological elegy like Antimachus, whose *Lyde* Callimachus scorned (fr. 398 Pf.); Callimachus' own *Hecale* would fit the bill well enough, for that matter. The critics are asking for prolix mythology, which gives Callimachus the cue for a withering retort. 'Kings and *battles*' is Virgil's variation, which newly brings epic into the picture.

[167] It suggests Callimachus' *leptos* and *leptaleos* (*Aet.* fr. 1. 11, 24). For *leptos* as a term of praise cf. Call. *Ep.* 27 Pf. 3 f. (on Aratus), Aratus 783 (the significance lies in an acrostic: the line begins with the word *lepte*; the first letter of the line and the four lines following it spell out the same word).

adjective, like 'rusticus', is so often a term of disparagement, and its antonym, 'urbanus', so often a term of praise. And thus throughout these opening sentences the equilibrium once again seems unsure, the balance tilting now one way, now the other.

In a passage such as this Virgil plays his game with a certain coolness and detachment, but in other places the sense of a precarious balance or—to revert to another metaphor—of a framework under pressure extends into the emotional heart of the poetry. When he departed from his Greek model by putting the land confiscations into his verse, he limited himself to making his herdsmen talk about their troubles: he did not bring soldiers or officials on to the stage. And yet this might have seemed an obvious step to take: Theocritus, for example, in his fifteenth Idyll, has some women of Alexandria talk about the festival of Adonis, but he then takes them out into the streets to see it in the flesh, bumping into passers-by and chatting to bystanders. But in the *Eclogues* the principal actions tend to take place off stage, and a remarkable number of the most important people do not even appear, but are merely spoken of: the young man who has saved Tityrus' livelihood in the first Eclogue, Alexis and Iollas in the second, Daphnis in the fifth, another Daphnis in the eighth, the poet Menalcas in the ninth. Sometimes the limits of the pastoral range have a slightly oppressive effect: Corydon in the second Eclogue and Gallus in the tenth are prisoners of love —at moments one may think, of self-love—obsessively turned in upon themselves. Sometimes, by showing us people and places subjectively, through the eyes of countrymen, Virgil creates a *fausse naïveté*: Corydon supposes the small-town Iollas to have the glamour of urbanity at his command; Tityrus describes Rome with thrilled amazement and his patron as a god. More generally, by suggesting a whole wide world of experience outside the range of the pastoral conception, Virgil gives a peculiar intimacy and tenderness to what he depicts within it. The orchard scene in the eighth poem is tender and touching through focusing on one small incident in one small life; so on a larger scale the *Eclogues* as a whole are touching because they enclose small particular areas of experience, with the greater areas beyond present by suggestion only. They do not represent, as does so much of the allegorizing pastoral written in the Middle Ages, the Renaissance and after, the world itself in microcosm, but a little world within the world.

Most poignantly, the pastoral world is vulnerable. Menalcas in the ninth Eclogue calls upon Varus for help, Tityrus in the first needs a patron to protect him. This theme was to appeal to the pastoral writers of the Renaissance, and they treated it mostly by bringing into the bucolic milieu grander men and women from outside: Calidore in the sixth book of *The Faerie Queene*, Pamela, Philoclea and their lovers in Sidney's *Arcadia*, the courtiers in *As You Like It*, Florizel and Polixenes in the fourth act of *The Winter's Tale*. The ladies and gentlemen envy the country folk their simplicity; the countrymen commonly need the aid or support of their more resourceful and sophisticated visitors. Virgil allows such figures to reach the edge of his field of vision but to come no closer, and thus achieves a distinctive delicacy of effect. The sounds of distant war are heard, but it is as important that they should remain distant as that they should be threatening. Here the generic idea of the frame under strain but holding coalesces with the poetry's emotional core. It is as though both the form of the poems and their content were like a rare seashell or a porcelain cup, beautiful because both fragile and unbroken. Ugliness threatens to burst into the forefront of the scene but never quite does so. An intruder has occupied Moeris' farm, but we do not see him; Meliboeus will trudge off into exile, but not until another day.

The tonal variations of the *Eclogues* extend into their treatment of the landscape and the life of the countryside. We have seen that they exhibit a geographical instability. The first, seventh and ninth poems are at moments set in Italy, as the place names tell us—Rome, Mincius, Mantua, and Cremona.[168] But we also seem to be in Greece: the herdsmen and their women all bear Greek names, and in the seventh Eclogue two of them are marked out as Arcadians.[169] The bees in the first Eclogue are from Hybla (in Sicily); in the eighth the Evening Star leaves Mount Oeta (in Thessaly); in the fifth Daphnis tames Armenian tigers and is mourned by African lions—but perhaps (we speculate) these are just quick dashes of decoration.[170] Matching these geographical mystifications is a fluctuation in the degree of naturalism with which the country and its people are portrayed. We have seen, again, that there are moments of quite sharp realism in Virgil's depiction of the rural scene; but at other times he is extravagantly anti-naturalistic. Theocritus in his first Idyll had made Thyrsis sing that jackals and wolves howled at the death of Daphnis; many cattle and even the lion in the forest lamented him.[171] The

---

[168] *Ed.* I. 26; 7. 13; 9. 27 f.   [169] *Ed.* 7. 4, 26.
[170] *Ed.* I. 54; 8. 30; 5. 27, 29.   [171] Theoc. I. 71–5.

universe of Thyrsis' song is a mythological realm much unlike the world in which he lives himself, but in imitating Theocritus Virgil dissolves the distinction between the shepherds' world and the world of fantasy where nature sympathizes with the men who inhabit it. At the same time he is more—and not, as one would expect, less—hyperbolical. The Daphnis of the fifth Eclogue, for all his wondrous acts, is no longer an established local deity or a mythological hero from a remote age, but someone who has been known to Mopsus and Menalcas themselves. None the less, no animal ate or drank when Daphnis died; the hills and woods tell of how even the lions have groaned for him; thorns and thistles spring up where violet and narcissus grew.[172] When he is taken into heaven, the wolves cease to prey on the flocks, the crags and copses sing aloud and the shaggy hills themselves shout to the sky for joy.[173] So too in the tenth Eclogue, the bushes, the rocks of Lycaeus and pine-clad Maenalus itself wept in sympathy with Gallus' plight.[174]

Through Virgil's example this motif of sympathizing nature was to become a part of the pastoral tradition, and modern scholarship sometimes cites it as an example of the pathetic fallacy. But in fact it is the antithesis of what Ruskin meant by the pathetic fallacy when he invented the term, and quoting Pope, he actually used an instance of the motif of nature's sympathy to demonstrate coldness and falsity:[175]

> Where'er you walk, cool gales shall fan the glade,
> Trees, where you sit, shall crowd into a shade . . .
> Your praise the birds shall chant in ev'ry grove,
> And winds shall waft it to the pow'rs above.
> But would you sing, and rival Orpheus' strain,
> The wond'ring forests soon should dance again,
> The moving mountains hear the pow'rful call,
> And headlong streams hang list'ning in their fall!

No lover could truly believe these words; but the pathetic fallacy, in Ruskin's sense, arises when the mind allows itself to be overborne

---

[172] *Ecl.* 5. 25–8, 38 f.   [173] *Ecl.* 5. 60–4.   [174] *Ecl.* 10. 13–15.

[175] Ruskin, *Modern Painters*, part 4 (= vol. iii), ch. 12 § 15; Pope, *Pastorals* 2. 73 f., 79–84. Pope begins the poem with the same motif, so much has it become embedded in the pastoral tradition: 'A shepherd's boy (he seeks no better name) | Led forth his flocks along the silver Thame . . . | Soft as he mourn'd, the streams forgot to flow, | The flocks around a dumb compassion show' etc. This passage is the more striking in that it cannot be explained, as the lines quoted by Ruskin might perhaps be, as a lover's playful fantasy: within the universe of the poem, nature's sympathy, despite the homely Oxfordshire setting, is a 'fact'.

by strong and genuine feeling into attributing to nature a sentience that it does not in reality possess: it is an instinctive rather than an artificial response. We shall do best to preserve Ruskin's understanding of his own term, which will help us to appreciate the range of ways in which the *Eclogues* apprehend the natural world. For the motif of sympathizing nature bears very little relation to the more familiar uses of the pathetic fallacy. It lies at one end of a spectrum: an extreme and obvious artificiality, in contrast to the patches of naturalism which we have met in other parts of the poems.

Virgil will sometimes juxtapose different and as we may feel almost incompatible pictures of the natural scene. In the first Eclogue Meliboeus describes Tityrus' land with a fair degree of realism—realism, at least, in the vulgar sense of stressing discomfort or inconvenience: it is a mixture of bare stone and reedy marsh.[176] But then the verse dissolves into cloudless idyll:[177]

> fortunate senex, hic inter flumina nota
> et fontis sacros frigus captabis opacum;
> hinc tibi, quae semper, vicino ab limite saepes
> Hyblaeis apibus florem depasta salicti
> saepe levi somnum suadebit inire susurro;
> hinc alta sub rupe canet frondator ad auras,
> nec tamen interea raucae, tua cura, palumbes
> nec gemere aëria cessabit turtur ab ulmo.

Happy old man, here among familiar streams and sacred springs you will court the shady coolness. Here, as ever, the hedge at your neighbour's boundary where the bees of Hybla feed full on the willow blossom will often by its gentle humming invite sleep to come, and there the woodman below the high rock will waft his song to the breezes, nor meanwhile will the hoarse wood-doves, your delight, nor the turtle-dove cease to moan from the lofty elm.

Conceivably the contrast could be explained in psychological terms: Meliboeus' envy of Tityrus' good fortune prompts him to belittle it until he is overwhelmed by a flood of homesickness. But one may doubt whether the portrayal of character is Virgil's chief intention, if indeed it is his intention at all: the reader's stronger impression is that the poem itself yields for a while to the pleasures of pure surface. The whole passage is carefully controlled in sound and in subtle variation of rhythm, but the later lines become more and more

---

[176] *Ecl.* 1. 47 f.   [177] *Ecl.* 1. 51–8.

openly onomatopoeic. Line 55 imitates the mesmeric humming of
the bees with its patterning of sibilants, liquids and nasals (and perhaps the trochaic caesura in the fourth foot, that rhythm shunned
by Hellenistic poets, adds to the sense of lullaby); the small touch of
pathetic fallacy in 'suadebit' is nicely judged—persuasive indeed.[178]
The word music of lines 57 and 58 needs no comment if they are
read aloud. 'Tua cura' is almost humorous in its mimicking of the
doves cooing; the impression of technical bravura is enhanced by
the fanciful syntax, adjective and noun being enclosed within the
adjective and noun to which they are in apposition ('raucae, tua cura,
palumbes').[179]

The poem (and the book) had begun with the pretty sounds of
piping: 'Tityre, tu . . .'.[180] Now, for a space, it reverts to pure melodiousness, and lingers there awhile. The sounds of bees and doves
and resonant song at a distance among the rocks could hardly be
more perfectly evoked.[181] But the poet surrenders any effort to penetrate or interpret: he is content for the moment simply to describe,
to bring the sounds of the summer landscape to the mind's ear. This
is poetry that courts an aural equivalent to the kind of praise which
the ancients so enjoyed bestowing on works of visual art—the statue
so lifelike that it seems to breathe. People sometimes talk of 'photo-
graphic realism'; here we have a moment of 'tape-recorder realism'.
Whereas the motif of nature's sympathy consciously denies the truth
of the physical world, this passage seeks to reproduce it. The *Eclogues*
have space for both approaches.

They display more artificiality than Theocritus but also more *verismo*:
Virgil develops his model in two apparently opposite directions. Yet
to say that some patches of the *Eclogues* are close to reality while

---

[178] Perhaps Virgil remembered Lucretius' 'autumno . . . suadente' (below, pp. 243 f.).

[179] This mannerism, especially favoured in the *Eclogues*, has been called the 'appositional
sandwich' and by O. Skutsch the *schema Cornelianum*, on the basis of a highly speculative
argument deriving its origin from Cornelius Gallus ('Zu Vergils Eklogen', *RhM* 99 (1956),
193–201, at 198 f.). *Durior Gallus*? It is not found in Hellenistic poetry; if it had been,
modern scholarship would be vocal. Some other mannerisms of Roman poets commonly
labelled 'Hellenistic' are in fact more characteristic of themselves than of the Greeks.

[180] *Ecl.* 1. 1. If it is asked why Virgil chose the name Tityrus, present but not prominent in Theocritus, the answer may simply be euphony. It should be remembered that *y*
sounds like *u* in French or *ü* in German. Experience suggests that it is worth adding that
the stress in 'Tityrus' falls on the first syllable.

[181] The passage inspired Tennyson's famous imitation (*The Princess* 7. 205–7): 'Myriads
of rivulets hurrying thro' the lawn, The moan of doves in immemorial elms, And mur-
muring of innumerable bees.'

others are fantastical is to give only part of the truth, for much in them is real and imaginary at the same time, as we learn from the very beginning when we meet two Grecian herdsmen in melodious discourse upon the woes of contemporary Italy. In some of the poems at least, the shepherds inhabit a world that is continuously both solid and visionary, both present and timeless. In the *Eclogues* as a whole Virgil creates a small universe that is at once real and artificial, strange and familiar, ordinary and magical. In the *Georgics* he was to find a way of fusing these opposing tendencies into an imaginative unity, so that the paradoxes which in the *Eclogues* were a literary brilliance become a means of exploring the depths of emotional experience. Though it is less than the full truth that some parts of the *Eclogues* are naturalistic, others imaginary, it remains the case that in these poems the *conceptions* of the real and the imaginary remain distinct: it is at least reasonable to suggest that the setting of several is and is not Italy, or that Menalcas is and is not Virgil. In the *Georgics*, by contrast, the setting is steadily Italy (unless we are transported for a while to some other part of the real world—Scythia, Noricum, or Greece), and it is the solid, actual Italy known to our own experience that is at once ordinary and magical, everyday and romantic: the physical landscape and the 'spiritual' or imaginative landscape have become one.

To find anticipations of the *Georgics* in the *Eclogues* comes as no great surprise; it is more surprising to find anticipations of the *Aeneid* in them. Virgil's epic is pervaded by a fascination with the sense of time, history and process, concerns which we might not expect to meet in his earliest poetry; yet they are to be found already in an unlikely place, the fourth Eclogue. This poem's strange and famous history as the Messianic Eclogue has sometimes disguised its lightness: it is courtly, rococo, high-fantastical. Elegantly, it combines three generic types: the encomium of a patron (in this case the consul, Pollio), the *genethliakon* or birthday poem, and by implication the epithalamium (this is indicated by two lines which echo the refrain from the wedding song chanted by the Fates in Catullus' *Peleus and Thetis*).[182] Naturally Virgil does not really believe that around (let us say) 20 BC oaks will start sweating honey and sheep turn purple in the fields. And yet despite these levities the poem does deal in its

[182] *Ecl.* 4. 46 f.; cf. Cat. 64. 327 etc.

oblique and whimsical way with a painfully immediate subject: the distresses of civil war and the longing for peace. Like the first and ninth Eclogues it soothes the sharpness of pain with the analgesic of fancy.

It is marked by a very high degree of unreality, in obvious ways, and yet the fantasy that it describes is rooted in an exactly measured historical context:[183]

> ultima Cumaei venit iam carminis aetas;
> magnus ab integro saeclorum nascitur ordo.
> *iam* redit et Virgo, redeunt Saturnia regna,
> *iam* nova progenies caelo demittitur alto.
> tu modo nascenti puero, quo ferrea primum
> desinet ac toto surget gens aurea mundo,
> casta fave Lucina: tuus *iam* regnat Apollo.
> *teque* adeo decus hoc aevi, *te consule, inibit,*
> Pollio, et *incipient* magni procedere menses;
> *te duce, si qua* manent sceleris *vestigia* nostri,
> inrita perpetua solvent formidine terras.

Now has come the last age of the Sibyl's song; the great line of the generations is born anew. Now the Virgin too returns, Saturn's realm returns, now a new offspring descends from high heaven. Pure Lucina, do you now favour at his birth the boy with whom the iron race shall first cease and a golden race arise throughout all the world: your Apollo now reigns. In your consulship, Pollio, in yours, this glory of the age shall begin and the great months shall start their progress; under your leadership, if any traces of our guilt remain, they shall be void and loose the earth from its continual fear.

'*Iam* redit et Virgo . . . *iam* nova progenies'—by that repeated 'now' our gaze is fixed, with an improbable precision, upon just this instant of history. The exact year is specified: 'te . . . te consule, . . . Pollio' —again the repetition, like an extra tap of the hammer, nails the exact moment. Uniquely in the *Eclogues*, we are given a date: it is in 40 BC that the wonder is to begin.[184] It will begin very soon, but not *quite* yet: the future tenses of 'incipient' and 'inibit' focus our

---

[183] *Ecl.* 4. 4–14.

[184] There is strong evidence that Virgil is thinking of the Treaty of Brundisium between Antony and Octavian (September, 40). The clue is that he is compelled to stress the child's conception rather than birth (*Ecl.* 4. 12, cf. 4. 61). It would be possible for a child to be conceived from the marriage of Antony and Octavia, arranged at Brundisium, while Pollio was still consul, but not for him to be born. The emphasis on conception, odd in a *genethliakon*, is otherwise inexplicable.

attention forward into the space between the moment of the poet's utterance and 31 December.

The nicety of those two verbs lies not only in their tense but also in the fact that they both describe inception: they introduce the poem's interest in continuous process. With an absorbed and fascinated attention Virgil watches the gradual development by which, little by little, the golden age is restored. 'Vestigia' in line 13 is a telling word: our sin will not endure but nor will it disappear in a twinkling; *traces* will remain for a while. The effect is enhanced by the delicate, tentative 'si qua'. '*Suppose* that *some* traces remain'—there is a hesitant, subtle searching for the degree of change or development. Virgil is the great master of the tiny word; we shall see what he can do with 'si' and 'si qua' in the *Georgics* and the *Aeneid*.[185]

The stages by which the golden age is re-established match the stages of the marvellous child's growth. Virgil tracks this growth through the poem: lines 18 ff. depict babyhood, 26 ff. boyhood or adolescence, 37 ff. manhood, accompanied by the full restoration of the golden age. Meanwhile the word 'iam' returns again and again: at lines 27 and 37, three times in lines 41–4 as the poet's enthusiasm gathers to its climax, and once more at 48. It is another of those little words which we shall see Virgil using to fine effect in the *Aeneid*.[186] Here in the Eclogue it conveys the sense of excitement and near expectation with which we await the new age's arrival: it is coming *now*. Yet it is significant too that he chooses the process word for 'now', 'iam' (often to be translated 'already') rather than the static 'nunc'; the adverb also enables us to feel the working of time, the distance between us and the completed golden age. It comes back for its last appearance in a small parenthesis, which interrupts a lofty invocation:[187]

> adgredere o magnos (aderit iam tempus) honores,
> cara deum suboles, magnum Iovis incrementum!

O enter upon your great honours (the time will soon be here), dear scion of the gods, great seed of Jupiter!

'O' is elevated and rhapsodical; the next line reverberates with the alliteration of *m* and culminates in a four-syllable ending, made the more monumental by the spondaic fifth foot, a rare licence for Virgil. Into this grandiose texture the little parenthesis thrusts itself with a

---

[185] See below, pp. 375 and 465.   [186] See below, p. 472.   [187] *Ecl.* 4. 48 f.

quick, darting eagerness. 'Aderit iam tempus'—each one of these
three plain words has its own weight. The glory *will come*, it will
come *soon*, but *time* will be needed to bring it to pass.

We can catch Virgil's concern for process again in an earlier
sentence:[188]

> at simul heroum laudes et facta parentis
> *iam* legere et quae sit poteris cognoscere virtus,
> molli *paulatim flavescet* campus arista
> incultisque rubens pendebit sentibus uva
> et durae quercus sudabunt roscida mella.

But as soon as you are now able to read the feats of heroes and your father's
deeds and to know what valour is, the fields shall gradually grow yellow
with the soft ear of corn, the reddening grape shall hang from wild
brambles and hard oaks shall sweat the dew of honey.

'Flavesco' is, as the grammarians say, an inceptive or inchoative verb:
not 'be yellow' but 'become yellow'. It is a significant clue to Virgil's
imagination that four inceptive verbs make their first appearances
in his work, two of them colour words, 'nigresco' ('grow black')
and 'rubesco' ('grow pink'). 'Flavesco' has appeared once before, in a
purely factual context in Cato's treatise on agriculture; this is its first
occurrence in poetry or high literature.[189] Its inceptive force is the
more keenly felt because it is qualified by 'paulatim'. The adverb
has a focusing effect: not just process but *gradual* process. Virgil's sentence is in a sense a statement about history, even though it is future
history and fantasy history. But characteristically this statement is
expressed through the use of the eyes, through a perception of nature's
changing appearance. When Isaiah, in a passage often compared to
this Eclogue, prophesies that the leopard shall lie down with the lamb,
the lion eat straw like the ox and the weaned child put his hand on
the cockatrice's den, he is certainly purporting to tell of future visible events, but we are not particularly encouraged to put them before
the mind's eye.[190] It is the idea of lamb and leopard together that
counts, not a picture of wool beside spotted fur. But by Virgil's
way of writing we are indeed invited to imagine the appearance of
those yellowing fields, to draw upon our own experience of seeing

---

[188] *Ecl.* 4. 26–30.
[189] 'Rubesco' at *Geo.* 2. 34 and then thrice in *Aen.*, 'nigresco' at *Aen.* 11. 824; 'flavesco'
first in Cato, *Agr.* 151. 2. 'Crebresco' and 'madesco' are also found first in Virgil.
[190] Isaiah 11: 6–8.

day by day, through the summer, the gradual transformation from green to gold. Although he is writing a fantasy, it is grounded upon the habit of being alert to the outward reality of the ordinary world around him.

We may learn something of Virgil's creative impulse from a few points of likeness between this passage and another which is in most repects extremely different—the death of Camilla in the *Aeneid*:[191]

> 'hactenus, Acca soror, potui: nunc vulnus acerbum
> conficit, et tenebris *nigrescunt* omnia circum . . .
> iamque vale.' simul his dictis *linquebat* habenas
> ad terram non sponte fluens. tum frigida toto
> *paulatim* exsolvit se corpore, lentaque colla
> et captum leto posuit caput, arma relinquens,
> vitaque cum gemitu fugit indignata sub umbras.

'Thus far, sister Acca, have I borne up; now the bitter wound dispatches me and everything around grows black with shadow . . . Now farewell.' Even as she was speaking she was letting go of the reins, gliding involuntarily to the ground. Then growing cold, she loosed herself gradually from out her body, and laid down her bending neck and the head now in death's power, letting go her weapons, and with a groan her life fled reluctant to the shades below.

The inceptive colour verb 'nigresco', coming as it does in Camilla's words, takes us inside the maiden warrior herself, so that we feel from within, and even see, her own experience of dying. Then the imperfect tense of 'linquebat' shows us that hers is a dying speech in a more literal sense than has been usual in epic verse. Homer's heroes, if they speak at all in their last moments, characteristically speak clearly and then die quickly, but Virgil watches the life ebbing from her as she utters. Death itself is not a point in time but a process; the adverb 'paulatim', again, plays an essential part, combining with 'exsolvit se' to present not death as a single instant but the loss of life as a slow, continuous dissevering. We may also detect traces of the amatory colour that has tinged her from the beginning: in Virgil's account she loosens herself from her body, almost as if it were a voluntary act; will-less, she flows to the ground; her neck bends slowly; she lays down her head, captured by death, in language which might perhaps be found in the discourse of lovers' pursuit and conquest. Only in the last line of the sentence does the

---

[191] *Aen.* 11. 823 f., 827–31.

tone of heroic indignation reassert itself, sweeping the languorous
swoon away. Since the scene is in most aspects a world away from
the *Eclogues*, the similarities—the inceptive colour verb, the fascination with process and the gradualness of process—give us an insight
into the abiding idiosyncrasies of Virgil's creative mind.

To return to the fourth Eclogue:[192]

> *pauca* tamen *sub*erunt priscae *vestigia* fraudis,
> quae temptare Thetim ratibus, quae cingere muris
> oppida, quae iubeant telluri infindere sulcos.
> alter erit tum Tiphys et altera quae vehat Argo
> delectos heroas; erunt etiam altera bella
> atque iterum ad Troiam magnus mittetur Achilles.

Yet a few traces of the old sinfulness will lie beneath; these will bid men
try the sea in ships, gird towns with walls and cleave furrows in the earth.
There will be a second Tiphys and a second Argo carrying chosen heroes;
there will be also another series of wars, and a second time will great Achilles
be sent to Troy.

These sentences reveal that Virgil is thinking not just of the idea of
a lost paradise but has specifically in mind the tale of the five races
of men in Hesiod's *Works and Days*.[193] First, Hesiod tells us, there
was a golden race of mankind, then a silver, then a bronze, then an
age of heroes, and lastly the present age of iron. What Virgil does—
and what, so far as we know, no one had done before—is to reverse
the story, to run the film backwards, as it were, back through the
age of heroes, represented by the Argonauts and the Trojan War,
until we reach the golden age again. In Hesiod's narrative the age
of heroes, interrupting the sequence of metals, is clearly an addition to the original myth; it is Virgil's idea of a second age of heroes
that shows him to have Hesiod's particular account in his mind.

In a sense Hesiod's myth describes an imagined process: it traces
the stages of man's decline. But it is a very limited sense, for the
story advances not continuously but in a series of jerks. First the
Olympian gods made the golden race of men, in the time of Cronos.
Then, after the earth covered over this race, the Olympians created
the race of silver. Then, because they would not sacrifice to the gods,
Zeus grew angry with them and buried them. When the earth
covered over this race too, Zeus the father made a third race, of

---

[192] *Ecl.* 4. 31–6.   [193] Hes. *Op.* 109 ff.

bronze. When the earth covered over this race too, Zeus made the fourth race, the heroes. They perished in their turn and have gone to the Isles of the Blest. And now is the age of iron.

Hesiod does not imagine a development but a series of destructions followed by new creations. Virgil not only abolishes the idea of destructions and creations but draws attention to the process of transition. Even 'running the film backwards' (perhaps that anachronistic metaphor may suggest how original he is) has this effect, for an abnormal movement sharpens our awareness of the normal movement that we commonly take for granted.[194] As time seems to reverse its course we feel more consciously the reality of its forward progress. Line 31 is especially alert to the sense of development through time: again we meet the telling word 'vestigia', now delicately qualified by 'pauca' and further modified by the subtle verb 'subesse' ('lie hid' or 'lie beneath'). Corruption cannot be erased in a moment of time: traces will remain, but not obviously; they will be few, and it may need a careful eye to spot their subterranean presence. In the midst of his fantasy Virgil's sense of the realities of historical process, and of the human heart, remains curiously nice. He may have had a line from Catullus' *Peleus and Thetis* in mind here: Prometheus, released from his chains and the torment of the eagle that gnawed his vitals, is present at the wedding, '*extenuata* gerens veteris *vestigia* poenae'.[195] Catullus' poem as a whole is filled with precise and loving observation of the external world, and here part of the fascination is that the wounds have faded but not entirely disappeared. As in the eclogue the healing process is almost but not quite complete. However, if Virgil drew on Catullus, he incorporated what he took into an imaginative pattern that is distinctively his own.[196]

[194] Strictly, of course, Virgil does not imagine time running backwards: he merely supposes some future events similar to past events but occurring in the reverse order. Such a prospect may seem hugely improbable (as Thucydides would agree) but it is not in itself impossible. Virgil's idea is, however, distinct from the cyclical idea of time, which supposes future events similar or identical to past events recurring in the same order. The cyclical idea is suggested at line 5, but modified later; the poet is not bound to a philosophic exactness.

[195] Cat. 64. 295. Virgil's immense admiration for this poem is sufficiently shown by the last episode of the *Georgics* and the fourth book of the *Aeneid*. We know that it was in his thoughts when writing the fourth Eclogue because of the allusion to the Song of the Fates.

[196] Virgil's manner of describing gradual process surely owes something also to the end of Lucretius' fifth book (especially 5. 1452 ff.). Here again his digestive imagination absorbs what it has taken into its own style of feeling.

Besides glancing back to Catullus we may track 'vestigia' forward into the *Georgics* as well. In the fourth Eclogue Virgil imagines justice, personified as the Maiden, returning to the earth again; in the later poem he recalls the departure of Justice at the end of the golden age:[197]

> extrema per illos
> Iustitia excedens terris vestigia fecit.

When Justice left the earth she planted her last footprints among them [country people].

In the Eclogue 'vestigia' was subtly qualified by 'pauca', here by 'extrema', and thus a refined melancholy tinges Virgil's praise of country life. No, the lost paradise is not still to be found in the countryside, but we may be just a little closer to it there, for though Justice has indeed left the earth, it was there that she planted her very last steps.[198] Once more we have a sense of process. Justice does not ascend vertically from the earth in an instant like a sky rocket, or like Christ in a medieval stained-glass window; instead we have an evanescence, as she flees into the countryside before disappearing altogether.

The Eclogue's sense of process, of the inevitability of gradualness, may tempt us further still into Virgil's later work. The passing thought at line 31, that traces of our sin will survive for a time before the golden age is entirely restored, adumbrates an idea that will be more fully explored in the sixth book of the *Aeneid*, as Anchises unfolds the great mystery of purgatorial pain:[199]

> quin et supremo cum lumine vita reliquit,   735
> non tamen *omne* malum miseris nec *funditus omnes*
> corporeae *ex*cedunt pestes, *penitus*que necesse est
> multa diu *concreta* modis *inolescere* miris.
> ergo exercentur poenis veterumque malorum
> supplicia *ex*pendunt: aliae panduntur inanes   740
> suspensae ad ventos, aliis sub gurgite vasto
> *in*fectum *e*luitur scelus aut *ex*uritur igni:
> quisque suos patimur manis. *ex*inde per amplum
> mittimur Elysium et pauci laeta arva tenemus,
> donec *longa dies perfecto temporis* orbe   745
> *concretam ex*emit labem, purumque relinquit
> aetherium sensum atque aurai simplicis ignem.

---

[197] *Geo.* 2. 473 f. (cf. *Ecl.* 4. 6).
[198] 'Vestigia' in the Eclogue is most naturally rendered as 'traces', in the *Georgics* as 'footprints'. This inconvenience of the English language should not disguise the similarity in the patterns of thought.   [199] *Aen.* 6. 735–47.

Indeed, even when life leaves them on their last day, not every evil nor all bodily plagues utterly depart from the poor souls, but it must needs be that many of these things, long set hard, become deep ingrained in them in strange ways. Therefore they are schooled by punishments and pay the penalty for their sins of old: some are hung up and stretched out empty to the winds, while the stain of guilt is washed out of others in a great tide of waters or burned out by fire: each of us suffers his own ghost-hood. Then we are sent forth into wide Elysium, and a few of us possess the happy fields, until the length of days, when the circle of time is complete, has driven out the hardened stain, leaving in purity the ethereal sentience and the fire of elemental air.

The high philosophic tone established at the beginning of Anchises' speech by many echoes of Lucretius is sustained through this passage. But Lucretius was a rationalist, and Virgil adds a haunting, uncanny note that is his own. Anchises expounds the doctrine that many things—sins and troubles, it would seem—grow so ingrained in us that they become part of us, part of our bodies even, so that they can only be purified out of us by the long, slow working of time. The strange image of the spirits hung up in the wind to dry conveys this marvellously,[200] but it is also brought out through Virgil's language. In line 738 the inceptive idea comes twice, with 'concreta', from 'concrescere', and 'inolescere'. 'Concretus' returns at line 746 to stress how deeply embedded sin can become and as part of a sentence in which each of the words 'longa', 'perfecto', and 'temporis', in different ways, brings out the sense of extended process. This sentence also hints at a providential purpose behind the sufferings of the dead: 'dies' when in the feminine gender is usually a special or appointed day, and 'perfectus' suggests a designed fulfilment. (We may reflect how much more easily a doctrine of purgatory can be extracted from Virgil than from the Bible.) From Lucretius Virgil learnt the force of repeated prefixes;[201] the idea of drawing out, of continuous gradual movement is evoked by a series of e- and ex- compounds: 'excedunt', 'expendunt', 'eluitur', 'exuritur', 'exinde', 'exemit'. These are balanced by verbs with in- prefixes and by adverbs that express deep inwardness: 'funditus', 'penitus', 'inolescere', 'infectum'.

The brief though penetrating perception of the Eclogue has here grown into something more profound: Virgil's sense of history—

---

[200] Perhaps he thought of the clothes hung up to dry at Lucr. 1. 305 f.
[201] See below, pp. 216 f.

that is, his sense of development, of the continuous action of cause and effect in the life of the world—is now combined with a sharp insight into human nature. He tells us a truth about ourselves: that what we experience and what we do, our sorrows and our sins, become us, part of our character and figuratively at least part of our substance, and cannot be detached from us. Such things can only be removed by a slow purification, a reversal of the process by which they became gradually ingrained. Such a view of the human condition has an appeal to the ethical and religious temper; small wonder that some of the Church Fathers loved Virgil so. The fourth Eclogue touches only lightly on this idea, but it might claim to be Messianic in this also, that here Virgil contemplates for the first time the possibility and pain of healing sin.

PART THREE

Lucretius

CHAPTER 5

A Conversion Experience:
Energy and Delight

And sooth it seems they say: for he may not
For ever die, and ever buried be
In baleful night, where all things are forgot;
All be he subject to mortality,
Yet is etern in mutability,
And by succession made perpetual . . .

(Spenser)

The force that through the green fuse drives the flower
Drives my green age . . .
The force that drives the water through the rocks
Drives my red blood . . .

(Dylan Thomas)

Baigne-toi dans la Matière, fils de l'homme.—Plonge-toi en elle,
là où elle est la plus violente et la plus profonde! Lutte dans
son courant et bois son flot! C'est elle qui a bercé jadis ton
inconscience;—c'est elle qui te portera jusqu'à Dieu!

(Teilhard de Chardin)

The world's function is to exist and to act with inexhaustible
energy, imitating in endless variety the riches of God's own absolute vitality.

(Austin Farrer)

In the course of the first century BC two men transform the poetic
perception of nature: Lucretius and Virgil. Lucretius was known to
Virgil when he wrote the *Eclogues*, but does not yet seem to affect
him in more than a superficial way.[1] The *Georgics*, by contrast, are
saturated in the older poet's influence. To study Lucretius' revolution is to enter into a subject which is of the highest interest for its

---

[1] An example would be the Lucretian noises at *Ecl.* 6. 31 ff., echoes of phrases from
De Rerum Natura designed to give a quick flavour of scientific or cosmological verse.

own sake; but it may also show us both Virgil's indebtedness and the fullness of his originality.

Since Lucretius' purpose is to expound the materialist philosophy of Epicurus, his opening is astonishing not only in its scale and splendour but in its theme:[2]

> Aeneadum genetrix, hominum divumque voluptas,
> alma Venus, caeli subter labentia signa
> quae mare navigerum, quae terras frugiferentis
> concelebras, per te quoniam genus omne animantum
> concipitur visitque exortum lumina solis: 5
> te, dea, te fugiunt venti, te nubila caeli
> adventumque tuum, tibi suavis daedala tellus
> summittit flores, tibi rident aequora ponti
> placatumque nitet diffuso lumine caelum.—
> nam simul ac species patefactast verna diei   10
> et reserata viget genitabilis aura favoni,
> aeriae primum volucres te, diva, tuumque
> significant initum perculsae corda tua vi.
> inde ferae pecudes persultant pabula laeta
> et rapidos tranant amnis: ita capta lepore   15
> te sequitur cupide quo quamque inducere pergis.
> denique per maria ac montis fluviosque rapaces
> frondiferasque domos avium camposque virentis
> omnibus incutiens blandum per pectora amorem
> efficis ut cupide generatim saecla propagent.—   20
> quae quoniam rerum naturam sola gubernas
> nec sine te quicquam dias in luminis oras
> exoritur neque fit laetum neque amabile quicquam,
> te sociam studeo scribendis versibus esse
> quos ego de rerum natura pangere conor   25
> Memmiadae nostro, quem tu, dea, tempore in omni
> omnibus ornatum voluisti excellere rebus.
> quo magis aeternum da dictis, diva, leporem.
> effice ut interea fera moenera militiai
> per maria ac terras omnis sopita quiescant.   30
> nam tu sola potes tranquilla pace iuvare
> mortalis, quoniam belli fera moenera Mavors
> armipotens regit, in gremium qui saepe tuum se
> reicit aeterno devictus vulnere amoris,
> atque ita suspiciens tereti cervice reposta   35

---

[2] Lucr. I. 1–43.

pascit amore avidos inhians in te, dea, visus,
eque tuo pendet resupini spiritus ore.
hunc tu, diva, tuo recubantem corpore sancto
circumfusa super, suavis ex ore loquelas
funde petens placidam Romanis, incluta, pacem.   40
nam neque nos agere hoc patriai tempore iniquo
possumus aequo animo nec Memmi clara propago
talibus in rebus communi desse saluti.

Mother of Aeneas' race, pleasure of men and gods, nourishing Venus, you who beneath the gliding stars of the sky fill with yourself the sea that bears the ships and the land that bears the crops, since by you every kind of living things (5) is conceived and when come forth looks upon the light of the sun: it is you, goddess, you whom the winds flee, the clouds in the sky flee you and your coming, for you the intricately working earth puts forth sweet flowers, for you the expanses of the ocean smile and the sky, made peaceful, shines with light spread abroad. (10) For as soon as the spring day's face is manifested, and the generative breeze of the west wind is unloosed and grows strong, first the birds of the air demonstrate you and your entering-in, struck hard in their hearts by your force. Then the herds, gone wild, bound over the rich meadows (15) and swim across the racing rivers, so does each one, taken by your charm, follow you desiringly where you proceed to lead them. Indeed, over seas and mountains and tearing rivers, the leafy homes of the birds and the verdant plains, you, striking sweet love into the breasts of all, (20) make them, in desire, reproduce their races according to their kind. And since you alone control the nature of things and without you nothing comes forth into the bright shores of light and nothing becomes glad or lovely, I desire you for my helper in writing these verses (25) which I strive to compose about the nature of things for our Memmius, whom you, goddess, have wished to excel at all times, graced with every quality. And so grant the more an everlasting charm to my words, goddess. Bring to pass that meanwhile the savage works of warfare (30) fall asleep and become calm over all seas and lands. For you alone can benefit mortals with quiet peace, since it is Mars mighty in battle who governs the savage works of war, he who often casts himself back into your lap, conquered by the eternal wound of love, (35) and looking up, with his curving neck thrown back, feeds his greedy eyes with love, gaping upon you, goddess, while as he lies back, his breath hangs on your lips. As he lies back upon your hallowed body, do you, goddess, pour yourself around him from above and pour sweet petitions from your lips, (40) seeking, glorious one, quiet peace for the Romans. For in this time of trouble for the fatherland neither can I do this work with untroubled mind nor can the noble offspring of the Memmii be wanting at such a crisis to aid the common good.

This Venus is a complex symbol. Invoked to aid the poet in his epic endeavour, she acts as an equivalent to the Muse.[3] As parent of Aeneas' race she is, like her lover Mars, an ancestor and patron of the Roman people.[4] As 'hominum divumque voluptas' she represents the Epicurean pleasure principle.[5] She is nature, or the energy that moves nature—'quae . . . rerum naturam sola gubernas'—[6] the force that through the green fuse drives the flower. What she is not is one of the deities of the Epicurean system.[7] Epicurus holds that atoms and empty space comprise all that exists. He was not an atheist: he believed that the gods existed and even that people could have authentic experience of them; but they are made of matter, like everything else that exists, play no part at all in the creation and government of the universe, and dwell in perfect peace and calm, entirely indifferent to the doings of humanity.

So the nature that is so passionately celebrated here is not in any way numinous or god-filled, but simply an immense physical machine; yet it is described in terms of a god's agency. In this Lucretius is both old and new: like earlier poets, he feels that he can only do justice to his stronger feelings for nature by using the language of deity, but now it is nature itself—the actual physical reality of winds and waters, plants and animals, the actual operation of spring accord-ing to scientific laws—that inspires the poet's feelings of awe and ven-eration and apparently almost ecstatic enthusiasm. His Venus is not found like Sappho's Aphrodite or the gods of Colonus or Theocritus' nymphs of Cos through or within or behind or beyond nature:[8] she is the working of nature itself. The activity of atoms—that is what we are to adore. He does not describe a specially chosen, distinctive or beautiful place—indeed there is no description of particulars at all—but the ordinary functioning of nature in all places and in every year. The objects of common experience—winds and meltwaters and beasts rutting—are to excite our reverence. Others—like the Stoic Lucilius Balbus in Cicero's dialogue—[9] ask us to admire the world

---

[3] Lines 24–8.   [4] Lines 1, 40 ff.   [5] Line 1.   [6] Line 21.

[7] Lines 44–9, identical to 2. 646–51, explain the nature of the gods according to Epicurean doctrine. Already in the Renaissance Marullus saw that they were an interpolation in Book 1 from Book 2, where they fit perfectly. The authenticity of these lines in Book 1 has been defended by a number of more recent authorities, but they produce utter incoher-ence: Lucretius cannot ask a god to pay attention to him on the grounds that gods pay no attention to mankind. (We need not posit a mocking interpolator: the lines will have been written in the margin as a cross-reference, and as so often, have found their way thence into the text.)

[8] See above, pp. 34 ff., 39 ff., 50 ff.   [9] See above, pp. 110 f.

as the creation of a wise providence; but that is a far cry from inviting us to come to all that is around us, to the totality that is the world,
with a spirit of worship. This is a new way of looking, a new vision.

The enormous vehemence, even violence, attributed to the common aspect of nature would be remarkable in any case; at the beginning of a poem devoted to expounding Epicureanism it is startling.
For the goal of the Epicurean adept was *ataraxia*, freedom from disturbance of mind, and the eternally passionless existence of the gods
was the model for humanity to imitate as best it could. How are
we to reconcile Lucretius' dynamism with the calm towards which
the disciple should aspire? The exploration of this puzzle, posed at
the very start, should draw us into his imaginative understanding of
the world and our relation to it.

Lucretius found the activity of atoms as we find the sea, soothing in its everlasting restlessness. As the theory of atoms unfolds, we
shall learn that one of their basic and universal properties is motion.
And Venus too is seen above all as activity: not so much nature as
nature's operation. The idea of energy and action is present in the
very first lines, at first inconspicuous but growing rapidly in force.
From the outset Venus is procreative: 'genetrix'. She is a mother, a
theme sustained by 'alma', 'nurturing', in the second line. Only much
later shall we discover the full importance of nature's motherhood
in the poem; but the more specific idea of generation or giving birth
is swiftly developed. 'Genus', in the fourth line, is in itself a neutral,
colourless word, 'kind' or 'type'; in this context, with 'genetrix' before
and 'genitabilis' and 'generatim' to follow, it springs into new life:
the various kinds of live beings are things procreated.

Other details of style or language suggest a world stirring, moving, active. On one level 'naviger' and 'frugifer' in the third line are
orotund compound adjectives, with a touch of Ennius' archaic flavour, thus implicitly announcing the paradox that this poem, formally didactic, has an epic ambition. But we may also feel that the
-fer and *-ger* terminations have come alive and are working: the sea
propels ships, the earth bears or brings forth crops.

In the next lines the ideas of conception and birth become more
explicit; and the sound and shape of the sentence reinforce the sense
of energy, even urgency. The heavy, obvious alliteration will soon
prove to be a basic feature of Lucretius' style. Once again, this has in
part a generic function, declaring that though the subject is physics and
philosophy, this didactic matter is to be set forth with the cyclopean
grandeur of epic poetry as practised by the forefathers of Latin verse.

Further, the alliterations express moral and intellectual energy. Robust and forceful rather than graceful, they suggest, like the manifold repetitions, cumbrous connectives and prosaic turns of phrase that Lucretius rams into his poem, the vigorous and remorseless seriousness needed to thrust through the complicated and recalcitrant subject-matter. And similarly they convey the energy of the physical world itself. 'Concipitur'—with its four plosive consonants the word's sound is crisp and brisk in itself, and its effect is increased by the way that it echoes, in sound and in exact metrical value, 'concelebras', which stands in identical position in the line above. And that alliteration of *c* is further extended by the hammering repetition in 'quae . . . quae . . . quoniam . . .' Lucretius is a master of what might be called irrational assonance. There is a kind of natural, sometimes imitative assonance that we immediately understand: we appreciate at once why the letter *r* represents the braying of trumpets, the letter *s* the softness of sleep or the sibilance of serpents. It is less obvious why an alliteration upon the letter *m* should represent the multitudinousness of matter or the immensity of the universe. But in *De Rerum Natura* it does so: by repetition and force of association Lucretius connects sound and signification.[10] The letter *c* may not seem inherently more energetic than several others. What Lucretius does is to alliterate it in two emphatically placed words which speak of filling, creating, and rejoicing, and to surround them with further forceful repetitions of the *k* sound. We learn of dynamism from the sense of the words; we hear dynamism in the pattern of sounds; meaning and assonance enhance each other.

Grammar also contributes to the effect. Lucretius is the great master of the prefix: 'con-', 'dis-', 'in-', 'ex-', 're-', 'per-'—these innocuous syllables come to express the unresting force of atomic movement, the pulls and pushes, the collisions, penetrations, tearings apart.[11] Several times he draws the parallel between the infinite number of meanings that can be created from rearranging the alphabet's

---

[10] In English the master of the irrational correspondence between sound and sense is Hopkins. 'Glory be to God for *dappled* things— | For skies of *couple*-colour as a brinded cow; | For rose-moles all in *stipple* upon trout that swim . . .' (*Pied Beauty*). Why is it that the *-apple*, *-upple*, *-ipple* sounds seem the just representation of the *poikilia*, the pied beauty, that Hopkins celebrates? Do we start to think of other words—'ripple', 'supple'? Similarly, the thrush's song 'does so rinse and wring | the ear' (*Spring*). Again, the *-in* sound in 'rinse' and 'wring' (and we also hear 'ring') seems to express purity, lucidity, astringency. Is it something intrinsic to the sound quality, or does Hopkins create such associations by his style of writing? Whatever the means, the effect is not in doubt.

[11] Two good examples of the expressive force of prefixes are 4. 916–19 and 4. 956–61.

few letters and the limitless number of diverse objects created by the rearrangement of atoms.[12] So the similarities and differences between (for example) such words as '*coniectus*', '*eiectus*', and '*distractior*' do in quite a strong sense mimic the wrenchings and jostlings of the elementary particles.[13] Moreover, the constant repetition of these prefixes and their very ordinariness convey the ceaseless activity of ordinary matter always and everywhere. The repeated 'con-' in the fourth and fifth lines of the exordium, the very first of the innumerable prefixes that are to flood the *De Rerum Natura*, marks the modest beginning of a large idea. What is creation, says the Epicurean philosophy, but the coming together of pieces of matter? What is death but their drawing apart? These are simple, natural processes, and therefore not to be feared. 'Con-', 'dis-'—in the simplicity of the syllables lies a moral lesson.

'Te, dea, te . . . tuum, tibi . . . tibi . . .'[14] In formal terms these repetitions follow the conventions of hymn or prayer. This is an aretalogy, that is, a recital of the god's deeds or virtues which precedes the call for his aid. At the goddess's epiphany the poet attributes emotions to inanimate nature—'fugiunt venti'—and the earth puts forth her flowers as at the *hieros gamos*; we can find precedents for this as far back as the *Iliad*.[15] But the parallels serve to point up the newness of Lucretius' idea; for he is saying that the emotions and passions which earlier poets derived from the supernatural should rather be sought in the plain physical facts of nature itself.

Thanks to the context we also hear in the repeated invocation of the goddess, in the hammer-beat repetition of the letter *t*, that energetic pressure already suggested in the preceding lines. A brilliant touch confirms the impression: 'fugiunt'.[16] The winds and clouds do not straightforwardly delight in Venus' arrival, they flee her: she is formidable, alarming. The verb also fixes our thoughts upon movement: even with clouds, Lucretius is concerned not with how they look but with what they do.

The next two and a half lines move towards a calmer, perhaps more conventionally charming picture of the spring, but even here the note of movement and activity is heard. The earth pushes up flowers, light is spread abroad; quietly the prefixes 'sub-' and 'dis-'

---

[12] Lucr. 1. 196 f., 823–9, 907–14; 2. 686–99, 1013–22. Cf. P. Friedländer, 'Pattern of Sound and Atomistic Theory in Lucretius', *AJP* 62 (1941), 16–34 (reprinted in C. J. Classen (ed.), *Probleme der Lukrezforschung* (Hildesheim 1986), 291–307).   [13] Lucr. 4. 956–61.
[14] Lines 6–8.   [15] See above, pp. 26 f. (and cf. below, pp. 245 f.).   [16] Line 6.

are working, energizing. The adjective 'daedalus' makes earth into an inventor, an artificer; even the sky is 'placatum' (pacified), not merely peaceful, its calm the result of action. The use of the pathetic fallacy is telling, and rather subtle. 'Fugiunt', though startling, brings this device closer to the perceived reality of nature than is usual; for whereas gentle breezes or threatening skies (to take two commonplace examples of the pathetic fallacy) plainly owe their epithets largely to what human beings find comfortable and convenient, so that the personifications seem imposed upon nature from outside it, we know that the clouds are driven by the winds, and that the winds themselves are in rapid motion, impelled, we infer, by some antecedent natural force. The smiling of the sea in the eighth line is less original, but well fitted to its context. The preceding clause, 'tibi suavis daedala tellus summittit flores', is poised on the borderline between literal truth and the pathetic fallacy. 'Daedalus' need not mean more than 'various' or 'formative', and it is little or no divergence from the facts of Epicurean physics to say that the earth drives the flowers upwards; yet in this place we shall hardly fail to sense a personification in the words, with the earth as an inventor and maker sending forth its creations in response to Venus' coming. 'Placatum' sustains the pathetic fallacy, but without strain, for it is natural to speak of weather calming down.

'Nitet' is literal, 'rident' metaphorical, but the words seem to share one emotional field of force. In short, though Venus herself is a striking personification, manifestly symbolic, the subordinate uses of the pathetic fallacy seem to grow naturally from the facts of the natural world. And the pathetic fallacy, as the poem will reveal, is not just an agreeable decoration for a purple passage; it is fundamental to Lucretius' way of describing all matter.

From the tenth line onward the impetus begins to gather. The west wind appears, not as the usual pretty zephyr, but in a metaphor which is both sexual and formidable. The very breeze has a kind of animal vigour: it grows stronger ('viget'), it is procreative ('genitabilis'), most strikingly it is unbarred as from a cage or prison; in 'reserata' is briefly indicated the untamed and dangerous aspect of the sexual impulse. Then the goddess is once more addressed directly, with renewed alliteration in 'te . . . tuumque', and now the note of near violence grows louder. In this setting 'initus' will mean more than 'approach'; it will suggest entry, penetration; like the numen of a true god, she will fill the birds' hearts, as she filled the fruitful earth through the 'concelebras' of the fourth line.

The birds are struck hard by her force: 'perculsae', a vehement word. Equally fierce is the phrase 'tua vi', the stressed monosyllable at the end of the line producing a clash of ictus against accent, so that those last two words are jabbed out against the flow of the metrical rhythm. 'Vis' is to be a leitmotiv in *De Rerum Natura*. Lucretius loves to use the alliteration of *v* to depict violence or destruction (Virgil will do the same, but with more restraint). For example:[17]

> principio venti vis verberat incita pontum . . .
>
> nec validi possunt pontes venientis aquai
> vim subitam tolerare: ita magno turbidus imbri
> molibus incurrit validis cum viribus amnis.

First the force of the wind, aroused, lashes the ocean . . . Nor can the strong bridges sustain the sudden force of the advancing water, so turbid with heavy rain is the river as it rushes against the piers with strong power.

When Lucretius speaks of man or mind or matter he is fond of such phrases as 'vis animai', 'animi vis', 'hominis vis', 'virum vi', 'ponderis . . . vi', 'vis . . . materiai';[18] for, once again, is not the essence of life the capacity to exert force upon atoms, the basic property of the atoms themselves the capacity to act and be acted upon? Especially does he love to end a line with 'vis', the clash of stress against metrical accent always emphatic. Virgil, like Catullus before him, uses such line endings very sparingly, for special effect: to do otherwise would be to lose subtlety and economy.[19] That was not Lucretius' way: in keeping with his pursuit of an epic ruggedness, complete with quasi-formulaic repetitions of lines and phrases, he does not disdain to achieve his effects by sheer accumulation. The constant reiteration of 'vis' is in itself an effect of 'vis': the poet hammers his idea home. The first appearance of the word in the exordium is another instance of his introducing an idea which will gain a wider significance within the poem as a whole.

'Concelebras', we saw, was picked up by 'concipitur' in the succeeding line, a word of the same metrical value in the same position, extending the alliteration and pressing the significance of the prefix. Lucretius now repeats the trick, 'persultant' echoing 'perculsae', while the driving, penetrative energy implicit in the prefix 'per-' is further reinforced by the crude vigour of the blatant alliterations in

---

[17] Lucr. 1. 271, 285–7.
[18] Lucr. 3. 397; 3. 450 and 5. 563; 4. 1040; 1. 728; 1. 1078; 1. 1051.
[19] There are only two such lines in Catullus, 64. 315 and 68. 19. Famous examples in Virgil are *Geo.* 1. 181 and *Aen.* 5. 481.

'persultant pabula laeta'; throughout this sentence there is an insist-
ent repetition of the plosive or velar consonants *p*, *t*, *c*, and *q*. The
note of violence swells in the meaning of the words too. 'Ferae
pecudes' is a taut oxymoron, lost in translation, for 'pecudes' are
domestic animals, and 'ferus' is 'wild' or 'savage': in the spring even
tame creatures become untamable.[20] And inanimate nature seems to
respond. The primary meaning of 'laetus' here is 'fertile' (indeed
'pabula laeta' will become a recurrent phrase in the poem), but in
this place the word's other meaning, 'joyful', is bound to be heard:
once more the language seems to make the facts expand naturally
into the pathetic fallacy, and the fields join in the universal exultation.[21] 'Rapidus' is an equally telling epithet, for Lucretius feels its
origins in the root which derives the verb 'rapio', 'seize':[22] the idea
of speed is combined with that of tearing or snatching, and the lust
to grip and clutch seems to spread from animals into the landscape
itself. This notion may be implicit merely in the 'rapidos . . . amnis' of
line 15, but soon, with the gathering momentum, it becomes explicit in the 'fluviosque rapaces', the grasping rivers, of two lines later.
In such a setting even commonplace words become alert and vigorous. We catch the suggestion of compulsion in 'capta' and 'inducere'.[23]
The repeated 'cupide' goes beyond desire to greed or lust.[24] When
it recurs, it is placed next to 'generatim'; the juxtaposition highlights
the sexual element in the 'gen-' root, now sounding for the fourth
time in twenty lines. 'Incutiens . . . per pectora' revives the ideas of
smiting and penetration that were in 'perculsae corda';[25] once again
this dramatic conception will prove according to the atomic theory
to be strict scientific fact. The idea of penetration and impulsive force
continues also, through both sound and meaning, in the sequence
'per maria . . . per pectora . . . propagent'.[26]

   Sex and violence—it would be hard to find another such explosion of these forces in Latin verse. Many years later the exiled Ovid,

---

   [20] Line 14. This is to take 'ferae' as an adjective in agreement with 'pecudes', having
predicative force: 'the domestic animals go wild and . . .' Bailey argues that 'ferae pecudes'
are two nouns in asyndeton, 'wild beasts and domestic animals'. The best argument against
this is its poetic inferiority. It might be added that the usage seems harsh (Bailey produces
no exact parallel, despite his claim) and that lush meadows are not the province of wild
beasts.
   [21] Virgil will make much of the dual meaning of 'laetus', as we shall see in Ch. 7.
   [22] Compare Virgil's description of the river Oaxes 'rapidum cretae', scouring the chalk
along its banks (*Ecl.* 1. 65).
   [23] Lines 15 f.   [24] Lines 16, 20.   [25] Lines 19, 13.   [26] Lines 17, 19, 20.

daring to twit an angry Augustus, will suggest that the list of licentious literature dangerous for the virtuous wife to pick up might include the poem beginning 'Aeneadum genetrix'.[27] He spoke truer than perhaps he intended: that elegantly naughty poet never celebrated sensual passion with half Lucretius' gusto.[28]

This is a revolution in the depiction of nature. The 'love of nature' originates, as we have seen, in a liking for the domesticated, the cultivated, and the comfortable; and despite the changes in the centuries between Homer and Lucretius, it would be hard to find a precedent for an evocation of the natural world either so dynamic or so independent of man's presence and convenience—and this to open a poem which will expound the mild quietist Epicurus. Lucretius startles by the recurrent suggestion of violence, or something very like it; and even without such rejoicing words as 'rideo', 'laetus', 'lepos', and 'blandus amor', we should hardly doubt that the poet is revelling in what he describes.[29] Should there remain any shadow of uncertainty, he will soon remove it. It is because Venus' powers are such, he explains, and because nothing joyful or lovable comes into being without her that he invokes her aid in the composition of his poem;[30] he prays that she will give his words 'lepos', and 'lepos', we recall, is the force that takes all living things captive and compels them to follow her wherever she leads.[31]

The significance of Venus and the relation of the exordium to the rest of the poem have been regarded as a painful interpretative crux. It would be better to feel the strangeness not as a problem to be solved or a difficulty to be surmounted, but as a penetrating poetical idea to be absorbed and enjoyed. Still, it will be expedient to approach the issue in academic spirit as a question in need of an answer, and that answer can be sought in two ways: by looking at the development of the exordium itself, and by relating the exordium as a whole to the later philosophical argument.

What sense can be made of the picture of Mars and Venus? How can it be made to cohere with the rest of the proem? These have

---

[27] *Tr.* 2. 261 f.

[28] Compare Auden, to Byron, on Jane Austen: 'You could not shock her more than she shocks me, Beside her Joyce seems innocent as grass' (*Letter to Lord Byron*). It is the hard eye and the lack of self-consciousness that strike home so.

[29] Contrast Virgil's treatment of animals' sexual desire in *Geo.* 3. We might also contrast Lucretius' own diatribe on love and sex in his fourth book; but that problem is beyond the scope of this study.

[30] Lines 21 ff.   [31] Lines 28, 15.

seemed maddeningly puzzling questions. Rather, not a puzzle but a deliberate paradox. Let us consider the seemingly discordant elements in what Lucretius says. First, what he depicts is a union between the two deities. This scene is, of course, a representation of the sexual act (within the bounds of decorum required by high poetry), a sensual celebration of coition which forms a fitting climax to the sexual imagery that has pervaded the previous praise of Venus in the spring. That much is immediately evident; but there are also two other implicit ideas which strengthen the sense that it is in the combination and co-operation of the two divinities that peace and security are to be found. First, into the complex texture of the proem is woven a patriotic theme, recurrent in various guises. Epicurus, celebrated at the start of the third book as a father of mankind, at the start of the fifth as a god, is here presented as a Greek, 'Graius homo';[32] Lucretius describes his own task as to illumine the dark discoveries of the Greeks in Latin verses.[33] Ennius appropriately finds his way into this part of the poem, where he figures as the man who first brought down from Helicon the crown that was to win fame among Italian peoples.[34] For both the epic poet and his philosophical successor, then, the task is one of bringing the achievements of Greek intellect and imagination into the possession of the Roman race. The patriotic theme has also a more political aspect. Venus is besought to bring peace to the Romans at a time of national distress; moreover, in the very first words of the poem she is addressed as mother of Aeneas' race, in allusion to one of Rome's two foundation myths. After such an opening, the name of Mars is bound to evoke the other foundation myth, the more especially as the god is shown in the act of coition: every Roman knows that Mars is the father of Romulus.[35] So in the union of Mars and Venus we see the father and mother of the Roman people brought together. Indeed, as she both pours her body around him and pours forth her pleas for the Romans to have peace,[36] he seems for a moment near to becoming a symbol for the bellicosity in the Roman character.

---

[32] Lucr. 1. 66.   [33] Lucr. 1. 136 f.   [34] Lucr. 1. 117–19.

[35] Mars was an old and authentic part of Roman state religion, whereas Venus seems to be an Italian spring spirit (as the only third-declension noun in -us, -eris that is not neuter, she looks suspiciously like a deified abstraction, similar to Lympha or Mens Bona). Lucretius therefore has to spell out her place in the national mythology (developed from her identification with Aphrodite); in Mars' case, there was no need.

[36] Lines 38–40.

Secondly, Lucretius draws upon a pre-Socratic symbolism. Mars seems close to the abstract principles of war, strife, destruction, Venus to the principles of creation, peace and love. Now Empedocles had held that the universe is governed by two principles, Love and Strife, and illustrated his theory by the myth of Ares and Aphrodite, their union representing the principle of Love, their separation by Hephaestus the principle of Strife (according to the traditional story, told in the *Odyssey*, the pair were caught in adultery by Hephaestus, Aphrodite's husband).[37] We shall return to this allegory shortly; for the moment let us note simply that it is the uniting of the two deities that symbolizes the principle of Love.

There is strong cause, therefore, for supposing that it is the partnership or combination of the two principles represented by Mars and Venus that Lucretius means to stand for that happy state which he desires. But at the same time there are other reasons at least as strong for thinking it to be the victory of Venus over Mars that he wants. She alone is prayed to, she it is who governs the whole of nature, in her operations not only the peace but also the energy of the universe are comprised. The poet pleads for an end to war throughout the world and for that peace which only she can provide; if Mars and Venus stand in part for war and peace, then what he seeks is a triumph of the goddess over the god. The picture of the divine union confirms it: Mars is conquered by the wound of love. He lies back, looking upwards at his conqueror, while she pours herself upon him from above. He appears as the dependant, hanging upon her mouth, feeding upon her beauty; and though Venus is the petitioner, asking him to grant the Romans peace, she seems none the less comfortably in control of the situation.

The contradictions, real or apparent, in Lucretius' picture can only be deliberate. And indeed the sexual metaphor is admirably suited to exploit the paradox. For here is the strongest and completest experience of union known to us; yet poets and lovers have been recurrently drawn to the language of wounds, conquest and surrender. The picture of Mars is an image at once of activity and passivity, of ardent lust ('pascit', 'avidos', 'inhians') and of satiety. Consider his pose, 'tereti cervice reposta' (with rounded neck thrown back):[38] 'teres' is a nicely untranslatable word, combining the ideas of smoothness

[37] Emped. fr. 17 etc. (with Eustathius cited by Munro on Lucr. 1. 41–3); Hom. *Od.* 8. 266–366.   [38] Line 35.

and roundedness. Catullus uses it of Ariadne's stomacher, taut to her
body and encircling it;[39] Virgil borrowed from Lucretius to describe
the wolf suckling Romulus and Remus on Aeneas' shield, 'tereti
cervice reflexa':[40] the adjective suggests both the smoothness of the
metal on which the animal is represented and the curvature of her
neck as she turns it to lick the babies at her paps. The turn of the
neck is probably Virgil's own addition to the older poet's idea, though
Botticelli's *Mars and Venus*, derived indirectly from Lucretius through
Politian, has the god sprawled with his neck bent a little to one
side as well as thrown backward, the perfect image of prostration.
This painting may serve to raise another question about Lucretius'
meaning. Though its contrast between Venus, cool, collected, fully
clothed, and the nude figure of the exhausted and sleeping god
differs in some respects from the Latin poem, it beautifully retains
the original idea that here is not only love-making but a subduing
of the male deity by the female. Now Botticelli's Mars is plainly a
representation of post-coital exhaustion; the question is whether this
idea is present in Lucretius too.

Epicurus' analysis of pleasure was complex and its details are controversial. One part of it concerns us here: his distinction between
kinetic pleasure and catastematic (that is, fixed or permanent) pleasure. Kinetic pleasure is the gratification of some desire: eating to
assuage hunger, drinking to allay thirst, copulating to satisfy the
sexual urge. Catastematic pleasure results from a state of contemplation untroubled by any active desire. Kinetic pleasure necessarily arises
from the sense of dissatisfaction or incompleteness: it is only when
someone is thirsty that he can enjoy the kinetic pleasure of slaking
thirst, only when he is lustful that he can enjoy the pleasure of sex,
and so on. Kinetic pleasure, therefore, imperfect and impermanent,
is inferior to catastematic. This conclusion may surprise the *homme
moyen sensuel*; but it is notorious that hedonist philosophers have tended
to be people who place a rather low value on pleasure as ordinarily
conceived: those who have been more keenly pricked by the goads
of pleasure have felt more urgently the need to subordinate it to an
austerer imperative. Epicurus, for his part, taught that men should
try to free themselves from physical desires to the best of their ability; given their material nature, complete success would not be possible, but the gratification of desire was to be seen as means to an
end: catastematic pleasure was the goal.

[39] Cat. 64. 65.   [40] *Aen.* 8. 633 ('with rounded neck bent back').

It seems likely that along with many other ideas an inkling of the Epicurean doctrine of pleasure is woven into the complex texture of Lucretius' proem. If we examine the whole movement of the first forty lines or so, we shall see that they act out the achievement of peace through energy, calm through passion. Perhaps we can even see the same movement, on a small scale, in the sequence that runs from lines 6 to 9: first the urgency—the flight of winds and clouds, the earth thrusting up the flowers—then the calm—the smiling waters and the shining, pacified sky. The lusts of the animals find their satisfaction: such is the implication of the words 'saecla propagent', with which Lucretius leaves them. The sexual metaphor is caught up again and encapsulated in the image of Mars and Venus that crowns the whole exordium. It is tempting to see in it a suggestion specifically of post-coital satiety, a completion of the generative impulse in calm; this would not only fit the rhetorical shape of the exordium, which moves to its goal in the image of the two deities, but would also, as we shall see, fit Lucretius' poetical interpretation of the nature of the universe according to the atomic theory. There need be no embarrassment, at any rate, about finding such a suggestion in a passage which also describes the god's eager desire. In the higher genres of classical poetry the sexual act is always represented indirectly, and it would be prosaic as well as prurient to enquire what stage of the love-making is being described: Lucretius' image embraces the whole act. Certainly both desire and fulfilment are comprised within his picture.

Taking the exordium as a whole, then, we find good reason to suppose that the contradiction which it appears to contain is not a casual inconsistency but a paradox carefully sustained. The next question, therefore, is what significance lies in the paradox, and whether it coheres with Lucretius' main argument. Let us return briefly to Empedocles, for one may suspect that in his symbolism there was a similar inconsistency. It is clear that on one level he represents Love as the good principle, as opposed to Strife: Love is the force by which the constituents of physical bodies come together and cohere, and it is thus the force that creates and gives birth; men call it Joy, he says, and also Aphrodite.[41] Strife, by contrast, is the force of dissolution and thus of death. On the other hand, he is also reported as having made the union of Ares and Aphrodite symbolize his principle of Love,[42] and this would seem to make good sense in

---

[41] Emped. fr. 17. 24 D.   [42] See above, n. 37.

terms of his system. He anticipated Democritus and Epicurus in holding that the constituents of matter could neither be created nor destroyed. New creation, therefore, could only come about through rearrangement of the existing stock of matter. On such a theory Strife ought to be as necessary to creation as Love, for without Strife there would be no change, none of the dissolution required to make fresh creation possible. Thus creativity would appear as the product of a harmonious relation between Love and Strife; in mythological terms, a union between Ares and Aphrodite.

Since Empedocles survives only in fragments, we cannot say how he resolved the apparent inconsistency in his scheme, or whether he noticed it, and so we do not know how far his idea is developed or transformed in *De Rerum Natura*. However, we can consider its force within Lucretius' poetic realization of Epicurus' system. Lucretius is a seeker after fixity and certainty. In his proem he already presents Epicurus as the man who has voyaged in spirit through the infinite,[43]

> unde refert nobis victor quid possit oriri,
> quid nequeat, finita potestas denique cuique
> quanam sit ratione atque alte terminus haerens.

From where victorious he brings back to us the knowledge of what can come to be and what cannot, and indeed on what principle each thing has its power delimited and its deep-set boundary-stone.

The ideas of limit and permanence are deeply important to Lucretius: the last two of these lines will return three more times before the poem is ended.[44] His language has both a patriotic resonance and a religious tone, for the stone of the god Terminus was sited, immovable by immemorial tradition, within the temple of Jupiter on the Capitol, the rocky hill symbolic to the Romans of the heart of the city and its perennial duration.[45] So 'terminus' here not only speaks of boundaries and limits but expresses fixity and centrality. And in the first paragraph of philosophical argument, after the proem has been completed, the word 'certus', 'fixed', will be sounded again and again.

For the Epicurean the physical world is everything that is the case: there is no supernature, no metaphysics. It is appropriate, therefore,

---

[43] Lucr. 1. 75–7.   [44] Lucr. 1. 595 f.; 5. 89 f.; 6. 65 f.

[45] For the Capitol as a symbol of indefinite duration, bound in with Roman and religious sentiment, compare Hor. *Carm.* 3. 30. 8 f. and Virg. *Aen.* 9. 448 f.

that Lucretius characteristically attaches his words expressing limit and certitude not so much to ideas and doctrines as to physical objects and particles of matter. Yet the elements of matter are unceasingly active and change continuous; what fixity can be found in nature? But therein lies the drama of his conception: on the microscopic scale a perpetual dance of atoms, in whose energy he delights; in the universe as a whole, immutability. No new atom can ever come into being, none can be destroyed or altered; the total sum of matter in the universe, though infinite, is thus fixed and changeless. If we look on the very largest scale or on the very smallest the physical nature of the universe is eternal; it is what lies in between these two scales that is subject to continual alteration. And there is another form of immutability upon which Lucretius lays much stress: the laws that govern change are themselves changeless. Birds and beasts and plants and men are born and perish; but the modes of their coming into being and the shapes of the atoms from which they are composed remain everlastingly the same. Rightly then can the poet speak of the 'certa . . . semina rerum':[46] the things themselves are constantly changing, but the nature of the 'seeds' from which they are constituted is fixed. Lucretius portrays a world that is 'etern in mutability'; and like Spenser after him he will take the sequence of the seasons to illustrate the interplay of change and changelessness, for what more natural or satisfying illustration could there be?[47] Spring is always giving way to summer and summer to autumn, but the rhythm of change is eternal.

It is a thrilling conception of the world, with a range and diversity unknown before, at once fascinated by minuscule detail and revelling in the boundlessness of void and matter. No one has relished infinity quite like Lucretius, who characteristically converts enthusiasm into assonance, resonating immensely: within his sound world the letters *m* and *n* come to evoke the magnificence of limitless multiplicity and endless space. But at the same time he is newly alert for the tiny, distinctive observation, *le petit fait signicatif*, for it is through the small details of the perceptible world that the unseen workings of the atoms are discovered. We can now grasp why Venus, in all the apparent contradictoriness of her nature, is such a superb symbol of the Epicurean universe. Empedocles seems to have seen Love simply

[46] Lucr. 1. 176.
[47] Lucr. 1. 174 ff. Cf. *The Faerie Queene* 3. 6. 47 ('etern in mutability'); ibid. 7 ('The Mutability Cantos'), esp. 7. 2.

as the force that coalesces, Strife as the force that dissevers. Lucretius' view is more paradoxical and more profound. He sees that the creative force needs to have the characteristics of Strife: it is the actions of atoms that tear, strike, collide, and penetrate. Action, indeed, is too mild a word: violence is at the heart of creativity, and violence he provides. Moreover, the creation of one thing is always the destruction of another, so that Love and Strife (if we may retain Empedocles' terms for a moment) are inextricably intertwined. They are, as we might say, married together; and similarly, Lucretius 'marries' Venus to Mars.

The world as a whole is a balance of creation and destruction, Love and Strife; but at the same time it is the triumph of Love over Strife, Venus over Mars. For the totality of the universe is creative; this is exemplified by the eternally beautiful rhythm of the seasons and the annual recurrence of spring. Rightly then can the whole operation of nature be called Venus. Equally, the total sum of the universe is fixed and secure: the immutable whole, in contemplating which lies the philosopher's pleasure, is the sum of innumerable energies, Peace is the totality of innumerable Wars. Ultimately, Peace contains and comprises War; and so Venus conquers Mars and soothes him with soft words and pours herself above and around him.

The Venus of Lucretius is thus multiformly expressive. The sexual act, dramatized in one way by the description of spring, in another by the image of Mars and Venus, takes us through energy into peace; for it is through the gratification of lust—which is itself in physical terms nothing but the effect of colliding particles—that the peacefulness of satiety is attained. That is a journey from energy to peace in terms of time: first the activity, then the repose. But the sexual imagery also displays in simultaneity the complex relation between violence and peace. We have seen that sexual love may be described as both union and conquest, victory and equality; we can now see the paradox of passion as an image of the paradox of the universe —a symbol which unfolds the drama, beauty, and complexity of reality.

Lucretius has a further reason for beginning with Venus. From the start she is a complex symbol, not only the force of nature and the personification of pleasure but the mother of the Romans and the poet's muse; complex, however, in a special sense, which can be brought out by a comparison. Propertius was to write a poem on the Battle of Actium in which Phoebus would figure both as the god of poetry and as the patron deity overseeing Augustus' victory.[48] That was an ingenuity, alluding in the person of a single god to both the elegances of Hellenistic poetry and the splendours of imperial success; but the ingenuity lies precisely in finding a link between two things naturally separate. Lucretius' complexity is of quite another kind. It is the essence of his demonstration that the diverse things symbolized by Venus cohere into a unity. In due course he will show this through scientific exposition: the movement of atoms is the source of all activity and of all sensation; alike it sends the flowers up through the earth, forms the poet's words and stimulates the sense of pleasure. But before appealing to our reason Lucretius will first seek to enthral our imaginations, and Venus, far from being an ornament loosely attached to the front of his work, is part of his strategy of persuasion, a captivating symbol of a cosmic truth. If oratory is the art of persuasion, this poem is the largest and greatest work of oratory in the Latin language. The rhetorical theorists spoke of 'captatio benevolentiae': the orator's task was to begin by enlisting his audience's sympathy on his side of the case. Lucretius' design is that we shall the more readily yield to his demonstration of the truth because we already want to believe him.

The very use of epic scale and language is part of his argument and method of persuasion. Epicureanism was regarded by its opponents as a peculiarly drab philosophy. Cicero, for example, though well aware that it was not the cult of self-indulgence which it was sometimes caricatured as being,[49] finds it an ignoble philosophy, since it sets up pleasure rather than virtue as the criterion for action. His approach to these questions may strike us as rather dilettante: he seems to select his beliefs rather as one might a suit of clothes, often seeming less interested in an unflinching search for the truth than in choosing a philosophy fitting for an honourable Roman gentleman. But Cicero's approach, we may suppose, was commoner among the educated than Lucretius': what was noble and high sounding must also be right. Simply on the practical level, if Lucretius wanted to convert his contemporaries, he would need to impress upon them the fineness and dignity of his creed. There was also, one suspects, another reason why some people might shrink from Epicureanism, though it may not be put explicitly into words: that it is a system which sucks all the beauty and magic out of the world. There are no gods

[48] Prop. 4. 6.   [49] The grossest travesty is Cicero's own, in his *In Pisonem*.

or spirits immanent in Epicurus' world, no room, it might appear, for wonder or mystery. We have seen how persistently, in various guises, the appreciation of nature was linked to an apprehension of the numinous; and the existence of the numinous—at least within the workings of nature as perceived by our waking senses—is something that Epicurus denies.

Lucretius counters these feelings. We can see this on a small scale in details of language. Take the facts of Epicurean physics. The universe is nothing more than so much matter, infinite in quantity, but neither created nor destructible: it is just so much bulk—in Latin, 'moles'. Moreover, it is simply a giant mechanism. What could be more prosaic than that? But put together these sober facts, and behold, we have a resonant phrase of epic sound: 'moles et machina mundi'.[50] As a description of the universe that is strictly correct according to Epicurean theory, and yet it is reverberant with Ennian dignity. On a larger scale, he can take the mechanical process that we call spring, employ Venus as a symbol, not as a literal goddess, and reveal that the energy inherent in matter itself can be a source of beauty and excitement. He can demonstrate how readily the conceptions of high poetry may be adjusted to fit Epicurean doctrine: he takes Homer's description of Olympus, and by a close paraphrase shows how close is this work of epic imagination to the facts according to his master.[51] Indeed, he might claim to have trumped the *Odyssey*: Homer locates the blessedness of the gods in their serenity, and that serenity is deeper and fuller on Epicurus' account than anything Homer conceived. He can elevate the facts of nature by clothing them in the language of fertility cult: father sky and mother earth.[52] He can take Epicurus himself, in sober reality a pacific character, who sat quietly thinking or writing in his garden at Athens, and present him as an epic hero, an Odysseus of the spirit, who voyaged far beyond the flaming walls of our cosmos and travelled over the whole immensity of the universe; or as a conquering warrior—an Achilles perhaps, or a Roman *triumphator?*—who brings back victory and tramples falsehood beneath his feet.[53]

Caught up in all this elevation is some language that is startlingly prosaic. Take the word 'ratio'. Perhaps Lucretius could not have avoided it altogether, but how he revels in it, repeating it again and again,

[50] Lucr. 5. 96.   [51] Lucr. 3. 18 ff.; Hom. *Od*. 6. 42 ff.
[52] Lucr. 1. 250 f.   [53] Lucr. 1. 72 ff.

forcing it into his text through such phrases as 'qua ratione' ('there-fore'), where reason is not the topic immediately under considera-tion. Or take the recurrent phrases by which he articulates the stages of his arguments: not only 'principio' and 'nonne vides . . .?' but such ostentatiously lumpish forms as 'quapropter' and 'quare etiam atque etiam'. Such cumbrousness is no unconsidered accident but a means of expressing the recalcitrance of his subject-matter, an expres-sion too of his struggle with the 'patrii sermonis egestas'. Normally he avoids Greek terminology, but when he first mentions the poverty of his native tongue he makes an exception, and a pretty grotesque exception it is too:[54]

> nunc et Anaxagorae scrutemur homoeomerian
> quam Grai memorant nec nostra dicere lingua
> concedit nobis patrii sermonis egestas,
> sed tamen ipsam rem facilest exponere verbis.
> principio, rerum quam dicit homoeomerian . . .

Now let us also examine Anaxagoras' homoeomeria, as the Greeks call it, the poverty of our native language not allowing us to name it in our own tongue, though the thing itself is easy to set out in words. First, as for what he calls the homoeomeria of things . . .

To end a line with a word of six syllables is an extreme abnormal-ity, and lest we should miss the point, the word is repeated in a line gratuitously drab and ponderous.[55] Part of his poem's fascination is the fascination of what is difficult, and he advertises the awkward-ness of his task, the prosiness of the tools with which he must work. He could almost say, like Tacitus, 'nobis in arto . . . labor', 'mine is a narrow . . . task';[56] and like the historian he secretly delights in the constrictions against which he purports to chafe, using them to create a new kind of grandeur. The struggle with the difficulties of words and material, the awkwardnesses and jaggednesses become part of a new aesthetic; they have their own rough splendour. And the clumsinesses and prosinesses are enmeshed with language of quite another kind. 'Ratio' may seem an unpoetic topic, but Lucretius will keep working at it, putting it in grand or enthusiastic contexts until the reader is battered into yielding to reason the honour which the

[54] Lucr. 1. 830–4 ('patrii sermonis egestas' also at 3. 260).
[55] The word also requires a trochaic caesura in the fourth foot, producing a rhythm which is sparingly allowed by Latin poets (it is rare in Lucretius) but always avoided in Hellenistic verse ('Hermann's Bridge').   [56] *Ann.* 4. 32.

poet believes it should have. Here too the style becomes part of the argument; catching up the plain or the ponderous into an epic sweep and elevation, Lucretius asserts that the prose of Epicurus, rightly understood, is the proper stuff of high poetry. The 'poetic' and the 'unpoetic' are brought together: from one point of view the heavy, repetitious connectives are Lucretius at his most prosaic; from another they are a didactic poet's equivalent to the formulaic repetitions of heroic verse. And this new aesthetic serves a new way of looking at the world; *De Rerum Natura* is in part a glorification of the prosaic, the factual, the ordinary. We shall find him studying and admiring, with an intensity of interest not seen before, the commonplace and the everyday.

Generally Lucretius looks to epic poets as his literary forebears: Ennius and Homer are the names that he singles out. He seems usually indifferent to the didactic poets—he never mentions Hesiod or Aratus—with one conspicuous exception: he lavishes praise on Empedocles, even in the midst of criticizing his doctrine;[57] this tribute is in marked contrast to the sarcastic or dismissive way in which he handles most rival opinions. Furthermore, he pauses for a short digression on Empedocles' native Sicily, manifestly irrelevant to the matter at issue: its purpose is to underline Empedocles' importance by lingering over him for a while. Lucretius is bound to condemn his doctrine:[58] the praise is for a great poet.[59]

And indeed one can see in Empedocles' fragments a vehemence, energy and enthusiasm that Lucretius must have liked and from which he may have learned. We encounter a robust use of repetition and alliteration:[60]

> ἀλλ᾽ ἄγ᾽ ἄθρει πάσῃ παλάμῃ, πῇ δῆλον ἕκαστον . . .
> ἔκ τε γὰρ οὐδάμ᾽ ἐόντος ἀμήχανόν ἐστι γενέσθαι
> καί τ᾽ ἐὸν ἐξαπολέσθαι ἀνήνυστον καὶ ἄπυστον·
> αἰεὶ γὰρ τῇ γ᾽ ἔσται, ὅπῃ κέ τις αἰὲν ἐρείδῃ.

But come, observe with all your might how each thing is clear . . . For it cannot be contrived that a thing can come to be from what is not, and it is impossible and not to be heard of that what exists can be utterly destroyed; for wherever one may set a thing, there it will be always.

---

[57] Lucr. 1. 716 ff.   [58] As he does forthrightly at 740 ff.
[59] 'Carmina . . . divini pectoris eius' (the songs of his godlike heart, 731).
[60] Emped. 3. 9; 12 D.

It might be objected that we have already derived these features of Lucretius' style from Ennius: but indeed one of his achievements is to synthesize different sources or influences; he finds something in Empedocles that can be developed into an Ennian grandeur. For that matter, he will have observed that Empedocles himself could adapt an epic turn of phrase to his own purposes, imitating Homer's *nepios*, 'fool', placed in isolation at the beginning of a line: *nepioi: ou gar sphin dolikhophrones eisi merimnai* (Fools: for they have no far-considering thoughts).[61] Lucretius in turn will give the single sharp word of dismissal at the line's start more force by making it the culmination of a sentence:[62]

> quod si forte aliquis, cum corpora dissiluere,
> tum putat id fieri quia se condenseat aer,
> errat . . .

If anyone thinks that this happens at the moment when bodies have leapt apart because the air thickens, he goes astray . . .

> quippe etenim mortale aeterno iungere et una
> consentire putare et fungi mutua posse
> desiperest.

Indeed, to link what is mortal to what is everlasting and to think that they can feel together and act upon one another, is foolishness.

Empedocles also anticipates Lucretius in the unabashed, somewhat cumbrous use of repetition to ram points home and articulate the sections of an argument:[63]

> δίπλ᾽ ἐρέω· τοτὲ μὲν γὰρ ἓν ηὐξήθη μόνον εἶναι
> ἐκ πλεόνων, τοτὲ δ᾽ αὖ διέφυ πλέον ἐξ ἑνὸς εἶναι . . .
> καὶ ταῦτ᾽ ἀλλάccοντα διαμπερὲc οὐδαμὰ λήγει,
> ἄλλοτε μὲν Φιλότητι cυνερχόμεν᾽ εἰc ἓν ἅπαντα,
> ἄλλοτε δ᾽ αὖ δίχ᾽ ἕκαcτα φορεύμενα Νείκεοc ἔχθει . . .
> ᾗ δὲ διαλλάccοντα διαμπερὲc οὐδαμὰ λήγει,
> τῇ μὲν γίγνονταί τε καὶ οὔ cφιcιν ἔμπεδοc αἰών . . .
> δίπλ᾽ ἐρέω· τοτὲ μὲν γὰρ ἓν ηὐξήθη μόνον εἶναι
> ἐκ πλεόνων, τοτὲ δ᾽ αὖ διέφυ πλέον ἐξ ἑνὸc εἶναι . . .

I shall tell a twofold story: at one time they grew to be one only out of many, while at another time they grew apart to be many out of one . . .

---

[61] Emped. 11. 1 D.

[62] Lucr. 1. 391–3; 3. 800–2 ('desiperest' again at 5. 165 (abruptly ending a nine-line sentence) and 5. 1043).   [63] Emped. 17. 1 f., 6–9, 12, 16 f. D.

And these things never cease continually exchanging, sometimes all coming together into one through Love, sometimes being borne apart through Strife's hatred . . . but insofar as they never cease continually interchanging, they exist always unchanged in the cycle . . . I shall tell a twofold story: at one time they grew to be one only out of many, while at another time they grew apart to be many out of one . . .

The repetition of *allote* is combined with a contrast which sets *sun-* . . . *eis hen hapanta* against *dikh'hekasta*. This somewhat resembles Lucretius' habit of contrasting prefixes such as 'con-' and 'dis-', though Empedocles is less emphatic.

Empedocles also enjoys a sort of rough vigour, in a style that recalls the later poet. Strife grows great in the limbs; he leaps to his prerogatives, at a time fixed by a broad oath.[64] The earth displays a shaggy might.[65] And there is joy within the operations of nature. The sphere (important in Empedocles' cosmology) rejoices in its circular solitude.[66] Love is called by the names Joy and Aphrodite.[67] Moreover, Empedocles describes the cosmic cycle in terms of the metaphors of birth, nurture, and death:[68]

> δοιὴ δὲ θνητῶν γένεcιc, δοιὴ δ' ἀπόλειψιc.
> τὴν μὲν γὰρ πάντων cύνοδοc τίκτει τ' ὀλέκει τε,
> ἡ δὲ πάλιν διαφυομένων θρεφθεῖcα διέπτη.

Double is the birth of mortal things, double their dying; for the coming together of all things gives birth to the one and destroys it, the other is nurtured and flies apart as they again grow apart.

Yet the comparison with Empedocles' verse also suggests that Lucretius (so far as we can judge) has greatly developed such hints and conceptions as he may have found there. First, he has fused the ideas of joy and vigour with the sexual metaphor. There are a few words directly descriptive of delight in the exordium of *De Rerum Natura*, but mostly the jubilation is implicit: Lucretius does not so much tell us about it as make us feel it through his way of writing. The gain in intensity and conviction is great. Further, he extends the sexual idea so that it underlies his entire exposition of Epicurean physics. Several basic terms of his technical vocabulary are metaphors taken from living things and their mechanisms of reproduction: 'semina', 'genitalia corpora', 'corpora prima'. In this he is different from

---

[64] Emped. 30 D.   [65] Emped. 27 D.   [66] Emped. 27–8 D.
[67] Emped. 17. 24 D.   [68] Emped. 17. 3–5 D.

Epicurus, whose terms provide a plain description—*atomos* means
that which cannot be cut or divided—different too from succeeding
Latin philosophers, who do not choose to take up his vocabulary.
Strictly speaking, we are correct to call Lucretius' terms metaphors,
and yet as the poem unfolds we hardly feel them that way; he makes
us apprehend elementary matter as 'seeds' and 'bodies' in a sense
that seems close to the literal. This is very different from the way
in which metaphorical language usually develops when it is taken
into a technical vocabulary. When the modern scientist talks of particles as 'bodies', the metaphor falls dead from his lips; Lucretius absorbs
such words into his scientific discourse without blunting their original meaning. It is significant that in the first book, after some two
hundred lines, when the physical argument is well under way, he
returns to Venus and the vocabulary of the invocation: 'daedala tellus',
'alit', 'generatim':[69] he demonstrates how closely, after all, the praise
of Venus is bound into the picture of the world presented by the poem
in its entirety. He also delights in language that blends the elements:[70]

> largus item liquidi fons luminis, aetherius sol,
> irrigat assidue caelum candore recenti
> suppeditatque novo confestim lumine lumen.

Likewise the generous source of liquid light, the airy sun, continually floods
the sky with fresh brightness and immediately supplies the place of light
with new light.

Fire, air, and liquid movement flow in and out of one another, conveying a sense of the whole as a great unity. Similarly, the world is
unified in its active, generative character: the sexual passions of the
beasts are an instance of a drive that extends through all creation,
animate and inanimate alike.

The picture of spring at the beginning of the work, therefore, is
a particular instance of the working of the living world, and the living world is a particular instance of that operation of atoms which
extends through the entire universe. Accordingly, nature acquires in
Lucretius' scheme an importance which it has never had before. The
visible created world is the base upon which his entire structure of
imagination and belief is founded. No longer is nature an occasional
refuge, a source of refreshment or relaxation from time to time. We
are to revere nature for its own sake, and from nature itself we are

---

[69] Lucr. 1. 225–9.   [70] Lucr. 5. 281–3.

to draw that religious feeling to which nature had previously been more or less an adjunct. We are still to feel love and veneration, but philosophically, scientifically, for earth and its products in their strictly physical and perceptible forms. And it will not be enough simply to adore; nature must also be studied with an accuracy new to poetry. 'Nonne vides'—'iamne vides'—'Do you not see? . . . do you *now* see?'—Lucretius' jabbing, reiterated questions must be given their full weight of meaning—'see' not just in the sense of 'understand' but literally as well. In Epicurus' philosophy, sense-perception is the basis of all knowledge, practical and theoretical; and in Lucretius' poem the argument of the eye acquires a new importance. He is, as no poet had been before, one for whom the detail of the visible world exists; he has, as we shall see, a talent for the minute observation, for picking out the quirks and quiddities and odd particularities of things. That is a poetic and a personal gift, but at the same time it is something to which his philosophy directs him, for that atomic theory argues in part from the exact scrutiny of minutiae. Out of Epicureanism Lucretius created a way of apprehending the world that is both loyal to his master and highly individual: his philosophical beliefs led him on the one hand to a rapturous celebration of nature in general and to a sense of scale and immensity, on the other hand to an intimate and precise study of small or ordinary things. It is to a large extent the double character of his vision —the combination of grandeur and homeliness, of the general and the particular—that impresses. If he had found the grandeur alone, it might have come to seem merely cloudy; if we had only the particular observations, we might have praised his eager minuteness without feeling that he had incorporated it into a personal vision. His achievement is both to see the world as it is and to interpret it, and to make the seeing and the interpretation part and parcel of each other. Science is not the enemy of poetry but its friend, and Platonism and Stoicism, which might seem more 'poetic' philosophies, could not in practice have furnished the stuff of the poem Lucretius wrote. Epicurus' teachings were divided into physics, moral doctrine, and canonics. Lucretius' attention is predominantly on the first of these: he will write about the real world, and the moral idea will grow out of solid, perceptible fact. In this the *Georgics* was to follow him.

Lucretius' first passage of scientific argument, rhetorically and poetically subtle in itself, will also be important to us for its relationship to Virgil.[71] The basic argument is simple enough. Nothing can be created out of nothing, for if this were not so, every kind of being could come into existence from any source whatever, and 'nothing would require a seed'. For example, humankind might arise from the sea, fishes from the dry land, and birds might burst into being in the midst of the sky; similarly, there would be no natural laws of growth, so that little babies might turn into young men in an instant and bushes spring from the ground without warning. Since we know from the evidence of our senses that none of these things can happen, it follows that things must be formed from determinate materials according to determinate laws.

We have noted that it is Lucretius' strategy of persuasion to work upon our emotions as well as our reason: we are not only to believe in Epicurus' teachings but to want to believe in them. He expects us to accept Epicurean doctrine because we are persuaded that it is true, but we are also to understand that it is wholesome and desirable, a philosophy that we should wish to take to ourselves. It is the more striking, then, that he should hint at a poetic and mythological tradition which seems at first to make his claim about the laws of nature unattractive, even if true. Let us look closer.

Lucretius is making play with the common motif of *adunata*, impossible things. Poets exploit the theme in diverse ways. It can be used to underline the extravagant or fantastic nature of what is being said: the rivers are flowing backward to their sources, sing the chorus of Euripides' *Medea*; honour is coming to the race of women.[72] It may ratify an oath or promise: Virgil's shepherd declares that deer shall feed in the sky, the seas shall cast their fish upon the shore, the Parthian shall drink from the Saône and the German from the Tigris before he forgets his benefactor.[73] The theme may give voice to despair: now may the wolf flee the sheep (says the heartbroken lover in the eighth Eclogue), oaks bear golden apples, tamarisks ooze amber and screech-owls vie with swans—since his own world is turned upside down.[74] Ovid turns the theme to the purposes of comedy: in consequence of the great deluge *adunata* become literally true, with fish

---

[71] Lucr. 1. 159 ff.   [72] *Med.* 410 ff.
[73] *Ecl.* 1. 59–63. Burns's 'Till a' the seas gang dry, my luve' is a classic example of this use of the *adunaton*. The classical influence is direct in Gay's libretto for Handel's *Acis and Galatea*: 'The flocks shall leave the mountains, The woods the turtle dove, The nymphs forsake the fountains, Ere I forsake my love.'   [74] *Ecl.* 8. 52–5.

caught in elm-trees, ships grazing the tops of vineyards, an anchor dropped down in a green meadow.[75]

And *adunata* are a feature of that imaginary lost paradise, the golden age, as Virgil shows us in his fourth Eclogue: when the golden age returns, the goats will come from pasturage, their udders swollen, of their own accord; cattle will not fear lions; corn will grow without need for men to cultivate it; grapes will hang from brambles, oaks ooze honey; there will be no need to hoe or prune or plough. Every soil shall bear every kind of crop; in Virgil's own words, 'omnis feret omnia tellus' (Every land shall bear every thing). That is in the world of fantasy; the reality is expressed in down-to-earth terms in the *Georgics*: 'nec vero terrae ferre omnes omnia possunt' (Nor indeed can all soils bear all things).[76] Here Virgil is echoing the very passage of Lucretius that we are considering:[77]

> nec fructus idem arboribus constare solerent,
> sed mutarentur, *ferre omnes omnia possent.*

Nor would the same fruits be constant to particular trees, but they would change, and all trees would bear all fruits.

Virgil echoes both Lucretius and his earlier self: in the robust tones of Lucretian realism (the thumping rhythm created by the self-contained fourth-foot spondee is one that he commonly avoids) he denies the existence of the fancy that he had once indulged. And Virgil has surely read his master aright: Lucretius is implicitly denying the possibility of a golden-age world. He offers us momentary glimpses of a paradisal, or apparently paradisal, state of things, only to snatch them from our sight. Fruits growing upon every kind of tree would surely seem a blessing that we should like to enjoy (one may think of the clusters of grapes hanging from brambles in the fourth Eclogue). The theme returns, more extensively, a little later in Lucretius' argument:[78]

> postremo quoniam incultis praestare videmus
> culta loca et manibus meliores reddere fetus,
> esse videlicet in terris primordia rerum
> quae nos fecundas *vertentes vomere* glebas
> terraique solum *subigentes cimus* ad ortus.
> quod si nulla forent, nostro sine quaeque labore
> sponte sua multo fieri meliora videres.

---

[75] *Met.* 1. 293 ff.　　[76] *Ecl.* 4. 39; *Geo.* 2. 109.
[77] Lucr. 1. 165 f.　　[78] Lucr. 1. 208–14.

Lastly, since we see that cultivated ground is superior to uncultivated and returns better crops when worked, it is clear that there are first elements of things in the earth which we summon to birth by turning the fertile clods with the ploughshare and working the earth's soil. If there were not, you would see all things becoming much better of their own accord, without any effort of ours.

'Labor', as Virgil will emphasize, is what falls to man's lot with the disappearance of the golden age. The urgent alliteration in 'vertentes vomere', Lucretius exploiting the letter which he associates especially with force, and the idea of pressure and compulsion in 'subigentes' and 'cimus', stress the hard effort that is the farmer's life.[79] However, these stern truths would not apply but for those laws of nature which Epicurean physics reveals to us: things would grow better of their own accord, without any toil on our part. Now we may be driven to accept this as truth, but why should we desire to believe it? In different terms: what are Lucretius' rhetorical tactics here?

On the way to answering this question let us notice first the recurrence in this passage of two adjectives. In the space of fourteen lines, between 159 and 172, 'omnis' occurs seven times; between 164 and 192 'certus' occurs six times, twice in emphatic position at the end of the line, and its negative 'incertus' twice. The reverberance of these two words can be seen as part of what may be called Lucretius' religious spirit. It will be as well to clarify what is meant by calling Lucretius a religious man. Of course he was fiercely hostile to whatever the Latin language conveys by 'religio';[80] nor was he religious in the formal sense that Epicurus was religious. Epicurus enjoined his followers to perform prayers and sacrifices in the traditional manner, and this seems to have been a matter of genuine feeling on his part, not just a wish to avoid offending his fellow citizens. However, this mode of feeling was rather like that of the agnostic don who treasures Latin grace at high table, or the man who regards weddings and funerals in church as part of the fitting order of things but attaches little or no structure of belief to such occasions. In this aspect of Epicurus' teaching—sentimental or traditional religion—Lucretius betrays no sign of interest, but his mind is deeply religious in a more important sense. This sense will have to be explained to

---

[79] 'Subigo' is found as an agricultural term in Cato (*Agr.* 161. 1) and Columella (2. 10. 21); the context in Lucretius reinforces the common sense 'subdue', break in'. Virgil uses 'subigo' with a similar suggestiveness at *Geo.* 1. 125: 'Before Jupiter no farmers worked the soil'—with the overtone of a struggle for mastery.   [80] Lucr. 1. 101.

a large extent ostensively, through observing the cast of thought that he develops through his first three books, culminating in the diatribe on death; indeed, one might almost say that he writes thousands of verses because his mode of apprehending our relationship to the world resists summary definition and can only be understood by being felt. But if a rough and ready definition of 'religious' is wanted, it might be said to describe whatever mode of apprehension, not necessarily theistic, the great living religions have in common.[81] Lucretius will tell us that at the contemplation of the truths of nature, revealed by Epicurus, 'me . . . quaedam divina voluptas | percipit atque horror' (A kind of divine pleasure and shudder grips me).[82] An awareness of the sacred (divinus), the feeling of being grasped by some power external to oneself (percipit), the strange blend of awe and joy—in all this we recognize what we call a sense of the numinous. Lucretius gets this not from the gods but purely by reflection upon the nature of things. Epicurus held that we can have authentic experience of the gods, especially in sleep, when the atoms of the body loosen one from another and the very fine particles which come off the gods' bodies can more easily penetrate their interstices and reach our minds. Lucretius duly records this as a fact of physics, but it has no emotional importance for him.[83] It is in nature itself, or the contemplation of nature, that sanctity resides.

Since it has been Lucretius' assertion, right from the beginning of his poem, that our veneration should not be for especially beautiful or consecrated places but for the ordinary and universal operations of nature, it is fitting that this idea should be developed through two such basic and simple Latin adjectives as 'omnis' and 'certus'. One part of the religious impulse is the search for wholeness, for an understanding of the totality of things; another is the desire for fixity among the changes and chances of a fleeting world. Lucretius offers to satisfy both, with a vision both of infinity and of strict limit; it is the power of his imagination to bring together boundlessness and boundaries impossible to cross. He explores the relation between these two conceptions; even the disposition of words within the metre helps to make his argument. We have already seen how the rhythm emphasizes one of these adjectives through the self-contained

---

[81] This is not to turn Lucretius into *anima naturaliter Christiana*, or to claim that his cast of thought resembles that of any actual living religion (if anything, it would be more Buddhistic than Christian).

[82] Lucr. 3. 28 f.   [83] Lucr. 5. 1169 ff.

fourth-foot spondee: 'ferre | omnes | omnia possent'. 'Certus' receives the same treatment three lines later, the point driven home even more firmly by the hammering alliteration of the velar consonant *k*: 'at nunc seminibus *q*uia | *c*ertis | *q*uae*q*ue *c*reantur' (As it is, since all things are produced from fixed seeds).[84] There is an element of sternness (as there is in much religious teaching) in the stress upon fixed boundaries: one of Lucretius' tasks is to compel us to the knowledge of limitations upon us that we can never hope to transcend. But that knowledge, as he will reveal to us, above all at the end of his third book, is ultimately liberating. Virgil too was to learn that sternness has its own splendour; indeed in those lines of Lucretius about ploughing we seem to hear already the tone of the first Georgic.

To the imagery of sexuality and reproduction already established in the use of the terms 'semina' and 'genitalia corpora' Lucretius now adds a new element, bringing it into connection with the idea of fixity:[85]

> quippe ubi non essent genitalia corpora cuique,
> qui posset mater rebus consistere certa?
> at nunc seminibus quia certis quaeque creantur . . .

If each kind did not have bodies to generate it, how could a fixed mother remain constant for things? As it is, since all things are produced from fixed seeds . . .

'Mater'—it is the first, unobtrusive appearance of a word that will assume great importance as the poem advances. In a quiet way it begins to develop a theme that has been implicit from the first two lines of the poem, where Venus was 'genetrix' and 'almus'. Even here 'mater' cannot be simply neutral, but necessarily carries an emotional weight: motherhood must be something that we greatly value. And Lucretius shows us that its existence depends upon fixity and limit, since indeed for any living thing to have a mother is for it to be attached to one individual origin, distinct from all others. The sense of belonging, the sense of identity require that individuation, that differentiation of one thing from another which the myth of the golden age would purport to abolish: every mother is of necessity a 'mater certa'.

Let us think again of those babes who, if things could be created from nothing, would turn into youths in an instant. When we

[84] Lucr. I. 169.   [85] Lucr. I. 167–9.

consider the notion, does it not strike us, as Lucretius intends that
it should, as repellent, an assault upon our idea of what it is to be
a human being? The reality (he continues) is otherwise:[86]

> quorum nil fieri manifestum est, omnia quando
> paulatim crescunt, ut par est, semine certo
> crescentesque genus servant; ut noscere possis
> quidque sua de materia grandescere alique.

It is clear that none of these things happens, since all things grow gradually, as is natural, from a fixed seed, and as they grow, preserve their kind,
so that you can be sure that each thing grows and is nourished from its
own proper substance.

Here Lucretius studies process: partly through the inceptive verbs
'crescunt', 'crescentes', 'grandescere' (indeed 'crescunt', expanding
into 'crescentes', mimics syntactically the growth that the sentence
describes), partly through the adverb 'paulatim', which fixes our attention upon the process of development across time. In Virgil the sense
of process will be more fully explored; but when he first takes up the
theme, in the fourth Eclogue, we find him learning from Lucretius
and using the elements that we see here: the word 'paulatim' in association with inceptive verbs.[87]

In that poem Virgil displays a delight in process, and this too
he had surely learnt from the older poet, for Lucretius puts the
idea of growth in a context which, once again, gives it an emotional colouring. When he introduced the name of mother, twenty
lines earlier, he followed it with the phrase 'seminibus . . . certis',
continued the maternal imagery with the verb 'enascor' and then
produced the word 'materies', thereby implying an etymological link
with 'mater':[88]

> quippe ubi non essent genitalia corpora cuique,
> qui posset *mater* rebus consistere certa?
> at nunc *seminibus* quia *certis* quaeque creantur,
> inde *enascitur* atque oras in luminis exit,
> *materies* ubi inest cuiusque et corpora prima . . .

If each kind did not have bodies to generate it, how could a fixed mother
remain constant for things? As it is, since all things are produced from fixed
seeds, each thing is born and comes forth into the shores of light out of
that in which reside the thing's material and first bodies . . .

---

[86] Lucr. I. 188–91.   [87] See above, pp. 202 f.   [88] Lucr. I. 167–71.

We remember this as now, once again, he puts his picture of growth into connection with the emotive ideas of seed and fixity ('semine certo') and motherhood, implied in the word 'materia' and overt in 'ali'. 'Alere' (nourish) and its cognate adjective 'almus' form another of his key terms: Venus is hailed as 'alma Venus' in the poem's second line, her maternal function declared even before her sexual function is celebrated. And thus we learn that the process of slow and gradual growth is something for us to delight in: it is an essence of humanity.

There is another charm which seed, limit and fixity make possible:[89]

> atque hac re nequeunt ex omnibus omnia gigni,
> quod *certis* in rebus inest secreta facultas.
> praeterea cur | vere ‖ ros|am, frumenta calore,
> vitis autumno fundi suadere videmus,
> si non, *certa* suo quia tempore *semina* rerum
> cum confluxerunt, patefit quod cumque creatur,
> dum tempestates adsunt et vivida tellus
> tuto res teneras effert in luminis oras?

And accordingly, all things cannot be begotten by all things, because separate capacities reside in particular things. Besides, why do we see roses in spring, corn in the summer's heat, vines spilling forth at autumn's coaxing, if not because each created thing discloses itself when its seeds have gathered together at their own time, while the due season is at hand and the lively earth brings forth tender things safely into the shores of light?

Lines 174–5 are exquisitely made. The three limbs of the clause form a tricolon auctum, the two disyllables of 'vere rosam' being followed by the two trisyllables of 'frumenta calore', while the picture of autumn expands to fill a whole line; the phrases for spring and summer are chiastically arranged, in the pattern ablative accusative accusative ablative; thus the sentence dances, as does the verse, with the words shaped into the most lilting rhythm of which the hexameter is capable: a continuous alternation of dactyls and spondees enhanced by a weak caesura in the third foot. The blend of balance and variation perfectly expresses the combination of regularity and diversity that is the rhythm of the seasons. How delightful it all sounds, how enticing; and the emotional colouring deepens in the next line, with the personification of autumn persuading the vines to pour forth their abundance—a persuasive image indeed, coaxing the reader into

[89] Lucr. I. 172–9.

realizing the beauty of nature's laws. These are a pair of lines which the fanciest of neoteric poets might be proud to have written, which rival the most elegant moments of the *Georgics*, and they serve to show us how much a matter of deliberate choice is the rougher texture of verse that Lucretius more commonly provides. Here the style changes because the style is part of the argument: we are to see not only that the fixed laws of physics create variety but that variety is good.[90]

Lucretius follows this by exploring another aspect of his maternal image. The earth is 'vivida', procreative; the masterstroke here is the word 'tuto' (safely), which in combination with 'teneras' suggests a mother's protective care of the helpless new-born. 'In luminis oras', an expression that Lucretius will often use again, is one that embraces the whole natural world; he is talking of flowers and crops, yet in the context we surely think also of an emergence from the womb, and once more see nature in a light coloured by the experience of our own humanity. Throughout the entire passage there is, running beneath the overt argument, what may be called an emotional argument. It goes something like this. A magical world freed from the laws of

---

[90] Lucretius' style has usually been seen as deliberately rough and archaizing, but we should give consideration to another possible argument: the traditional view (it might be said) derives from hindsight: Lucretius was not to know how far Virgil would smoothe the hexameter, and if he did not adopt the latest refinements of some contemporary poets, that is nothing exceptional. E. J. Kenney's fine account of his language and metre (commentary on Book 3 (1971), 20 ff.) comes close to this position: 'If Lucretius' style, compared with that of Cicero, seems "archaic", that is no more than a summary and somewhat misleading way of saying that he adhered to certain usages and forms which were already being discarded in his own day because by doing so he was able to communicate what he had to say more directly and forcibly' (22). But the conventional view seems more or less justified. (1) Some of Lucretius' grammar, like the genitive ending in *-ai* and the elision of final *s* (as in 'omnibu' rebus'), is considered by Cicero to be old-fashioned. (2) Cicero's youthful translation of Aratus does use these forms, but the style of its hexameters is none the less closer to Virgil's—perhaps a quarter of a century before Lucretius wrote. (Judgement may be affected by dating, however: E. Courtney (*The Fragmentary Latin Poets* (Oxford, 1993), 171) suggests that *De Rerum Natura* should be placed in the later 60s.) (3) As Kenney himself points out (23), a passage of high pathos like that on Iphigenia contains not one verse-ending that is 'irregular' in terms of Virgilian practice. Passages such as that and the one now before us indicate that the roughnesses in Lucretius are consciously sought.

His style in part proclaims the epic dignity of his theme, by allusion to Ennius, in part his intellectual and practical toughness. The epic character and the down-to-earth character may seem opposites, but indeed it is one of his achievements to forge a style that asserts a connection between the two. It should be stressed that he does not 'affect the ancients', as Spenser does, for romantic or sentimental reasons; the antiquarian temper, latent in so many Latin poets, is in him quite absent.

physics, such as we find in pictures of the golden age, would not, upon reflection, be attractive at all. Nature's laws give us the sense of security that comes from the knowledge that things can be thus and not otherwise; at the same time, though apparently restrictive, they make possible variety and particularity. These things are beautiful in themselves, but they are also the necessary condition for that awareness of growth, origin, and individual identity which is part of the pleasure of being human.

Lucretius has made a great discovery: he has learned the beauty of imperfection. It is a discovery that was to be momentous for the young Virgil. Let us sum up the elements in Lucretius' picture. He views nature in terms of growth and process; variety and rhythm; the limits imposed by physical law; the emotional link between man and the world around him realized in his sense of belonging and of individual origin. All of this will be found again, with a difference of temperament and emphasis, in Virgil. Perhaps Virgil's most distinctive contribution to this nexus of feeling will be to link it with the patriotic idea. He will not use the maternal image with Lucretius' insistency, but he will show us that the metaphor implicit in the word 'patria' (fatherland) is not in his hands a dead one. The sense of belonging will be associated with Italy as a whole and with one's own locality or 'patria' within Italy; the idea of variety will be directed to the diversity of Italian landscapes, brought out by vignettes of Italian scenery, sharply particularized; the idea of parenthood will be enlarged into a sense of ancestry, of rootedness in a deep past, solemnized by the nation's history and institutions. Virgil's sense of these things is both original and profound, but without Lucretius it would not have been possible.

The ideas which Lucretius has thus adumbrated at the beginning of his argument are worked into the fabric of the poem, appearing in various contexts and combinations. The maternal metaphor soon returns in a bold image:[91]

> postremo pereunt imbres, ubi eos pater aether
> in gremium matris terrai praecipitavit . . .

Finally, the rains pass away, when father sky has shot them into the lap of mother earth . . .

---

[91] Lucr. 1. 250 f.

The metaphor is taken from the *hieros gamos*, the sacred marriage of sky and earth, which we have already met in Aeschylus and in connection with the deception of Zeus in the *Iliad*. It is more than a poetic flourish: Lucretius' choice of imagery is part of the argument, since his purpose is to show us that his philosophy has the kind of splendour and excitement that we associate with religious ritual and high poetry. When he describes the true nature of the gods in phrases taken almost directly from the *Odyssey*, he demonstrates the high beauty of the Epicurean conception; when he advises us to rebuke ourselves in terms which echo the words which Achilles speaks to Lycaon before killing him, he gives to the stern fact of mortality a consolatory grandeur.[92] Here, similarly, the image instructs us to regard with veneration the atomic activities which govern the world.

But it also gives a new twist to the parental metaphor. For this father and mother are the parents not of one or two individuals but of all natural processes; they are Zeus and Demeter (or in Roman terms, Jupiter and Ceres). In part their divinity teaches us to reverence the natural order; but since they are the father and mother of all plants and creatures, ourselves included, their presence suggests a kinship between all living things. Before, the maternal image brought out our sense of individuality; now it brings us into community with nature as a whole. It is a theme which Lucretius will enlarge as the poem proceeds.

For the moment he continues with these lines:[93]

> at nitidae surgunt fruges ramique virescunt
> arboribus, crescunt ipsae fetuque gravantur;
> *hinc* alitur porro nostrum genus atque ferarum,
> *hinc* laetas urbis pueris florere videmus
> frondiferasque novis avibus canere undique silvas;
> *hinc* fessae pecudes pingui per pabula laeta
> corpora deponunt et candens lacteus umor
> uberibus manat distentis; *hinc* nova proles
> artubus infirmis teneras lasciva per herbas
> ludit lacte mero mentis perculsa novellas.

But the bright crops spring up and the branches on the trees become green, the trees themselves grow and get heavy with fruit; thanks to this our kind and beasts after their kind are nourished, thanks to this we see flourishing cities bloom with children and leafy woods ring on all sides with the

---

[92] See above, p. 230, and below, p. 272.　　[93] Lucr. I. 252–61.

song of birds; thanks to this the herds, weary with fatness, lay down their bodies in the rich fields and the white milky stream trickles from their swollen udders; thanks to this the new offspring gambol wantonly on their tottering legs across the tender grass, their new little brains knocked sideways by pure milk.

The length and amplitude of the sentence match nature's abundance. The fourfold repetition of 'hinc' expresses the poet's urgent enthusiasm, but it is also expansive, the word recurring at ever larger intervals, first after one line, then after two, then after more than two and a half. The sentence explores diversity and unity. First come a series of dynamic verbs. The upward thrust of the crops (surgunt) answers to the downward thrust of god's rain (praecipitavit); the inceptive form of 'virescunt', echoed in 'crescunt', expresses process; 'fetuque gravantur' balances the theme of dynamism with the theme of heaviness, and develops the maternal idea through the image of pregnancy.[94] The imagery of the sentence has moved from conception (in gremium matris . . . praecipitavit) to pregnancy; now it moves from pregnancy to nursing (alitur) and thence to youth or boyhood (pueris); meanwhile the subject is moving from rain to plants, from plants to men and beasts, and thence to cities. Variety and unity are blent together: plants and animals, man and beast, nature and culture are all part of a cycle of growth, springing from the father's fertilizing rain. The community of all things is shown partly in the picture of the birds—instead of saying prosaically that birds sing in the woods Lucretius has the woods sing with birds, a phrase which suggests the harmony of nature animate and inanimate—but most strikingly in the language of line 255. The bold metaphor of cities flowering with children is reinforced by the adjective 'laetus'; its basic meaning, 'fertile', is strongly felt in the context.[95] Virgil will learn from this: the ambiguity in 'laetus'—both 'fertile' and 'glad'—will be a key to the Georgics; the metaphor of fertility and flowering will be used to bind civilization to the land in the Aeneid.[96] Here in De Rerum Natura the idea that the enlargement of cities is like the enlargement of crops and fruits, the product of rain falling upon soil, is arresting; it has a moral and emotional content, but it is also true to the facts of Epicurus' physics, because the rainfall is an atomic

---

[94] English translation cannot easily bring out the double meaning of the words: 'grow laden with fruit', 'grow heavy with child'.

[95] No doubt 'pueris' should be taken with 'florere' (flower with children), but we shall also hear it with 'laetas' (towns rich in children).   [96] See below, pp. 331 ff., 473.

process which, by setting in motion other atomic processes, leads ultimately to all these diverse effects.

The variety of nature is further explored in the latter part of the sentence. The creatures of the air, singing in the branches, are realized in a single line which is wholly dactylic, while the ruminants of the field, weary and heavy with milk, are introduced in a line of dragging heterodyne rhythm, and their description sprawls across more than two and a half lines, ending with the weight and ooziness expressed in the long syllables of 'manat distentis'; then energy comes back as Lucretius turns from the cows to their calves. The metaphor in 'perculsa' takes us back to the proem;[97] its fierceness, placed beside the homely, sentimental diminutive 'novellas', is curiously touching. The epithet 'merus' (pure, unmixed), usually and more naturally applied to wine rather than milk, glances at the idea of intoxication:[98] a faint hint of violence mingles with an implied and playful comparison of the calves' staggering movements to a drunk's progress. Again tenderness blends with force; we may think back to the beginning of the sentence, where the awesome might of nature's sexual act is conveyed by the rapid homodyne rhythm and shower of voiceless plosive consonants in 'terrai praecipitavit'.

The passage is plainly a purple patch; every reader understands that Lucretius' picture is meant to appear attractive and exciting. But the very expansiveness serves the purpose of a further emotional argument; for the paragraph ends,[99]

> haud igitur penitus pereunt quaecumque videntur,
> quando alid ex alio reficit natura nec ullam
> rem gigni patitur nisi morte adiuta aliena.

So all things that are seen do not perish altogether, since nature freshly makes one thing out of another, and allows nothing to be begotten without the help of another thing's death.

Here Lucretius says two things: first that there is no death; second, that without death there can be no birth. There is of course no contradiction, as he is talking about different kinds of death, but by his

---

[97] Lucr. 1. 13.

[98] This observation is pilfered from D. West, *The Imagery and Poetry of Lucretius* (Edinburgh, 1969), 6. 'Merum' is used as a noun to mean wine; that 'merus' as an adjective is strongly associated with wine is shown by Ovid's joke: 'He shuns wine and abstemiously enjoys undiluted water (meris . . . undis)' (*Met.* 15. 323, contrasted with 'mera vina' (undiluted wine) at 331). [99] Lucr. 1. 262–4.

form of expression change and changelessness are once more brought
pointedly together. The imperishability of atoms has already been
offered for our comfort; but now there is added to it a new kind
of consolation. The death of individual beings—that form of death
which is the necessary condition for new birth—has come to seem
part of a process which is good and pleasing; death is something in
which we, so to speak, have an interest. To put the matter in Epicurean
terms: we pursue pleasure, and affection for our kindred is a natural
source of pleasure to us. Friendship played a large part in Epicurus'
teaching, and Lucretius is showing us that we are 'friends of the earth',
bound to it by ties of kinship, since all living things have a common
parentage. This idea, implicit here, will be enlarged and made explicit
in the second book. Thus we are invited to accept, maybe even to
welcome, the mortality of individual creatures which is an essential
element in that life of universal nature of which we are a part.

Lucretius lays his schemes deep and matures them slowly. He is
not yet ready to confront us directly with the fact of our own mortality, but he is beginning to develop a complex of ideas which will
come to their climax in the diatribe on death in the third book.
That passage is of central importance to the entire work; but we
should equally notice that the themes which we have been tracing
find their way into the poem's ordinary texture. Thus in the course
of arguing for the indivisibility of atoms, he writes,[100]

> at nunc nimirum frangendi reddita *finis*
> *certa* manet, quoniam refici rem quamque videmus
> et *finita* simul *generatim* tempora rebus
> stare, quibus possint aevi contingere *florem*.

As it is, a permanently firm limit to division is ordained, since we see each
thing being made anew, and things having their definite times at which
they can attain the flower of their life, according to their kind.

There is no need to labour the ways in which this echoes earlier
ideas. Out of context, the sentence seems unremarkable; within the
poem it is resonant with emotional complexity. And so the ordinary business of the didactic poem is irradiated with a warmth of
feeling. This is done in part by building up a field of force around
common words; Virgil was to do the same in the *Georgics*.

We can see the fibres interwoven in Lucretius' poetic thought as
he moves the argument onward:[101]

[100] Lucr. I. 561–4.   [101] Lucr. I. 581–98.

at quoniam fragili natura praedita constant,
discrepat aeternum tempus potuisse manere
innumerabilibus plagis vexata per aevum.
denique iam quoniam *generatim* reddita *finis*
crescendi rebus constat *vitamque tenendi*,   585
et quid quaeque queant per *foedera* naturai,
quid porro nequeant, *sancitum* quandoquidem exstat,
nec *commutatur* quicquam, quin omnia constant
usque adeo, *variae* volucres ut in ordine cunctae
ostendant maculas *generalis* corpore inesse,   590
immutabili' materiae quoque corpus habere
debent nimirum. nam si primordia rerum
commutari aliqua possent ratione revicta,
incertum quoque iam constet quid possit oriri,
quid nequeat, *finita* potestas denique cuique   595
quanam sit ratione atque *alte terminus haerens*,
nec totiens possent *generatim* saecla referre
naturam mores victum motusque *parentum*.

But once bodies are supposedly endowed with a breakable nature, it is inconsistent to imagine that they could have endured for eternity, when harried across the ages by an infinite number of blows. Again, since there is a limit to their growth and maintenance of life established for things according to their kind, and since it stands ordained by the decrees of nature what each kind can and cannot do, and nothing is changed, but rather all things remain constant to such an extent that the diverse birds all in their due order show that the speckles marking their kind are on their bodies, then they must undoubtedly also have a body of unchanging matter. For if the first elements of things could be overcome and changed in some way, it would also now be uncertain what could come into being and what could not, and indeed on what principle each thing had its power delimited and its deep-set boundary stone, nor could the generations so often reproduce after their kind the nature, habits, way of living, and movements of their parents.

The first of these sentences conveys the poet's feeling for time and multiplicity and the immense scale of the universe in both spatial and temporal terms; the favourite alliteration upon *m* and *n* and the vast adjective 'innumerabilibus', spreading across half a line, express his delight in the contemplation of these infinitudes. From infinity he moves characteristically to limits ('finis' in 584, echoed by 'finita potestas' in 595). This idea is made more vivid by the legal metaphor in 'foedera' (586), and further fortified by 'sancitum' in the next line, a word drawn from the area where law and religion meet.[102] The emotive blend of the legal and the sacral is heard again in 'alte terminus haerens' (596), a phrase reverberant with the powerful feelings of the proem.[103] As we have learnt by now, those apparent opposites, limit and limitlessness, are bound together by the theme of immutability; this first appears explicitly at 588 (nec commutatur quicquam, quin . . .), to be echoed in 'immutabili'' and 'commutari'.[104] At once (and again this is characteristic of Lucretius' pattern of thought) immutability is exemplified in the variety of the living world (variae volucres), and this variety is brilliantly visualized in the speckles on the birds' bodies; no illustration could more sharply bring out that union of diversity and fixed law which is the paradoxical glory of the world. 'Generalis' here echoes 'generatim' in 584; literally we may translate 'after their kind', but within the complex of associations formed by the poem, words with the *gen-* root suggest also birth, process, generation (a suggestion here reinforced by 'crescendi' and 'vitamque tenendi' in the next line). 'Generatim' returns at 597, rounding off the section by bringing it back to its starting-point. And yet we do not simply end where we began, for the paragraph closes, forcefully, with the emotive word 'parentum'. The idea of parenthood, which may well have seemed to lie beneath the paragraph as a whole, at last breaks the surface.

It should be stressed that this is a paragraph of ordinary, straight-forward argument. Perhaps only 'foedera', 'sancitum', and 'alte terminus haerens' have obvious metaphorical colour, but it is enough to awaken, so to speak, the metaphors dormant in such words as 'corpora' and 'generatim'. We sense Lucretius' pleasure in the world beneath his largely descriptive surface, but largely because of the setting within the poem as a whole. Some thoughts and phrases in this paragraph pick up earlier ideas, others look forward to later books. The argumentative passages and the purple patches are interdependent in establishing a distinctive vision of the world.

---

[102] Perhaps the excessive alliteration of *qu*, together with the genitive in -*ai*, imparts an antique religious flavour.

[103] The whole line is repeated from I. 77, discussed above.

[104] Lines 591, 593.

CHAPTER 6

A Conversion Experience:
The Conquest of Death and the
Pleasures of Life

Ich beschwöre euch, meine Brüder, bleibt der Erde treu and
glaubt denen nicht, welche euch von überirdischen Hoffnungen
reden!

(Nietzsche)

I count poetical vision and even amatory passion the friends of
religion . . . the lover and the poet at least look at something
and see it. And the chief impediment to religion in this age, I
often think, is that no one ever looks at anything at all: not so
as to contemplate it, to apprehend what it is to be that thing,
and plumb, if he can, the deep fact of its individual existence.

(Austin Farrer)

Lucretius' second book proclaims more loudly some of the emotional arguments introduced in the first. Whereas the first book
describes the nature of atoms, the second deals with their movement, and after an introduction celebrating the blessings of philosophical wisdom, the poet sets out the book's purpose. The reader,
now immersed in Lucretius' thought world, quickly recognizes much
that is familiar: the idea of compulsive force, the spawning of procreative imagery, the delight in immensity (expressed in the assonance
of nasal consonants), the combination of flux and permanence:[1]

> nunc age, quo motu *genitalia* materiai
> corpora res varias *gignant genitas*que resolvant
> et qua *vi* facere id *cogantur* quaeque sit ollis
> reddita *mobilitas magnum* per *inane meandi,*
> expediam . . .

[1] Lucr. 2. 62–6.

Come now, I shall set out by what motion the generative bodies of matter beget diverse things and break apart those that have been begotten, by what force they are compelled to do this, and what speed of travelling through the great void is granted them . . .

There must be void in between the atoms, he explains, since we see all things diminish and as it were flow away in the long lapse of time.[2] A melancholy truth, might we think?—but mark how he continues:[3]

> cum tamen incolumis videatur summa manere
> propterea quia, quae decedunt corpora cuique,
> unde abeunt minuunt, quo venere augmine donant,
> illa senescere at haec contra florescere cogunt,
> nec remorantur ibi. sic rerum summa novatur
> semper, et inter se mortales mutua vivunt.
> augescunt aliae gentes, aliae minuuntur
> inque brevi spatio mutantur saecla animantum
> et quasi cursores vitai lampada tradunt.

And yet the sum of things is seen to remain untouched, for the reason that when bodies depart from a thing, they diminish the thing from which they go and benefit with increase that to which they have come, compelling the former to grow old and the latter correspondingly to flourish, and yet do not linger there either. Thus the sum of things is ever made new, and mortal beings live by mutual exchange among themselves. Some races increase, others lessen, and in a short space the generations of living things change and like runners hand over the torch of life.

The first of these sentences is essentially descriptive and practical; yet there are touches in it which imply an emotional response to the facts which it presents. 'Incolumis' (safe, unharmed) suggests the idea of security with which Lucretius has invested the fact of the universe's ultimate indestructibility, 'donant' (bestow) the beneficence of nature's flux. The inceptive form of 'senescere' and 'florescere' reminds us of his pleasure in process. The first of these verbs is most naturally applied to human beings, the second to plants; in combination they reassert the unity and interdependence of all living things, animate and inanimate alike. And they come in a sequence of lines which grow in emotional force: repeating the idea factually expressed in the line before, they give it a new warmth. This repetition has a subtle effect. Line 73 follows the movement of the atoms:

---

[2] Lucr. 2. 67–70.   [3] Lucr. 2. 71–9.

first they leave one object, then they attach themselves to another. Line 74, as a matter of course, falls into the same pattern; yet because of the metaphor which it contains, the natural order seems to be reversed. It is natural to speak of rise and fall, growth and decay; such is the rhythm of all mortal things. Lucretius reverses the order: age comes first, then the flowering of fresh growth. This gives a wonderful buoyancy to the verse; instead of the dying fall which we might expect, old age is seen merely as a beginning, the source of new youthfulness. Life's transitoriness had not been put in a setting of such vigour since Homer likened the generations of men to those of leaves: the wind scatters them, but the forest buds and puts forth more, when the season of spring comes round again.[4] Other poets who took up Homer's simile and developed it rested in autumnal reverie, saying nothing of spring's return; Lucretius alone joins Homer in asserting that though men perish, man is immortal. But as yet he is still easing us gradually towards the acceptance of death, a state of mind from which we may naturally recoil: he is not yet talking specifically about humanity, but about all living things.

Fired with enthusiasm, he now enlarges his theme's emotional content: 'sic rerum summa novatur | semper . . .' In the luxurious flow of the phrase across the line-ending, to conclude triumphantly upon the emphatic 'semper', how he exults in the glory of the world's everlasting freshness. We should remember the phrase: it will be echoed in a climactic place.[5] That 'semper', placed as it is, ends the clause not gently but with a new access of force, so that the verse surges onward into the even more dramatic idea that is to follow. The movement of thought has seemed entirely easy and natural, and yet in the course of a very few lines Lucretius has said two startlingly different things about the 'summa rerum': first that it remains unchanged; second, that it is always new. There indeed is the grand paradox of atomism. Of course, a more prosaic writer could resolve it easily enough by saying that the totality of atoms does not change but the subordinate parts of that totality do. But Lucretius has chosen to seek out the paradox, to dramatize the freshness of eternity; it is a superb stroke that the word 'semper' is detached from the idea of perennity and given to the idea of change. In the old mythology immortal youth was the unique privilege of the gods; now our own world possesses it.

---

[4] Il. 6. 146–9 (quoted below, p. 659, with references to variations on the theme by later poets).   [5] See below, p. 269.

Furthermore, the eternal newness is bound up in the great co-operation of all living beings: 'inter se mortales mutua vivunt'—no translation can fully convey the sense of unity and community which these words imply. We are being prepared to feel that we have an interest of a sort in the mortality of everything that has life. At line 77 Lucretius picks up the theme of line 74. His thought follows a chiastic pattern: he moves from fall and rise to rise and fall, adding that life is only for a short space of time. But this more familiar turn of thought is purged of its natural melancholy, partly because of what has gone before, partly because he presses forward to end his sentence on an energetic note. 'Mutantur' echoes 'mutua', two lines above; our mutability, not naturally welcome to us, is made to feel more attractive because it is the necessary condition for the community and interdependence of life as a whole. And while the sound of 'mutua' is echoed in 'mutantur' the emotional idea implicit within it is developed in the extraordinary and brilliant metaphor with which Lucretius concludes. The relay runner wants to hand on his torch as quickly as he can: he is glad for his own race to be over, so that his team may win. Lucretius suggests to us (what he will not say directly) that we too are part of a team, that we can as it were desire our own extinction so that the totality of which we are part may survive and flourish.

Already it may be apparent that Lucretius is bringing his feeling for the natural world into connection with his project to defeat the dread of death; but we must wait until the third book for the threads to be drawn together. Meanwhile in the second book he continues to embed his emotional argument within his scientific exposition. As he begins a practical discussion of the shapes of atoms, we hear some larger resonances:[6]

> nunc age iam deinceps cunctarum exordia rerum
> qualia sint et quam longe distantia formis
> percipe, *multigenis* quam sint *variata* figuris . . .

Come now, learn next of what kinds the beginnings of all things are and how far they differ in form and how they are diversified by shapes of various sorts . . .

In the last of these lines quantity, creative activity, and variety are meshed together through 'multi-', 'gen-', and 'variata', and these themes continue to surface in the lines that follow; thus 'copia tanta',

---

[6] Lucr. 2. 333–5.

'such abundant quantity' at 338. Soon he starts to illustrate his argument from organic life: from human beings, fish, flocks, herds and
birds.[7] He is beginning to talk explicitly about mankind (at 67 ff.
he talked very generally, about all living things, and it was left to us
to apply the moral to our own species if we chose), but the reference to the human race is still light and brief; he passes straight on
to other creatures, and it is on birds that he prefers to expand:[8]

> et variae volucres, laetantia quae loca aquarum
> concelebrant circum ripas fontisque lacusque,
> et quae pervulgant nemora avia pervolitantes . . .

And the diverse birds which throng the gladdening wetlands, around banks,
springs and lakes, and which people pathless forests, flitting through them . . .

We have already met the 'variae volucres' in the first book,[9] and
here as there they are well chosen for their purpose, because we can
think both of the diversity of their species and the varied dapplings
of their bodies; Virgil will remember these words and their implications.[10] Next Lucretius at last makes explicit what he so suggestively
implied in the first book, that difference and variety are necessary
for the sense of motherhood—for the mother to know her offspring,
and the offspring its dam:[11]

> quorum unum quidvis generatim sumere perge,
> invenies tamen inter se *differre* figuris.
> nec ratione alia proles cognoscere *matrem*
> nec *mater* posset prolem . . .

Then go and take any one of these, of some particular kind, and you will
still find that they differ in form one from another. In no other way could
the mother know its offspring or the offspring its mother . . .

Lucretius goes on to illustrate his point in one of his best-known
passages, depicting a cow searching piteously for her lost calf; the
passage is extended a little beyond what is strictly necessary for the
argument, but it is none the less held within a paragraph of sober
scientific exposition, and it strengthens the emotional case by engaging

---

[7] Lucr. 2. 342 ff.   [8] Lucr. 2. 344–6.   [9] Lucr. 1. 589.
[10] 'variae . . . volucres' come at *Aen.* 7. 32 f. The same words are at *Geo.* 1. 383. 'aut
arguta lacus *circumvolitavit* hirundo' (Or the twittering swallow flits around the ponds) at
Geo 1. 377 might owe something to a memory of Lucr. 2. 346; Virgil is usually thought
to have filched this line unaltered from Varro Atacinus, but see the doubts of H. D. Jocelyn,
'Ancient Scholarship and Virgil's Use of Republican Latin Poetry II', *CQ* NS 15 (1965),
126–44, at 139 f.   [11] Lucr. 2. 347–50.

our feelings on behalf of the force and pathos of motherhood.[12] Just
before he describes the cow, he alludes again to mankind, but still
briefly and in passing: mother and offspring recognize one another,
he observes, 'just as men do'.[13] And as he leaves the cow, another
of the ideas implicit in the first book comes to the surface: that motherhood is caught up with the notions of familiarity and belonging:[14]

> nec vitulorum aliae species per pabula laeta
> derivare queunt animum curaque levare:
> usque adeo quiddam *proprium notumque* requirit.

Nor can the sight of other calves in the rich pastures divert her mind or
lighten it of its grief: so much does she seek for something that is her
own and known to her.

Later in the book he binds together the themes of earth and parenthood, of the interplay between universality and particularity, of
seed, fixity, growth, and maternity; the repetitions of 'omnis' and
'certus' recall the first book:[15]

> . . . per *terras omniparentis.*
> quorum nil fieri manifestum est, *omnia* quando
> *seminibus certis certa genetrice creata*
> conservare genus *crescentia* posse videmus.
> scilicet id *certa* fieri ratione necessust.
> nam sua cuique cibis ex *omnibus* intus in artus
> corpora discedunt . . .

. . . throughout the lands, parents of all things. But it is evident that none
of these things happens, since we see that all things are born from fixed
seeds and a fixed mother, and can preserve their kind as they grow. Clearly
this must come about in a fixed manner. For the bodies proper to each
thing pass away from all of its food and are absorbed into its frame . . .

Taken on its own, this seems a passage of routine scientific argument; it gains its emotional significance from its place within the
architectonics of the whole poem.

   Such passages prepare the way for one of the most remarkable
episodes in the book. Though Lucretius integrates his emotional theme
into his rational argument with great skill, one may still feel that this

---

[12] He also seizes a chance to prick the superstitious: the calf has been the victim at a
sacrifice. He cannot press the point: Epicurus approved the outward show of conventional
religion.   [13] 'Nec minus atque homines', 2. 351.
[14] Lucr. 2. 364–6.   [15] Lucr. 2. 706–12.

paragraph stands out a little oddly in its context; its importance to him goes well beyond the requirements of his scientific exposition:[16]

> denique caelesti sumus omnes *Semine* oriundi;
> omnibus ille idem *pater* est, unde *alma* liquentis
> umoris guttas *mater* cum *terra* recepit,
> *feta parit* nitidas fruges arbustaque *laeta*
> et genus humanum, *parit omnia* saecla ferarum,
> pabula cum praebet quibus *omnes* corpora pascunt
> et dulcem ducunt vitam prolemque propagant;
> quapropter merito *maternum* nomen adepta est.
> cedit item retro, de terra quod fuit ante,
> in terras et quod missumst ex aetheris oris,
> id rursum caeli rellatum templa receptant.

Last, we are all sprung from heavenly seed; we have all that one father from whom the nourishing mother, the earth, receives the liquid drops of moisture and then teeming brings forth the healthy crops, the vigorous trees and the human race; she brings forth all the races of wild beasts, affording the food with which they nourish their bodies, draw the goodness of life, and beget their offspring; for which reason she has rightly obtained the name of mother. Likewise, that which was before from the earth, returns to the earth, and that which was sent from the shores of the sky is taken back again and the temples of heaven once more receive it.

Despite this passage's dense and complex texture, there is probably no need to analyse it in great detail because most of its many interwoven strands are by now familiar to us. A few points may be singled out. The picture of father sky and mother earth echoes the metaphor of the first book, drawn, as we have seen, from the religious sphere.[17] This is now brought together with the idea of unity and community celebrated earlier in the second book. But now Lucretius dares to speak directly of 'us'; and this takes the emotional argument much further forward. We all have the same father and mother—in other words, we are all one single family—and 'we', it transpires, are not the human race alone but all living things, beasts, crops and trees. It is hardly possible to overstate the strangeness and boldness of this idea in Lucretius' time. 'We are all children of one heavenly father'—the almost biblical flavour of the sentiment is coincidental; and yet there is a sense in which it is not altogether an accident. Like the early Christians Lucretius conveys two ideas: that

---

[16] Lucr. 2. 991–1001.   [17] Lucr. 1. 250 f.

each of us individually has a kind of heavenly ancestry; and that collectively we are members of one community, family or 'church'. Lucretius, however, goes further in giving us a kinship not just with humanity but with all life. We are sprung of heavenly seed, and what has come from heaven is taken back into it again—this sounds for a moment closer to Plato than to Epicurean materialism. Later in the paragraph Lucretius warns us to grasp the physical facts,[18]

> neve putes aeterna penes residere potesse
> corpora prima quod in summis fluitare videmus
> rebus et interdum nasci subitoque perire.

. . . And so that you may not think that what we see floating on the surface of things and sometimes being born and perishing on a sudden abides in the possession of the eternal first bodies.

This language, which seems momentarily to suggest the superficiality of sense impressions, could almost fit the Platonist idea that the phenomena accessible to our senses are but temporary modes of an eternal, absolute being. While maintaining Epicurus' doctrines, Lucretius none the less advances to seize imaginative and spiritual areas hitherto occupied by philosophies antithetical to his master's. We have already met his religious sense and his sense of unity or community; now he brings them together, and combines them with a materialist philosophy. The amalgam is radically new.

Line 998 will be echoed twice in the fifth book, where the theme of the earth's motherhood returns once more, and with stronger emphasis than ever:[19]

> linquitur ut merito maternum nomen adepta
> terra sit, e terra quoniam sunt cuncta creata.
>
> quare etiam atque etiam maternum nomen adepta
> terra tenet merito, quoniam genus ipsa creavit
> humanum atque animal prope certo tempore fudit
> omne . . .

It remains that the earth has rightly obtained the name of mother, since out of the earth all things have been created . . . Therefore, again and again, the earth has rightly obtained and keeps the name of mother, since she herself created the human race and almost at a fixed time brought forth every animal . . .

[18] Lucr. 2. 1010–12.   [19] Lucr. 5. 795 f., 821–4.

Between these two sentences Lucretius expounds his origin of species: the strange theory that wombs grew from the ground and out of these creatures were born. The earth then opened its pores and gave forth a sap very like milk, just as a woman is filled with milk when she has given birth. And so the maternal theme comes to its culmination in the revelation that the earth is our mother in a sense that is very nearly literal. In the *Aeneid* Virgil will value the idea of manhood growing out of the land, but he will have to transmute it into metaphor.[20] A little later Lucretius describes the hardihood of early man, formed as he was from the hard ground:[21]

> at genus humanum multo fuit illud in arvis
> durius, ut decuit, tellus quod dura creasset,
> et maioribus et solidis magis ossibus intus
> fundatum, validis aptum per viscera nervis, . . .

The human race then in the fields was much harder, as was fitting, since the hard earth had created it, and it was built up with bigger and more solid bones inside, bound together by strong sinews passing through the flesh . . .

In the *Georgics* Virgil will again value the closeness of this bond between tough men and tough nature; since he has not Lucretius' physical theory to account for it, he mythologizes it: mankind is hard because made from the hard stones which Deucalion and Pyrrha threw behind them.[22] Myth takes the place of science; but within the myth it remains true that man is literally made out of the landscape. Virgil does all that he can to preserve the drama, strength and intimacy of Lucretius' conception.

In the fifth book Lucretius returns also to spring and the rhythm of the seasons:[23]

> it vér ét Vénus, ét Véneris praenuntius ante
> pennatus graditur, Zephyri vestigia propter
> Flora quibus mater praespargens ante viai
> cuncta coloribus egregiis et odoribus opplet.

Spring comes, and Venus too, and Venus' winged harbinger advances before them; for whom mother Flora, coming close on the steps of Zephyrus, strewing all their path before them, fills it with glorious colours and scents.

He personifies freely; and the tone, part fanciful, part quaint, anticipates the exquisite mythologizing of Horace's spring ode to Sestius,

---

[20] See below, pp. 472 f.   [21] Lucr. 5. 925–8.
[22] *Geo.* 1. 62 ff.   [23] Lucr. 5. 737–40.

Solvitur acris hiems.[24] Venus as the spring recalls the poem's beginning.[25] Though pretty and decorative, Lucretius' idea here still has
force in it: there is a stress on six of his first seven syllables, enhan-
cing the eager alliteration of *v* and *t* and the springing, dancing rhythm
of mingled spondees and dactyls. Mother Flora presses on the steps
of Zephyrus: the good lady is caught up in the happy energy.

But this time Lucretius is not concerned with the spring alone. His
purpose is to show that things are brought to birth 'certo . . . ordine',
in fixed sequence,[26] and he passes on to the other seasons. In the
first book the interchange of spring, summer and autumn was evoked
seductively, the poet needing, thus early in his argument, to cajole
us into sharing his affection for the natural world;[27] now there is a
robuster realism. The heat of the summer is parching, and Ceres is
dusty (another matron seen in a mildly undignified light); autumn
leads on to wind and storm and finally to Winter, whose teeth, in
a last quaint personification, chatter with the cold.[28] The tone is realist, but the note of affection can still be heard underneath. And he
ends by sounding another leitmotiv once more, bringing us back
to the unity of rhythm and fixity, change and changelessness, even
tolerating a weak last line for the sake of the emphasis:[29]

> quo minus est mirum si certo tempore luna
> gignitur et certo deletur tempore rursus,
> cum fieri possint tam certo tempore multa.

So it is less wonderful if the moon is born and blotted out again at a fixed
time, since so many things can come about at a fixed time.

Before following Lucretius' strategy to persuade us that death is
not an ill through to its culmination in the third book we might
pause to appreciate his intellectual originality. The great weakness of
Epicureanism was not, as is sometimes said, that it was equivocal in

---

[24] *Carm.* 1. 4. If Horace thought of Lucretius, it would be a pleasant irony that the
robust forebear directed him to a delicacy of fancy lighter than is usual with him.

[25] Though not too much should be made of this. In the proem Lucretius conflates Venus
the spring goddess with Venus the force of nature as a whole. Venus at the beginning is
a marvellously complex symbol, but once we have got beyond the first book she has served
her turn, and Lucretius does not need her again. The Venus of the fifth book merely picks
up, briefly, one element from the Venus of the opening; we are not to overload this engaging passage by importing into it further significances. Venus in the fourth book stands
simply for sexual desire. To suppose that the flat Venus of Book 4 in some way 'corrects'
the deep, subtle and complex Venus of Book 1 is to suppose Lucretius a bungler.

[26] Lucr. 5. 735.   [27] Lucr. 1. 174 f.

[28] Lucr. 5. 741–7.   [29] Lucr. 5. 748–50.

its attitude to pleasure, half insisting on the centrality of physical experience, half recoiling from it.[30] The fact that Epicurus placed a comparatively low value on what the man in the street considers to be pleasure may be surprising, but it is not illogical. Epicurus holds that we live in an imperfect world, that we are creatures liable to pleasure and pain, that we have potentially disorderly appetites, and that we must make the best sense we can of the situation in which we find ourselves. Given these premisses, the conclusion that we shall live best by moderating our physical appetites and developing purely mental pleasures is in no way contrary to reason. Some may think this approach to life pusillanimous, a failure of nerve; others may reckon that whether it be right or wrong, the idea that the greatest happiness is to be found in the absence of pain and a calm of mind fortified by the pleasures of friendship and memory is neither ignoble nor obviously absurd.[31]

Epicurus' problem was rather to account for altruism. His project to convert man to true philosophy and thus bring him happiness seems plainly altruistic, and this cannot readily be fitted into a system in which each individual pursues his own pleasure. It is hard to see what answer Epicurus could have given to the problem other than to say that the philosophic man gets pleasure from persuading other people of the truth; it would simply be a coincidence that what the philosopher finds agreeable is also beneficial to others. This would be a very weak response, the more so since Epicureanism is centrally concerned with motive, and the motive of the philosophic missionary remains clearly altruistic; even if it is true that the philosopher gets pleasure in the process, that pleasure would be a by-product, not the mainspring of his action. Epicurus does not have the concept of the greatest happiness of the greatest number, which, however problematic in practice, does offer to reconcile a hedonist view of human ends with a concern for others; for him the self, within its limits, is dominant and absolute. No one has reasonable

[30] For this claim, see e.g. the thoughtful article of P. de Lacy, 'Process and Value, an Epicurean Dilemma', *TAPA* 88 (1957), 114–26.

[31] Age may influence judgement. At the age of 20 Epicurus' idea of happiness might seem wildly unreal, at 40 not unreasonable, at 90 plain common sense. Experience will also have its effect. Convalescence after serious illness can produce moments of pure felicity that seem at the time to surpass any kinetic pleasure. (Beethoven's *Heiliger Dankgesang* (on recovery from illness), containing perhaps the finest realization of pure serenity in art, seems to express this feeling.) It is a mental experience inseparable from bodily experience, a gratitude for being an animal.

grounds, it appears, to consult anyone's happiness except his own. This dominance of the self also makes it harder to combat the dread of death: if life is pleasurable and if our own pleasure is the only good that we may rationally consider, it is difficult to see that we should not regret our life's termination. Epicurus did essay some hedonist arguments against the dislike of death; Lucretius echoes them, but he has also, as we shall see, a further strategy of his own.

Already in his second book he is trying to ease the problem of altruism, and ultimately the dread of death, by breaching the wall between the self and everything outside it. We are to see ourselves as part of a greater whole whose mutability, mortality and perennial newness we may enjoy. He cannot directly say, 'You should think of other people', because his philosophy gives him no reason so to argue. He cannot directly say, 'If you would only feel yourselves to be part of nature as a whole, you would face your extinction more cheerfully', because one cannot command a person into a feeling.[32] What he can try to do is to present the facts in so captivating a light that our feelings may be changed. His belief is that reality may be apprehended in a poetic and imaginative way, and through poetry and imagination become conformable to our desire. This is a belief that can be enforced not by assertion (which is why no paraphrase of Lucretius can convey his meaning) but only through poetic creation itself. It is commonly said that the poetry and philosophy in Lucretius are inseparable; which seems usually to mean that his philosophical arguments are expressed in skilful verse and diversified by splendid set-pieces in praise of nature or Epicurus. That much is true, more or less, but it is a limited truth, for his poem is one of those rare cases where the medium genuinely is the message: Lucretius transforms Epicureanism by revealing it as a poetic faith, and there could be no way of doing this other than by writing a poetic masterpiece. While remaining wholly faithful to his master, he radically reinterprets him; which is in itself an intellectual feat of no mean order. The force and novelty of this project seem to go unrecognized; so far are the philosophy and the poetry in practice studied apart.

[32] He later admits the problem: people have differing temperaments, and these have physical causes—the shape of the atoms that make up their *animus*; how then can reason prevail over their characteristic emotions: anger, timidity, passivity, or whatever? His answer (3. 319–22) is hurried and flimsy: reason cannot do everything, but in practice it does enough to enable us to live the philosophic life. Here he is dutifully following one of Epicurus' arguments, but his brevity may indicate some discomfort.

Epicurus says that death is nothing to us;[33] Lucretius adds the implication that our own deaths will be the less inclined to distress us if we experience our lives as part of a greater life which is ever safe, strong and new. Among more recent philosophers, this cast of thought most suggests Spinoza, whose pantheist metaphysics declare that the pains, changes, and chances of our world are to be held of no account because they are all modes of an eternal, impassible God. Lucretius, for his part, displays us as part of a continuum, temporary phenomena within an eternal, changeless, impassible order which we are to venerate, as though it were a god, in a spirit of worship. Certainly, he would have regarded almost everything in Spinoza as nonsensical and obscurantist; the oddity of their likeness may bring out his originality. But within the ancient world itself there is another comparison to be drawn: his distinctive tone is heard also in Stoicism, most conspicuously in Marcus Aurelius some two centuries later: 'By the changes of the parts of Universal Nature the whole world continues ever young . . . Now what tends to the advantage of the Whole is ever altogether lovely and in season; therefore for each individual the cessation of his life is no evil . . . rather it is good because it is in due season for the Whole . . . Whenever you feel something hard to bear, you have forgotten . . . the great kinship of man with all mankind . . .'[34] With the teachings of Epicureanism Lucretius fuses a mental disposition more characteristic of Stoicism. His new apprehension of Epicureanism could have come entirely from within himself or it could have been a conscious annexation of a Stoic cast of mind—for our purposes it does not matter which.[35] In either case, it must be stressed that he is not unfaithful to his master. His project may be seen as an attempt—brilliant if ultimately unsuccessful —to heal the greatest weakness in Epicurus' philosophy or as the fusion of Epicureanism with a new imaginative apprehension of the world. From each of these viewpoints his originality is profound.

We have been investigating the place of nature in Lucretius' scheme of things; but this itself cannot be fully understood until it is related to his central project, to free us from the fear of death. These two subjects may not seem to have much obviously in common; but indeed

---

[33] *KD* 2, echoed by Lucr. at 3. 830.   [34] Marc. Aur. (tr. Farquharson) 12. 23, 26.
[35] This issue is also independent of the question whether any of Lucretius' attacks on other philosophers are aimed at the Stoics. D. Furley argues persuasively that they are not ('Lucretius and the Stoics', *BICS* 13 (1966), 13–33, reprinted in C. J. Classen (ed.), *Probleme der Lukrezforschung* (Hildesheim, 1986), 75–95).

it is one of his achievements to bring them into connection. The task he has set himself is formidably difficult—if the truth be told, impossible. It is convenient, as a kind of shorthand, to talk about the fear of death, but in reality Epicurus, and Lucretius as his disciple, want to go much further: not only to remove the dread of death, but to convince us that our deaths should be a matter of simple indifference to us. This is, on the face of it, a very implausible claim. Epicureanism maintains that human existence is good and that it is wholly extinguished by death. Someone who accepts these premisses may well agree that he has no cause to be frightened by death. But if death is the irrevocable loss of something good, it still seems to be an ill, even if it is an ill that may be faced calmly. Yet Epicureanism goes beyond the claim that we should not fear death; it asserts that we should not even dislike it. Lucretius will have known, as a matter of simple, observable fact, that Epicurus had not persuaded the bulk of mankind that their deaths did not matter to them; he believed that the master's arguments were valid, but he saw that they had not taken effect. Could he, the good disciple, present them in a more persuasive light?

He devotes the greater part of his third book to proving that the mind and soul are material and perishable. This done (as he supposes), he can turn to the conclusion: that we have no cause to be concerned by the fact that we shall die: 'nil igitur mors est ad nos neque pertinet hilum' (So death is nothing to us and matters not a jot).[36] He applies some forensic skill to the suggestion that this conclusion follows simply, as a matter of course. Modern editors have to divide the text into paragraphs, and they naturally mark a new one at this point; commentators explain that here begins the last grand section of the book. Yet Lucretius, who did not have to mark paragraphs, has so arranged matters that we feel no clear break at this point as we are reading: the previous section ends with no peroration, but with a couple of more or less casual points. It is as though we could punctuate thus:[37]

> adde furorem animi proprium atque oblivia rerum,
> adde quod in nigras lethargi mergitur undas;
> nil igitur mors est ad nos . . .

Note too madness as peculiar to the mind and its forgetfulness of things; note also that it sinks into the dark waters of lethargy; so death is nothing to us . . .

---

[36] Lucr. 3. 830.   [37] Lucr. 3. 828 ff.

This is the technique of an assured debater. It is also the proper expression of a larger idea: that our conquest of the fear of death grows, as it were organically, out of a right understanding of the natural world and how it is constructed.

However, Lucretius is of course well aware that the conclusion does not follow self-evidently from the premiss: it must be argued for. And indeed the last part of the book does contain a number of arguments directed to this end, some of them impressive. But the most casual reader must notice that much of the time the poet seems to be trying to overbear us with a kind of grand indignation rather than by logic, and that where the indignation is loudest there are arguments which appear to fail for all too obvious reasons. The poet considers how nature might chide man if she had a voice to speak with. Why lament, mortal? If you have enjoyed your past life, why do you not withdraw like a banqueter full fed with life, to sleep calmly and in safety?[38] The analogy fails for a very plain reason: the feaster retires happily to sleep because he expects to wake again to further pleasures; man dreads death because he expects it to bring all pleasure to an end. Later Lucretius tells us that we can remember the great men who have died—Ancus, Xerxes, Homer, Democritus, Epicurus himself—and then ask ourselves, 'Will you then shrink from dying? will you protest?'[39] This is barely an argument at all: if an experience is disagreeable, it is not made agreeable by the information that good or important people have also undergone it. The point is made plain if we think in terms of physical rather than mental pain: which of us would feel the toothache less if told that Julius Caesar or Francis of Assisi had been a fellow sufferer?

The reader may also note the settings in which these 'arguments' (if such they be) are put. In the former instance the words are given to an imagined speaker, in this case Nature; the rhetoricians called the device prosopopoeia. A function of this device can be seen in Cicero's defence of Caelius, where it is brilliantly used. The orator has set himself an awkward task: he wants to call traditional morality in aid by exciting the jury's indignation against the dissolute lives of Caelius' enemies, especially his former mistress, Clodia; at the same time he must excuse Caelius' association with this raffish circle by appealing to the jury's worldly wisdom. Prosopopoeia helps him to bring off the trick. He imagines the lady's ancestor, Appius Claudius

[38] Lucr. 3. 931–9.   [39] Lucr. 3. 1025 ff.

the Blind, rebuking her degeneracy in tones of sonorous indignation; but then he tries a different tack.[40] Perhaps this archaic, shaggily bearded figure seems too much of another age? If so, let us proceed in more urbane style. 'I shall do away with this uncouth, almost rustic old gentleman'—and Cicero turns instead to quotations from the New Comedy. He has treated Appius Claudius with respect, yet with an affectionate irony; he has had his moral outburst, yet kept it between inverted commas; he can feel for what the old man has said, without absolutely being committed to it.

In a curious way Cicero and Lucretius are here mirror images each of the other. Cicero cannot afford the forensic orator's usual indignation, and so turns to prosopopoeia; the figure in Lucretius' prosopopoeia is likened to a forensic orator: 'What can we reply, except that Nature is bringing a fair suit and setting out a true case in her speech?'[41] The forensic metaphor serves to show how far we have departed from the ordinary tones of philosophical discourse; and the use of prosopopoeia licenses the departure. Nature's castigation is just, the poet tells us; yet he can remain in his own person the coolly reasonable man, leaving her to do the bullying. Like Cicero, he can endorse the sentiments without being wholly committed to their tone. Similarly the 'argument' that we should not make a fuss about death since greater men than us have died is one which we, Lucretius' audience, can rehearse to ourselves;[42] he does not put it forward in his own person.

What then is his purpose? He does not conceal the fact that remonstrance at times takes the place of philosophical proofs; rather he draws attention to it: 'Rightly would she [Nature] rebuke and chide a man.'[43] Let us look back to the start of his argument. The fact that we shall not exist after our deaths, he claims, is no more disturbing than the fact that we did not exist before our births. Indeed, if one considers the variety of atomic movement and the infinite time that has already passed, it seems quite likely that the atoms from which we are now made have been arranged in the same combination before; but since there is no continuity between those past beings and our present selves, the matter does not trouble us.[44]

The argument is straightforwardly rational, and yet Lucretius colours it:[45]

---

[40] Cic. *Cael.* 33 f., 36 f.   [41] Lucr. 3. 950 f.   [42] Lucr. 3. 1024.
[43] Lucr. 3. 963.   [44] Lucr. 3. 832–61.   [45] Lucr. 3. 854–6.

> nam cum respicias immensi temporis omne
> praeteritum spatium, tum motus materiai
> multimodis quam sint . . .

For when you look back at the whole past extent of limitless time, and
then consider how manifold the movements of matter are . . .

The language is purely descriptive, with every word functional—indeed
its philosophical force depends on its being purely descriptive—yet
it is resonant with the emotional tone that three books have gradually
developed. The appeal to multiplicity and immensity, accompanied
by the poet's favourite *m* alliteration, reminds us of the spiritual splendour in which these conceptions have been clothed. Behind the rational
argument we catch the overtones of an emotional argument: that we
should enjoy the nobility of seeing ourselves as one small part of the
immense processes of nature. And thus the reverberant conclusion
to the paragraph,[46]

> mortalem vitam mors cum immortalis ademit

Once immortal death has taken away mortal life

is more than just an epigram or paradox. The immortality of death,
enhanced again by the *m* alliteration, associates an event which we
may naturally dread with that immutability upon which our spirits
have been invited to repose, and helps us to reconcile us to our extinction by investing it with a sombre glory.

Let us now look at a later part of the diatribe. Bringing Nature's
grand rebuke to a close, Lucretius continues his forensic metaphor,
but now joins to it another theme which looks back to an earlier
part of the poem:[47]

> iure, ut opinor, agat, iure increpet inciletque.
> cedit enim rerum novitate extrusa vetustas
> semper, et ex aliis aliud reparare necessest . . .

Rightly, I think, would she plead her case, rightly chide and upbraid. For
the old ever gives way, pushed out by the newness of things, and each
thing is necessarily created out of others . . .

The logic may seem weak. Certainly we cannot resist the law of
nature: but if that law is unpleasant, the fact that it is inescapable
cannot make us like it.[48] Nature's rebuke would be entirely fitting

---

[46] Lucr. 3. 869.   [47] Lucr. 3. 963–5.

[48] True, it was a commonplace of consolation that you should accept such-and-such
because there was nothing you could do about it. But Lucretius is in the business of chal-
lenging received attitudes.

if it were bidding us yield to the will of a God who had a claim upon our gratitude and obedience; but Epicureanism has no place for such a god. Yet Lucretius from his very first lines has told us to come to the natural world in a spirit of worship and veneration; and now in lines 964–5 he echoes the passage where he developed that spirit into an awareness of each creature's place in one great whole: in the second book he delighted in the eternal freshness of the world, made possible by the ceaseless process of ageing and renewal, and expressed his enthusiasm by letting a clause flow exuberantly over the end of the line to conclude with an emphatic 'semper', before the sentence surged onward again.[49] Here in the third book is the same construction, and the same 'semper'. In the second book he went on to show the community of all life; now he can use the memory of that revelation to give his argument an emotional resonance. 'Materies opus est,' he continues, 'ut crescant postera saecla' (Matter is needed for coming generations to grow).[50] In itself that is a bald truism, but if he has succeeded in making us enter his imaginative world, it has a persuasive force. An appeal to necessity may be factual merely or persuasive. If the kulak is told, 'You will have to work hard for the five-year plan to be fulfilled', he will accept the truth of the statement but may have no interest in the five-year plan whatever. If he is told, 'You must work hard if your children are to be fed', he will recognize not only a statement of fact but an appeal to his own wishes: he has an interest in his children's health. In the present case Epicurean physics provide the facts; Lucretius' imaginative vision of community adds the persuasion, by giving us an interest of a kind in the generation which will succeed us.

He comes back to another legal metaphor:[51]

> sic alid ex alio numquam desistet oriri
> vitaque mancipio nulli datur, omnibus usu.

Thus one thing will never cease to arise out of another, and life is given to none as freehold, to all for usufruct.

The idea in the second of these lines was a commonplace before Lucretius, though he gives it an admirably epigrammatic concision, lost in translation.[52] Of its nature it seems a sardonic reflection; we might compare Horace's treatment of a similar theme in his ode to

---

[49] Lucr. 2. 74 ff., discussed above.   [50] Lucr. 3. 967.   [51] Lucr. 3. 970 f.

[52] The commentators cite examples. The force of Lucretius' version lies partly in its terseness, partly in the exactness of the legal metaphor, which is accurately conveyed in English only by the term 'usufruct', laboured though it sounds.

Postumus, *Eheu fugaces*. The years slip away, the poet tells his friend:
when you are dead, your heir will squander the fine vintages that
you have so carefully preserved.[53] 'You can't take it with you when
you go'—the sentiment, in itself, is obvious enough. Lucretius' originality is to put this dour thought in a context which gives it almost
a hopeful air: it is because new things never cease to come into being
that we have life only as usufruct. The legal metaphor makes us think
of our heirs: for the childless Horace they are merely usurpers; but
if, with Lucretius, we can feel the kinship of all life, we can have a
natural interest, once again, in the happiness of our successors.

Nothing can make the argument of the banqueter logically water-
tight, but that is not Lucretius' purpose; this idea too gains emotional and persuasive force both from its immediate context and from
its place in the poet's larger imaginative world.[54]

> nam si grata fuit tibi vita anteacta priorque
> et non omnia pertusum congesta quasi in vas
> commoda perfluxere atque ingrata interiere,
> cur non ut plenus vitae conviva recedis
> aequo animoque capis securam, stulte, quietem?

For if the life that is past and gone has been grateful to you and all its
blessings have not, as though collected in a jar full of holes, run away and
perished unvalued, why do you not leave like a banqueter full fed on life
and with calm mind embrace a rest free of care, you fool?

Aristippus held that the only thing to be taken into account was the
pleasure of the moment; Epicurus was not content with this, and
tried to give a significance to past experience by valuing the pleasures of memory; Lucretius follows him, but seems to want to go
just a little further. Half seen behind his words is an idea more religious than strictly philosophical: that the good life is a unity, a whole,
the sum of its parts. If you have lived your life well, its blessings
have not flowed away through the holes in the vessel; presumably
they are still held there. A feaster is still full when he retires; and
he has been fed (we may suppose) upon a rich variety of courses.
Let us look on to Nature's second outburst:[55]

> sed quia semper aves quod abest, praesentia temnis,
> imperfecta tibi elapsast ingrataque vita
> et nec opinanti mors ad caput adstitit ante
> quam satur ac plenus possis discedere rerum.

---

[53] *Carm.* 2. 14.   [54] Lucr. 3. 935–9.   [55] Lucr. 3. 957–60.

But because you always crave what is not to hand and despise what is, your life has slipped away incomplete and unvalued, and death has come to stand at your head before you thought it, and before you can depart glutted and full fed.

'Imperfecta' is the striking word here: the philosophical life differs from the life of the unenlightened in that when it comes to an end it is in some sense 'complete'. And this adjective is linked to another: 'ingratus'. Here is a thought stressed in Nature's rebukes: 'ingratus' has already come at 937 and 942, 'gratus' at 935. There should be no place for gratitude in Epicurus' system, since there is no one to be grateful to, but the prosopopoeia comes to the poet's aid: he cannot tell us that we ought to be thankful, but Nature may. However, his imaginative recreation of Epicurus' philosophy throughout the poem prevents us from taking Nature's claim on our gratitude simply as a momentary metaphor. It coheres with the larger vision: at the very beginning we venerated Nature; to praise we are now to add thanksgiving. The feaster is described as 'conviva', a guest, and the context gives the word a new edge: Nature has been our host, and guests, we may reflect, ought to be thankful to their providers. Lucretius does venture to refer passingly to man's ingratitude in his own person, and here in connection with two other ideas he has used before: the variety of the seasons and the metaphor of the vessel full of holes:[56]

> deinde animi ingratam naturam pascere semper
> atque explere bonis rebus satiareque numquam,
> quod faciunt nobis annorum tempora, circum
> cum redeunt fetusque ferunt variosque lepores,
> nec tamen explemur vitai fructibus umquam,
> hoc, ut opinor, id est, aevo florente puellas
> quod memorant laticem pertusum congerere in vas,
> quod tamen expleri nulla ratione potestur.

Then to be always feeding the ungrateful character of the mind, to fill and yet never satisfy it with good things, as the seasons of the year do for us, when they come round again, bringing their diverse products and charms, and yet we are never filled full with the fruits of life—this, I believe, is meant by the story of the girls in the flower of their youth pouring water into a perforated vessel which cannot be filled up by any means.

[56] Lucr. 3. 1003–10.

This complex of motifs is significant. The metaphor of the vessel suggests that the value of life is cumulative: in the case of a good life the vessel is gradually filled up. The variety (and regularity) of the seasons cannot be enjoyed at a single moment: they are the sum of experiences collected over time, a whole made up of many parts. We have seen before how the rhythm of the seasons contributes to Lucretius' larger vision. He sees nature as a whole, and each individual life as a whole, and here those two ideas are felt together. Epicureanism is concerned with pleasure; Lucretius cannot easily instruct us to be pleased by something; but he can hope to make us pleased by it through the imaginative power with which he presents it, and thus he can hope to transform Epicureanism by irradiating it with a new vision, while yet remaining faithful to the master.

The Book of Job faces the problem of suffering, but the argument is cut short by the voice of God: How little you are! who are you to question the divine order? Lucretius faces the problem of death; as a rational philosopher, he must not cut short the argument, but he does want, like the author of Job, to introduce a divine voice, not arguing but by grand rebuke enforcing the spirit of acceptance. It is in these terms, and these alone, that the prosopopoeia makes sense as part of Lucretius' total strategy: on to the philosophy is grafted a religious spirit of worship, self-discipline, and submission. And thus his moral and aesthetic purposes, his poetry, and his philosophy, become inseparably one, for the argument itself is that there is poetry in the philosophy, that the master's teaching is to be imaginatively apprehended as a thing of poetic and spiritual beauty.

Lucretius goes on to bring out the note of self-discipline more strongly. As the diatribe proceeds, we come to realize that the prosopopoeia was a transition, a half-way stage preparing for an even bolder move: for Nature's rebuke is followed by an even more surprising voice, that of the reader himself: 'hoc etiam *tibi tute interdum dicere possis*' (From time to time you may say this to yourself).[57] There is a satirical edge to the words with which we are to chasten ourselves, yet the tone is grand and resonant with ancient splendours; Ennius is echoed, and Homer.[58] As we have seen, there is no real argument here, for Lucretius has another purpose. He presents the

---

[57] Lucr. 3. 1024.
[58] These echoes come in the first two lines. Line 1025 is a quotation, with minimal alteration of Enn. *Ann.* 137 Sk. Line 1026 echoes Achilles' rebuke to Lycaon, *Il.* 21. 107.

great declamation as a spiritual exercise, something that we are to use regularly and repeatedly (interdum); the emphatic 'tibi tute' stresses the inward nature of the discipline. We are to contemplate the saints and heroes: Ancus and Scipio; the poets, and Homer, king of poets; Democritus; and Epicurus himself.[59] These men are far above us, and yet not entirely so, for they have all died, which is the common lot of all humanity. That is no new reflection, but it gains a new strength and beauty if we have absorbed Lucretius' feeling for the universal kinship: we are one with Homer and Epicurus in a sense that goes beyond the flat fact that they have died as we shall. Glory and humility are here combined; and that combination too, perhaps, has the religious character. At this climactic point Epicurus is named, for the only time in the entire poem; and yet he who is elsewhere hailed as saviour, father and god, is here presented merely as a man like others. Despite the grand rhetoric there is also a simplicity of tone: 'ipse Epicurus obit . . .'[60] 'Obeo' is a word that belongs to the ordinary register of language; Lucan was to conjure a similar effect from it when he began Cato's obituary of Pompey with an eloquent plainness: ' "Civis obit," inquit . . .' ('A citizen has died,' he said . . .).[61] Lucretius uses the word again in the book's last paragraph —'nec devitari letum pote quin obeamus'—thus linking our own fate to that of mankind's greatest benefactor.[62]

Lucretius commonly likes to end a book or section quietly, not at a climax.[63] The last part of his diatribe, less striking rhetoric, continues to suggest his larger themes. If men saw aright, he says, they would set aside their affairs, and strive to learn the nature of things:[64]

[59] Lucr. 3. 1025–44. Scipio is perhaps not a saint; and Lucretius includes Xerxes (1029–33), neither a saint nor a hero. He is combining two themes: the mortality of all men, great and little; and the vanity of earthly power and glory faced with the fact of death. For the second theme especially, compare Juvenal 10. Lucretius is indeed the first to strike the note of high declamatory satire of which Juvenal was to make himself the master.
[60] 'Epicurus too died . . .' (1042).
[61] Lucan 9. 190. On the tone of 'obeo' see R. O. A. M. Lyne, Words and the Poet (Oxford, 1989), 108 f.
[62] Lucr. 3. 1079, 'Nor can death be avoided, but die we must'.
[63] Compare the proem of the first book, which gradually descends towards the more matter-of-fact, or the quiet conclusion to the diatribe at the end of the fourth. Contrast Virgil's technique in the Georgics of ascent to a concluding climax: the proem and the end of the first book, the laus Italiae in the second, the proem of the third.
[64] Lucr. 3. 1073–5.

temporis aeterni quoniam, non unius horae,
ambigitur status, in quo sit mortalibus omnis
aetas, post mortem quae restat cumque manenda.

since the issue in question concerns the state for eternity, not for one hour—
the state in which mortals will pass all time that remains to be expected
after death.

The expression here is a little odd from the Epicurean point of view, and would seem to come more accurately from a philosopher who believed in a life after death;[65] Lucretius' tolerance of the oddity seems to import the religious sense that a man's inner life here and now has an eternal significance. 'Manere' here seems to signify 'await' or 'expect', but the word also means to remain or abide, and these connotations allow the period to end with another suggestion of perennity. Three lines later, Lucretius declares, 'certa quidem finis vitae mortalibus adstat' (A fixed term to life awaits mortals)—a simple phrase, but within this poem full of resonance.[66] We have seen that the words 'certus' and 'finis' are woven into a nexus of feeling about sure and eternal laws within which we are encouraged to find security and consolation. Through the significance with which he has charged these simple terms he may fleetingly hint that we can find even in the sure fact of our mortality a sort of comfort and safety.

And so Lucretius has given nature a new centrality in human experience: not only is it to be reverenced for itself, but it is the key to man's right understanding of his place in the world, his life and his death. 'Nature' is a notoriously slippery concept, but the looseness of the English word may conveniently cover the range of Lucretius' imagination. He begins with the spring—nature at its most obviously appealing—but moves outward to encompass all life and beyond that the entire universe of things, both organic and inorganic. Virgil's scope is less vast: in the *Georgics* it will be organic nature and landscape that chiefly excite him. The mode of his love and veneration for nature, and the morals he draws from it, are in many ways different from Lucretius, but without Lucretius' example it is unlikely that he would have made nature central to a long

[65] Formally, it can be reconciled with Epicureanism by saying that the open question, for the man who has not yet turned to philosophy, is what state awaits him throughout eternity after his death; the correct answer, supplied by Epicureanism once he has studied philosophy, is, 'None: death is followed by complete non-existence.'

[66] Lucr. 3. 1078.

poem of such passion and seriousness. What makes the *Georgics* so enormously different from the didactic poems of the Hellenistic age is the combining of imaginative depth with moral intensity; and that is another inheritance from Lucretius.

We have seen that much of Lucretius' celebration of nature is in general terms, and here too he may have influenced his successor; though there is precise observation in the *Georgics*, as there had been in the *Eclogues*, it is surprising how much of the poem is generalized (in the *laus Italiae*, for example, there are very few lines of actual description). But Lucretius is also a master of detail. Though the materialism of Epicurus' philosophy might seem to suck the poetry out of the world, we have seen that in one respect it was the best philosophy for a poet, through the primacy which it gave to the senses and the importance which it attributed to observation, including minute observation. If Lucretius had been a Stoic, he would not have had the same cause to explore the curious detail of the world.

In his poem two influences seem to come happily together. Something of its character must be attributed to the spirit of the age. In the poetry of the first century BC we find the search for the *petit fait signicatif*, a new apprehension of detail, of things and of moments of time; we meet it in Catullus, in the *Eclogues*, in the Augustans; perhaps we might have met it in the lost poets of the late republic. Lucretius is indeed one of the makers of this spirit, but it is unlikely that he made it alone. However, philosophy is another influence on this aspect of his poem. He studies the effects of attrition: the ring on the finger thin through wearing (thin underneath, 'subter'—a nice exactitude), the stone hollowed by dripping water, the hands of bronze statues rubbed down by the touch of passers-by.[67] We might judge this poetry characteristically Roman, did we not know that the argument and some of the examples derive from the Eleatic philosopher Melissus of Samos.[68] Perhaps the accident of Lucretius' philosophical interests gave a chance impetus to what became distinctively Roman.

But we must still attribute most of his flair for detail to his own poetic temper. His stabbing questions, 'nonne vides . . . ?', 'iamne vides . . . ?', 'Do you not see? . . . do you now see?', press home his demand that we use our eyes properly. He is a man for whom the visible world exists, passionate to see things as they are. This urge applies

---

[67] Lucr. I. 311 ff.
[68] Melissus B 8 D. Bailey, on Lucretius ad loc., suggests that the argument became a commonplace of the atomic school.

to actions and experiences as well as things. He notices how children deliberately make themselves giddy, and remembers how it felt.[69] Indeed, he seems to have had an especially affectionate interest in children. He observes how when their father comes home, they compete to reach him first, running ahead of their mother: 'oscula . . . *praeripere*' (to snatch the first kisses) the detail is in the verb's prefix.[70] And thus your children, he adds in a lovely phrase, touch your heart with a silent sweetness, 'tacita pectus dulcedine tangent'.[71] In a repeated simile he compares the unphilosophic to children afraid to go into the dark[72] and likens his verses to the honey smeared round the cup of bitter medicine to induce the child to drink it.[73] He even advances the unexpected theory that in man's early history children civilized their parents, softening them by their charming ways.[74] They broke the grown-ups' proud spirit, 'ingenium fregere superbum'; the phrase is affectionately ironical.

Breaking through convention to the actuality of experience he describes dreams as they are, and not as the poets had described them; he reports the discontinuities of dreams, the reworking of waking experience within them, the falling dream.[75] But above all his acuity is directed to the sights of waking life. He can capture a tiny instant of time, as with a high-speed camera, noting the split second after the starting-gates are thrown open before the horses burst out.[76] He studies the iridescence of the dove's neck, wrestling with the *patrii sermonis egestas* to convey the truth of hue and sheen through a mixture of colour adjectives and the names of jewels: 'pyropus' (garnet) and 'zmaragdus' (emerald).[77] He watches to see how colour changes as a dyed cloth is pulled apart into shreds;[78] he observes how the

---

[69] Lucr. 4. 400 ff.   [70] Lucr. 3. 895 f.

[71] '[After death no more] will they touch your heart . . .' (3. 896). This sentence, however, is among those with which the unenlightened address us. They tell us that we should feel death as a misery, and we are to reject that view; none the less, the detail in 'praeripere' and the loveliness of the phrase that follows show that they are appealing to what Lucretius himself sees as a beauty of human experience. On Lucretius' tactics here see Jenkyns, *Three Classical Poets* (London, 1982), 130, and on the later part of the paragraph, which grows satirical as it proceeds, D. West, *The Imagery and Poetry of Lucretius* (1969), 28 f.

[72] Lucr. 2. 55–8 (= 3. 87–90, 6. 35–8).   [73] Lucr. 1. 936 ff.

[74] Lucr. 5. 1017 f.

[75] Lucr. 4. 818 ff., 962 ff., 1020 ff. Realistic dreams are rare in ancient literature, but not unknown. The dream of Ilia from Ennius' *Annals* (38 ff. Sk) has some of the inconsequence of dreams as we know them. At *Aen.* 12. 908–12 Virgil adapts one of Homer's similes (*Il.* 22. 199–201) to make it closer to a familiar type of frustration dream (interestingly, he speaks about what 'we' experience in sleep). For dreamlike quality in *Aen.* 6, see below, p. 451.   [76] Lucr. 2. 263 ff.

[77] Lucr. 2. 801 ff.   [78] Lucr. 2. 826 ff.

awning flapping over the theatre on a sunny day makes the audience below ripple in its own colours (the verb 'fluitare', to flow, hence to move with a wavery motion, is repeated—is there a hint of watery or even submarine light?).[79] Playing with the words 'canus' and 'candens', he picks out the mixture of hoariness and glossiness in a stormy sea:[80]

> ut mare, cum magni commorunt aequora venti,
> vertitur in canos candenti marmore fluctus.

As the sea, when strong winds have stirred its expanse, turns into hoary waves with gleaming sheen.

He warns us that the mind falsifies the evidence of the senses, so that we seem to have seen what we expected to see and not what we really saw.[81] His examples of optical illusions seem to have been commonplaces of the philosophical schools, and indeed they are not particularly remarkable in themselves, but they contribute to the poem's sense that it is searching earnestly for the truth of sense experience. Like a camera Lucretius records the visual image as the eye receives it, and not as the mind corrects it: the effects of perspective, with the lines of a colonnade receding to a point; the refraction of light under water.[82] He reports that when we look at towns from afar, their square towers seem to be rounded.[83] That too was a stock example in the schools; more surprising is his claim that sheep grazing or lambs gambolling on a distant hillside appear as a single white blur on a green background.[84] This could be personal enough for us to wonder if he might have been short-sighted.

As some of these examples suggest, this collecting of things seen leads him towards a feeling for the world's curiousness. He looks into a shallow puddle in the street and sees the reflections in it, as deep as the heaven is high above him.[85] We find in him two apprehensions which will become profoundly important for Virgil; that the familiar is strange and that the familiar is wonderful. In Virgil this sense is usually implicit, but Lucretius draws the moral directly. Consider the clear, pure colour of the heaven, he says, and all that it contains, sun and moon and travelling stars; if men were now

---

[79] Lucr. 4. 75 ff.

[80] Lucr. 2. 766 f. Translation loses something of his force and precision. He takes two common poetic words for sea and squeezes their full weight of meaning out of them: 'aequor' (plain, expanse), the sea as level surface, 'marmor' (gleam, marble), the sea as shining surface. [81] Lucr. 4. 462 ff.

[82] Lucr. 4. 426 ff., 438 ff. [83] Lucr. 4. 353 ff.

[84] Lucr. 2. 321 f. [85] Lucr. 4. 414 ff.

seeing these things for the first time, how marvellous they would appear, how much beyond belief beforehand. They should be objects of wonder; but as it is, people are dulled by a satiety of sight, and no one bothers to look up into the shining spaces of the sky.[86] 'Mirabilis', 'mirandus'; the words of wonder are repeated. Early man, he tells us, laughed and smiled at simple pleasures, because everything was strong in newness and wonder (omnia quod nova tum magis haec et mira vigebant).[87] Conversely, the curse of modern man, unless he be enlightened by philosophy, is a restless boredom which can find satisfaction neither in town or country, at home or away.[88] Part of this poet's mission is to revivify the eye and freshen experience.

Some of his alertness to the external world is a love of nature in the straightforward sense: an affection for country life and landscape. In the *Georgics* Virgil distinguishes himself from Lucretius: the scientific intellect on the one hand, the country-lover on the other.[89] But that is not the whole truth. At the start of his second book Lucretius extols the virtues of philosophy: what need of wealth and grand palazzi? We expect him to contrast the pomp of riches with the pleasure of pure contemplation. But no: the sentence turns in another, more sensuous direction:[90]

> neque natura ipse requirit,
> *si non* aurea sunt iuvenum simulacra per aedes
> lampadas igniferas manibus retinentia dextris,
> lumina nocturnis epulis ut suppeditentur,
> nec domus argento fulget auroque renidet
> nec citharae reboant laqueata aurataque templa,
> cum tamen *inter se* prostrati in gramine molli
> propter aquae rivum sub ramis arboris altae
> non magnis opibus iucunde corpora curant,
> praesertim cum tempestas arridet et anni
> tempora conspergunt viridantis floribus herbas.

Nor does nature herself feel a lack, if there are no statues of youths about the house carrying fiery torches in their right hands to supply light for banquets by night, if the building does not shine with silver or gleam with gold nor panelled and gilded rafters echo to the lyre, so long as people can lie in company on soft grass by a stream under the branches of a tall tree and refresh their bodies delightfully at no great cost, above all when the weather smiles and the season of the year sprinkles the greenery with flowers.

---

[86] Lucr. 2. 1030–9.   [87] Lucr. 5. 1404.   [88] Lucr. 3. 1060 ff.
[89] *Geo.* 2. 490 ff.   [90] Lucr. 2. 23–33.

The contrasting pleasure turns out to be a sociable life (notice 'inter se'), one of leisure in the countryside in the springtime, with shade and water and greenery—the good life as we shall see it again in the *Eclogues*. In the *Georgics* too, when he praises country life in contrast to urban opulence, Virgil will follow the shape of Lucretius' rhetoric, borrowing his 'si non':[91]

> *si non* ingentem foribus domus alta superbis
> mane salutantum totis vomit aedibus undam . . .
> at secura quies et nescia fallere vita . . . (etc.)

This comes shortly before he draws the distinction between Lucretius and himself; but Lucretius (as he well knows) has been there before him.

In Lucretius' pictures of the countryside we can detect both 'pastoral' and 'georgic' notes (as they may, anachronistically, be called). His 'pastoral' passages are perhaps evidence of a new sensibility, as they contain trace elements of feelings that are not especially well suited to the Epicurean case. Early man inhabited what Lucretius sees as the youth and springtime of the whole world, 'novitas . . . florida mundi';[92] their life and landscape are evoked in some well-known lines:[93]

> at sedare sitim fluvii fontesque vocabant,
> ut nunc montibus e magnis decursus aquai
> claru' citat late sitientia saecla ferarum.
> denique nota vagis silvestria templa tenebant
> nympharum, quibus e scibant umori' fluenta
> lubrica proluvie larga lavere umida saxa,
> umida saxa, super viridi stillantia musco,
> et partim plano scatere atque erumpere campo.

But rivers and springs summoned them to quench their thirst, even as now the downrush of water from high mountains calls loud and far to the thirsting tribes of beasts. Then too they occupied the woodland haunts of the nymphs, which they discovered from their wanderings, and from which they knew that running streams of water issued to wash with abundant flow the wet rocks, the wet rocks, dripping over green moss, and to splash and burst out here and there over the level plain.

The pathetic fallacy slips in, as the springs and rivers draw men to them with the enticing 'vocabant', suggesting perhaps the actual sound

---

[91] *Geo.* 2. 461 ff.; see below, pp. 371 ff.   [92] Lucr. 5. 943.
[93] Lucr. 5. 945–52.

of running water. More strikingly, men haunt the dwelling-places of the nymphs. Of course it is open to the rational Lucretius to explain this as a shorthand for the places where they believed the nymphs to dwell; none the less we seem to sense a pleasure in the thought of impalpable presences being part of the idyll. It is not, as in early Greek poetry, that the divine presence is important in itself; these nymphs enhance a secular pleasure, and decorate the rural scene.

Later Lucretius describes the invention of the pipes:[94]

> inde minutatim dulcis didicere querelas,
> tibia quas fundit digitis pulsata canentum,
> avia per nemora ac silvas saltusque reperta,
> per loca pastorum deserta atque otia dia.

Then little by little they learnt the sweet plaints which the pipe pours forth when pressed by the players' fingers, the pipe discovered among the pathless woods and forests and glens, among the shepherds' lonely haunts and bright repose.

A delight in melancholy, implied in the oxymoron of 'dulcis . . . querelas', sets a tone that we might think more characteristic of Virgil than Lucretius. And this pleasurable plaintiveness resounds through a landscape of lovely loneliness (avia, deserta); as it happens, this note of romantic solitude is hardly to be heard in the *Eclogues*, except the last of them. We may feel that Lucretius does anticipate Virgil, though, in the mingling of physical landscape and mental experience. 'Per loca . . . atque otia'—the grammar yokes the two nouns together, but the one is concrete, the other abstract; place and emotion fuse. The adjective 'dius' is strikingly unexpected; this strange, elusive word, with its connotations of brightness and divinity, irradiates the simple life with a momentary hint of sanctity. Lucretius had used it earlier to describe pleasure, already identified in the poem's first line with the goddess Venus: 'dux vitae dia voluptas' (divine pleasure, the guide of life).[95] We are not far here from the 'divini gloria ruris' of the *Georgics*.[96]

This landscape is lonely, but it is visited by shepherds; Lucretius takes no pleasure, as Virgil does at moments, in a wilderness from which man is wholly absent. The vast areas of the world which are useless to man are a sign of its faultiness; of course, the argument was too good for an Epicurean to miss. But it would be sufficient

---

[94] Lucr. 5. 1384–7.
[95] Lucr. 2. 172. 'Dius' comes once only in Virgil, at *Aen.* 11. 657, in a passage examined in Ch. 13.   [96] *Geo.* 1. 168.

for this argument to point (as he does) to the arctic and torrid zones and the waste expanses of the sea; as it is, he adds rocks, mountains and forests to his tally of the earth's imperfections:[97]

> principio quantum caeli tegit impetus ingens,
> inde avide partem montes silvaeque ferarum
> possedere, tenent rupes vastaeque paludes
> et mare quod late terrarum distinet oras.

First, of all that the vast stretch of the sky covers, part has been greedily occupied by mountains and forests full of beasts, part is held by rocks and waste marshes, or the sea which holds the shores of different lands far apart.

It will be left to Virgil to use the long, cold sounds of line 202 to evoke the beauty of crags and waters and woods haunted by creatures of the wild.[98] Taming the hills and cutting back the forest are for Lucretius not only signs of progress but a source of aesthetic enjoyment; in this he is still at one with the poet of the *Odyssey*:[99]

> inde aliam atque aliam culturam dulcis agelli
> temptabant fructusque feros mansuescere terra
> cernebant indulgendo blandeque colendo.
> inque dies magis in montem succedere silvas
> cogebant infraque locum concedere cultis,
> prata lacus rivos segetes vinetaque laeta
> collibus et campis ut haberent, atque olearum
> caerula distinguens inter plaga currere posset
> per tumulos et convallis camposque profusa;
> ut nunc esse vides vario distincta lepore
> omnia, quae pomis intersita dulcibus ornant
> arbustisque tenent felicibus obsita circum.

Then they tried one way after another of cultivating their dear little patch of land and watched wild fruits grow tame in the earth through kindly treatment and gentle tilling. As the days passed, they forced the woods to retreat further up the mountain and surrender the land below to tilth, so that they might have meadows, ponds, streams, crops and fertile vineyards on hills and plains, and that a blue-grey belt of olives might run between, making a clear line, spreading over swell, hollow and plain; just as now you see the landscape picked out with diverse charms, since men embellish it, interspersing it with pretty orchard-trees, and occupy it, planting fruitful shrubs around it.

---

[97] Lucr. 5. 200–3.

[98] *Ed.* 10. 14 f.; *Geo.* 2. 469 ff. Whereas 'silvae ferarum' are an inconvenience to man in Lucretius' view, at *Geo.* 2. 471 Virgil celebrates 'saltus ac lustra ferarum' as one of the charms of country life—if the line is not an interpolation (see below, p. 371).

[99] Lucr. 5. 1367–78.

But there is also much here that looks forward to the *Georgics*. In the prettiness of 'dulcis agelli', with its sentimental diminutive, we catch an affection for the soil. In the personifications of 1368–9, likening the farmer's work to breaking in animals or bringing up children, we recognize what will become one of Virgil's favourite techniques. 'Fructusque feros mollite colendo,' he will write, echoing these very lines (Tame the wild fruits by cultivating them).[100] Lucretius also recognizes that cultivation diversifies the scene: it is because of man's work that all things are 'vario distincta lepore'. This is a theme that Virgil will richly develop.

Lucretius' love of force, energy, and vigour invades this part of his imagination also. This too was to influence Virgil; the spirit of the *Georgics* would have been rather different without it. We have already met Lucretius describing how at the origin of humanity hard men were born out of the hard earth, and seen how eager Virgil was to preserve this idea, though he has to substitute myth for science. Later, Lucretius links man's hardness to his capacity for toil; he explains that the male sex was the first to work wool, before abandoning it in favour of more arduous labour:[101]

> agricolae donec vitio vertere severi,
> ut muliebribus id manibus concedere vellent
> atque ipsi pariter *durum* sufferre laborem
> atque opere in *duro durarent* membra manusque.

Until the stern fathers turned it to scorn, so that they were ready to leave it to women's hands and themselves to share in putting up with hard toil and hardened their limbs and arms by hard effort.

He likes the robustness of these early countrymen; even their recreations, as he depicts them, were hard and energetic. 'Agrestis enim tum musa *vigebat*,' he declares (Then the rustic muse grew to strength);[102] the verb is characteristic, and will be repeated at the end of another sentence only a few lines later.[103] He enjoys their rustic dances,

> Lifting heavy feet in clumsy shoes
> Earth feet, loam feet, lifted in country mirth
> Mirth of those long since under the earth
> Nourishing the corn.

---

[100] *Geo.* 2. 36.

[101] Lucr. 5. 1357–60. Line 1359 is under suspicion. Giussani bracketed it, supposing 1359 and 1360 to be alternative versions by Lucretius. Or possibly 1359 is a marginal gloss which, in altered form, has got into the text (it is similar to line 1272). But the cumbrousness is not out of character for this poet.

[102] Lucr. 5. 1398.   [103] Lucr. 5. 1404; quoted above, p. 278.

Merriment led them to garland themselves, 'and advance moving their limbs heavily, out of step, and with heavy foot thump mother earth':[104]

> atque extra numerum procedere membra moventis
> *duriter* et *duro* **térram péde pél**lere mat**rem**.

'Whacking mother'—that personification gives the line a roughly comic edge which Horace will pick up, along with the sound and rhythm, when he has his countryman thump his feet upon the ground in a dance of jubilant vindictiveness:[105]

> gaudet invisam pepulisse fossor
> **tér péde terram.**

The ditcher delights to beat the hated earth thrice with his foot.

Lucretius' picture of *duritia* and energetic effort is almost entirely favourable. An exception (we naturally suppose) comes in the paragraph in which he lists the world's imperfections:[106]

> quod superest arvi, tamen id natura *súa ví*
> sentibus obducat, *ni vis humana* resistat
> *v*itai causa *v*alido consueta bidenti
> ingemere et terram pressis proscindere aratris.
> si non fecundas *v*ertentes *v*omere glebas
> terraique solum subigentes cimus ad ortus,
> sponte sua nequeant liquidas exsistere in auras . . .

As for the rest of the land, nature would still cover it over by her own force, if human force did not resist, well used to groaning over the strong mattock for livelihood's sake and to cleaving the earth with ploughs pressed deep. If we did not by turning the fertile clods with the ploughshare and subduing the soil of the earth summon the crops to birth, they would not be able to come forth into the clear air of their own accord . . .

Yet there is much in this that we associate with some of his most exuberant passages: the vigour, the *v* alliterations, the enjoyment of the clash of opposing forces (brought out here by the repetition 'vi . . . vis . . .'). It is revealing that lines 210–11 are taken, with minimal alteration, from the first book, where the feeling is of a stern delight in man's energy and power.[107] And even here, where he is showing the world's imperfections, the paragraph comes round to end on a note which, familiar enough from the poem elsewhere, is most unexpected in this context:[108]

---

[104] Lucr. 5. 1401 f.   [105] *Carm.* 3. 18. 15 f.   [106] Lucr. 5. 206–12.
[107] Lucr. 1. 211 f.   [108] Lucr. 5. 233 f.

> quando omnibus omnia large
> tellus ipsa parit naturaque daedala rerum.

since for all the earth itself brings forth all bounteously, she and nature
the intricate fashioner of things.

Cheerfulness keeps breaking in. Lucretius is aware of the austerity
of toil and perhaps of the ambivalence of *duritia*, but without strong
feeling; Virgil will develop these things much further. We should
not underestimate Virgil's ambivalence on these themes, but we ought
also to remember that he is looking back to a poem in which they
are seen for the most part in a favourable light, and sometimes with
enthusiasm.

Lucretius showed Virgil how to write a large poem: at a time
when there seemed to be a danger of literary exhaustion, he discovered a new, broad field where it might be feasible to take the
Greeks on and beat them at their own game. He also showed how
a great poem could be written without any people in it. Now Virgil
may have distrusted his own capacity to create character. The vir-
tual absence of 'characterization' in the usual sense from most of
his poetry is used by him to create effects which could hardly have
been made in any other way. Part of the *Eclogues'* elusiveness is that
instead of being offered clear pictures of countrymen—like Horace's
Ofellus, let us say, or Ovid's Philemon and Baucis[109]—we hear mysterious voices coming from persons half disembodied, or find a world
in which a god, a poet, and a pigman may converse with one another.
The *Aeneid* has hardly any characters in the sense that the *Iliad* has
characters—that is, individuated personalities with different tempers
or kinds of behaviour, like Achilles, Agamemnon, Odysseus, Diomedes,
and Ajax. There is psychological acuity, certainly—keen observation
of how people act and think—but not much individuation, the creation of distinctive personalities who, once met, can be recognized
again in different circumstances. This absence, though it creates some
poetic problems, is related to some of Virgil's best and most original
effects. It assists his subjectivity: the concern not so much to let us
see Aeneas plain as to see with him, to enter into his thoughts and
feelings. It assists the prismatic effect, which often shows us Aeneas,
Dido, or Turnus not in a clear, bright light but in the changing light
of other figures—Hector, Achilles, Nausicaa, Calypso, and so on. But
it is arguable that Virgil created strength out of weakness: perhaps

---

[109] Hor. *Serm.* 2. 2; Ov. *Met.* 8. 618 ff.

he had small talent for individuation. Achates, notoriously, is a mere cipher, Ascanius mostly lifeless, and if the truth be told, Turnus not quite interesting enough to bear the emotional weight laid upon him. Dido stands as the great exception, yet even with her Virgil seems less interested in delineating an individual than in studying and entering into the emotions of pride, honour, and passion.

Now characters might be thought necessary to any truly great poem. If Virgil, for whatever reason, would not create characters in the conventional sense, he faced a problem. The 'solution' in the *Aeneid* is of a unique and extraordinary kind, and it may have been years before he found it. Meanwhile Lucretius demonstrated how a poem of heroic scale and quality might be achieved without characters, indeed without any people in it at all. In the event the *Georgics* will not be quite so austere; but Orpheus, Eurydice, Aristaeus, and the gardener of Tarentum gain some of their poignancy as individual human beings who break into a poem that has hitherto done without them.

There is, moreover, a kind of resilience in Lucretius which may have been inspiriting to a poet of different temper. Certainly Virgil is generous enough in the *Georgics* to praise Lucretius for an unlikeness to himself. Lucretius' beliefs denied him the consolations derivable from a providential understanding of the world—and indeed there was good polemic to be got out of the world's imperfections —but absent from him is that *mal du siècle* which so infects most writers of the late republic. On the one side we meet restlessness and decadence, exhibited in the confused, untidy lives of Catullus and others of his milieu and in their puzzled, undirected half-rebellions against the society which gave them the privileges which allowed the luxury of dissidence. On another side we find an alarmed awareness that the old order was cracking up, and we hear despondent laments over moral failure, from Cicero, from Sallust, with even Catullus joining in at the end of his *Peleus and Thetis*. Languor and pessimism were both parts of the spirit of the age, the responses of different temperaments to the condition of Rome. Cicero disliked the posturings of the neoterics, but their verse and style of life were as much the product of the times as his own gloom and anger. It is an oddity of the late republic that its vitality coexists with— and paradoxically, is in part created by—a pervasive listlessness. The lowering sense of decline was strong enough to persist in the era of Augustus, when one would expect a more facile optimism, and to emerge in Horace and Livy. The more notable, then, is the lack of this feeling in Lucretius. To be sure, he attacks the competitive struggle for power and office,[110] but that was a permanent and traditional part of Roman life, not a new form of corruption, besides being a regular object of philosophic criticism. The common contrast of the present with a morally superior past does not seem to hold much interest for him. The old countrymen who grumble about things not being what they were are treated with a grave humour.[111] When the vine planter complains how the virtuous men of old, 'antiquum genus . . . pietate repletum', put up with life on a narrow plot, at a time when each man had less land to support him, his complaints miss the point.[112] It is no use wearying heaven with complaints ('caelumque fatigat'—an ironic phrase since the true cause of agricultural decline is that the natural order is slowly growing weary and running down);[113] it is not moral decline but physical facts that account for the soil being less productive than it was. 'Nec tenet omnia paulatim tabescere' (Nor does he grasp that all things gradually waste away)—yet even this thought Lucretius seems not to take too much to heart. Far more characteristic of him are those assertions which we have examined of the world's continued freshness and vitality.[114]

Certainly he observes the spoilt restlessness of modern life—the *taedium vitae* of the man who rushes from town to country villa and back to town house again, haste and listlessness combined[115]—but he regards such behaviour as an absurdity, a state of mind unknown to the philosopher. He lacks the sense that all life is flawed or haunted; he does not luxuriate in melancholy or hear the *lacrimae rerum*. 'Medio de fonte leporum | surgit amari aliquid quod in ipsis floribus angat' (in the midmost fountain of delights something bitter wells up to strangle them among the very flowers)[116]—his famous words may

---

[110] Lucr. 2. 11 ff.; 3. 59 ff.   [111] Lucr. 2. 1164 ff.   [112] Lucr. 2. 1168–72.

[113] Lucr. 2. 1169. 'caelum' is Wakefield's emendation of the manuscripts' 'saeclum'.

[114] Virgil uses 'antiquus' 47 times, often with strong evocative force, Lucretius 9 times only. Four of these cases refer pejoratively to the false superstitions of the past (2. 610, 5. 13, 5. 86, 6. 62); one refers to the crude weaponry of primitive man (5. 1283); and one passage, discussed above, lightly mocks the farmer who praises the good old days (2. 1170). In two places 'antiquus' merely means 'previous' (2. 900, 5. 871), and the comparative adverb 'antiquius' is once used neutrally to mean 'older'. Lucretius never uses 'antiquus' as a term of praise; in a Latin poet that is striking.

[115] Lucr. 3. 1060 ff.   [116] Lucr. 4. 1133 f.

seem to catch a certain Virgilian mood better than almost any one line in Virgil himself; but whereas in Virgil they might express a truth about the human condition, in their actual place they merely describe the fate of the unenlightened, unphilosophical man. The spirit that calls 'carpe diem', 'gather ye rosebuds', the banqueter troubled at the feast by the shadow of mortality—to Lucretius this is mere foolishness.[117] Vehement, noisy and passionate he may certainly be, but with a largeness, exuberance, robustness. There is something hugely healthy about him. The 'mala mentis gaudia' that appear before Aeneas in the underworld, that terrible sickness of the spirit, seem unknown to his experience.[118]

Through his sense of everlasting newness and universal community he weaves a sense of delight and confidence into his poem's fabric. Thus he describes the workings of the 'summa', the totality of things:[119]

> efficit ut *largis avidum* mare fluminis undis
> *integrent* amnes et solis terra vapore
> fota *novet* fetus summissaque gens animantum
> *floreat* et *vivant* labentes aetheris ignes . . .

It causes the rivers to restore the greedy sea with the generous flow of their streams, the earth, cherished by the sun's heat, to renew its offspring, the race of living things to spring up and flourish, and the fires that glide through the sky to live . . .

This is essentially a report on physical fact, in a passage of busy argument, but through the pattern built up by such words as 'largus', 'integro', 'novo', 'floreo', 'vivo'—'avidus' too, in view of his delight

---

[117] Lucr. 3. 912 ff.

[118] *Aen* 6. 278 f. These observations concern Lucretius' poetic personality, not that unknown, the historical Lucretius. Jerome's story that *De Rerum Natura* was written in the intervals between madness is usually rejected nowadays, as is probably right. If it could be shown to be true, we should still want to say that the poem as a whole shows no sign of it (one or two passages might conceivably be excepted). The works of some people who have been intermittently or permanently mad do show signs of obsession or disorder (Smart, Dadd, Ruskin); but who would guess Wolf's history from his music, or Hölderlin's from his verse? There is no general rule about whether the insanity of the creator is reflected in his art.

From purely internal evidence it is plausible enough to suppose that Lucretius was highly emotional; it is not even implausible to fancy that a stridency at times betrays some subconscious insecurity. But such speculations would not imply madness, or even neurosis.

[119] Lucr. 1. 1031–4.

in the urgency of appetite—he creates a feeling of celebration. This feeling becomes pervasive, so that when he writes, for example:[120]

> namque aliud putrescit et aevo debile languet,
> porro aliud succrescit et e contemptibus exit.

For one thing rots and withers, weak with age, while another grows up and leaves its scorned origins.

which is strictly little more than a statement of a truth known to everyone by experience, we become aware none the less of an emotional pressure behind it. 'E contemptibus', 'out of the spent and unconsidered earth', as a later poet will put it—we feel this recovery of strength to be not only a fact but an invigoration to the spirit. Now remarkably Lucretius applies this sense of newness and energy to the age in which he himself lives. In the fifth book he evokes a time, centuries ago, when the earth was young; it is a theme naturally handled in the language of happiness. But earlier in the same book he has told us that he believes our universe to be still new, and to our surprise he links this cosmological supposition to the state of contemporary culture—the works of art and intellect. Things are getting better, he declares; various arts are on the rise and being made more polished; there are improvements in seafaring, musicians are composing new works of beauty, the true philosophy is a recent discovery, and Lucretius is the very first to present it in Latin.[121] In both cultural and social terms such blitheness is unusual. Where else in Latin poetry shall we meet the cheerful, unforced assumption that the present age is a good time to live in? Hardly anywhere, except, oddly, in Ovid.[122] And where is that burden of the past that haunts so much of Roman literature? A few lines earlier Lucretius has observed that poets tend to write about the Theban and Trojan Wars.[123] For most Latin writers that would be a withering observation; one may think of Virgil's complaint that all themes are already hackneyed.[124] But Lucretius feels no oppression: he slips the remark in casually, in the middle of an argument about the origins of earth and sky; and when he goes on to note that he is the first to handle his subject

[120] Lucr. 5. 832 f.   [121] Lucr. 5. 330–37.
[122] Ov. Ars Am. 3. 121–8. The demands of imperial panegyric are quite another matter. Anchises foretells that Caesar Augustus will found a golden age (Aen. 6. 792 f.). The extravagance of the claim makes it almost meaningless; but in any case Virgil presumably imagines that this fabulous time, like the conquest of the Indians and Garamantes (794), is still in the future as he writes.
[123] Lucr. 5. 326 f.   [124] Geo. 3. 4.

in Latin, it is not aggressively or with a wealth of literary allusion, but straightforwardly, with a sort of pleased surprise.[125]

Virgil, by contrast, is keenly self-conscious about his predecessors, and bears the burden of the past, but it is perhaps because he was so different in temper from Lucretius that Lucretius' robustness was so valuable to him. There are conflicting impulses in him: on the one hand a search for delicacy and high finish, on the other an ambition for great themes and big scale. He faced both a technical and an imaginative problem. The technical difficulty was to find a path beyond the *Eclogues*, exemplifying as they did a perfection that could neither be repeated or carried further. Where might the matter and manner for a larger poetry be found? Lucretius supplies an answer: in didactic verse. The imaginative challenge for the poet was to develop his vision of the world and man's place in it. Not even Virgil could have succeeded with a work of two thousand lines in the *Eclogues'* tone. Lucretius pointed the way to a confident vigour that escaped glibness and self-deception. It is not that Virgil will lose his refinement and sensitivity; rather, he will incorporate something of the Lucretian tone into a complex texture.

We are easily tempted to find in our favourite writers what we want to find, to attribute to them interests and attitudes close to our own. Virgil reads his predecessor too attentively to fall into this trap: alone among classical authors he praises Lucretius not as poet but as philosopher. Now *De Rerum Natura* is the best philosophy in classical Latin, superior to Cicero and Seneca in strength of purpose and quality of argument; yet these others never think to cite him as a source. There had been no truly didactic poem since the fifth century: Aratus and Nicander only pretend that their purpose is to give instruction about weather-signs, agriculture or snake-bites, just as Virgil will only pretend to teach farmers how to farm. So eccentric is the project of genuinely doing philosophy in verse that Cicero, who admires Lucretius as a poet, never mentions him in his philosophical works.[126] But for Virgil Lucretius is

---

[125] Lucr. 5. 336 f. Lucr. 1. 921 ff. (1. 926 ff. = 4. 1 ff.) is more assertive, but significantly he claims that his poetry is wholly new, whereas others—Ennius, Virgil, Horace, Propertius —say that they have inherited the role of some Greek poet, or been the first to imitate him in Latin.

[126] Praise of Lucretius: Cic. *Ad Q. fr.* 2. 9. 3. *Tusc. Disp.* 1. 10 f. may be a dig at the poet: Cicero suggests that to attack the fear of torment by the monsters of the underworld is to flog a dead horse. If he has Lucretius in mind here, he treats him with scorn.

the man who understands, who has mastered physics and overcome fear and fate.[127]

It is sometimes said that Virgil 'answers' *De Rerum Natura*, defending the case that the gods govern the world.[128] Thus Lucretius argues that the gods cannot have planned the world, because such large areas of it are unfit for human beings. Virgil looks at the matter the other way round: though the torrid and arctic regions are uninhabitable, the beneficence of the gods has granted mortals two zones in which they may live.[129] But if this is meant as a response to Lucretius' case, it is in philosophical terms nugatory. He has produced a strong argument, and it is a poor rebuttal, as Virgil must have known, to answer that the gods have shown some kindness. So it seems better to say that Virgil declines to tackle so formidable an intellect, and rather than answering him, simply prefers to talk in different terms, especially since this is what he suggests himself in the second Georgic. Twice he ducks the direct challenge to Lucretius, slipping sideways. May the Muses teach him the workings of nature; but if he has not the capacity, may he love the woods, streams and valleys of the countryside. Happy the man who has understood the causes of things and trodden the fear of death beneath his feet; but fortunate too is he who has known the country gods.[130] Each time the philosophic poet is met by a contrast—not a contrast that declares him to be wrong, but one that escapes into a different order of experience. Very different is Lucretius himself, who firmly insists that false belief is false, however seductive. Virgil surely knew that we should be able to compare him with Lucretius, and notice what he has failed to say.

Virgil reflects the influence of Lucretius in countless details of style and language. At first sight it is surprising that he risked drawing so much from so recent a poet, and one who wrote in his own language; this was an altogether different proposition from following Theocritus, Alcaeus, or Callimachus, and there is nothing else quite like it in Latin. Yet the risk could be run, partly because Virgil's temper remains so unlike Lucretius', partly because he could outdo even so great a predecessor in technical mastery, both on the

---

[127] *Geo* 2. 490–2 (and by implication 475 ff.).

[128] On Virgil's relationship to Lucretius, much discussed, see especially V. Buchheit, *Der Anspruch des Dichters in Vergils Georgika* (Darmstadt, 1972), 55 ff. and *passim*, and P. Hardie, *Virgil's Aeneid: Cosmos and Imperium* (Oxford, 1986), 158 ff.

[129] Lucr. 5. 200 ff.; *Geo.* 1. 233 ff.　　　　[130] *Geo.* 2. 475 ff., 490 ff.

small scale in his manipulation of the hexameter and on the large in his command of form. But we may suppose that he is so ready to acknowledge his debt by external signs because of Lucretius' effect upon the inwardness of his poetry. When Lucretius explored the pathless tracts of the Muses and drank from untasted springs, he opened up a new territory for his successor, transforming the vision of nature, giving it a fresh importance in man's understanding of himself, while at the same time displaying an enhanced interest in little things. Small wonder that he liked to call the earth 'daedalus', for in that adjective are both the large and the small at once, both the limitlessly diverse fertility of nature's creation and its multiplicity of detail, as well as that pleasure in variety and complexity—what the Greeks called *poikilia*—which was to be congenial to Virgil's cast of mind.[131] Our broad survey of literary history has suggested that across the centuries the Greeks had moved towards a greater interest in nature for its own sake. But Lucretius could not have been fore-told; the originality, indeed eccentricity of his project, together with his use of philosophical sources which made exact observations of minute particulars, enlarged the possibilities for a successor shrewd enough to learn from him. Had Lucretius not lived, Virgil would still have written nature poetry—after all, the influence of *De Rerum Natura* on the *Eclogues* is superficial—but much of it would have been rather different. But indeed Virgil is the supreme example in literature of a writer for whom imitation was a spur to the keenest originality.

There is a last and broader influence to be considered. Following his master Epicurus, Lucretius offers man salvation. No one, as far as we know, had used didactic poetry to this end before; we have lost Parmenides and Empedocles, of course, but it is most unlikely that these Pre-Socratics were concerned with the sort of salvation that the Hellenistic schools dealt in. Here the *Georgics* follows Lucretius, and it is this, more than anything, that sets Virgil's poem a world away from Aratus and Nicander: though it is not, like Lucretius', directly about salvation, it learns from him to use the didactic method, the investigation and presentation of fact, as a means of developing a vision of the world that offers to give sense and coherence to human existence. And Virgil was to carry this conception of poetic purpose

---

[131] 'daedala tellus', Lucr. 1. 7, 1. 228; cf. 'natura daedala rerum', 5. 234. Lucretius also uses the adjective in three further places.

on into the *Aeneid*, which is in the business of redemption in a way
that Apollonius and Ennius are not, nor of course the *Iliad* and *Odyssey*,
for all their deep moral importance.

Yet the *Aeneid* is not a religious poem in the fashion that *De
Rerum Natura* is; Lucretius' proffered salvation is inward and spiritual,
Virgil's is external and secular. This is not because his mythological
machinery is a fiction, which he can manipulate to his convenience:
the examples of Dante and Milton show that the free invention of
supernatural detail can serve a fully religious end. It is rather that
Lucretius offers salvation to each individual privately, through a right
understanding of nature, whereas Virgil grounds his hope in man-
made institutions: city and empire. Lucretius was able to incorporate
men and their cities into his vision, seeing them as part of a single
natural order: cities are fertile and flower with young people, even
as the woods sing with birds; all are products of one atomic flux.[132]
We shall see that when Virgil explored nature, patriotism, and identity, he was able to inherit this vision and enhance it, but he could
not quite manage to give city and empire the same philosophical
and emotional foundation.

However, he surely saw the need to give his vision of man and
world a philosophical and religious grounding. Anchises in Elysium
begins his revelation with a grand cosmology which echoes Lucretius
in style and gestures towards Stoicism in its content; it would be
belittling to the poet to suggest that he meant this as no more than
a decorative frontispiece, like the pretty cosmogony, again coloured
with Lucretian tone, that opens Silenus' song in the sixth Eclogue.[133]
Virgil wants to unite nature and culture, to see history and human
society as part of a great universal order, but he fails, albeit very
grandly: Anchises' cosmology remains awkwardly detached, and we
cannot satisfactorily relate the nurturing spirit of which he speaks
either to the Jupiter who rules in the rest of the poem or to the
historical vision of Rome's progress.[134]

Insofar as he seeks for a salvation in the institutions of this world
Virgil takes over part, but only part, of Lucretius' vision, and here

---

[132] Lucr. 1. 255 f.   [133] *Aen.* 6. 724 ff.; *Ecl.* 6. 31 ff.

[134] As F. Solmsen has pointed out, Virgil's theology properly requires the future heroes
of Rome to be second-class souls, inferior to those that by merit have been released from
the cycle of rebirth ('The World of the Dead in Book 6 of the *Aeneid*', *CP* 67 (1972),
31–41, at 38 (= Harrison, 208–23, at 219)). His concealment of this embarrassment is a
triumph of technique, masking a flaw in imaginative coherence.

he is far from *anima naturaliter Christiana*. But there is a last irony: Christianity itself was to develop an established church, monarchically governed, and after Constantine the idea of a Christian empire. Virgil's epic could seem concordant with this idea, and may even have influenced it; if so, his praise of empire, a worldly side of his imagination, contributed to the making of the Christian church.

PART FOUR

The *Georgics*

CHAPTER 7

An Italian's Experience:
Earth and Country

Bénie sois tu, âpre Matière, glèbe stérile, dur rocher, toi qui
ne cèdes qu'à la violence, et nous forces à travailler si nous voulons
manger.

(Teilhard de Chardin)

Dryden said that the *Georgics* was the best work of the best poet;[1]
and if that be a slight exaggeration, we might at least agree that no
poem on such a scale has come so close to perfection. The third
book, masterly in technique, does not quite achieve the same quality of inspiration as the others, and a severe criticism might find that
a small blemish. The second and fourth books reach the greatest
heights, but if the first book alone had survived, it would suffice
to establish the *Georgics* as one of the very finest achievements of
classical poetry. Though it yields more and more upon each re-
reading, it is not essentially a difficult work, and it has not been
much misunderstood—or not until recently. Yet there are some difficulties in talking about it. The first is that so much of the merit
and indeed meaning of the poem resides in the details and their
accumulation that any description which falls short of being a commentary is likely to be inadequate. This book may seem, following a
track printed with the spoor of many large beasts, to fall into the trap
of dwelling on the purple patches at the expense of the didactic
sections which make up the greater part of the poem; but it will
indeed give space to examining the didactic texture, and it will try
to show how the different elements in the work relate to each other.
Certainly any interpretation of the *Georgics* is false which turns the
didactic parts into padding between the bits that really matter. A

---

[1] In the dedicatory letter to Lord Chesterfield prefixed to his translation of the *Georgics*.

second difficulty arises from one of the work's glories. This is the most superbly constructed of all larger poems. It is also very grandly constructed: it equals and probably surpasses all other poetry in the building of immense paragraphs. These virtues are hard to discuss and illustrate, especially on the printed page; none the less, this account will attempt also to examine the poem's architectonics and explain how its shape and scale help to form its meaning.

The metaphor of structure derives originally from building, and in some respects the construction of the *Georgics* well fits the analogy with architecture, where we look for the balancing of mass and proportion. The poem is carefully symmetrical. The four books hardly vary in length;[2] the first and third begin with long proems and end abruptly, with violent passages lacking words of conclusion; the second and fourth books have short introductions and short paragraphs to round them off. In a broad sense—and only in a broad sense— the poem's tone too is given a symmetry, the first and third books being predominantly strenuous and serious, the second and fourth expansive and relaxed.[3]

When we talk of a building's structure, we speak literally; when the term 'structure' is applied to music, it becomes a metaphor. Poetry is, like music, an experience in time, and the principles of literary form are in many ways closer to those of music than to those of the visual arts. To be sure, architecture itself commonly offers an experience in time—the interior of a cathedral is to be understood by moving around it, not by standing at a single point, and the builder of a palace may achieve his effects by taking the spectator up a staircase or walking him through a sequence of rooms—but the distinction between auditory and visual experience remains important. When we look at the façade of a building, we expect to find that it is symmetrical, or if not symmetrical, that the masses on the right-hand side, though differently disposed, answer to those on the left. But the larger a musical form is, the less it is likely to meet such canons of balance or proportion: the last phrase of a tune may respond to its beginning, but we have no natural expectation that the last movement of a symphony will recapitulate the material or match the

---

[2] The third book is 566 lines long, the last book only one line shorter (4. 338 is spurious). Line numbering was not introduced until the 17th cent., and even so near an approach to exact equality will not have been planned.

[3] So B. Otis, *Virgil: A Study in Civilized Poetry* (Oxford, 1963), 151.

size of the first, or that the last notes of a movement will echo its opening. The form or structure of a work of auditory art may rather be a matter of development or evolution, and poetry is at root an auditory art.[4] Paradoxically, composers seem readier than writers to think of themselves as architects; a metaphor does not lack explanatory or inspirational force because it is a metaphor. Rather, the paradox suggests that when thinking of a large poem's structure it may be helpful to bear both the architectural and the musical analogy in mind; and this is perhaps especially true of the *Georgics*.

The *Eclogues* seem consciously 'closed' both in their limited range of content and in their form, though even in these poems Virgil has ways, as we have seen, of undercutting his closing devices. But in the *Georgics* Virgil dares the experiment of what we might call open structures. On one level each book is beautifully complete and self-contained, its internal structure built up with consummate elegance, and the books are related to each other, both through likeness and through contrast, with a 'classical' neatness and balance; in these respects the work's construction is 'architectural'. But counterpointing this neatness—and indeed made possible by it—is a different tendency. This is most obviously seen in the startlingly abrupt endings of the first and third books, the noise and fury suddenly shut off when at their loudest and harshest. The end of the first book is especially bold: as it describes, in metaphor and simile, a world out of control, the very last line mimics the anarchy by the hectic irregularity of its rhythm (a weak caesura in the third foot without the strong caesura in the fourth which would normally follow it, producing a coincidence of ictus and accent in all but the second foot, so that the verse hurtles forward):[5]

> saevit toto Mars impius orbe,
> ut cum carceribus sese effudere quadrigae,
> addunt in spatia, et frustra retinacula tendens
> fertur equis auriga neque audit currus habenas.

The unholy War-God rages throughout the whole world, as when chariots burst out from the barriers, gathering speed with each lap, and the driver, tugging the harness to no avail, is borne along by the horses, and the car does not hearken to the reins.

---

[4] We might reflect that poetry had existed for thousands, perhaps tens of thousands of years before writing was invented. On the longest view, it is only very recent poetry that has been recorded at all.   [5] *Geo.* I. 511–14.

Perhaps no book in any poem ends with such precipitous confusion. However, we may say that in a formal view Virgil creates a structure that in its totality seems controlled and assured, since the endings of the first and third books behave similarly and in one sense each is well prepared because it caps an immense paragraph of obviously climactic bravura; and yet the expressive effect is different. But indeed it is the formal control that makes the fierce dissonance of the expression at such a point possible: in the first book above all, the near hysteria of the conclusion might, we feel, collapse into neurotic chaos if the larger structure of the poem lacked the strength safely to contain it. And thus the tension between the structure and the expression becomes itself a type of expression, dramatic and moving. The firmness of Virgil's framework is demonstrated by the freedom that it allows him within it: he can afford to end the book with so vivid a representation of impassioned disorder because the poem as a whole will restore a final balance of proportion and feeling. The third Georgic reinforces the moral: its sudden and savage ending with the plague in Noricum is modelled on *De Rerum Natura*, which ends with the plague at Athens, but at least in terms of poetic organization Virgil improves upon his pattern. Lucretius' conclusion, for all its force, is an aesthetic misjudgement, not because it is abrupt or horrific, but because these things, in his treatment of them, seem arbitrary;[6] Virgil realized that the wilder the beast, the stronger should be the fencing around it. In the *Aeneid* he will show that even in a very long poem a sudden ending may be an entire success, but this is perhaps the most brilliantly organized piece of construction anywhere in his epic: Jupiter recapitulates the grand themes that he announced in the first book; what there was prophecy is now achieved, or ready for achievement, through Aeneas' victory and Juno's conversion; the story is complete, the issues resolved, and the poet is free to storm through a coda unmatched for velocity and force.

---

[6] Lucretius' ending is philosophically puzzling—no really satisfactory explanation has been offered—and the philosophy and poetry of *De Rerum Natura* are so much a unity that the intellectual and aesthetic problems cannot be entirely separated; but this would be too large an issue for the present occasion, even if a solution were to hand. Transposition of lines may lessen the literary fault—the last line in the transmitted text seems especially unhappy in its important place—but cannot remove it. The length of the last book and the disposition of the whole work discourage the speculation that the poem is incomplete. Interesting attempts to resolve the problem have been made recently by D. Clay, *Lucretius and Epicurus* (Ithaca, 1983), 250 ff., and C. Segal, *Lucretius on Death and Anxiety* (Princeton, 1990), 228 ff.

At the end of the second Georgic the closing paragraph, a mere two lines long, is carefully casual:[7]

> Sed nos immensum spatiis confecimus aequor,
> et iam tempus equum fumantia solvere colla.

But we have traversed a boundless plain on our course, and it is now time to unyoke the horses' steaming necks.

No violence or passion here; indeed, these lines, in their quiet way, resolve the dissonance at the end of the first Georgic. Again, there is a metaphor drawn from horses, and the resemblance is lightly reinforced by verbal parallels: in each book 'equus' appears in the last and 'spatium' in the penultimate line. But whereas the horses before were careering out of control, now they have obediently fulfilled their day's work.[8] The style of this ending answers to the themes of the whole book. The second Georgic celebrates fertility and flowing abundance, and form matching content, the lyric fecundity seems as though it might flow on almost for ever, did not the poet gently interpose, 'But it's time to stop.' The essence of this book is expansiveness; but expansiveness is also a quality of the work as a whole, expressed through its construction—construction in this case of the musical type, an evolution through time. The *Georgics* sets itself in a relationship to Hesiod's *Works and Days*, as the *Eclogues* to Theocritus and the *Aeneid* to Homer, but with this difference, that it is only the first book which parallels the Greek model.[9] Like the butterfly cracking open its chrysalis, the poem breaks out of its hard archaic casing and expands gloriously into three more glitteringly variegated books.

The last of these presses forward into areas of style, subject, and experience unattempted in the earlier parts. Hitherto the *Georgics* has had no people in it, but now Virgil's account of the old gardener of Tarentum brings an individual into the poem for the first time.[10] Formally, this passage is a pendant, or a transition; expressively, it leads the poem in a new direction, preparing the way for more individuals, Aristaeus, Orpheus, and Eurydice, and for the human drama

---

[7] *Geo.* 2. 541 f.

[8] For another resolution in the second book of a dissonance at the end of the first see below, p. 361. For a dissonance at the end of the first book resolved at the end of the fourth see Jenkyns, 'Virgil and the Euphrates', *AJP* 114 (1993), 115–21.

[9] As Virgil indicates in the poem's very first line; see below, p. 325.

[10] *Geo* 4. 125 ff.

that will burst forth in the last half of the book. And this conclusion breaks out of the poem's bounds in other ways too: it introduces mythology and narrative—and a new style also, the elaborately plangent pathos known to us from Catullus' neoteric manner and from the *Eclogues*—a tone which until now has been kept out of the *Georgics*. Another individual who begins to emerge from the shadows is Virgil himself. Where he presents himself in the first half of the poem, his personality is usually hidden by the bardic robes in which he has wrapped himself. 'Pity with me the country people who know not the way', 'I sing Ascraean song through Roman towns'—the voice is as public and vatic as Horace's when he declares, as priest of the Muses, 'Odi profanum vulgus et arceo.'[11] Reticence replaces Hesiod's chatty self-disclosures, and any kind of appeal to personal experience is rare. 'Vidi equidem,' he says, (I have myself seen), but all that follows is a way of treating beans.[12] 'Vidi' comes twice more in the first book, but the observations are such as any Roman in the countryside might have made: seeds rotting, autumn storms.[13] He includes within the praise of country life late in the second Georgic some lines about his capacities and his hopes for his work; but it is still Virgil the author and hardly at all Virgil the man that he is presenting here, and the limited sense of self-disclosure is yet further muffled by a language which blurs the distinction between poet and simple countryman.[14] In the proem to the third book the pose is as vatic as ever, but an individual, though hardly a private, note is newly brought in by the appearance of Mantua and the River Mincius. Finally, in the fourth book, the Corycian gardener is introduced as a personal memory, and in the poem's very last lines we are surprised by details unprecedented in a *sphragis*: the time, place, age and past work of P. Vergilius Maro.[15]

A sense of the poem's evolutionary construction may help in understanding the place of the story of Aristaeus. This is a famous puzzle, though it has perhaps troubled those who write about Virgil more than those who read him. Scholars have been perplexed to

---

[11] *Geo.* 1. 41, 2. 176; Hor. *Carm.* 3. 1. 1 and 3.   [12] *Geo.* 1. 193.

[13] *Geo.* 1. 197, 318. 'This is not autobiographical but didactic, emphatically asserting the veracity of the detail which follows' (R. Thomas on 'vidi' at 1. 193).

[14] *Geo.* 2. 475 ff.

[15] *Geo.* 4. 125 ff., 559 ff. Nicander begins his *Alexipharmaca* (1–11) by indicating that he is writing from Colophon to a friend in Cyzicus. Such was the sort of *sphragis* that Virgil had as his model, but he says much more and says it at the end. The effect is thus of an expansion in the degree of self-disclosure.

explain what a long narrative is doing at the end of a didactic poem, and have hunted for a 'meaning'; numerous solutions have been offered, but most seem arbitrary, many seem implausible, and all accuse one another by their diversity.[16] One interpretation appears to have remained widely influential. Virgil (it is suggested) celebrates the beauty of art and laments its limitations; Orpheus, the poet, the aesthete, is contrasted with Aristaeus, the practical man of action; Orpheus, though deeply sympathetic, fails, for art and love cannot prevail over death, while Aristaeus gains his end; and thus Virgil dramatizes the idea that art, which means so much to himself, is lovely but ineffectual, whereas the unromantic Aristaeus succeeds.[17] That is an eloquent conception, but it is not Virgil's. Orpheus' art is not ineffectual: it can amaze the house of the dead, paralyse Cerberus and stop Ixion's wheel. Nor is he a dreamy aesthete but a man of action who dares to penetrate the underworld, like the heroes Hercules and Theseus and (in a poem not yet written) Aeneas. His only mistake, to look back at his wife, breaking the condition that Proserpina had imposed, is made solely because he loves too much; that is a failure neither of art nor of enterprise.

So we are left without a 'meaning' for the story of Aristaeus—at least without a meaning in the sense of an allegory or a message or a summation of the poem as a whole. Perhaps the search for such a meaning is misguided. Let us consider what we may reasonably infer. It is extremely improbable that Virgil's first readers had some key to his purpose that is lost to us; if modern critics' ingenuity cannot find it, the likelihood must be that it never existed. Possibly if more poetry survived from the mid-century, it would illuminate some points of detail; but it is very hard to imagine how the possession of (say) Cinna's *Zmyrna* and Calvus' *Io* could resolve the central problem of exegesis. And possibly they would make scant difference at all.

[16] In two pages of savage urbanity Griffin surveys seventeen interpretations produced over a period of twelve years (*Latin Poets and Roman Life* (1985), 163 ff.). He has not put a stop to the game. R. O. A. M. Lyne is able to believe that the story symbolizes the Battle of Actium (*Horace: Behind the Public Poetry* (New Haven and London, 1995), 46). Some may be surprised to learn from Ross that Orpheus, lover and singer, who is not represented as doing any kind of work apart from making music, should represent ' "scientific poetry", which is to say intellectual understanding of the world' (p. 226). Do you object that 'control of nature through intellectual understanding' (p. 227) suggests, if anyone, Aristaeus rather than Orpheus? Ross has the answer for you: Aristaeus 'is ultimately equivalent to Orpheus' (p. 229).   [17] Griffin, *Latin Poets and Roman Life*.

The story of the neoteric poets is familiar enough. They produced a number of mythological poems of medium length; besides the *Zmyrna* and the *Io* we know of Cornificius' *Glaucus*, and the surviving example is Catullus' *Peleus and Thetis*. Modern scholarship has fixed on this kind of poem the label 'epyllion', a useful term, though notoriously unsatisfactory because it smuggles in the implication that these works are in some relationship to epic.[18] Given our ignorance, the label may also seduce us into assuming that these poems were fairly similar, whereas in truth they have perished so entirely, Catullus apart, that we know almost nothing about them.[19] We do know enough about Catullus, though, to realize that he was original in everything he did. No one again tried to write love poetry in hendecasyllables; that was a game which could only be played once. Each of his longer pieces is an experiment of some kind, and in two of them, 64 and 68, he took the risk of writing a work without any one dominant theme. In the sixty-fourth poem the myth of Ariadne is placed inside the account of Peleus and Thetis' wedding, and takes up half the length of the work. We should not want to say that it was 'about' either Ariadne or Peleus and Thetis; the poem refuses to focus upon a single subject. In itself the story within a story is as old as Homer; and it is a device that Callimachus used in his *Hecale*. Catullus' originality is a matter partly of proportion, partly of tone. No longer is the inset story subordinate; indeed, it seems to be the emotional heart of the poem. The piece is full of bright scenes and decorative surfaces; the style is glossy, self-aware in its display, conscious of the poem as artefact; and Ariadne herself is literally a work of art, for even within the fiction of the poem she is not a living presence but an embroidered figure on a tapestry. Yet despite the mannerism and the high polish, the work is mysteriously moving: it creates a new aesthetic, in which the sheen of the surface is not a barrier to poignancy but the means of its expression.

---

[18] *Epyllion* means 'little word' and its present use as a literary term is without classical Greek authority. Though this is well known, the idea of a relationship to epic seems to linger on, encouraged perhaps by the beliefs that the neoterics worshipped Callimachus and that Callimachus was hostile to epic poetry. The first of these suppositions is exaggerated and the second wrong.

[19] Three lines of *Zmyrna* are extant, six of *Io*. It is an easy but insecure assumption that the works of friends or acquaintances will be similar. See the judicious observations of E. J. Kenney in 'Doctus Lucretius', *Mnem.* ser. 4, 23 (1970), 366–92, at 368, citing the Bloomsbury Group as a comparison. How much does *The General Theory of Economics* have in common with *Mrs Dalloway*? And who belongs? Does Forster? does Eliot?

The nearest parallel to this in Greek literature is Theocritus' first Idyll, a dialogue between Thyrsis and a goatherd, each of whom presents a 'work of art'. The goatherd describes a cup carved with fabulous skill; Thyrsis sings the jewel of his repertoire, the song of Daphnis' death. Callimachus does not affect this aesthetic: he is a scholar, a learned poet, clever perhaps, allusive maybe, but not a virtuoso of style or tone. Catullus, for his part, was not an *érudit*, though some modern scholars, reluctant perhaps to believe that a great poet could be much unlike themselves, seem to imagine that Catullus and his friends were learned people—as though these young men about town, after a hard day's wine and love-making, liked nothing better than to relax with a volume of etymology or mythography. The application of the word 'doctus' to poets and their acquaintance has perhaps misled; in some of these contexts it means something like 'educated', 'cultivated', or 'of educated taste'.[20] It is true that Cinna's *Zmyrna* had a reputation for obscurity,[21] but obscurity and allusiveness are not the same as learning, and even if Cinna was learned in the manner of a Hellenistic scholar poet, the distinctiveness of his reputation suggests that the other new poets were not. *Peleus and Thetis*, after all, is not obscure, though it is unusual; the more weight we give to Cinna's reputation for difficulty, the more we must distinguish him from his famous friend.

Peleus and Thetis, then, seems to be essentially an original and personal achievement. It is a work of the innovator and experimenter who wrote Poems 65 and 68 and love poems in scazons and hendecasyllables. Did he have imitators? The style would not have been easy to copy: the neoterics may have had some quirks of diction or prosody in common—Cicero noted their fondness for spondees in the fifth foot of the hexameter—[22] but one can no more decide to write with glittering beauty than one can decide to master the

---

[20] We hear of 'doctus . . . Catullus' at [Tib.] 3. 6. 41. Catullus does put on a momentary show of learning, referring to an obscure cult, when he calls Minerva/Athena the goddess of Itonus at 64. 228 (this, preposterously, from the mouth of Aegeus, king of Athens, Minerva's own city). It is a gesture towards Callimachus, a playful and momentary pretence of erudition, which he makes no attempt to sustain.

[21] Suetonius, *Gramm.* 18: the grammarian Crassicius made his name by explicating it. According to Catullus (95. 1 f.) it took nine years to write, a claim which was already taken literally by Quintilian (10. 4. 4) and has been by many scholars since. It is likely to be a humorous exaggeration; if true it would be another instance of Cinna's unusualness: few poets would care to fuss over a piece of moderate length for so long.

[22] Cic. *Att.* 7. 2. 1.

Hammerklavier Sonata.[23] To follow Catullus in this required a virtuoso who was his equal or superior; someone, that is, like Virgil. But apart from style, there is also the question of construction. If we had *Io* and *Zmyrna* and *Glaucus*, would we find that each one of them consisted of a story within a story, with the inner story occupying as least as much space and emotional weight as the other? It seems very implausible. And indeed the likenesses between Catullus' poem and Virgil's go further still. In each case the two stories have no previous connection, but are brought together by a transparently flimsy and artificial link: in Catullus Ariadne happens to be the subject of the embroidery on the bridal bed of Peleus and Thetis, in Virgil Eurydice happened to be running from Aristaeus when she was fatally bitten by a snake. Contrasts between the inner and outer stories, not made explicit, are lightly implied: in Catullus between passion within marriage and passion outside it, between a happy love and an unhappy, in Virgil between recovery from a loss and a loss that is not recovered.[24] Even one of the dislocations which are a feature of Catullus' aesthetic is imitated by Virgil. In *Peleus and Thetis* Ariadne will gulp her last sobbing words, we are told; a flowing speech of eighty lines follows. In the Georgic Proteus, the old man of the sea, delivers his tale reluctantly, rolling his eyes and grinding his teeth; yet there is no harshness in the telling, but some eighty lines of exquisitely melodious plangency. Virgil does not imitate the older poet's metrical idiolect, for technically he was indeed superior to his model: whereas Catullus favours end-stopping, Virgil exploits the resources of enjambment to the full, and whereas Catullus constructs a great many lines with a word of three long syllables after the caesura, Virgil is much more various. Nor does he follow Catullus in affecting the fifth-foot spondee. But in terms of the aesthetic he is Catullus' disciple—that is, in achieving high

---

[23] A pair of lines and one other single line are all that survives of *Zmyrna*. The couplet (fr. 6 Courtney) is lumpishly expressed.

[24] The likeness between the two poems may extend further and more subtly: in each are oppositions which prove less simple than at first they seem. *Peleus and Thetis* seems to present a contrast between a happy and an unhappy tale, but at the end of the Ariadne episode we learn that Iacchus is about to bring her a new love, and a more glorious one—the love of a god. The fourth Georgic seems to present a contrast between the birth of a new swarm of bees and the fate of man, for whom there is no rebirth after death. And yet Eurydice is almost brought back from the dead: it is only because Orpheus breaks Proserpina's command and looks round at her that she is not restored. The apparent contrast between humanity and nature's everlasting power of renewal is imperfect.

pathos through self-conscious artifice, a bravura manner and an elaborated beauty of sound and expression.

We have good reason, then, to believe that for the story of Aristaeus, Orpheus, and Eurydice Virgil has attached himself to a single poet, as elsewhere to Hesiod, Theocritus, and Homer. That is not to say that there are no references to others: the *Odyssey* is laid under contribution for Aristaeus' encounter with Proteus, the *Iliad* for Cyrene and her nymphs, and no doubt if more neoteric poems had survived, we should pick up echoes here and there. But the essential relation, we may suppose, is with *Peleus and Thetis*, and this being so, it should shed light upon this part of the *Georgics*. Catullus' poem has no central theme, almost no meaning beyond itself, no message available to be easily cashed out. (It does end with some moralizing reflections upon the wickedness of mankind, but these should be regarded as a coda, distinct from the rest of the poem.) It offers art if not for art's sake then for the sake of sentiment and beauty. Now it is in principle possible that Virgil took Catullus as his model only to turn his themes and ideas to a radically new purpose, but it seems pretty clear that this is not the case, since no one has been able to find a message or moral that is not improbable or wholly subjective. One of the charms of *Peleus and Thetis* is that it keeps surprising the reader by taking him in new directions: we do not expect the story of Peleus to divert so quickly and lengthily to the story of Ariadne, or Ariadne's laments to end with the arrival of Iacchus, or the wedding song to be sung by the Fates, with a grim picture of the future Trojan War, or the poem to conclude with a denunciation of the crimes of mankind. Like Catullus, Virgil develops his poem as it advances: the Roman 'Works and Days' of the first Georgic expands into four whole books, the fourth book finally flowers gloriously into neoteric mythology that blithely resists the anxieties of the commentators.

The proof of the pudding is in the eating. The truth is surely that readers have not felt that the story of Aristaeus and Orpheus is out of place or awkwardly introduced, however puzzled they may have been by its function. Virgil has taken a chance and pulled it off. Whereas we may feel some loss of control at the end of *Peleus and Thetis*, Virgil seems to retain complete mastery of his material. Formally speaking, the Aristaeus episode is justified as explaining the origin of *bougonia*, the birth of a swarm from the corpse of an ox, and so tightly controlled is his structure that the formality suffices. At the end of the *Georgics* he seems to take off into free flight, but it is the discipline of his form that makes that easy freedom possible.

Did Virgil believe in *bougonia*, or is it for him a fantasy with poetic possibilities? We cannot be sure, but the question raises the issue of truth and invention in the *Georgics*. Earlier he has insisted that he is not writing fiction (non . . . carmine ficto),[25] and as we shall see, it is crucial to the poem that it is about the real countryside, the real Italy. And yet he combines this essential veracity with a cheerful insouciance about the details. (There is a parallel of a kind with the *Aeneid*, where he explores the idea of history with an intensity and seriousness that deters him not at all from using bold fabrication and anachronism. Similarly, he plants lofty hanging woods on the barren coast of Tunisia—false (as he must have known) as a picture of the African shore, keenly truthful as a representation of landscape and man's apprehension of it.)[26] A good instance of his technique can be seen in the second book, only a few lines after his denial that he writes fiction:[27]

> nec modus inserere atque oculos imponere simplex.
> nam qua se medio trudunt de cortice gemmae
> et *tenuis* rumpunt tunicas, *angustus* in *ipso*
> fit nodo sinus; huc aliena ex arbore germen
> *in*cludunt udoque *docent inolescere* libro.
> aut rursum enodes *trunci resecantur*, et *alte*
> *finditur* in *solidum cuneis* via, deinde *feraces*
> plantae immittuntur: *nec longum tempus*, et *ingens*
> exiit ad caelum ramis *felicibus* arbos,
> *miratas*tque novas frondes et non sua poma.

Nor are the methods of grafting and budding the same. For where the buds push out from the bark and break their fine sheaths, a narrow slit is made right on the knot; here they insert a shoot from an alien tree and teach it to grow into the moist sapwood. Alternatively, knotless trunks are cut back, a path is cleft deep into the core with wedges, and then the fruitful slips are put in. It is not long before a mighty tree has shot up heavenwards with prosperous branches, wondering at its unfamiliar leaves and fruits not its own.

---

[25] *Geo.* 2. 45.

[26] On Virgil's anachronisms see W. Kroll, *Studien zum Verständnis der römischen Literatur* (Stuttgart, 1924), 178–84, and F. H. Sandbach, 'Anti-Antiquarianism in the *Aeneid*', *PVS* 5 (1965–6), 26–38, reprinted in Harrison, 449–65.   [27] *Geo.* 2. 73–82.

Other authorities knew three or even four methods of grafting;[28] Virgil cut them down to two for the sake of symmetry and contrast. He represents budding as a sensitive operation: the sheaths are thin, the slit narrow, the cut must be made precisely on the knot. He depicts gradual process through the inceptive verb 'inolescere'; the impression of careful exactitude is enhanced by the repetition in the verb 'inolescunt . . . includere'—we seem to be close beside the husbandman, observing the delicate incision—as also by the pathetic fallacy of 'docent', with its implication of watchful nurturing. By contrast, crown-grafting is portrayed as a rude, rugged business: trunks are cut back, wedges are driven deep into the thickness of the wood, the scions are robust, and whereas the slips inserted by budding had to learn to assimilate themselves, these grafts grow with a speed and scale that provoke astonishment.

Of course, the distinction between the two means of grafting is quite unreal: no one could graft successfully if he went about the business with the rough vigour which Virgil attributes to his second method. He knows it, and he does not care. Only a pedant would object to the poet's licence, which is entirely characteristic of the way in which he quietly vivifies his more unemphatic passages of agricultural instruction. The contrast between the subtle and the rude kinds of grafting has its own charm, and for Virgil that is enough. No one will understand or appreciate the *Georgics* who cannot allow the poet this much freedom.

Virgil's invention in matters of detail has a consequence for the interpretation of the poem. The view has been canvassed that he plants falsehoods in the text deliberately: the reader (so it is maintained) is intended to pick these up and thereby acquire a larger mistrust of the poet's veracity. But even if he had wanted to play this curious game, his method, which allows him such ample latitude in minor matters of fact, would have prevented it. One might add that those who believe in Virgil's lies usually want to wrench the poem in a pessimistic direction: warned of his mendacity, we are to doubt the passages of praise and joy. Yet the most blatant fabrications in the *Georgics* are the majority of those portents that follow the death of Julius Caesar (near the end of the first book) and the plague in

---

[28] Mynors ad loc.

Noricum at the end of the third.[29] The believers in Virgil the liar
strain at gnats and swallow camels.[30]

Another issue of interpretation in the fourth book may introduce
us to the question of the character of the poem as a whole. It has
often been held that the bees are symbolic, though there has been
less agreement on what they might be symbols of. This is a classic
example of how a misguided idea lingers on once it has got into
the bloodstream of scholarship. The older notion was that the bees
represented an ideal human society.[31] Later critics have seen that this
cannot be right; but rather than getting rid of the idea of symbolism altogether, some have tried to salvage it by proposing that the
bees might stand for some different kind of human organization. Yet
the text gives no warrant for any such interpretation, and indeed
the notion that the bees symbolize any human society can be ruled
out for various reasons, some of them strikingly simple.

First, the bees have no sexuality.[32] That is not true of any human
society, nor could it be true of any that is to endure for generations,
as the bees' does.[33] Second, the bees are likened to little Quirites,
Roman citizens; yet only a few lines later we learn that not even
Egyptians, Lydians, Parthians, or Medes show such devotion to their
king: once he perishes, their community collapses.[34] Stalwart Romans
and servile orientals—these are incompatible forms of society, and

[28] Mynors ad loc.
[29] 'It matters little for the *Georgics* whether or not this plague really occurred (and it
seems likely that it did not . . .).' This from Thomas (on 3. 474–7), who elsewhere keeps
an eagle eye out for Publius' porkies.
[30] We must also remember, of course, that some of Virgil's inaccuracies are due to limited knowledge or wrong belief. In other cases ignorance or conflicting opinions may have
made poetic licence the easier. We do not know whether Virgil realized that some of his
grafts were impossible; we do know that the ancients did not understand the biological
principles in question. Columella declares that any slip can be grafted on to any tree
provided that the barks of the two species are not dissimilar (5. 11. 1; *Arb.* 26. 1). Pliny
knows of an experiment—he saw it himself—in which a tree was grafted with many
different fruits, and bore walnuts, grapes, pears, figs, pomegranates and apples (*Nat. Hist.*
17. 120). That is impossible: either Pliny is lying or he was gulled. (The tree did not
live long, he adds: was someone destroying the evidence, or did the insertion of boughs
already laden with fruit do too much damage?) Whatever the case, the anecdote indicates
what an ancient naturalist could believe and expect his readers to believe. Virgil's grafts
are modest by comparison. And indeed Pliny takes him seriously, twice citing him on this
subject (17. 100, 105).
[31] Examples are cited by Griffin, *Latin Poets and Roman Life*, 165 f. His refutation is brisk
and decisive: how could Virgil hold up as an ideal model an impersonal, collectivist society without sympathy or understanding for art and love?   [32] *Geo.* 4. 198 f.
[33] *Geo.* 4. 208 f.   [34] *Geo.* 4. 201, 210–18.

no one thing can symbolize both at once. If Virgil's bees are real bees, there is no problem. 'Quirites' is a metaphor, and the reference to orientals a comparison. In some respects the bees are like human beings, in some not; at one moment they may suggest Romans, at another the unquestioning obedience of the east.[35]

On these grounds alone a symbolist interpretation of the fourth Georgic is to be rejected, but there are other reasons why it obstructs our appreciation of the poem. The whole of the *Georgics*, as we shall see, presents the beauty and value of nature, and of the smallest facts of nature, for their own sakes; and Virgil reasserts this idea—surely in the clearest terms—right at the start of the fourth book. He tells Maecenas that he is going to set forth 'admiranda tibi levium spectacula rerum' (the show of a tiny world at which you shall marvel)[36] —sights, that is, which are to excite our admiration for themselves. He does not say that the bees stand for large and lofty affairs; on the contrary the edge and vividness of his argument are that he is

[35] Griffin wants the bees to put us in mind of early Roman society. This influential interpretation is compatible with an understanding of the bees that falls short of full symbolism, but despite the elegance and panache with which it is put forward, there are very strong arguments against it even in a modified form. (1) There is nothing in the text to suggest that Virgil has *early* Rome in mind at all. (2) The comparison to eastern monarchies is much more extensive and explicit than any reference to Rome. The bees have a 'city', 'homes' and so on, but these are likenesses to human organization in general. Specific reference to Rome seems to be limited to the single word 'Quirites'; elsewhere the bees are depicted as (for example) armies under rival kings. (3) The bees' sexlessness remains an obstacle to their evoking any society in a sustained way, let alone manly Rome. (4) Griffin himself observes that the bees' society is 'impersonal, collective, Stakhanovite, without art' (166). Early Rome had art, though it may not have been distinguished art. No ancient society, not even the Spartans', was collective in the sense familiar to us from the dictatorships and police states of the twentieth century. The epithet 'Stakhanovite' is witty—too witty, for it should alert us to the anachronism being imposed here: no Roman could have regarded a communistic ideal and grinding industrial toil as characteristic of his nation's past. Early Rome is a city of great individuals: Curtius, Horatius, Lucius Brutus.

Griffin maintains that Virgil here adumbrates an idea that he will develop in the *Aeneid*: that the Romans have to renounce art for the sake of their task of conquest and government. This in turn rests upon a misinterpretation of a famous passage, the climax of Anchises' speech (*Aen.* 6. 847–53). Anchises says not that the Romans will have no art but that others (the Greeks) will practise the arts *better*. Virgil could not be meaning him to say that the Romans would never have any arts, because (first) it would be an absurd untruth and (second) he includes forensic oratory, which Cicero had brought to great heights. (The implied judgement is rather that however fine Cicero may be, Demosthenes is yet finer.) He could not even have wanted to suggest that the Roman must give up the 'aesthetic life', an existence given over wholly to the arts and graces of civilization, for if that had been his purpose, he would not have mentioned forensic oratory, pre-eminently a part of the public life of the man of action. [36] *Geo.* 4. 3.

dealing with 'light matters', and yet we are to wonder at them.[37] Here again Virgil appears one for whom the visible world exists. As he explains,[38]

> in tenui labor; at tenuis non gloria, si quem
> numina laeva sinunt auditque vocatus Apollo.

My field is slight, but not slight the glory, if the adverse powers permit and Apollo hears my prayer.

It is hard to make much sense of this if Virgil is embarking upon allegory and the bees stand for anything other than themselves. The point is in the paradox: the theme is indeed miniature, and yet it has its own splendour; 'gloria', as we shall discover, is an echo from earlier in the poem, in which the paradox has been embodied.

To return to Virgil's preceding words:[39]

> admiranda tibi levium spectacula rerum
> magnanimosque duces totiusque ordine gentis
> mores et studia et populos et proelia dicam.

I shall set forth in due order the show of a tiny world at which you shall marvel—great-hearted chiefs and the customs, concerns, tribes and battles of an entire race.

No sooner has he introduced the bees—as bees—than he is decorating them by metaphor and analogy. And for the next two hundred lines the hive will be recurrently likened to a human polity, with words like 'city', 'town', 'house', 'penates', and 'lar'.[40] But the charm of this is precisely that the bees are not human; the technique is one that Virgil has favoured in earlier books, as for example when a vintage is described as a king or as standing up in deference to a superior.[41] When the bees are called 'wee Quirites', the verse is freshly and momentarily lit by an amusing thought that seems to have flashed newly across the poet's mind.

Virgil likes to look at things from a bee's eye view, often with lightly humorous effect. He refers, for example, to the 'ingens oleaster'; now the olive does not strike one as a huge tree—unless, of course, one is a bee.[42] A few lines later we are told to hurl 'great

---

[37] Line 3 is hard to put into English. 'Of a tiny world' for 'levium . . . rerum' is borrowed from Fairclough's Loeb translation, but the sense 'light matters' needs also to be felt; otherwise Virgil's point is blunted, and the tang of paradox lost.

[38] *Geo.* 4. 6 f.   [39] *Geo.* 4. 3–5.

[40] *Geo.* 4. 193, 178, 209, 155, 43.   [41] *Geo.* 2. 98.

[42] *Geo.* 4. 20 'huge wild-olive'. At 4. 273 the ironic hyperbole 'ingentem . . . silvam' (mighty forest), of a plant that grows in a clump, has a similar effect, though the bees are in the background here.

rocks' into the waters where the bees resort, for them to settle on.[43] How big are these rocks? We turn to Virgil's source, Varro, and find that they are 'sherds' and 'pebbles'.[44] The pond, Varro says, should be two or three fingers deep; Virgil turns it into a sea, elevating it yet more by the grandiose metonymy 'Neptunus'.[45] When the bees are compared to Cyclopes, the simile is especially piquant because it is tiny insects who are being likened to these giants.[46] But the humour does not exclude seriousness, or even solemnity. We are bidden 'admirari'—to admire in the modern English sense as well as to marvel—and at once Virgil is pointing to the great spirits of these minute creatures.[47] That is a quaint thought, but it is also respect-ful. So again, and more explicitly, in the battle of the bees, where the two kings 'ingentis animos angusto in pectore versant' (have vast passions tossing in their narrow breasts)[48] Virgil can present human-kind to us as at once great and little,[49] and now he will treat these insects in the same way: their battle is impressive while it lasts, but we may end it by sprinkling a handful of dust.[50] He gains by an alternation of vision, studying the bees sometimes empathetically, from their own viewpoint, sometimes with a godlike remoteness. That may enlarge our understanding of our place in the scheme of things. As we govern our bees, now cherishing them, now tearing off wings, killing the defeated king, or preventing their fickle spirits from unprofitable play, we can reflect that we are treating them as Jupiter in the first book treated us, with an impassive severity, cruel maybe, perhaps incomprehensible to its victims, yet not without a purpose.[51] From which we may learn something of what it is to be human.

In considering the general character of the *Georgics* we should beware of being caught by an easy fallacy: that poets have a particular 'view of life' and that they express the whole of it throughout their works.

---

[43] 'grandia conice saxa', *Geo.* 4. 26.   [44] Varro, *Rust.* 3. 16. 27: 'testae aut lapilli'.
[45] Varro, ibid.; *Geo.* 4. 29. Thomas, noting that the metonymy of Neptune does not occur in the *Aeneid*, suggests that Virgil might have avoided it there as a poetic cliché. If so, this would give a touch more satiric edge to his usage here.   [46] *Geo.* 4. 170–5.
[47] *Geo.* 4. 3 f., cited above.   [48] *Geo.* 4. 83.
[49] See e.g. below, p. 382.   [50] *Geo.* 4. 87.
[51] *Geo.* 4. 106 f. (removing the king's wings), 89 f. (killing the king), 105 (preventing play). Clipping or cutting off the wings was regular practice (Mynors on 103–8), but Mynors notes (on 90) that bees would in fact kill an unsuccessful queen themselves; so Virgil has chosen to make the bee-keeper harsher than he needed to. On the other hand we are to keep the bees to their task not only by immobilizing the king but by creating gardens that breathe enticing scents (109 ff.). So too perhaps does the divine power send upon us benisons and pain. (On Jupiter's purpose, see below, pp. 335 ff. and Appendix.)

Now it may be doubted whether most people have a clear and consistent view of life. Almost everybody believes that life is good —suicide is reckoned to be the product of madness or sickness—but we are inclined to lay weight at some times upon life's hardships and at another upon its blessings. So too with artists: it is really not surprising or paradoxical that the same man should compose one joyful and one tragic symphony, or write both *A Midsummer Night's Dream* and *King Lear*. There is another consideration too: an artist, composer, or writer may 'try out' a particular view of things; one might contemplate Milton's pair of poems, *L'Allegro* and *Il Penseroso*. Even a work on the very largest scale may be a construction—an experiment—in this sense: Wagner's *Ring* creates an entire human and cosmic order which is evidently to its maker a fiction, an idea of how things might be, not of how they are. We could indeed reflect on how far even the *Aeneid* might be understood on these terms.

Even if an individual poem does proclaim a distinctive vision of life, it does not follow that this is expressed in every part of it. If one part of the *Georgics* is serene or horrifying, we should not immediately assume that it conveys Virgil's sense of the entire world, and we can ask what the emotional character of a particular passage may owe to aesthetic considerations of form, variety or balance (which is not to say that the emotion in question must be factitious). The third Georgic will illustrate the point. The plague that fills its last hundred lines balances the terrible conclusion of the first book. That earlier passage was indeed at the heart of Virgil's concern for himself and his nation, but this is not. We should probably not be far astray in calling it a rhetorical set-piece, but even those who may find such a description too cool should allow that Virgil is not portraying a widespread or regular characteristic of the world; it is significant that he keeps the plague well away from Italy, in a Slovenian obscurity.

A similar moral may be drawn from this book as a whole. The subject is livestock, but here (as elsewhere) Virgil is selective: he deals fairly briefly with sheep and goats, and says nothing about pigs or chickens, all of which would have given the book a much different flavour if they had been allotted a larger part. It is evident that his stress on the violent and aggressive sexual passions of horses and cattle is selective in its turn; he knows, and his readers should know, that he could have dwelt upon peaceful ruminants or tractable herbivores had he so chosen. Equally, it would be rash to assume from his treatment of livestock that he supposes the human experience of sexual feelings to be universally unhappy and obsessive. All crea-tures, he declares in a sombre passage, are driven by love into the same frenzy of passion, beasts and birds and fishes and man also.[52] Yet there is a bleak magnificence in this vision of our own and our fellow creatures' vehemence and ferocity that is not without its dark appeal.[53] But even if we should find Virgil's picture here unrelievedly grim, it is not his whole picture: the last part of the poem will be dominated by a story of love and fidelity within marriage. Orpheus' history is a pathetic one, certainly, but the pathos resides in our sense that what he has lost was so good.

What is sure, from the second book and from the *Eclogues*, is that he was content, in the right place, to give a far rosier picture of country matters and the countryman's life. And indeed he indicates as much within the third book itself. Good spirits bubble up irre-pressibly as he breaks into an idyllic celebration of the shepherd's day —an idyll more extended than anything in the *Eclogues*. 'Carpamus', he calls, let us take to the fields, for he cannot resist joining in him-self, and he leads us out through the dewy cool of a summer morn-ing, on into a shady valley beneath the spreading boughs, a refuge from the noonday heat, and back home through a moonlit evening, as the birds once more take up their song.[54] Within the structure of the book, this lyrical interlude is short enough, but within the life of the countryman (if we listen to Virgil attentively) the space it occupies is large.

[52] *Geo.* 3. 242 ff.
[53] Virgil is writing under the shadow of Lucretius. Predominantly we are likely to feel that he has wrenched the excitement of Lucretius' invocation to Venus in a more savage direction; yet the memory of the earlier poet may remind us of the thrill that he found in the energy of violence. There is space for a range of response, depending on the mood or temperament of the reader. Or looking at the two poems as wholes, we might say that Virgil inverts the scheme of his model. Lucretius treats sexual passion exuberantly in his first book, savagely in his fourth; Virgil treats sexual love savagely in his third book but will 'redeem' it in his last.
Curiously enough, it is immediately after his paragraph on the wildness of sexual desire that Virgil remarks how time is fleeing irrecoverably while he lingers on details, captivated by love of his subject (284 f.). Perhaps he indicates that he is indeed enthralled by the force of physical passion, but it seems most natural to take his words as looking back over the book or the poem as a whole. On this account the preceding paragraph comes as an interruption, powerful and significant, but in some sense a diversion from the main flow of the discourse.
[54] *Geo.* 3. 322–38; 'carpamus' at 325. The verb is finely chosen, for though 'carpere iter' is, as Mynors says, 'little more than poetic diction for *ire*', in the context the word suggests the eagerness with which we pluck or grasp the delights of country existence. Compare Horace's 'carpe diem' (*Carm.* 1. 11. 7) and see Mynors ad loc.

Nor is this the only place in the book where cheerfulness breaks through. When he begins to describe the life of the Scythians in the frozen north, it sounds pretty miserable: never does the sun disperse the gloom of their perpetual winter, their clothes stiffen on their backs, the icicles harden on their beards, they have to take an axe to their wine.[55] But gradually the sheer oddity of this exotic world becomes more prominent than its discomforts. The cattle perish, big oxen stand around in frozen stillness (that still sounds wretched enough); the stags are so deep in snow that the tips of their antlers hardly stick out (this is starting to become quaint, and almost comic).[56] And now a gathering liveliness carries the story onward: the natives have no need to hunt these animals, but simply hew them down where they stand, and bring them home with loud shouts of rejoicing. In caves below the ground they build enormous fires—whole elms are thrown on to the hearth—and pass the night at play, merrily drinking their strange bitter liquor.[57] The jollity of this gains hugely in force from the way in which it has surged up from the chill and gloom. It is a good example of Virgil's 'musical' construction: the paragraph evolves—or modulates—as it proceeds. Yet when it is complete we realize how solidly the 'architecture' is made: the new turn given to the mood is held within a controlling structure. The paragraph is brought to a culmination through two favourite techniques of Virgil: the enrichment of texture through proper names, and last of all, to round the whole thing off, a patterned line—in this case virtually a golden line: 'et pecudum fulvis velatur corpora saetis.'[58]

Understandably, people want to know what the meaning or message of the *Georgics* may be; does Virgil, they ask, draw from nature a hopeful or a desponding moral? But if he is writing about the real world, he is dealing necessarily with a great variety of different phenomena, and he may not offer any simple answer.[59] It is

---

[55] *Geo.* 3. 356–66.   [56] *Geo.* 3. 368–70.   [57] *Geo.* 3. 371–80.

[58] 'And [this race] clothes their bodies in the tawny bristles of beasts' (*Geo.* 3. 383; the proper names cluster thick in the two preceding lines). The 'golden line' follows the pattern adjective adjective verb noun noun. The genitive 'pecudum' is adjectival in force; the conjunction 'et' is too light to make much difference. A variant on the golden line marks a lesser, midway culmination at 366 (noun adjective verb adjective noun).

[59] Compare D. Furley's suggestion that 'the question so often posed about Lucretius' history of civilization, "primitivist or progressivist?", is quite beside the point' ('Lucretius the Epicurean', in *Lucrèce* (Entretiens Hardt 24 (Geneva, 1978)), 1–27, at 9). Both Lucretius and Virgil examine complex phenomena with a fascinated absorption in the facts which ought to exclude simple schematization.

perhaps worth pausing to consider what our own attitudes to nature are. Some of us would claim to love nature, almost all of us would agree that we draw pleasure and refreshment from nature, both animate and inanimate—earth and waters, animals and plants. We are all, more or less, friends of the earth; or in a drabber jargon, we are concerned about the preservation of the environment. It seems perverse, inhuman—or rather non-human—not to enjoy the natural world and to think it good.[60] But we combine this compelling sense with the awareness that nature can be harsh and destructive: through flood, famine, earthquake, and disease.[61] We might reasonably start at least with the expectation that Virgil felt similarly; that the *Georgics* will show us the cruelties of nature and the toil which may be needed to draw a livelihood from the soil, as well as the charms of country life and the rewards of effort; but that undergirding the whole, at all events, will be a sense of the goodness and delightfulness of the natural world. Only the poem itself can show whether this expectation will be fulfilled, but it would perhaps be surprising if Virgil devoted four books and several years of his life to the assertion that the country is unappealing and the countryman's life unremittingly depressing. Such propositions may seem banal and obvious; but they have lately been doubted.

Like Lucretius, like the *Eclogues* at moments, the *Georgics* asserts the significance and value of the everyday objects of perception; it shows things as ordinary and special at one and the same time. Lucretius had declared that the usual appearance of the world, if only our vision had not been dulled by familiarity, would strike us with wonder and amazement;[62] Virgil inherits this apprehension but adds a new idea: glory.[63] His sense of the fascination of the commonplace is conveyed in part through an equivocation over the nature of his theme: is it grand or is it humble? Sometimes farming seems a modest enough

---

[60] 'Too much green and badly lit' was the comment of one wit (was it Wilde?) on the countryside. Sheer implausibility gives the remark its salt: it seems impossible to consider grass and trees aesthetically displeasing.

[61] It is wrong to call such things perversions of nature; they are of course part of nature. After Darwin, we are also keenly aware of all species' struggle for survival. That was not felt by the ancient world in the same way. It may also seem obvious to us that nature is 'red in tooth and claw', but it struck the 19th cent. with the force of a fresh shock.

[62] Explicitly at 2. 1028 ff.

[63] 'Gloria' comes twice only in Lucretius, once dismissively, and never in connection with the natural world: the glory of kingship brings no profit to the body (2. 38); Epicurus' glory is borne up to heaven (6. 8).

topic. In the second book he expresses the hope that the Muses may teach him astronomy, geography, and geology—the stars, the passage of sun and moon, earthquakes and tidal waves, the causes of variation in the length of day and night. But if he should be unequal to these great matters (he adds), may he enjoy the countryside, the woods, the streams in the valleys—'inglorius'. And that unexpected adjective stands out the more because Virgil—with what was to become a favourite trick of Juvenal's—brings the sentence to a sudden stop with a fourth-foot dactyl.[64] Yet even here the self-deprecatory note is not the whole story. In a way he defers to the master of scientific poetry, Lucretius; yet as the verse proceeds and his exaltation of country life develops, he seems to assert an equality with his great predecessor.[65]

The tone at the very end of the poem is carefully studied:[66]

> haec super arvorum cultu pecorumque canebam
> et super arboribus, Caesar dum magnus ad altum
> fulminat Euphraten bello victorque volentis
> per populos dat iura viamque adfectat Olympo.
> illo Vergilium me tempore dulcis alebat
> Parthenope studiis florentem ignobilis oti,
> carmina qui lusi pastorum audaxque iuventa,
> Tityre, te patulae cecini sub tegmine fagi.

Thus I sang about tending fields and flocks and about trees, while great Caesar thundered in war beside the deep Euphrates and victoriously bestowed laws upon willing peoples and scaled the path to heaven. At that time I, Virgil, was nurtured by lovely Parthenope and blossomed in the pursuits of inglorious ease, I who sported with the songs of shepherds and in the boldness of youth sang of you, Tityrus, beneath the cover of a spreading beech.

'Inglorious ease'—it sounds diffident enough; yet one may detect an ambivalence. Great Caesar and modest Virgil each receive the same amount of space—four lines; and as the paragraph sweeps forward, we may reflect that it is the poet in his privacy, not the public man, who occupies the climax.[67] We may also remember the proem to the work, so loud and long in the ruler's praise, yet ultimately calling on Caesar to join Virgil in pitying the countryman; or the

---

[64] *Geo.* 2. 475–86 ('inglorius' at 486). On Juvenal and the fourth-foot dactyl see Jenkyns, *Three Classical Poets* (London, 1982), 171–3.
[65] For a fuller account of this complex passage, see below, pp. 373 ff.
[66] *Geo.* 4. 559–65.   [67] As is observed by Griffin in a very fine analysis, 177 f.

praise of Italy in the second book, where the climax moves on from Caesar to the land itself and lastly to the poet's own triumph.[68]

The memory of these earlier places allows a light irony to play over his urbane humility; and not these alone. Out of an unemphatic passage about making ploughs and baskets springs the phrase 'divini gloria ruris' (the glory the divine country offers).[69] English translation is liable to impoverish the Latin words. 'Gloria' is a word that most naturally belongs to the public or military sphere, and there is the tang of paradox in its application to country matters: basketmaking has indeed been a symbol of poetic slenderness in the *Eclogues*.[70] And 'divinus', 'god-filled' or 'sanctified by deity', is the more striking from the ordinariness of the context: we are not in the middle of a rhapsody about the loveliness of the landscape. The two words, 'divinus' and 'gloria', neither very remarkable in itself, play together, each irradiating the other with hints of splendour and the numinous.[71]

Is Virgil's work then ample or slender? We have already lighted on the words in which he suggests that it is both: 'in tenui labor; at tenuis non gloria, si . . .'[72] There is a characteristic fluctuation back and forth as he moves from modesty to a pride which is in turn qualified by a note of hesitation in the conditional clause. In the previous book he had declared,[73]

> nec sum animi dubius verbis ea vincere magnum
> quam sit et angustis hunc addere rebus honorem.

Nor do I doubt how great a task it is to master these things in words and to bring distinction in this way to narrow matters.

The task is to exalt the everyday: these matters are indeed 'narrow', but 'honos'—again a word with a public resonance—can be brought to them. Virgil's admirer Tacitus saw the point, though in following the poet he does away with his exquisite haverings. 'Nobis in arto

---

[68] *Geo.* 1. 41—note 'mecum' (with me), 2. 170 ff.
[69] *Geo.* 1. 168. [70] *Ecl.* 10. 71.
[71] The line as a whole presents some difficulty of interpretation; see Mynors ad loc. As far as 'the glory of the divine country' goes, it is pretty clear that the primary meaning is 'the opportunity of glory offered (to you) by the country'. Mynors notes that when 'divinus' conveys 'a general sense of excellence', it is 'normally applied to people'. Perhaps the slightly unusual application here may justify us in hearing, as an overtone, the suggestion that glory is possessed by the countryside itself. Cf. T. E. Page, 'The "divine country" has a "glory" . . . which it can bestow'; Huxley, ' "The glory of the heaven-blest land" '.
[72] *Geo.* 4. 6. [73] *Geo.* 3. 289 f.

et inglorius labor,' he announces, 'My work is narrow and without glory'.[74] With this last adjective he diverges from Virgil—or would do, did we quite believe him. We suspect, rather, that a sardonic irony plays over the contrast that he draws between his gloomy task and those earlier historians who had the agreeable labour of recounting conquests and triumphs; we know that he would not really prefer to be Livy, and he knows that we know. His relentless sombreness glows with its own dark splendour.[75] In their different styles both Tacitus (though he denies it) and Virgil draw an aesthetic value from the very 'narrowness' of their themes. Virgil's talk of the glory of modest matters links to that feeling for simple objects and scenes found already in the *Eclogues*: he writes about ants, birds' nests, geese, crops, mice, moles, cows—all ordinary things—but a sort of sanctity hangs somehow about them. Lucretius had described his own poetic achievement in terms of a metaphor adapted from Callimachus: 'iuvat integros accedere fontis | atque haurire' (I delight to approach those untouched springs and drink deep of them). At the climax of his praise of Italy Virgil, borrowing Lucretius' language in his turn, makes a significant change of adjective: 'ausus *sanctos* recludere fontis' (daring to unseal the *sacred* springs).[76]

Some people see the subject of the *Georgics* as abstract: they suppose that the poem is about moral order, peace and abundance, or the hopes of such things, or (if they favour a pessimist interpretation) the frustration of these hopes. The Farmer, who may even be dignified with a capital letter, his work and his surroundings form (on this account) a metaphor or symbol by which these lofty matters may be represented.[77] But this is to get the poem back to front; indeed, to mistake it fundamentally. For one thing, if the land and

---

[74] *Ann.* 4. 32.

[75] Tacitus' admirer catches his note: 'The design has imposed a pessimistic and truculent tone, to the almost complete exclusion of the gentler emotions and the domestic virtues' (R. Syme, *The Roman Revolution* (Oxford, 1939), p. viii). That purports to be apology, but author and reader collude in the understanding that it is nothing of the kind.

[76] Lucr. 1. 927 f.; *Geo.* 2. 175.

[77] A lucid expression of this point of view: 'The poem argues piety, order, peace, productiveness, *life*—in reaction to chaos, destruction and war. It does so through the metaphor of the Farmer.' This is then qualified: '"Metaphor" is slightly to overstate; or to oversimplify.' (R. O. A. M. Lyne, in T. Woodman and D. West (eds.), *Quality and Pleasure in Latin Poetry* (Cambridge, 1974), 47–66, at 47.)

Ross (p. 14) notes acutely, 'My impression is that much in our current views of the poem is the result of reading for the message of the digressions, then finding that message metaphorically presented by the didactic content.' His discussion on pp. 12–14 is valuable.

its work stood for some abstraction, we should have to suppose that the mass of often exact agricultural detail, which can certainly not be cashed out in metaphorical terms, was so much decoration, a diversion from the *Georgics'* central purpose—an incredible conclusion, and ruinous to the poem's value. Rather, Virgil writes about the real life of the real land; in one place he says directly that his subject is the earth, not fiction.[78] Now it might perhaps be argued that he has romanticized the Italian countryside and suppressed some unpleasant realities (latifundia is absent, and slavery almost invisible),[79] and some may wish to go on from this to criticize him for complacency or disingenuousness.[80] But whatever the merit or otherwise of such arguments, they have no bearing on the meaning of the poem as such, only on the modern reader's possible response to that meaning. Virgil does not take abstractions—political ideas or moral values—as his starting-point and proceed to exemplify them figuratively through the depiction of rural life. The whole movement of the poem, both in its general conception and, as we shall see, in individual passages, is in the opposite direction. Jupiter, we learn early in the first book, has made the battle of existence difficult; and therefore man must be versatile, hard-working, and creative. The land of Italy is of such and such a kind; and therefore we should love it. A virtue of the *Georgics* is that its moral and political idea grows naturally, almost it may seem casually, out of the solid facts of geography, biology, and history; and this helps to make Virgil's moral vision, whether or not we ultimately approve it, deeper and more serious than that of any of his contemporaries. In a complex passage in the second book he draws a double contrast: between the philosopher and the countryman; between Lucretius and himself. This doubleness assimilates the poet's concerns to those of the farmer: the business of both is with the too too solid earth. Happy is the man who has been able to know the causes of things and trample the terrors of the underworld beneath his feet; but fortunate

---

[78] *Geo.* 2. 45.

[79] The ninth day of the month is propitious for runaways at 1. 286; the poet and his readers probably assumed that the ditcher and the vine-dresser at 2. 264 and 417 were slaves; the workers mentioned in one or two other places may be hired hands or slaves or a mixture of the two. On Virgil and slavery, see above, pp. 15 f.

[80] Yet Virgil is under no obligation to describe all country life everywhere. M. S. Spurr demonstrates that what Virgil usually has in mind is a substantial villa estate ('Agriculture and the *Georgics*', *GR* 2nd ser. 33 (1986), 164–83, at 171–5; the article is reprinted in I. McAuslan and P. Walcot (eds.), *Virgil* (Oxford, 1990), 69–93).

too (Virgil adds) is he who has known the country gods, Pan and Silvanus and the Nymphs' sisterhood.[81] Whatever his limitations in logical or speculative thought, he implies, he knows and understands the land of Italy; here at least the ground is firm beneath his feet. He is thinking in part of the beliefs and sentiments that spring out of the land—those rural deities—but also of the physical appearance of the landscape itself. For he has just expressed the hope that if he lacks the capacity to understand nature's workings—the movements of the heavens, the causes of earthquakes and so forth—he may at any rate love the woods and rivers of the countryside.[82] This for him is the original experience, the foundation on which perhaps, if the Muses are kind, some abstract ideas and values may be built. It is interesting to see that when Martial wanted to put a name to this poem, he called it 'Italia'; for him at least its subject was a real land, a particular place.[83]

All this part of the second Georgic is radically ambivalent: modesty and pride, melancholy and enthusiasm are indissolubly fused. And so too with Virgil's attitude to his master: even as he draws out the difference between Lucretius and himself, he is acknowledging the depth of his debt. It was Lucretius who had shown how didactic poetry could also be romantic poetry; but he had generated excitement by the way in which enthusiasm and exaltation leapt out from apparently dry or uninspiring beliefs and subject-matter; in him the poetry is, in a sense, dependent on the prose. Virgil would not rival his intellectual force and energy, but he did learn from him the value of letting his romance and rhapsody spring from the prose of everyday life and experience. Like Lucretius, he writes about 'res', things.

As the *Georgics* is like and unlike Lucretius, so it is like and unlike the *Eclogues*. Nature, landscape and sense of place are all topics already present in Virgil's first work, and this would help to confirm, were confirmation needed, that these themes, deeply interesting to him for their own sake, are part of the root conception of the *Georgics*, not metaphors or illustrations of moral ideas. But as we have seen, the less comfortable side of country existence, like so much in the *Eclogues*, is present there only at the edge of the field of vision. Corydon watches others toiling at the harvest but is at leisure himself; Meliboeus has business on hand, but for the sake of entertainment will postpone it for the moment; rain will fall heavily but not until

---

[81] *Geo.* 2. 490–4.   [82] *Geo.* 2. 475–86.   [83] Mart. 8. 55. 19.

after the poem's end. Menalcas in the fifth Eclogue and Thyrsis in the seventh sing briefly of winter, but meanwhile the sun is shining and they are at rest in the shade.[84] In the *Georgics*, however, where the nominal model is no longer Theocritus but dour, practical Hesiod, the toughness of the farmer's life is much more often before our eyes. In one smelly detail he goes beyond Hesiod: as Cicero noticed, the Greek poet does not mention manure, but in the first book Virgil tells us not to be squeamish about spreading the dung thick, and even in the more idyllic second has us scattering muck around our cuttings.[85] Aware that he risks an airy prettiness, he determines to make a show of being down to earth.

In the poem's very first lines, if we attend to him, he shows us how he conceives spiritual values growing out of practical realities:[86]

> Quid faciat laetas segetes, quo sidere terram
> vertere, Maecenas, ulmisque adiungere vitis
> conveniat, quae cura boum, qui cultus habendo
> sit pecori, apibus quanta experientia parcis,
> hinc canere incipiam. vos, o clarissima mundi
> lumina, labentem caelo qui ducitis annum;
> Liber et alma Ceres . . .

What makes the crops flourish, beneath what star it is fitting to turn the soil, Maecenas, and to join vines to elms, what attention cattle need, what care is needed for keeping a flock, what practice for keeping thrifty bees—here I shall begin my song. O ye most radiant lights of the firmament, who lead the gliding year through the heaven; O Bacchus and bounteous Ceres . . .

Lucretius had begun with an exordium of unprecedented complexity, part addressed in epic style to Venus, part in the didactic manner to a contemporary, Memmius. We have seen that Venus herself is a complex figure, not only standing in place of the Muse but representing natural process itself, so that she bears upon both the poem's form and its content. Besides the goddess and the patron, Epicurus is praised in one section of the exordium and Ennius is named in another; both a philosophical and a literary ancestry are established. This is the model for the complex nature of Virgil's own proem,

---

[84] *Ecl.* 2. 10 f., 7. 17, 7. 60, 5. 70, 7. 49–52.

[85] Cic. *De Sen.* 54; Virg. *Geo.* 1. 80, 2. 346 f. Mynors notes on the first passage that handling muck was more noisome for the ancients, since they carried it not as we do in a vehicle but either on a stretcher or in a basket on a man's back. He also cites Columella 2. 15. 2, where dung is scattered broadcast, like seed. [86] *Geo.* 1. 1–7.

various in tone, addressed successively to Maecenas, a group of twelve gods and Caesar, and ranging over such diverse fields as practical farming, religious feeling, and that blend of moral and political sentiment with personality cult which we may choose to call Augustanism.

Since Lucretius is the model, the striking differences between the two openings are significant. *De Rerum Natura* begins with a blaze of splendour; we might have expected Virgil to devise something comparably arresting. In his other works, after all, he grips the reader at once: in the *Eclogues* by the exquisitely melodious pipings of 'Tityre tu', in the *Aeneid* by a dense, weighty energy.[87] But the first lines of the *Georgics* may seem, momentarily, a little flat. The tone is plain; the poet does not even try to commend his subject, in the usual way. This is the more surprising in that ancient poems were sometimes referred to by their opening words; yet no one would wish to speak of the *Quid faciat*.[88] Martial refers to the *Aeneid* in this style, but we have noticed that he prefers to call the *Georgics* 'Italia'.[89]

Though Virgil owes so much to Lucretius, in one respect he does the reverse of what his model did. Lucretius has a subject that may seem dry, dull, and impersonal, and must infuse it with life, joy, and enthusiasm. He was, as we have seen, a genuinely didactic poet, the first since the fifth century; Virgil was not. The danger for Lucretius was that the poetic element would be crushed by the mass of scientific and philosophical argumentation; the danger for his follower was that the didactic pose might come to seem winsomely literary, a mere peg upon which to hang a romantic celebration of the land. So Lucretius begins with a prayer to a goddess in whom he cannot literally believe; so Virgil begins with a terse practicality that is something of a show.

'Quid faciat . . . , Maecenas . . .'—it is revealing that we hear this tone again at the start of Horace's first Satire: 'Qui fit, Maecenas . . .'[90]

---

[87] The *Iliad*'s beginning is more wonderful even than Virgil's, but where he is new is in combining immediate forward thrust with a sense of monumental mass. In a different form the *Aeneid* exemplifies Tovey's observation on the opening of Beethoven's Ninth Symphony, that the composer 'achieves his evidences of gigantic size in a passage which is, as a matter of fact, not very long'.

[88] Servius produces four lines which he alleges were written by Virgil to stand at the head of the *Aeneid*. E. J. Kenney has noted, as one more argument for their spuriousness, that Virgil would not have wanted readers to refer to 'that incomparable poem, the *Ille ego*' (*CR* ns 20 (1970), 290).   [89] Mart. 8. 55. 19.

[90] 'How does it come about, Maecenas, that . . .' (*Serm.* 1. 1. 1). The resemblance is indeed striking; there is no way of knowing which poet was first.

When Horace gave his collection of *Odes* to the world, he framed it with two fulsome addresses to his patron, scion of ancient Etruscan kings, his protector, his delight.[91] In the *Satires* the desire to laud Maecenas must give way to the generic demand: the bare vocative, with no flattering phrase in apposition to amplify it, demonstrates that in this work the Muse will travel on foot.[92] Virgil likewise begins by speaking to his patron in conversational style, without adornment, but as one man to another. It is in keeping with this brisk down-to-earth manner that he gets through the subject-matter of his four books in as many lines; every word is functional, except perhaps 'parcis', the bees' epithet, and even this maintains the no-nonsense tone, for thrift is a plain virtue, and it will be required of men also. Yet even when writing with apparent straightforwardness, Virgil's control is exact and refined: a series of enjambments ensures that the summary only of the fourth book ends where a line ends, and the resistless forward flow is encouraged by a further subtlety which blurs the boundary between the first and second books: the two elements of the first book, crops and star signs, are syntactically separate, but the second element is syntactically linked to the summary of the second book by the verb 'conveniat', governing both clauses.

The first line alone does a great deal of work—as we should expect from Virgil. The first words of the *Aeneid* are thick with significance. 'Arma virumque . . .'—in an instant Virgil has summed up his theme, alluded to epic in general and to Homer in particular, and presented his hero as a new Achilles and a new Ulysses. The first line of the *Eclogues* establishes the notes of melodiousness, ease, and refinement, and introduces a name drawn from Theocritus. So comparably the dry, factual character of the *Georgics'* opening marks the didactic genre, and it also, as Servius observed, contains a specific allusion, for Virgil describes the subject of the first book, unlike that of the others, in two clauses, corresponding to the division of Hesiod's poem into *Works* and *Days*. The vocative 'Maecenas' functions as another generic indicator: Hesiod harangues his brother Perses, and his Roman counterpart will also find an individual to buttonhole (it is notable that as he addresses Maecenas for the first time in his poetry, he gives no indication whatever that the man is his patron;

---

[91] *Carm.* 1. 1. 1 f., 3. 29. 1; 3. 30 follows as a *sphragis*. The first three books of *Odes* form, of course, a single collection, the fourth book being a separate and later production.

[92] 'Musaque pedestri' (*Serm.* 2. 6. 17).

the kowtowing is deferred to the next book).[93] Memmius performs
the same function in Lucretius' exordium: after the invocation of
Venus has advertised the poem's epic aspect, the call to this individual
Roman shows it to be didactic as well. Both Lucretius and Virgil
follow Hesiod in speaking personally to their chosen addressee in
some places while using the second person singular with a general
reference at others:[94] 'nudus ara, sere nudus', 'quaecumque premes
virgulta per agros | sparge fimo pingui'—such rough commands were
not for the aesthete of the Esquiline.[95]

So the plainness of style and content at the beginning of the
poem is not as innocent as it may appear; but it is valuable above
all in preparing the way for a stroke of genius. At the start of the
fifth line—'hinc canere incipiam'—come the first hints of a greater
amplitude of expression: the alliteration of *n* and *c* adds a little to
the sonority, though the vowels remain clipped and colourless, and
'canere', 'sing' implies something richer than the bare exposition we
have had so far. There follows a strong stop; and then suddenly, unpredictably, in the middle of the line, there is a lifting of the tone, and
the verse soars upwards into a glorious invocation of the gods. 'vos
o . . .'—two long *o*'s signal the new grandeur, and the *l*'s, *m*'s and *n*'s
in the next line and a half deepen the sonority. Brevity of expression
gives way to an enormous, apparently endless sentence (it runs on
continuously to the end of line 42—probably the longest sentence
in Latin poetry); the move from Maecenas to the gods is a move
from an unadorned vocative to one preceded by the poetical and
hymnic 'o', from singular to plural, from human to divine. This surge
of poetic splendour is aesthetically of very great charm, but it is also

---

[93] Contrast the fulsome deference of 2. 39–41, and compare '*o decus, o famae merito
pars maxima nostrae,* | *Maecenas*' (O my pride, O by right chief sharer in my fame, Maecenas)
with Horace, *Carm.* 1. 1. 1 f., '*Maecenas* atavis edite regibus, | *o* et praesidium et dulce
decus meum' (Maecenas, scion of ancient kings, O my protection and my dear pride). Virgil
names Maecenas once and once only in each of his four books, twice in the second line
and twice in the forty-first—even for this poem a markedly exact symmetry. 3. 41 advertises the poet's subordinate status: 'tua, Maecenas, haud mollia iussa' (your commands, by
no means light); at 4.2, as at 1.2, the address is plain.

[94] Of course there are substantial differences. Perses is an important figure in *Works and
Days*; also the target of some abuse. Memmius vanishes from vast tracts of *De Rerum Natura*,
while Virgil is even more restrained, though more orderly, in his references to Maecenas.
Some have thought that Memmius is, like Maecenas, a patron, but the absence of gratitude or more than perfunctory praise, as well as the warning note of 1. 102 ff., is against
this. Perhaps acting as a generic signpost is what has earned him immortality.

[95] 'Plough and sow when you are stripped down' (1. 299, echoing Hes. *Op.* 381); 'Sprinkle
any young trees that you plant on your land with rich dung' (2. 346 f.).

a method by which the poet expresses his meaning through the shape of his structure. He tells us from the beginning—or rather he shows us—that the celebration of nature should grow out of the facts of nature, that the glory we may hope to draw from the 'rus divinum' is to come from attending to the way the farmer goes about his work.

We may come to appreciate Virgil's technique—both its power and its refinement—from considering how to punctuate him. Rightly understood, the invocation of deities is momentarily checked by a parenthesis:[96]

> et vos, agrestum praesentia numina, Fauni
> (ferte si|mul Fau|nique || ped|em Dryadesque puellae:
> munera vestra cano) . . .

And you, Fauns, gods at hand to help countrymen (Fauns and Dryad maidens, come step together: it is your benisons that I sing) . . .

No other interpretation of the sentence structure will be found to work satisfactorily.[97] And indeed the interruption has much charm: it adds an attractive variation to the long line of invocations, the epanalepsis (Fauni . . . Fauni . . .) and parenthesis evoke for a moment the grace of the bucolic style—for example,[98]

> 'Tityre, dum redeo (brevis est via), pasce capellas,
> et potum pastas age, Tityre, et inter agendum
> occursare capro (cornu ferit ille) caveto.'

'Tityrus, until I return (short is the road), feed my goats, and when they are fed, lead them to drink, Tityrus, and as you lead them, take care not to get in the he-goat's way (he butts with his horn).'

—the rhythm dances (the movement of line 11 is very similar to Lucretius' line describing the rhythm of the seasons),[99] the words themselves are an invitation to the dance.[100] The parenthesis is just one among Virgil's methods of diversifying his successive invocations

---

[96] *Geo.* 1. 10–12, as in Mynors's Oxford text.

[97] For a characteristically sensitive but unconvincing attempt to expound the structure with a full stop in the middle of 12, see Klingner, 186. One consideration: after the poet has addressed Liber and Ceres with the words 'vestro si munere' (if by your bounty, 7), it is intolerable that the sentence should come to its climax (or rather anticlimax) with the statement 'munera vestra cano' (I sing your bounties, 12). These last words need to be subordinated and addressed to the Fauns and Dryads alone: 'Come along, you Fauns and Dryads, it is your bounties *too* that I am singing about.'

[98] *Ecl.* 9. 23–5.   [99] Lucr. 1. 174.

[100] Probably, despite Mynors's argument that 'ferte pedem' merely means 'come'.

(for example in the varied placing of proper names); they would repay a close study.[101]

From lines 5 to 23 the poet calls upon a series of deities; from 24 to 42 he invokes the future deity, Caesar. Some editors place a full stop at the end of 23; this has the merit of articulating the syntactical structure, but it undoes a remarkable subtlety, which consists in disguising the nature of that structure until almost the end of the paragraph. Lines 21–4 display an obvious regularity which, by its contrast with the variations that have come before, is itself a form of variety: each line begins with a monosyllable to which '-que' is attached. Moreover, lines 21–3 are all end-stopped, so that when the clause in line 24 spills over into the succeeding lines, we seem to have a familiar crescendo construction with the appeal to Caesar as its natural climax:[102]

> *dique* deaeque omnes, studium quibus arva tueri,
> *quique* novas alitis non ullo semine fruges
> *quique* satis largum caelo demittitis imbrem;
> *tuque* adeo, quem mox quae sint habitura deorum
> concilia incertum est, urbisne invisere, Caesar,
> terrarumque velis curam, . . .

and all gods and goddesses whose care is to protect the fields, you who nourish the new plants that grow unsown, and you who send down on the crops abundant rain from heaven; and you, Caesar, whom some company of the gods will include in due time, but which is uncertain—whether you choose to watch over cities or prefer to look after lands . . .

For many more lines we shall continue to assume that the new subject, like all those that have preceded it, governs 'adsis' (come), the sole main verb that we have hitherto met in the sentence, slipped into the middle of the list of deities at line 18. But by a technique similar to enharmonic modulation in music, the 'tu' of line 20, heard at first as governing 'adsis', comes at last to govern four other main verbs instead. That consummation is long delayed, the sentence being stretched out still further by two more parentheses, one almost two lines, the second almost four lines long,[103] until finally four strong imperatives in only three lines, like a return to the tonic key, hammer the paragraph home to its majestic conclusion:[104]

---

[101] It is not easy to agree with Klingner that the passage is 'feierlich monoton'; on the contrary, sprightly and various.   [102] *Geo.* I. 21–6.

[103] *Geo.* I. 34 f. and 36–9.   [104] *Geo.* I. 40–2.

> *da* facilem cursum atque audacibus *adnue* coeptis,
> ignarosque viae mecum miseratus agrestis
> *ingredere* et votis iam nunc *adsuesce* vocari.

Grant me an easy passage and favour my bold enterprise, and pitying with me the countrymen who know not the way, approach and even now become accustomed to be called upon in prayer.

Here, at the ceremonial and festive start of his poem, Virgil lavishes his resources of structural imagination and control on a passage where he has, in a sense, almost nothing to say. When he comes to unleash these powers of both strength and refinement on a theme that speaks to the deep places of his spirit, in the *laus Italiae* of the second book, the result will be supremely magnificent and consummately beautiful.

Returning to the fifth line, we can see Virgil using two techniques: he elevates the tone after a dry beginning; and he makes a sudden new start in the middle of the line. Each technique can be found again, with various effect, in the *Aeneid*. The eighth book opens with seventeen brisk, largely factual lines which summarize the Italians' preparations for war. The passage is full of activity, full of names: Turnus, Latinus, Messapus, Mezentius, Ufens, Venulus, Diomedes. At the start of line 18 the topic is instantly and brusquely dismissed: 'Talia per Latium' (such were the events in Latium)—a sentence of only three words, and too terse to spare room for a verb. Then suddenly, in mid-line, the poet switches from bustle and multitudes to Aeneas, alone and at night, anxiously pondering his troubles. He is introduced at once in his most grandiosely mythic form as 'Laomedontius heros', the hero, scion of Laomedon. And out of the night, out of the stillness comes quiet and grey the mysterious vision of the god Tiber, all the more effective for the contrast with the dryness of the paragraph before. In such a place we see that Virgil is a master of the sudden as much as of the gradual transition.

We might compare some early lines in the second book:[105]

> sed *si* tantus amor casus cognoscere nostros
> *et* breviter Troiae supremum audire laborem,
> *quamquam* animus meminisse horret, luctu*que* refugit,
> incipiam.

But if you have such a passion to learn of our experiences and briefly to hear the last agony of Troy, although my spirit shudders to remember and has shrunk back in grief, I will begin.

[105] *Aen.* 2. 10–13.

Aeneas shrinks from reliving the horror of the past. That reluctance is expressed in a sentence that seems unwilling ever to reach the point, as four subordinate clauses follow one after another. But when the main clause arrives, it contains one word only, 'incipiam', reminiscent of 'hinc canere incipiam' in the Georgic, but with a new bluntness and urgency. And immediately Aeneas plunges into a remarkably concise and rapid account of how the Greeks built the wooden horse. The unexpected change of pace—in direct contrast to the opening of the eighth book, a change from slowness to speed—is poetically attractive, but it also serves a psychological end: Aeneas so recoils, we feel, from telling his story, that he can only manage it by kicking aside his unwillingness and diving straight in.

Virgil's powers of postponement are most elaborately developed at the beginning of the seventh book. We expect him to open the second half of his poem with a new invocation; so he does, but it is delayed for more than thirty-five lines. First we are to hear about the death of Aeneas' old nurse, then of the Trojans' night journey along the coast of Latium, then of a new sunrise; and only after this does he invoke the Muse Erato, announcing that he is about to embark upon a larger theme.[106] This invocation culminates, at the start of line 45, with the words 'maius opus moveo' (I essay a greater task)—plain words, bald, lapidary. The sentence ends in mid-line, and abruptly the poet leaps headlong into his new story:

> Rex arva Latinus et urbes
> iam senior longa placidas in pace regebat.

King Latinus, now old, ruled over lands and cities calm from long peace.

Editors incline to begin the sentence 'Rex arva etc.' on a new line, leaving a broad swathe of white space; typographically that is almost too exciting, but it makes the point. The phrase 'maius opus moveo' is nothing in itself, but the sudden plunge into narrative isolates it, giving it simple monumental force; at the same time the unanticipated plunge into a new tone and subject imparts fresh impetus to what follows: it is as though a pent-up force has broken out.

The great leap upward in the fifth line of the *Georgics* has an expressive function, indicating how the enthusiasm in the poem grows out of its basis in solid, sober fact; but that idea is already present, in

---

[106] *Aen.* 7. 37 ff. Apollonius Rhodius opens the second half of his *Argonautica* with a fresh invocation, addressed to Erato (3. 1). By choosing the same Muse, Virgil underlines, for those who know the earlier poem, the perversity of his own procedure.

germ, in the very first line, with the single word 'laetus'. One of its meanings, probably its original meaning, is 'flourishing' or 'fertile'; in these senses it is a practical, simple word. Servius notes that 'laetamen' was a common word for dung, and Cicero observes that metaphor is so common a part of ordinary language that even country folk say 'laetas esse segetes'.[107] So Virgil opens with plain, factual Latin, and yet this first adjective in the poem—the first word of any colour at all—is pregnant with larger significance: it will come back again and again as the word proceeds, occurring thirty-three times in all. Since it also means 'joyful', it unites within itself practical reality and emotional warmth. Virgil's approach to personification is a far cry from the Psalmist's 'The valleys also shall stand so thick with corn, that they shall laugh and sing.'[108] There the pathetic fallacy is extravagantly on display; here, by contrast, we may feel the quiet stirring of a personification that is felt as potential, latent beneath the surface signification of a word like the seed hidden in the soil.

When Virgil tells those sheep-farmers whose interest is in wool to avoid 'pabula laeta' (lush meadows), the adjective obviously has no emotional significance;[109] and there are more places where we realize the meaning to be primarily and perhaps exclusively descriptive.[110] In other cases, while the surface or literal meaning must clearly be 'fertile', the word seems to be striving toward some further significance: for example, 'at quae pinguis humus dulcique uligine laeta' (land that is rich and enjoys a sweet moisture).[111] The oozy squelchiness of the u's and i's reinforces the literal sense of 'laeta', and a few lines later mud is called 'felix', Virgil choosing another epithet which begins by meaning 'fertile' and shifts to meaning 'happy'.[112] But just before this we have been hearing about lands that 'rejoice' in the olive, as part of an unambiguous personification.[113] Thus 'laetus' and 'felix' have been unobtrusively put in a context where, however robustly they may be used (mud and slime are not romantic), their metaphorical potential can be strongly felt.

In another place it seems impossible to say whether the literal or the metaphorical meaning is uppermost:[114]

[107] Cic. De Orat. 3. 155, Orat. 81. He assumes that 'joyful' is the original meaning of the word; the truth may well be the other way around.   [108] Ps. 65. 14.
[109] Geo. 3. 385.   [110] e.g. Geo. 1. 69, 101 f., 325.
[111] Geo. 2. 184.   [112] Geo. 2. 188.
[113] Geo. 2. 181 (gaudent). The farmer has won over some cussed soil: the hill-slopes are 'maligni' (grudging), by nature (179).   [114] Geo. 2. 362–5.

> ac dum prima novis adolescit frondibus aetas,
> parcendum teneris, et dum se laetus ad auras
> palmes agit laxis per purum immissus habenis,
> ipsa acie nondum falcis temptanda . . .

While the early youth of the new leaves is growing towards maturity, one should spare their tenderness, and while the shoot thrusting into the clear air with reins loosed presses happily up towards the sky, it is too soon to set the knife's edge to them . . .

'Laetus' is here part of a complex of words, 'prima . . . aetas', 'adolescit', 'teneris', which are literally true of the plant, while at the same time clearly comparing its care metaphorically to a child's education. A little earlier 'joyful' had seemed to be the primary meaning:[115]

> ver adeo frondi nemorum, ver utile silvis,
> vere tument terrae et genitalia semina poscunt.
> tum pater omnipotens fecundis imbribus aether
> coniugis in gremium laetae descendit, et omnis
> magnus alit magno commixtus corpore fetus.

Spring aids the leaves of the groves, spring aids the woods, in spring the earth swells and calls for generative seeds. Then heaven the almighty father descends in fruitful showers into the lap of his glad consort, and in his greatness mingling with her great body nourishes all growth.

The tone evokes Lucretius, his phrase 'genitalia semina', his favourite verb 'alo' and the heavy alliterations of 327 all contributing to the effect. Indeed 325 f. are adapted from *De Rerum Natura*:[116]

> postremo pereunt imbres, ubi eos pater aether
> in gremium matris terrai praecipitavit.

But Virgil's modifications are interesting. The first line and a half quoted are wholly literal, but then 'genitalia semina', as in Lucretius himself, suggests the analogy with sexual procreation, and 'poscunt' unobtrusively introduces the pathetic fallacy. The last words of the sentence thus form a pivot between the previous clauses and the three lines to come, so that the transition to the metaphor that follows is smooth and natural. And unlike Lucretius, Virgil has not felt the need to spell out that the 'coniunx' represents earth; the double sense of 'laetus' does that for him. As we have seen, there is also an allusion here to cult, to the *hieros gamos* or sacred marriage of sky

---

[115] *Geo.* 2. 323–7.   [116] Lucr. 1. 250 f., quoted and discussed above, pp. 245 f.

and earth. Thus myth, metaphor, reality all seem close to one another
here, and the adjective 'laetus', its dual meaning rooted in the history of the Latin language, plays its part in binding the different
levels of discourse together, by helping to make the image of father
sky and mother earth seem deeply and simply natural. In the course
of the *Georgics* the meaning of 'laetus' moves along a spectrum ranging from 'fertile' at one end to 'joyful' at the other. It may not be
important, it may indeed be impossible, to identify a particular point
along the spectrum in any one context; what matters is that by its
repeated use, sometimes conspicuous, sometimes unobtrusive, it is
worked into the fabric of the verse and assists in unifying the different elements out of which the poem is made.

Lucretius had found—and it was a new discovery—that he could
take the plainest adjectives, 'omnis', 'certus', 'magnus', and by context and repetition import to them a weight of poetic significance.
Virgil, whose mastery and flexibility of technique enabled him to
achieve almost any tone except perhaps pure simplicity, does not
operate in the *Georgics* with adjectives as wholly colourless as these,
but he did take from Lucretius a sense of the force that ordinary
epithets can potentially carry, though whereas Lucretius repeats common adjectives for their strength of meaning, Virgil does so rather
for diversity of effect. 'Laetus' is one such, 'durus' (hard) another. The
charm of 'laetus' is that it fluctuates between two meanings; with
'durus' the meaning is not in doubt, and the fascination is rather in
the word's changing emotional charge. Sometimes the word has little
or no evaluative content; if Virgil tells us that a hoe, axe or ploughshare is 'durus', our passions are not much engaged.[117] When he
calls the Scipiones 'duros bello' (hardy in war), he is praising them;
when the ploughman, 'durus arator', tears the nightingale's unfledged
chicks from their nest, every reader hears in the epithet the tone
'unfeeling', 'hard-hearted'.[118] The word is common, and it would be
unlikely for a poet to write two thousand lines without using it at
all; some of its occurrences in the *Georgics* may be casual, and have
only a local effect. But in other places 'durus' seems to contribute
to the poem's larger moral vision, and in such places, where the
emotional or evaluative force seems most significant, it is not clearer
but more hidden, perhaps more ambivalent. 'Dicendum et quae sint
duris agrestibus arma' (I must also tell of the hardy countrymen's

---

[117] *Geo.* 2. 355, 4. 331, 1. 261.   [118] *Geo.* 2. 170, 4. 512.

tackle).[119] The word for 'tackle', 'arma', has hitherto meant 'weapons';[120] 'durus' implies respect for the countryman's toughness, but
in strengthening a little the hint of a military metaphor, it adds to
the suggestion that the farmer's work is a battle. Lucretius had said
that early man was harder because he had been born out of the hard
earth;[121] that assertion gains power because, according to his scientific
theory, it is literally true. Virgil wants to inherit this sense of intimate
relationship between man and earth; not sharing Lucretius' science,
he works through mythology instead. This is where 'durus' first appears
in the poem.[122]

> continuo has leges aeternaque foedera certis
> imposuit natura locis, quo tempore primum
> Deucalion vacuum lapides iactavit in orbem,
> unde homines nati, durum genus.

From the beginning nature laid these everlasting laws and provisions upon
definite places, from the time when Deucalion first cast stones into the
empty world, whence men were born, a hard race.

If we are unconscious of Lucretius' influence here, we may lay more
weight on those words which speak of limit, restriction and compulsion. If we know Lucretius, we may remember the value that he
found in the very facts of law and fixity, and the pleasure he took
in the vigour of man's hardness.[123] Virgil is not telling us exactly
what to think: he is showing us, albeit in part through mythology,
the world as it is, and implying that we are emotionally engaged with
the facts of the world, but he allows us some space—not unlimited
space—for our own response: in some moods we may feel more
the severity implicit in the hardness of stone-born man, in others the
strength.[124] The mistake is to think that if he shows us some aspect

---

[119] *Geo.* 1. 160.

[120] 'Arma' in this sense is a calque of the Greek *hopla*, which was commonly used of
gear as well as weaponry. The calque, first met here, may be Virgil's invention, fitted to
this particular context.   [121] Lucr. 5. 925 f.

[122] *Geo.* 1. 60-3. Compare too *Geo.* 2. 341: earthborn man arose from the hard fields
(duris . . . arvis)—a line with a clear echo of Lucr. 5. 925 f.

[123] See above, pp. 239 ff., for Lucretius' use of 'certus', the word with which Virgil
ends line 60.

[124] At *Aen.* 9. 603 the Italian warrior Numanus Remulus is loud in praise of his people as a 'durum . . . genus', and he goes on to 'quote' a line of the *Georgics* (607). His
sentiments would have a strong bearing on the present passage if, as some think, they were
the poet's own; but that may be doubted (see below, p. 416). Numanus would be an
enthusiastic, but not an ideal reader of the *Georgics*.

of the world that is less than wholly perfect, some difficulty that offers a challenge, he is despondent or without hope. In the love poetry of his century the woman becomes a more solid presence than she has been before, a personality capable of difficulty, resistance, and complexity, and this, far from making her less lovable, makes the passion for her fuller than ever. Virgil's treatment of the land may be likened to this. In the *Aeneid*, Italy is not purely lovely: it exudes mephitic vapours and conceals infernal wrath. In the *Georgics* the land is generous and stubborn, recalcitrant and yet educable; it has, so to speak, acquired a fuller 'personality'. And like Lesbia and Cynthia, nature thus becomes the object of a larger emotion. The word 'durus' should interest and engage us. It is soon to return in a passage of crucial complexity, as in another mighty paragraph Virgil surveys the divine purpose and the growth of human civilization.[125]

He approaches these broad themes through one of his elegant transitions. Once again, this has an expressive as well as a structural function, showing how his grandest reflections grow from his consideration of the farmer's everyday business. So he begins with some practical nuisances:[126]

> nec tamen, haec cum sint hominumque boumque labores
> versando terram experti, nihil improbus anser
> Strymoniaeque grues et amaris intiba fibris
> officiunt aut umbra nocet. pater ipse colendi
> haud facilem esse viam voluit, primusque per artem
> movit agros, curis acuens mortalia corda
> nec torpere gravi passus sua regna veterno.

However, though the toil of men and oxen has wrought this in turning the earth, the tiresome goose and Strymonian cranes and bitter-fibred succory are not unable to cause trouble nor shade to do harm. The Father himself has willed that the way of husbandry should not be easy, and he first set ingenuity to stir the fields, sharpening mortal hearts with anxieties and not allowing his realm to grow slothful in heavy lethargy.

The second sentence, starting as it does in mid-line, and so soon after a new topic has been broached, at first seems a passing comment; a line or two more must pass before we guess how largely it

---

[125] *Geo.* I. 118–159 ('durus' at 146). The whole passage has been much debated, and especially 145 f. The controversy deserves a full scrutiny; there is also a danger that the passage may come to seem not poetry to be interpreted but a problem to be solved. Detailed argument for the interpretation here offered is therefore left to the Appendix at the end of this book.   [126] *Geo.* I. 118–24.

is likely to expand.[127] Virgil next turns to describe man's vanished paradise. The golden age appears in all three of his works; in each case the picture is different, and in each he combines a story of decline and a story of advance.[128] Modern scholarship has coined the terms soft primitivism—the idea that the early life of man was blissful—and hard primitivism—the idea that it was poor and bleak. Virgil begins with the soft conception: at first there was no farming and no property; the earth bore all that was needed freely, honey grew on leaves, wine flowed everywhere, men shared in common with one another. Then Jupiter abolished all this; he put poison into snakes, commanded wolves to prowl abroad, stirred up the sea and took away fire.[129] So far this is the traditional picture of a paradise lost, but Virgil now grafts on to it the hard-primitivist idea, with its progressive conception of human history. He has already hinted that Jupiter's harshness is not without a purpose, in speaking of the god's 'sharpening' human hearts—a subtle choice of language, suggesting keenness mixed with pain—and forbidding his realm to grow lethargic through sloth. Now the idea of a stern providence becomes explicit:[130]

> ut varias usus meditando *extunderet* artis
> paulatim, et sulcis frumenti quaereret herbam,
> ut silicis venis abstrusum *excuderet* ignem.

So that practice might by taking thought hammer out the various crafts, little by little, and seek the blade of corn in the furrows; so that it might strike forth the fire hidden in the veins of flint.

The verbs of hammering and striking, their rough vigour enhanced by the repetition of the prefix *ex-*, are reminiscent of Lucretius, with his delight in rude force and energy; the close similarity in rhythm and syntax between the first and last of these lines also has a certain robustness.[131] The next ten lines, driven forward by a succession of words for 'then' or 'now',[132] convey the thrust of man's advance: the

---

[127] Elsewhere some of Virgil's best known moralisms are indeed brief asides from the didactic business: 1. 199–203 (on the tendency of all things to decline, with a comparison to the rower upstream who is swept back if he relaxes for a moment—again a thought that begins in mid-line); 3. 66–8 (wretched mortals find that their best days are the first to fly; age, trouble, and death follow—this a momentary interruption of a discussion of stockbreeding). [128] *Ecl.* 4; *Aen.* 8. 314 ff. See pp. 199 ff., 493–6.

[129] *Geo.* 1. 125–32. [130] *Geo.* 1. 133–5.

[131] Every word break is at the same metrical point; verb and object are identically placed; every foot except for the third has the same rhythm. Such lack of variation is not typical of this graceful poet.

[132] 'tunc . . . tum . . . tum . . . iam . . . tum . . . tum . . .' (*Geo.* 1. 136, 137, 139, 141, 143, 145).

invention of boat-building, navigation, trapping and hunting, fishing, iron-working. And so (we may suppose) to the climax:[133]

> tum variae venere artes. labor omnia vicit . . .

Then divers arts came. Toil conquered everything . . .

—the sentence seems complete, and the voice will naturally pause an instant at the end of the line. But the poet is about to surprise us: the sentence continues, and with a sour twist:

> labor omnia vicit
> improbus et duris urgens in rebus egestas.

Toil conquered everything, unkind toil, and the pressure of need in hard circumstances.

The catalogue of man's inventions suggested a gathering enthusiasm. His labours have been victorious, and that truth remains, but now our view of the achievement is given a harsher turn. 'Egestas' signifies a pinching deprivation; the word cannot, like 'paupertas', indicate a modest but decent state.[134] But this cruel pinch has had good consequences; the picture of man's success is not abolished but qualified by a certain severity. The primary signification of 'durus' is here pejorative: 'hard' in the sense of 'painful', 'difficult'. Yet the ambivalence embedded in the word and the resonances set up by its first use in the poem should be allowed to linger: hardness in things offers a challenge, hardness in people is toughness, strength.

The line's other adjective, 'improbus', so emphatically placed, so surprising, has its own distinctive flavour. In terms of force and diction, this word had a wide range. It could appear in the rhetoric of high tragedy—Dido will apostrophize love as 'improbe Amor'[135] —but it might also be used quite lightly, and in ordinary speech. Horace tells the story of Philippus, a gentleman who is so charmed by the sight of the humble auctioneer Vulteius Mena cleaning his nails outside a barber's shop that he sends his slave to invite him to dinner; the slave comes back saying, 'negat improbus' (The wretched fellow refuses).[136] The tone of this must be 'the blasted man says no' or 'the ruddy man says no'; plainly 'improbus' expresses light annoyance (maybe even humorous annoyance), not moral blame.

Virgil was himself ready to exploit this side of the word:[137]

---

[133] *Geo.* 1. 145.   [134] As Servius observes; see Appendix.
[135] *Aen.* 4. 412. Some nuances are lost to us. One might ask, tentatively, if a ghost of ordinary language does not survive even here. Is the tone (not of course the diction) of 'Love, you bastard' just hinted at?
[136] *Epist.* 1. 7. 63.   [137] *Geo.* 1. 388 f.

> tum cornix plena pluviam vocat improba voce
> et só|là in síc|cà sé|cùm spatiatur harena.

Then that villain the raven calls full-throatedly for rain and stalks alone by
itself along the dry sand.

In the second line the alliteration of *s* and *c*, and the three words
each beginning with the same letter, each of two long syllables, and
each in heterodyne position straddling three successive feet wittily
mimics the raven's strutting gait, while 'secum' especially may suggest a self-importance in the bird. 'Improba' adds a pennyworth to
the tone of amusement by implying a smiling pretence of impatience
at the tediousness of the raven's cawings, their persistence evoked
by quaint alliteration, in this case of *p* and *v*.

A similar flavour must lurk in 'improbus anser', the 'rascally' or
'wretched' goose, in the discussion of farmyard nuisances.[138] Pests were
indeed a serious matter to the ancient farmer,[139] but serious matters
may be handled with a light touch, and it is perverse to deny that
Virgil derives some amusement from just this theme a little later in
the book. If you do not prepare your threshing-floor carefully, he
warns us, divers pests will 'mock' you;[140] and he responds with a
little gentle mockery in his turn:[141]

> saepe exiguus mus
> sub terris posuitque domos atque horrea fecit,
> aut oculis capti fodere cubilia talpae,
> inventusque cavis bufo et quae plurima terrae
> monstra ferunt, populatque ingentem farris acervum
> curculio atque inopi metuens formica senectae.

Often the tiny mouse has made his home under the ground and established his granaries, or the sightless moles have dug their bedrooms, and
the shrew [*or* toad] and the many creatures that the earth engenders are
found in chinks, and the weevil and the ant, anxious about her needy old
age, ravage an enormous pile of grain.

---

[138] Most find playfulness in the phrase; Thomas stands in stern opposition.

[139] Compare K. Thomas, *Man and the Natural World* (London, 1983), 274 f. (on early
modern England): 'It is easy now to forget just how much human effort went into war-
ring against species which competed with man for the earth's resources. Most parishes
seem to have had at least one individual who made his living by catching snakes, moles,
hedgehogs and rats . . . Every gardener destroyed smaller pests, and it was usual for the
gardening-books to contain a calendar like the one drawn up by John Worlidge in 1668:
"January: set traps to destroy vermin. February: pick up all the snails you can find, and
destroy frogs and their spawn. March: the principal time of the year for the destruction of
moles. April: gather up worms and snails. May: kill ivy. June: destroy ants. July: kill . . .
wasps, flies." And so on throughout the year.'

[140] *Geo.* 1. 181 (inludant).   [141] *Geo.* 1. 181–6.

'Exiguus mus'—the stressed monosyllable at the line's end produces a famous piquancy.[142] The singular number, applied to all the pests except the moles, makes each of them into an individual, bringing a touch of charm. The notion that one tiny mouse should be constructing those granaries adds a little quaintness to the personification. 'Oculis capti' is a phrase of some formality; 'monstra' seems in the context rather a portentous term. The use of 'populare' (ravage), here apparently first applied to animals,[143] suggests the grave humour with which the battles of bees will later be described. The singular number makes the vastness of the devastation sound the more improbable, and turns the ant, fussed about her old age—another unrealistic personification—into a momentary, miniature 'character'. To spell these things out may be to labour the delicacy of the original. Virgil sketches lightly; but the touches are felt.

The censure in 'improbus anser' is not deeply meant. Virgil is serious about the nuisance of geese and weeds, but he can handle the matter with a certain wryness. Nor is it an accident that the adjective should return at the rhetorical climax: he wants a tone that can link the practicalities of the farmyard to the large thoughts about the human lot which grow out of it. As we hear of man's success the dour voice of the farmer breaks in again: the adjective's effect is empathetic, and the tone—not of course the diction—is something like 'darn hard work' or 'bloody hard graft'. The story of steady technical advance has been shaken a little, but for a line or two more it continues to surge forward, with Ceres teaching men to plough:[144] the picture of a god guiding humanity to fresh discoveries recalls the work's proem.[145] But new capabilities bring new woes: mildew and weeds—thistles, darnel, and barren oat.[146] Virgil's technique is polyphonal. With 'improbus' and 'duris urgens in rebus egestas' the account of progress is given a twist of austerity; it presses on, but then is twisted again, and a gloomier note starts to predominate as the theme descends once more to the practical problems of farming. And thus, seemingly without effort, Virgil has come back

---

[142] The phrase is already praised by Quintilian, who says that the monosyllable has imported charm (addidit gratiam, 8. 3. 20). 'Would commentators be so amused,' Thomas asks, 'if we did not have the subsequent and famous line of Horace, *parturient montes, nascetur ridiculus mus, A. P.* 139?' (Mountains shall labour, and an absurd mouse be born.) The answer is yes: Horace has picked up Virgil's touch of humour but spoiled the best of the effect by amplifying Virgil's understatement.

[143] R. F. Thomas ad loc.   [144] *Geo.* 1. 147 f.

[145] e.g. *Geo.* 1. 5–7 (Ceres showing how to grow corn and Liber revealing wine), 1. 18 f. (Minerva finds the olive, Triptolemus invents the plough).   [146] *Geo.* 1. 150–4.

to his starting-point. Birds, weeds, the shadow of overgrowing trees
—each of these nuisances, introduced at the start of the paragraph,
returns at its end, and the practical solution to them is laid down:[147]

> quod nisi et adsiduis herbam insectabere rastris
> et sonitu terrebis avis et ruris opaci
> falce premes umbras votisque vocaveris imbrem,
> heu magnum alterius frustra spectabis acervum
> concussaque famem in silvis solabere quercu.

So unless you harry the weeds with persistent hoe and frighten the birds
with noises and suppress the shade that darkens the landscape and call for
rain in prayer, ah me, you will eye another's great big heap to no avail,
and allay your hunger by shaking oak-trees in the woods.

It sounds a bit gloomy, but farmers do grumble, and if we attend,
we shall hear that what the muttering voice is saying is that the harm
threatened by pests and shade can be overcome (if you are idle, you
will indeed go short, but the good farmer piles up a big store). The
tone at the end is ironic and not to be taken too solemnly. The pictures of the lazy farmer gaping at the neighbour's heap and shaking
acorns from the trees are quaint and bantering;[148] the 'heu' (ah me)
is humorously grave.[149]

Taken as a whole, the passage integrates the earthy and the lofty;
it is masterly in its use of complex, flexible rhetoric, various in tone.
The paragraph describes a great parabola, beginning and ending with
the same commonplace bothers.[150] The opening topic leads to a remark
about Jupiter's severity, which proves to be much more than a remark,
as out of it springs a great vision of human progress which rises to a
climax, twists, turns, and falls again, back from god to man, from past
to present, back too to that familiar tone of wry, dour irony which
was never quite absent even when the declamation was at its height.

---

[147] *Geo.* I. 155–9.

[148] Acorns, notice: not the food that the hungry would actually go for, but a traditional
commonplace about the diet of primitive hardship.

[149] If that 'heu' were wholly serious, it would be a bad error of taste and proportion.
For a similar use of 'heu', compare Tibullus 2. 3. 2 and 49.

[150] It is a misjudgement to mark a new paragraph at line 147, as Geymonat and Thomas
do, masking the poetic architecture.

CHAPTER 8

An Italian's Experience:
Land and Nation

One generation passeth away, and another generation cometh:
but the earth abideth for ever.

(Ecclesiastes)

The splendid days of Augustus and Trajan were eclipsed by a
cloud of ignorance; and the barbarians subverted the laws and
palaces of Rome. But the scythe, the invention or emblem of
Saturn, still continued annually to mow the harvests of Italy . . .

(Gibbon)

Another adjective which 'tells' in the *Georgics*, as it does already in
Lucretius, is 'varius'.[1] The word itself is not used as a leitmotiv in
the poem, as to an extent 'laetus' and 'durus' are, but the topic of
variety concerns the second book especially, where 'varius' sounds
immediately after the eight introductory lines of invocation to the
god Bacchus: 'principio arboribus varia est natura creandis' (Firstly,
the nature by which trees may grow is diverse).[2] This theme will
pervade the book.[3] On one level, Virgil explores the variety of the
physical landscape; he enjoys examining the different kinds of soil
and terrain, and considering what can best be grown on each. Such
discussion is the expression of the interest in the quiddity of particular places and landscapes that we have found growing in Virgil's
predecessors and shall meet again in his younger contemporaries; he
gives the sentiment a new solidity by linking it so naturally to the
practical problems of agriculture. But while more down-to-earth than
before, he becomes at the same time more cerebral. This double
development is especially impressive: it broadens his whole field

[1] On 'varius' in Lucretius, see above, p. 251. 'Varius' in the *Aeneid* will be discussed
on p. 470.
[2] *Geo.* 2. 9.
[3] Variety as a theme in Book 2 is especially stressed by B. Otis, *Virgil: A Study in
Civilised Poetry* (Oxford, 1963), 149, 163 f.

of imaginative vision. The early paragraphs of the second book are preparing the way for his praise of Italy or *laus Italiae*,[4] in which he will describe the variety of many different nations: he sees Italy as just one element in the wonderful diversity of a much wider world. So he is doing more than using his senses to observe what is immediately around him; he is also reflecting upon his country in a keenly self-conscious way. Then he narrows the range of his gaze to celebrate the variety within Italy itself. Here there is a kinship with the local patriotism to which Cicero gives voice and which reappears, influenced by Virgil, in the Augustan poets; here is a connection too with that Italian patriotism whose origins we have examined, though his pan-Italian spirit is not picked up by later poets but remains distinctive of himself. He is particularly original in combining both the local and the Italian tendency, in showing unity in diversity, and finding the identity of Italy to be the product not of uniformity but of variety. Indeed we shall see that this idea is presented almost as a discovery freshly made: the pace quickens as the poet seems to awaken to the realization that diversity is in itself a source of glory, that what begins as a problem for farmers—the variety of terrains limits what can be grown on each—is transformed into a revelation filled with emotional and patriotic meaning.

Patriotism has become a chilly word in English, but it will have to be used in default of a better. *Patria* is expressive for Virgil in part because it can be used, like *patrie* in French, for locality as well as nation. When he says 'divisae arboribus patriae' (trees have their different homelands)[5] he is talking about different nations—Arabs and Indians and denizens of the steppes—but his words also carry as an undercurrent the sense of local loyalty and identity for which English has no single term, but which we can represent by borrowing a German word. 'Trees have their different *Heimaten.*' It is curious that the English have no straightforward equivalent to *Heimat*, since they certainly have the concept. At all events, we shall appreciate Virgil better if we recognize that his exploration of 'patria' is concerned with the interlocking of kinds of belonging which range from sense of nation to sense of home.

His patriotism differs from his contemporaries' in this also, that it is a patriotism of a peculiarly self-conscious kind. Self-consciousness

---

[4] The useful label *laus Italiae* (praise of Italy) or *laudes Italiae* (the glory of Italy) is commonly applied to lines 136–76. It will here be applied to lines 109–76, the whole of which must be taken as a unity, for reasons which will become apparent.   [5] *Geo.* 2. 116.

is a term which must serve to cover what is in itself a complex of ideas. First, there is Virgil's sense of history, which suddenly blossoms forth, as we shall see, in the middle of the *laus Italiae*, bringing new width and depth to our understanding of what Italian patriotism means. He interweaves this with a geographical self-consciousness also, at which we have glanced in considering the theme of variety: Italy is seen first from the outside, in contrast to other countries, India, Media, Ethiopia, and the rest. But in this context such geographical self-consciousness too is one part of a more general self-consciousness that pervades the whole of his imaginative life: a capacity to look at the familiar as though it were strange.

Half hidden beneath the surface of the *laus Italiae* runs a transformed and subtilized version of that much used motif, the *adunaton* or impossibility. It already suffuses the early parts of the second Georgic, breaking above the surface at least three times in the first hundred lines. As so often in this poem Virgil learns from Lucretius, taking from him here the idea that the ordinary workings of nature should fill us with delight and enthusiasm; yet he appears to turn on its head the older poet's picture of the impossibility of a nature without laws. Lucretius says that the kind of fruit growing on each species of tree cannot change;[6] Virgil seems to say that it can:[7]

> quin et caudicibus sectis (*mirabile* dictu)
> truditur e sicco radix oleagina ligno;
> et saepe alterius ramos impune videmus
> vertere in alterius, mutatamque insita mala
> ferre pirum et prunis lapidosa rubescere corna.

Moreover, when the trunk is cleft, (a marvel to relate) an olive root thrusts itself from the dry wood; and often we see the branches of one tree turn with impunity into those of another, the pear transformed bear grafted apples and stony cornels redden on the plum.

The wit of this is that he writes as though he had escaped into a realm of fantasy, and yet what he is describing is the familiar process of grafting.[8] A glory of the *Georgics*, above all of this book, is to combine a sense of wonder and a sense of solidity. The idea of nature as a source of marvels will soon return, in a passage already quoted:[9]

---

[6] Lucr. 1. 165 f.   [7] *Geo.* 2. 30–4.

[8] The plum cannot be grafted on to the cornel. For the ancients' wildly exaggerated beliefs in the possibilities of grafting, see above, Ch. 7, n. 31.

[9] *Geo.* 2. 80–2 (above, p. 308). For speed of growth (nec longum tempus) in an 'impossible' world compare Lucr. 1. 186 f.

nec longum tempus, et ingens
exiit ad caelum ramis felicibus arbos,
*miratast*que novas frondes et non sua poma.

Since the words 'wonderful' and 'marvellous' have weakened in English,
it should be stressed that Virgil means 'miratast' and 'mirabile dictu'
in a strong sense: a common agricultural technique can seem as
enthrallingly exotic as the impossibilities discussed by Lucretius, if we
have the imagination to look at the known world with fresh eyes.

In the fourth Eclogue Virgil described such *adunata* as grapes
hanging on brambles with the return of the golden age and oaks
oozing honey.[10] Grafting likewise makes the most unpromising plants
provide food:[11]

> inseritur vero et fetu nucis arbutus horrida,
> et steriles platani malos gessere valentis,
> castaneas fagus; ornusque incanuit albo
> flore piri glandemque sues fregere sub ulmis.

The rough arbutus is grafted with a walnut shoot, barren planes have
borne sturdy apple-boughs, and beeches have borne chestnuts; the ash
has whitened with the pear's pale bloom and pigs have crushed the acorn
under elms.

We must not suppose Virgil to be claiming that the countryside of
Italy is a golden world (indeed towards the end of the book he clearly
repudiates this notion);[12] it is of prime importance that he asserts,
and in this part of his poem, the realism of what he is describing:[13]

> ades et primi lege litoris oram;
> in manibus terrae. non hic te carmine ficto
> atque per ambages et longa exorsa tenebo.

Come, and skirt the edge of the near shore; the land is on hand. I shall
not hold you here with invented song, amid tangles and long preludes.

'In manibus terrae', word for word 'on hands earths'—it is an admirably
terse phrase, with three meanings. First, it sustains the metaphor of
the previous line: we are in a boat, but land is close at hand. But it
also means, straightforwardly, 'Terrains (or soils) are the subject now
in hand.' And this sense implies a third, almost literal signification:

---

[10] *Ecl.* 4. 29 f.   [11] *Geo.* 2. 69–72.
[12] For refutation of the view that Virgil claims Italy to be a golden world (a view on which
the theory of 'Virgil's lies' is largely based) see below, pp. 359 f.   [13] *Geo.* 2. 44–6.

we have got earth on our hands; as it were, dirt under the finger-
nails. When Virgil gives this real world a colouring of the golden
age, he anticipates a method which he will much develop in the
Aeneid, where he likes to take a person or place or idea, and walk
round his subject, so so speak, looking at it from different angles or
in different lights, watching a different facet of the prism catch the
sun. At one time or another we see Aeneas in the light of Achilles,
Hector, Paris, Jason, Theseus, Hercules, Augustus. This does not
mean, as some suppose, that Aeneas represents or is 'identified' with
Augustus or Achilles, or that the poet is flashing simple moral sig-
nals at his readers: 'Aeneas is like Jason here; condemn him. Turnus
is like Hector here; approve him.' The *Aeneid* is a morally serious
poem, and these points of likeness should start our enquiry, not end
it: we shall have to make our own judgement on whether the comparison of Aeneas to some other figure is more significant for the
resemblance or the difference. Such comparisons, explicit or implied,
suggest one light in which a character can be or has been viewed;
there may be others. (These lights may even be deceitful: when Aeneas'
enemies call him a Paris, suggesting that he is a selfish seducer, they
travesty the facts.)[14] And so with the golden-age colouring here in
the *Georgics*: it is not a flight from reality but the evocation of one
mood or spirit in which real facts may be contemplated.

Virgil does indeed take some care to incorporate into the first
part of the second Georgic phrases to link it to what has gone before.
Into one paragraph he slips two lines recalling the theme of work
so prominent in the first book:[15]

> scilicet omnibus est labor impend*endus*, et omnes
> cog*endae* in sulcum ac multa mercede dom*andae*.

For sure, toil must be spent on all, and all must be forced into the furrow and tamed at the cost of much effort.

The amount of effort needed is emphasized by the repetition in
'omnibus . . . omnes', the three forceful gerundives, and the expressive rhythm of 'impendendus', three long syllables and then the drop
to the short syllable followed by a slightly unexpected pause in the
middle of the fifth foot: the word itself seems to overhang, to 'impend'.
But in the context we feel more the bracing vigour of the work than
its toilsomeness. The farmer is winning: he 'compels' and 'subdues'.

---

[14] *Aen.* 4. 215 (Iarbas), 7. 321 (Juno).   [15] *Geo.* 2. 61 f.

And in the next lines nature answers humanely, harmoniously, and with matching energy: olives and vines 'respond', trees come to birth.[16] This might have been said about the crops of the first Georgic; or the labour of viticulture might have been commanded here in sterner tones. Virgil probably thought of Lucretius: the exuberance of nature depicted at the start of *De Rerum Natura* contrasts with the progressive enfeeblement of natural forces described in the second book, which ends with the vine-grower grumbling that the land no longer gives such increase as earlier generations enjoyed. It may be uncertain how to reconcile what Lucretius says in these two places, but that problem is not our present concern. Virgil takes up the contrast, but softens and subtilizes it, presenting severe determination and vigorous acceptance as areas in a spectrum of moods that shade toward one another.

A similar moral may be drawn from a slightly earlier place:[17]

> quare agite o proprios generatim discite cultus,
> agricolae, fructusque feros mollite colendo,
> neu segnes iaceant terrae. iuvat Ismara Baccho
> conserere atque olea magnum vestire Taburnum.

So come, ye farmers, learn the culture proper to each kind, and soften the wild fruits by cultivation, and let not the earth lie idle. It is a delight to sow Ismarus with Bacchus' vine and to clothe great Taburnus in the olive.

'Neu segnes iaceant terrae'—we have heard that tone of voice before. Farmers are now being exhorted to treat the land with the kind of hard purpose which Jupiter imposed upon man and nature: he did not wish his realm to grow slothful and lethargic.[18] But this time the sentiment is instantly followed by the firm verb 'iuvat', 'it is a delight'; the farmer's work is still work, but now seen not as a struggle but as a pleasure. The sentence well illustrates Virgil's technique of variation. Each of the noun phrases contains two nouns ('Ismara Baccho', 'olea . . . Taburnum') arranged in the chiastic pattern *abba*, accusative preceding ablative in the first phrase, ablative coming before accusative in the second. Each phrase is enlivened by a personification, but the first time it comes in the noun ('Baccho'), the second time through the pathetic fallacy in the verb 'vestire' (clothe). The two place names are also contrasted: 'Ismara' takes us to the remote

---

[16] *Geo.* 2. 64 (respondent), 65 (nascuntur), 68 (nascitur).
[17] *Geo.* 2. 35–8.   [18] *Geo.* 1. 124.

and wild region of Thrace and into the literary world of Homer (Odysseus gives Ismaric wine to the Cyclops);[19] Taburnus, a mountain in Samnium, making its first appearance in a Latin text, brings us home to the Italian heartland and a life not seen through literary spectacles. In miniature this is the movement made across twenty lines and more in the *laus Italiae*, from romantic lands far away to our own familiar territory.

Such refinements vivify the passages in which Virgil is or pretends to be dealing with the poem's ordinary business. The verse flows in an easy and graceful fashion, but it is not casual, nor is it meant to seem so.[20] It is easy in the sense that travel in a Rolls-Royce is easy; we are borne along by a superlatively tuned poetical machine, and we are meant to appreciate the beauty of the engineering, conscious of the craftsmanship that has gone into its making. Maybe such writing, for the exceptional poet capable of it, carries the danger that technique will outstrip imagination, leaving a lifeless efficiency, and perhaps that danger is felt at a few moments in the *Aeneid*. But the Rolls-Royce manner (if one may call it that) does not fail in the *Georgics*, where the extraordinary quality of the quieter passages is a high but still more a rare achievement.

The first hundred lines of the second Georgic prepare the way for the *laus Italiae* by evoking a new mood of quiet exaltation suffused with a sense of suppressed excitement. This sense is awakened in several ways. From time to time we feel a more personal pressure behind the efficient elegance that forms the poem's ordinary stuff. We have already seen the theme of wonder breaking three times above the surface. At 35 ff. we have heard men and the earth alike being stirred into activity (quare agite o . . .).[21] The verse is tremulous with expectancy: the vowel sounds are light, the rapid dactyls are made to quiver the more by the double elision in the first foot. The tone is not simply one of brisk practicality, for the note of

---

[19] *Od.* 9. 196–8.

[20] The effect of Virgil's balance and variation has been divergently understood. G. Williams, on *Aen.* 7. 759 f., believes that one effect of variation is 'to create the sense of casual ease, almost of impromptu composition, that yet makes the final result seem inevitable' (*Tradition and Originality in Roman Poetry* (Oxford, 1968), 724). By contrast, A. Parry rightly stresses the formality that coexists with the note of grief ('The Two Voices of Virgil's *Aeneid*', *Arion* 2 (1963), 66–80, at 66 f., reprinted in *The Language of Achilles and Other Papers* (Oxford, 1989), 78–96, at 78–80). The conscious enjoyment of technique should be as much part of the aesthetic response in such places as it is with (say) Bernini's St Teresa.

[21] Quoted above, p. 346.

elevation is also there: 'o . . . agricolae'. That call will be echoed, more rhapsodically, at the book's other end: 'o fortunatos nimium, sua si bona norint, | agricolas . . .'[22] The slow swooping cadence of that famous phrase is significantly different from the modest bustle of awakening at line 35. But as Virgil will say at the book's close, we have traversed a vast distance;[23] and we have earned the right to look back reflectively over what we have come to understand. Line 35, by contrast, marks a beginning.

'Quippe solo natura subest' (for natural force lurks in the soil).[24] This tersely suggestive phrase encapsulates the spirit of this part of the poem. Nature is conceived as a kind of force, latent in the soil like the seed of a plant; it is hidden below the surface, but it is also dynamic. The root meaning of the Latin word 'natura' as bringing to birth, as creativity, seems to come alive: nature is also native power.[25] The dynamism is brought out by the context in which the phrase is placed:[26]

> sponte sua quae se tollunt in luminis oras,
> infecunda quidem, sed laeta et fortia surgunt;
> quippe solo natura subest.

Those plants which raise themselves into the shores of light of their own accord are infertile, but flourishing and strong; for natural force lurks in the soil.

'Sponte sua' and 'laeta et fortia' suggest both harmony and vigour; the verbs 'surgunt' and 'se tollunt' are strong and thrusting. Verbs and phrases describing drive and movement recur in this part of the poem: 'sponte sua veniunt' (come of their own will), 'surgunt' (rise), 'pullulat' (sprout multiply), 'se subicit' (spring up), 'sequentur' (follow).[27] Other verbs attribute a sort of alertness to nature, as though it were bubbling with eager life: 'exspectant' (await), 'respondent' (respond).[28] Virgil has learnt, once again, from the opening of *De Rerum Natura*. Wisely, he does not attempt to rival the tremendous energy of that passage, but characteristically chastens Lucretius' boisterousness. Here the force of nature is still felt, but kept in check;

---

[22] *Geo.* 2. 458 f., discussed below, p. 375.   [23] *Geo.* 2. 541.   [24] *Geo.* 2. 49.
[25] The literary ancestry shows how Virgil assimilates. His phrase is modelled on Hom. *Od.* 9. 135, *epei mala piar hup'oudas* (for fatness lies abundantly under the soil), where, however, lacks the dynamic idea. The vocabulary echoes Lucr. 3. 273, 'latet haec natura subestque' (this nature lies hidden and below), where the subject is not the soil and growth is not in question.   [26] *Geo.* 2. 47–9.
[27] *Geo.* 2. 11, 14, 17, 19, 52.   [28] *Geo.* 2. 27, 64.

the charm of his method lies in the delicate balance between vigour and restraint.

The first lines of the book set the tone, showing once more how such formal matters as the length of a sentence or a paragraph can serve an expressive purpose.

> Hactenus arvorum cultus et sidera caeli;
> nunc te, Bacche, canam, nec non silvestria tecum
> virgúl|ta èt pró|lèm tár|dè cres|centis olivae.
> huc, pater o Lenaee: tuis hic omnia plena
> muneribus, tibi |pampine|o gravi|dus au|tumno
> floret ager, spumat plenis vindemia labris;
> huc, pater o Lenaee, veni, nudataque musto
> tinge novo mecum dereptis crura coturnis.
>   Principio . . .

Thus far tillage of fields and the stars in the sky. Now I sing of you, Bacchus, and with you of the woodland copses too and the progeny of the slow growing olive. Come hither, O father, God of the Winepress: all things here are full of your bounty, for you the field flowers, heavy with autumn's tendrils, and the vintage froths in full vats; come hither, O father, God of the Winepress, pull off your buskins and with me dip your bare legs in the new must. Firstly . . .

All is brisk and bright. Instead of the huge majesty of the first book's invocation, all we need is eight lines, and then down to business. The first note struck is one of practical, even prosaic recapitulation, but a single line is enough to sweep away that Hesiodic stuff (no time for a verb), and at once the poet turns to hail the wine god, indeed to hail him three times, such is the force of his enthusiasm, with the simple 'Bacche' soon replaced by the resplendent 'pater o Lenaee'. He revels in the processes of nature, the slow heterodyne movement of the third line pointing up the olive's slow growth, the bizarre rhythms of 'pampineo gravidus autumno', with its fifth-foot spondee and lack of third-foot caesura communicating the heavy fecundity of the vineyard at harvest time. In the first Georgic the gods were addressed from afar, with pomp; now god and man are bound together in unceremonious harmony. Virgil ended his proem by calling upon Caesar to feel compassion for farmers, 'mecum', 'with me';[29] the contrast between that passage and the effect of 'mecum' at the end of the new invocation is amusing. It is a pity to miss the jollity

---

[29] *Geo.* I. 41.

of Virgil's picture of god and poet taking their boots off and clamber-
ing into the vat together. People sometimes think that Virgil lacked
a sense of fun; it is not so.

As we approach the *laus Italiae*, a comparison with another poet
may help to suggest the originality of sensibility that Virgil brought
to it—provided, of course, that the comparison is not pushed too far.
In his *Lines Composed a Few Miles above Tintern Abbey* . . . Wordsworth
contrasts two attitudes towards nature. First he recalls the feelings
that he had experienced in his early twenties:[30]

> For nature then
> (The coarser pleasures of my boyish days,
> And their glad animal movements all gone by)
> To me was all in all.—I cannot paint
> What then I was. The sounding cataract
> Haunted me like a passion: the tall rock,
> The mountain, and the deep and gloomy wood,
> Their colour and their forms, were then to me
> An appetite; a feeling and a love,
> That had no need of a remoter charm,
> By thought supplied, nor any interest
> Unborrowed from the eye.

The passionate adoration of nature recollected here does not suggest antiquity, but it has this at least in common with the 'Greek'
view as described by Ruskin,[31] that it sees nature as it is. There can
be hardly any question of the pathetic fallacy, though in a very mild
form it just creeps in with the adjective 'gloomy'. There is no question at all of using the associative power of the mind (there is no
need of 'a remoter charm, By *thought* supplied, nor any interest,
Unborrowed from the eye'). Indeed, so immediate and all-absorbing is
the experience that it seems scarcely possible to make poetry of it
at all ('I *cannot paint* What then I was'); someone in such a frame
of mind can no more transfer his passion into words than he can
analyse his emotions in the act of making love.

But Wordsworth finds that now, five years later, he has changed:[32]

> That time is past,
> And all its aching joys are now no more,
> And all its dizzy raptures. Not for this
> Faint I, nor mourn nor murmur; other gifts
> Have followed; for such loss, I would believe,

---

[30] *Tintern Abbey* 72–83.   [31] See above, pp. 22 f.   [32] *Tintern Abbey*, 83–111.

Abundant recompense. For I have learned
To look on nature, not as in the hour
Of thoughtless youth; but hearing oftentimes
The still, sad music of humanity,
Nor harsh nor grating, though of ample power
To chasten and subdue. And I have felt
A presence that disturbs me with the joy
Of elevated thoughts; a sense sublime
Of something much more deeply interfused,
Whose dwelling is the light of setting suns,
And the round ocean and the living air,
And the blue sky, and in the mind of man:
A motion and a spirit, that impels
All thinking things, all objects of all thought,
And rolls through all things. Therefore am I still
A lover of the meadows and the woods,
And mountains; and of all that we behold
From this green earth; of all the mighty world
Of eye, and ear,—both what they half create,
And what perceive; well pleased to recognize
In nature and the language of the sense,
The anchor of my purest thoughts, the nurse,
The guide, the guardian of my heart, and soul
Of all my moral being.

And yet this is not so much the pathetic fallacy in Ruskin's sense—
that is, a half instinctive attribution of sentience to insentient
nature—as a conscious faith that nature contains a meaning. The
man who calls a wood gloomy or a wave indolent will admit readily enough, if challenged, that there is no possibility of trees suffering depression or sea-water amending its behaviour; Wordsworth is
seeking after something else, something more unusual. This thing
is impalpable, resisting definition of its very nature, so that to paraphrase or explicate Wordsworth's idea is necessarily to alter it. We
may find that Virgil's sense of nature stands to that of his predecessors in a relation comparable to that between the older and younger
Wordsworth (remembering always that the younger Wordsworth's passion lacks an ancient equivalent). Virgil too is aware of 'something
interfused'; for him too the appearance of the world is related in
some way to the life of humanity; nature has something like a moral
character and an expressive force. Most interesting of all, perhaps,
for comparison with Virgil is Wordsworth's idea of the senses both
half creating and perceiving; one of the new splendours of the *laus*

Italiae is the way in which it is the eye itself at its most acute that reveals the human meaning of the physical landscape; the historical associations are not something imposed adventitiously upon the natural scene. This is not to claim that Virgil's understanding of nature is close to Wordsworth's; most obviously, he has no equivalent to the English poet's implicit pantheism, and though in the *Aeneid* he becomes concerned to instil into the landscape a sense of the numinous, that is not part of his purpose in the *laus Italiae*, except perhaps vestigially in its final lines. Indeed, although prayer and the country gods are present in the *Georgics*, there is very little sense in them of the gods within nature itself. Here Lucretius' magnetism is felt: like *De Rerum Natura*, and unlike the *Aeneid*, the *Georgics*, because for the most part it does not find the divine within nature, finds other kinds of human and spiritual meaning there.

A hundred lines or so into the second book Virgil reaches the subject of soils and terrains, an important topic but not obviously exciting. It will take him further than we could have expected:[33]

> nec vero terrae ferre | omnes | omnia possunt.
> fluminibus salices crassisque paludibus alni   110
> nascuntur, steriles saxosis montibus orni;
> litora myrtetis laetissima; denique apertos
> Bacchus amat collis, Aquilonem et frigora taxi.
> aspice et extremis domitum cultoribus orbem
> Eoasque domos Arabum pictosque Gelonos: 115
> divisae arboribus patriae. sola India nigrum
> fert hebenum, solis est turea virga Sabaeis.
> quid tibi odorato referam sudantia ligno
> balsamaque et bacas semper frondentis acanthi? . . .

Nor indeed can all soils bear all plants. Willows are born by rivers, alders in heavy marshland, barren ashes on rocky mountains; shores are the most flourishing ground for myrtle groves, while Bacchus loves the open hillsides and yews love the North Wind and the cold. Look too at the globe tamed by men tilling its farthest limits, at the Arabs' eastern home and the painted Gelonians: trees have their different homelands. Only India bears black ebony, to the Sabaeans only belongs the stem of frankincense. Why need I tell you of balsams oozing from scented wood and the pods of the evergreen acanthus? . . .

---

[33] *Geo.* 2. 109–119. The whole of the *laus Italiae* will be quoted in the following pages, broken into sections for the convenience of the reader, who may none the less prefer to have a text in front of him.

And thus imperceptibly the *laus Italiae* has begun, with the most seam-
less of all Virgil's transitions. In the case of the disquisition on Jupiter's
purpose and human progress in the first book it was still possible,
at least in retrospect, to mark the point at which the practical farming stopped and the moral excursus started; here it is not. There is
no determinate point at which the instruction ceases and the celebration begins. Once again, the character of this transition, besides
its elegance, has an expressive function: poetic patriotism is seen to
grow organically out of the realities of using the land. Line 109 has
a robust ponderous rhythm, produced by the self-contained spondee
of the fourth foot; as we saw earlier, its second half is taken, with
the change of one letter, from a crucial passage of Lucretius.[34] Virgil
aligns himself with Lucretius' view of nature as impressive for the
very reason that it is rational and obedient to scientific laws; and at
the same time he turns aside from the picture of a golden age, in
which, as he has told us in the fourth Eclogue, 'omnis feret omnia
tellus' (every land shall bear everything)—here the rhythm is significantly more elegant.[35] But the very absence of a golden age from
Italy (we shall learn) and the very limitations of the country prove
ultimately a source of delight and glory, for the sense of place and
distinctiveness that these limitations make possible, the devotion to
one's own 'patria', the ability to locate one's origins and emotions
in one particular corner of the world are such precious gifts. The
topic that Virgil is now about to handle has already been treated,
more briefly, in the first book. Tmolus produces saffron, he says there,
India ivory, Sabaea frankincense, and so on;[36] the resemblance to lines
116 ff. in the present book is obvious. But in the earlier book he continues, in lines already quoted, with the restrictions and requirements
that nature has imposed; man is accordingly a 'hard race'.[37] In the
second Georgic Virgil looks at the same circumstances in a fresh
light: the facts that before seemed tough and demanding now inspire
enthusiasm and excitement. Much of the sense of brightness and
enlargement conveyed by this book is created by such transmutation of themes met before: we see those sunlit uplands opening up
before us.

The rough texture of 109 is not allowed to persist; a gesture towards
Lucretian ruggedness is enough. Lines 110 f. advance smoothly and
steadily towards a more ornamental form of expression: each of the

---

[34] Lucr. I. 166.   [35] *Ed.* 4. 39.   [36] *Geo.* I. 56–9.   [37] *Geo.* I. 60–3.

three clauses that make up these two lines contains two nouns the first is decorated by no epithets, the second by one (crassis), the third by two (steriles, saxosis). By lines 112 f. the poetical machine is cruising at full power: 'litora myrtetis laetissima' is a graceful variation upon the previous clauses; whereas before the trees were in the nominative case (salices, alni, orni) and the terrains in the dative (fluminibus, paludibus, montibus), the pattern is now reversed 'Laetissima' starts to add more colour because of the potential personification in the word's double meaning: it signifies 'flourishing but may suggest 'glad'. Then the next two clauses make the personification fully explicit in the verb 'amat'. Each of them is decorated with a proper noun, which forms the subject in the first case, the object in the second (Bacchus . . . Aquilonem). We have already observed such variations and incidental graces as the poem's common currency, a means of animating subjects not inevitably entertaining; and so here they hide rather than suggest that a purple passage is on the way. 'Divisae arboribus patriae'—in retrospect we shall appreciate that this begins to open out a new and deeper theme, linking the diversity of physical landscapes to the multiplicity of local loyalties in Italy; but when we first read it, it seems no more than another of the many personifications enlivening what purport to be the more routine passages of agricultural instruction. (One might compare the way in which a little sparkle is added to a list of wines in the previous paragraph: Tmolian and even King Phanaean himself stand up out of respect for Aminnean vines.)[38] So too with the catalogue of eastern lands: only gradually do we perceive that these are not just one or two more examples of different terrains suitable for trees but are taking the poem's argument into new areas.

One rhetorical question leads to another, then to a third; there is one line for the Ethiops, one for the Chinese; then, as the paragraph broadens out, two lines for India, nine for the Medes:[39]

> quid tibi odorato referam sudantia ligno
> balsamaque et bacas semper frondentis acanthi?
> quid nemora Aethiopum molli canentia lana,   120
> velleraque ut foliis depectant tenvia Seres?
> aut quos Oceano propior gerit India lucos,
> extremi sinus orbis, ubi aëra vincere summum
> arboris haud ullae iactu potuere sagittae?—

---

[38] *Geo.* 2. 97 f.   [39] *Geo.* 2. 118–39.

et gens illa quidem sumptis non tarda pharetris.   125
Media fert tristis sucos tardumque saporem
felicis mali, quo non praesentius ullum,
pocula si quando saevae infecere novercae,   128
auxilium venit ac membris agit atra venena.   130
ipsa ingens arbos faciemque simillima lauro,
et, si non alium late iactaret odorem,
laurus erat; folia haud ullis labentia ventis,
flos ad prima tenax; animas et olentia Medi
ora fovent illo et senibus medicantur anhelis.   135
    sed neque Medorum silvae, ditissima terra,
nec pulcher Ganges atque auro turbidus Hermus
laudibus Italiae certent, non Bactra neque Indi
totaque turiferis Panchaia pinguis harenis.

Why need I tell you of balsams oozing from scented wood and the pods of the evergreen acanthus? why of the Ethiopians' groves growing white with soft wool, or of how the Seres comb fine fleeces from leaves? or of the forests that clothe India, that farthest corner of the world, nearer Ocean, where no arrow shot can reach beyond the tree's airy top? (And yet that race is not slack when they take up the quiver.) Media produces the tart juice and lingering flavour of the beneficent citron, than which nothing is more efficacious, if cruel stepmothers have poisoned the cup, to bring help and drive the black venom from the limbs. The tree itself is huge and very like a bay in appearance, and if it did not spread another scent abroad, it would be a bay; its leaves do not drop in any wind, its flower clings exceptionally strongly; the Medes use it to freshen the breath of malodorous mouths and cure the asthma of the old. But neither the Medes' forests, that richest land, nor fair Ganges and Hermus turbid with gold, can vie with Italy in glory—not Bactra nor the Indians nor all Panchaia, fat with incense-bearing sands.

The vegetation of eastern and southern lands is described in terms that once more suggest the motif of the *adunaton*: wool growing on trees, branches that sweat, laurels that are not laurels, gigantic in size and with leaves that never drop.[40] As in Alice's Wonderland, things are the wrong size—the Indian tree, too, higher than arrow can reach (with the quaint addition that the Indians are pretty good with the bow). Propertius was to give the game away in an agreeable poem

[40] Latin usage permits the shift from the subjunctive of 'iactaret' to the indicative of 'erat', which slightly sharpens the edge of paradox. Line 133 is cunning. Virgil may be taken, prosaically, as saying that the tree is evergreen (and evergreens do drop their leaves). But his way of putting it suggests a leaf that no wind can detach; which sounds magical. Italy itself is soon to be treated in a similar way.

which is his tribute to Virgil's *laus Italiae*. Writing to his friend Tullus, who has been serving abroad, he thinks of his life in Cyzicus on the Propontis, and fancies that he may nurse a desire to travel in yet more exotic regions. And yet, 'omnia Romanae cedent *miracula terrae*' (All these wonders shall yield to the land of Rome).[41] The odd phrase 'Romanae . . . terrae' appreciates what the *laus Italiae* is soon to reveal to us: Virgil's fusion of Rome and Italy, culture and nature, city and earth.[42] As the younger poet also recognizes, the things which Virgil describes are indeed 'miracula', sights to provoke amazement; more subtle than Propertius, he does not say so directly, but lets us feel the wonder for ourselves.[43] The mood is complex: faintly discernible in Virgil's picture is the ghost of that feeling, found before in Lucretius, that a world in which the laws of nature were suspended, where fish might grow from the ground and fruits grow on any tree, would be not paradisal but unpleasing.[44] Wondrous though exotic lands may be in his account, they are also bizarre; we are being made ready to feel that Italy is, in a sense, the more 'natural' place.

None the less, an ambivalence lingers: Virgil is not simply saying, 'Foreign countries are pretty odd; see how much better Italy is.' The woolly trees of China and Ethiopia are described in terms reminiscent of the golden age, when, as we learn from the fourth Eclogue, grapes grow on briars and oaks exude honey;[45] the Indian trees higher than arrow-shot inspire awe; Media's healing fruit is a blessing that any land should be glad to possess. And yet . . . 'Sed neque Medorum silvae . . .'—that 'sed' is the mightiest conjunction in Latin literature, as the catalogue of exotic lands that has gone before is suddenly revealed to be, in effect, merely the first limb of a colossal period.[46] 'Sed' here is powerful in part because it newly opens to our vision the immensely broad scale upon which Virgil is writing; powerful also because it is astonishing, and in a way implausible, that Italy should surpass things so splendid. And so 'ditissima terra', far from being a makeweight to fill out the hexameter, is emphatic: Media is the richest of lands, and yet Italy's glory surpasses it. We see here

---

[41] Prop. 3. 22. 17.　　　[42] Compare too 'Romana per oppida' at *Geo*. 2. 176.

[43] Greek ethnographers loved to report *thaumata*, 'marvels'. They are so keen an interest in Herodotus' survey of foreign peoples that he troubles to begin his account of Lydia by saying that (with one exception) it lacks *thomata* (1. 93).

[44] See above, pp. 241–5.　　　[45] *Ecl*. 4. 29 f.

[46] This is why we should not think of the *laus Italiae* as starting at 136; the line is a middle, not a beginning.

a pattern of thought characteristic of Virgil and recurring in him
with variations of emphasis and effect, whereby he praises one thing
and then turns to set it against the praise of another, not usually to
diminish either but to give weight to the merits of each. We shall
meet it at the heart of the *Aeneid*, where Anchises asserts the superiority of the Greeks in arts and sciences before unfolding Rome's
great purpose.[47] We shall find it (in significantly distorted form) at
the start of the praise of country life later in this book. We have
detected it in the last sentence of the poem, where Virgil moves
from Caesar to himself, and despite the parade of modesty leaves
us with a signature as conspicuous as the 'Vincent' scrawled at the
bottom of Van Gogh's paintings. He will move from Caesar to himself at the end of the *laus Italiae* also, not of course to make Caesar
smaller, but to pile climax upon climax. In the *Aeneid* Anchises' concession to the Greeks will add a weight of solemn significance to
the sterner Roman task; here in comparable fashion, though in more
exuberant spirit, the assertion of Italy's supreme glory is the more
deliberately made for the recognition that she does without wonders
and blessings that are so great.

The shape of the sentence running from 136 to 139 conveys glorious confidence and abundance. It works towards a climax with the
emphatically placed words 'laudibus Italiae certent', and yet the verse
continues to pour on copiously with yet more romantic names, Bactra,
India, Panchaia, for another line and a half. A part of Virgil's self-
consciousness, to be most fully realized in the *Aeneid*, is his sensitivity to the overtones of proper names: we are to feel the touch
of incongruity in the name Italy enisled in the midst of such alien
and exotic places, three coming before, three after. Still the element
of *adunaton* is to be caught in the language. 'Auro turbidus' is virtually an oxymoron: the very mud or silt of Hermus is gold. 'Turiferis
. . . pinguis harenis' is another resplendent paradox: in Arabia even
the sands—thin soil, as the farmer knows—breathe the fatness of
luxurious scents. Arabia itself is called Panchaia, the name of the
happy island about which Euhemerus wrote in his philosophical fantasy. The resonance here has been well compared to that of Eldorado
in later times;[48] that is to say, we are still in the real world, or in a
place that has been supposed to belong in the real world, but to a
part of it half lost in the mists of distance and fable.

---

[47] *Aen.* 6. 847–53.   [48] By Sidgwick, quoted by Page ad loc.

The next sentence is founded upon the same pattern of thought, but this time it comes in a distorted form:[49]

> haec loca non tauri spirantes naribus ignem
> invertere satis immanis dentibus hydri,
> nec galeis densisque virum seges horruit hastis;
> sed gravidae fruges et Bacchi Massicus umor
> implevere; tenent oleae armentaque laeta.

No bulls breathing fire from their nostrils have ploughed this land for the sowing of a gigantic dragon's teeth, nor has a field of warriors bristled with helmets and serried spears, but teeming crops and Bacchus' Massic juice have filled it; olives and prosperous herds possess it.

The underlying idea is, 'Italy cannot rival the strange and magical crops that spring up in the world of Greek myth, but on the other hand she has more solid and comfortable agricultural virtues.' The distortion is this: the poet, his confidence and enthusiasm rising as the paragraph proceeds, has given a rhetorical twist to the first limb of the sentence. Whereas the marvels of the east were related in language which made no attempt to diminish their glory, the marvels of heroic legend are now presented in terms that make them appear somewhat sinister and unappealing.[50] Italy is now triumphing more easily and serenely over less happier lands. The praises sound louder:[51]

> hinc bellator equus campo sese arduus infert,   145
> hinc albi, Clitumne, greges et maxima taurus
> victima, saepe tuo perfusi flumine sacro,
> Romanos ad templa deum duxere triumphos.
> hic ver adsiduum atque alienis mensibus aestas:
> bis gravidae pecudes, bís | pòmis utilis arbos.   150
> at rabidae tigres absunt et saeva leonum
> semina, nec miseros fallunt aconita legentis,
> nec rapit immensos orbis per humum neque tanto
> squameus in spiram tractu se colligit anguis.
> adde tot egregias urbes operumque laborem,   155
> tot congesta manu praeruptis oppida saxis
> fluminaque antiquos subterlabentia muros.

---

[49] *Geo*. 2. 140–4.
[50] We shall find a similar pattern of distortion at 2. 461 ff.; see below, pp. 372 f.
[51] *Geo*. 2. 145–57.

From here comes the war horse, carrying itself erect across the plain; coming from here, Clitumnus, white herds and the bull, that noblest victim, often bathed in your sacred stream, have led Rome's triumphs to the temples of the gods. Here are constant spring and summer in months that are not its own: twice the cattle breed, twice the tree affords its fruits. But ravening tigers and the lion's savage brood are not here, nor does monkshood deceive the unhappy gatherer, nor does the scaly serpent dart huge spirals across the ground and wrap so mighty a length into a coil. Think too of all those noble cities and the effort in their works, of all the towns piled up by men's hands on precipitous rocks and rivers gliding beneath ancient walls.

By 149 f. the tide of enthusiasm is flowing so strongly that it is now Italy herself that is celebrated in language recalling conventional descriptions of the golden age. Now a man is not on oath when composing a patriotic panegyric, and indeed the *laus Italiae*, like the praise of country life later, is meant to feel exuberant, transported by its own enthusiasm. Yet Virgil keeps his exaggerations within careful bounds (Shakespeare, through the mouth of John of Gaunt, is much more extravagant in praise of England). And here especially it must be stressed that Virgil recalls the golden age; he does not say that Italy actually still enjoys it. The first Georgic very plainly shows that Italy is not a golden world; and Virgil will deny it again, if we attend to him properly, at the end of this very book.[52] It would be silly for him, as a matter of consistency, to assert here what he elsewhere denies; it would be silly, as a matter of logic, to maintain that there were perpetual spring *and* perpetual summer;[53] it would be silly, as a matter of fact, to claim that there is no winter in Italy. What he does is altogether more subtle: he remains in the real world but colours its surface with a golden lustre. The element of *adunaton* is now transferred from far climes to Italy itself: how strange and magical is our own land, if we have the wit to see it. The two halves of line 149 are complementary. In the second half Virgil clearly avoids saying

---

[52] *Geo.* 2. 473 f., 536 ff. See below, pp. 379 f.

[53] 'Ver' most often seems to be 'early summer'; classically it is the season when the roses bloom (as at 4. 134). So probably here, while 'aestas' is 'high summer'. For Cicero too 'ver' is the time of roses, 'aestas' harvest time (*Verr.* 2. 5. 27, 29). Virgil implies that Italy has a long season of bloom (the roses of Paestum flower twice at 4. 119) and that summer's warmth lingers late in the year. But the *patrii sermonis egestas* means that 'ver' is also used for early spring, the season when the snows melt, as in Hor. *Carm.* 1. 4. (the 'ver' at *Geo.* 1. 313 may not be exactly the same season as the 'ver' at 2. 323 ff.). English use of 'spring' presents somewhat similar difficulties, though it does not go as late as 'ver' (no roses).

that summer is perpetual: the phrase 'alienis mensibus', though it carries with it associations of an imaginary world in which the laws of nature are overturned, signifies on the literal plane that summer lingers on, not that it is endless. 'Adsiduus' in the first half of the line must similarly mean something like 'persistent';[54] 'perpetuus', which would scan identically, would be the obvious word if Virgil had really wanted to say that summer never ends; he eschews it.

In the fourth book the old gardener of Tarentum is treated similarly. While sullen winter was still splitting the rocks, he would be culling the hyacinth and chiding the summer for its delay.[55] It sounds like a miracle, close to the fantasy of the golden age; but Virgil has ingeniously picked the small corner of Italy which enjoys a winter climate closer to that of North Africa than to the rest of the peninsula, as an isothermic map reveals.[56] The spring flowers of the Galaesus valley, blooming while the Apennines behind are still locked in bitter cold, represent an idyll, but not an impossibility. The old fellow was the first to squeeze frothing honey from the comb, the first to pick roses in spring and apples in the autumn; his thorns bore plums and all his blossoms turned to fruit.[57] Again this is not magic, though it may have that sound, but skill: he was good at grafting, and had green fingers.[58]

At 151 ff. the pattern of 140 ff. is gracefully inverted. In the first passage Virgil told us, 'Italy may not have the fierce marvels of mythological Greece, but she is rich in produce'; now he tells us, 'She is rich in produce, but she does not have fierce creatures.' In the former case a touch of awe at the wonders of other places lingered on, competing with the rising sense of Italy's superiority; now the animals and poisons of foreign lands are shown in a light that makes them wholly unattractive. The repetition 'bis . . . bis . . .' in line 150 is another token of gathering enthusiasm: the second 'bis' gains a pressure of extra emphasis through its heterodyne position in the second part of the foot. And here, once more, the words seem to describe a breach in the ordinary laws of nature, yet do not do so.

---

[54] For 'adsiduus' in this sense cf. e.g. Lucr. 5. 252 and 341.   [55] *Geo.* 4. 135 f.

[56] F. Braudel, *The Mediterranean and the Mediterranean World in the Age of Philip II*, tr. S. Reynolds, i (London, 1972), 235. Horace notices the long summers and warm winters of Tarentum (*Carm.* 2. 6. 17 f.); Seneca treats the mildness of its winters as common knowledge (*Dial.* 9 (= *Tranq.*). 2. 13).   [57] *Geo.* 4. 134–46.

[58] One might compare, from the other end of Italy, the old man in Olmi's film, *L'Albero degli Zoccoli*, whose tomatoes are always the first to ripen—because he is passionate about growing tomatoes.

Meanwhile, in lines 143 ff., the emotional and associative content has been growing more complex. By mentioning crops, herds, wine, and olives Virgil binds the *laus Italiae* to the overall theme of the *Georgics*, and indeed to the particular subjects of this book. The phrase 'Massicus umor' introduces the first of the Italian proper names that will multiply in the later parts of the panegyric. Virgil has been looking at the diversity of the world and Italy's place in it; now he begins to narrow and concentrate his focus, gradually revealing the diversity within Italy herself. Massic wine and the originally Greek god Bacchus (143) represent the cultivated, Hellenized country of Campania; the Umbrian river Clitumnus (146), on the other hand, takes us to the old Italic heartland of the Apennines (146). As the great encomium moves onward, Virgil will come to speak of the works of man in Italy (155 ff.) and finally of the Italian peoples themselves (166 ff.); here from 143 he subtly and almost imperceptibly begins the process of enmeshing the natural character of his country with its historical and political greatness. The idea of human effort enters at 143, with corn and vines—grown by men, but in any number of lands. The herds of 144 (armenta) have more specifically Italian associations. Italy was supposed to be especially rich in cattle: Gellius calls it 'armentosissima', and antiquarians linked its name with 'vitulus' (bullock), and the Greek *italos*, 'ox';[59] during the Social War the allies issued a denarius showing a bull, symbolic of Italy, trampling the Roman wolf.[60] The warhorse (145) alludes to Rome's military greatness; the white herds of Clitumnus are Italian in a still more individualistic way, both for their distinctive and unusual colouring and for their special role in the ceremonial religion of Rome.[61]

At 148 Rome herself is named for the first time since the conclusion of the first book. The memory of that almost hysterical passage enhances, by force of contrast, our sense of the serene pomp with which the City now reappears. It enters as the culmination of a sentence, and in the nobly formal shape of a line held within a noun and its epithet—suitably enough for a phrase describing the

---

[59] Gell. 11. 1. 1 f.   [60] See above, p. 79.

[61] Of 'tuo perfusi flumine sacro' (147) commentators note that the use of possessive adjective and epithet together is characteristic of earlier Latin poetry, comparing Enn. *Ann.* 26 Sk and Lucr. 1. 38. The line of Ennius, 'teque, pater Tiberine, tuo cum flumine sancto' (you, father Tiber, with your sacred stream), surely in Virgil's mind here, is more closely imitated at *Aen.* 8. 72. Perhaps the old-fashioned tone imparts a sacral feeling, besides being a first hint of the antiquity of Italian tradition and belief, a theme to be developed in the later part of the panegyric.

formality of a national celebration. The triumph had an extraordinary emotional appeal to the Roman mind: Juvenal finds himself declaring, in the very satire which mocks the vanity of military glory, that had Marius died on the day of his triumph, he would have been the happiest of mortals; Horace powerfully finishes his Cleopatra Ode with the word 'triumpho', so that at the end of a poem which has seemed to concentrate upon the Egyptian queen, it is the idea of traditional and patriotic ceremony that reverberates in the memory.[62] Here too the word 'triumphos' seems to set the final seal upon a climactic line; but as with those other highly patterned lines, 139, 157, 171, any one of which seems formal and splendid enough to round off a paragraph, the illusion that we have reached a pause is only momentary, and the verse surges on with the copiousness of enthusiasm, and on again.

As the Clitumnus flows out of Umbria to mingle its waters with the Tiber, and its cattle descend from their native soil to their sacrificial death upon the Roman Capitol, we may feel Virgil already suggesting to us what he will make explicit at 167 ff., that Roman greatness has grown out of the Apennines, the ancient backbone of Italy. To call this symbolism would be misleading. It is not that the landscape symbolizes Roman history: landscape and history, agriculture and patriotism are indissolubly mingled. The fertility of the soil and the Roman lust for glory both go to the making of the 'bellator equus'. There is so much evoked in lines 143 ff.: the Greek, Roman, and old Italian elements of a single but complex nation, the sense of particular locality and of pan-Italian patriotism, the fecundity of the land, the traditions of its people, rural landscape and urban temples, pastoral life at home and conquest abroad, the ancient sanctity of Clitumnus and the elaborated civic religion of Rome. We should not try to distinguish cause and effect or mark a boundary between the literal and the imaginative: the physical and 'spiritual' qualities of the land are blended into one.

Not only nature but the civilizing work of man also has gone to the making of the Italian landscape; Virgil first tells us so explicitly at 155. At this moment he enlightens the verse with a new and unexpected brilliance. Hitherto in the *laus Italiae* he has not written about the land descriptively: he has told us about crops and herds, Clitumnus and Rome, spring and summer, rather than trying to put them before our mind's eye. Set descriptions, as in the *Aeneid*, and

---

[62] Juv. 10. 276 ff. (contrast 10. 133 ff.); Hor. *Carm.* 1. 37. 32.

even little vignettes of landscape such as the *Eclogues* offer, have been striking for their absence; now for the first (and for that matter the last) time in this panegyric Virgil realizes his sense of place in two sharp visual depictions. Lines 156–7 appear always to be taken as a picture of a single scene, but this is surely not so. The first line depicts the hill-towns of the Apennines, as everyone recognizes, but these are by their nature far removed from rivers, which do not glide beneath them; indeed, rivers are inconspicuous in the Apennine landscape altogether.[63] The second line would fit Rome (low-lying, outside the Apennine chain, and not piled up on rocks), but as a typical landscape it suggests much more the cities of the northern plain: Pavia, Placentia, Verona, and Virgil's own Mantua. He is asserting the diversity within his land, and insisting that the totality of Italy embraces the scenery of its old frontier, and even beyond, in what was so recently Cisalpine Gaul.

The picture in line 156 may seem to this day distinctively Italian. Horace had already described Anxur, 'impositum saxis late candentibus' (sited on rocks that gleam afar).[64] This momentary glimpse has a touch of particularity: in four words Horace seizes Anxur's distinctiveness, the abrupt site, the way the rocks catch the sun, even at a distance. But there is an element in Virgil's imagination absent from Horace; with his curious and characteristic blend of detachment and emotional engagement he invites us once again to see the familiar as though it were strange and wonderful: 'congesta manu' —how extraordinary are our Italian towns, if only we have eyes to see; to think that human hands could heap up habitations on such precipitous crags. This way of seeing is typical of his imagination; but perhaps we should also recall, in this instance, that he was a child of the plain. When he first left his native patch the Apennine hill-towns will have been as novel to him as they are to the modern visitor from a northern land.

In purely formal terms line 157 is a *tour de force*, a hexameter of only four words arranged in a chiastic pattern.[65] 'Subterlabentia' is

---

[63] The modern reader may find line 157 a better description of France or Germany than of peninsular Italy.   [64] *Serm.* 1. 5. 26.

[65] 'Subterlabentia' should not be written as two words (so Mynors in his Oxford text, though the lemma in his commentary suggests that he changed his mind). If 'subter' were a preposition and not part of a compound verb, it would have to go closely with 'antiquos', and instead of a line of classic calm and balance we should have an eccentric line in which the caesura was weakened by the close connection between the preposition and the adjective. But this is not the place for oddity. 'Subterlabor' is not found before Virgil, and is probably his own admirable coinage. It occurs first at *Ed.* 10. 4, where all editors print it as a single word.

serene both in rhythm and content. The energy and effort of the two lines before pass away into a line that is deeply and timelessly calm. Men toil and build and are gone, becoming part of the past; the ancient walls remain, and the river flows by for ever. We have seen how the Romans were warmed by the word 'antiquus';[66] yet it is simple enough. Part of the beauty and indeed serenity conveyed by Virgil's line is owed to the simplicity of his means. 'Moribus antiquis res stat Romana virisque,' Ennius wrote;[67] and a combination of durability, morality, manpower, and national identity found in distinctive and traditional institutions underlies the *laus Italiae*. Where Virgil differs from Ennius is in seeing these qualities embodied in the Italian landscape of town and river, so that the mind's imagining and solid reality fuse. This consideration brings us back to the position of these lines within the structure of the *laus Italiae* as a whole. As we have seen, at line 155 Virgil speaks directly, for the first time in the panegyric, about the civilizing work of man, and the rest of the *laus Italiae* will prove to be, in one sense or another, moral and political. By a stroke of genius he chooses just this moment, as he is moving towards more abstract themes, to show us his country pictorially. Our understanding of what it is to be an Italian is in every way deepened: it is through an appreciation of history and man's achievement that we come to see the landscape fully; it is through seeing the landscape that we appreciate our national history and achievement. 'Antiquus' here has been described as 'chiefly a pictorial epithet',[68] but who shall say whether the mind 'perceives' that antiquity or 'half-creates' it? The abstract and sensuous experiences have become indivisible. Line 157 evokes a sense of time and history, of change and changelessness. The durability of man's work and the perennity of nature merge into a harmonious whole. All human things are subject to decay, we may suppose, and yet those walls, the work of human hands, have stood there, unaltered, for so long; the waters slip past ceaselessly, always different and always the same. This is not the creation of a spiritual landscape but the 'spiritualization' of a real landscape; and it has all—river as much as masonry—become instinct with the 'music of humanity'. These lines inaugurate a new era in the western imagination.

After the momentary stillness of line 157 the pace quickens with a series of rhetorical questions:[69]

---

[66] See above, pp. 117 f.
[67] *Ann.* 156 Sk (The Roman state rests upon traditional manners and men).
[68] By Conington ad loc.   [69] *Geo.* 2. 158–72.

an mare quod supra memorem, quodque adluit infra?
anne lacus tantos? te, Lari maxime, teque,
fluctibus et fremitu adsurgens Benace marino?   160
an memorem portus Lucrinoque addita claustra
atque indignatum magnis stridoribus aequor,
Iulia qua ponto longe sonat unda refuso
Tyrrhenusque fretis immittitur aestus Avernis?
haec eadem argenti rivos aerisque metalla   165
ostendit venis atque auro plurima fluxit.
haec genus acre virum, Marsos pubemque Sabellam
adsuetumque malo Ligurem Volscosque verutos
extulit, haec Decios Marios magnosque Camillos,
Scipiadas duros bello et te, maxime Caesar,   170
qui nunc extremis Asiae iam victor in oris
imbellem avertis Romanis arcibus Indum.

Or shall I tell of the upper and lower seas that wash Italy? or of its mighty
lakes? of you, greatest Larius, and you, Benacus, rising with a roar of waves
like the sea? Or shall I tell of harbours and the barrier brought to the
Lucrine Lake and the loud roar of the resentful sea, where the ocean is
thrust back and the Julian waters resound afar and the Tyrrhenian surge
pours into the basin of Avernus? This same land has revealed in her veins
streams of silver and mines of copper and has most amply flowed with
gold. This land has brought forth a keen race of men, Marsians and Sabine
stock, the Ligurian inured to adversity and the Volscians with their pikes;
it has brought forth the Decii and Marii and great Camilli, the Scipiones
tough in war and you, most mighty Caesar, who, now victorious on Asia's
farthest bounds, keep the cowed Indian from the towers of Rome.

Virgil has alluded to Campania, Umbria, and Rome; now he moves
north towards the Alps. In his time there was no part of the civilized world that could rival northern Italy for large and beautiful
lakes; so in part lines 199 f. represent an accurate appraisal of his
country's peculiar glories.[70] But Larius and Benacus—the Lakes of
Como and Garda—had until lately been part of Cisalpine Gaul, so
that he is also indirectly making a political point. These lines further enlarge our patriotic understanding; they recognize the full and
newly established extent of the variety contained within the unity

[70] The immense width of the southern part of Garda makes it in bad weather the stormi-
est of the Italian lakes; so as with Mincius, Virgil is seizing upon a distinctive characteristic of these waters. It is interesting that he expands on Garda and the Lucrine Lake, two
places that he, born in Mantua and living in Naples, will presumably have seen. By contrast, Larius is merely 'maximus' (if he means that it is the largest Italian lake, he was mistaken). Earlier he has named Clitumnus, but unlike (for example) Carducci and Mynors,
he is not moved to celebrate the beauty of its springs; probably he had not seen them.

that is Italy. The succeeding lines increase the political content by bringing the achievements of the Julian family to this book for the first time. Virgil's mastery of transition is again in evidence: the movement from rivers to seas, from seas to inland waters, from inland waters to the engineering works around Avernus and the Lucrine Lake seems natural and almost effortless. Man-made marvels and the marvels of nature sit side by side. The element of *adunaton*, which was so strongly felt at 149 f., is still perceptible: Benacus, though only a lake, heaves and roars as though it were an ocean; the Tyrrhenian Sea pours over to an inland basin; precious metals seem to flow from the soil like water. The parallelism between lines 165 and 167 suggested by the repetition 'haec . . . haec' continues to harmonize man and nature: tough men and tough metals alike seem to grow out of the rugged landscape. Such phrases as 'genus acre', 'adsuetum malo', and 'duros bello' link what might be called Virgil's Roman and Italian themes. We recall how 'durus' was applied in the first book to mankind in general and to countryfolk in particular;[71] now it describes the martial Scipios, 'duros bello', but just at the point where the robustness of Italian country peoples is being admired. The austerity of country life and the power of endurance in war are seen to be intimately linked. The listing of four different Italian peoples maintains the theme of diversity within unity; the allusion to the 'veru', their distinctive weapon, is a small individualizing touch.[72]

Once again the transition, from metals to men, from Italian hill peoples to Roman heroes, and from Roman heroes to Caesar, is superbly assured. And once again Virgil shows his feeling for the associative qualities of proper names. As with Italy at 138, encircled by the names of exotic places, so here we should feel the distinction between the contemporary leader Caesar and the resonantly familiar names of the heroes of the past. The distinction is sharpened by the way in which the plurals of line 169 f., loosely and extravagantly conveying the abundance with which the land brought forth the great men of old, yield to the sudden singular of 'Caesar'; the unexpected vocative, too, particularizing and immediate, marks the passage from hazily realized past to vivid present, while Caesar's contemporaneity is further emphasized by 'nunc' and 'iam' in 171. And yet Virgil makes the distinction only to override it, for again he makes a political assertion: that the living Caesar is indeed fitly to be ranked with

---

[71] *Geo.* I. 63, 160.   [72] As again at *Aen.* 7. 665, 'veruque Sabello' (the Sabine dart).

the national heroes of long ago. By another fine stroke of invention Virgil links Caesar with the theme of the panegyric as a whole. At 136 ff. Italy was compared and contrasted with eastern lands in terms of their physical appearance; now that we have learnt so much more about the relation between landscape and human history, the comparison is repeated in political and military terms. We meet here a sense of geography—of place and distance—that Virgil also develops, as we shall see, at the end of the first Georgic and in the proem to the third. In line 171 we are out in the farthest orient (*extremis Asiae . . . in oris*); in line 172 we are back in the heart of the Roman citadel itself. Even the word-order of 172 is geographically expressive: Rome is at the centre, and the unwarlike Indian at the extremities.[73]

With the entry of Caesar we expect the *laus Italiae*, like the exordium of Book 1, to come to its climax and conclusion; but no, the verse surges forward still further. Now that the distinctive identity of Italy has been expressed in both physical and political terms, Virgil can tie the many threads of his thought together as he finally invokes the land itself.[74]

> salve, magna parens frugum, Saturnia tellus,
> magna virum: tibi res antiquae laudis et artem
> ingredior sanctos ausus recludere fontis,
> Ascraeumque cano Romana per oppida carmen.

Hail great mother of crops, Saturn's land, great mother of men: for you I enter upon a matter and craft esteemed from of old, venturing to unseal the sacred springs, and sing Ascraean song through Roman towns.

'magna parens frugum, . . . magna [parens] virum'—in the parallelism between these two phrases the way that a people's identity is rooted

---

[73] If the Indian is unwarlike, what virtue is there in Caesar keeping him from Rome? Of the arguments advanced by those who think that Virgil undercuts his *laus Italiae*, this is the one which deserves consideration, though it ought to be unbelievable that he should spoil the finest panegyric ever written for the sake of a jibe which would be in political terms ungrateful, even risky, and in aesthetic terms cheap. The crispest, decisive answer comes from E. Fantham (reviewing Thomas's commentary, *CP* 86 (1991), 163–7, at 165), who shows from Livy that to call the defeated 'imbellis' may either honour (1. 12. 8) or belittle (9. 19. 10) the victor. We might reflect, too, that the mythic appeal of the 'Dunkirk spirit' and the 'damned close-run thing' would not have struck much of a chord with the Romans. The eighth Aeneid displays Augustus at Actium triumphing with godlike ease over the frightened east. (Servius suggests that 'imbellem' is proleptic: Caesar's power renders the Indians unwarlike. The objection to this is that orientals were unwarlike by convention, but possibly Virgil floats loosely between the stock idea that the Indians are naturally unwarlike and the thought that they feel unwarlike once they face a Roman chief.)

[74] *Geo.* 2. 173–6.

in its native soil is more firmly than ever proclaimed. In this context 'Saturnia' is profoundly and multiply suggestive. Virgil is not
asserting that the miraculous world of the golden age survives in
Italy; for an Italian, after all, Saturn was a genuine native deity, not
a moral or poetical symbol. He is at moments almost a 'patron saint'
of Italy: Ennius already uses 'Saturnia terra' as a synonym for Italy,
and when Evander in the eighth Aeneid says that 'Saturnia tellus'
has often changed its name, he means that Italy has changed its
name not that paradise has.[75] Saturn will have suggested several things
to Virgil's contemporaries. His name appears to be of Etruscan derivation; he was an agricultural deity, invoked against blight. Antiquarians
(wrongly) drew the name's etymology from the root which produces
'sata' (crops). He became identified with the Greek Kronos, ruler
of the gods until he was overthrown by his son Zeus, and in the
Eclogues Virgil has already had him reigning in that golden age which
Zeus or Jupiter destroyed; hence too the story in the *Aeneid* that
when defeated by Jupiter he fled to Italy, establishing another kind
of 'golden age' there.[76]

Bearing all this in mind, we can see how rich in associations his
name is here. It evokes a complex of ideas: fecundity, moral virtue, national glory, numinousness, the immemorial depths of Italian
history, the blessedness and changelessness of country life. Sundry
phrases in lines 173–5 bring out the various aspects of the complex emotion contained within the words 'Saturnia tellus'. 'Frugum'
stresses fertility, 'virum' patriotic pride; the idea of motherhood in
'parens frugum' and 'parens . . . virum' seems to suggest both the
intimacy of man's link with nature, which nurtures him, and, more
particularly, the strength of the tie that binds his loyalty and affections to one especial spot of earth. 'Antiquae laudis' roots the greatness of Italy in her long past, which in the context we are invited
to trace back beyond Rome, beyond Jupiter even, to primeval Saturn.
'Ars' close to 'antiquus' implies the changeless continuity of the farmer's
work, that ancient skill.[77] In this setting 'sanctos . . . fontis', that significant adaptation of Lucretius' 'integros . . . fontis',[78] suggests not just
the conventional apparatus of poetic inspiration—Muses and suchlike
—but the divine aura that rests upon the countryside itself, an aura
enhanced by Saturn's associations with a world of primal, god-filled

[75] Enn. *Ann.* 21 Sk; *Aen.* 8. 329.   [76] *Ecl.* 4. 6 (cf. 6. 41); *Aen.* 8. 319 ff.
[77] 'Ars' is the worker's craft (cf. 1. 133), not the art of didactic verse.
[78] Lucr. 1. 927.

innocence. Virgil reveals the depth in ordinary things: he shows us an experience of the world growing out of the deeps of religious tradition, the solidity of the earth, the dark abyss of distant time.

No one had written like this before, and Virgil may have known it, for he seems to feel, as we do, that he has earned the right to end by celebrating his own achievement. For he has still not finished, not quite. We had thought that Caesar must be the climax, or if not Caesar, the land; but there is still one more object of praise to come: the poet himself. It is a bold step, the more so since he here eschews the graceful self-deprecation that we find at the end of the poem. He seems to raise himself to an equality even with Caesar, for the idea of motion implicit in 'Romana per oppida' (itself a paradoxical phrase which unites the great city with the municipia of Italy) suggests a triumphant progress. He too has brought back spoils from the east: not slaves or treasure but Ascraean song. Bold though it is, his self-confidence seems entirely fitting at the conclusion of so jubilant a passage; his proud signature sets the seal upon the great declamation. It shows his command of structure that he, the master of transition, should not try to soften the change of mood, theme and pace in the next lines:[79]

> nunc locus arvorum ingeniis, quae robora cuique,
> quis color et quae sit rebus natura ferendis.

This is the place to discuss the character of soils, the strength of each, its colour and native capacity for growing things.

The practical tone (again, no verb) has a resumptive character; it presupposes that we have paused, before returning to business and a less exalted manner. The full stop at the end of 176 is perhaps the mightiest stop in Latin literature, and appropriately so; we have reached a climax so immense that it demands a huge fermata at the close.

When Virgil buckles down again to his didactic task, the little personifications suggested in the first two lines are quickly developed, as he tells us about cussed soils cheering up when the olive grows on them.[80] We are back to the familiar techniques by which he enlivens his drier topics. And yet as we read the poem through continuously, we ought to feel that something has changed. As far as its content goes, the paragraph which he has now newly begun might come almost anywhere in this book. Yet coming where it does, the sense of

[79] Geo. 2. 177 f.   [80] Geo. 2. 179–81.

something human interfused in the landscape conveyed by 'ingeniis', the connectedness of strong earth and strong men suggested by 'robora', the particularity in 'cuique'—all these things will be coloured by what we have learnt in the sixty lines before. Had the *laus Italiae* survived as a fragment, we might have guessed that it ended the poem or the book. But as it casts its light forward on Virgil's continuing exposition, we may appreciate why it does not.

Since Virgil has paused, we might pause with him, and reflect on his achievement. He has discovered an area of imaginative experience which becomes through him part of the inheritance of western man, and which will best be expressed again, after him, in the nineteenth century. As an example we might take Henry James's novella *The Passionate Pilgrim*, in which the hero, a visiting American, climbs the Malvern Hills, from where he looks down upon 'the complex English earth'. That pregnant phrase speaks of the appearance of fields, hedgerows, villages, and coppices, but at the same time alludes also to the long history and elaborate social evolution which have gone to the making of that picture. Virgil is the originator of this species of feeling; it is he who first finds how the mind's eye and the literal eye may work together, so that landscape may give us an understanding of our past and our identity, and history enhance our apprehension of the visible scene.

His conception is not only aesthetic but also in the broad sense political. He appreciates that sentiment and imagination are constituents of the national idea; in other words, that they are a political necessity.[81] Further, he realizes the use of what one might call concentric loyalties; Burke is his descendant when he asserts that attachment to the 'subdivision' or 'little platoon' is not the enemy of a larger goodwill, but the first link in a series leading outward to the love of country and of mankind.[82] In our own world the nation-state is the overwhelmingly dominant object of common allegiance. For the ancient Greeks it was different: their loyalty was to a smaller political unit, the city-state, and more widely, to that part racial, part linguistic, part territorial, part cultural idea, Hellas. For the Romans

[81] This consideration has an immediate relevance today. The European Union's present travails owe much to an élite's either being unaware that union cannot succeed without a community of sentiment among the peoples composing it or else believing that juridical and constitutional change will of themselves bring such a community of sentiment into existence. Virgil would be useful reading in the chancelleries of Europe.

[82] From *Reflections on the Revolution in France*, quoted at the head of Ch. 3. Burke was referring to class rather than local loyalty, but the principle is the same.

the focus was Rome, conceived either as city or empire. Virgil cannot of course invent the idea of the nation-state, but the extent to which he anticipates it is remarkable. What he celebrates as a focus of common loyalty is the shared experience over time of people inhabiting a large continuous area of land, diverse in character but with its diversity contained by an overarching unity.[83] That is the modern sense of nationhood, more or less, with the exception that the nation-state is a juridical and administrative entity in a way that ancient Italy was not. No one had written about Italy like this before, nor would anyone in antiquity quite do so again: when the Elder Pliny, for example, dilates on Italy's beauties, he merely burbles indiscriminate praise, limping in the master's footsteps, without his feeling for nature and history interfused.[84] Virgil's idea, or complex of ideas, adds a new element to the imaginative inheritance of humanity and entitles him to rank among the makers of the modern mind.

Unlike the *laus Italiae*, the praise of country life is not approached by a subtle transition. It begins with an exclamation, unconnected to the lines immediately before, and appears to be exactly what it is, the opening of a long peroration to end the book:[85]

> o fortunatos nimium, sua si bona norint,
> agricolas, quibus ipsa procul discordibus armis
> fundit humo facilem victum iustissima tellus.   460
> *si non* ingentem foribus domus alta superbis
> mane salutantum totis vomit aedibus undam,
> nec varios inhiant pulchra testudine postis
> inlusasque auro vestis Ephyreiaque aera,

[83] The idea of unity in diversity has become instinctive: 'This land is your land, this land is my land, | From California to the New York Island'—and so on. Some years ago Edward Heath gave a lecture in Oxford, mostly a sober survey of practical politics. But as a peroration he felt the need for a vision of Britain—our quiet villages and crowded city-centres, our bustling market-towns and windswept moorlands—or words to that effect. It was not particularly well done—indeed there drifted into the mind the image of a great white flightless bird, flapping its wide wings vainly in an unavailing effort to get off the ground—but the significant thing is that it was attempted at all.

[84] Pliny, *Nat. Hist.* 3. 39–42.

[85] *Geo.* 2. 458–74. Line 471 is here tentatively deleted. It has never been suspected and appears in the early manuscripts; and 'saltus et lustra ferarum' sounds Virgilian. But 'non absunt' is a flat and pompous anticlimax after the enjambment, and 'non absunt illic' provides an entire half-line of stodge, which is not like Virgil (it would not surprise in Lucretius). The paragraph runs better if the line is removed; if that is agreed, it is hard to see why Virgil should have included it. Perhaps someone thought that the sentence needed a verb. But the main verb can be understood for 467–70, just as it must be for 471–3 in the text as it is transmitted.

alba neque Assyrio fucatur lana veneno,   465
nec casia liquidi corrumpitur usus olivi;
at secura quies et nescia fallere vita,
dives opum variarum, *at* latis otia fundis,
speluncae vivque lacus, *at* frigida tempe
mugitusque boum mollesque sub arbore somni,   470
[non absunt; illic saltus ac lustra ferarum]
et patiens operum exiguoque adsueta iuvantus,
sacra deum sanctique patres; extrema per illos
Iustitia excedens terris vestigia fecit.

Oh too happy, if they recognize their own blessings, the farmers for whom
far from the clash of arms the earth herself, most fairly, pours from the
soil an easy sustenance! If no house with proud portals disgorges from all
its halls a mighty tide of morning visitors, and people do not gape at doors
inlaid with fair tortoiseshell or raiment tricked out with gold or bronzes
of Ephyra, and the usefulness of clear olive-oil is not affected by cassia—
still, theirs is rest without anxiety and a life that does not know deceit,
rich in manifold resources, theirs is ease in broad demesnes, caves and living lakes and cool vales and the lowing of oxen and soft sleep beneath the
trees and young men accepting of toil and inured to small means and worship of the gods and revered greybeards; Justice left her last footprints among
them as she passed from the earth.

The underlying pattern of the rhetoric in 461 ff. is indicated by the
first words 'si non' and the later 'at . . . at . . . at'. The shape of the
thought is this: '*Although* the country has not got the splendours of
the city, at least it can still claim certain charms of its own.' That is
to say, the underlying shape is one that assumes it to be a conventional or at least common view that the attractions of the country
cannot match those of the town. Something of Corydon's mood
hovers in the background: the country may be rough and inelegant,
and yet . . .[86]

But this rhetorical pattern is distorted, wrenched in another
direction: 'Although the country has not got the (rather vulgar and
wearisome) splendours of the city, it can still claim (very large) charms
of its own.' It is a sophisticated technique of persuasion: the writer
purports to be making concessions to the opposite point of view,
but quietly takes them back in the act of giving them. Part of Virgil's
bland elegance here is that though he makes his meaning plain—no
one doubts that the city comes badly out of the comparison—there

[86] *Ecl.* 2.

is strictly speaking not a single word which overtly and unambiguously condemns urban life. 'Ingens' and 'altus' are words commonly used to import a little grandeur or elevation to a description;[87] 'superbus' is an epithet which can be neutral or favourable, though we suspect a pejorative tone here. The verbs of spewing and gaping (vomit, inhiant) encourage us to think of a human orifice, and to think of it with distaste; the language suggests the greed and ugliness of the urban mass, but it remains suggestion merely.[88] 'Fuco' and 'venenum' at 465 are simply descriptive in their literal signification—'stain' and 'dye'. Naturally we shall hear a darker overtone—'taint' and 'poison' —but Virgil achieves a suave suggestiveness by placing words which are formally neutral in a context which appears to shed an unpleasing light upon them. Even 'corrumpo' does not necessarily imply disapprobation: the word is used, though rarely, without pejorative force to describe the mingling or breaking down of matter. After six lines entirely free of elision come for contrast two lines containing three elisions of the same syllable, 'inlusasque auro', 'Ephyreiaque aera', 'neque Assyrio'. The clogging of the metre and the exotic, even baroque epithets ('Ephyreian', meaning 'Corinthian', is freighted with the apparatus of learning) seem in the context to imply that a superfluity of pompous encrustation is the townsman's idea of magnificence. But still this is suggestion, not statement.

As we have seen, the pattern of thought underlying 461 ff. has already appeared in the *laus Italiae*. It is to come twice more, and on these occasions without distortion of the rhetorical shape, in the peroration's next limb. First, the poet indulges his own hopes:[89]

> me vero primum dulces ante omnia Musae,   475
> quarum sacra fero ingenti percussus amore,
> accipiant caelique vias et sidera monstrent,
> defectus solis varios lunaeque labores;

> . . . .

---

[87] Though with such common words grandeur is bought at a cheap rate. Virgil does nothing to make the city's scale appealing.

[88] We should tread delicately here. Latin 'vomo' is seldom well translated by English 'vomit'; the English word is perhaps always unpleasant, but 'vomo' can be neutral, even impressive. The passages leading into the amphitheatre were called 'vomitoria'; in Ennius (*Ann.* 453 Sk) Tiber 'vomit' its waters into the sea (two comparisons already made by Macrobius (*Sat.* 6. 4. 3) in discussing this very passage). 'Vomo' is used by Lucretius of Etna's fiery eruption (1. 724) and at *Aen.* 8. 681 of the flames breaking from Augustus' joyful temples at Actium. The poet's suavity here in the *Georgics* lies in choosing a word which does not have to be disagreeable.   [89] *Geo.* 2. 475–8, 483–6.

> *sin* has *ne* possim naturae accedere partis
> frigidus obstiterit circum praecordia sanguis,
> rura mihi et rigui placeant in vallibus amnes,   485
> flumina amem silvasque inglorius.

But for my part, first and above all may the sweet Muses, whose sacred emblems I bear, smitten with a mighty love, accept me and show me the stars and the pathways of heaven, the diverse eclipses of the sun and the moon's travails; . . . but if the blood about my heart is cold and blocks me from reaching these aspects of nature, may the countryside and the running streams in the valleys delight me, may I love the rivers and woods, in obscurity.

The poet aspires to understand the workings of natural science, but the note of uncertainty is soon heard ('sin . . . ne' is similar to 'si non' at 461): if his power of intellect should prove insufficient, may he at least love the countryside's outward charms, 'inglorius'. To be sure, an irony hangs around this surprising epithet, but some part of the self-deprecation is truly meant. For the rhetorical pattern returns yet again:[90]

> felix qui potuit rerum cognoscere causas
> atque metus omnis et inexorabile fatum
> subiecit pedibus strepitumque Acherontis avari:
> fortunatus et ille deos qui novit agrestis
> Panaque Silvanumque senem Nymphasque sorores.
> illum non populi fasces, non purpura regum
> flexit et infidos agitans discordia fratres . . .

Happy he who has been able to learn the causes of things and has trodden beneath his feet all fear and inexorable fate and the roar of greedy Acheron. Fortunate too he who has known the country gods, Pan and old Silvanus and the sisterhood of the Nymphs. He has not been turned from his course by the emblems of public office, the purple of kings or discord stirring brother to disloyalty against brother . . .

The reference to Lucretius, pretty clear at 477 ff., is now inescapable.[91] A poet who wished to convey an unruffled sense of superiority

[90] *Geo.* 2. 490–6.
[91] Virgil does not name Lucretius, just as Anchises does not name the Greeks at *Aen.* 6. 847 ff., nor Lucretius Epicurus in any of his three encomia (1. 62 ff., 3. 1 ff., 5. 1 ff.). Perhaps we do not quite understand the reason for these silences, but we may find them impressive, without exactly knowing why. Maybe they are a tribute to fame: no need for a name, we all know who is meant. Maybe there is a sense of reticent awe, like the idea in some cultures that god may not be named. In the present case we should perhaps also consider the game whereby the author looks back to the *protos heuretes* or founding father of his genre: we pretend that Hesiod is the model, even though Lucretius matters so much more.

might hesitate to invite his readers to measure him against so formid-able a rival. After the grandiose 'din of Acheron' does not 'fortunatus et ille' steal forward with a kind of quietness, a shyness? We have already noticed that Virgil ducks the direct challenge to Lucretius, and shows us as much: we expect him to set *De Rerum Natura* against his own poem, but he slips sideways, setting it instead against the countryman's life.

Three times, then, in less than forty lines he has followed a sim-ilar movement of thought: the suggestion of some lack or loss or incapacity, and then the responding note, 'and yet . . .' One beauty of this pattern of ebb and counterflow is that it does not insist on a pat answer: does the proffered consolation balance the loss or out-weigh it or compensate for it in part only? The mixture of regret and gladness may also vary from one place to another: each will invite a fresh response.

And in the present case we may fancy that we hear other notes of yearning. 'O fortunatos nimium, sua si bona norint, | agricolas' —the shape of this exclamation, together with something of the mood, is drawn from Catullus' *Peleus and Thetis*:[92]

> o nimis optato saeclorum tempore nati
> heroes . . .

O heroes born in an era of time too much desired . . .

Virgil has picked up not only 'o' and 'nimis' but the sweep of the phrase across the end of the line to conclude after the first syllable of the second foot; the effect is especially marked in the earlier poem, where the apostrophe comes after a succession of end-stopped clauses. Virgil differs, though, in slipping a tentative conditional clause into the middle of his effusion (sua si bona norint). Once again, the little 'si' has a significant effect. His 'nimium' follows Catullus. In *Peleus and Thetis* the wisp of melancholy is unmistakable: Catullus is looking out of the uninspiring present back to a vanished age of romance and glamour, and the hint of excess—'age *too much* desired' —enhances his sense of loss. For Virgil, on the other hand, the good life of the country still exists; and yet in his 'nimium' too, coming as it does after the slow spondees and bare open vowels of 'o for-tunatos', we may hear the note of romantic nostalgia linger. Both where he remains with his model and where he departs from him, there is a touch, a light touch of melancholy tone.

[92] Cat. 64. 22 f.

And another follows at 473 f., for in the very act of saying that Justice left her last footprints in the country, he is asserting—subtly but without ambiguity—that she is no longer to be found there: the golden age is long gone.[93] That idea is picked up in almost the last lines of the book:[94]

> *hanc* olim veteres *vitam* coluere Sabini,
> *hanc* Remus et frater; sic fortis Etruria crevit
> scilicet et rerum facta est pulcherrima Roma,
> septemque una sibi muro circumdedit arces.   535
> *ante* etiam sceptrum Dictaei regis et *ante*
> impia quam caesis gens est epulata iuvencis,
> aureus *hanc vitam* in terris Saturnus agebat;
> *necdum* etiam audierant inflari classica, *necdum*
> impositos duris crepitare incudibus ensis.   540

This is the life that the old Sabines pursued of yore, and Remus and his brother too; thus, for sure, Etruria grew strong and Rome became the fairest of nations, one city which threw a wall around her seven strong-points. Before the Dictaean king yet held the sceptre and before a sinning race feasted on slaughtered bullocks, this was the life that golden Saturn led upon the earth; men had not yet so much as heard the trumpet blow, nor yet swords ringing, laid on hard anvils.

Even by Virgil's standards, this is a passage masterly in its polyphonic refinement and control. For many lines now he has been depicting country life as the good life—'hanc . . . vitam', he declares at 532, gathering up this theme, and the 'hanc' is quickly repeated, with a kind of exaltation. And 'hanc vitam' returns at 538, in association with Saturn, evoking for us the changelessness of country ways across immense tracts of time and a kind of continuity even with the golden age, so that the rural idyll is tinged with an aureate lustre. A glorious peroration—and yet at some moment it should dawn on us that somehow we have been slipping back through layer after layer of the past—back to the Sabines of old, back beyond them to Romulus and Remus, beyond even them to Jupiter, the Dictaean king, and, with Saturn, to a time that is older even than he.

Almost without our realizing how it has happened, or even that it has happened, an exquisite nostalgia has overspread the verse. This has been achieved partly by a subtle shift of tenses. For many lines,

---

[93] Compare *Ecl.* 4. 6, where the Virgin (Justice) returns with the returning of the golden age. 'vestigia' is a telling word; see above, p. 206.   [94] *Geo.* 2. 532–40.

up to 531, Virgil has been using present tenses, describing the charms of country existence as they remain to this day. At 532 he moves to past tenses: this is the way the old Sabines lived, this is how Rome grew great. But this is a past which has survived into the present: the Sabines are still good countrymen, and Rome is still great. Line 538, which introduces Saturn, slips into the imperfect tense; now we have come to a past which has not survived: his life on earth is over and done with. In a way this line still describes a continuity, but at the same time it tells of a remote and irremediable loss. Most unusually, Virgil twice begins and ends a line with the same adverb, 'ante . . . ante', 'necdum . . . necdum'. Each of these repetitions is emphatic, and each drags the line across into the next with languorous cadence. 'Before', 'not yet'—the weight upon the words stretches out time, bringing out the immensity of the distance that separates us from Saturn's golden era. The first 'ante' is also reinforced by 'etiam': 'even before'. These were days before men ate meat, before there were swords and trumpets; so the poet tells us, by these details too showing how vastly far and different was the golden age from our own. The end of the second book returns, albeit very briefly, to the theme that dominated the end of the first: war. That symmetry brings home to us that we now live, beyond all question, in an age when swords are hammered out upon the anvil and trumpets blown. Unobtrusively, too, the slaughtered bullocks of 537 look forward to the stockbreeding which will be treated in the next book. In each case, Virgil shows us the difference between the conditions of the golden age and our own.

He also weaves into his rhapsody the theme of hard work. The dragging heterodyne spondees of 513 convey the effort of pulling the plough through the inert earth: 'agricola incúr|vò tér|ràm dimovit aratro.'[95] The next line picks up the hint: 'hinc anni *labor*' (From here comes his year's work). And there is no pause, the poet soon adds, using words that also mean 'there is no rest', while the repetition 'aut . . . aut . . . aut' enforces the message that there is always more to be doing:[96]

> nec requies, quin aut pomis exuberet annus
> aut fetu pecorum aut Cerealis mergite culmi,
> proventuque oneret sulcos atque horrea vincat.

[95] 'The farmer has been sundering the earth with the curved plough.'
[96] *Geo.* 2. 516–18.

Without pause the season teems either with fruits or with the flocks' off-spring or with sheaves of Ceres' blade; it loads the furrows with increase and overflows the barns.

Winter at least, we might hope, would permit a little ease—why, even the first book allows the farmer to be lazy then—but no, there is olive-oil to be pressed.[97] Even on feast days, amid the drinking and the sprawling on the grass, the shepherds will still be energetic: their very sports toughen them for work or practise them in the arts of war:[98]

> ipse dies agitat festos fususque per herbam,
> ignis ubi in medio et socii cratera coronant,
> te libans, Lenaee, vocat pecorisque magistris
> velocis iaculi certamina ponit in ulmo,
> corporaque agresti nudant praedura palaestra.

He himself keeps holiday and stretched on the grass, where there is a fire in the middle and the company wreathe the bowl, he calls on you, God of the Winepress, with a libation, and sets up a target on an elm for a competition with the speeding javelin among the masters of the flock, or else they bare their hardy bodies for a rustic wrestling-match.

A familiar word reappears, and now in intensified form: 'praedurus' (very tough), comes here alone in the *Georgics*. It is revealing that the Italian Numanus Remulus in the ninth Aeneid, expressing what might crudely be called the outlook of the first Georgic, though with a coarseness of spirit foreign to Virgil himself, praises his country's youth, hardy in toil and inured to scanty living, in a line taken with two insignificant variations from this part of the second book.[99] The severe vigour of the first book has not been denied or forgotten in the second but absorbed into a new mood and spirit.

Throughout the praise of country life, then, idyllic though it is, there runs an awareness of the imperfection in the world as we know it. Yet to extract this one element from a complex sensibility is of course artificial and one-sided. To such notes of hesitancy or humility as there may be in the opening lines the 'at . . . at . . . at' of 467 f. responds with gathering enthusiasm. If there is a diffidence in 493 f., it fades and merges into the great sweep of 'illum non populi fasces . . .' The last lines recall that we live in a world where trumpets blare

[97] *Geo.* 2. 519 (leisure in the winter: 1. 299).   [98] *Geo.* 2. 527–31.
[99] *Geo.* 2. 472; *Aen.* 9. 607. See below, p. 416.

and battles rage, but in the very act of making a comparison with the end of the previous book, Virgil enforces a hopeful contrast. No longer is a chariot out of control the image in the final line, but the horses' harness peaceably undone;[100] no longer does universal anarchy threaten, but the countryside is strong enough to outlast the transient might of empires, 'res Romanae perituraque regna'.[101] In the first book the Persians and Germans inspire alarm; in the second, though the Dacian may be on the march, the countryman can afford to ignore him.[102]

And the very notes of regret or hardness may themselves be ambivalent. Justice has departed from among mankind, but the countryside is closer to the unfallen world than anywhere else; and since we all know that if there was ever a paradise on earth, it is lost, to say even so much as this is to say a great deal. Besides, the earlier parts of the second book have taught us that toil is not merely a burden; it can bring the pleasures of energy; and this lesson remains as the farmer's labours are enmeshed in the final idyll. But it is now the very abundance of nature that makes those labours ceaseless: 'nec requies, quin aut pomis *exuberet* annus . . .' To say that the second book presents a delight in vigour and successful effort as a compensation for toil is to put the matter too simply, for in Virgil's vision toilsomeness and delight are not separable: the sheer hardness of the work is not a regrettably necessary diminution of the pleasure but an essential part of it. There are some gratifications possible only in a fallen world.

Which brings us to a subtle consideration. We have found that when Virgil describes how Justice left the earth, he draws upon Hesiod but alters him: no longer a simple departure but a gradual dissevering.[103] It would be unnatural to suppose that he presents this as a purely detached observer: we feel that he not only shows us process but enjoys it. And this spreads over into another kind of enjoyment: like Lucretius, Virgil recognizes the beauty of imperfection. He is so delicately aware of imperfection that he cannot help but delight in his perception of it. How should he not rejoice in the world's imperfection when he has shown us how precious are the variety and particularity, the sense of place and the sense of belonging, which imperfection makes possible? Here corn will grow but

[100] *Geo.* 1. 514; 2. 542.
[101] *Geo.* 2. 498, 'the affairs of Rome and kingdoms that will pass away'.
[102] *Geo.* 1. 509; 2. 497.   [103] See above, pp. 204 f.

not the vine, here the vine but not the olive—the loss of paradise is the cause, a loss which alone can give us that pride of home and nation, that delight in the diversity of nature both in Italy and in the wider world beyond, which the poem celebrates.

The very notes of regret or melancholy have something of satisfaction in them. Catullus has gazed back towards the age of heroes with a thick, voluptuous nostalgia; in borrowing from him, Virgil refines the quality of the emotion. He is less luxurious, less knowingly escapist and artfully self-indulgent than his great predecessor. Catullus soaks himself in the pleasures of the cultivated imagination, well aware that he is dealing with fiction, and not pretending otherwise; Virgil preserves the pleasures of the imagination but fuses them with his perception of the solid world about him. He evokes an ecstasy of yearning, a passion of melancholy delight.[104] We meet here a paradox of the human imagination: the passion *is* the pleasure, the melancholy *is* the joy, and we would misrepresent that area of experience which Virgil has discovered and explored if we tried to tease the emotions apart. Perhaps we may dare a remote analogy. At the end of *The Song of the Earth* Mahler leaves a major sixth floating, unresolved above the tonic triad of C, endlessly yearning, endlessly serene. That, in a very different age and medium, is not so far from the Virgilian note.[105] The mood cannot be precisely defined, but moods, after all, are to be experienced, not explained.

The praise of country life comes to an end, at 540, with a patterned line, in fact the so-called golden line.[106] That formality indicates the end of the paragraph, so that the two lines still to come are marked off as a tiny paragraph of their own:[107]

> sed nos immensum spatiis confecimus aequor,
> et iam tempus equum fumantia solvere colla.

But we have traversed a measureless expanse on our course, and it is now time to loose the horses' steaming necks.

---

[104] A writer in *The Collins Guide to English Parish Churches* says of Isel in Cumberland, 'This is a perfect English harmony of man and nature . . . All around stretches a lost landscape of pasture and river. *O fortunatos nimium . . .* !' A *lost* landscape—Virgil's tone seems to be caught instinctively.

[105] Before Mahler, Delius concluded his *Mass of Life* also with an unresolved major sixth; Mahler ends with the word 'ewig', Delius with 'Ewigkeit'. The two composers seem to have come to their idea independently; yet anyone would suspect intertextuality.

[106] Two nouns, each with its adjective, and a verb, arranged in the form aa||vnn.

[107] *Geo.* 2. 541 f.

After the soft nostalgia that has spread across the verse, it is fitting that the book should end so simply and gently. The great rhapsody fades into a diminuendo; the golden line rounds it off; and in the final couplet it is quietly folded into its box and put away.

We should believe that Virgil means what he says. The second Georgic is rather less than half the length of most books of Lucretius, but it is colossal: the extent of the spiritual adventure is indeed immense, and for all his brevity and quietness at the close Virgil properly recognizes how much he has done. Perhaps the absolutely supreme achievements of the human imagination are imperfect; but there are also a few moments in art where the creator seems to be 'on song' and for the while apparently infallible—happy in inspiration, flawless in proportion, carried along by an invention that wells up endlessly fresh. To this rare class belong the second act of *Figaro* and the later chapters of *Pride and Prejudice*—and the second book of the *Georgics*. Since antiquity it has been believed, on understandable but inadequate grounds, that Virgil composed very slowly.[108] One might rather fancy that he wrote the second Georgic fast.

We have met an interest in process already in the fourth Eclogue. In the *Georgics* Virgil begins to enlarge this into a further sense: of the sheer length and scale of time, the complexity of development, the many 'superpositions of history'. This feeling is to be most fully expanded in the *Aeneid*, but it emerges in the *laus Italiae* and more visibly in the praise of country life; most conspicuously, though, at the end of the first Georgic and in the proem of the third.

The finale of the first book is wild, on the edge of panic. Hideous portents stalk the earth; the cycle of civil misery seems endless. Then comes a sudden stillness:[109]

---

[108] Donatus' Life claims that Virgil worked on the *Georgics* by composing a good number of lines a day and then whittling them down to a very few (*Vit. Verg.* 22). This process is not easy to envisage and looks like the fabrication of a scholiast who, taking Augustan poetry to be a nine-to-five job, has stolidly divided the number of lines in Virgil by the years of his active life. But literature is not to be measured by the Persian chain, as Callimachus said (*Aet.* 1. fr. 1. 17 f.), and poets were not required to be voluminous. Ennius, Ovid and Lucan were copious, and Lucilius could write 'two hundred lines an hour standing on one leg' (Hor. *Serm.* 1. 4. 9 f.); but Virgil wrote more than Lucretius, Catullus, Horace, Propertius, Tibullus, or Juvenal. Artists differ too much for generalizations to be authoritative, but most of the best will be found, in cases where we have knowledge, to have worked at times with great speed.   [109] *Geo.* 1. 493–7.

> scilicet et tempus veniet, cum finibus illis
> agricola incurvo terram molitus aratro
> exesa inveniet scabra robigine pila,
> aut gravibus rastris galeas pulsabit inanis
> grandiaque effossis mirabitur ossa sepulchris.

The time will surely come when in those lands the farmer working the earth with his curved plough will find lances eaten away by scaly rust or will strike with his heavy hoe against empty helmets and wonder at the big bones in the tombs he has dug up.

Even in the midst of passion Virgil retains his self-consciousness, and with a strange detachment observes his own time through other eyes, and from very far. For he has projected himself not a few years into the future but an enormous distance: drawing on the idea that the world is slowly losing its vigour,[110] he has travelled to a time so remote that the human race has shrunk and our bones seem big; he may also imply that the farmer who digs up the remains of the Roman dead may no longer understand their significance, so wide is the expanse of time between. The splendour of this is that we appear both great and little; mighty in the eyes of a wondering posterity, yet diminished by distance, the causes of our passions forgotten (the emptiness of the helmets seems symbolic). And this paradox is enmeshed with another: we see the transience of mortal affairs, and yet an indestructible continuity: the farmer keeps on ploughing. Line 494 offers a momentary note of hope; it is no accident that it will return, with the change of one word, in the second book's praise of country life.[111]

In climactic passages it is characteristic of Virgil, as we shall discover, to widen the range of his vision in opposite directions at once. Here, having studied the present from a very remote future, he returns to the present, from where he views the very remote past: with another abrupt leap of thought he traces the woes of his day not, as we might expect, to the late republic or to the growth of empire, nor even to Romulus, but right back to Troy, and within Troy not even to the crime of Paris but back to Laomedon's treachery at the city's first origins:[112]

---

[110] Homer's Diomedes and Aeneas can hurl a stone such as two men today could not lift (Hom. *Il.* 5. 302–4, 20. 285–7); Hector is only slightly less powerful (12. 445–9). Compare too the end of Lucretius' second book. Columella begins his treatise by protesting at the common opinion that the earth's strength is waning.

[111] *Geo.* 2. 513.   [112] *Geo.* 1. 501 f.

satis iam pridem sanguine nostro
Laomedonteae luimus periuria Troiae.

Long now have we atoned enough for the perjury of Laomedon's Troy.

Next, having enlarged his vision in terms of time, he enlarges it spatially. Hitherto his mind has been concentrated upon Rome and Italy, with a battery of proper names evoking the ancestral, sacred heart of things:[113]

di patrii Indigetes et Romule Vestaque mater,
quae Tuscum Tiberim et Romana Palatia servas . . .

Indigites—gods of our country—and Romulus and mother Vesta, you who guard the Tuscan Tiber and the Roman Palatine . . .

But now his eye moves outward, to the warfare raging all over the globe: 'tot bella per orbem' (there are so many wars across the globe), 'saevit toto Mars impius orbe' (unholy Mars rages across the entire globe).[114] He looks north and east, to the edges of the earth: 'hinc movet Euphrates, illinc Germania bellum' (from this side Euphrates stirs warfare, from that side Germany).[115] Then Italy having been seen in relation to the world as a whole, our gaze immediately contracts again, and having studied extremities, we study closeness: towns near to one another, 'vicinae . . . inter se . . . urbes', take up arms amongst themselves.[116]

Curiously, Virgil mentions the Euphrates thrice only, and each time six lines from the end of a book.[117] Each time Caesar is near at hand: the romantic orient and the far-flung empire are part of the apparatus of praise. At the end of the *Georgics* the poet enjoys the juxtaposition of home and distance, setting public Caesar thundering by the Euphrates against private Virgil snug in Naples. 'Me . . . dulcis alebat | Parthenope' (I was being nurtured by lovely Parthenope)—by turning Naples into a nymph, and one who feeds him like a mother, he points up the contrast between closeness and a vaguely conceived remoteness.[118] We have seen that his ending is both modest and proud; we can add that it is both intimate and immensely spacious. At the end of the eighth Aeneid he magnifies Caesar's triple

[113] *Geo.* 1. 498 f.   [114] *Geo.* 1. 505, 511.
[115] *Geo.* 1. 509.   [116] *Geo.* 1. 510.
[117] This observation is owed to R. Scodel and R. Thomas, 'Virgil and the Euphrates', *AJP* 105 (1984), 339. The other places are *Geo.* 4. 561, *Aen.* 8. 726. For a fuller discussion of the significance than is given here, see Jenkyns, 'Virgil and the Euphrates', *AJP* 114 (1993), 115–21.
[118] *Geo.* 4. 563 f.

triumph by pressing outward to almost every limit of the known world: Euphrates is displayed beside the Rhine and the Araxes; Africans and Nomads from the Sahara are there, Dahae from beyond the Caspian, the Morini from western Gaul, 'the furthest of mankind'.[119] It is a noisy passage; but this time the trappings of exoticism have become rather conventional.

In the proem of the third Georgic Virgil describes in elaborately symbolic terms the future work that he supposedly intends to write in praise of Caesar. Imagining the great man's victories, once more he presses to the diverse limits of the world: the Britons, the Ganges, Mount Niphates in Armenia.[120] So far this is again conventional. Britain was fabulously obscure. For Catullus the shaggy Britons were the furthest of mankind; he had already paired them with the Indians, from the other end of the earth.[121] With an extravagance of despair, Virgil's Meliboeus imagines dispossessed farmers being driven to exile in Africa, Scythia, or among the Britons, a people separated from the whole world.[122] Poets want conquerors to conquer poetic countries. Horace expects Augustus to add the Britons and Persians to the empire;[123] he is not much interested in actual or likely battles, such as the nasty little war being fought in Spain. Caesar himself was not immune from the glamour of the ultimate: his *Res Gestae* record the farthest reaches to which armies under his auspices had penetrated, even though he had been nowhere near these places in person.[124]

But these evocations of elsewhere become more pointed in the third Georgic from the context in which they are placed; for they follow the poet's declaration that he will bring the Muses from their Grecian mountain to his own 'patria'—which proves to mean his *Heimat*, not Rome but Mantua. And the local and particular feeling of this is developed in the individualized picture of the Mincius, which draws out those features that distinguish it from other rivers.[125] Thus near and far, home, nation, and empire, the sharply realized and the vaguely conceived, are incorporated into the one exordium. And here too the spatial expansion is accompanied by an expansion in time. Virgil envisages his poem pushing into the past, further than Rome, further than the Trojan War, to the first beginnings of Troy and even to the gods beyond that; for it will include[126]

---

[119] *Aen.* 8. 724–8.   [120] *Geo.* 3. 25, 27, 30.   [121] Cat. 11. 2, 11 f.
[122] *Ed.* 1. 64–6.   [123] *Carm.* 3. 5. 3 f.; cf 1. 35. 29 f.   [124] RG 26.
[125] See above, pp. 147 f.   [126] *Geo.* 3. 35 f.

> Assaraci proles demissaeque ab Iove gentis
> nomina, Trosque parens et Troiae Cynthius auctor.

The offspring of Assaracus, the names of the people sprung from Jupiter, father Tros and the Cynthian, the founder of Troy.

There is the sense here of different layers even within this very distant past: not only Assaracus' descendants but his father too. The repetition in 'Tros . . . Troiae' and the coming to rest on the word 'auctor' conveys the sense of pressing on deep and deeper into ancient time.

In the sixth Aeneid Virgil will rework these lines. The hero comes to Elysium to be shown his posterity, but as is characteristic of this poet, the temporal vision widens in both directions. He is to see a more distant future than ever before, but first he sees a more distant past:[127]

> hic genus antiquum Teucri, pulcherrima proles,
> magnanimi heroes nati melioribus annis,
> Ilusque Assaracusque et Troiae Dardanus auctor.

Here is the ancient line of Teucrus, a fairest stock, great-hearted heroes born in better years, Ilus and Assaracus and Dardanus, founder of Troy.

Virgil is adapting both his earlier self and a line of Homer: *Ilos t'Assarakos te kai antitheos Ganumedes* (Ilus and Assaracus and godlike Ganymede).[128] Whereas the words in the *Iliad* record an ancestry without evoking a sense of distance, Virgil insists on oldness (antiquum); Assaracus, as in the Georgic and elsewhere in the *Aeneid*,[129] is a talismanic name; the name of Ilus comes alive as an eponym—the parent of Ilium—and Homer's Ganymede disappears to be replaced by another eponymous hero, Dardanus, founder of the Dardan race (Tros in Virgil's earlier poem had the same effect). And once more he ends with first beginnings: 'auctor'.

The proem of the third Georgic looks back to an immeasurably long gone past, but with its concluding words it looks into the future, again across an immense tract, as Virgil declares that his intended poem will carry Caesar's fame as far into time to come as Caesar himself is far from the first origin of Tithonus, a figure who in turn was commemorated in myth for his enormous age.[130] Once more he brings out the gigantic scale of his temporal vision, and once

---

[127] *Aen.* 6. 648–50. [128] *Il.* 20. 232.
[129] e.g. *Aen.* 1. 284. [130] *Geo.* 3. 46–8.

more he thrusts in both directions, future and past. The *Aeneid* was to turn out very different from the poem projected here; the promised narrative of Caesar's battles was never written. It is the more revealing, therefore, that Virgil has already conceived the idea of a poem linking the present with a very old and foreign past—a past, moreover, which is itself an accumulation, stratum upon stratum. But indeed such things were at the roots of his imagination.

PART FIVE

The *Aeneid*

CHAPTER 9

A Trojan's Experience:
The Wanderings of Aeneas

Je n'eus besoin pour les faire renaître que de prononcer ces noms:
Balbec, Venise, Florence, dans l'intérieur desquels avait fini par
s'accumuler le désir que m'avaient inspiré les lieux qu'ils désig-
naient . . . Les mots nous présentent des choses une petite image
claire et usuelle . . . Mais les noms présentent des personnes—
et des villes qu'ils nous habituent à croire individuelles, uniques
comme des personnes—une image confuse . . .

(Proust)

To go to the supreme is a wandering, a wandering afar, and
this wandering is a returning.

(Tao liturgy)

The first book of the *Aeneid* has an exploratory air. In this it differs from the *Odyssey*, which opens with Zeus himself laying out
the moral rules, and the *Iliad*, which moves rapidly to the heart
of the action, so rapidly indeed that it does not pause to give any
motive for Agamemnon's first fatal error, his insulting of the Trojan
priest Chryses.[1] The first Aeneid has its grand set pieces too, but
predominantly it gives the impression of introducing themes and
motifs which will be enlarged and developed as the poem proceeds.
We have already considered one such theme: the investigation of
landscape and man's place within it. Later in the poem Virgil
will present various human settings or societies—Latinus' palace, the

---

[1] When Achilles and Agamemnon clash, we are indeed interested in their opposing wills
and distinct characters. But to ask why Agamemnon insults Chryses is to fall into the 'docu-
mentary fallacy'. The question has no answer: the poet sweeps it aside, pressing on to the
heroes' quarrel. There is a sort of kinship to the first scene in *King Lear*. That has a dry
formality: the story is set going briskly, and we cannot get far by interrogating the king's
motives at this point. The playwright presses forward, sketching the origins of Lear's tragedy
simply, because his concern is intensely focused on its consequences.

Italian countryside, Evander's town—giving to each its own tone or atmosphere. He has the gift of surrounding people and places and moments of experience with a distinctive and impalpable aura, and in the Italian books of the *Aeneid* this style of feeling is brought to bear on his senses of nature, history, and national identity. But in the first book it irradiates a somewhat different scene, Aeneas' encounter with the disguised figure of his mother Venus.

The hero meets a maiden (or so it seems) in the midst of a wood; she appears to be a huntress.[2] Her maidenliness is stressed: 'virginis os habitumque gerens et virginis arma | Spartanae'.[3] If not a Spartan girl, then she resembles Thracian Harpalyce, when her running leaves horses tired and outstrips the swift river Hebrus. She carries a bow, her hair floats loose in the breeze, her legs are bare, her costume girt high. A picture of fresh girlhood, we might think, and yet not quite, for Aeneas senses (we do not know how) that she is surely a goddess. Are you a nymph? he asks; or the sister of Phoebus? It is a natural question, since she has been described in terms which suggest the standard representation of Diana. She denies that she has such distinction: it is the custom, she replies, for Tyrian maidens to carry the quiver and tie purple boots high on their calves. The picture thus continues to be pretty and seductive: this is the second time in a few lines that we have been invited to look at her legs. Finally, turning her rosy neck, her hair breathing forth ambrosial scent, she disappears; and Aeneas realizes what we have known from the first, that this is Venus, his mother.[4]

The atmosphere of this passage is not easily described, and that might almost be said to be its purpose: Virgil has created a strange and elusive mood. On the surface is a pleasing picture of lithe, athletic maidenhood: youthful vigour, youthful limbs. Yet somehow he has surrounded it with a bloom and radiance that slip naturally into a sense of a divine aura: when Aeneas insists that he is looking at a goddess, we are not surprised, although we have been given no reason why he should be able to penetrate Venus' magical disguise. But overlaying this blithe charm are other tones. There is a feeling of impalpable loss, as Aeneas meets and yet does not meet his mother, known to us throughout the scene, but consciously recognized by the hero himself only as she vanishes, and he is left asking why she

---

[2] *Aen.* I. 314 ff.
[3] *Aen.* I. 315 f., 'wearing the face and garb of a maiden, bearing a Spartan maiden's weaponry'.   [4] *Aen.* I. 402 ff.

deludes him with false appearances and will not let him even clasp her hand in his—a cool enough gesture between mother and son, by any reckoning.[5] And to mystery is also added a spirit of the uncanny, since this apparently chaste nymph is actually no such thing: not adolescent, but a mother; not virginal, but the goddess of sexual desire. A sexy virginal mother, your own mother—it is a troubling thought. There is something faintly sinister and slithery in this, a tone that is to become stronger as Virgil slides from this episode to the scene in which Aeneas first catches sight of Dido. He spies upon her unobserved, as he has been made supernaturally invisible; there is a hint of the sinister in this also.[6] It is now she who is likened to Diana, leading the dance on the banks of the Eurotas—again a touch of Sparta—or on the ridges of Cynthus, with a thousand Oreads about her.[7] Dido is proud, chaste, and prosperous; but when we reflect that the seeming Diana whom Aeneas saw before proved to be the goddess of sexual passion, we may shudder.

Virgil adapts the simile and indeed his whole scene from the episode in the *Odyssey* where the hero, shipwrecked, naked, and hidden in the bushes, watches Nausicaa and her handmaidens washing clothes and playing ball.[8] This is the first depiction in European literature of happiness, simple happiness. And no tragedy is to destroy it: there will be nothing more than a gentle poignancy at the parting, delicately understated in the telling.[9] The possibility of Nausicaa being seduced by Odysseus simply does not arise. Dido's case is very different. In terms of the poem's reworking of the *Odyssey*, she has to sustain in her single person the roles not only of Nausicaa, but also those of Calypso, Circe, and Penelope;[10] in a sense the formidable literary weight that she has to carry is part of her tragic burden, and she collapses beneath it. An element of her pathos is that she is a Nausicaa who has been made vulnerable, a Calypso and a Circe but without the divinity that she needs to sustain those roles. Circe can

---

[5] *Aen.* 1. 407–9. The 'failed embrace' is a motif that will return; see below, p. 559.

[6] *Aen.* 1. 439 f., 494 ff.

[7] *Aen.* 1. 498–502. Virgil's model here, a Homeric simile, already has a touch of Sparta in it, for it describes Artemis on Mount Taygetus or Erymanthus (*Od.* 6. 103). Virgil preserves the Spartan element, but his passion for rivers leads him to replace Taygetus with Eurotas.

[8] *Od.* 6. 110 ff. Odysseus' vulnerability is in contrast to Aeneas' supernaturally engineered security.　　　　　　　　　　　　　　　　　　　　　　　　[9] *Od.* 8. 457 ff.

[10] Not to mention the roles of Hypsipyle and Medea from Apollonius' *Argonautica* and of Ariadne from Catullus 64.

part from Odysseus with good cheer; Calypso grieves, but she is not destroyed by her grief, nor—since Odysseus never learns why she lets him go—is she humiliated, as Dido will be, before her lover. Dido has Nausicaa's sweet youthfulness, Calypso's passion, Circe's latent barbarousness, but without their resources.

What is more, she is so situated by Virgil that we can see her as a would-be Penelope, without Penelope's hopes or fulfilments. She is faithful, at least in intention, to an absent husband, but to one who is dead and can never return. She wishes to be Aeneas' wife and the mother of his child, but she has no Telemachus, and soon even the hope of a 'little Aeneas' is to be snatched from her.[11] She is besieged by suitors but without the hope of rescue, since her besiegers include not only the resistible Iarbas but the irresistible Aeneas himself; Virgil's metaphorical structure, surrounding her with images of a city invested and captured, makes the hero into both friend and enemy.

By implicitly comparing Dido to Nausicaa, and by associating the comparison with the epiphany of Venus in the form of a maiden huntress, Virgil presents her, on this her first appearance, as very young. This can easily be forgotten. Perhaps because she is a widow, perhaps because of her command of heroic rhetoric in the fourth book, perhaps because of her later career in the European tradition as an operatic heroine, she is often seen, or so one may suspect, as a lady of maturity and some amplitude of figure, ripely mezzo-soprano in utterance. That was not Virgil's conception. Not only is she likened to Diana and Nausicaa here, but she will be seen later in terms that recall Apollonius' Medea, who is not the virago of Euripides but a young woman invaded by a passion beyond her powers of resistance.

Venus' epiphany is the first evocation of the feminine in the *Aeneid*, and it reaches forward to later episodes in the poem. It leads towards our first sight of Dido, whose presentation is in turn caught up with the women of the *Odyssey*. It leads ultimately to Camilla, another light-foot maiden, whose femininity Virgil will enmesh with his sense of Italy and its landscape.[12] And it leads to Creusa's farewell, which blends human intimacy with an exploration of time, history, and national consciousness. In her speech proper names become important; but this is another theme which originates in the first book, and it is there that we must first examine it.

---

[11] 'parvulus Aeneas', *Aen.* 4. 328 f.   [12] See below, pp. 564 ff.

The great game of playing with proper names, of handling them
to feel their weight and significance, is set in motion by the father
of gods and men himself. Jupiter unfolds the future to his daughter
Venus:[13]

at puer Ascanius, cui nunc cognomen Iulo
additur (Ilus erat, dum res stetit Ilia regno),
triginta magnos volvendis mensibus orbis
imperio explebit, regnumque ab sede Lavini   270
transferet, et Longam multa vi muniet Albam.
hic iam ter centum totos regnabitur annos
gente sub Hectorea, donec regina sacerdos
Marte gravis geminam partu dabit Ilia prolem.
inde lupae fulvo nutricis tegmine laetus   275
Romulus excipiet gentem et Mavortia condet
moenia Romanosque suo de nomine dicet.
his ego nec metas rerum nec tempora pono:
imperium sine fine dedi. quin aspera Iuno,
quae mare nunc terrasque metu caelumque fatigat,   280
consilia in melius referet, mecumque fovebit
Romanos, rerum dominos gentemque togatam.
sic placitum. veniet lustris labentibus aetas
cum domus Assaraci Pthiam clarasque Mycenas
servitio premet ac victis dominabitur Argis.   285
nascetur pulchra Troianus origine Caesar,
imperium Oceano, famam qui terminet astris,
Iulius, a magno demissum nomen Iulo.
hunc tu olim caelo spoliis Orientis onustum
accipies secura; vocabitur hic quoque votis.   290
aspera tum positis mitescent saecula bellis:
cana Fides et Vesta, Remo cum fratre Quirinus
iura dabunt; dirae ferro et compagibus artis
claudentur Belli portae; Furor impius intus
saeva sedens super arma et centum vinctus aënis   295
post tergum nodis fremet horridus ore cruento.

But the boy Ascanius, to whom the surname Iulus is now added (he was
Ilus, while the state of Ilium stood firm in power), shall accomplish in
authority thirty great circles of the revolving months, and shall move his
sovereignty from its seat at Lavinium and fortify Alba Longa with great
might. Here the kingdom shall then remain throughout three hundred years
under Hector's race, until the royal priestess Ilia, pregnant by Mars, shall

[13] *Aen.* i. 267–96.

give birth to twin offspring. Then Romulus, resplendent in the tawny hide of the wolf his nurse, shall take the race to him and build Mars' walls and call the people Romans after his own name. To their empire I set no boundary or period: I have given them dominion without end. Indeed, harsh Juno, who now with terror wearies sea and earth and sky, shall change her judgement for the better and with me shall cherish the Romans, masters of the world, the people of the toga. Such is my pleasure. As the years slip by, the time shall come when the house of Assaracus shall impose servitude upon Phthia and glorious Mycenae and shall hold sway over conquered Argos. From this fair line shall Trojan Caesar be born, whose power shall be bounded by Ocean, his fame by the stars—Julius, a name descended from great Iulus. In happy assurance you shall duly receive him into heaven, laden with the spoils of the east; he too shall be invoked in prayer. Then shall warfare be set aside and the rough ages soften: hoary Faith and Vesta and Quirinus with his brother Remus shall issue laws; the gates of War, grim with iron and close-fitted bars, shall be shut; within unrighteous Rage, sitting upon cruel weaponry and bound behind the back with a hundred brazen knots, shall roar hideously with bloody mouth.

Aeneas' son now has three names, presented one after the other within a line and a half: Ascanius, Ilus, Iulus. The repetition in 'Ilus . . . Ilia' has the effect of lightly stressing the 'Trojan-ness' of the old name, and marking the distinction in tone between Ilus and the new name Iulus, with its obviously Roman associations. The next names, Lavinium and Alba Longa, evoke the remote prehistory of Rome; three hundred years pass quickly by, and we seem to have left Troy far behind, when we are suddenly pulled back to the past by the phrase 'gente sub Hectorea'. This would be a slightly illogical phrase even for the Trojans of Aeneas' time, since Hector was never ruler of Troy, and his son's slaughter left him without descent; applied to Italians centuries after his death it is—though mildly yet plainly—paradoxical. Hector's is of all Trojan names the one most firmly rooted in a particular time and place; he has no significant existence in legend beyond Ilium and the plain and the Achaean siege. Hector, Hector is the name that echoes in the sixth book at the moment of Misenus' death—[14]

> Hectoris hic magni fuerat comes, Hectora circum
> et lituo pugnas insignis obibat et hasta.

He had been the companion of great Hector, by Hector he would face battle, notable for both his trumpet and his spear.

[14] *Aen.* 6. 166 f.

—and appropriately so; for Aeneas is now preparing to journey through the underworld that the future may be revealed to him, and it is symbolically apt that at this time a link with his Trojan past should snap.

The paradox implicit in 'gente sub Hectorea' is resolved, so to speak, in the next line with the bringing together of Mars, that emphatically Roman deity, and Ilia, a priestess with a Trojan name. It is from the union of Troy and Italy, almost literally, that the founder of Rome shall be born. The proper names in the next lines require no comment: 'Romulus . . . Romanos . . . Romanos . . .' And not only is Rome here, but Roman *mores*: we are reminded that this is the people of the toga. After these lines of resonant imperial patriotism, we may have thought that Troy was left behind, but Jupiter has a surprise in store for us: the house of Assaracus, he declares, shall conquer Phthia, Mycenae, and Argos. To describe Rome's conquest of Greece thus is epigrammatic in effect: to say that Trojans will beat Greeks is like saying that lambs will pursue wolves. But that is not the whole story. In part, the lines are an expression of Virgil's sense of history: there is a pattern of recurrence, and yet change; history repeats itself, and yet is transformed. And he also infuses a sense of time passing: 'veniet *lustris labentibus* aetas . . .' But that is still not all: it is not the house of Priam or Hector which is said to conquer the Greeks, though some such phrase might sharpen the epigram, but the house of Assaracus—once more that mysteriously talismanic name, used in the *Georgics* to evoke an immeasurably remote past, and to be used again in the sixth Aeneid.[15] Here as elsewhere Virgil looks further back into the past just at the point where he looks further into the future. We see three layers of history at once: Rome in the second century, the generation of the Trojan War (the three Greek cities named, the homes of Achilles, Agamemnon and Diomedes, enforce the remembrance of that time upon us), and Troy three generations earlier still.

The historical perspective enlarges, and with it the suggestion of paradox. If it was odd to call the people of Alba Longa 'gens Hectorea', it is odder still to think of figures from the comparatively recent past like Aemilius Paulus, conqueror of Greece, as 'domus Assaraci'. And yet within the fiction of Rome's Trojan origins, it is strictly accurate, and that is its charm. The paradox comes to its climax with

[15] See above, p. 385, and below, p. 460.

the appearance of great Caesar himself: to think that this Roman
of Romans, the very man who will ascend to heaven laden with
the spoils of the orient, should prove to be a man from the east.
Virgil preserves the epigrammatic pointedness; his syntax eludes
the bland correctness of some phrase such as 'of Trojan descent',
and makes Augustus himself a Trojan, 'Troianus . . . Caesar'.[16] The
handsome line 288, held monumentally between the pair of nouns
'Iulius . . . Iulo', sums up and resolves the succession of paradoxes.
In this line we seem to see the whole history of the Roman destiny across vast tracts of time. With the first word we feel Jupiter,
from the time of Aeneas and Assaracus, gazing forward to the time
of Virgil and Augustus; Virgil, with the last word, gazes back from
the present to the distant past. 'Nomen Iuli' in 288 echoes the
words 'cognomen Iulo' twenty-two lines before. This echo, and the
monumental structure of the line, impart an air of massive finality.
But as with the *laus Italiae* in the *Georgics*, that impression is delus-
ive: the verse surges vigorously onward, bursting the bounds that
have sought to confine it. That air of finality, however, does not
go for nothing. Now that we have seen the full shape of the historical process that leads from Trojan Iulus long ago to the hero
of modern Rome, the paradoxes dissolve. The tensions felt below
the surface from the conflicting tugs of association in Trojan and
Roman or Italian names need be felt no more. Troy is subsumed in
Rome, and the names that reverberate in the final sentence, 'cana
Fides et Vesta, Remo cum fratre Quirinus', are Roman; Roman
to the core.

The names in Jupiter's speech are only one element in a complex texture, nor perhaps are they used as subtly as in some parts
of the *Aeneid*, but already we can see Virgil's use of proper names
bound in not only with his sense of place but with time and history as well. The poem will explore this nexus of interlinked feelings as it proceeds. That the play with time and names is not just
a superficial matter to Virgil but at the heart of his imagination is
suggested by its appearance in passages of high emotion; for
example, in Anchises' lament for the early death of Marcellus, as yet
unborn:[17]

---

[16] 'From this fair line shall Trojan Caesar be born' is a rendering of line 286 which preserves the pointedness of the Latin syntax; 'Caesar shall come to birth, Trojan in his fair
origin' might be more natural English.   [17] *Aen.* 6. 872–9.

quantos ille virum magnam Mavortis ad urbem
campus aget gemitus! vel quae, Tiberine, videbis
funera, cum tumulum praeterlabere recentem!
nec puer Iliaca quisquam de gente Latinos
in tantum spe tollet avos, nec Romula quondam
ullo se tantum tellus iactabit alumno.
heu pietas, heu prisca fides invictaque bello
dextera!

What lamentation will that field send forth to Mars' great city! what exequies you will see, Tiber, when you glide past his newly built tomb! No child of Trojan race shall so much exalt his Latin ancestors by his promise, nor will the land of Romulus ever boast so much in any of her offspring. Alas for his virtue, alas for his old-fashioned honour and hand unconquered in war!

Part of the pathos is that this youth, dead before his prime, should reincarnate the qualities of old Rome. The passage is filled with words redolent of antiquity; early history, ancestors, traditional virtues. But all this creates a complex, curious time pattern: Marcellus, far in the future, will recall the distant past, and most of that past is a long distance in the future from the viewpoint of Anchises and his son.

We might for a moment entertain the idea that the effect is merely incidental: Virgil, for reasons both poetic and politic, wished to commemorate Marcellus, and to represent him as a repository of traditional values, but within the epic poem he could figure only in a vision of futurity. Further reflection, however, reveals the poet's careful purpose. In the show of heroes as a whole, Anchises is made to peer into the far future with something less than a full certainty.[18] He is not sure whether Aeneas Silvius will reach the throne of Alba Longa:[19]

Silvius Aeneas, pariter pietate vel armis
egregius, si umquam regnandam acceperit Albam.

Aeneas Silvius, outstanding also in virtue and in arms, if he shall ever win the governance of Alba.

He ventures the question whether the souls of Julius Caesar and Pompey will attain life in the world above:[20]

[18] On the incomplete vision in Anchises' listing of future towns at 6. 773 ff., see below, p. 400.
[19] Aen. 6. 769 f.   [20] Aen. 6. 828 f.

> heu quantum inter se bellum, *si lumina vitae*
> *attigerint,* quantas acies stragemque ciebunt . . .

Alas what a great war they will stir up between them, if they reach the light of life, what battle and slaughter . . .

and passionately he pleads with his descendant to refrain from civil war. For a moment he even toys with the vain hope that Marcellus might break the bonds of fate: 'heu, miserande puer, *si qua* fata aspera rumpas!'[21] For most of the time Virgil must make Anchises, for reasons of plot and structure, speak out with accuracy and authority; it is the more remarkable, therefore, that the note of uncertainty is made to intrude. We may contrast the pageant revealed by the witches to Macbeth, a remorseless chronological procession of future kings. Shakespeare wishes to emphasize the fixity of doom, Virgil to suggest the slight blurriness that must come over our vision of any time other than our own.

Within the lament for Marcellus itself, Virgil draws quiet attention to the temporal oddity. Anchises' paradoxical position, far from diminishing the emotional force, increases it; there is an additional poignancy in the curious time structure that allows an ancestor to mourn for his unborn descendant. The old man himself gently makes the point:[22]

> purpureos spargam flores animamque *nepotis*
> his saltem accumulem donis . . .

Let me scatter bright flowers and heap my descendant's spirit with these gifts at least . . .

For an instant Marcellus appears in the guise of one of those youths by the banks of the Styx, laid upon the pyre before their parents' eyes.[23] The element of paradox has already been brought out a few lines earlier. Every Roman schoolboy knew that the Trojans came before the Latins in their national story: Virgil had shown the progression from Troy to Italy in the natural order in the very first lines of Anchises' disquisition on the Roman future:[24]

---

[21] *Aen.* 6. 882, 'Ah, pitiable boy, if only you might somehow break the harsh decrees of destiny!' [22] *Aen.* 6. 884 f.
[23] *Aen.* 6. 307 f. (At 884 Anchises uses the word 'nepos', which can mean both 'grandson' and 'descendant'; English translation obscures this.)
[24] *Aen.* 6. 756–7, 759.

nunc age, *Dardaniam* prolem quae deinde sequatur
gloria, qui maneant *Itala* de gente nepotes,

. . . .

expediam dictis . . .

Come now, I shall expound what glory will attend Dardanus' line, what
descendants of Italian race are to come . . .

But the odd expression at 875 f. about a boy of Trojan family exalt-
ing his Latin ancestors seems to imply a reversal of proper historical
order; the language is deliberately epigrammatic. And this does not
exhaust the ingenuity of the lines, for as we listen to the names reverberating though the sentence, we realize that Virgil has resolved the
paradox in the very act of stating it. 'Iliaca . . . Latinos . . . Romula'—
while the syntax of the sentence seems to set chronology topsy-turvy,
the sequence of proper adjectives in the order of their appearance
asserts the true progress of the destined people; from Troy to Latium,
and from the union of Trojans and Latins to the birth of Rome.[25]

This passage shows that point and epigram—wit in the widest sense
of the word—need not be the enemies of strong feeling. In Virgil at
his best, the head and the heart are at one. This is as it should be:
Housman spoke at best a very partial truth when he proclaimed that
poetry's peculiar function is to transfuse emotion, not to transmit
thought.[26] It is a fallacy, in the first place, to suppose that emotion
and intellect are opposites; the strongest and deepest emotions, in
life as in art, are informed by the activity of mind. Lust can be mind-
less; love never. And in any case, poetry will ring false unless it is
the product of the whole personality; the thinking man who pretends not to think sins against his own spirit (the consequences may
indeed be seen in a certain vapidity in some of Housman's own verse).

What happens after Virgil is that intellect and emotion start to
dissever. We can easily imagine how Seneca or Lucan or even Ovid
would have laboured the paradox of a Trojan with Latin ancestry or
a dead ancestor lamenting his unborn heir; and we know too well
how the smart epigram, in such hands, tends to inhibit the pathos.
Anchises, in a silver epic, would have explained the oddity of his situation in some neat phrase; and as we admired the poet's ingenuity,

---

[25] Line 876 includes the first use of 'Romulus' as an adjective. Virgil employs it perhaps because though he is talking about the land, he wants to bring out the sense of historical process, and the adjective will remind us of Rome's founder.
[26] 'The Name and Nature of Poetry' (1933); *Selected Prose*, ed. J. Carter (Cambridge,
1961), 172.

we should have felt that Anchises was stating his situation rather than experiencing it. The contrast between Virgil and his successors tells us not that there is no point or epigram in him but rather that he keeps these tendencies beautifully unobtrusive: they can enter into passages of great solemnity because they are an integral part of an alertness in the perception of experience that embraces thought and feeling alike.

Virgil allows himself the flicker of a smile even over Anchises' prophecy:[27]

> hi tibi Nomentum et Gabios urbemque Fidenam,
> hi Collatinas imponent montibus arces,
> Pometios Castrumque Inui Bolamque Coramque;
> haec tum *nomina* erunt, nunc sunt sine *nomine* terrae.

These men, you must know, will build Nomentum and Gabii and the city of Fidena, they will plant on the hills the citadel of Collatiae, Pometii and Castrum Inui and Bola and Cora; these will then be names, though they are now lands without a name.

The last line exploits the common use of 'nomen' to mean 'fame': Anchises implies that the towns he lists will acquire a certain import-ance. But we hear a further resonance; for who would attribute eminence to Castrum Inui, Bola, and Cora?—these places will in turn sink into dimness, becoming names merely. The patriarch is conscious of knowing so much more than his son, but we for our part are conscious of knowing so much more than he, and we may be momentarily amused at his proud parade of these undistinguished places. Propertius saw the point: in a poem much influenced by the *Aeneid* he includes Gabii and Fidenae among examples of once notable towns that have fallen into emptiness or obscurity.[28] But there is a serious side to Virgil's irony: here is one glimpse among many of history's multiple layers, as our thoughts are guided to a time before Gabii existed, a time when it was important, and a time when it has lapsed into insignificance once more. Perhaps we catch a similar wryness in his verse when he shows us Italy arming for war:[29]

> quinque adeo magnae positis incudibus urbes
> tela novant, Atina potens Tiburque superbum,
> Ardea Crustumerique et turrigerae Antemnae.

Indeed five great cities set up anvils and make new weapons, mighty Atina and haughty Tibur, Ardea and Crustumeri and towered Antemnae.

---

[27] *Aen.* 6. 773–6.   [28] Prop. 4. 1. 33–6; see below, p. 610.
[29] *Aen.* 7. 629–31.

What are these great cities? It is a small world in which they can seem mighty; and what indeed is 'haughty Tibur' now but an agreeable retreat from the summer heat of Rome, its hillside dotted with the exurban residences of the well-to-do?[30] This is a mode of irony that has room for affection, maybe even for a touch of pleasant melancholy: we might perhaps compare Hardy's picture of Shaftesbury, once crowned by abbey, mansions, and many churches, now a sleepy market town.[31]

So fascinated is Virgil by names that he uses no less than four of them for the Tiber. In ordinary discourse the river was called Tiberis, but this form appears only once in the Aeneid, in the catalogue of Italian forces, to indicate the area from which some of the soldiery come;[32] and probably the reason for its use in this place is simply that neither of his usual forms will fit the context. These are Thybris and Tiberinus; and with only two exceptions, the first of them is used in speech, the second in narrative.[33] Tiberinus is the river's sacral name: it was used in cult—'Father Tiber, to whom the Romans pray'—and is found on dedicatory inscriptions. Thybris is a literary and Graecized name, flaunting its Greekness in the consonant *th* and the vowel *y*; the likelihood is that it was Virgil himself who introduced it into Latin verse.[34] So when the characters in the poem utter this name, we hear them speaking in an accent unlike ours; we realize that they belong to a time and world different from our own. This is most pointed in the eighth book, when Aeneas sees a vision of the river god: Virgil calls him Tiberinus, but the deity introduces himself as Thybris, and Aeneas then prays to 'Thybri . . . genitor'. Virgil is here adapting a line of Ennius, who naturally

---

[30] It is interesting to find that Florus, dilating on a similar theme (1. 11), uses some of the same names as Virgil: 'Cora (who would believe it?) and Alsium were objects of terror . . . One blushes to say it, but we celebrated a triumph over Verulae and Bovillae. Prayers were spoken on the Capitol before an attack on Tibur, now a weekending place (suburbanus), and that agreeable summer retreat, Praeneste.' Bovillae is among the names used by Propertius in this context (4. 1. 35).

[31] *Jude the Obscure*, pt. 4, sect. 1.   [32] *Aen.* 7. 715.

[33] Thybris occurs 16 times, Tiberinus (as a noun) 5. In addition, 'Tiberinus' appears twice with 'flumen', where it is either an adjective or a noun in apposition, and once certainly as an adjective; all these appearances are in narrative. The adjective 'Thybrinus' appears once, in speech.

[34] Thybris is not found in poetry before the *Aeneid*, unless [Virg.] *Cat.* 13. 23 is earlier. Horace and Propertius use only 'Tiberis' and 'Tiberinus'. Thanks to Virgil's example Thybris becomes standard in Ovid's *Metamorphoses* and in later epic poets. In them the form has simply become a piece of high diction; the contrast with the care of Virgil's usage is instructive. (For a detailed discussion of his sources, and his originality, in treating the god Tiber, see A. Momigliano, 'Thybris pater', *Terzo contributo alla storia degli studi classici e del mondo antico* (Rome, 1966), ii. 609–39.)

used the words 'pater Tiberine'; but Aeneas invokes not father
Tiberinus, as a Roman would, but father Thybris—because it is the
name he has been given.[35]

Virgil uses Thybris outside speech only once, in the eighth book,
when the river calms his stream to ease the Trojans' passage up to
Evander's city.[36] It is, as we shall see, an intensely subjective passage:
Virgil is much concerned to see the event through the Trojans' eyes,
and that may be the reason why he permits the form Thybris, to
which he has given a subjective character, in this place. The one
appearance of Tiberinus in speech is indeed significant: by that name
Anchises, lamenting Marcellus' early death and the loss to Rome,
apostrophizes the river beside which his tomb will stand.[37] This exception is telling, for it shows that Anchises' prophetic powers have projected him into the future, and into a Roman setting, where the
sacral name is now known and appropriate. Virgil's one use of the
fourth name, Albula, is also pointed, for it comes as part of a speech
in which Evander explains how names change with the coming of
new peoples. Albula is an old name, a 'true' name, now lost; and
thus it becomes part of the poet's exploration of the depths of time
and the processes of history.[38]

Tiber appears as early as the second book, while Aeneas is still
in Troy, in his vision of his lost wife Creusa, from which we may
learn indeed how in this poem names and places become a vital
part of the way in which Virgil understands human experience. Here
the public and the private are tightly intertwined. Creusa's last message of personal consolation to her husband must take the form of
large prophecy; conversely, that prophecy's tone is affected by the
intimate setting in which it appears. Grand and informal, grief-stricken
and comforting, spare and gentle, a parting and yet not a parting,
the scene is full of implied paradox; and in the paradox is the pity.[39]

> ausus quin etiam voces iactare per umbram
> imple*vi* clamore *vi*as, maestusque *Creusam*
> nequiquam ingeminans *iterum iterum*que vocavi.   770
> quaer*enti* et tectis urbis s*ine* fine ru*enti*
> infelix simulacrum atque ipsius umbra *Creusae*
> visa mihi ante oculos et nota maior imago.

[35] *Aen.* 8. 72; Enn. *Ann.* 26 Sk.
[36] *Aen.* 8. 86. *Aen.* 7. 151 is only an apparent breach of the rule, because indirect speech
is implicit: the Trojans learn 'that this river is called Thybris'.
[37] *Aen.* 6. 873.   [38] *Aen.* 8. 332.   [39] *Aen.* 2. 768–94.

obstipui, steteruntque comae et vox faucibus haesit.
tum sic adfari et curas his demere dictis: 775
'quid tantum insano iuvat indulgere dolori,
o dulcis coninux? non haec sine numine divum
eveniunt; nec te comitem hinc portare *Creusam*
fas, aut ille sinit superi regnator Olympi.
longa tibi exsilia et vastum maris aequor arandum,   780
et terram Hesperiam venies, ubi Lydius arva
inter opima virum leni fluit agmine Thybris.
illic res laetae regnumque et regia coniunx
parta tibi; lacrimas dilectae pelle *Creusae.*
non ego Myrmidonum sedes Dolopumve superbas   785
aspiciam aut Grais servitum matribus ibo,
Dardanis et divae Veneris nurus;
sed me magna deum genetrix his detinet oris.
iamque vale et nati serva communis amorem.'
haec ubi dicta dedit, lacrimantem et multa volentem   790
dicere deseruit, tenuisque recessit in auras.
ter conatus ibi collo dare bracchia circum;
ter frustra comprensa manus effugit imago,
par levibus ventis volucrique simillima somno.

Indeed, daring to hurl my cries into the darkness, I filled the streets with
my shouting, and in my sorrow with vain repetition called 'Creusa' again
and again. As I searched and rushed endlessly in frenzy through the city's
houses, the unhappy phantom and shade of Creusa herself appeared before
my eyes, an image larger than her wont. In my amazement my hair stood
up and my voice stuck in my throat. Then she spoke thus and took away
my cares with these words: 'O dear husband, what use is it to give way
so much to crazed grief? These things do not come about without the
will of the gods; it is not permitted you to carry Creusa hence as your
companion, nor does the great lord of lofty Olympus allow it. You must
go through a long exile and plough a vast expanse of sea; you will come
to the land of Hesperia, where Lydian Tiber flows with gentle advance
through fields rich in men. There prosperity and a kingdom and a royal
bride are provided for you. Dry your tears for the Creusa you have loved.
I shall not see the proud homes of the Myrmidons or Dolopes, not I, nor
go to be a slave to Greek ladies, who am of Dardanus' stock and Venus'
daughter-in-law; but the great mother of the gods keeps me back on these
shores. Now goodbye, and guard your love for the son we share.' When
she had spoken these words, she abandoned me weeping and wanting to
say many things, and drew away into the thin breeze. Thrice I tried there
to throw my arms around her neck, thrice the image, clasped in vain, escaped
my hands, like the light winds, most like to winged sleep.

A parting and not a parting. An element of Aeneas' sorrow is that amid the chaos of the fallen city he lost his wife without knowing when or how, and as he tells us himself, he never saw her again: 'nec post oculis est reddita nostris'.[40] When the vision of Creusa appears, it is in some degree unlike the living woman, larger in stature, and filling the hero with such speechless awe as a god's apparition might inspire: his hair stands up and his voice clings to his throat, just as it will do when Mercury comes to him in Carthage.[41] Creusa can be seen and heard, but when Aeneas tries to embrace the vision, there is nothing there.

But for all this, we can hardly imagine her simply as a hallucination, divinely inspired. The spirit of loving resignation compels us to the sense that it is Creusa herself who is speaking. The pathos of her situation is that it is she, the lost wife, who comforts her husband with the knowledge that a new bride awaits him elsewhere. The pathos of Aeneas' situation is that he seems briefly to be so close to her; like the scene with Venus in the first book, this is an encounter which at the last moment fails to be an encounter. There is speech, but no reciprocity: just as Aeneas is about to answer, 'multa volentem dicere', Creusa is no longer there, and the joy of touch and solid flesh is denied. So near and yet so far; the ambivalence, and even the contradictoriness, of Aeneas' account is of the essence.

As often in Virgil, we feel a tremulous balance between powerful opposing forces. This is reflected even in the diction which leans towards both everyday speech (the supine form of 'servitum') and an epic elevation ('o dulcis coniunx', 'regnator Olympi'). The emotional colour suggests the same delicate, mysterious poise. Aeneas tells us, before Creusa has spoken a syllable, that her words consoled him, taking away his cares; and when she has finished, he is left weeping. Both emotions, the tears and the comfort, are to be taken seriously. Line 775 will be twice repeated later in the poem, each time before a prophecy; this is one of Virgil's small gestures to the formulaic language of Homer.[42] But this does not mean that the words are meaningless, and in any case this is their first appearance: as we listen to Aeneas telling his story, we do not yet know that we are to hear the sentence again. Besides, to ignore the element of hope and encouragement is to belittle Creusa. She is not a self-conscious

[40] *Aen.* 2. 740 ('and she was not restored to my sight again').
[41] *Aen.* 4. 279 f. Line 774 is repeated at 3. 48, when Aeneas hears the dead Polydorus speaking out of a tree.　　　　[42] *Aen.* 3. 153, 8. 35.

martyr, advertising her own generosity of spirit; part of the episode's greatness is that we are persuaded of her sincerity and unselfishness. She means to help her husband, and to a degree she achieves her end. Often enough he will feel the severity of the divine command: many a time the quest for Hesperia will seem a weary and unending labour. Significantly, that is not how Creusa presents it here. Unlike Apollo or the Penates in the next book, she does not command Aeneas to Italy; the new land is shown to him calmly, as a fact: 'you will come to Hesperia', not 'you must . . .' Nor does she reveal the war that he will have to fight, as Anchises and the Sibyl do. There will be exile and sea to endure, that she does not disguise, but his Italian kingdom she sees as an end to trouble, a place of repose after much toil. Carefully she avoids the note of passion. Her language suggests long shared experience, the adjectives combining restraint with deep emotion: 'o *dulcis* coniunx', '*dilectae* pelle Creusae'. Her last words are of her son. Later we shall be able to liken, but also to contrast, the last words of Dido's first denunciation, concerning the son who does not exist, the 'little Aeneas' who will never be born to her.[43] Indeed, Virgil sets up a series of contrasts between the hero's secure, fruitful marriage to Creusa and his affair with Dido, childless, outside the bonds of custom and tradition, with neither party understanding the other's mind and character.

Creusa does understand. The epithet 'dilectae' is a masterstroke: she tells Aeneas not that she loves him, but that he loves her. She can speak with the serenity of trust and confidence: she knows the quality of his affection for her and can simply take it for granted, without making much of it. This is one of literature's greatest tributes to married love. The noun to which the epithet is attached, 'Creusae', illustrates the complexity of emotional tone. This name, heard for the first time only at line 562, echoes through the latter part of this book: nine times we hear it, and every time at the end of a line.[44] The name echoes, likewise, through the stricken city, as Aeneas calls it again and again. Lines 768–71, filled with resonant sounds and the constant repetition or near repetition of syllables, mimic the hollow reverberance of the hero's cries; and by another

---

[43] *Aen.* 4. 327–30.
[44] In Homer Aeneas' wife is Eurydice. One of Virgil's reasons for changing the name is surely for the sake of repeating it at the line end, another to avoid confusion with the Eurydice of the fourth Georgic. If the same name appeared in *Geo.* 4 and *Aen.* 2, scholars would certainly have elaborated connections between the two passages.

kind of imitation the name enters the poem more frequently than ever: four times in only sixteen lines between 769 and 784. And thus the 'Creusam . . . Creusae' of the wife's speech seems to answer the 'Creusam . . . Creusae' of the husband's immediately preceding narrative: we feel with Aeneas, clinging to the name when the substance is gone, both in Troy long ago and now again in Carthage, as he 'renews his sorrow' to entertain the admiring queen.

Yet Creusa's own intention is quite other: to soothe grief, not to prolong it. 'You will have a royal bride to replace *me*'—that might have been too painful, and perhaps self-pitying. Instead, with a tender austerity, she puts herself into the third person for the greater part of her speech, until she can turn to the better part of her fortune. Thus the same words, echoing her name, contain both grief and consolation, depending whether we hear her speaking them or Aeneas now repeating them. Literally, of course, he cannot forget Creusa— is he not recalling her to Dido now?—but the poem will be able to set her aside. For two hundred and fifty lines she has been a constant presence, but after this Aeneas will never mention her again; she does not appear in the underworld, and the hero does not think to look for her. To be sure, Virgil had reasons of poetical economy for leaving her out: a meeting with his wife would weaken the force of Aeneas' encounters with Dido and Anchises, and would retrospectively remove the finality from the scene in the second book; it is also conceivable that Virgil had not yet thought of Creusa's death when he wrote his underworld episode. But her absence seems to go unremarked by commentators and unresented by readers, and that testifies to the coherence of Virgil's imagination: we feel, even if we are not consciously aware of it, that Creusa, unlike Dido, is over and done with; her ghost, so to speak, is laid. Indeed, we shall hear of her once more only, and that from Ascanius' lips in the sole book from which Aeneas is absent:[45] Creusa dead does not haunt the hero's memory as Dido and Anchises do, or as Sychaeus does his widow, and that is not a clumsiness on Virgil's part, but a nice sense of the proper limits of pathos. This is a quality that does not diminish but rather sharpens the poignancy. It is touching that Creusa should seek to dismiss herself from Aeneas' remembrance; it is doubly touching that, in a sense, she succeeds. And there is a deeper, a moral fitness: a good marriage is complete, and its memory need not perturb the spirit.

---

[45] *Aen.* 9. 297 f.

Such is the background against which we must set her prophecy. Aeneas' experience is a mysterious combination of opposites, not only loss and gain, but the strange and the familiar together: Creusa is both wife and ghost, intimate and yet so far removed. In such an atmosphere the promised land is appropriately presented to the reader's imagination too as both strange and familiar, at 781 f. Nothing is said of Rome: Aeneas will not hear that name until he reaches Anchises in the underworld, and then never again, and thus Virgil uses the withholding of a word from his hero to shape his central climax: Rome is in one sense the hero of the *Aeneid*, and perhaps Virgil recalled how Lucretius had withheld the name of his hero, Epicurus, until its single climactic appearance at his central point, near the end of his third book.[46] Italy, even, is an absent name: we see the new country through Creusa's eyes, as Hesperia, the land in the west, and the adjectives in the previous line, 'longus' and 'vastus', have stressed how far it is. Both Hesperia and Thybris are names of Greek formation; Creusa, the first person in the poem to mention the Tiber, does so in a guise that reminds us that it is an alien, a stranger to Italy who is speaking. In another place, or in another poet, we might be content to label the word as poetic diction; although we do not yet realize how much play Virgil will make with the river's various appellations, already we should appreciate from the context that it has a good deal more significance than that.

Virgil likes to see things subjectively, through his characters' eyes, but counterpointing this empathy is his habit of reminding us that we know many things which his characters do not. The names in the present passage are complex in effect because while we are conscious, by empathy, of how they are likely to strike Creusa and Aeneas, we are also aware that they have a further and different resonance for ourselves. Ennius had given the idea of Italy an epic elevation when he wrote, 'est locus Hesperiam quam mortales perhibebant';[47] and here too, certainly, familiar places are invested by the Grecian names with a literary dignity. And so we see our own Italian home in a doubly unfamiliar light: with a romantic gloss upon it, and at the same time as a remote and foreign land. Our feeling of seeing the familiar as strange is increased by the epithet attached to the Tiber, 'Lydian'. This refers to the legend that the Etruscans originated in

[46] Lucr. 3. 1042.
[47] *Ann.* 20 Sk, 'There is a place which mortal men used to call Hesperia'.

Asia Minor, but whereas with another poet it might once more be enough to note the learned allusion and leave it at that, here the adjective has an emotional force as well. Its transference from race to river creates a hint of paradox or oxymoron, for people can migrate and geographical features cannot. It is weird indeed that the great river of the Italian heartland should receive this oriental epithet, for are not homely, manly Italy and the languid east poles apart? That is how the Augustan or Italian reader may react, while Creusa, for her part, means to hearten Aeneas by impressing upon him the opposite idea: that this far distant land is in a sense 'close to home' after all.[48] Meanwhile the words 'opima virum' stir yet further associations.[49] Virgil's language hints at the mysterious connection between the soil and the people who dwell upon it: good land, good men. It is a note that has been heard in the *Georgics*, and in Lucretius, and it will be heard again later in the *Aeneid*. Here it counterbalances the strangeness and elegance of 'Lydius . . . Thybris' with the sentiment of tradition, solidity, patriotism, and deep roots.

Even the sound of the verse helps to shape Virgil's meaning. Up to the end of line 780 Creusa has a severe message to impart, and the prophecy of Hesperia that follows can have little emotional appeal in itself to a Trojan. And yet the gentle tones in which the Tiber is depicted—especially the limpid sounds of *l* and *y*—begin to give the new land a certain charm; we are indeed lapped in soft Lydian airs. Then comes a climax with the glad tidings of line 783, the firm slow rhythm reinforced by the strong but not excessive alliteration of the letter *r*, before the lapse back to the delicate lyric pathos of 'lacrimas dilectae pelle Creusae'. The description of Tiber and Hesperia stands between defeat and success, and its complex ambivalence makes the transition between the two. The episode as a whole fluctuates between hope and sorrow; its elusive mood is epitomized

---

[48] It is far from sure that Catullus called Lake Garda 'Lydiae lacus undae' (lake of Lydian waters), in his poem on Sirmio (31. 13)—'lucidae' (D. Guarinus) or 'limpidae' (Avantius) might be more probable—but if 'Lydiae' should be right, we could mark the distinction between him and Virgil. Catullus has the *doctrina*, but not the sense of strangeness and wonder, the feeling for the associations of proper names, that Virgil can bring out.

[49] 'It is most improbable that *opima* should be taken closely with *virum* (on the analogy of e.g. *dives opum*, 22) as some commentators have suggested'; so Austin, ad loc. This seems too sceptical. The syntax is supported by the analogy cited, the sentiment by other passages in Virgil and Lucretius. But in any case grammatical nicety is beside the point: even if it be right formally to translate 'fertile fields of manly folk', the shape of the sentence will still suggest the overtone, 'fields fertile in men'.

in the lines on Italy, with their blend of exile and enchantment, home and far romance.

Creusa's farewell is among Virgil's most beautiful inventions; moreover, it is presented with a simplicity and transparency that is seldom among his effects. The very greatest poets have sometimes achieved an extreme plainness at the heart of complexity. We meet it amid the orotundities of *Paradise Lost* ('she plucked, she ate'), in Shakespeare quite often ('undo this button', 'put out the light', 'good night, sweet prince'). So too Achilles on Patroclus, bare and blank: *ton apolesa*, 'I have lost him'.[50] Aeschylus, who developed perhaps the densest idiolect ever used by a great poet, none the less has Cassandra end with a line utterly drab and flat: *kai tout'ekeinou mallon oiktiro polu*, 'And I pity this much more than that'.[51] Out of its place it seems pointless; in its place it is a marvel. Virgil's technical mastery, flexible, sophisticated, and expressive, every rift loaded with ore, hardly ever allows him quite this sort of plainness. But Creusa's farewell, for all its subtlety and multiplicity of tones, has also a humane straightforwardness, and her 'iamque vale' might be called Virgil's most Shakespearean moment.

The *Iliad* is famous for its even-handedness. The Trojan War is not presented as a struggle of Greeks against barbarians, or Europe against Asia. The two sides seem to have the same culture: they speak the same language, use the same weapons, worship the same gods. Though the Achaeans are in the right in the quarrel, and their opponents in the wrong, the poet seems to show no partisanship or racial preference, and the Trojans are made at least as sympathetic as their enemy. This was not, however, the fashion in which the scholiasts of late antiquity and Byzantium always saw the text: for some of them Homer was a 'philhellene', ready to belittle the Trojans in various small ways. Their arguments seem unpersuasive, though there are modern scholars who have been ready to credit them.[52] For our immediate purpose

---

[50] Hom. *Il.* 18. 82.   [51] Aesch. *Ag.* 1330.

[52] The issue is judiciously examined by E. Hall, *Inventing the Barbarian* (Oxford, 1989), 21 ff., who concludes (rightly) that distinctions between the two sides are negligible. Perhaps the best claim for a cultural difference between Achaeans and Trojans concerns Priam. He has great numbers of sons, many by concubines, but from a few passages (*Il.* 8. 305, 21. 85, 22. 48) he appears to be polygamous. Otherwise, men in the *Iliad* are, in the strict sense, monogamous always. If he is indeed polygamous, he is unique among Trojans. Some may think his many sons give him an oriental quality, but their function is (at least primarily) to provide spear-fodder: their deaths culminate in the killing of Hector, whom Priam, his senses warped by grief, calls his only son.

the most interesting question is one which is not certainly answerable: how did Virgil himself read the *Iliad*?[53] Luckily the matter is not of great moment, since even those readiest to believe that Homer marks distinctions between the two peoples will agree that he marks them lightly, and that they are for much of the time forgotten. If Virgil thought that he found a sense of cultural difference or variety in Homer, it is something that he developed in his own way, though still for the most part unobtrusively, without strong emphasis.

It is no longer straightforwardly the case that both sides have the same gods. The Olympians, with Jupiter as supreme, are worshipped by all; but the Trojans also have their local goddess Cybele.[54] And unlike the various Italian deities mentioned in the later books of the *Aeneid*, who remain, very effectively, obscure and shapeless presences, buried in the dark depths of time and ancestral memory, she is even brought into the tenth book to play a part in the action. The cult of Cybele had been brought to Rome in 204 as part of the effort to defeat Hannibal, she had acquired a festival in the Roman calendar, the Megalensia, and Augustus incorporated her into his religious programme, but she retained an exotic flavour, and the two great poets of the previous generation had both, in different ways, depicted her ecstatic Asiatic cult, accompanied by dancing eunuch priests, with a mixture of shock and excitement: Lucretius in his second book, Catullus in his *Attis*.[55] Virgil might have chosen to play down her alien character, following his master Augustus, but he does not; indeed he makes Numanus Remulus in the ninth book express scorn for the cult, a voice from the Italian heartland. So when Creusa, almost at the end of her speech, tells us that the 'great mother of the gods' is keeping her back in her native shores—the first hint in the poem that the Trojans worship anything other than the familiar Graeco-Roman pantheon—we receive a slight stab of surprise.[56] We are

---

[53] Hall, *Inventing the Barbarian*, 24, notes that most of the scholia which comment on barbarian characteristics in the Trojans are of Byzantine date, and come out of a world obsessed with the barbarian peril. That, and a reluctance to believe that so sensitive a literary intelligence would have (as we may think) misread the *Iliad*, encourage one to believe that Virgil did not interpret it as a philhellene text.

[54] Virgil never in fact gives her this name. He once uses the metrically useful variant Cybebe (10. 220); elsewhere, she is identified by periphrasis, as 'the great mother of the gods' (2. 788), 'the Berecynthian mother' (6. 784, 9. 82) or 'the mother of Ida' (9. 619 f.).

[55] Lucr. 2. 600–45; Cat. 63. Cf. T. P. Wiseman, 'Cybele, Virgil and Augustus', in T. Woodman and D. West (eds.), *Poetry and Politics in the Age of Augustus* (Cambridge, 1984).

[56] *Aen.* 2. 788.

reminded, once more, of the great gulf, of both time and space, between Troy and Italy. Creusa will stay behind: she will always be a Trojan, and nothing more. Aeneas will go on; and the changing relationship between him and the gods of Italy will become an important theme.

Moreover, the clothes, gear, customs, and language of the Trojans are different from those of the other peoples whom they meet. This distinctiveness of theirs is something to which Virgil gives just the right degree of prominence, not stressing it, but working it into the fabric of his verse by a number of passing allusions. The Greek Achaemenides is terrified at the sight of men in Trojan costume bearing Trojan weaponry; he can recognize them even from afar.[57] Andromache, a little earlier, was also astonished by the sight of Trojan arms.[58] When Aeneas sends an embassy to Latinus, a messenger reports to the king that men in unknown costume (ignota in veste) are approaching.[59] The full significance of this theme comes out in the final reconciliation between Jupiter and Juno: the queen of the gods hammers it home with passionate alliteration:[60]

> ne vetus indigenas nomen mutare Latinos
> neu Troas fieri iubeas Teucrosque vocari
> aut *v*ocem mutare *v*iros aut *v*ertere *v*estem.

Do not command the native Latins to change their ancient name or become Trojans and be called Teucrians or, men as they are, change their language or alter their dress.

Juno gets her way; and this has the effect of reminding us that it is the Trojans' garb which is, from our own viewpoint, odd and foreign. This effect is the clearer because it picks up motifs that have appeared earlier in the poem. For one thing, there is the matter of Aeneas' hair-oil. It offends Turnus:[61]

> da sternere corpus
> loricamque manu valida lacerare revulsam
> semiviri Phrygis et foedare in pulvere crinis
> vibratos calido ferro murraque madentis.

Grant me to lay low the body of this eunuch Phrygian, to rend and tear apart with my strong hand his breastplate, and to foul in the dust his hair crimped with hot iron and dripping with myrrh.

---

[57] *Aen.* 3. 596–8.   [58] *Aen.* 3. 306–8.   [59] *Aen.* 7. 167.
[60] *Aen.* 12. 823–5.   [61] *Aen.* 12. 97–100.

It has previously offended Iarbas:[62]

> et nunc ille Paris cum semiviro comitatu
> Maeonia *m*entum *m*itra crinemque *m*adentem
> subnexus, rapto potitur . . .

And now that Paris with his eunuch train, his chin and dripping locks wound about with a Maeonian headdress, enjoys what he has snatched . . .

Now Iarbas is a savage (there is something barbaric even in the grossness of his alliterations), though oddly pathetic in his violent, impotent passion; and Virgil has warned us, only a few lines before his speech begins, that rumour mingles lies and malice with the truth.[63] We are not to take him literally; nor Turnus. Clearly it is untrue that Aeneas and his company are eunuchs or unmanly (there is pathos, indeed, in the feebleness of Turnus' self-deceiving abuse: sexual jealousy of a sexless man!). Nor is it just to represent Aeneas' dalliance with Dido as morally equivalent to Paris's seduction of Helen, an adulterous violation of hospitality (Juno, still more outrageously, calls Aeneas a Paris on the basis of his engagement to Lavinia, a woman he has not even met; which shows that not even a great goddess can be trusted).[64] The presentation of Aeneas as a second Paris is, in part, an example of Virgil's technique of viewing his hero subjectively, in different lights, some of which may be luridly and deceitfully coloured. More importantly, it shows Virgil's psychological understanding. Frustration leads to self-deception; Iarbas, Turnus, even Juno seize, half deliberately, half unconsciously, upon some element of truth and then distort it. Iarbas works himself up into a state of self-righteousness; Turnus, desperate to recover his confidence, picks up the language of cheap propaganda and addresses it to himself. Virgil understands how men's minds work, and by this sympathetic knowledge he makes both Turnus and Iarbas, in different degrees, at once distasteful and touching.

The element of truth in their diatribes (we are invited to infer) is that Aeneas does oil his hair; and though the Trojans are hardly effeminate in the sense that Turnus and Iarbas would like to believe, they do worship Cybele, and presumably with eunuchs as priests. As late as the tenth book, after he has prayed to the nymphs of Laurentum and been accepted into Italy by the god Tiber, Aeneas can still pray to the Great Mother, and, as the narrative shows us,

---

[62] *Aen.* 4. 215–17.   [63] *Aen.* 4. 188.   [64] *Aen.* 7. 321.

rightly so.[65] Yet it is significant that he should be described, in the words introducing his prayer, as 'Tros Anchisiades', the Trojan, the son of Anchises.[66] We are seeing a side of Aeneas that belongs to his past, and to another country; a side of the Trojans that is to be purged out of them.

These small touches are enhanced by Virgil's taking the step that Homer does not take and presenting the Trojan War as a struggle of Europe against Asia. The growth of panhellenic propaganda in the fourth century had long ago encouraged such an attitude in Greece; and in Rome Catullus had called Troy the common grave of the two continents, 'commune sepulcrum Asiae Europaeque'.[67] Ilioneus in the seventh book, Juno in the tenth describe the Trojan War in the same terms; and when Aeneas tells Venus that he has been driven from Europe and Asia the phrase has a similar effect.[68] Virgil never uses the name of Europe except in these three places, for contrast with the rival continent. Originally Asia was of a much more limited area, a usage preserved in the Roman province named Asia, and to this day in the phrase Asia Minor. Virgil exploits the double reference: the kingdom of Troy can be called Asia in a more or less literal sense, and yet the name suggests an almost limitless immensity. At the death of Priam it sets the seal upon a sentence of monumental summation:[69]

> haec finis Priami fatorum, hic exitus illum
> sorte tulit Troiam incensam et prolapsa videntem
> Pergama, tot quondam populis terrisque superbum
> regnatorem Asiae.

This was the end of Priam's destiny, this the close that fell to his lot, as he saw Troy in flames and Pergamum in collapse, he who had once been the potentate of Asia, proud in his many peoples and lands.

Again, the very first words of the third book:[70]

> Postquam res Asiae Priamique evertere gentem
> immeritam visum superis, ceciditque superbum
> Ilium et omnis humo fumat Neptunia Troia . . .

---

[65] *Aen.* 10. 252 ff.   [66] *Aen.* 10. 250.   [67] Cat. 68. 89.

[68] *Aen.* 7. 224, 'Europae atque Asiae'; 10. 91, 'Europamque Asiamque'; 1. 385, 'Europa atque Asia pulsus'.   [69] *Aen.* 2. 554-7.

[70] For translation, see below, p. 426. It is interesting that in each of these places the adjective 'superbus' comes to the poet's mind.

As Aeneas sets out upon his odyssey, we are made to feel that not a city or a nation only but a whole world almost has collapsed behind him. These passages demonstrate, once more, the complexity of associative force that Virgil can get out of names: set against Europe, Asia sounds alien, oriental, and remote; but the romantic tragedy of a whole continent falling in ruins invests it with a kind of Wagnerian glamour.

Virgil's fullest treatment of the oriental motif comes with the speech of Numanus in the ninth book:[71]

> non pudet obsidione iterum valloque teneri,
> bis capti Phryges, et morti praetendere muros?
> en qui nostra sibi bello conubia poscunt!   600
> quis deus Italiam, quae vos dementia adegit?
> non hic Atridae nec fandi fictor Ulixes:
> *durum* a stirpe genus natos ad flumina primum
> deferimus saevoque gelu *duramus* et undis;
> venatu invigilant pueri silvasque *fatigant*,   605
> flectere ludus equos et spicula tendere cornu.
> at patiens operum parvoque adsueta iuventus
> aut rastris terram domat aut quatit oppida bello.
> *omne aevum ferro teritur*, versaque iuvencum
> terga *fatigamus* hasta, nec tarda senectus   610
> debilitat viris animi mutatque vigorem:
> canitiem galea premimus, semperque recentis
> comportare iuvat praedas et vivere rapto.
> vobis picta croco et fulgenti murice vestis,
> desidiae cordi, iuvat indulgere choreis,   615
> et tunicae manicas et habent redimicula mitrae.
> o vere Phrygiae, neque enim Phryges, ite per alta
> Dindyma, ubi adsuetis biforem dat tibia cantum.
> tympana vos buxusque vocat Berecyntia Matris
> Idaeae; sinite arma viris et cedite ferro.   620

Are you not ashamed, twice conquered Phrygians, again to be pent by siege and rampart and to use walls to keep death away? Look at these people who are using war to demand marriage with us! What god, what madness has brought you to Italy? There are no sons of Atreus here, no lie-spinning Ulysses: a race tough from the root, we bring our sons early

---

[71] *Aen.* 9. 598–620. Numanus' antecedents are discussed by N. M. Horsfall, 'Numanus Remulus: Ethnography and Propaganda in *Aen.* 9. 598 ff.', *Latomus* 30 (1971), 1108–16, reprinted in Harrison, 305–15. On this topic, and on Aeneas and Italy more generally, there are good observations by F. Cairns in *Virgil's Augustan Epic* (Cambridge, 1989), ch. 5.

to the rivers and toughen them in the fierce ice and waters. Our boys stay awake at night and weary the woods with their hunting; their sport is to guide their horses and aim arrows from the bow. Our young men, inured to toil and accustomed to scant living, either tame the earth with harrows or shake towns in war. Our every age is worn with iron, and turning our spears we weary our bullocks' flanks; nor does the slowness of old age enfeeble the strength of our spirit or impair our vigour: we press the helmet on our white hairs, it is ever our delight to carry off fresh spoil and live on booty. You have clothes embroidered with saffron and gleaming purple, idleness is your delight, your pleasure is to indulge in dancing; your tunics have sleeves and your bonnets have ribbons. O Phrygian women truly—not even Phrygian men—go through high Dindyma, where you are used to the pipe giving you its double-issuing song. Timbrels are calling you and the Berecynthian flute of the Mother of Ida; leave weapons to men and yield to iron.

The poet has informed us, just before the speech begins, that it will contain a mixture of good and bad, 'digna atque indigna relatu';[72] as a signal to the reader this is less subtle than is Virgil's wont, but he is evidently anxious not to be misunderstood. He has also told us in advance that Numanus is about to be killed, and by Ascanius at that, a mere boy; which casts an ironic shadow forward upon the speaker's boastful sense of superiority. And another sardonic shadow is cast back upon his invective when Ascanius slays him: it is Numanus, the advocate of dour Italian toughness, who has proved to be full of idle words, and the Trojan who is laconically brief:[73]

> 'i, *verbis* virtutem inlude superbis!
> bis capti Phryges haec Rutulis responsa remittunt.'
> hoc *tantum* Ascanius.

'Go, mock courage with arrogant words! The twice captured Phrygians send back this answer to the Rutulians.' Ascanius said this only.

The substance of Numanus' abuse is much like that of Turnus and Iarbas: a loose association of luxury, peculiar clothes, sloth, effeminacy, and the cult of the Great Mother. And we return the same verdict: distortion and wishful thinking, but with an element of truth somewhere.

So there is, here too, a certain doubleness in the way we are invited to regard the Trojans. Fundamentally we are with them, we know that justice and destiny are on their side; but tugging against this

---

[72] *Aen.* 9. 595.   [73] *Aen.* 9. 634–6.

feeling is the suggestion—not much more than a hint, but distinctly perceptible—that there hang about the Trojans qualities which are faintly distasteful. Where this passage differs from the others is in combining this fairly simple tension with another which is emotionally deeper and more complex. Line 607 is taken, with two small modifications, from the second book of the *Georgics*; Virgil probably hoped that some of his readers would notice the echo.[74] But without that recognition his meaning can still be grasped; what we pick up in any case is the language of Italian conservatism: the familiar idea that it was the old, hardy, frugal life of the Italian countryside that made Rome great. One interpretation sees Virgil as here echoing his earlier work to a pessimistic end: we see a character who uses the tough, admirable language of the *Georgics* killed by an outsider, and (it is argued) our sense of Italian patriotism is outraged.[75] But Virgil's purposes are subtler.

Numanus is not a modern Roman or an Augustan but a Rutulian of the heroic age, and Virgil's historical sense makes him realize that this character should not speak just like Sallust or Horace or indeed the poet of the *Georgics*. As he rants on, a harsher, more primitive note enters. He exults in banditry; and even if there is a soft, oriental streak in the Trojans, his philistine contempt for the arts and graces of life is something which we can hardly approve. Virgil assuredly did not.

But suppose we take lines 603–11 on their own and ask how they affect us before Numanus moves on from sturdy patriotism to sneering at a lesser breed. There is much, surely, to earn our admiration: young men courageous and energetic, old men still vigorous in mind and body—how can we not applaud? And our approval will not be moral alone; because of the association of such discourse with Italian patriotism, we feel an emotional stirring at the roots of our national consciousness. 'Durum . . . duramus . . .'—that key word from the *Georgics* echoes again through this speech. Yet our reaction, even to the earlier part of Numanus' speech, is not one of simple enthusiasm. The word 'durus', as we have seen, has its rough and even cruel side: it is inherently ambivalent. But that is not all. As we look closer, we see that this is not the chastened but firm patriotism of the *Georgics* after all, but something of coarser fibre. 'Fatigant . . .

---

[74] *Geo.* 2. 472.
[75] R. O. A. M. Lyne, *Further Voices in Vergil's Aeneid* (Oxford, 1987), 200–6, esp. 202.

fatigamus'—another repetition, and one with an overtone of brutality to it. That impression is confirmed by Numanus' callous attitude to children and animals alike, and his thoughtless pleasure in the destructiveness of war. 'We first take our sons to the rivers and harden them in the fiercely icy waters'—well! 'Cold baths before breakfast', 'made me the man I am'—that sort of harsh complacency is hardly the voice of the *Georgics*. The curious resemblance of lines 603 ff. to sentiments conventionally attributed in more recent times to a dim blimpishness is in a sense an accident; and in a sense not. The kind of smug insensitivity that disguises itself as manliness is recurrent in human nature. Numanus turns out, somewhat surprisingly, to be rather a realistic figure.

What Virgil has done is to excite a complex emotional reaction. We have not only mixed feelings about the Trojans, but mixed feelings of a different sort about the Italians, and these perhaps of a more testing kind. It looks as though we shall be able to enjoy the easy warm throb of patriotic sentiment, and then we are denied—no, half denied—that pleasure. This casts an interesting light back upon the *Georgics*, suggesting how easily the Augustan values of robust simplicity might lapse into crudity, how finely judged is Virgil's blend of sternness and enthusiasm. Perhaps no other Roman patriot entirely escapes the danger, not even a figure as sophisticated as Horace, who tends, on the national theme, to wrap himself in an easy, off-the-peg nobility. But the *Georgics* somehow fails to give offence, not because the patriotism is a pretence and Virgil covertly critical of Augustus, but because of the largeness of his moral imagination. He can feel deeply and still be willing to inspect the nature of his emotions, experiencing them within, observing them from without.

Here in the *Aeneid* it is not that Numanus' attitudes are worthless: he does say things 'digna . . . relatu', after all. We do feel the patriotic tug at the heart, but we also feel that his values are inadequate. This doubleness is compressed into the brilliant phrase, 'omne aevum ferro teritur', which means so much more than its speaker intends. We share his pride in the strength and valour of Italy, but beyond this we sense the Virgilian awareness of imperfection, of a golden age lost, with all the complexities of sensibility which that involves, and we feel too in those rasping words—rasping in sound and sense— that there is a hardness of heart in Numanus, that the iron (to seize a metaphor from another place) has entered into his soul. Patriotism of his kind is not enough. What will be needed is a blending of the

Trojan and Italian virtues, a purging out of Trojan and Italian flaws. And that, the *Aeneid* tells us, is more or less what will come about. The complex, many-sided presentation of these peoples is thus an expression of Virgil's historical sense. Remulus is not an Augustan in fancy dress, nor is Aeneas: a process of development will be needed to transform the values of their epoch into those of Augustus' age. The seeds of Virgil's own values are there, as the echo of the *Georgics* teaches us, but they will need time for growth and careful husbandry. And this is a hopeful picture of history: Virgil finds not only change but progress.

If he sees both sides of a question or a quarrel, this does not mean that he espouses a moral relativism. In real life it is not the high-principled but the morally insecure or unimaginative man who does not dare to see things from the other person's point of view. Some-one brought up on the values of liberal democracy who goes abroad and lives under a dictatorship may well, if he has imagination, start to appreciate why a system that he deplores should be successful, even popular. But that does not mean, or should not mean, that his own convictions are weakened. And so with Virgil's poetry: his sympathy with different viewpoints does not amount to a diffused, evasive benevolence—'much to be said on both sides', and that is all. What impresses is the combination of broad imaginative sym-pathy with firm conviction. Turnus is sympathetic, but wrong; the making of Rome is costly, but a great adventure none the less.

Numanus calls the Trojans 'Phrygians'. That is correct. Aeneas himself can describe his company as coming to the altar veiled in Phrygian garb or pray to the Great Mother to lend her Phrygians aid.[76] But this label does tend to be used especially by the Trojans' enemies, partly no doubt because of the two Greek sounds in the word, *ph* and *y*, partly perhaps because it seems to be particularly associated with Cybele. Numanus, moreover, twice uses the Greek nominative plural form 'Phryges'; coming from the mouth of this Italian chauvinist, it has the effect of fancy language held in quota-tion marks, so to speak, and spat out scornfully. By careful repeti-tion Virgil accumulates a penumbra of association around the name of Phrygia. Aeneas relates that Andromache gave Ascanius a Phrygian cloak (*Phrygiam . . . chlamydem*); the very obviously Greek origin of the word 'chlamys' and the reminder of the Trojans' distinctive style

---

[76] *Aen.* 3. 545; 10. 255.

of clothing help to bring out their oriental side at this moment.[77]
'Let Dido serve a Phrygian husband,' Juno tells Venus—a subtle piece
of psychology on Virgil's part, for Juno is purporting to be friendly
and co-operative, but we feel her extreme bitternesss forcing its way
through, in her own despite, in the contemptuous adjective.[78] Turnus
plays effectively upon racial feeling by spreading the story that the
Phrygian stock is being mingled with Latin; he calls Aeneas 'Phrygius
tyrannus', the Grecian formation of the noun again drawing attention to his rival's foreignness.[79] Those who want to represent Aeneas
as a soft seducer, a second Paris, think in terms of Phrygia. So Amata
to Latinus:[80]

> mollius et solito matrum de more locuta est,
> multa super natae lacrimans *Phrygiis*que hymenaeis:
> 'exsulibusne datur ducenda Lavinia Teucris,
> o genitor, nec te miseret nataeque tuique?
> nec matris miseret, quam primo Aquilone relinquet
> perfidus alta petens abducta virgine *praedo*?
> an non sic *Phrygius* penetrat Lacedaemona pastor,
> Ledaeamque Helenam Troianas vexit ad urbes? . . .'

She spoke softly and in the usual way of mothers, weeping much over the
marriage of her daughter and the Phrygian: 'Is Lavinia being given to Trojan
exiles to wed, O father, and have you no pity for your daughter and yourself? Have you no pity on her mother, whom that faithless brigand will
desert when the first north wind blows, carrying off the girl and making
for the deep waters? Was it not thus that the Phrygian shepherd wormed
his way into Sparta and bore Helen daughter of Leda away to the cities
of Troy?'

So too the prayer of Amata and the Latin women to Minerva, in
very similar language: 'frange manu telum *Phrygii praedonis* . . .'[81] And
as we have seen, Turnus also tries to stain Aeneas with the taint of
eastern effeminacy by calling him a Phrygian eunuch.[82]

In choosing names for foreign peoples Virgil did not have the
resources of modern English-speakers. Our language, in its colloquial
and lower registers, is immensely rich in racial nicknames, affectionate,
neutral, disparaging, offensive. Latin offers no equivalent to this:
when the Romans wished to denigrate the Greeks—and they often
wished to denigrate the Greeks—they could not do better than the

---

[77] *Aen.* 3. 484.   [78] *Aen.* 4. 103.   [79] *Aen.* 7. 579; 12. 75.
[80] *Aen.* 7. 357–64.   [81] *Aen.* 11. 484.   [82] *Aen.* 12. 99.

diminutive 'Graeculus'. In our own experience some names have an emotional field of force around them intrinsically. A simple case is the patriotic and poetical synonym: Albion, for example. This name has long been obsolete, but when it could still be used, it could not be used neutrally: it carried with it certain associations and implied a certain tone. Latin too has a few such poeticisms: when Virgil uses the name Ausonia for Italy, it signifies patriotism and the grand manner. But such prefabricated pomp has little depth. More interesting are names which without having associations that are intrinsic, have certain emotional tendencies. 'England' is an instance. This is a strictly descriptive label for some fifty thousand square miles of southern Britain. Now any patriot anywhere hears the name of his native land with some emotion: the Frenchman's heart quickens at the name of France, the Mongolian's (one presumes) at the name of Mongolia. But the name of England seems to go beyond this, and to be not entirely within the power of the people who use it. Imperialist poets and politicians on the hustings have found themselves speaking of England although they have known that Britain would be a more accurate label, besides being less troublesome to the sensitivities of the Scots and Welsh. They have known that England is a descriptive term, which does not accurately denote what they are talking about, but they have been in thrall to the power of the word.[83] The travails of Irish nationalism are instructive: at one time the name Eire was promoted, but it is now largely avoided, because it lacks resonance for the Irish themselves.[84] Every Irishman is stirred by the name of Dublin, few by Baile Atha Cliath.

This kind of feeling for names is characteristic of old countries: time is needed for names to acquire a patina. This is true even of poeticisms: the nineteenth-century attempt to establish Columbia as a lofty synonym for the United States (like Caledonia) and even to make Columbia an allegorical figure (like Britannia) was a failure. Stephen Vincent Benét's poem *American Names* expresses an envy of European names and the 'magic ghost' that they guard. He crams his verse with American names in the hope that they may work upon

---

[83] One might try this experiment. 'Some corner of a foreign field That is for ever Britain' does not sound right. 'Some corner of a foreign field That is the United Kingdom' would be hopeless. The United Kingdom has trade statistics, Britain has an Empire and Railways, but England is home.

[84] Significantly it is used by some Unionists in Northern Ireland when they want to annoy the Republic.

the imagination in a similar way, but too many of them wear their picturesqueness merely on the surface: Medicine Hat, Deadwood, Lost Mule Flat.[85] They have not yet gained the evocativeness supplied by history and shared experience. The authentic romance of the American land is of another kind: vastness, the frontier, the new, the unknown. Against this may be set the European idea, for which Virgil speaks and which he in part creates, that the land is known and has been known for generations, that men and the earth have made their history together.

It is perhaps a sign of the oldness which the Romans felt in themselves, distinguishing them from the Greeks,[86] that a few of their names start to acquire emotional associations. If an Augustan poet mentions the Medes or the Marsians, it is likely that he means to evoke eastern softness by the one, virile austerity by the other. If he sets the two names side by side, his purpose becomes even clearer. 'sub rege Medo Marsus et Apulus . . .' Horace writes, and without reading another line, we know what his point will be: to think that these manly mountain-bred soldiers, of all people, should bow to an oriental despot.[87] Horace does not tell us that the Marsians are rugged, or that the Medes are soft. He does not need to; the associations of the proper names do it for him.

We may not be greatly impressed by this example; nor when Horace goes on to wheel out the stage properties of Roman tradition and religion: the 'ancilia' or sacred shields, and eternal Vesta. The use of words with natural associations clinging to them can be a substitute for a live poetic language.[88] But Virgil's way of exploiting the associations of proper names is distinctive: his subjective or empathetic method means that he can feel the associative penumbra and yet criticize it. He *explores* words. He can turn the words round to look at them from different angles: as we have seen, the word 'Phrygius' feels one way on Juno's lips, another on the lips of Aeneas. And thus the use of proper names, like the use of associative words such

---

[85] Of all his names, perhaps only Nantucket has been around long enough to resonate as he wants. But all such judgements are subjective. (Yet when one thinks of the evocative names he might have chosen: Kentucky, Chattanooga, Ozark . . .)

[86] See above, p. 117.   [87] *Carm.* 3. 5. 9.

[88] Orwell observes of Housman ('Inside the Whale'), 'His poems are full of the charm of buried villages, the nostalgia of place-names, Clunton and Clunbury, Knighton, Ludlow, "on Wenlock Edge", "in summer time on Bredon".' And he loses patience with Rupert Brooke's *Grantchester*: 'a sort of accumulated vomit from a stomach stuffed with place-names'. The judgement is too harsh, but the warning is salutary.

as 'durus', rather than producing sentimentality or patriotic self-satisfaction, serves a breadth of sympathy and understanding. Also remarkable is the extent to which Virgil creates his own penumbra of associations. Let us consider the word 'Phrygius' again. How is it that we become aware of the slightly contemptuous edge to it? Not from the study of dictionaries or parallel passages but from reading the *Aeneid* itself. Perhaps no one before had given 'Phrygius' the kind of timbre that it has in Virgil,[89] but the interesting thing is that it makes no difference whether anyone had or not: the shape and style of the poem itself are what make us feel a word like 'Phrygius' as we do. Lucretius had created a field of force around certain simple adjectives, giving them a special life and energy within the universe of his poem; Virgil now does something similar with names. We are taken into his own imaginative world, drawn to feel about names and peoples and places in a Virgilian way, just as we are made to feel about time, space, size, objects in a Virgilian way. Everything takes on a Virgilian colour.

Virgil may use the 'natural' associations of words or he may create his own mesh of associations. New subtleties arise when he combines both these things, stirring the emotions both of recognition and surprise. We have found this with the name Hesperia: he takes over the existing resonance of the word, but adds his own resonances which partly supplement, partly go against the inherited nuances. Sometimes the clash between the expected 'stock response' and the new context can be quite sharp:[90]

> en huius, nate, auspiciis illa incluta Roma
> imperium terris, animos aequabit Olympo,
> septemque una sibi muro circumdabit arces,
> felix prole virum; qualis Berecyntia mater
> invehitur curru Phrygias turrita per urbes
> laeta deum partu, centum complexa nepotes,
> omnis caelicolas, omnis supera alta tenentis.

See, my son, glorious Rome, founded under his auspices, shall match the earth in empire, Olympus in spirit; this single city shall enclose with a wall seven citadels, blessed in the men who are her progeny, like the Berecyntian mother who is borne in her chariot with her battlemented

---

[89] A possible anticipation might be Cicero's *Pro Flacco*, with its repeated sneers at Phrygians, Mysians, and Lydians (3, 17, 40, 41, 65). But his aim is to belittle Asia generally, and all its peoples are grist to his mill: one name seems to be as good (or bad) as another.

[90] *Aen.* 6. 781–7.

crown through the cities of Phrygia, glad in the gods who are her children, embracing a hundred descendants, all dwellers in heaven, all denizens of the heights above.

The passage and the two dozen or so lines leading up to it are heavy with Roman sentiment, and at this point national pride swells larger than ever, with Virgil going so far as to see the city as like a universal mother; but at the same moment, just when the Roman tone is loudest, he makes the startling comparison with Cybele, giving to the iconography of personified Rome herself an oriental flavour. Once again, Virgil's subjectivity enables him to produce a curiously double effect. Anchises is talking to Aeneas, and entering into their point of view we see unfamiliar Rome being put in a light which a Trojan can understand and warm to; but entering into the attitudes of Virgil's contemporary readers we see the familiar iconography of Rome presented as something strange. But not only as strange: for while we feel the oddness, we feel also a stirring at the deep, familiar heart of patriotism. 'Felix prole virum' . . . 'mater' . . . 'laeta' . . . 'partu' . . . —motherhood, manliness, fertility, and the sense of national identity—that profound complex of ideas which means so much to Virgil, which we find in Creusa's speech, in the introduction to the catalogue of Italian forces in the seventh book, and above all in the *Georgics*, is here too, worked into the fabric of the verse. So perhaps it was too simple, after all, to speak of the oriental element being purged out of Aeneas' descendants. Instead we are offered a subtler version of the process of development: not the straightforward elimination of such things as the worship of Cybele but their transmutation into something that can blend with Italian institutions, seemingly so different in character. Here we see the hopeful aspect of Virgil's vision. On every side there are good qualities that go to the making of Rome and later Italy. We are given a vision of change and development that is also a vision of progress.

A passage such as this suggests that some at least of the feelings about Troy that Virgil implies are not the most obvious ones to occur to a Roman gentleman. A Roman would be proud to claim Trojan ancestry (Varro traced the origins of aristocratic families in Aeneas' companions) and we may presume that such pride was normally untroubled by any diffidence about foreign blood or oriental tendencies. The legendary origins of the Romans make a theme that Virgil handles sometimes straightforwardly, sometimes with a special pointedness. A passage from the fifth book will serve as an illustration.

As he lists the competitors in the boat race, he links them to their descendants:[91]

> Sergestusque, domus tenet a quo Sergia nomen,
> Centauro invehitur magna, Scyllaque Cloanthus
> caerulea, genus unde tibi, Romane Cluenti.

And Sergestus, from whom the Sergian house takes its name, sails in the great Centaur, and in the blue Scylla sails Cloanthus, whence comes your family, Roman Cluentius.

That seems brisk and uncomplicated. But just a few lines before Virgil has introduced the same theme in slightly different terms:[92]

> velocem Mnestheus agit acri remige Pristim,
> mox Italus Mnestheus, genus a quo nomine Memmi . . .

Mnestheus drives on the swift Pristis with its eager oarsmen, soon to be Italian Mnestheus, from whose name comes the family of the Memmii . . .

'Mnestheus . . . mox Italus Mnestheus'—the repetition draws attention to the name. It is of very obviously Greek form—unlike, say, Sergestus—a matter to which Virgil again draws attention by putting the adjective 'Italus' beside it. Dissonant against the Italian and Roman tone is the small stress on Mnestheus being an outsider; and at the same time Virgil slips in his theme of change and transformation: the outsider will become an Italian, 'one of us'. This is not a passage of great significance or great quality, but it serves to show how Virgil's themes are worked into the texture in minor passages. In such a context the adjective 'Romane' with 'Cluenti' no longer seems otiose: we feel a small brief prick of pointedness.

Behind the poem, then, we may sense two simple Roman sentiments: pride of birth, including Trojan ancestry; and pride of race, including a certain condescension towards most humanity east of the Adriatic. Virgil subjects them to a critical scrutiny, and yet he can also absorb and adapt them, simple as they are, to serve a deeper purpose. Partly this is because in his conception Italy and Troy are not so much opposites as distinct. He takes Italy and the complex of ideas and emotions around it; he takes Troy and the complex of ideas gathered around it too; and he sets them side by side, playing with them, now bringing them closer together, now drawing them apart.

---

[91] *Aen.* 5. 121–3.   [92] *Aen.* 5. 116 f.

Troy and Italy together form not a painful discord but an intriguing dissonance, and a dissonance that resolves into consonance, for Trojan and Italian qualities prove to be not antipathetic but complementary; ultimately they will be merged. Virgil creates an atmosphere such that when we get a juxtaposition like 'Troes | Italiam' or 'Latium Teucri', to take two very minor examples from early in the tenth book, we feel a tiny passing piquancy.[93] We are not told how to react to the words but we are made to feel that they have an import, a weight; we are invited to think about them, to sense that they are energized and active in the poet's imagination. And Virgil can also make use of both those Roman sentiments because they contribute to his historical view. We detect Roman characteristics in the Trojans, and yet we feel that a great distance separates us from them. Thus in his hands the casual incompatibilities of common sentiment become the material of a solemn paradox: the Trojans are both like us and unlike us; across a vast tract of time we become aware of both change and continuity.

The theme of the Trojans' transformation and the creation of a new Italy is broad and monumental; it is given a more personal and immediate application in the experience of Aeneas himself. Virgil has two motifs. The first is the idea of Aeneas gradually becoming more of an Italian. This is not explicitly said, but it is the more effective for being left implicit; we shall find it emerging naturally from the imagery and from the way he himself speaks and acts. The idea of becoming Italian is momentarily glimpsed in other characters too. Mnestheus is not an Italian but will in course of time become one; Evander, a Greek who speaks of himself as an Italian, has already done so.[94] But Virgil also develops a quite different motif: Aeneas and his people have been of Italian descent all along, since Dardanus, the founder of the Trojan race, himself came from Italy; this strange notion, not found before Virgil, is probably his own invention, devised for the particular purposes of this poem. We shall find that these two themes enable him to bring out both change and continuity: he can stress now one, now the other, or both at once, looking at the matter from different angles, with that shifting, enquiring gaze so characteristic of his vision.

The third book begins with Aeneas emphatically the Trojan, the Asian:[95]

***

[93] *Aen.* 10. 31 f., 58.   [94] See below, p. 554.   [95] *Aen.* 3. 1–12.

Postquam | res *Asiae Priami*que evertere gentem
immeritam visum superis, ceciditque superbum
Ilium et omnis humo fumat Neptunia *Troia*,
diversa *exsilia* et desertas quaerere terras
auguriis agimur divum, classemque sub ipsa
Antandro et *Phrygiae* molimur montibus Idae,
incerti quo fata ferant, ubi sistere detur,
contrahimusque viros. vix prima inceperat aestas
et *pater* Anchises dare fatis vela iubebat,
litora cum *patriae* lacrimans portusque relinquo
et campos ubi *Troia* fuit. feror *exsul* in altum
cum sociis natoque || pen|atibus | et mag|nis || dis.

After it pleased the gods to lay low the power of Asia and Priam's innocent people, after proud Ilium fell and all Neptune's Troy smokes from
the ground, we are driven by signs from the gods to seek distant places
of exile and empty lands. Just below Antandros and the peaks of Phrygian
Ida we build a fleet, unsure where destiny may lead us or where it may
be granted us to settle, and we muster our men. Scarcely had early summer begun when my father Anchises was bidding us spread our sails to
destiny; weeping, I leave the shores and harbours of my homeland and
the plains where once was Troy. I am borne an exile into the deep, with
my comrades and son, with the Penates and the Great Gods.

Every name for Troy and things Trojan is heard, clung to pathetically,
in these opening lines: 'Asia', 'gens Priami', 'Ilium', 'Troia', 'Phrygius',
and again 'Troia'. To the name of 'pater Anchises' the word 'patria'
forms a pitiful echo in the succeeding line. Aeneas leaves Troy, he
insists himself, as an exile. This is no voyage of discovery, in his eyes:
he can think not of what he is going to, only of what is past and gone.

Yet even here the poem may offer an ambivalence. 'Troy is
finished'—that is the message; Aeneas opens with a self-contained
spondee, terse and forceful: 'postquam'. But while this thought means
only irreparable loss to the hero, it has another signification for us: we
hear that a chapter is ended, that the Asian destiny of Aeneas' people
has come to an end; a new and—we may suppose—a greater stage is
about to begin. There is thus a dramatic irony in his words; not a
tragic irony but rather the reverse. His statement is not grimmer than
he supposes but more hopeful. So, at the start of the hero's wanderings, Virgil gives us an example of that double vision which is to recur
throughout the *Aeneid*, counterbalancing his famous empathy: we are
conscious that the characters in the drama hear one thing, ourselves
another.

The double vision is brilliantly developed at the climax of the paragraph. The extraordinary rhythm of line 12, combining a spondaic fifth foot with a stressed monosyllable at the end and the absence of a strong caesura in either third or fourth foot, is without parallel in Virgil except where the line is echoed in a later book:[96] this is therefore a line that draws attention to itself. It comes just at the point where the word 'exsul' has picked up the 'exsilia' of line 4. What Aeneas is telling Dido is that he has lost his home and country, but he has salvaged a few precious fragments from the wreckage: his son, his followers, his gods. These gods are hugely important to him, the context shows us, because they are deities of the Trojan nation and of his Trojan home.

But we are bound to hear another message. Virgil echoes a line of Ennius: 'dono—ducite—doque—volentibus cum magnis dis' (I grant and give them—take them—the great gods being willing).[97] Even if the reader does not recall the passage, he may still catch in the rugged rhythm, bizarre in terms of Virgil's own practice, the accents of Latin poetry's rude forefather. In other words, Aeneas' Trojan nostalgia comes through to us in tones suggestive rather of robust ancestral Italy. The very gods in question reinforce this feeling, but here Virgil differs from the older poet. In Ennius the speaker is Pyrrhus, a Greek, and by 'magni di' he presumably means 'the mighty gods' in a quite general and unspecific sense. But for Virgil these words are a name or title, and characteristically he explores the name's effect in a foreign mouth. The nature of the 'magni di' remains obscure, but they seem to be national and Italic in character; they are associated with, and may be identical to, the Penates: 'magnis diis' was the inscription on the base of a statue in the temple of the Penates on the Velia. Indeed, the word 'penates' too carries similar associations in this place. Here we need a little caution. The Romans habitually found Latin equivalents for the names of Greek gods; we expect Virgil to turn Zeus into Jupiter, Aphrodite into Venus, and draw no moral from this whatever. So although the lares and penates were important in Roman domestic and public religion, when a poet uses these words he may be doing no more than saying 'household gods' in Latin, using the only vocabulary he has for the purpose. It is the context in which Virgil puts the word 'penates' that makes us feel its paradoxically Roman flavour. Habitually he takes words and names,

[96] *Aen.* 8. 679. [97] *Ann.* 190 Sk.

ordinary enough in themselves, and interrogates them, bringing out the fullness of their significance. And the effect of this habit is cumulative, so that when we meet 'lar' or 'penates' again, as when we meet 'Italia' or 'Phrygius', we are ready to find the words charged, as it were with electricity. We sense a little stab of shock when Juno in the first book and Venulus in the eighth speak of Aeneas bringing his 'defeated penates' to Italy;[98] we detect the small tension of associations pulling in contrary directions when we hear of the 'lar of Troy' or the 'lar of Assaracus' (in each case that feeling is increased by the introduction of the so Roman name of Vesta, the national mother invoked with Romulus and the Indigites as one of the ancestral gods in the passionately patriotic close of the first Georgic:[99]

> Pergameumque *Larem* et canae penetralia *Vestae*
> farre pio et plena supplex veneratur acerra.

He worships the Lar of Pergamum and the shrine of hoary Vesta in prayer with a full censer and the due offering of meal.

> 'per magnos, Nise, *penatis*
> *Assaraci*que *larem* et canae penetralia *Vestae*
> obtestor . . .'

'I adjure you, Nisus, by the great Penates, by the Lar of Assaracus and the shrine of hoary Vesta . . .'

The irony, the doubleness of vision at 3. 12 are to be picked up again much later, when Virgil describes the Battle of Actium depicted upon Aeneas' shield:[100]

> hinc Augustus agens *Italos* in proelia Caesar
> cum patribus populoque *penatibus et magnis dis*,
> stans celsa in puppi, geminas cui tempora flammas
> laeta vomunt patriumque aperitur vertice sidus.

On one side was Caesar Augustus leading the Italians into battle with the fathers and the people, with the penates and the Great Gods. He was standing on the lofty poop; his glad brow pours forth a double flame and his father's star shines out on his head.

The repeated phrase is so forceful and so odd that Virgil must surely have intended his readers to notice the echo and ponder its significance. As we do so, we become aware of a formidable continuity:

---

[98] *Aen.* 1. 68; 8. 11.   [99] *Aen.* 5. 744 f.; 9. 258–60; cf. *Geo.* 1. 498.
[100] *Aen.* 8. 678–81.

despite the vast tracts of time that divide them, Augustus is the heir of Aeneas, both the descendant of his loins and his destined successor as leader of the race, and he is carrying across the seas to war the same gods that Aeneas carried so many centuries before. And yet what a change also: for Augustus leads Italians to battle against the forces of the east, reversing Aeneas' role.[101] One particularly subtle touch is that Aeneas travels 'cum . . . nato', with his son: the word looks forward to the next generation, to the future. Augustus comes to Actium 'cum patribus', 'with the fathers', that is, with the senate; the word looks back to the past. Thus each of these lines looks towards the other, the one reaching forward to Roman prehistory, the later line enjoying the sense of accumulated tradition.

From the earlier line alone we should already feel that even in the Trojan Aeneas, and even before he has reached Latium, there are seeds of Roman-ness—seeds of which he is himself unaware. None the less, upon the surface it is plainly the abidingly Trojan side of Aeneas that is insisted upon in the first lines of the book. But soon Virgil will begin to balance against this his other motif: Aeneas the Italian. This is a darker, stranger theme, and it is developed, appropriately, in two divine and oracular utterances. First the voice of Apollo:[102]

'Dardanidae duri, quae vos a stirpe parentum
prima tulit tellus, eadem vos ubere laeto
accipiet reduces. antiquam exquirite matrem.
hic domus Aeneae cunctis dominabitur oris
et nati natorum et qui nascentur ab illis.'

Hardy sons of Dardanus, the same land which first bore you from your ancestors' stock shall welcome you on your return to her rich breast. Seek out your ancient mother. This is where the house of Aeneas and the sons of your sons and those who are sons to them shall hold sway over all lands.

This is one of those passages in which Virgil enlarges the historical perspective in both directions: we look back to the far past (*antiquam . . . matrem*) and simultaneously forward to the far future: the repetitions in 'nati natorum . . . nascentur' seem to press onward to

---

[101] Though this is to simplify somewhat: see below, p. 556.
[102] *Aen.* 3. 94–8. It is disputed whether Virgil himself invented Dardanus' Italian origin. V. Buchheit, *Vergil über die Sendung Roms* (Heidelberg, 1963), 151 ff., argues that he did; the opposite view is maintained by N. M. Horsfall, 'Corythus: The Return of Aeneas in Virgil and his Sources', *JRS* 63 (1973), 68–89, at 74 ff.

immensely distant times. And here again is that complex of associated ideas—toughness, fertility, ancestry, earth, antiquity, motherhood—which binds together nature, time, and national identity: 'duri', 'parentum', 'prima', 'tellus', 'ubere laeto', 'antiquam'. The message contained in Apollo's command is not simply factual: through the imagery of parenthood and maturity, with even a mother's breasts suggested in the words 'ubere laeto', the Trojans are tied emotionally to something with which, on the conscious level, they have no emotional links at all. Aeneas is an exile, and yet he is not an exile. He will not be like an emigrant to America or Australia, starting afresh on virgin soil in a new world: instead, mysteriously, he will come home upon an alien shore. Virgil surrounds this conception with a kind of uncanniness: it is almost as though the sense of *déjà vu*, that brief puzzling feeling that people have at odd moments—'somehow, sometime I have been here before'—has been broadened out into the experience of the race as a whole.

This is the first occasion on which Aeneas is clearly told that his people's future home will be their place of ultimate origin, but to us the idea is not entirely new, for in the first book he has told Venus, 'Italiam quaero patriam' (I seek my country [*or* fatherland] Italy).[103] We might hardly notice the paradox, or might take 'patria' as being a little loosely used—'I am seeking a home [*or* my future country] in Italy'—had not Virgil drawn attention to the oddity by making Aeneas explain, just a couple of lines earlier, that he is carrying with him penates rescued from his fallen city. Once again, Virgil interrogates an ordinary word, making it yield up its full significance. 'Patria' is literally 'fatherland', and strange as that meaning may seem in this particular context, it is strictly correct. Thus, so early in the poem, Aeneas the Trojan and Aeneas the Italian are set side by side.

But at the time of Apollo's utterance Aeneas has not yet heard the name of Italy, and indeed his father hastens to misinterpret the god's meaning. There is some subtlety in the way that Virgil makes Anchises both understand and misunderstand the divine voice:[104]

> tum genitor veterum volvens monimenta virorum
> 'audite, o proceres,' ait 'et spes discite vestras.
> Creta Iovis magni medio iacet insula ponto,
> mons Idaeus ubi et gentis cunabula nostrae.
> centum urbes habitant magnas, uberrima regna,

---

[103] *Aen.* I. 380.   [104] *Aen.* 3. 103–15.

maximus unde pater, si rite audita recordor,
Teucrus Rhoeteas primum est advectus in oras,
optavitque locum regno. nondum Ilium et arces
Pergameae steterant; habitabant vallibus imis.
hinc mater cultrix Cybeli Corybantiaque aera
Idaeumque nemus, hinc fida silentia sacris,
et iuncti currum dominae subiere leones.
ergo agite et divum ducunt qua iussa sequamur:
placemus ventos et Cnosia regna petamus. . . .'

Then my father, pondering the records of the men of old, said, 'Listen, ye chiefs, and learn what hopes are yours. Crete, the island of great Jupiter, lies in the midst of the open sea, and therein are Mount Ida and the cradle of our race. They dwell in a hundred great cities, most fertile domains, whence Teucer our earliest father, if I duly remember what I have heard, first sailed to the shores of Rhoeteum and chose that place for his kingdom. Ilium and the citadel of Pergamum had not yet arisen; the people lived in low valleys. From here came the mother who dwells on Cybelus, the bronze cymbals of the Corybants and the grove of Ida, from here came the devout silence at her rites and yoked lions passed under the mistress's chariot. So come, and let us follow where the gods' commands lead us. Let us appease the winds and make for the domain of Cnossos.'

Despite his error, Anchises responds in the right spirit to the prophecy's emotive content, picking up the ideas of antiquity, fertility (uberrima regna), and motherhood (gentis cunabula); and he is able to evoke a past, remote world, enticingly strange and romantic. It is a world of din and silence; of lions, but of lions tamed. This is a kind of primitivism, but its wild, exotic, half-abandoned character is far removed from the primitivisms of Italy to be unfolded in later books: the pastoral world of Tyrrhus and his neighbours, the country-gentlemanliness of Evander, the woodland chastity of Camilla, the sombre archaic splendours around Latinus. These distinctions suggest Virgil's command of tone, and the variousness of the world which he invites us to explore.

Aeneas' companions follow Anchises in responding to the call to seek for a rootedness in a distant past: 'Cretam proavosque petamus,' they cry.[105] Aeneas himself echoes the mood: 'et tandem antiquis Curetum adlabimur oris.'[106] But his instincts at this stage are half right, half wrong:[107]

---

[105] *Aen.* 3. 129. For the word 'proavus', cf. above, p. 117.
[106] *Aen.* 3. 131.   [107] *Aen.* 3. 132–4.

ergo avidus muros optatae molior urbis
Pergameamque voco, et laetam cognomine gentem
hortor amare focos arcemque attollere tectis.

So eagerly I set to work on the walls of the longed-for city and call it
after Pergamum; I press my people, delighted by the name, to love their
hearths and to build a citadel to protect their homes.

'Hortor amare focos'—that is right, the sense that simply to find a
spot to settle in is not enough, that what a people requires is to be
bound emotionally to their place of local habitation. What, though
of his followers, glad that he has named the new city after Troy? On
the one hand, Virgil persistently conveys to us the power of words
and names, and the Trojans' sentiment is one to which he is keenly
sympathetic. On the other hand, we shall see this book developing
in a way that exposes the inadequacy or incompleteness of such an
attitude. Italy will be both old and new. The Trojans must go back,
certainly—Apollo has shown us that—but they must also go forward.
So far they have only grasped half of the message. We easily come to
think of Aeneas' special destiny, and the elaborate divine apparatus
used to expound it, as an artificial construct, remote from reality.
It is that, in part, but it is also a heroicized version, grander and
simpler than in life, of an element in everyone's experience. For each
of us, our past is a part of ourselves; but the past is also a foreign
country, from which we are constantly travelling with every minute
that goes by. We can never undo the past; and we can never recover
it. Virgil's sense of time and history is not simply something loftily
theoretical; it is part of his understanding of the human condition,
and his sympathy with it, and in some degree Aeneas' experience
illuminates our own. It would be a gross distortion to say that Aeneas
is a symbol of every man; rather, he is like every other man in that
he is a unique individual in unique circumstances, and interesting
to us for that reason, as other fictional heroes—Emma Bovary, say,
or Pip, or Anna Karenina—are interesting. He is both exceptional
and representative, both a myth and a man. This has sometimes been
misunderstood, as for example by those who have seen him as a pup-
pet of destiny (a view now out of fashion). Mercury commands him
to leave Dido, and he quickly obeys, though he would rather stay.
We ourselves do not have divine messengers appearing before us, but
we are all familiar with the conflict between duty and inclination.
A moral imperative, whether delivered by a god or by conscience,

is in a sense compelling, but it is in obeying it (or refusing to obey it) that we experience our freedom as moral beings. The man who obeys speedily is not less free than the man who hesitates longer, but is in all probability a better person. The essential though not the invariable characteristic of Aeneas, as the recurrent epithet 'pius' tells us, is goodness; and this gives the poet a formidable problem, for the portrayal of virtue is notoriously difficult. (It is commonly said that fictional characters with flaws are 'more human', but this is not so: St Francis is not less human than the rest of us. The truth is rather that imperfection is so much easier to represent.) Some have felt that Virgil fails to overcome the difficulty, and that his hero is stiff or dull. But if this is so, it does not alter the nature of his conception; though Aeneas is a great hero with a peculiar destiny, his experiences may be interpreted in common human terms, not only the acute conflict between love and duty but also the ordinary texture of his emotions as he wanders the Mediterranean world.

The Penates, appearing in a vision by night, repeat and clarify to him themes adumbrated by Creusa and Apollo.[108]

> 'mutandae sedes. non haec tibi litora suasit
> Delius aut Cretae iussit considere Apollo.
> est locus, Hesperiam Grai cognomine dicunt,
> terra antiqua, potens armis atque ubere glaebae;
> Oenotri coluere viri; nunc fama minores   165
> Italiam dixisse ducis de nomine gentem.
> hae nobis propriae sedes, hinc Dardanus ortus
> Iasiusque pater, genus a quo principe nostrum.
> surge age et haec laetus longaevo dicta parenti
> haud dubitanda refer: Corythum terrasque requirat   170
> Ausonias; Dictaea negat tibi Iuppiter arva.'

[108] *Aen.* 3. 161–71 (the speech begins at line 154). There is an inconsistency between the second book where Creusa tells Aeneas that he will come to Hesperia, and the third, where he has no idea where he is going to until the Penates tell him. Though the inconsistency is minor, it can hardly be argued away: there is no reason given why Aeneas should doubt or forget Creusa's words, and though 'Hesperia' is a vague term (and Tiber perhaps quite unknown to Aeneas), it cannot cover Crete. The obvious explanation is that Virgil composed Creusa's speech after most or all of the third book, and did not live long enough to remove the inconsistency in the course of revision. Two plausible working assumptions are that Virgil would not have significantly altered Creusa's farewell, a masterpiece; and that he would not have removed the conception, fundamental to the structure and meaning of the third book, that Italy should emerge gradually out of obscurity. We may reasonably proceed in the belief that Virgil's final text would not have been far from the one we have. (It may be impertinent to instruct Virgil's ghost, but a line or two after 101 explaining that Aeneas forgot Creusa's prophecy in the excitement of the moment would remove the difficulty.)

'You must change your abode. Delian Apollo has not urged these shores upon you or bidden you settle in Crete. There is a place which the Greeks call by the name Hesperia, an ancient land, potent in arms and in the richness of its tilth. Oenotrian men once worked it; now the tale is that their successors have called their nation Italy from their leader's name. This is our proper abode, here Dardanus and father Iasius arose, from whom our race takes its origin. Come, rise, and gladly bring these words, not to be doubted, to your aged father: He must seek for Corythus and the land of Ausonia; Jupiter denies you the territory of Dicte.'

We have heard four of these lines, 163–6, before: Ilioneus uses them in his speech of embassy to Dido.[109] But we must once again distinguish our own experience from that of the characters: though these words may come to us as an echo, they come to Aeneas now with the force of a revelation, and for us too they acquire a greater emotional depth in their new setting.[110] After Creusa and Apollo, we feel the more forcefully the binding power of that tangle of earth and oldness, fertility, motherhood and strength in battle—all superbly brought out in 164, a line of brief and simple words, each one driving home a new point with magnificent terseness. The words 'ubere glaebae' adapt Homer's phrase, *outhar aroures*, but the complex and intimate imagery with which Virgil has surrounded them strengthens and deepens the simple Greek metaphor.

As in Creusa's farewell, the emotionally binding words are balanced by others which are emotionally distancing. The qualities of subjectivity and alienation in the name 'Hesperia', delicately implicit before, are now explicitly spelled out: 'Hesperiam *Grai cognomine dicunt.*' Indeed Virgil perhaps labours the point a little, making Anchises pick it up when he exculpates himself for misinterpreting the prophecy:

---

[109] *Aen.* I. 530–3.

[110] Perhaps Virgil would not have let the passage stand in both places when he revised the poems. We may ask for which place it was originally written. Heinze, who held (implausibly) that the third book was planned late in the composition of the *Aeneid* (86–95), maintained that the lines were first written for Book 1 (89 n.); the opposite view was forcefully argued by J. Sparrow, *Half-Lines and Repetitions in Virgil'* (Oxford, 1931), 93 f. The latter possibility is indeed more likely: it is not appropriate for Ilioneus to lecture Dido on Italian antiquities, and a little odd for him to praise the fertility of a land that he has never seen. Heinze claimed that it was unfitting for the prophetic Penates to talk about 'fama'; but in terms of Virgil's conception of time and change it is entirely apt. The Penates, who for Virgil himself are ancestral native gods, have not yet reached Italy and are not even confident in their knowledge of it. So too Aeneas, who will become an *indiges* (12. 794 f.), an Italian god, does not at first know the rivers of Latium (7. 137 f.), including the river Numicus (7. 150), with which his cult will be associated.

'sed quis ad *Hesperiae* venturos litora *Teucros* | crederet?' (for who would suppose that Teucrians would come to the shores of Hesperia?).[111] The feeling of remoteness that Virgil has imparted to this place name gives an edge of paradox to the Penates' surprising assertion, 'hae nobis propriae sedes'. 'Hae' is emphatic, underlining the strangeness; indeed the whole brief clause is forcefully economical, once again, with a pressure of significance felt behind every one of those four words. Aeneas has introduced these gods as 'Phrygian penates', and that too is paradoxical and complex in its effect.[112] Aeneas means 'my native gods'—he adds that he had rescued them from the flames of Troy—and in a sense the Italian reader shares his feelings: the Penates are indeed 'my native gods', an Italian cult. But the reader is separated from Aeneas in finding the adjective 'Phrygius' bizarre, attached to an indigenous cult of his own land. The paradox is sharper than in the case of the games Virgil plays with the Great Mother, for in actual life, outside the fiction of the poem, the cult of Cybele was indeed an import from the east, whereas the Penates had never been Phrygian but were primordially native.

As so often, while Virgil thinks about places he is thinking about time also. In order that we may watch time passing and working its changes, he slips a single aorist in among a number of present tenses: 'Oenotri col*uere* viri; *nunc* fama . . .' But it is not the movement of time alone that concerns him; as with his view of names and places, he studies too the subjectivity with which any man (or god even) observes it. Italus, to whom allusion is made in 166, is a person very dimly perceived; in the seventh book we shall find that he is a faint ancestral figure even in relation to the aged Latinus, and his place in the line of kings is wrapped in obscurity.[113] But the Penates are so unimaginably old that to them even he is a newcomer. 'Fama est' seems to suggest the immense spaces that separate Troy from Italy: the Penates cannot be sure about something that has happened so far away. These evocations of high antiquity are matched by the introduction of Dardanus and father Iasius. The first of these is a favourite of Virgil's in such contexts, from the *Georgics* onwards; commentators have puzzled over why he should have given such prominence here to the little known name of the second. Perhaps his charm lies in his very obscurity: Virgil may want the earliest forebears to be a little hazy with distance.

---

[111] *Aen.* 3. 186 f.   [112] *Aen.* 3. 148.   [113] *Aen.* 7. 178; see below, p. 487.

The words of the Penates both set Aeneas at a distance from the idea of Italy and draw his sentiments towards it. This doubleness is matched—and here too the scene resembles Creusa's farewell—by a mood which strangely blends severity and joy. There is a bleak solemnity in the two word sentence, 'mutandae sedes'. They will not let him rest; they warn him that long toil lies still ahead. But the essential note is one of stern comfort: they 'take away his cares', their speech being preceded by a line identical to the one introducing Creusa's farewell.[114] And whereas Creusa's concern is with her son, her husband and herself, the divine vision reaches further, and the Penates, amplifying Apollo's words, look on beyond Aeneas' own life to the splendours of the Roman empire.[115] Characteristically, though, Virgil binds a promise of glory and the command to labour into a single sentence, 'tu moenia magnis | magna para longumque fugae ne linque laborem'; toil cannot be dissevered from glory.[116] As they uproot him from Crete, the Penates bid him rejoice, 'surge age et haec *laetus* longaevo dicta parenti | haud dubitanda refer . . .', and momentarily we may feel that this is the hardest command of all.[117] Still, he does rejoice: 'perfecto *laetus* honore | Anchisen facio certum remque ordine pando.'[118] That echo of the Penates in the hero's own voice has its effect; Italy is starting to seem a genuine enticement, and we feel that he has already travelled some distance, spiritually as well as physically, since he lost his wife in Troy. Indeed, his danger now is that he may rejoice too soon; later Helenus will warn him that the Italy he imagines to be so close is still far away.[119] It adds to the pathos of his situation later, as he meditates dispiritedly upon the ever receding fields of Ausonia,[120] that not long before they had seemed within his grasp.

After he has torn himself reluctantly from Helenus' city, Aeneas and his company sail past the Ceraunian cliffs and come ashore for the night to sleep: 'sternimur optatae gremio telluris ad undam'.[121]

[114] *Aen.* 3. 153 (= 2. 775).   [115] *Aen.* 3. 158–60.

[116] *Aen.* 3. 159 f., 'Do you build mighty walls for the mighty, and do not abandon the long effort of exile'.

[117] *Aen.* 3. 169 f., 'Come, arise, and gladly bring to your aged father these tidings, not to be doubted'.

[118] *Aen.* 3. 178 f., 'After completing the rite, I gladly tell Anchises, and recount the matter to him in due order'.

[119] *Aen.* 3. 381 ff.   [120] *Aen.* 3. 496.

[121] *Aen.* 3. 509 ('We stretch ourselves out by the water in the lap of the longed-for earth').

What he means, as the next lines make clear, is that the sailors are glad to be on dry land again; and yet, as so often, Virgil means much more (he uses similar language to describe the Trojans' landfall after the storm, in the first book).[122] 'Optatae gremio telluris'—in three Latin words all the longing for home, for roots, for mother earth is contained. It is characteristic of Virgil to make the passing phrase pregnant with a deeper significance; characteristic too that his style of apprehending experience is established not only through the big set pieces but by an accumulation of momentary effects. So too his feeling for the possibilities of proper nouns is developed through a multitude of small touches. For example: 'Corythum terrasque requirat | Ausonias.'[123] Ausonia is an obvious name in the context, but not the obscure Corythus. However, we shall learn later that it was 'from the Etruscan abode of Corythus' that Dardanus set out for Phrygia;[124] Virgil is making an ancestral link between Troy and Italy. Besides, the name contains those Greek sounds *y* and *th*, while Ausonia, by contrast, is a name resonantly old-Italian. And yet these two goals, Corythus and Ausonia, sounding so different, are one and the same. Once again, in Aeneas' experience and in our own, Virgil makes the strange familiar and the familiar strange.[125]

From time to time we are made aware of the double vision, of how we see differently from the actors in the drama. Thus, 'Actiaque Iliacis celebramus litora ludis' (We throng the Actian shore with Trojan games).[126] Aeneas does not know, of course, that his descendant will win a great battle in this place; what is more, the way we have been made to think about things Trojan gives a small ironic pressure to 'Iliacis' (typically, Virgil jams the two proper adjectives up together). How curious that the Battle of Actium—that great victory, as we shall learn in the eighth book, of Italy over exotic barbarians—should be celebrated according to the customs of that eastern city Troy. And yet in another way the oddity is no oddity at all. Just as alien Hesperia is on a deep, half-hidden level not alien at all, so the fact of the Aeneadae unknowingly celebrating an Italian victory in Trojan fashion is not inappropriate. (We might compare that Roman institution,

---

[122] *Aen.* 1. 171 f.   [123] *Aen.* 3. 170 f.   [124] *Aen.* 7. 209.
[125] Corythus occurs four times in the *Aeneid* (the other two places are 9. 10 and 10. 719). In Book 3 and perhaps Book 10 it appears to be the name of a place, in the other two cases the name of a man, though in every instance it is used as a way of designating a place ('the cities of Corythus', etc.). N. M. Horsfall, *JRS* 63 (1973) at 70, argues that Corythus is a place-name in every case.   [126] *Aen.* 3. 280.

the 'Troy game', which will be commemorated in the fifth book.) And so the picture of change and continuity is recalled to us in a passing phrase.

This example may strike us as a little laboured: why should the Trojans choose to hold games at this particular moment? We can hear the mechanism creaking as Aeneas hastens to supply a reason: they were relieved to have slipped past so many Greek cities and eluded their enemies.[127] We are not persuaded that this explanation is given for the benefit of Dido and the Carthaginians; Aeneas, we may feel, is looking nervously over his shoulder towards posterity, the readers of this poem. Subtler are Anchises' words, 'nate, Iliacis exercite fatis' (Son, troubled by Ilium's destiny).[128] The context suggests that the old man says more than he knows: after all, there is no Ilium any more; Aeneas' heart is still in Troy, he is still too tightly bound to an irrecoverable past. And yet Anchises means no reproach: in calling his son a man tried or troubled by Trojan destiny, he means only to offer sympathy. It is we who feel a doubt.[129]

When Aeneas prays to Apollo, he addresses him as a national god, referring to his cult at Thymbra in the Troad:[130]

> da propriam, Thymbraee, domum; da moenia fessis
> et genus et mansuram urbem; serva altera Troiae
> Pergama, reliquias Danaum atque immitis Achilli.

Grant us, god of Thymbra, a home to be our own; grant us in our weariness walls and descendants and a city that will abide; preserve as Troy's second Pergamum these remnants that have survived the Greeks and pitiless Achilles.

Even as he looks forward to the future, asking for a 'city that *will* abide', he is trying to hang on to the past, to recreate what no longer exists as closely as possible to what was before. 'Troiae Pergama'— that strange double phrase makes Aeneas seem to cling to Troy, Troy; and then almost immediately follows 'Danaum', introducing yet a third form of the Trojan name. But Aeneas' nostalgia is nothing to Helenus' thoroughgoing effort to live entirely in the past. As Andromache explains:[131]

---

[127] *Aen.* 3. 282 f.   [128] *Aen.* 3. 182.

[129] Anchises' shade uses the same phrase at 5. 725, where no overtone seems intended. It is the context within the third book which suggests the questioning note.

[130] *Aen.* 3. 85–7.   [131] *Aen.* 3. 333–6.

> morte Neoptolemi regnorum reddita cessit
> pars Heleno, qui Chaonios cognomine campos
> Chaoniamque omnem Troiano a Chaone dixit,
> Pergamaque Iliacamque iugis hanc addidit arcem.

At Neoptolemus' death part of the kingdom passed in turn to Helenus, who gave the name Chaonian to the plains and called the whole land Chaonia from Chaon of Troy, and put a Pergamum and this citadel of Ilium on the heights.

'Troiano . . . Pergamaque Iliacamque'—again three forms of the Trojan name in quick succession, but that is not all: 'Chaonios . . . Chaoniamque . . . Chaone . . .'—the grinding repetitions suggest an obsessive clinging to names when the substance is gone. The sentence as a whole is almost indigestible, so densely is it clotted with proper nouns and adjectives. But surely that is Virgil's intention.

Andromache's words might seem to labour the point sufficiently; but although we have heard something about Helenus' mimic Troy already, we are to hear yet more:[132]

> procedo et parvam Troiam simulataque magnis
> Pergama et arentem Xanthi cognomine rivum
> agnosco, Scaeaeque amplector limina portae . . .

I advance and recognize a little Troy, a little Pergamum that mimics the great one and a dry brook with the name of Xanthus; and I embrace the doorway of the Scaean Gate . . .

The reader may start to protest that Virgil is laying it on too thick, with an obviousness and overemphasis untypical of him. Now it may be the case that in this book Virgil handles the themes of names and places without the exceptional power and subtlety found in Creusa's farewell, in the seventh and eighth books, and in the second Georgic. It must also be allowed that in the third book as a whole there is some diminution of the poet's usual brilliance: as Aeneas works perfunctorily through a selection of Odysseus' old adventures, we may start to notice the disadvantages of Virgil's method and reflect how much better suited primary epic is to this sort of thing. However, the wearisomely reiterated emphasis upon the Trojans' attachment to their past is not a blemish but has its proper function. As we are taken over and over Helenus' forlorn enterprise, we surely find ourselves thinking how feeble it is. Virgil has implied as much, with a

---

[132] *Aen.* 3. 349–51 (cf. 302–5).

nice obliquity: as Aeneas first approaches the city, he observes the waters of 'falsi Simoentis' and the empty tomb of Hector (inanem).[133] His primary meaning is that he saw a mimic Simois and a ceno- taph, and the words need mean no more than this; but we catch beneath the words' descriptive surface a hint of falsity and futility.

Mostly, though, Virgil works not through hints but by letting us feel for ourselves the inadequacy of Helenus' scheme. The Trojans, for their part, are delighted with what they see, and Aeneas gladly embraces the Scaean Gate;[134] it is we who decide that the old man is weakly 'living in the past'. After all, we think, the original Troy was a great and mighty city; the new Troy is a toytown, a 'parva Troia' as Aeneas himself admits, noticing too that a dry stream-bed has to do duty for the river Xanthus.[135] So when Helenus ends his enormous speech, 89 lines in all, which has carried us away from Epirus to Italy and the wars to come, with the name of the lost city, it comes with massive emphasis, but also oddly contrary to expecta- tion: 'vade age et ingentem factis fer ad aethera Troiam' (Go your way and by your deeds lift great Troy to the sky).[136] Yes and no, we say: in a sense the future will apotheosize the old Troy, but in another and surely stronger sense it will abolish it: after all, what Roman ever seriously thought of the national achievement as reflecting glory upon a town in Asia Minor? Helenus feels one way, we another, and perhaps we should sense a similar distance between ourselves and Aeneas when in reply he looks forward to his descendants by the Tiber making Hesperia and Epirus one Troy in spirit.[137] Some, says Servius Auctus, have taken this as a reference to the foundation of Nicopolis by Augustus. Perhaps; but we might also, or instead, detect an irony, for to any educated Roman what Epirus meant first and foremost in Roman history was Pyrrhus' invasion. Aeneas' ring- ing exhortation here resembles his still more fervent promise in the first book that he will remember and praise Dido for ever:[138] it is a pledge destined to be fulfilled imperfectly or not at all. We warm to his enthusiasm, aware none the less of the limits of his knowledge and understanding. 'Epiro Hesperiam'—Virgil presses together the

---

[133] *Aen.* 3. 302, 304.   [134] *Aen.* 3. 351 f.

[135] *Aen.* 3. 349 f. Virgil perhaps had one eye on the pretentious gardens of certain rich Romans; the mimic Xanthus and Simois recall Cicero's mockery of contemporaries who gave names like Nile and Euripus to the artificial watercourses which they had made on their own property (*Leg.* 2. 2, quoted in Ch. 3).   [136] *Aen.* 3. 462.

[137] *Aen.* 3. 500–5.   [138] *Aen.* 1. 607–10.

two names, each of which has a meaning as a Greek word: 'main-land', 'western land'. That juxtaposition hints once more at the sub-jectivity of the hero's view: it is still from an easterner's standpoint that he looks towards his future home.

The significance of all this is to draw us imaginatively into the quest for Italy. We are not for the most part lectured upon the majesty of Jupiter's plan; we learn it ourselves by responding to the shape and language of the poem. We admire the hero's *pietas*, his devotion to his home as to his family and people, but we realize that this sentiment of loyalty and affection must change and develop if it is not to collapse into a pusillanimous nostalgia. The *Aeneid* observes this development. The consequence is that in the dazzling paradox which seals the poem's structure, Juno comes in a strange way to seem right after all: on the level of the domestic politics of Olympus, Jupiter's consent to the abolition of the Trojan language and customs is a gracious concession to his defeated queen, but within the scheme of human history it appears as the right and necessary resolution of the poem's conflict. There has been much rough hewing; but even the apparent obstacles in the path of destiny have proved to have a shaping purpose after all.

The idea of Italy is a dynamic concept, dimly adumbrated at first, growing in force and clarity. We, the readers, hear the full tale of destiny in the first book, where Virgil arrays himself in deepest purple for the purpose; Jupiter, no less, is his mouthpiece. Aeneas' experience is different. Creusa foretells an ultimate resting-place and a good marriage; no more. Apollo's prophecy, splendid though it may be, is brief; and still the name of Italy has not been heard. Even the Penates, enlarging considerably upon Apollo's terseness, approach this name with an odd obliqueness. Not until the sixth book does Aeneas attain to the length and definiteness of historical vision that we were given in the first. There Jupiter presented 'Caesar . . . Iulius' —the title Augustus is not yet heard—as the culmination of the his-torical process.[139] Through the next four books and more nothing further is heard of him, until Anchises reveals him in Elysium:[140]

> hic vir, hic est, tibi quem promitti saepius audis,
> Augustus Caesar, divi genus . . .

This is the man, this is he, whom you so often hear promised to you, Caesar Augustus, the god's son . . .

---

[139] *Aen.* 1. 286–8.   [140] *Aen.* 6. 791 f.

The long silence both articulates the poem's construction and forms its meaning: it makes the passage climactic, a resolution long awaited, as the glorious title Augustus sounds for the first time; it presents the man through the structure of the poem as a whole, through both its statements and its reticences, as the summation of the Roman story.[141]

We shall find, however, that even in Elysium Aeneas cannot fully understand what he sees; nor when he is shown that other vision of the future, the shield. But though he does not see the future perfectly (after all, no one can), he does grow in knowledge and understanding. The third book represents part of his voyage of discovery, literal and metaphorical. There is a sense of progress, of advance towards a goal, however fitful and unsteady. The way that the idea of Italy grows is reflected in a pattern of repetitions, once the place has been hesitantly identified by the Penates. 'Hesperiam . . . Hesperiae', says Anchises; 'Italiam . . . Italiam', comes from Celaeno; 'Ausoniae . . . Ausoniae', from Helenus; then finally from Aeneas hinself, when the promised land has been sighted at last, 'Italy, Italy, Italy':[142]

> iamque rubescebat stellis Aurora fugatis
> cum procul obscuros collis humilemque videmus
> Italiam. Italiam primus conclamat Achates,
> Italiam laeto socii clamore salutant.

The dawn was now reddening and had put the stars to flight, when afar we see dim hills and low Italy. 'Italy,' Achates is the first to shout; my men greet Italy with joyful cry.

From a poet schooled in neoteric elegance we might expect a polyptoton, a variation of case endings such as Catullus supplies in his *Peleus and Thetis*:[143]

> tum *Thetidis Peleus* incensus fertur amore,
> tum *Thetis* humanos non despexit hymenaeos,
> tum *Thetidi* pater ipse iugandum *Pelea* sensit.

Then Peleus is said to have been inflamed with love for Thetis, then Thetis did not disdain a wedding with a mortal, then the father himself saw that Peleus should be joined to Thetis.

---

[141] 'The man whom you often hear promised'; it is not clear why Augustus should be so described. Though it is possible to rationalize (perhaps when Anchises haunted Aeneas' dreams at Carthage, he told of the great man to come?), the attempt is like trying to count Lady Macbeth's children. The dynamics of the poem as we have it are what matters: this is the first time we see the promise made to Aeneas, and on any account this is presumably the first time that he has actually heard Augustus' name.

[142] *Aen.* 3. 185, 253 f., 477–9, 521–4.   [143] Cat. 64. 19–21.

But such graces are not for Virgil at this moment; instead, a rock-like monumentality. Nor, alternatively, is there variation in the positioning of the repeated 'Italiam' within the line or sentence. The three words stand like big square blocks, the first isolated at the start of the line, the first following immediately after a bare asyndeton, while the third repeats the line position of the first and the sentence position of the second. Italy is anchored in the text solidly, weightily.

Depite this solidity, the lines convey a glorious sense of liberation. After the brisk level narration which has now been running for some time, after the quiet undramatic tone of 522 with its low land and dim hills, 'Italy' bursts out at the start of the new line like a sudden explosion. Small wonder that it is echoed and re-echoed. The whole passage is indeed beautifully handled, and effective on several levels. In the first place, it vividly evokes the experience of landfall: when land is first seen from far out at sea, it does indeed appear dim and low upon the horizon. The word order and the disposition of the sentence within the metrical scheme contribute too to the effect: something obscurely seen, yes land (can it be?), yes—Italy. And Virgil conveys the mental as well as the visual experience: that line of hills is so faint and unremarkable to the outward view, and yet it means so much. Virgil's feeling for not just the appearance but the inner significance of natural scenes comes through once more in yet another form; and it comes from a simple, lifelike recreation of how people do feel when they first sight their goal at the end of a long voyage: there is a thrill inspired by the very contrast between the littleness of what the eye sees and the import of what the mind supplies, a small spurt of animated inner knowledge.

Moreover, the adjectives of 522 are carefully chosen to suggest a metaphorical as well as a literal significance, and there is an irony in the promised land first appearing in such a guise. In a way, it is true that Italy is 'lowly' and 'humble', for as yet it has not the famous cities and heroic renown of Greece or the Trojan kingdom; in a way, it is not true, for this will become, as we cannot forget, the greatest of lands. We may compare the irony with which we observe Aeneas at the site of Rome, a place which we are able to regard at one and the same time as engagingly modest and awesomely great. This is, of course, not a bitter but an amused, warming, patriotic irony, from which we derive a wry, knowing pleasure. And perhaps it also serves, in the third book as in the eighth, to remind us of Virgil's historical theme: as a humble Italy is set before our eyes (to our surprise at first, though the idea is to be much refined and elaborated in later books), we reflect that if such a description has come to seem agreeably incongruous, it is through the immense operations of time.

But for Aeneas and his people, immediately, there is an unkinder irony at work. When he does finally land upon Italian soil, it proves to be Greek territory, and the poetical structure makes us share the experience of the actors. We too feel the flatness of disappointment; we look for Virgil to pull out all the patriotic stops at this point, but our expectations are cheated: after 521–4 there follows no further climax. From Aeneas comes no prayer of thanksgiving to the gods of the locality, such as we meet in the seventh and eighth books;[144] instead, he sets dutifully about the unappealing task of worshipping Juno, his enemy, and then without taking pause (haud mora) he is off upon the sea again.[145] The whole scene feels oddly brisk and unsatisfying; but surely Virgil meant it to feel that way.

Quitting the shore they have so rejoiced to see, tired and lost, the Trojans drift into danger:[146]

> interea fessos ventus cum sole reliquit,
> *ignari*que *viae* Cyclopum adlabimur oris.

Meanwhile in our tiredness, when the wind has left us along with the sun, not knowing the way we drift towards the shores of the Cyclopes.

'Ignari viae' is yet another of those passing phrases that leave a larger reverberance behind. Significantly, Virgil had used the very same expression at the climax of the proem to the *Georgics*, in a context where it is clear that a symbolic meaning lies behind the literal sense. He summons Caesar to his aid:[147]

> da facilem cursum atque audacibus adnue coeptis,
> ignarosque viae mecum miseratus agrestis
> ingredere et votis iam nunc adsuesce vocari.

Grant me an easy passage and favour my bold enterprise, and pitying with me the countrymen who know not the way, approach and even now become accustomed to be called upon in prayer.

Just as the 'way' that the farmer needs to learn is more than a matter of agricultural technique, so the 'way' that Aeneas must seek is more than a route across the sea: it is the path of duty and destiny, a path only gradually revealed, and easily lost amid temptations and discouragements. 'Ignarique viae'—the pathos, and the excitement, of Aeneas' situation flower in that pair of lonely words.

---

[144] *Aen.* 7. 135 ff., 8. 71 ff.   [145] *Aen.* 3. 543 ff. ('haud mora', 548).
[146] *Aen.* 3. 568 f.   [147] *Geo.* 1. 40–2.

CHAPTER 10

Beyond Experience: The Underworld

Nur immer zu! wir wollen es ergründen,
In deinem Nichts hoff' ich das All zu finden.

(Goethe)

When we surveyed the development of Greek poetry, we found a growing interest in nature for its own sake, and we saw this process taken even further by Lucretius. No one should doubt that for Virgil likewise nature, landscape, and things seen were greatly valuable in themselves. Yet in much of his poetry he shows rather little interest in exact description. Propertius gives individualized pictures of Assisi and Mevania in his fourth book;[1] here indeed he follows the example of Virgil's depiction of the river Mincius,[2] but nowhere else in the *Georgics* is there again such a particularized evocation of a known Italian landscape. Ovid at times observes with acuteness and precision: a live coal going out, the curvature of a bird's wing, the true colour of a woman's hair;[3] Juvenal is a master of visual detail, Apuleius an exquisitely refined painter in words.[4] All these writers are inheritors of that passion for the perceptible world which Lucretius and Virgil put at the heart of their poetry; but Virgil himself is less interested than they in exact depiction.

He is more intently concerned with the significance of things seen, with their effect upon the observer. Even perhaps in the case of the 'still life' in the second Eclogue the contrasting textures of fruits and nuts are as much felt as described: though the various flowers 'paint' a picture—the poet's own word—he is primarily engaged with the idea of apprehending difference, more than with specifying just what the differences are.[5] The rivers flowing beneath ancient walls at the heart of the *laus Italiae* are wonderfully vivid, but in a sense they are not a picture but a generalization: we are to do much of the

---

[1] See below, pp. 613 f.   [2] *Geo.* 3. 13–15.   [3] See below, pp. 627–9.
[4] On Juvenal's descriptive power see Jenkyns, *Three Classical Poets* (London, 1982), 173 ff.
[5] *Ecl.* 2. 45 ff.; see above, pp. 148 ff.

imagining, drawing upon a multiplied experience of the Italian land-scape. This is one of the greatest moments of crystallization in all poetry, but it does not crystallize into a single image; whereas when Propertius describes Mevania, or Juvenal an earlobe distorted by the weight of an earring, we know with something like precision what we are to see.[6] Virgil's walls and rivers, as we discovered, take much of their power from the placing of the phrase within the paragraph and within the structure of the poet's thought.

It may be useful to make a distinction between vividness through description and vividness through evocation. Of course the boundary between these two is not precise, especially since the most detailed description in words is vague in comparison to pictorial art. That is in the nature of the media. When we look at a picture we are automatically 'told' an indefinitely large number of facts: that there is a tree to the left of the house, that the house stands above a lake, that the lake is such and such a shape, and so on. The writer cannot multiply such facts indefinitely, even if he wants to; but in any case he will be wise not to weary the reader with insignificant detail, with 'too many particulars of right hand and left'.[7] Still, despite the necessary incompleteness of all verbal description, the distinction between description and evocation has its value. Virgil's mastery of evocation enables him not only to present natural objects and scenes with a minimum of actual descriptive fact, but also to occupy an area which lies uncertainly between the outer world and interior emotion, where we may even be unsure whether we have to do with perceptible scenes and objects at all. Aeneas' visit to the world of the dead takes us beyond experience, and yet Virgil can use it as a means of exploring the strange dark places of the perceiving or half-perceiving mind.

Paradise Lost offers two famous phrases which might baffle the logical and emotionless mind of a Martian: 'No light, but rather dark-ness visible'; 'Dark with excessive bright thy skirts appear.'[8] The painter asked to represent such scenes might well decline; and the second indeed is designed to represent the ineffable, beyond all depiction: God himself. Yet our own experience tells us that these phrases are very vivid. One has only to compare Bentley's notorious rewriting, 'No light, but rather a transpicuous gloom.' The illustrator cheers

---

[6] Prop. 4. 1. 123; Juv. 6. 459.   [7] Jane Austen's phrase, quoted in Ch. 2.
[8] *Paradise Lost* 1. 63; 3. 380.

up at once: that he can of course depict. But we know that Milton's vividness has been lost. Perhaps we have not exactly seen darkness visible, but we seem to have met it in some corner of experience. Paradox, for that matter, may be part of the quite ordinary observation of nature, the still water below trees, for example, dark and yet transparent, black and yet brown and green. The painter finds formulae to put these things on canvas, but those ingenious patches of colours, those dashes of white, are only translations of what we have seen, they are not the thing itself. Our experience of depth and surface, darkness and translucency has been ordered and interpreted. And thus a verbal description that cannot be simply cashed out in pictorial terms may oddly be more vivid, because it leaves a space for the spectator's experience, with all its natural unclarity. A verbal art which aspires to the condition of a photograph will leave something out, because it forgets that things are seen not objectively but through a subjective pair of eyes. I am not a camera.

If this applies to the observation of straightforwardly natural scenes or objects, it will be all the more true of a region that lies between the natural and the imagined worlds, or maybe belongs to both. Such is Milton's Hell, a place and a state of mind. We may perhaps want to think of Virgil's underworld in similar terms. He does not give his realm of the dead a rigid geography, as Dante will do, but he does indicate that it is a real place, not a symbol or allegory. It has a specific location, below Cumae. Aeneas' journey through the underworld takes place in real time: when he leaves Deiphobus, the poet notes that it is past midday in the world above.[9] And he feels the need to explain the brilliant light of Elysium: the subterranean paradise has its own sun and stars.[10] This is not his happiest invention —such small-scale, artificial illumination seems like stage-lighting, inevitably inferior to the light of common day—but the fact that he includes it suggests his concern to make the underworld, within the fiction of the poem, actual. These prosaic details do perhaps help to prevent the story collapsing into mere metaphor, with literary allusion and precedent usurping the place of experience; there was a risk of that from the sheer range and disparateness of Virgil's sources.

His ultimate model was the eleventh book of the *Odyssey*, itself a curious mélange of ideas drawn from different places. It begins with necromancy; the spirits of the dead come up from below,

[9] *Aen.* 6. 535 f.   [10] *Aen.* 6. 641.

drink the blood of slaughtered animals, and thereby acquire enough substance to converse with the hero. But this conception seems to slide into that of *katabasis*, the hero's descent into the underworld. Predominantly the notion is that the life of the dead is miserably attenuated, an idea summed up in the declaration of Achilles' ghost that he would rather be a landless peasant upon earth than be king of the dead.[11] Yet at the end, in a passage already suspected as an interpolation in antiquity, we have a quite different conception. The dead no longer come up to taste the blood: we see them in the depths of Erebus, where sinners are punished and the virtuous dead continue in the activities that most delighted them on earth.[12] The islands of the blest have, as it were, been conveyed underground. For our immediate purposes it does not matter whether these oddities are the result of interpolation, multiple authorship or the weaving together of different strands by one ingenious poet. Whatever the case, the same conclusion holds: that out of a certain amount of inconsistency in his model Virgil developed the idea of a realm whose nature seems to fluctuate, sometimes appearing as a solid place beneath the ground, north of Naples, sometimes as an expression of inner experience. But his apprehension of ordinary nature, constantly alive to its imaginative or 'spiritual' dimension, helps him to achieve this blend of the abstract and the actual.

Some have thought that his underworld is purely a symbol or a dream.[13] But if this were so, Virgil would have left out his explanatory mechanisms: he would not have measured Aeneas' journey in space and time or accounted for the light of Elysium. Above all, it is essential to the human drama that there should be other focuses of consciousness besides Aeneas in the underworld. It must be Palinurus, not the figment of another's imagination, who hears the Sibyl's grim warning, whose darkness is lightened just a little by the news of the everlasting fame he shall receive.[14] And the spirit encountered in the Mourning Fields must be Dido, Dido herself. We learn that her sorrows do not leave her even in death;[15] this has no meaning unless

---

[11] *Od.* 11. 489–91.   [12] *Od.* 11. 568 ff.

[13] The fact that Aeneas leaves by one of the gates of dreams (6. 893 ff.) has doubtless encouraged such views. No fully satisfactory explanation of this scene has yet been offered. Some interpretations are prosaic; the more imaginative ones usually founder because they do not explain why, when there are two gates of dreams, it is the gate of false dreams through which Aeneas passes.

[14] *Aen.* 6. 373 ff.   [15] *Aen.* 6. 444.

she has an existence independent of Aeneas. But quite apart from this explicit statement, the terror and beauty of the scene depend on her continued suffering. She keeps her eyes on the ground as he pleads his case, not looking at him; at last—'tandem'—she tears herself away.[16] Evidently she is still in love with him; one word tells us that, and it is enough. What struggle has it cost her not to reply to him? (There is none of the eloquent denunciation that we heard in the fourth book. She cannot trust herself once she speaks, and therefore she says nothing.) Poor Sychaeus, her husband, consoles her in the shadows; how effective is his consolation? These questions get no answers, but they are poignant none the less, and for them to arise Dido (and Sychaeus) must be actual.

It is hardly less important for Aeneas' own experience that he should meet the actual Dido. For she snubs him. Now conscience and vain regret can affect one in various ways, but they cannot exactly snub one. It is essential to this scene—whether or not we detect Aeneas' conscience or remorse within it—that it should be a personal encounter, and one which leaves him in a slightly foolish position, gazing ineffectually after the woman who has scorned him. In plain, vulgar terms Dido, both here and in the fourth book, has upstaged him. Part of the pathos of his position in both places is that he is not only grieved but is also left looking obscurely undignified: on some level this woman has got the better of him. Part of the loneliness of his position in the sixth book is that he has indeed met someone from whom he might have won a response and has failed to do so; it matters greatly that he has been defeated not only (if at all) by remorse or the irrevocability of time but by her. Aeneas is alone: his failure of emotional contact here will be matched by his failure of physical contact in Elysium, when he thrice embraces Anchises' wraith, and there is nothing there.

Indeed the insubstantiality of all the people in the underworld depends for its effect on that underworld itself being actual. If you stab someone in a dream, it does not matter whether he bleeds or vanishes; but if you meet a ghost on the stairs today in your waking life and it walks straight through you, that is a tale worth the telling. So it is with the Greek warriors who squeak or flee at the sight of Aeneas; that is a striking event because they really are Greek warriors.[17] So too when Charon's boat creaks and leaks under Aeneas'

---

[16] *Aen.* 6. 469 ff. ('tandem', 472).   [17] *Aen.* 6. 489 ff.

weight: the dour comedy of that scene depends on the vessel having some solidity but only just enough.[18] And so with Anchises: the scene is one to ravish the senses, and yet within it he is spirit only.

In the early parts of the sixth book, even before Aeneas enters the world of the dead, Virgil prepares for its mysteries. Misenus has died suddenly, and the Trojans go to cut down timber for his pyre. 'Itur in antiquam silvam'—a simple action, simply expressed.[19] Yet the impersonal, passive verb reacts with the adjective to become darkly, multiply suggestive. The passing into the wood becomes an archetypal act, the Trojans' business becomes every man's experience— 'Mi ritrovai in una selva oscura.' Perhaps we reflect that thus men have entered the wood for generations, or we contemplate the contrast between man's brief passage through the trees and their massive, unmeasured duration. 'Itur in *antiquam* silvam, stabula *alta* ferarum'[20]—'altus' is vague, suggesting both the trees' loftiness and the profundity of the forest's interior; as the line is completed, the two adjectives combine to evoke indeterminate extension of height and depth and time. Virgil had a model in some fine lines of Ennius, which begin, 'incedunt arbusta per alta, securibus caedunt' (They advance through the high trees, and cut them down with axes).[21] The comparison shows how Virgil's mood is all his own, though created by very simple means; even as ordinary an epithet as 'altus' gains a large and solemn significance.

We are soon to approach a place where reality and unreality, the palpable and the impalpable will seem to blend together. Again Virgil's mastery of transition is in evidence: his world of the dead will be alien to ordinary experience, and yet it seems to grow out of it and speak to it. The suggestiveness of 'itur in antiquam silvam' is itself prepared. Before he learns of Misenus' death, Aeneas hears from the Sibyl that the underworld is thick with woods. From this thought she slides to the golden bough, which is to be discovered in a wood above ground, in the world of the living; but it grows on a dark tree with dim shadows around it, and it is sacred to 'the Juno of the underworld'.[22] All of this can be taken literally: this is a real wood.

---

[18] *Aen.* 6. 412–14.
[19] *Aen.* 6. 179 (with barbarous literalness, 'There is a going into the ancient wood').
[20] '. . . the high (*or* deep) lairs of beasts'.
[21] *Ann.* 175 ff. Sk. Both Ennius and Virgil have a more remote model in Hom. *Il.* 23. 114 ff. (the preparations for Patroclus' funeral).   [22] *Aen.* 6. 131 ff.

And yet it seems to be merging into the underworld, moving towards mystery. 'alte vestiga,' the Sibyl commands—plain enough language again, but once more suggestive: the depth of the forest and the penetration of the exploring mind fuse.[23] Later, as Aeneas searches for the bough, he speaks of the rich branch that darkens the fertile ground: 'ubi pinguem dives opacat | ramus humum.'[24] Here too the words evoke paradox and mystery. The wealth of the precious metal seems bound in with the richness of the soil, nature and culture blending; 'dives' and 'pinguis' are juxtaposed. It is not sunlight that fertilizes the soil but an obscurely enriching darkness. The bough itself is paradox, organic and metallic, nature and artefact. The solemn play of words that evokes it, 'aura . . . auri' (breath of gold), dissolves its solidity into air.[25]

The preparations for Aeneas' descent are elaborate, the place itself specified: the jagged cave, the lake, the wood, the mephitic vapours.[26] But in the event we never see him make his journey: Virgil turns aside to invoke the gods of the underworld,[27] and when he resumes his narrative after four lines Aeneas and the Sibyl are already below: 'ibant . . .' (they *were* going . . .). This abrupt jump from one place to another has the inconsequence of a dream. So too at the end of the book when they leave through the gate of ivory: we do not know how the Sibyl parts from Aeneas, but suddenly she is no longer there, and he finds himself near his ships, with no mention of the hard ascent threatened earlier in the book.[28] The significance of this is not that the realm of the dead is indeed a dream or a psychological state but rather that it is a part of reality which may at moments feel surreal or insubstantial. As he opens his account of the underworld, Virgil sustains a distinctively strange and elusive atmosphere for some twenty lines and more; he then starts to shift the tone.

He begins with a very strange simile:[29]

> ibant obscuri sola sub nocte per umbram
> perque domos Ditis vacuas et inania regna:
> quale per incertam lunam sub luce maligna
> est iter in silvis, ubi caelum condidit umbra
> Iuppiter, et rebus nox abstulit atra colorem.

---

[23] *Aen.* 6. 145, 'Track (it) deeply'.   [24] *Aen.* 6. 195 f.
[25] *Aen.* 6. 204.   [26] *Aen.* 6. 237–41.   [27] *Aen.* 6. 264 ff.
[28] *Aen.* 6. 893 ff. (cf. 128 f.).   [29] *Aen.* 6. 268–72.

They were passing in the dark, in the lonely night, through the shadows, through the empty house of Dis and his insubstantial realm, like a journey made in woods beneath the grudging light of a fitful moon, when Jupiter has hidden the sky in shadow and black night has stolen the colour from things.

Most similes differ from this one in being unlike the thing to which they are compared. That may sound paradoxical, but it is a demonstrable truth. Take a simple form of Homeric simile: a fighter likened to a lion. In most ways a man does not resemble a lion: he walks on two feet, talks, marries, wears clothes, cooks his food and worships gods; he does not have fur, claws, a tail or a mane. The use of similes is usually to clarify or focus by picking out the one respect, or the few respects, in which two unlike things are like. The man is like a lion because he is fierce, leaps forward, has foam on his jaws, or whatever. There may be several points of comparison, but they will be far fewer than the points of difference. Often it is the case that the more complex or individual the simile, the greater the unlikeness. Homer's Simoeisius is very unlike a poplar, except in the few respects that matter to the poet at the moment of his death; Ajax is very unlike a donkey in a field; Apollo is very unlike a child knocking over a sandcastle.[30] These differences between the comparison and the thing compared do not mean that the simile must be narrow or limited in effect: the simile of the child and the sandcastle shows us much about the gods—their power, destructiveness, indifference, frivolity. Suppose that we substituted a simile that was more like: Apollo destroyed the Achaean wall like a strong man demolishing an earthwork. That is not only dull, but tells us less about Apollo. (In the case of Homer unlikeness commonly has a further expressive effect: most of the *Iliad*'s similes are drawn from nature or peacetime activities, and the horror or cruelty of war is shown through a contrast with a world of creativity, craftsmanship, life, and natural growth.)

Furthermore, the picture within the simile itself is usually clear and expressed in straightforward language. If the simile's function is to order and interpret experience, that is fitting. The picture of child and the sandcastles illuminates Apollo's action because it is so plain. We recognize the scene, and through the clarity of that recognition we find the points of likeness in those very dissimilar agents, playful

[30] *Il.* 4. 482 ff., 11. 558 ff., 15. 361 ff.

child and destroying god; through the picture of an action which we can readily understand and imagine we come to a fuller appreciation of an action that is altogether larger and more mysterious. Again, this does not mean that similes are not suggestive; rather, the suggestiveness depends to some extent on the clarity. It is because the sight of the boy kicking over his castle is so easily grasped in itself that the imagination is free to work, to reflect on how children feel and behave, and thus to learn something about the gods.

The same considerations can be applied to Virgil's use of simile. It is true that he has a liking for the 'multiple-correspondence simile', that is, one in which there are a considerable number of points of resemblance, explicit or implied, between the image and the thing compared.[31] Such similes are not rare in Homer, as it happens, but in the *Aeneid* they are commoner and typically more elaborate in their development. But in even the most elaborate the essential unlikeness is not much affected. Aeneas likens himself watching the fall of his city to a shepherd; the correspondences multiply, but when all is said and done, he is not a shepherd, he is not on a rock, it is not a flood that is destroying Troy; and without such unlikenesses the simile would have little point.[32] Multiple correspondences do tend to bind the simile tightly to the thing compared, but that is a different matter. Perhaps there is even a danger that they may be too tightly constricting, telling the reader too firmly how to interpret and leaving the imagination less room to play freely around the idea. But however many the correspondences, the greater unlikenesses remain in such similes; what of one in which there is hardly any unlikeness at all?

That is what we meet as we enter the underworld. Aeneas and his guide travel through woods in the darkness and the poet tells us that they were like travellers through woods in the darkness. And the picture within the simile is itself blurred or obscured in several ways. The moon is 'incertus'. The language, usually straightforward in similes, is here figurative, using personification and the pathetic fallacy: 'maligna', 'Iuppiter . . . condidit', 'abstulit'. (Malignancy indeed: those verbs suggest, without quite being explicit, a kind of jealousy or hostility in the natural world around Aeneas at this

---

[31] The classic study is D. West, 'Multiple Correspondence Similes in the *Aeneid*', *JRS* 59 (1969), 40–9, reprinted in Harrison, 429–44.
[32] *Aen* 2. 304 ff., admirably analysed by West.

moment.) The baffling impersonality of 'est iter' leaves us wondering who is passing along this difficult path and why. The scene is a depiction of negatives: a light that is virtually no light, a sky that is hidden from sight, a colour taken away.

Later, when Aeneas meets Dido's wraith, Virgil offers another image:[33]

> inter quas Phoenissa recens a vulnere Dido
> errabat silva in magna; quam Troius heros
> ut primum iuxta stetit agnovitque per umbras
> obscuram, qualem primo qui surgere mense
> aut videt aut vidisse putat per nubila lunam,
> demisit lacrimas dulcique adfatus amore est . . .

Among them Phoenician Dido, her wound still fresh, was wandering in the great wood. When the Trojan hero first stood near her and recognized her, dim in the shadows, like one who sees or thinks he sees the moon rising through the clouds when the month is new, he shed tears and spoke with tender words of love . . .

By this time some of the terrible vagueness that haunts the hero's first encounter with the underworld has been resolved; the simile is also more conventional in that it compares unlike things; still, Virgil sustains a careful dimness and continues something of the earlier atmosphere by returning to the wood, the obscurity and that uncertain moon. He has adapted an image from Apollonius' *Argonautica*, where Lynceus spies Heracles in the distance, 'As a man at daybreak sees or thinks he sees the moon through haze.'[34] Though Virgil's words are so similar, his effect is very different. There are clarity, space, and buoyancy in Apollonius' image: fresh light, extreme distance, a world that we know and in which we can feel at ease. Indeed, the simile is to demonstrate the very keenness of Lynceus' vision, whereas Virgil evokes mist and darkness and a troubling loss of clear perception.

The blurring of the comparison and the thing compared is wonderfully effective in the earlier simile of the woodland journey. This is not how similes normally behave, but then we have left the normal world for one where the literal and the figurative cannot always be surely distinguished. On one level Virgil is conveying the sense experience of darkness or uncertain light: he depicts in words a scene of twilit gloom such as a painter might depict on canvas. But

---

[33] *Aen.* 6. 450–5.　　　[34] Ap. Rh. 4. 1479 f.

this depiction of unclarity shades into another idea: an uncertainty not simply about whether things can be perceived or not but about whether they exist at all or which order of existence they belong to. And these two uncertainties provoke a further uncertainty: a doubt as to which of the two uncertainties we are experiencing. The simile, by failing to interpret experience in the expected fashion, deepens the ambiguity about what level of reality we are encountering.

Even the boundaries between the animate and the inanimate start to lose their firmness. Aeneas will find men and women who have lost their bodily substance; they at least are still people, with self-consciousness. But before he sees these ghosts of the dead he passes among ghostlike things that may not be ghosts at all but mere abstractions, Grief, Woes, Age, Fear, and so on.[35] And while these animate or apparently animate beings fade towards insubstantiality, conversely the realm of the inanimate seems to be striving towards sentience. In the woodland simile the light was grudging and night stole the colour from things. Later, Aeneas reaches the Lugentes Campi, the Mourning Plains (the Latin is so phrased that it is as though the landscape itself were lamenting);[36] later still,[37]

> devenere locos laetos et amoena virecta
> fortunatorum nemorum sedesque beatas.

They came to the glad land, the pleasant greenery of the happy groves and the blessed abodes.

Glad places, happy woods, and blessed abodes—after such language, when Anchises speaks of 'laeta arva' we shall feel the double pull of the adjective: 'arva', fields, will awaken the root sense 'fertile', familiar from the *Georgics*, while the memory of 'locos laetos' and other personifications will seem to infuse the ground itself with feeling.[38] Similarly, when Deiphobus speaks of 'tristis . . . domos' (grim abodes), we may wonder if 'tristis' merely connotes visual gloom or reaches further, hinting at a sadness or malignancy, once more, in the very landscape.[39] And what of the 'tacitum nemus' (the silent wood), beside the Styx? is it perhaps 'holding its leaves in silence' like the expectant forest in Euripides' *Bacchae*?[40] A prosaic criticism might say that such phrases are merely compressed, standing for 'plains occupied by those that mourn' or 'groves where the blessed dwell'.

---

[35] *Aen.* 6. 273 ff.   [36] *Aen.* 6. 441.   [37] *Aen.* 6. 638 f.
[38] *Aen.* 6. 744. On 'laetus' in the *Georgics*, see Ch. 7.   [39] *Aen.* 6. 534.
[40] *Aen.* 6. 386 (Eur. *Ba.* 1084 f.; see above, p. 39).

Such explications are correct, on one level; but Virgil has put these phrases in a setting where they hint at more.

At the beginning of the underworld a vivid representation of darkness and emptiness, as we know them through our sense perceptions, merges into the representation of things that cannot normally be perceived, such as Toil, Sicknesses, and Sleep.[41] 'Perque domos Ditis *vacuas* et *inania* regna' maintains a fine ambiguity between physical space that has no contents and something that can hardly be put into words: a space for non-existences, absences or lacks—Fear, Hunger, Need—perhaps even a non-spatial experience altogether, a realm of negatives, of not-being.[42]

'Not-being' may seem an exaggeration. Are these nouns not personifications, embodying abstractions, of a fairly familiar type? After all, we learn that the Sicknesses are pale and Fear and Hunger shapes terrible to behold, 'terribiles visu formae'.[43] But though we hear that the shapes looked frightening, we are not shown how they looked. There is a horror of vagueness: the narrative resists clear apprehensibility for a while, so that it is almost a relief when Discord, concluding the catalogue of abstractions, appears with the conventional apparatus of personified monstrosity: snakes for hair and ribbons stained with blood.[44] The strangeness of Virgil's technique can be seen by comparison with other poets. He includes among the abstractions Sleep who is kin to Death.[45] This pair go back to Homer, but in the *Iliad* they are 'people' who can be bribed with the promise of a golden throne or a fair maiden, or used to carry a dead warrior back to his native land; Virgil turns down the chance of these engaging embellishments.[46] Ovid's personifications are fully realized in physical form, with picturesque details: Hunger is wan, shrunken, and emaciated; Sleep keeps nodding off.[47] These figures were to be the ancestors of Spenser's allegories and Milton's Death. Silius, in a close imitation of Virgil, makes Age querulous and has Envy throttle her own neck.[48] If Virgil himself eschews these macabre charms, it is surely because he has a different purpose, to occupy the uncertain territory between the experience of the senses and the experience of the mind. Are we seeing these abstractions, with Aeneas,

---

[41] *Aen.* 6. 273 ff.   [42] *Aen.* 6. 269, 276.   [43] *Aen* 6. 275, 277.
[44] *Aen.* 6. 281 f.   [45] *Aen.* 6. 278.
[46] *Il.* 14. 231, 238 ff.; 16. 454 ff., 681 ff. Sleep and Death are twin brothers in both Homer and Hesiod (*Th.* 756); Virgil prefers the vaguer 'consanguineus', 'kindred'.
[47] *Met.* 8. 799 ff.; 11. 610 ff. (esp. 619 ff.).   [48] Sil. It. 13. 583 f.

or are we inhabiting for a moment the obscure, inner regions of his instinctual, pre-rational psyche? (It is an advantage for Virgil that, unlike the modern editor, he does not have to choose between majuscule and minuscule letters.) A psychological understanding of the passage is further suggested by one or two small touches. Hunger is 'malesuada Fames' (counselling evil); what unutterable horrors are implied by that rare adjective?[49] Most disturbing of all are the 'evil joys of the mind' (mala mentis | Gaudia).[50] The other abstractions are evils by definition, but joys should be good; the line-ending makes a tiny pause, so that the noun comes with a small stress upon its unexpectedness. What corrupt or perverse passions are wrapped within this opaque phrase? Seneca tried to rationalize it: Virgil's language, he suggested, was eloquent but inaccurate, for nothing bad is a joy; clearly the poet has confused joys with pleasures, which people do pursue at the cost of harm to themselves.[51] But how shallow this bland, sensible logic seems beside Virgil's glance at the dark places of the soul.

The appearance of Discord marks the beginning of a gradual shift towards the more plainly physical, which is at the same time a shift towards traditional mythology; Virgil's mastery of transition is once more in evidence. Discord is still an abstraction, but her snaky hair recalls Medusa, preparing the way for the fee-fi-fo-fum monsters of Greek story who are soon to follow, Briareus, the Chimaera, Gorgons, Harpies, and the rest. These names—they are hardly more—lead on in turn to Charon on the banks of Acheron, a scene which expands into picturesque detail, with mud and whirlpools belching sand. The move from nothingness to a fully physical mythology is now complete. Between Discord and the first of the mythological figures comes the first solid object that we see in the underworld, the elm:[52]

> in medio ramos annosaque bracchia pandit
> ulmus opaca, ingens, quam sedem Somnia vulgo
> vana tenere ferunt, foliisque sub omnibus haerent.

In the middle an elm, shadowy, huge, spreads its boughs and aged limbs. They say that empty Dreams hold to it as their abode and cling under all the leaves.

But though the elm is (presumably) solid, the description resists clarity: 'opaca, ingens' merely produces a large vagueness. The Dreams

[49] *Aen.* 6. 276.   [50] *Aen.* 6. 278 f.   [51] *Epp.* 59. 3.   [52] *Aen.* 6. 282–4.

clinging beneath the leaves are a brilliant stroke: we can hardly resist imagining a mass of spectral, batlike forms. And yet do we see them? Does 'vanus' imply a statement about the nature of dreams—that they are empty—or does it suggest that these apparent beings are non-beings, unrealities? The poet will not even commit himself to the presence of these entities in any sense: 'ferunt' (men say) that they are there. What of Aeneas himself? Does he see them or think he sees them? We do not know.

The vagueness of 'ulmus opaca, ingens' as description is enhanced by the looseness of the syntax and the dark, reverberant sound. Virgil uses this pattern of words several times. Closest to the present passage is Achaemenides' account of the man-eating Cyclops' dreadful cave, 'intus opaca, ingens'. Fama is 'monstrum horrendum, ingens', Latinus' palace is 'tectum augustum, ingens', Turnus picks up a 'saxum antiquum, ingens'.[53] This Virgilian quirk shows again that his way of apprehending ordinary sights and objects enables him to move along a spectrum that passes from plain physical perception to circumstances where things are incompletely perceived (because the scale is too vast, or the light too dim) and even to an area where it grows unclear whether the senses are at work at all or entirely the imagination.

At one end of the spectrum is the rock in the twelfth book. The pair of straightforward epithets suggests a manner of experiencing the world such that even with an object as big, solid and ordinary as a lump of stone, the historic imagination is at the ready. The way in which the sentence unfolds—the noun followed by one adjective, then repeated with two—'picks up' the rock, so to speak, and examines it, searching for the significance in a simple thing:

> nec plura effatus saxum circumspicit ingens,
> saxum antiquum ingens . . .

Saying no more, he looks round and sees a huge stone, a huge, ancient stone . . .

Achaemenides' phrase brings out the vividness of his experience, which requires a certain vagueness in the sense-perception. The Cyclops' cave is full of blood and bones—that is gruesome enough in a predictable way—and then comes the obscurity of 'opaca, ingens'. Fear

---

[53] *Aen.* 3. 619, 'shadowy within, huge'; 4. 181, 'a monster, ghastly and huge'; 7. 170, 'a house venerable and vast'; 12. 897, 'a stone, ancient, huge'.

tries to blot out what it has seen; the mind takes refuge in a sort of nebulous vastness. Paradoxically we see the nightmarishness of the cave more vividly through entering into Achaemenides' experience of trying not to see. (One might compare Virgil's treatment of Tartarus: there were obviously spectacular effects to be had by taking the hero through this place of torment, as Dante's *Inferno* shows, but that is not Virgil's way; instead, Aeneas hears of it from the Sibyl, and we feel the horror of its being kept in a dim dreadful distance.) Latinus' palace is a place where visual perception is necessarily unclear. It has a hundred lofty columns; naturally the eye cannot take them all in. And here, as we shall find later, the sense impression and the imaginative impression come not as rivals or alternatives but blend into each other; the palpable and the impalpable fuse.[54]

And so to the elm: all that we have learnt or felt about woods is now gathered into the presence of a single tree. As with the golden bough, it has no known precedent; the modern reader may think of those great symbolic trees of the northern imagination, Yggdrasil and the World Ash. Fortuitous though these comparisons may be, they do suggest a capacity in Virgil to create objects or symbols with a mythic, archetypal quality. Sometimes seen as an entirely calculating, hypereducated poet, he also has the power to dig down to the deep, instinctive roots. Why should dreams be clinging in swarms to the dark undersides of an elm-tree's leaves? There is no rational explanation, but we know that Virgil's invention 'tells'.

The combination of elm and dreams, unrealities attached to an object, is part of the transition from abstractions to the monsters of Greek myth. These latter are existences with (we suppose) the power of consciousness but without solidity, 'tenuis sine corpore vitas'.[55] But they seem solid enough for Aeneas to draw his sword against them, whereas we do not hear of him taking a weapon to Grief and Care, and could hardly imagine it. However, Virgil is still using words that might seem ambiguous between existence without material solidity and the illusion of existence: 'umbra' and 'forma' each twice, the latter coming the second time in a negative phrase, 'cava sub imagine formae', 'under the hollow semblance of shape'.[56] From this indeterminate kind of existence, actual, visible, but without bulk and suggestive of illusion, the final transition is made to an area

---

[54] See below, p. 486.   [55] *Aen.* 6. 292, 'thin lives without body'.
[56] *Aen.* 6. 289, 294, 289, 293.

where physical qualities are to the fore: the slime, the river, and the grotesque appearance of Charon.

Scholars have from time to time tried to divide Virgil's under-world into sections differentiated by the character of their source material: popular, mythological, Homeric, philosophical, or what-ever.[57] But the poetry resists such compartmentalization: though one type of source or influence may be especially prominent in a par-ticular area of the narrative, Virgil interweaves the strands he has drawn from diverse places. And thus the region of the blessed, though in one sense sharply different from what has gone before, grows out of it as a seemingly natural development. At the same time, by bind-ing together his imagination of the concrete and the abstract, he creates a huge sense of enlargement and liberation when we reach Elysium. The mythology does not disappear: it remains the frame-work, but is now seen as part of a greater whole. It is not true that the underworld can be apportioned into two sections, the first con-cerned with the past, the other with the future, though it may fairly be said that there is a greater stress on the past earlier, and on the future in the later stages. When Aeneas enters Elysium, the entire historical perspective widens: he will see further into time to come than ever before, right up to the poet's own day, but first and imme-diately he sees further back into the past than before, to figures ancient not only to us but even to himself:[58]

> hic genus antiquum Teucri, pulcherrima proles,
> magnanimi heroes nati melioribus annis,
> Ilusque Assaracusque et Troiae Dardanus auctor.

We have already observed how Virgil adapts a line of Homer to con-vey a thrust back to a remote antiquity. And this temporal expan-sion is matched by an expansion in terms of space. Tartarus was a prison, and its characteristic was fixity, summed up in the terrible words telling of Theseus, 'sedet aeternumque sedebit'.[59] By contrast, the happy existence is space and free movement: as Musaeus declares, in the first words that Aeneas hears from a blessed spirit, 'nulli

---

[57] For discussion and criticism of this approach, see F. Solmsen in 'The World of the Dead in Book 6 of the *Aeneid*', *CP* 67 (1972), 31–41, reprinted in Harrison, 208–23.

[58] *Aen.* 6. 648–50, translated and discussed above, p. 385.

[59] *Aen.* 6. 617, '. . . sits and shall sit for ever'. Dante shares this conception: goodness is energy, and therefore Satan, the lowest evil, is fixed in frozen immobility. Contrariwise, Milton's Satan is energetic and resourceful, and therefore so formidable a foe.

certa domus' (None has a fixed home).[60] For the hero himself movement has at last become simple: before the journey was hard, as Anchises tells him, but now Musaeus will set him on an easy path, 'facili iam tramite sistam'.[61] There is more in that 'iam' than the speaker knows: through our own sense that the path has finally been made smooth, after so much endured, we feel the relief, and the achievement.

And there is yet a third kind of enlargement, in knowledge and understanding. Hitherto the Sibyl has been terse, or spoken with a seeming reluctance, as Virgil has indicated through such phrases as 'pressoque obmutuit ore', 'breviter fata est Amphrysia vates';[62] but now Anchises will pour forth revelation. And this abstract enlightenment is matched by a literal radiance, in sudden contrast to the shadows in which Aeneas has wandered so long: 'largior hic campos aether et lumine vestit | purpureo' (Here an ampler air clothes the fields in rosy light).[63] And just as the mental enlightenment is paralleled by the physical brightness, so conversely the physical light has a metaphorical or imaginative dimension, being infused with suggestions of the pathetic fallacy: 'largior' hints at this, with its connotations of generosity, abundance, and vigour. Lucretius had seen the quality of this adjective when he called the sun 'largus . . . fons luminis' (the generous fountain of light), surrounding the phrase with words expressing flow, quantity, and perennity, and giving light the weight and immediate apprehensibility of liquid.[64] Here in the *Aeneid* the sense of a kindness in the air itself is created by the combination of 'largior' with 'vestit' (clothes), not a new metaphor, but especially effective here.[65] After the long darkness, the sudden radiance feels so warming, so enveloping, that it may well seem to have the density of clothing. After regions where even bodies proved to lack substance, the contrast is telling with a place where even the air gives an impression of solidity. And in a realm where the bounds between metaphor and actuality, animate and inanimate are always

---

[60] *Aen.* 6. 673. It is very hard to depict paradise without insipidity; Milton too uses movement to help bring off the trick (*Lycidas* 178–80): 'There entertain him all the saints above, | In solemn troops, and sweet societies | That sing, and singing in their glory move . . .'
[61] *Aen.* 6. 688, 676.
[62] *Aen.* 6. 155, 'she spoke, and fell silent, lips tight'; 6. 398, 'the Amphrysian prophetess spoke briefly'.
[63] *Aen.* 6. 640 f.
[64] Lucr. 5. 281–3, quoted above, p. 235.
[65] Austin ad loc. cites examples of the metaphor from Lucretius and (repeatedly) Cicero's *Aratea*. The association of purple with fine raiment is not easily conveyed in translation.

liable to blur, it is fitting that the landscape itself should be 'moral-ized' and suffuse benevolence.

How is a poet to portray paradise without making it seem vapid, dull, or pompous? Virgil's answer is to depict a mixture of cere-mony and informality. There is dignity and splendour, but also young men playing games, and picnics, and shady groves and meadows beside fresh waters, where the banks swell into cushioning shapes.[66] This is ennobled pastoral. In the fifth Eclogue the shepherd Daphnis was taken into Olympus; now the pastoral idea itself is apotheosized. Eridanus flows through the wood; the presence of this legendary river, later identified with the Po, as by Virgil himself in the *Georgics*, blends myth and reality, the mysterious and the known.[67] There is even a various landscape, not only level grass and sand and a laurel grove but hills and deep valleys and 'summa cacumina', which would seem to mean 'peaks' or 'mountain tops' or at least a high ridge falling steeply to the vale below.[68] Even in the land where life is easy Virgil's imagination requires the blessed existence to be set in a beautiful and diverse scenery, although those high hills may sound strenuous.

His picture of Elysium grows out of the old idea that the fortu-nate dead enjoy the pastimes that most pleased them when alive. Thus in the *Odyssey* Heracles is seen feasting with fair-limbed Hebe, Minos the good king is judging, Orion is hunting; and in a fragment of Pindar, 'Some enjoy themselves with horses and sports, some with draughts, some with lyres.'[69] But there is something in Virgil which we do not quite find in any Greek account: the apo-theosis of the ordinary or modest. Lucretius had described the life of herdsmen as an idyll of food and music and repose on the grass by running water, touching it with sanctity in the phrase 'otia dia'.[70] Virgil too had learnt to irradiate simple things, simple experiences. Elysium is as the mirror-image of this: a transfigured world suffused with the ordinary. His way of apprehending the real world, known through daily experience, has now given him the capacity to human-ize this imaginary world without diminishing its quality of mystery, otherness, and splendour.

---

[66] *Aen.* 6. 642 f., 656 f., 673–5. [67] *Aen.* 6. 659 (cf. *Geo.* 1. 481–3).
[68] *Aen.* 6. 642 f., 658, 676, 679, 703, 678.
[69] *Od.* 11. 568 ff., 601 ff.; Pi. fr. 114 Bowra.
[70] Lucr. 5. 1384 ff., quoted above, p. 280.

CHAPTER II

A Trojan in Italy: Latinus' Kingdom

> O Mensch! Gib acht!
> Was spricht die tiefe Mitternacht?
> 'Ich schlief, ich schlief—
> Aus tiefem Traum bin ich erwacht:—
> Die Welt ist tief,
> Und tiefer als der Tag gedacht . . .'
>
> (Nietzsche)

> *Wanderer.*
> Allwissende!
> Urweltweise!
> Erda! Erda!
> Ewiges Weib!
> Wache, du Wala! erwache!
>
> (Wagner)

The second half of the A*eneid* begins strangely:[1]

> tu quoque litoribus nostris, Aeneia nutrix,
> aeternam moriens famam, Caieta, dedisti;
> et nunc servat honos sedem tuus, ossaque nomen
> Hesperia in magna, si qua est ea gloria, signat.

You too, Caieta, Aeneas' nurse, have in dying given an everlasting fame to our shores; and even now the honour paid you clings to your resting-place, and in great Hesperia, if such renown be anything, your name marks your bones.

The grand invocation to the Muse is postponed, and Virgil starts instead with a tiny incident—a paragraph of a mere four lines. Moreover, there is a small breach of epic decorum in the very first line: 'litoribus *nostris*' (*our* shores). The epic poet is conventionally objective—one may read Homer through from end to end without ever hearing that the poet is Greek. Only once again in the *Aeneid*

---

[1] *Aen.* 7. 1–4.

will Virgil speak in the first person: in the passionate lines of the ninth book where he assures the dead Nisus and Euryalus that if his songs have any power their names will endure as long as the Capitol.[2] That is an emphatic passage; here, however, the first person is slipped in almost casually. The seventh and eighth books are those in which, above all, Virgil unfolds to us the land of Italy. Quietly he lets us know, at the very start, that we are not to view this ancient landscape dispassionately: we are to be engaged with it and its people, for this is our own land, it is familiar.

But almost at once the pendulum swings back in the other direction, as 'litoribus nostris' is balanced by the contrasting 'Hesperia in magna'. And now we see Italy not through our own but through Caieta's eyes. Virgil is here treating a theme which is common enough in classical poetry: in Apollonius' *Argonautica*, for example, Jason presses Medea to help him with these words:[3]

In future time I will render thanks to you for your help, as is right and proper for those who live far off to do, giving you a fair name and glory; the other heroes too will celebrate you, when they return to Greece, as will their wives and mothers . . .

But Virgil has infused this theme with a new subjectivity and pathos. It does not cross Jason's mind—nor, it would seem, Apollonius'—that Hellas is nothing to Medea; but Virgil understands that if we desire renown, we do not desire it as a piece of real estate, from which profit may be drawn no matter where it is situated. For Caieta Hesperia is, as it was for Creusa, an alien shore, a land away in the west, far from the Trojan home.[4] In the *Georgics* Virgil made us see the familiar as strange; the effect here is quite different, and yet curiously similar: for through new means he is once again enlarging our experience by making us look with a fresh eye upon customary things. And again there are both detachment and commitment; we feel the shore to be our own, and yet we look upon it with the eye of a stranger.

The mood is elusive: on the one hand, the tone is sonorous, the language grand: 'Aeneia nutrix', 'aeternam . . . famam', 'Hesperia in magna'. But into the midst of these resonant affirmations a small parenthesis is pressed shyly forward: 'si qua est ea gloria'. On the surface that is an understatement: everlasting fame in a mighty nation— is there any glory in that? Of course there is.

[2] *Aen.* 9. 446–9.   [3] Ap. Rh. 3. 990–4.   [4] See above, p. 407.

And yet we hear another note also. The very simplicity of the modest parenthesis (its plain diction in contrast with the sonorousness around it), the questioning note of 'si' (we may recall how subtly that little conjunction was used in the second Georgic),[5] the humble rank of Caieta herself (no great hero this, merely Aeneas' old nurse, a slave), the tininess of the paragraph as a whole—all these make the mood feel tentative, hesitant.

Virgil later uses a similar phrase, in the words which Aeneas speaks over Lausus' dead body:[6]

> teque parentum
> manibus et cineri, *si qua est ea cura*, remitto.

I hand you back to the spirits and ashes of your fathers, if such a care is anything to you.

Here the voice of doubt is plain. Will the victor's generosity mean anything to the dead man's shade?—Aeneas does not know. And as we read of Caieta's distinction, we may think back to two others who have also recently received the honour of giving their names to promontories. Misenus is buried with pomp and ceremony, but his dust has no sense of them: 'cineri *ingrato* suprema ferebant'.[7] Palinurus is promised 'aeternum nomen', like Caieta's 'aeterna fama', and he rejoices that land is to bear his name; yet this too is an ambivalent passage. He has just heard from the Sibyl that there can be no remission of his innocent suffering. She offers him the tidings that a cape will commemorate him as comfort in his hard lot, 'duri solacia casus'. His cares are taken away and pain is driven from his heart 'parumper', for a while.[8] The happiness is real, but how long will it last?

There are certainly differences between Caieta's death and each of these other passages. We know ashes to be insensible; that does not mean that Misenus' spirit has no afterlife. Aeneas is genuinely doubtful whether the dead Lausus has any care for the fate of his corpse; but that Caieta is much honoured there can be no doubt. If we press for an answer to the question implied in the words 'si qua est ea gloria', there can be only one: yes, there is renown. Palinurus, we may recall, with much greater cause for grief than Caieta, did none the less rejoice that his name would endure. But to press so hard is to be false to the spirit of these lines. Their ambivalence is

---

[5] See above, p. 375.   [6] *Aen.* 10. 827 f.
[7] *Aen.* 6. 213, 'They were paying the last rites to his ungrateful ashes'.
[8] *Aen.* 6. 376–83.

of a subtle kind. Virgil does not retreat into an easy agnosticism: the note of affirmation remains, but it is shadowed by a delicate pathos. What is the worth of honour in far Hesperia to poor Caieta? The question is not trivial; but the honour abides none the less.

We have heard nothing of Caieta hitherto, and we shall never hear of her again; her very unimportance, matching the littleness of the passage as a whole, is a part of the pathos. Still, her death has a special significance for Aeneas. Gently, almost imperceptibly, his last link with his Trojan past is dissevered. He has lost Creusa; he has just taken leave of Anchises for ever; and now this other guardian of his childhood, his nurse, has perished. Of his family only Ascanius remains, and Virgil uses him to represent rather the future than the past, while Aeneas' companions have small emotional significance within the poem. His experience of Italy is about to begin, and as we shall discover, it will prove not a static experience but a process: he will grow into Italy. That process is still in the future; at present Italy is still an alien shore. But at this moment he finds himself alone as never before, his father and his surrogate mother lost to him at almost the same time; orphaned in all but name, he stands emotionally empty, ready for the discovery of a new kind of ancestry in a new land.

One and a half lines see Caieta buried; the sea falls calm, and Aeneas sets sail.[9]

> aspirant aurae in noctem nec candida cursus
> luna negat, splendet tremulo sub lumine pontus.
> proxima Circaeae raduntur litora terrae,   10
> dives inaccessos ubi Solis filia lucos
> adsiduo resonat cantu, tectisque superbis
> urit odoratam nocturna in lumina cedrum
> arguto tenuis percurrens pectine telas.
> hinc exaudiri gemitus iraeque leonum   15
> vincla recusantum et sera sub nocte rudentum,
> saetigerique sues atque in praesepibus ursi
> saevire ac formae magnorum ululare luporum,
> quos hominum ex facie dea saeva potentibus herbis
> induerat Circe in vultus ac terga ferarum.   20
> quae ne monstra pii paterentur talia Troes
> delati in portus neu litora dira subirent,
> Neptunus ventis implevit vela secundis,
> atque fugam dedit et praeter vada fervida vexit.

[9] *Aen.* 7. 8–24.

The breeze blows on into the night, nor does the bright moon forbid voyaging, and the sea shines in the quivering light. Closely they skirt the shore of Circe's land, where the wealthy daughter of the Sun makes her unapproachable groves resound with her unceasing song, and in her proud halls burns scented cedar to turn it into nocturnal light, as with whistling shuttle she sweeps across the fine web. Here could be heard the growls and anger of lions chafing at their chains and roaring in the late night hours; bristling boars and bears in their cages raged and the shapes of great wolves howled—creatures whom Circe with her potent herbs had changed from the likeness of men and clothed in the features and hides of beasts. Lest the good Trojans, borne into harbour, should suffer such weirdness or draw close to this dreadful shore, Neptune filled their sails with favouring winds, gave them their escape and carried them past the seething shallows.

Yet once more Virgil's masterly control of transition is in evidence. The sixth book has ended in mystery, with the passing of Aeneas and the Sibyl through the gate of false dreams and her sudden, unexplained disappearance. By postponing the invocation which we might have expected at the beginning of the book Virgil lets the atmosphere of wonder linger on.[10] Even something of the underworld's strangeness remains a while: the Trojans approach Latium by night, and as in the sixth book, the travellers pass through darkness before emerging into a radiance of peace and light.[11] The moon lights them upon their way: we shall hardly forget how evocatively Virgil used the moon in the sixth book to conjure up the mysterious troubling half light of the world of shades.[12] Circe herself seems to partake of this underworld atmosphere. The good Trojans, 'pii Troes', sail past her in safety; the mention of their virtue at this point implies that she can only turn men into beasts by working upon their lusts and passions. Like the great sinners of the underworld, her victims suffer for their wrongdoing; and like those great sinners, we may not see them face to face; instead, they are kept obscure, in a dark and awful distance. The very form of the narrative enhances the atmosphere; the episode of Caieta, so tiny, so tentative, assists a mood tremulous with wonder and expectancy.

Even without Virgil's subtle preparations, the Trojans' passage up the Latian coast would be strange and wondrous enough; the

---

[10] The repetition of the name Caieta, first as a place, then as a person, in 6. 900 and 7. 2, strengthens the link.
[11] The dawn rises at 25 ff.　　[12] See above, pp. 453 f.

moonlight trembling upon the waters, the impenetrable forest, songs and rich odours from a source unseen, the roaring of lions, the howling of bears, wolves' ululations—this is familiar, homely Latium turned strange indeed. In Conrad's story *Youth* Marlow describes the east: 'Suddenly a puff of wind, a puff faint and tepid and laden with strange odour of blossoms, of aromatic wood, comes out of the still night —the first sigh of the East on my face . . . The scented obscurity of the shore was grouped into vast masses, a density of colossal clumps of vegetation, probably—mute and fantastic shapes.' With no knowledge of the orient, with an apprehension of the exotic derived from imagination, not personal knowledge, Virgil yet has access to archetypal human experience: he knows the rightness of combining darkness and scents (aromatic wood—even that detail is common to Virgil and the so different Conrad) and shoreline and the density of forests. Literature and experience worked together upon Virgil's imagination, but if we seek a Homeric ancestry for this passage, it is not so much to the tangled scrub around Circe's palace that we should turn as to Ogygia, Calypso's isle.[13] Though both Circe and Calypso sit at their looms and sing as they work, in the *Odyssey* it is Calypso alone who burns scented cedar, as does Virgil's Circe. But it is less in the individual details that Calypso inspired Virgil than in the expressive use of landscape. In the *Odyssey* Calypso's surroundings merge into her own nature in a way that Circe's do not. Heavy with perfume, thickly embowered in trees, Calypso's cave breathes an atmosphere strange, remote, and passionate. Calypso's name presents her as the Concealer; the name of Latium was derived by Varro from 'latere', to lie hid, an etymology to which Virgil refers in his eighth book;[14] an association of ideas, conscious or unconscious, may have been working on him here. Of course there are many differences between the two poets: the sombre sonority of line 13, with its synaesthesia of scent and sight, is more thickly sensuous than anything in Ogygia; the cry of beasts replaces Homer's birdsong; the long *u* sounds that recur especially from line 15 onward enhance a scene more uncanny and sinister than in the *Odyssey*. But for Virgil emulation and invention go hand in hand.

The sun rises and the Trojans see the mouth of the Tiber for the first time:[15]

---

[13] See above, pp. 29, 30 (Circe singing at the loom, *Od.* 10. 221–3; Calypso likewise, with scented cedar burning, 5. 59 ff.).

[14] *Aen.* 8. 323 (Varro is cited by Servius ad loc.).　　[15] *Aen.* 7. 25–36.

iamque rubescebat radiis mare et aethere ab alto   25
Aurora in roseis fulgebat lutea bigis,
cum venti posuere omnisque repente resedit
flatus, et in lento luctantur marmore tonsae.
atque hic Aeneas ingentem ex aequore lucum
prospicit. hunc inter fluvio Tiberinus amoeno   30
verticibus rapidis et multa flavus harena
in mare prorumpit. variae circumque supraque
adsuetae ripis volucres et fluminis alveo
aethera mulcebant cantu lucoque volabant.
flectere iter sociis terraeque advertere proras   35
imperat et laetus fluvio succedit opaco.

And now the sea was reddening with the sun's rays and saffron Aurora
from the high heaven was shining in her rosy chariot, when the winds
fell and every breath suddenly sank down and the oars struggle in the sluggish waters. Here Aeneas looks from the sea upon a vast forest. Through
it with fine flow Tiber, yellow with much sand and with swirling eddies,
bursts out into the sea. Around and above the diverse birds that haunt the
banks and river bed were soothing the air with their song and flying through
the forest. Aeneas orders his companions to change their course and turn
their prows to land, and joyfully enters the dark river.

Characteristically Virgil brings up the dawn gradually.[16] It is characteristic too that he takes a subjective stance: 'Aeneas . . . prospicit'
—we are to share the hero's experience, see through his eyes. The
familiar thus becomes strange in a double fashion. History makes
it strange: for this huge forest, empty of humanity, is on the site of
Ostia, which Virgil's readers know as one of the most busy and
populous spots in all Italy. And geography too has a transforming
power, since this familiar coastline is for Aeneas the Trojan the first
sight of *terra incognita*. It is easy for us to miss Virgil's originality here,
for we have been brought up on the annals of exploration, with
the first sightings of a new world or a savage shore. Virgil's reading
cannot have offered him anything much resembling African travels or
the discovery of the Americas; yet he turns the Latian coast into a
mysterious jungle, with father Tiber, like some Congo or Limpopo,
bursting through the trees from out of an unknown interior.[17]

[16] 'Rubesco', found once in the *Georgics* and thrice in the *Aeneid*, is one of five inceptive verbs that appear first in Virgil. On his use of inceptive verbs of colour, see above,
p. 202.
[17] This effect will be more pronounced still in the eighth book; see below, p. 535.

The effect is conjured by a few unobtrusive touches. The dawn glitters with the formal panoply of Greek mythology and literary culture. The Italian shore is dark and dense (the darkness of the river at line 36 evokes the thickness of the forest); and there seems to be no sign of a human presence. The blend of radiance and sombreness, Grecian and Italic, the glamour of poetic civility and the glamour of the undiscovered, creates an atmosphere of impalpable romance. 'Varius' is an epithet that Virgil likes to apply to bright contrasts of colour;[18] the strict meaning in the present passage is 'birds of various kinds', but in the picturesque context the use of the adjective seems to hint at a splash of semi-exoticism (the word recurs, indeed, in the jungly description of the river Tiber in the eighth book).[19] This is further enhanced by lines 33 f.—the birds soothing the air with their song—with its lush mixture of synaesthesia and the pathetic fallacy.

Woodland and darkness are related as part of a complex of images and ideas, fertile in associations, which will be developed in the course of the Italian books. The paragraph ends, unexpectedly, with an adjective, 'opaco'. But this lack of light is not frightening or threatening, for balancing 'opaco' is another adjective, 'laetus'. Somehow this inspissated darkness is safe and consoling: it is as if Aeneas has come home. And so indeed he has: this is the land of his earliest ancestors and, as he declares after the portent of the tables, 'hic domus, haec patria est.'[20] We have seen the familiar as strange; but also, entering into Aeneas' experience, we feel the opposite as well: to him there is something deep, mysteriously familiar about this landscape never seen before. Later in the book Juno says of the Trojans, 'optato conduntur Thybridis alveo | securi pelagi atque mei' (They are sheltered in the longed-for bed of the Tiber, safe from the sea and me).[21] 'Condere' is a word of several meanings, to hide, to found, to bury. Enhanced by the context created by scenes and images in the earlier part of the book, this sentence evokes darkness, safety (this is made explicit by the word 'securi'), a firm rootedness in the physical

---

[18] 'varios . . . colores' is found at *Ed.* 4. 42, *Geo.* 1. 452, *Aen.* 4. 701, 5. 89; cf. *Ed.* 9. 40 and *Geo.* 2. 463, where colour effects are evidently indicated.

[19] *Aen.* 8. 95. 'variae volucres' is Lucretius' phrase (1. 589, 2. 344) and has already been adopted by Virgil in the *Georgics* (1. 383). (In each case Lucretius has the adjective and noun together and Virgil separates them, a nice illustration of the difference in style between the two poets.)

[20] *Aen.* 7. 122 (Here is our home, this is our fatherland).   [21] *Aen.* 7. 303 f.

substance of Italy. 'Alveus' is closely related to 'alvus', 'womb'; the 'fluminis alveus' was mentioned at line 33 just before Aeneas' entry into the mouth of the dark river. It is surely not fanciful to feel the safe, ancestral darkness into which he passes as womblike, and it is appropriate to the mixture of strangeness and familiarity in his experience, for the womb is the most intimate home that we have ever had, and the most unknown.

The Italy that Virgil unfolds in the seventh and eighth books is, like the Italy of the *Georgics*, diverse, though this time the emphasis falls more especially on the diversity of the peoples who inhabit it than on the variety of soil and landscape. The wild forest gives way to the city of Latinus, where the stress is on wealth, grandeur and a civilization rooted in a long past. Latinus' rustic subjects, Tyrrhus' family and their neighbours, live by contrast in a style and setting that have affinities with the *Eclogues*; Evander's Pallanteum has its own different and distinctive atmosphere, a blend of simplicity and heroic dignity. Evander's people import one kind of Greekness into their new land, blurred at the edges and merging into the old Italy; the city of Diomedes down in the south presents a Greekness of another kind, freshly arrived and still sharply separate.

This pleasure in diversity spreads into the catalogue of Italian forces that concludes the seventh book. In place of the dry unyielding uniformity of his model, Homer's catalogue of ships, Virgil seeks a delicate fluctuation of tone, from Grecian to native, from grand to modest, from realism to fantasy.[22] Some of the warriors are given origins out of Greek mythology, but Caeculus' followers are rustic and primitive, while Clausus is all-Italian, of ancient Sabine blood, the ancestor of Roman aristocrats. Ufens and his men are reivers, rough sons of the soil, whereas Umbro, a priest gifted with magical powers, is decorated with a fantasy out of pastoral: when he dies, the woods and lakes of Italy will weep for him.[23] It is not that the various elements of ancient Italy are sharply separated; rather there is a blend, with different aspects highlighted in different places.

As he introduces this human geography of Italy, Virgil associates it, characteristically, with the theme of time and history:[24]

[22] This is analysed by R. D. Williams, 'The Function and Structure of Virgil's Catalogue in *Aeneid* 7', CQ NS 11 (1961), 146–53.
[23] *Aen.* 7. 678 ff., 706 ff., 744 ff., 750 ff.   [24] *Aen.* 7. 641–6.

> pandite nunc Helicona, deae, cantusque movete,
> qui bello exciti reges, quae quemque secutae
> complerint campos acies, quibus Itala iam tum
> floruerit terra alma viris, quibus arserit armis;
> et meministis enim, divae, et memorare potestis;
> ad nos vix tenuis famae perlabitur aura.

Now open Helicon, goddesses, and begin the song of what kings were stirred to war, what troops followed each to fill the field, with what men the nurturing land of Italy flowered even then, with what weaponry it blazed; for you remember, goddesses, and you can recall; to us there wafts barely a thin breeze of tale.

This invocation too imitates the catalogue in the *Iliad*:[25]

Tell me now, Muses who have your homes on Olympus (for you are goddesses, you are present, and know all things, while we hear report only and know nothing), who were the leaders and lords of the Danaans.

But the mood is very different. Homer is lucid, factual and absolute: the goddesses are present and know everything; men know nothing. Virgil softens the distinction between omniscience and ignorance. His Muses remember and recollect; for them, as for us, these events are way back in the past. We, for our part, do in some sense have an experience of past history: that breeze is light, but we can feel it.

It is this brilliant metaphor of the breeze that most transforms Homer's idea. On the one hand it suggests the remoteness of this ancient time: it has had to travel so far that it is faint, and it only just reaches us: 'vix', 'tenuis'. That reflection evokes a cultivated melancholy of which there is no trace in Homer's words. And yet that soft air on our faces is surely inviting; we are enticed into enjoying the romance of the past and finding a charm in the very fact that it is so distant and hazily known.

Virgil's sense of history is more robustly expressed in the preceding lines. The two little words 'iam tum' convey both change and continuity. They assert the distance of this early age—how striking that *already* Italy should be flourishing with brave men—but at the same time we recognize in these warriors of a time long gone a people that we know: they are our people, the good old Italians praised in the *Georgics*, by Horace, and in a hundred and one other places. And as in the *Georgics*, Virgil also binds the people to their

---

[25] *Il.* 2. 484–7.

earth. 'Floruerit terra alma viris'—every one of those words is alive and working. The Lucretian adjective 'almus' joins with the idea, also from Lucretius, of the land 'flowering' with men as with plants and crops. But distinctively Virgilian is the further fusion of this communion of man and nature with time, history and nationhood. This nexus of sentiments, already adumbrated in the third Georgic, will be developed in the books that follow.

A feeling for the mingled romance and obscurity of the past has already been suggested in the passage which first introduces Latinus:[26]

> rex arva Latinus et urbes
> iam senior longa placidas in pace regebat.
> hunc Fauno et nympha genitum Laurente Marica
> accipimus; Fauno Picus pater, isque parentem
> te, Saturne, refert, tu sanguinis ultimus auctor.

King Latinus, now old, ruled lands and cities in a long peace. We are told that he was born of Faunus and the Laurentine nymph Marica; Faunus' father was Picus, who claims you, Saturn, as his parent; you are the ultimate originator of the line.

'Accipimus', 'refert'—we are *told* that Latinus was the son of Faunus and Marica; Picus *claims* Saturn as his father. To say that Virgil is taking a formula from the Alexandrian poets, whose concern for 'scholarship' led them to note that they spoke with the authority of tradition, is at best a half truth: he picks up the Hellenistic motif only to transform it, for the weight here is not upon certainty or authority but rather on the distance of the past and the unclarity with which we perceive it.[27] We shall find that his whole presentation of Latinus is marked by his mastery of a controlled imprecision.[28]

Latinus, as we meet him in the *Aeneid*, is essentially Virgil's own creation; all other sources present him in a very different light. The name occurs earliest in Hesiod's *Theogony*, where he is the son of Circe and Odysseus; when we first find him linked to the Aeneas legend, in the third-century historian Callias, he marries one of the newly arrived Trojans and has three sons by her.[29] The sources more

---

[26] *Aen.* 7. 45–9.

[27] Virgil may have been influenced by Catullus 64. That poem, which recurs to what 'they say' ('dicuntur' (are said) comes as early as the second line), already delights in the remoteness of legend (see further Jenkyns, *Three Classical Poets* (London, 1982), 99).

[28] 'Controlled imprecision', 'calculated imprecision'—the phrases are W. R. Johnson's, and so apt that plagiarism becomes a duty.

[29] Hes. *Th.* 1011 ff.; Callias ap. Dion. Hal. *Ant. Rom.* 1. 72. 5 (= *FGH* 564. 5).

or less contemporary with Virgil—Livy, Strabo, and Dionysius of
Halicarnassus—broadly agree: Latinus pledges Lavinia to Aeneas, and
they ally to make war upon the Rutulians.[30] Livy mentions a variant
of the story in which a war between Trojans and Latins precedes the
alliance of Aeneas and Latinus and conflict with Turnus.[31] In Strabo
and Dionysius' accounts Latinus is killed in battle; this had also been
Cato's story.[32] Much later Ascanius wages war on Mezentius.

The general picture is clear. Virgil alone places Latinus in the opposite camp from Aeneas throughout the war; only Virgil and Livy do
not have him killed in battle, and Virgil alone sweeps him away from
the battlefield altogether; he also makes him aged, which is surprising
in a man with a single nubile daughter. Moreover, the curious genealogy with which he supplies Latinus is presumably his own invention. He has compressed a series of two or more wars into a single
campaign only a few days in length; that was only to be expected,
for reasons of narrative economy. But the other changes require a
different explanation.

One of the sorrows of Aeneas' situation is that he seems, in the
words of the old cliché, to see history repeating itself. A second Achilles
awaits in Latium, as the Sibyl grimly tells him.[33] That is but half the
story, as we know and as Aeneas will learn: Turnus, the second Achilles,
will prove in the end to be a second Hector, doomed to defeat at
Aeneas' hands, while Aeneas himself will not only conquer but see
Trojans and Italians bound together in an eternal peace.[34] Still, on
the immediate view the cycle of suffering seems to keep turning
ever onward, and it is part of the hero's burden that wherever he goes
he brings unintended destruction with him. By coming to Carthage
he causes Dido's death—and he never meant to; by killing Silvia's
stag, his son will set off war in Latium—and he never meant to; a
succession of lovely and admirable young men will perish—Lausus,
Euryalus, Pallas, Turnus, the maiden Camilla also—and it all seems
so wasteful and unnecessary. Aeneas has mourned Hector's death; soon
it will be his task to slay the new Hector, Turnus. All these things

---

[30] Livy 1. 1–3; Strabo C 229 (= 5. 3. 2); Dion. Hal. *Ant. Rom.* 1. 57–9.

[31] Livy 1. 1. 6. (Two notes in Servius (*in Aen.* 1. 267, 4. 620) cite Cato for another
variant in which Aeneas first fought Latinus before joining with him to fight Turnus. But
the version in our Augustan prose sources, more or less, is attributed to Cato by Servius
in Aen. 6. 760 and cited by Servius auctus, without attribution, *in Aen.* 1. 259. There may
be some garbling here.)   [32] Serv. locc. cit.

[33] *Aen.* 6. 89.   [34] *Aen.* 12. 504.

are only sorrows to him, of course, because he is himself admirable, a man of reflective compassion; it is a subtlety of the poet's to bring us to a sympathy with his hero by the way in which he writes of other people.

Let us now look at Latinus too through Aeneas' eyes. The ruler of a powerful kingdom, the possessor of a great and civilized city, having reigned in peace for so long only to see death and destruction brought upon his country in the time of his old age, he is bound to recall Priam. Perhaps we shall ourselves think as much of Homer's Priam as of Virgil's. In the *Iliad* we are reminded of Troy's past prosperity and tranquillity: as Achilles chases Hector around the walls of the city they pass the troughs where the women of Troy used to wash their shining robes, in the time of peace, before the Achaeans came.[35] And in their first and final encounter, Achilles tells Priam,[36]

We hear tell that you too, *old man, had fortune formerly*; in all the land that Lesbos out to sea, the realm of Macar, and Phrygia inland and the boundless Hellespont contain, they say that you, *old man*, exceeded all in *wealth and sons*. But now that the heavenly gods have brought this woe on you, you have always *fighting and the killing of men* around your *city*.

Now Aeneas has himself told us of great Priam's humiliation, and with much pathos;[37] it will be no joy to him to bring grief upon the old Italian. The similarity in circumstance between the Trojan and Latin kings enhances our sense both of Latinus' misfortune and of Aeneas' ungrateful lot.

Not that the similarities should be pressed too far. We shall hardly fail to think of Priam as we read of Latinus; but Virgil does not seek to prolong the comparison. The elderly king seems an obvious vehicle for pathos; we might have seen him, like Priam, feebly trying to buckle on his old armour in a sad attempt to die as a warrior (after all, other sources have him killed in battle); but Virgil passes by these opportunities, and indeed brusquely removes him from the action before the war begins, not to appear again until the eleventh book. For Virgil has other purposes in making Latinus an old man; and these are barely compatible with using old age to portray, as he does with Priam, the ultimate weakness of the human condition.

[35] *Il.* 22. 153 ff.   [36] *Il.* 24. 543–8.   [37] *Aen.* 2. 506–58.

In all versions of the story except this, Latinus is an actor in the drama like the others, on the same level as Turnus, Aeneas, and the rest. Virgil works differently: the *Aeneid* builds Latinus up into a figure around whom there gathers the spirit of religious awe: ancient, sacral, remote. We are induced to feel that his name is the eponym of the entire Latin race; he belongs, we fancy, with those other eponymous heroes, the mysterious Italus and father Sabinus, whose carven effigies stand within his palace in the company of Saturn, Janus, and Picus.[38] Thus Latinus, too, seems to find his proper place alongside gods or deified ancestors; three times, indeed, he is called 'pater'.[39] Literally, of course, he is no demigod: despite his divine ancestry, he is as fully and as merely human as Turnus or Aeneas; nor is he literally the father of the Latin race, since he has but one child, and her unmarried. What tells, though, is the aura with which he is surrounded.

This semi-divine aura may explain why he plays so strangely little part in the events that follow. Some have thought that he is meant to be portrayed, naturalistically, as complacent or ineffective, but though this may seem to explain away a difficulty, it can hardly be right: the whole thrust of Virgil's presentation is in another direction. Yet after the numinous majesty which has surrounded him earlier in the book his conduct when Turnus and the shepherds come to him demanding war seems unexpectedly weak. However, it does not look as though Virgil meant it to seem so. The king is honoured with a simile implying unconquerable strength: he is like a sea-cliff, unmoved by the howling waves that beat against it; the cliff holds firm; the foam-drenched crags and rocks around roar, but to no avail.[40] Then Virgil adds a transparently awkward 'verum' (but): once Latinus finds that he has no power to overcome the crowd's blind determination, Juno's will directing the outcome, he declares that he is broken by destiny, borne down by the storm, and with a dire warning to Turnus of his sin and coming punishment, to the people of the suffering that they will reap, he withdraws.[41] As a whole, the scene does not quite cohere, and the awkwardness is surely because Virgil has wanted to preserve Latinus' majesty and authority while shielding him from a share of responsibility for an unjust war. Earlier he has shown him unmoved by Allecto, when Turnus and Amata are overwhelmed by her power; here too he seems at pains to suggest that

---

[38] *Aen.* 7. 177–82.   [39] *Aen.* 7. 92, 612; 11. 410.
[40] *Aen.* 7. 586–90.   [41] *Aen.* 7. 591 ff.

the wrong is Turnus' doing, that the king is overwhelmed by an irresistible force ('We are broken by destiny'), that he is somehow apart, detached from a ruler's normal task of guiding events. He says no more:[42]

> nec plura locutus
> saepsit se tectis rerumque reliquit habenas.

Saying no more he enclosed himself in his house and abandoned the reins of government.

'Saepsit se tectis'—in that terse but evocative phrase we feel him to be abstracted from the world of everyday and lifted on to another level, wrapped in the obscure splendours of his temple-palace, mysterious and remote. This motif of tenebrous withdrawal returns when he refuses to open the gates of war in accordance with custom:[43]

> abstinuit tactu pater aversusque refugit
> foeda ministeria, et caecis se condidit umbris.

Father Latinus refrained from touching [the gates], turned away, shrinking from the loathsome office, and buried himself in the blind darkness.

Such is the complex of mood and imagery which Virgil has built up that such simple words as 'pater' and 'condere' now reverberate with a solemn significance.

When Latinus is silent or absent, he is magnificent; it is when he must take action that Virgil seems less at ease. There is again a certain oddity about Latinus' later appearances, though on these occasions the difficulties are better disguised. In the eleventh book he summons a council and makes his own proposals for peace in a lengthy speech, but he remains a strangely static, immobile figure, fixed like an icon upon his throne:[44]

> sedet in mediis et maximus aevo
> et primus sceptris haud laeta fronte Latinus.
> .   .   .   .
> praefatus divos solio rex infit ab alto . . .

Latinus, greatest in age and first in royal authority, sits in the middle with no gladness on his brow . . . First addressing the gods, the king begins from his high throne . . .

---

[42] *Aen.* 7. 599 f.   [43] *Aen.* 7. 618 f.   [44] *Aen.* 11. 237 f., 301.

Despite his speech he seems less to take part in the debate than to watch over it from a distance. 'Advise,' he concludes his address, as though he had made no proposal of his own. Drances and Turnus proceed to their quarrel; suddenly news arrives that the Trojans and Etruscans are advancing; Turnus rushes from the palace and the council breaks up, unconcluded. Thus the nature and extent of Latinus' authority are a matter which remains undefined; his response is yet again a solemn and obscure withdrawal:[45]

> concilium ipse pater et magna incepta Latinus
> deserit ac tristi turbatus tempore differt . . .

Father Latinus himself abandons the council and his grand designs and puts them off, disturbed by the sombre moment . . .

At the start of the last book he is restored to the semblance of almost godlike impassibility: he presses peace upon Turnus but with a strange lack of ordinary human urgency; the words prefacing his speech have overtones of divinity (the archaic 'olli' and the stress upon his placidity recall lines introducing the speeches of Jupiter): 'olli sedato respondit corde Latinus . . .' (Latinus answered him with placid spirit . . .).[46] He does grieve, however; later he will rend his garments and foul his grey head with dust;[47] the divinity that seems to hedge him is a matter of suggestion rather than actuality.

Whatever the minor discomforts in Virgil's handling of Latinus later, in the first half of the seventh book he represents him superbly: here, once more, time, history, patriotism, and sense of place interact with a profound suggestiveness. Italy as a whole is an ancient land, and even Turnus, though young and fiery, has his power embedded in generations long gone by. At his very first appearance he is described as 'avis atavisque potens':[48] it is characteristic of Virgil that even in so small a phrase as this we feel the impulse to press ever further back into the past, from 'avi' to 'atavi' (literally 'grandfathers' to 'great-great-great-grandfathers'). But it is Latinus above all who directs our vision back to primordial times. His great age places him in a generation which must seem even to Aeneas to belong to the past; none the less, no sooner have we met him than we descend steadily deeper into the past, stage by stage, as we trace Latinus' ancestry backwards, from Faunus to Picus, from Picus to Saturn:[49]

---

[45] *Aen.* 11. 469 f.   [46] *Aen.* 12. 18 (cf. Jupiter at 1. 254 f.; 12. 829).
[47] *Aen.* 12. 609–11.   [48] *Aen.* 7. 56.
[49] *Aen.* 7. 47–9, translated above, p. 473.

hunc Fauno et nympha genitum Laurente Marica
accipimus; Fauno Picus pater, isque parentem
te, Saturne, refert, tu sanguinis ultimus auctor.

We have seen that in other places where Virgil is uncovering layer
after layer of the past he comes finally to rest upon the word 'auctor'.[50] Here the backward thrust through time is reinforced by the
adjective 'ultimus'. And indeed we have been carried back to a deity
so ancient that he is a generation older than Jupiter himself, the god
elsewhere styled 'father of gods and men'.

The ancient and the Italic go hand in hand. Virgil does away with
Ulysses and Circe as parents for Latinus and substitutes a lineage
primordially native. Faunus, Picus, and Marica are all Italian deities
for whom there is no Greek equivalent.[51] Saturn had long been
identified with the Greek Cronos, and strictly, as Evander will tell
us in the next book, he came to Italy as an exile from Olympus.
But that is something of which we shall hardly be conscious here;
Saturn was, after all, an Italian agricultural god in origin, and in the
Aeneid as in the Georgics he is associated in a particular intimacy with
the Italian earth.

The dimness of historical memory, the darkness of the past may
seem to be mere metaphors; but in this book it remains part of Virgil's
art that metaphor and actuality flow in and out of one another. Italy,
as a nation rooted in its past, is full of metaphorical darkness; but it
is rich in a real, physical darkness also. Faunus is a god of the woodland; his very name, repeated in the context of shadowy, primordial ancestry, imports a certain opacity, and not many lines later the
darkness becomes actual and deep.[52]

at rex sollicitus monstris oracula Fauni,
fatidici genitoris, adit lucosque sub alta
consulit Albunea, nemorum quae maxima sacro
fonte sonat saevamque exhalat opaca mephitim.
hinc Italae gentes omnisque Oenotria tellus 85
in dubiis responsa petunt; huc dona sacerdos

---

[50] Geo. 3. 35 f., Aen. 6. 648.
[51] Faunus in the Aeneid is kept sharply unlike Pan, who is indeed excluded from the
poem, except for a passing mention at 8. 344. In earlier works there was no need for such
nicety: the Fauni of Ecl. 6. 27 and Geo. 1. 10 f. are clearly the Greek Panes with an Italian
name. The distinctiveness with which Faunus is treated in the Aeneid may be seen by
comparison with Ovid's handling in the Fasti (see below, p. 621).
[52] Aen. 7. 81–95.

cum tulit et caesarum ovium sub nocte silenti
pellibus incubuit stratis somnosque petivit,
multa modis simulacra videt volitantia miris
et varias audit voces fruiturque deorum   90
conloquio atque imis Acheronta adfatur Avernis.
hic et tum pater ipse petens responsa Latinus
centum lanigeras mactabat rite bidentis,
atque harum effultus tergo stratisque iacebat
velleribus: subita ex alto vox reddita luco est . . .   95

But the king, troubled by the omen, approaches the oracle of his prophetic
father Faunus and consults the woods below high Albunea, which, mightiest of forests, resounds with its sacred spring and in the darkness breathes
out fierce sulphur. Here the Italian peoples and all the Oenotrian land seek
pronouncements in times of doubt; when the priest has brought offerings
here and lain on the outspread skins of slaughtered sleep in the silent night
and sought sleep, he sees many phantoms flitting in mysterious ways and
hears diverse voices and enjoys converse with the gods and speaks to Acheron
in lowest Avernus. Then too father Latinus himself, seeking an oracle, duly
sacrificed a hundred woolly sheep, and resting on their hides he lay on the
strewn fleeces. A sudden voice came from the deep wood . . .

The scene is set not only in a forest, but at night. And there is a
darkness of a third kind also: of the underworld and its chthonic
powers.

Virgil commands subtle shifts of tone. Whereas the darkness at the
mouth of the Tiber was safe and consoling, the darkness of Albunea
is uncanny and awe-inspiring, with its sulphurous vapours, ghosts,
and weird voices. Yet both darknesses are related, for both are woodland darknesses, mysteriously ancestral, and associated with an Italian
patriotism. Latinus consults his father: if it is not pressing the hinted
womb imagery in the earlier passage too far, perhaps this is a male
darkness as the former was a female darkness. Faunus remains unseen,
without form or shape: his words come disembodied out of the night,
introduced by an ambiguous phrase which seems momentarily to
suggest that the grove itself is speaking: 'subita ex alto vox reddita
luco est'. And indeed Faunus, as an Italian god, is not a divinity like
the Olympians with a crisp contour and a clearly defined personality: he is a spirit immanent in the grove. In this phrase landscape
and ancestry, the past and the soil blend fabulously together; to consult the earth and to consult the ancestors are one and the same
thing. Virgil emphasizes that Albunea is an oracle for all Italy; and

he associates it with chthonic forces, with those powers embedded literally within the Italian land itself.[53]

By sliding from the darkness of the Tiber to the darkness of Albunea Virgil enlarges our understanding of our patriotism and our native country. The earth and the ancestors are not just warmly cosy; we learn that those bonds and emotions which seem to us most tightly intimate and familiar are at the same time deeply strange and unknown. And this truth of human experience, this complexity, Virgil marvellously conveys through the ambiguous imagery of darkness, which in his hands shifts to and fro between the safe and the uncanny. The scene at Albunea alone is emotionally complex, at once thrilling and alarming; Virgil realizes the religious sense so economically and suggestively described by Lucretius as both pleasure and shudder.[54] Other poets could invent spirit-haunted woods, crowded with the furniture of mystery and horror. Compared with, say, Lucan's handling of the theme,[55] Virgil's Albunea seems classically restrained. Yet Virgil makes these other treatments look like mere pantomime spookiness, because his mephitic glooms and nameless voices are bound in with ideas and experiences that we have ourselves to some degree apprehended: the past, the love of Italy, the delight and terror of religious awe.

We might not expect the fury Allecto to go to ground—literally —in the very heart of Italy, but such is Virgil's plan:[56]

> est locus Italiae medio sub montibus altis,
> nobilis et fama multis memoratus in oris,
> Amsancti valles; densis hunc frondibus atrum
> urget utrimque latus nemoris, medioque fragosus
> dat sonitum saxis et torto vertice torrens.
> hic specus horrendum et saevi spiracula Ditis
> monstrantur, ruptoque ingens Acheronte vorago
> pestiferas aperit fauces, quis condita Erinys,
> invisum numen, terras caelumque levabat.

There is a place in the middle of Italy beneath high mountains, celebrated and known to fame in many lands, the valley of Amsanctus; a wooded hillside, dark with thick leafage, hems it in on both sides, and in the middle a broken torrent roars with its rocks and twisting eddies. Here a

---

[53] It seems too that the strange ritual of incubation—sleeping on the sheepskins—though in sober anthropological fact a Geek practice, is meant to have the mysterious quality of an ancient indigenous rite.
[54] Lucr. 3. 28 f.
[55] Luc. 3. 399–425.   [56] Aen. 7. 563–71.

fearsome cave and the breathing-holes of savage Dis are to be seen, and
a vast chasm where Acheron bursts forth opens its pestilent jaws, wherein
the Erinys, hateful power, buried herself, lightening earth and heaven.

This passage, breaking into the episode concerning Tyrrhus and his
neighbours, counterbalances the prettiness with which the rural life
of Latium has been endowed. This adds to the diversity which is
fundamental to Virgil's picture of his country. It does not mean, of
course, that his admiration for Italy is somehow qualified or diminished. Rather he deepens, metaphorically and indeed literally, our
understanding of the land; a home that is seen to be undergirded
by dark and terrible chthonic powers is the more authentically and
more spiritually known.

Earlier we found trees and darkness associated together; we can
now begin to see how complex is the web of imagery in which
they are enmeshed—time, parentage, patriotism, the past, the sense
of place, religious awe. To which can be added some vaguer concepts: height, depth, centrality. 'Altus' is such a favourite epithet of
Virgil's for woods and groves that we may be tempted to dismiss it
as a cliché or mannerism, like his excessive use of 'ingens'. Yet like
'ingens' it can be a part of his power to give a pregnancy to ordinary words and ordinary things. Lucretius before him had discovered
the power of simple adjectives, and he had used language in such a
manner as to convey his sense of the size and scale of things; Virgil
also learnt the force of simple epithets, and developed his own way
of conveying his sense of scale. We have already seen this in the sixth
book: 'itur in *antiquam* silvam, stabula *alta* ferarum.'[57] Here is the
sense of penetration into some deep, its dimensions extensive in both
time and space: the two epithets, 'antiquus' and 'altus', react upon
each other. So too the centre of Latinus' palace:[58]

> laurus erat tecti *medio* in *penetralibus altis*
> sacra comam *multos*que metu servata per *annos* . . .

There was a laurel in the middle of the palace, in the deep interior, with
sacred foliage, preserved by awe through many years . . .

Again, the size and the age of the place are ideas obscurely intertwined. We feel that we have to penetrate far into the building, far
into the past, to reach its secret, sacred heart. In view of the later and
fuller description of the palace, it is significant that it should appear,

---

[57] *Aen.* 6. 179; see above, p. 450.   [58] *Aen.* 7. 59 f.

at its first mention here, to be far from conventionally domestic: right at its centre there is 'metus', a religious dread. There is a parallel with Virgil's treatment of the ancestral darkness: the inmost part of the home is also numinously unknown.

Virgil's sense of dimension and its significance reaches to small passing phrases: it is part of the texture of his sensibility. Allecto tells Latinus,[59]

> et Turno, si *prima* domus repetatur origo,
> Inachus Acrisiusque patres *mediae*que Mycenae.

Turnus too, if the first origin of his house be sought for, has as ancestors Inachus and Acrisius and the heart of Mycenae.

'Domus' is both home and family in this context; the search for Turnus' origins ('repetatur' is a significant word: we must scrutinize, we must penetrate) is a quest through a distance both spatial and temporal. And the goal is not just Mycenae but 'mediae Mycenae'; by so modest an adjective, linking the ideas of ancestry and centrality, Virgil enforces the sense that a man is fixed and grounded in the experience of his forebears.

Later, Allecto sounds her horn to rouse the shepherds to conflict: a voice of the underworld, 'Tartarea vox':[60]

> qua protinus omne
> *contremuit* nemus et silvae insonuere profundae;
> audiit et Triviae longe lacus, audiit amnis
> sulpurea Nar albus aqua fontesque Velini,
> et *trepidae* matres pressere ad pectora natos.

At this [voice] every wood forthwith trembled and the depths of the forests resounded; Trivia's lake too heard afar, the river Nar heard, white with sulphurous water, and the springs of the Velinus, and frightened mothers pressed their children to their breasts.

The phrase 'silvae profundae' is from Lucretius, who in turn drew it from Homer's *batheies hules*.[61] Alien to Homer, though, is the association of the woodland and its depth with fear and trembling. This combination seems peculiarly Virgilian; yet it too comes in Lucretius' lines:[62]

[59] *Aen.* 7. 371 f.   [60] *Aen.* 7. 514–18.
[61] Lucr. 5. 41; Hom. *Il.* 5. 555.   [62] Lucr. 5. 39–41.

ita ad satiatem terra ferarum
nunc etiam scatit et trepido terrore repleta est
per nemora ac montis magnos silvasque profundas; . . .

The earth as it is teems so abundantly with wild beasts and is filled with
trembling terror through woods, great mountains and deep forests . . .

But Virgil knew how to make what he found in Lucretius part of
his own sensibility; and besides, there are fine differences of tone
between him and his master. 'Contremuit' is a verb of primarily visual
application, 'insonuere' a verb of sound (the resonance of *m*'s and
n's, subtler than in Lucretius, enhances the effect); 'contremuit' hints
at the pathetic fallacy and at the feeling of fear, but could be taken
in a simply literal sense (only at 518, with the 'trepidae matres', is
the idea made explicit). This inexplicitness, combined with the
echoing sound, conjures up a wide vague spaciousness within the
forests; then Virgil brings in the Italian proper names, accompanying
them with suggestions of both direness and beauty: the lakes and
springs on the one hand, the sulphur and Trivia, dread goddess of
the underworld, on the other. Add to all this the presence of Allecto,
and we have a sense of the numinous which is the more effectively
conveyed for being suggestion only. The numinousness, and the
romantic mixture of delight and dread in this evocation of the Italian
scene, are qualities which we do not find in Lucretius' words.

Unlike Lucretius, Virgil does not mention high mountains in this
place, but they will come in the description of Amsanctus.[63] Here again
are the elements of a romantic spirit-haunted landscape, along with the
din of waters, the exhalations from the lower world, the thickness
of woods, the sense of Italy; here too, height and depth are blended
in with the idea of centrality, expressed through the repeated 'medio'.
The middle of *Italy*, our own land—once more we come to the
heart of the home, and meet there the deep and the undiscoverable.

Virgil uses the word 'augustus', other than as a proper name, twice
only in the *Aeneid*, both times in the same area of the seventh book,
and in association with Latinus.[64] The word belongs to the register
of religious language, and the Romans frequently linked it with
'augur' and its cognates: Ennius declared that Rome was founded

[63] *Aen.* 7. 563–71.
[64] *Aen.* 7. 153, 170. As a proper name he also uses it twice (*Aen.* 6. 792; 8. 678). Before
the *Aeneid* he employs it only at *Geo.* 4. 228 (where, however, the variant reading 'angus-
tam' is also possible).

'augusto augurio'.[65] The name Augustus was translated into Greek as *Sebastos*, 'reverend', even 'awe-inspiring'. Latinus' very walls have this quality: 'augusta ad moenia regis'.[66] Once more we press back far into the past: Latinus, old himself, sits on a throne far more ancient still: 'solio medius consedit *avito*.'[67] Here, as at line 36, Virgil unusually ends a paragraph with an adjective; and here again the adjective is of strong significance. Once more, too, antiquity is obscurely and suggestively linked to the idea of centrality: the words 'medius' and 'avitus' play against each other. Rooted to his throne within the depths of his many-columned home, Latinus seems, as the ambassadors are commanded to approach, almost like the cult-statue within a shrine; when he utters, it is with a godlike calm: 'placido prior edidit ore.'[68] But before he speaks, Virgil describes his palace in lines within which the nexus of imagery is grander, and also more complex, than ever:[69]

tectum augustum, ingens, centum sublime columnis 170
urbe fuit summa, Laurentis regia Pici,
horrendum silvis et religione parentum.
hic sceptra accipere et primos attollere fascis
regibus omen erat; hoc illis curia templum,
hae sacris sedes epulis; hic ariete caeso 175
perpetuis soliti patres considere mensis.
quin etiam veterum effigies ex ordine avorum
antiqua e cedro, Italusque paterque Sabinus
vitisator curvam servans sub imagine falcem,
Saturnusque senex Ianique bifrontis imago 180
vestibulo astabant, aliique ab origine reges,
Martiaque ob patriam pugnando vulnera passi.
multaque praeterea sacris in postibus arma,
captivi pendent currus curvaeque secures
et cristae capitum et portarum ingentia claustra 185
spiculaque clipeique ereptaque rostra carinis.
Ipse Quirinali lituo parvaque sedebat
succinctus trabea laevaque ancile gerebat
Picus, equum domitor, quem capta cupidine coniunx
aurea percussum virga versumque venenis 190
fecit avem Circe sparsitque coloribus alas.
   tali intus templo divum patriaque Latinus
sede sedens Teucros ad sese in tecta vocavit,
atque haec ingressis placido prior edidit ore . . .

---

[65] *Ann.* 155 Sk. On 'augustus' and 'augur' etc., both deriving from the family of 'augere', see further Fordyce on *Aen.* 7. 153.   [66] *Aen.* 7. 153, 'the king's reverend walls'.
[67] *Aen.* 7. 169, 'takes his seat in the middle on his ancestral throne'.
[68] *Aen.* 7. 194.   [69] *Aen.* 7. 170–94.

His house, venerable, immense, lofty with a hundred columns, stood on the city's height, the palace of Laurentine Picus, shuddersome with woods and the awe of the ancestors. Here it was auspicious for the kings to receive the sceptre and to raise their fasces for the first time, this temple was their council-house, these seats were for their sacred feasts, here after killing a ram the elders were wont to sit along the undivided tables. Moreover, the images of the ancient forefathers in order, carved from old cedar, Italus and father Sabinus the vine-planter, still holding his pruning-hook in effigy, and aged Saturn and the statue of two-faced Janus stood in the hall, along with other kings from the beginning who had suffered the wounds of war fighting for their fatherland. There hung besides on the consecrated door-posts many weapons, captured chariots, curved axes, crests of helmets, the massive bars of gates, javelins, shields, and beaks torn from ships. Holding the Quirinal staff and girt in a short chasuble there sat, bearing the sacred shield in his left hand, Picus himself, the horse-tamer; whom his bride Circe, seized by desire, struck with her golden wand and transformed by potions, making him a bird and sprinkling his wings with colours. Within this temple of the gods, seated on his ancestral throne, Latinus summoned the Trojans into the house to his presence, and when they entered, with serene countenance first addressed them thus . . .

In the first lines of the paragraph the physical and the spiritual fuse. 'Horrendum silvis et religione parentum'—the wood is solid enough, but the 'horror' resides also in something else wholly impalpable, the spirit of the ancestors. The application of 'horrendum' is also effectively vague: the spectators shudder—and may we perhaps fancy a shudder in the trees and the 'religio' themselves?[70] The description is vivid not for its clarity but in the very way that it baffles the eye: 'augustum, ingens'—the words resonate immensely, but create no picture. The hundred lofty columns block the gaze in every direction and, we must suppose, shut out the light. (Not until much later is the palace described as dark in so many words;[71] characteristically Virgil works indirectly, through suggestion and overtone.) There seems to be no distinction made between interior and exterior: tall pillars and ancient trees, the work of nature and the ancient work of man, merge strangely together. Twice Virgil tells us that the place is a temple.[72] The word falls naturally and comes as no surprise; for before telling us explicitly, he has already made us feel, by atmosphere and

---

[70] Lucan puts the shudder unambiguously into the wood (3. 410 f.): 'non ullis frondem praebentibus auris | arboribus suus horror inest' (Though the trees present their leaves to no breezes, a shudder of their own is in them).

[71] *Aen.* 7. 619.   [72] Lines 174 and 192.

suggestion, that temple and palace, nation and religion, are one. The mention of the 'parentes' introduces yet another theme also, that of ancestry: it is superfluous to pick out the many phrases following which point back to the earliest origins of the race.

The ancestors import another kind of dimness. Who are these 'other kings' and where did they rule? We were told before that Latinus was himself the founder of the city.[73] Who are Italus and Sabinus? They played no part in the genealogy which Virgil provided earlier in the book; indeed we have heard nothing of them before and shall hear nothing again. Even Picus, so prominent in this paragraph and Latinus' grandfather in the genealogy, has no further existence in the *Aeneid*. In principle it would be possible to fabricate a family tree which fitted Italus and Sabinus into Latinus' ancestry,[74] but that is not Virgil's way: it is of the essence that those ancient kings remain obscure. Virgil broke with the tradition of epic poetry by giving the different races gods of their own: Faunus is a specifically Italian deity, Cybele a Trojan, though of course the Olympians are shared by all. But the native Italian gods presented a difficulty. Most had little or no mythology attached to them and some were divinized forms of things or abstractions: the gods invoked by Varro at the start of his *Res Rustica* include Earth, Mildew, Fresh Water, and Happy Outcome. Many of the native gods had long had Greek equivalents found for them: even Venus, who philologically looks as though she should be a neuter noun, could be identified with the Greek Aphrodite and achieve full femininity. In the process, however, such gods lost their distinctively native flavour, at least within literature: Jupiter, Juno, and the rest naturally function in the *Aeneid* as part of a universal Graeco-Roman pantheon. It is possible in certain cases to put some mythological flesh and blood upon the wraith-like figures of the native gods: Ovid will tell the story of Vertumnus and Pomona in his *Metamorphoses*, of Anna Perenna (for example) in the *Fasti*,[75] and by scratching around among the antiquarians we can get a little more information—not much—on Italus and Sabinus. But Virgil takes another path. It was not enough for him to name Italian gods and heroes; their quality must be distinctively Italian also.

---

[73] *Aen.* 7. 61. Virgil might perhaps have chosen to remove the direct conflict between this line and 171 in revision.

[74] 'Clear evidence of lack of revision' (Fordyce on line 178). That possibility can seldom be excluded (cf. the previous note), but everyone has two grandfathers and four great-grandfathers. [75] Ov. *Met.* 14. 623 ff.; *Fasti* 3. 523–696.

Myth and legend are accordingly cut to a minimum. Italus and Sabinus remain entirely unexplained: Virgil might have told us that the one was king of the Oenotrians (or in an alternative version, a Sicilian), and that the other was the son of Sancus; but he forbears. The exotic story of Picus' transformation into a bird, told in full by Ovid,[76] is reduced to a mere three lines—a splash of bright colour against the sombre background of the temple, and like the wood-pecker itself, a flash of brilliance that is gone as soon as seen. In the eighth book Evander will tell us just enough about Saturn to explain Virgil's distinctive notion of the golden age in Italy, but more remains opaque; his wife, Ops, is never mentioned, and we are given no idea of how he ceased to rule in Latium and what has become of him since. Virgil left himself space for an ample narrative of Italy's legendary past; he chose to fill it not with an Italian god or hero but with the Graeco-Roman figure of Hercules. Above all, the Italian gods in the *Aeneid* do almost nothing. Phrygian Cybele steps from the shadows in the ninth book to plead with Jupiter and turn the Trojan ships into sea-nymphs;[77] but from Saturn we hear never a word and from Faunus only six lines of oracular utterance in the darkness. The nearest Faunus comes to action is in the last book when Turnus prays to him, along with Earth, another deity with-out clear shape or form, to hold fast within his sacred olive stump the spear which Aeneas has driven into it. Nor did the hero call on the god's aid in vain, we are told—at least until Venus intervenes to restore the spear to Aeneas.[78] That is the limit of Faunus' activity in the poem. Of course Virgil does not give a full or authentic pic-ture of Italian religion, past or present: there will be no rough Vediovis or Mutunus Tutunus to abrade the polished surface of the verse, nor indeed any of the traditional festivals, Floralia, Compitalia, and the like. What he does instead is to suggest an Italian quality, and this by allowing his Italian deities to be half seen, no more. This approach is peculiar to the *Aeneid*: for Horace Faunus is a Latinized Pan or satyr, lusting after the Nymphs, and Ovid will make him the protagonist of a ribald tale.[79]

We have seen the thrust back into the past in the description of Latinus' palace; but that does not exhaust the temporal complex-ity of the passage. For while Virgil looks back in time he is at the

[76] Ov. *Met.* 14. 312 ff.   [77] *Aen.* 9. 80–106.   [78] *Aen.* 12. 766–87.
[79] Hor. *Carm.* 3. 18; Ov. *Fasti.* 2. 303–58. Faunus was a god of flocks as well as of woods; Virgil excludes the former role, keeping him in the shadows.

same moment looking forward, towards contemporary Rome. The form of the palace, and the uses and ceremonies attributed to it, are designed to call to mind the temple of Jupiter on the Capitol.[80] The epithet 'augustus', for all its venerable ring, has obviously acquired a peculiarly modern significance from the title newly taken by the first citizen (we may perhaps think of the house and temple on the Palatine as well as of the Capitol). A number of words point us, with an unexpected particularity, to the distinctive institutions of the Roman state: 'fasces', 'curia', 'patres'. The *ancilia*, the sacred shields supposedly entrusted to King Numa, had an especial significance, patriotic and religious, for the Romans: Horace names them as he seeks to stir up a spirit of national indignation at the thought of the defeated Italian soldiers who have dared to accommodate themselves to a life under Parthian sway.[81] Anachronistically Picus holds an *ancile*. Furthermore, he grasps a 'lituus', the staff borne in Virgil's day by the augurs, and wears the 'trabea', the tunic once worn by the kings and then by the consuls at certain high ceremonies; both objects were associated with Romulus, also called Quirinus, and the surprising adjective 'Quirinalis' reinforces the association. In such a context the many spoils of war displayed within the temple will not fail to call to mind the unparalleled victories of Rome.

It is perhaps no accident that the figure most heavily laden with the trappings of later Rome is Picus, the strangest of them all, whose bizarre metamorphosis and vast antiquity are matched by the quaintly archaic alliteration, recalling Ennius, in the lines describing him: 'quem *c*apta *c*upidine *c*oniunx | aurea percussum *v*irga *v*ersumque *v*enenis | fecit avem'. We are left in no doubt that this is an old, odd world very unlike our own; and yet it insistently recalls more recent times. Thus, once more, we feel both change and continuity in the operations of time; the past is so foreign—and so familiar. On this occasion, whereas the push backward into a further past is openly expressed, the glances forward to Rome are indicated by suggestion only. That is effective: we are first to feel for ourselves the links between ancient Latium and modern Rome, and only later in the book will the continuity of long tradition be blazed forth to the sound of trumpets:[82]

---

[80] See W. A. Camps, 'A Second Note on the Structure of the *Aeneid*', *CQ* 53 (1959), 53–6, at 54.

[81] Hor. *Carm*. 3. 5. 5–12.   [82] *Aen*. 7. 601–15.

mos erat Hesperio in Latio, quem protinus urbes
Albanae coluere sacrum, nunc maxima rerum
Roma colit, cum prima movent in proelia Martem,
sive Getis inferre manu lacrimabile bellum
Hyrcanisve Arabisve parant, seu tendere ad Indos   605
Auroramque sequi Parthosque reposcere signa:
sunt geminae Belli portae (sic nomine dicunt)
religione sacrae et saevi formidine Martis;
centum aerei claudunt vectes aeternaque ferri
robora, nec custos absistit limine Ianus.   610
has, ubi certa sedet patribus sententia pugnae,
ipse Quirinali trabea cinctuque Gabino
insignis reserat stridentia limina consul,
ipse vocat pugnas; sequitur tum cetera pubes,
aereaque adsensu conspirant cornua rauco.   615

There was a custom in Hesperian Latium, which the cities of Alba in due
course held sacred, as Rome, greatest of nations, does now, when they
first rouse Mars to battle, whether they are readying their hands to bring
tearful war to the Getae, the Hyrcanians, or the Arabs, or else to make
for the Indians, to follow the dawn and to reclaim the standards from the
Parthians. There are two Gates of War (so men call them), sanctified by
war and the dread of fierce Mars; a hundred bolts of bronze and the everlasting strength of iron close them, and Janus their guard never leaves the
threshold. When the vote of the Fathers is firmly fixed on war, the consul, conspicuous in the Quirinal robe and girt in the Gabine manner, himself unbars these doors so that the threshold screeches, himself summons
battle; then the whole army follows the call, and the brazen horns join in
blaring their hoarse assent.

This passage repeatedly echoes the description of Latinus' palace. Here
again 'religio' sanctifies the city's great buildings and the nation's pride
in war, and Janus stands by the threshold. Here too are the 'patres'
and the 'Quirinal robe'; and yet these echoes bring out the change
as well as the continuity, combining the stability of tradition with
the evolutionary force of history; for the 'patres' are no longer a
monarch's counsellors but the sovereign senate of Rome, and the
trabea, seen before upon a god's son, the husband of an enchantress,
now clothes the consul's solidly republican form. Both passages are
concerned with time, history, and the nation; but this one answers
to the earlier one like the reflections in a mirror, its explicit thrust
forward through the centuries complementing the thrust backwards
in the account of the palace. In 601 ff. we feel the inexorable progress

of history and the many layers of the past. Virgil begins with ancient Latium, and indeed with Latium seen through Trojan eyes: '*Hesperio in Latio*'. And even this primeval state is a nation long established: the paragraph opens with the firm round monosyllable 'mos', 'tradition', that concept so resonant in the Roman spirit. From Latium we pass in sequence of time to the Alban towns, from them to Rome, and then on to an allusion unique in the *Aeneid* for the precision of its reference to a political issue immediate at the time Virgil was writing: the demand that Rome recover the standards lost by Crassus when the Parthians won the Battle of Carrhae.[83] At one end early Latium, at the other a matter that was buzzing in the politics of the 20s, and in between a vast distance of time and mood, through which we pass, stage by stage; and yet the same tradition endures.[84]

> hoc *et tum* Aeneadis indicere bella Latinus
> more iubebatur tristisque recludere portas.

Then too Latinus was bidden according to this custom to declare war on Aeneas' people and open the grim gates.

Like the 'iam tum' that will follow in the introduction to the catalogue, 'et tum' here at once binds us to the past and holds it separate.[85]

The sense of dynamism, movement, and process in these lines is the more forceful because, as elsewhere, the progress through time is complemented by a progress across the earth. From the Latian heartland we move outwards to the remotest parts of the inhabited world; or to look at the passage in another way, we move from the land of the west ('*Hesperio* in Latio') far into the east, to the Indians, and by the sound of it, even further (Virgil seems to be trying to trump even the climax of his *laus Italiae*). At one end lies Hesperia, the land of evening; at the other Aurora, the dawn, a journey long enough to match in spatial terms our voyage across the ages.

---

[83] This is the only appearance of the Parthians in the *Aeneid* except for an allusion to their poisoned arrows in a simile at 12. 857 f. They are here for Virgil's own purposes; we should not suppose that he had to fit the Parthians in somewhere to satisfy his patrons. Augustus could not know that he would be able to get the standards back; it must have been something of an embarrassment that his poets harped on the subject, but he could not check them without humiliation to himself. The ruler of the world was impotent against the unhelpful flattery of the loyal. Virgil seems to have been shrewd enough on this occasion to recognize, as Horace apparently was not, that conquest was out of the question: 'reposcere signa' is guarded language. Of course, it is conceivable that he wrote (or rewrote) these lines after Tiberius had recovered the standards in 20 BC; by negotiation, not force of arms. [84] *Aen.* 7. 616 f.

[85] *Aen.* 7. 645; see above, p. 472, and cf. 8. 349 f. (below, p. 551).

A nice genealogy discovers that Aeneas and Latinus are second cousins, each being a great-grandson of Saturn. The significance of this fact is that it goes unnoticed: Virgil employs genealogy not nicely but for its affective force. In the next book it will suit him to have Aeneas laboriously explain Evander's kinship to the Trojan race; in the present book both Latinus and the Trojan ambassador Ilioneus dwell upon the origins of Dardanus in Italy; but of the more immediate link between the Latin and Trojan leaders there is not a word. Instead, Virgil uses genealogy to keep the two peoples apart. Latinus stresses that his people are Saturn's nation;[86] and Ilioneus in reply begins by addressing him as 'genus egregium Fauni'; but Virgil makes him continue with an extreme stress on Troy's connection with the god who took Saturn's place:[87]

> consilio hanc omnes animisque volentibus urbem
> adferimur pulsi regnis, quae maxima quondam
> extremo veniens sol aspiciebat Olympo.
> *ab Iove* principium generis, *Iove Dardana* pubes
> gaudet avo, rex ipse *Iovis* de gente suprema:
> *Troius Aeneas* tua nos ad limina misit.

Purposely and with willing hearts do we all come to this city, driven from the realm which was once the greatest that the sun saw in his journey across the whole expanse of heaven. From Jupiter is the origin of our race, Dardanus' people rejoice in Jupiter as their ancestor, of Jupiter's highest descent is our king himself: Aeneas the Trojan has sent us to your door.

Troy and its leader appear in the clarity of an Olympian daylight, bound firmly to the new order; Latinus has been associated with the old order, and wrapped in a rich Italian gloom.

This separating of Latins and Trojans is one more expression of Virgil's loving particularity. The Trojans are, like the grand urban civilization of Latinus or the sweet rusticity of the Tyrrhidae, like Etruscans, Rutulians, and Arcadians, one of the diverse elements from which the future Italy is to be formed; and Virgil delights in the diversity of these elements, affectionately exploring the distinctive quality and spirit of each. But on this occasion he has a more sombre purpose also. The romance and virtue of Latinus' kingdom make it sad that the old order must give way to the new. Saturn has already gone from Italy; Faunus in the last book will prove ineffective against Venus and Aeneas, a new goddess and a new man. And not just a

---

[86] *Aen.* 7. 202 f.   [87] *Aen.* 7. 213, 216–21.

new man but an outsider. For in one sense, Latinus' side is 'our' side. Even before the description of the king's palace, when the Trojan ambassadors first see the Latin city, its august masonry, its lofty roofs and towers, the flower of its youth exercising themselves in archery, horsemanship, and athletics before its walls,[88] we understand that this polity, primeval though it be, is also a foreshadowing of the future Rome. And as the news reaches the king that men in garments of an unknown kind are approaching,[89] we are quietly reminded once more that these Trojans are foreigners, with manners unlike Italian habits of life. A double vision is at work again. We see Latinus' walls and towers through the wondering eyes of the approaching Trojans; and at the same time we see with our own eyes 'our' city, Rome, transformed by antiquity and romance. It is a little like those ideal towns that decorate the shining distance in the paintings of Memling and Van Eyck, remote, fabulous, and yet of a style recognizably formed from the Flemish cities of that day.

The Trojan strangers do not have an instinctive empathy, as we do, for Italian things. They will indifferently cut down Faunus' sacred olive tree, and Faunus will be powerless to punish them. In all this time and place are again imaginatively intertwined; things old and Italian give way to what is Trojan and new. And how shall we not feel for this Italian defeat? This passing away of ancient splendours and sanctities, like the shattering of rural Italy's childlike peace later in the book, shows the cost of Jupiter's purpose, the loss and the sorrow. This sense of loss is the more poignant in that the name of Saturn is associated with the golden age. It will be left to Evander in the next book to make that association explicit, but it is clearly present by allusion in Latinus' words:[90]

> ne fugite hospitium, neve ignorate Latinos
> Saturni gentem haud vinclo nec legibus aequam,
> sponte sua veterisque dei se more tenentem.

Do not shun our hospitality, and be well aware that the Latins are Saturn's people, just not because of bonds or laws but freely disciplining themselves in the manner of that god of old.

But justice must be done to Virgil's subtlety. In the first place, the Italy to which Aeneas comes is no longer in the golden age; and second, the golden age that did once exist in Italy, according to the

---

[88] *Aen.* 7. 160–5. [89] *Aen.* 7. 167. [90] *Aen.* 7. 202–4.

Aeneid, was a golden age of rather a special kind, different from the paradisal world described in the fourth Eclogue and the first book of the *Georgics*.[91]

It should be plain enough that the Italy which the Trojans find is not a golden world. Latinus' palace bristles with the memorials of war; Ufens and his tribe delight to live off banditry; Etruria has risen against its sadistic tyrant; Evander is constantly at war with his neighbours.[92] Some have thought that Virgil had two different conceptions, which he did not resolve: that the Latins who have lived in long peace and the Latins who keep fighting with the Arcadians cannot be reconciled. But there is no inconsistency. 'Pax' is security, a freedom from destruction within the state; it is not 'peacefulness', and indeed is quite a tough concept, from which the idea of force of arms is seldom far distant:[93] *si vis pacem, para bellum*. The Pax Romana, like the later Pax Britannica, was maintained by armies who were constantly skirmishing with native tribes. The 'pax' upon which the Roman is to impose 'mos' in the sixth book is bound up with the subjection of the nations and the crushing of the proud.[94] Even Augustus' restoration of a golden time is to be accompanied by a vast extension of the empire; by what means the poet does not specify.[95] Latinus' peace is like the peace of Augustus: not the absence of war but security at home, buttressed and dignified by warfare abroad.

Lest there should be any doubt, in the eighth book Evander explains directly that the golden age has gone: when Saturn was king in Italy, those were the times which men call golden; he ruled in peace until a tarnished age succeeded, with lust for war and greed of gain.[96] Then came Ausonians and Sicanians, and 'often the land of Saturn has laid aside her name'.[97] Since Saturn, in other words, the land has been called Oenotria, Ausonia, Italia. Evander's phrase places a huge bulk of history between Saturn and the present moment; so much has happened, so much changed since that golden time.

[91] On the golden age in Virgil's earlier poetry, see above, pp. 199 ff., 336. Cf. also I. Ryberg, 'Vergil's Golden Age', *TAPA* 89 (1958), 112–31.

[92] *Aen.* 7. 182 ff., 748 f.; 8. 481 ff., 55.

[93] 'To the Roman, peace was not a vague emollient: the word "pax" can seldom be divorced from notions of conquest, or at least compulsion' (R. Syme, *The Roman Revolution* (Oxford, 1939), 304). Augustus' own phrase, 'cum esset . . . parta victoriis pax' (when peace had been secured by victories), is expressive, and the word he uses for his military actions in Gaul, Spain, and Germany is 'pacavi' (*Res Gest.* 13, 26).   [94] *Aen.* 6. 853.

[95] *Aen.* 6. 791 ff.   [96] *Aen.* 8. 314 ff.   [97] *Aen.* 8. 329.

Not only is the golden age gone from the Italy of Latinus and Evander; Virgil's concept of what it was like even when it was still present differs from that put forward in the *Eclogues* and *Georgics*. However, we still need to think in terms of those two basic conceptions of the early life of mankind current in the ancient world, which modern scholarship has christened hard and soft primitivism:[98] on the one hand, the idea that the life of the first men was nasty and brutish, and humanity has progressed from that time through the discovery of the arts and sciences which make civilization possible; on the other hand, the idea that the human race lived at first in a paradise, and since that time, whether through divine indignation or mankind's own corruption, has declined into its present state.

The soft view appealed to that belief in decline which is so strong a feature in ancient thought generally and in Roman thought above all; but it must have struck the philosophic mind that the primal paradise was obviously a fairy story. And perhaps neither hard nor soft primitivism alone could do justice to the complexity of human history: wealth and civilization have brought progress and decline with them at one and the same time. A generation or two before Virgil Posidonius advanced a theory, known to us from Seneca's report of it, which combined elements of both the hard and soft concepts.[99] On his account, men originally lived virtuously and according to nature; this was the golden age, but instead of living in a communistic paradise, as in the traditional accounts, they put themselves under the guidance of one man, better than themselves: for it is natural for the inferior to submit to the superior. At this time government was in the hands of the wise; later, vices crept in, kingdoms were changed into tyrannies, and the need for laws arose; these in turn were devised by wise men. According to Seneca, the wise also devised all the arts of living: when men lived in caves and tree-trunks, they taught the means of building houses; and they invented mining, weaving, the techniques of farming, and so forth. At what stage in man's development Posidonius put these discoveries is not entirely clear.

Despite some uncertainties, two features stand out: the presence of wise rulers in the golden age, and the synthesis of hard and soft theories of primitivism. None of Virgil's golden ages is identical to that of Posidonius, but each of them is a personal modification

---

[98] A. Lovejoy and G. Boas, *Primitivism and Related Ideas in Antiquity* (Baltimore, 1935), 10. See also above, p. 336.   [99] Sen. *Ep.* 90 (Posidonius fr. 284 EK).

of traditional views. We cannot be certain that Virgil had read Posidonius (though we do know that his reading was exceptionally wide); nor can we achieve a full view of the intellectual currents of the time; but it is intriguing to watch him playing with different ideas of the golden age and developing a version that serves both a romantic vision and a moral seriousness.[100] In the fantasy of the fourth Eclogue a good ruler presides over the golden age restored; but in other respects Virgil takes over the traditional myth of paradise and decline, only runs it backwards. In the *Georgics* he combines the hard and soft ideas for the first time: the loss of paradise leads to an era of vigorous progress, and the whole process is part of a providential design; a new moral earnestness and complexity infuse the old story.[101] In the *Aeneid* the order of events is reversed. A period of savagery precedes the establishment of the golden age, and the subsequent decline seems to be partial only. As in the Eclogue, the golden age is connected with the advent of a good ruler; unlike both the Eclogue and the *Georgics*, however, the concept of a paradisal time, when the laws of nature themselves were quite different, disappears: Saturn's Italy was a good place, but it was not magical.

Virgil's synthesis, then, is distinctively his own; and it serves the particular purposes of the *Aeneid*. On the one hand, it is romantic. Here is the real Italy, which we can still recognize across the gulf of time. Saturn has gone, but the afterglow of his presence remains, the more especially since there hovers in Evander's speech an implicit comparison between Saturn and himself: both were driven from their homes in Greece; both came as exiles to Italy, where they established their own kingdoms. There is imperfection, but as Virgil had shown in the *Georgics*, an imperfect world is more lovable and more evocative than a perfect.

At the same time, the *Aeneid*'s version of the golden age is a part of his moral vision. This Italy may appear idyllic but it is not really so. The banditries of Ufens, Numanus' coarse praise of violence, the constant skirmishings between Evander and Latinus' peoples, Mezentius' brutality are wrongs which need righting; and Aeneas' triumph, bringing eternal peace between Trojans and Italians, will be a stage forward in the pacification of Italy. Even Tyrrhus and his neighbours are far from perfect: their life has a childlike charm, it is true, but like children, they are casually and foolishly violent, with

---

[100] There is the additional problem that Seneca's account of Posidonius may be contaminated by Virgil: he quotes from the first book of the *Georgics* three times and echoes a phrase from *Aeneid* 8.   [101] See above pp. 336 ff., and Appendix.

dreadful consequences for both the Trojans and themselves; they too need wise governance, and some of the blessings of civilization. We have seen how poignant is the cost of the Trojans' coming to Italy; we can now see that this is not the full story, the more particularly since Virgil has chosen to associate the golden age with the reign of a good king and the rule of law. In the short term, with the coming of war, there will be grief and destruction, and Virgil will realize these to the full; but in the long term there will be great gain. Even the Italian rites and traditions, which seem to be threatened with extinction, will not perish utterly, for in the marvellous reversal of the last book Juno obtains that the Trojan customs not the Italian shall be extinguished;[102] and indeed the whole way in which Virgil handles Faunus (say) or the symbols and ceremonies of Latinus' city presupposes that they still survive, potent upon the imagination of his readers. He has avoided both a glib optimism and a too easy gloom: we can see both Jupiter's providence and its cost.

The idea that law and leadership are necessary for the best happiness of mankind may strike some as a more mature view of the human situation than lamentations for a lost paradise. Moreover, since Saturn's disappearance, there has, on Virgil's account, been neither a steady decline nor a steady advance. The progress of history is not simple: Virgil suggests a diversity of phenomena, both good kings and bad. Furthermore, by modifying the traditional concept of the golden age, he keeps open the possibility that under a good ruler it might again return. In the fantastical fourth Eclogue Virgil could pretend to envisage the imminent return of paradise; in the more sober world of the *Aeneid* that would be grotesquely out of place, but the return of a golden age such as Evander describes would not be beyond the range of imagination. Indeed, we have heard about the golden age earlier in the *Aeneid*:[103]

> hic vir, hic est, tibi quem promitti saepius audis,
> Augustus Caesar, divi genus, aurea condet
> saecula qui rursus Latio regnata per arva
> Saturno quondam, super et Garamantas et Indos
> proferet imperium; iacet extra sidera tellus,
> extra anni solisque vias, ubi caelifer Atlas
> axem umero torquet stellis ardentibus aptum.
> huius in adventum iam nunc et Caspia regna
> responsis horrent divum et Maeotia tellus,
> et septemgemini turbant trepida ostia Nili.

---

[102] *Aen.* 12. 819 ff.   [103] *Aen.* 6. 791–800.

This is the man, this, whom you so often hear promised you, Caesar Augustus, child of a god, who shall again establish a golden age for Latium in those lands once ruled by Saturn, who shall extend his empire beyond the Garamantes and Indians—a land lies beyond the stars, beyond the yearly path of the sun, where Atlas, bearer of the sky, turns upon his shoulder the heaven, studded with blazing stars. Because of his coming the Caspian realms and the Maeotian land shudder even now at the gods' oracles, and the trembling mouths of the sevenfold Nile are in turmoil.

Behind the fantasy and the flattery we can recognize some of Virgil's recurrent themes. There is the extension of the time horizon in both directions; as Anchises looks the very furthest forward that he can possibly see (for as later ironists have observed, his vision is clear as far as the poet's lifetime but is blocked beyond it), he gazes back simultaneously to the earliest king in Italy that he could possibly name. Once more, too, the temporal extension is accompanied by a spatial extension, as the empire seems to be flung extravagantly beyond Garamantes and Indians to the stars. The Caspian and the Sea of Azov take us to a remote and semi-fabulous north, Indians to the east, Nile and the Garamantes to the far south.[104]

Virgil's idea of history is strongly linear, and this linearity is reinforced by his sense of greater and lesser spaces. Little Latium is a limited area, just one small corner of the earth (indeed, where Saturn lurked hidden, as we later learn),[105] but it is set against the whole world and the universe beyond. The vast expansion of empire from so small a core will be a linear process, the operation of many centuries. On the other hand, the idea of the golden age returning again may seem to suggest a cyclical view of history. There is no contradiction, however, for this scheme is not cyclical in the strict sense: it is not that history runs through the same sequence of events a second time; rather, Augustus brings about a restoration that comes as the climax of operations that have spread over hundreds of years. Anchises' speech offers a complex view: there are vast developments and changes described in it, but these are combined with a sense of the connectedness of history. The final achievement of Augustus and

---

[104] But no mention of the west or north-west. Horace openly expects Augustus to conquer the Britons (*Carm.* 3. 5. 2 ff.); that was not on the cards, and Virgil never predicts it. Instead, he here preserves a certain vagueness; the Romans were inclined to count anyone east of Suez as 'Indus', and 'Garamantes' could be used to cover most North African peoples; the Caspian and the Nile merely shudder. Though Virgil sounds as if he is foretelling vast conquests, he actually commits himself to little; even in the midst of extravagant and fantastical flattery, he retains a certain realism.   [105] *Aen.* 8. 323.

the Romans will grow out of what it is Aeneas' task to start here and now: already the ends of the earth are trembling, '*iam nunc* et Caspia regna | responsis horrent divum . . .'. Aeneas himself will not restore a golden age; he will not even found Rome. But he marks the start of a process. And like both Saturn and Evander he comes to Italy as an exile, to found a virtuous kingdom.

The seventh book looks to both past and future, and appropriately it gives an especial prominence to an aged man, Latinus, and a very young one, Ascanius, also called Iulus, the very name foreshadowing his Roman descendants. Twice in this book the Trojans perform an act of critical importance, and in each case the principal agent is not father Aeneas but his unwitting son.

The first of these acts is the 'eating of the tables', which reveals to Aeneas that a prophecy has been fulfilled and his people have reached their final home. It is told in an extraordinary passage:[106]

> Aeneas primique duces et pulcher Iulus
> corpora sub ramis deponunt arboris altae,
> instituuntque dapes et adorea liba per herbam
> subiciunt epulis (sic Iuppiter ipse monebat)
> et Cereale solum pomis agrestibus augent.
> consumptis hic forte aliis, ut vertere morsus
> exiguam in Cererem penuria adegit edendi,
> et violare manu malisque audacibus orbem
> fatalis crusti patulis nec parcere quadris:
> 'heus, etiam mensas consumimus?' inquit Iulus,
> nec plura, adludens. ea vox audita laborum
> prima tulit finem, primamque loquentis ab ore
> eripuit pater et stupefactus numine pressit.

Aeneas, his chief captains and the handsome Iulus lay their bodies down under the boughs of a tall tree and set out their feast; they place cakes of meal on the grass under the delicacies (so Jupiter himself inspired them) and heap the wheaten base with fruits of the field. It now chanced that when the rest of the food was consumed, as scarcity of eating drove them to direct their bites to scant Ceres, to violate with hand and bold jaws the circle of the fateful pastry and not to spare the flat cakes, Iulus said, 'Hey, are we eating our tables too?'—only that, as a joke. That speech, as they heard it, first brought the end of their travails, and his father at once caught it up from his mouth as he spoke, and checked his words, awestruck by the divine omen.

---

[106] *Aen.* 7. 107–19.

Lines 112–15 have been found sinister, the language suggestive of sacrilege; but if that was Virgil's purpose, we should have to agree with the censure that the passage has also received for being turgid and overblown.[107] However, both these judgements mistake the tone. The clue comes in the line and a half that follow: 'heus' is a colloquialism, and the construction of 'nec plura' and 'adludens', two little phrases hung on to the end of an already completed sentence, is equally foreign to normal epic style. The casual manner is deliberate, but Virgil would have known that it must be disastrous after a passage which he had intended to be either rhetorically grand or sombrely significant. It makes sense, however, once we recognize in those earlier lines a kind of elephantine playfulness. Classical poets being fond of metonymy, the paradoxical description of the goddess of increase as exiguous Ceres, though certainly epigrammatic, might elsewhere not strike the reader as exactly humorous;[108] it becomes so when taken with such grotesqueries as 'poverty of eating', the violating hands, the audacious jaws, the pitiless massacre of segments and the circle of the portentous scone; for after all what is Virgil describing in these bizarre phrases but the conclusion to a perfectly modest and ordinary meal alfresco, as innocent as the sublime picnic of the blessed in Elysium, depicted in the previous book? Epic comedy, some poets have felt, may appropriately be massive and robust: rough buffoonery kindles unquenchable laughter among Homer's gods, and the heavy jesting in the sixth book of *Paradise Lost* led Landor to declare that the first sin of the fallen angels was punning. But the *Odyssey* and even the *Iliad* in the twenty-third book are elegantly humorous, and Virgil too allows some sly touches to lighten at moments the *Aeneid*'s severity; surely his fun here is ponderous to serve a particular purpose. Let us consider further.

Ancient literature has rather little to say about childhood; though a baby appears in the sixth book of the *Iliad*, there is no child, as such, in the Homeric epics. Modern biographies dwell upon childhood experience, and of memoirs it is a commonplace to say that the early parts are often the best. In ancient lives, by contrast, there is little about the subject as a boy, and what there is tends to take the form of stiff anecdotes representing him as a smaller version of

---

[107] K. Reckford asks, 'Why is the nullification of Celaeno's threat described in terms better applied to some major sacrilege?' ('Latent Tragedy in *Aeneid* VII, 1–285', *AJP* 82 (1961), 252–69 at 261); Fordyce (on 110 ff.) finds the lines 'turgid and pretentious'.

[108] 'Exiguam Cererem' at Lucan 4. 96, though pointed (and pilfered), is not comic.

the adult that he is to become:[109] little Cyrus plays at being a king, organizing the other village children and punishing the one who disobeys; little Cato, already inflexible and harsh to flatterers, plays at being a prosecutor and conducting the condemned to prison; the only story told in the gospels about Jesus' childhood foretells his future mission, as the 12-year-old is found in the Temple, confuting the scribes and doctors of the law.[110] This attitude to childhood was encouraged by the idea, prevalent though not universal in antiquity, that everyone was born with a certain fixed *ethos* or character; circumstances might either encourage or hold back its open expression, but essentially it was innate. We, by contrast, are readier to believe that early experience may shape or permanently alter a person's character. More particularly, the modern idea of the child as possessing his own order of experience has come down to us from Wordsworthian romanticism, Victorian sentimentality, and (from a different angle) Freudian psychology. In antiquity the man who expresses a sense of the specific and separate character of childhood experience most strongly, at least before the fourth century, is probably Jesus. 'Except ye be converted, and become as little children, ye shall not enter into the kingdom of heaven'—it is hard now to recover the originality of that vision. Nor is it sentimental: the demand that we should 'receive the kingdom of God as a little child' implies that children have their own quality, not that they are innocent or perfect.[111] Indeed, Jesus watches how they sulk and bicker: 'Whereunto shall I liken the men of this generation? . . . They are like unto children sitting in the marketplace and calling one to another, and saying, We have piped unto you, and ye have not danced; we have mourned to you, and ye have not wept.'[112] Not many classical poets share this interest, Lucretius being a striking exception, as we have seen. In one place Juvenal observes the child's passion for imitation: the gambler's son plays at rattling a toy dice-box.[113] And here is Virgil, noticing that children like silly jokes, and producing the first specimen of child's humour in European literature: Iulus stands

---

[109] A striking exception, from late antiquity, is Augustine's *Confessions*.

[110] Hdt. 1. 114; Plut. *Cato min.* 1. 2, 2. 5; Luke 2: 41 ff.

[111] Matt. 18: 3; Mark 10: 15.

[112] Luke 7: 31 f. As another instance of his original conception of human relationships, Jesus is perhaps the only man in antiquity who is recorded as having friendships with women, independent of physical desire.

[113] Juv. 14. 4 f. Juvenal's interest in children finds expression in other places too: see Jenkyns, *Three Classical Poets*, 194–7.

revealed as the forebear of not only Caesar Augustus but Nigel Molesworth. This touch of naturalism is the more unexpected in that Virgil's treatment of the boy seems elsewhere somewhat uncertain: his age appears to fluctuate considerably.[114] It is sometimes said that a growth of interest in children during the Hellenistic period and after is indicated by their more frequent appearance in visual art (and even by the purchase of very young slaves as *deliciae*); in such cases, however, the child is viewed and enjoyed from outside, as a pet might be, or a comic slave or a quaint old woman. But Virgil, just for a moment, gets inside the childish mind.

Looking back over the whole episode, we can now see that the galumphing humour of lines 112–15 prepares the way for Iulus' rather clumsy joke. In terms of diction there are three tones in the passage. First comes the orotundity with which the meal is described, then the colloquial casualness of Iulus' remark, matched by the momentary looseness of the few words that follow it, and then one of those sudden liftings of tone at which Virgil excels. As in the fifth line of the *Georgics*[115] it comes unexpectedly and yet (as we feel) inevitably in the middle of the hexameter. 'Nec plura, adludens'— it is all so trivial, and yet (here is the wonder) that triviality brings the Trojans to the end of their troubles. The sense of amazed relief, impressed upon us by the changing pattern of the diction, is forceful and oddly touching. And as the diction changes, so does the subject: young Iulus is forgotten and father Aeneas takes command. Indeed our thoughts are drawn back one generation more: as Aeneas speaks, he twice recalls Anchises, each time calling him 'genitor',[116] just as he was himself called 'pater' at line 119. What meant so little to the boy means so much more to the experienced Aeneas and to Anchises' prophetic wisdom. As the poet presses back one generation, and then back again, we recognize a variation on one of his recurrent themes.

Ascanius comes to the fore again later in the book, when he goes hunting and shoots a stag, the pet of Silvia, Tyrrhus' daughter. The

---

[114] The child fondled by Dido in the first book would seem much younger than the young warrior of the ninth. Heinze (157 f.) suggested that he is 11 or 12 at Carthage, a year older in Latium. Or perhaps he could be imagined as about 15; but a discomfort persists. Virgil is sufficiently concerned with plausibility, however, to have Ascanius kill Numanus with an arrow shot, and then to withdraw from battle: in hand-to-hand combat the Italian must necessarily have won. (The idea recently canvassed that in having Ascanius use the bow Virgil means to belittle or cast moral doubt on him is a fantasy: on the contrary, he stands as a pattern of youthful virtue—cf. below, p. 581.)

[115] See above, pp. 329 ff.   [116] *Aen.* 7. 122 f., 134.

country folk are indignant; a brawl starts, people are killed, and a rustic mob rushes to Latinus, demanding battle. As an account of how the war began, this narrative has been both praised and blamed; Macrobius observed that the wounding of the stag was in itself 'leve nimisque puerile' (slight and too childish).[117] But for better or worse, Virgil surely meant it to be so. In the first place, the episode is 'puerilis' in a literal sense. Ascanius, whatever age we suppose him, is less than a full adult. At the story's centre are Tyrrhus' family. Silvia is evidently a child, since she plays with the deer as a pet, and her brother Almo, though the eldest of Tyrrhus' sons, is young enough to be called 'puer'.[118]

Moreover, this is a world which echoes something of the tone and spirit of the *Eclogues*. Virgil stresses that we are among country people: some form of the word 'agrestis' ends the line three times in this episode; the men are 'indomitae agricolae' (farmers unsubdued), and Allecto declares, 'spargam arma per agros' (I shall broadcast arms across the fields).[119] These rustics are also described as herdsmen: it is 'pastores' who hurry to Latinus; Allecto sounds a 'pastorale . . . signum' to arouse them; Galaesus, a casualty of the brawl, though also an arable farmer, has five flocks of sheep and as many herds of cattle.[120] 'Silvae' (woods) had been Virgil's symbol for pastoral, and the word replaces the more solemn 'lucus' in this part of the book. The stag wanders in the woods (errabat silvis), rather like a Corydon; and when he rests from the heat on a green river bank, he resembles the herdsmen in (say) the seventh Eclogue.[121] At the sound of the Fury's horn, 'omne | contremuit nemus et *silvae* insonuere profundae' (Every copse trembled and the woods resounded to their depths).[122] The very name of Silvia makes the word resound the more. It is evidently Virgil's own invention: 'bonum puellae rusticae nomen formavit', Servius observes, 'It was a good name that he devised for a country girl.'[123] A grimmer note is heard in the description of Allecto: 'pestis enim tacitis latet aspera *silvis*' (the fierce fiend lurks in the silent woods); but the tension between the charm of the country and its vulnerability had also been part of Virgil's pastoral idea; the words here recall the third Eclogue: 'frigidus, o pueri (fugite hinc!),

---

[117] *Sat.* 5. 17. 2 (Macrobius supposes that Virgil himself was aware of the problem, and looked for ways of overcoming it).
[118] *Aen.* 7. 487 ff., 532, 575.   [119] *Aen.* 7. 482, 504, 523, 521, 551.
[120] *Aen.* 7. 574, 513 ('a herdsmen's call'), 538 f.   [121] *Aen.* 7. 491, 495.
[122] *Aen.* 7. 514 f.   [123] Serv. *in Aen.* 7. 487.

latet anguis in herba'(Flee from here, my lads, a chill snake lurks in the grass).[124]

These two kinds of affect interact: the pastoral colouring and the centring of the story upon children. Literally, of course, this is not a society of children (Galaesus indeed is elderly), but it is a world in which it comes naturally to dwell out of proportion upon the very young. The whole scene acquires a childlike aura which can hardly be separated from the bucolic tone. Both have a sweetness, a prettiness about them that ventures perilously near to sentimentality (though we may find that Virgil has his own reasons for taking the risk). But there is another colour which is also given to these countryfolk. They are tough, 'duri . . . agrestes'—a tone more reminiscent of the *Georgics*, and one that will be heard again from Numanus later.[125] They are quick to anger:[126]

> improvisi adsunt, hic torre armatus obusto,
> *stipitis* hic gravidi nodis; quod cuique repertum
> rimanti telum ira facit. vocat agmina Tyrrhus,
> quadrifidam quercum cuneis ut forte coactis
> scindebat rapta spirans immane securi.

They arrive before they are expected, one armed with a stake burned to a point, another with a heavy, knotted club; anger makes a weapon of what each man finds as he searches. Tyrrhus summons the ranks, breathing mightily as he snatched up an axe, for he happened to have been cleaving an oak in four by driving in wedges.

Their weapons partake of their own rugged, perhaps clumsy character: significantly, when the word 'stipes' is repeated a few lines later it now bears the epithet attached before to the men themselves:[127]

> non iam certamine agresti
> *stipitibus duris* agitur sudibusve praeustis . . .

It was no longer a matter of a country brawl with hard clubs or scorched stakes . . .

This more robust colour shades into yet another. The name Silvia glances on one side towards the pastoral tone, but also in a more heroic direction, for Silvius will be a name in the royal house of Alba Longa, as Anchises has already declared:[128]

---

[124] *Aen.* 7. 505; *Ecl.* 3. 93.   [125] *Aen.* 7. 504; cf. 9. 603 ff.   [126] *Aen.* 7. 506–10.
[127] *Aen.* 7. 523 f.   [128] *Aen.* 6. 760–71.

ille, vides, pura iuvenis qui nititur hasta,   760
proxima sorte tenet lucis loca, primus ad auras
aetherias Italo commixtus sanguine surget,
Silvius Albanum nomen, tua postuma proles,
quem tibi longaevo serum Lavinia coniunx
educet silvis regem regumque parentem,   765
unde genus Longa nostrum dominabitur Alba.
proximus ille Procas, Troianae gloria gentis,
et Capys et Numitor et qui te nomine reddet
Silvius Aeneas, pariter pietate vel armis
egregius, si umquam regnandam acceperit Albam.   770
qui iuvenes!

That young warrior whom you see, leaning on the spear of valour, holds
by lot the place nearest to the light, and first will rise into the upper air
with an admixture of Italian blood. He is Silvius, an Alban name, your
last-begotten son, whom late your wife Lavinia will bear to you in your
old age and bring up in the woods, a king and the parent of kings, whence
our kin shall hold sway in Alba Longa. That next man is Procas, glory of
the Trojan race, then Capys and Numitor and he who shall revive you by
his name, Aeneas Silvius, outstanding like you in virtue and in arms, if
ever he shall attain the Alba that should be his to rule. What warriors!

The emphasis on the Silvii is strong; three other kings pass by in a
mere line and a half. Chronology is cast aside: Aeneas Silvius is the
son of Silvius, but Virgil has wanted these two names to frame the
entire list. We shall come back to the reasons for this stress; for
the moment we may note that it is firm enough for us to remember it when Silvia appears. This is an example of the poet's prismatic method: the light struck off one passage falls on another, and
the colours alternate, or merge. 'Silvis' at 765 is paradoxical beside the
sonorously heroic 'regem regumque parentem'; the grandeur of this
early monarch is softened by this unexpected note, perhaps pastoral,
perhaps mysterious and deep. Conversely, when the girl is named
in the seventh book, the heroic connotations of her name prepare
us to allow a kind of dignity to her people, those 'indomitae agri-
colae', ready, for all their simplicity, to challenge the armed Trojans
face to face. Later, as the towns of middle Italy arise, Virgil writes,[129]

vomeris huc et falcis honos, huc omnis aratri
cessit amor; recoquunt patrios fornacibus ensis.

The honour they paid to the share and sickle, all their love for the plough
has come to this; they temper again their fathers' swords in the furnace.

[129] *Aen.* 7. 635 f.

Honour to the humble share and sickle, love for the useful plough
—these are striking phrases, picking up a theme from the *Georgics* but
more sharply paradoxical than the lines which they partly echo:[130]

> non ullus aratro
> dignus honos, squalent abductis arva colonis,
> et curvae rigidum falces conflantur in ensem.

The plough receives none of its due honour, the fields grow ragged, for
the farmers are taken away, and curved sickles are forged into the stiff sword.

Virgil presents a kind of ennobled rurality, very different, for sure,
from the ennobled rurality of his Elysium, yet alike it in attributing
a dignity and loveliness to simple things.

How then may these various colours work upon our feelings,
how guide our wider understanding of the poem? The stag's death
is effective as a cause of the war because Virgil speaks upon several
levels: naturalistic, symbolic, moral. In naturalistic terms, he indicates
that a small act can entail huge consequence; a spark can destroy a
forest.[131] A girl in distress; an angry farmer and his neighbours, too
indignant to stop and think or await an explanation; a brawl that
turns into a fully armed skirmish before anyone quite knows how
(it is a subtlety of Virgil's narrative that he writes, 'It was no longer
a rustic conflict', before he has mentioned any exchange of blows
at all)—although Juno's agent Allecto fans the flames, the sequence
of events has a dreadful plausibility on a simple human level. In this
light, the *leve* and the *puerile* are not awkward but pointed: so slight
a cause, the result so grave.

But there is an imagistic as well as a naturalistic meaning.
This is not the first time in the poem that a deer has been used
symbolically:[132]

> uritur infelix Dido totaque vagatur
> urbe furens, qualis coniecta cerva sagitta,
> quam procul incautam nemora inter Cresia fixit
> pastor agens telis liquitque volatile ferrum
> nescius: illa fuga silvas saltusque peragrat
> Dictaeos; haeret lateri letalis harundo.

---

[130] *Geo.* 1. 505–7.
[131] Compare Gibbon's account of a real conflict: 'A blow was imprudently given; a sword
was hastily drawn; and the first blood that was spilt in this accidental quarrel became the
signal of a long and destructive war' (*Decline and Fall*, ch. 26).   [132] *Aen.* 4. 68–73.

Unhappy Dido burns and wanders all through the city in a frenzy, like a
deer struck by an arrow shot, when a shepherd hunting in the woods of
Crete has pierced her, unwary, from afar and left in her his flying steel,
unknowing; in her flight she traverses the forests and glens of Dicte; the
deadly shaft clings to her flank.

The simile, fine in itself, is the more forceful in that it crystallizes
earlier metaphors for Dido's love, the wound and the image of Aeneas
fixed in her breast.[133] As the fate of Latinus recalls that of Priam, so
now the fate of the Italian countrymen recalls that of Dido, partly
through the deer, partly through the hunt. Twice in the *Aeneid* a
hunting party is described, and in each case it sets in train the chief
crisis of one half of the poem, both times through a turn of events
designed by Juno, unforeseen and unintended by the human actors,
first when the storm brings Dido and Aeneas to the cave, and now
when Ascanius shoots the stag. As with Latinus and Priam, the recurrence of images and narrative pattern enforces a sense of the seemingly endless distresses through which Aeneas must pass on his way
to fulfilling his destiny; and there is also a further and more particular symbolism. The shepherd in the fourth book is 'nescius'; he
does not know where his arrow has landed. This detail has both an
immediate and a general application: it shows us Aeneas unaware
that Dido has fallen in love with him; and on a larger view, it suggests that his doom is to bring destruction with him without his
willing it. Dido, like the deer, is lovely and innocent; and Aeneas,
against his own desire, will become the occasion of her death.

The symbolism of Silvia's pet carries a similar implication. If Dido
was like a deer, this deer is conversely like a human being. It has
been brought up in Tyrrhus' family; it is even accustomed to the
master's table; it is combed and washed like a man ('pectebatque ferum',
'she used to comb this creature of the wild'—the paradoxical noun
shows the stag's distance from its natural animal character).[134] It reclines
by the river bank, like a shepherd; and when wounded it seems to
be striving for human speech: it is like one beseeching, 'imploranti
similis'.[135] The phrase that then follows, 'Silvia . . . soror' (sister Silvia),
seems to make her as much the stag's sister as the boys'; the animal
is 'part of the family'. And like the good citizen of Italy that it has
almost become, it knows its home: from its wandering in the woods
it would return nightly 'ad limina *nota*', to the familiar threshold;

---

[133] *Aen.* 4. 1 f., 4 f.   [134] *Aen.* 7. 490, 489.   [135] *Aen.* 7. 495, 502.

the epithet is echoed, pathetically, as the beast staggers home to die: 'saucius at quadripes *nota* intra tecta refugit'.[136]

Another small touch marks the symbolic purpose: Ascanius, as he shoots, is 'eximiae laudis succensus amore' (kindled with a passion for high glory).[137] The phrase seems a little excessive: the boy is hunting, after all, he sees a fine stag with good antlers, and naturally he wants to bring it down. But Virgil wants to recall the cost of glory: in its modest, pastoral way this incident takes up the theme sternly sounded by Anchises in the underworld when he catches sight of Lucius Brutus: this man will sentence his sons to death, driven by love of country and vast desire of glory, 'laudumque immensa cupido'.[138] There is, to be sure, a difference of kind as well as degree between Brutus' vast passion and Ascanius' sporting zeal: the liberator's act is a hard choice freely willed, while the boy has no hard decision to make. But his innocence is Virgil's point: the price of glory may not always be paid upon weighty and mature calculation; it can also be levied upon a man by forces beyond human control. Aeneas does not want to fight a war in Latium; his grief that he must kill Lausus sums up the sorrow of all the young deaths of the war, fair victims who might well be called 'forma praestanti' (of an excellent beauty), as is Silvia's stag.[139] But the Trojans, fathers of Italians yet unborn, must destroy Italian men and Italian things. Of this sombre truth a boy's sport is the foreshadowing, terrible in its slightness.

Both the realistic and symbolic sides of the episode carry a moral weight. The mixing of what might loosely be called the pastoral and georgic modes creates a certain complexity in the depiction of this people. Admiration and a kind of condescension are balanced against each other: we approve the simplicity and hardihood of this folk, yet with a sense of superiority. We may respect the innocence of childhood, but we know that we have outgrown childhood, and we should not have wished to continue children for ever. This doubleness of attitude appears in the description of Galaesus:[140]

> iustissimus unus
> qui fuit Ausoniisque olim ditissimus arvis:
> quinque greges illi balantum, quina redibant
> armenta, et terram centum vertebat aratris.

He who was most just and wealthiest in the fields of Ausonia in those days: five flocks of bleating sheep, five herds of cattle came home to him, and he turned the soil with a hundred ploughs.

---

[136] *Aen.* 7. 491, 500, 'But the wounded animal took refuge within the house it knew'.
[137] *Aen.* 7. 496.   [138] *Aen.* 6. 823.   [139] *Aen.* 7. 483.   [140] *Aen.* 7. 536–9.

Despite his wealth, Galaesus is evidently not a grandee like Latinus, or even an aristocrat like Evander: he belongs to the same society as the countrymen among whom he is killed, and if he is a magnate, he is one of an engagingly rural kind. Though he is a more dignified and substantial figure than the herdsmen of the *Eclogues*, there is in Virgil's account a hint of Corydon remaining:[141]

> despectus tibi sum, nec qui sim quaeris, Alexi,
> quam dives pecoris, nivei quam lactis abundans.
> mille meae Siculis errant in montibus agnae;
> lac mihi non aestate novum, non frigore defit.

I am despised by you, nor do you ask what I am, Alexis, how rich in flocks, how wealthy in snow-white milk. A thousand lambs of mine wander on the Sicilian hills; fresh milk does not fail me in summer, or in the cold.

(How naïve, the sophisticated reader observes, is the poor shepherd's boast.) From one point of view, Virgil dignifies a modest society: within his own community Galaesus is most wealthy and most just, and what Roman could have asked to be more? From another point of view, Virgil gives his wealth a quaintly rustic colour. His prismatic technique discovers both viewpoints. There is a risk, in handling such a theme, of a patronizing tone, or else of sentimentality. Virgil may hope to tread delicately between the two dangers.

Not only is the mixture of pastoral and georgic notes complex; there is a complexity within the georgic tone itself, epitomized in the ambivalent word 'durus'.[142] The ambivalence cannot be cashed out at a fixed value: in the *Georgics* it is absorbed into a predominantly confident tone; in the ninth Aeneid there is a stronger sense that the religion of toughness is inadequate. Indeed, the gap between the enthusiastic way in which Numanus dwells upon the word and the more doubtful note of the poet himself shows how its moral quality fluctuates. And so its appearance here rather raises a question than supplies an answer: how shall we regard this countryfolk's 'hardness'? Virgil's narrative explores this issue.

Let us consider the 'facts' of the matter. Ascanius is innocent (Virgil was not of course enrolled in a league against cruel sports, and the boy's hunting is no crime); Allecto, who goes about her work by exploiting human passions, acts not upon the Trojans but through the Italian shepherds. The most that she does in Ascanius' case is to

---

[141] *Ecl.* 2. 19–22.   [142] Cf. above, pp. 333 f., 416 f.

ensure that his arrow hits the mark;[143] she does not try to influence his mind. More generally, Virgil describes Allecto's interventions in such a way as to baffle attempts to allot simple blame. She slides serpent-like into Amata's being; is it the queen or the demon within her that leads and rages on Turnus' behalf? Turnus himself resists the fury until overborne by her more than human power; in what sense then is the anger that floods through him his own?[144] Virgil wants these questions to be riddling, because their obscurity corresponds to the difficulty of understanding the scope and limits of will and responsibility. How far are men answerable for what they do, how far the agents of causation external to themselves? But this at least may be said, that Allecto works for the most part with the grain of human passion, pressing upon her victims where they are already weak. She exploits Amata's maternal partisanship, Turnus' proud and wrathful temper; we cannot readily imagine her using Aeneas and Latinus in this way. With the country people, similarly, she fans a flame that it already alight: significantly, Tyrrhus and his closer neighbours have already picked up weapons, alarming if clumsy—stake, bludgeon, and axe—before she sounds her signal.[145] Her functions are to bring Tyrrhus and his friends on to the scene and to enlarge the skirmish by spreading the news more widely.

[143] That is, if 'nec dextrae erranti deus afuit' (the god was there to keep his hand from missing) at 498 refers to Allecto. If the 'deus' is Allecto, the fact that Ascanius hit the mark (though not apparently the fact that the stag he lighted upon happened to be Silvia's) was at least partly the goddess's doing. But it seems preferable to take the reference to 'deus' as little more than an epic manner of saying that Ascanius achieved his aim, with a cruel irony in the application of the language of auspicious success to a disastrous act. In this case, the divine malignancy is limited to exploiting the incident once it has happened.

[144] It must be conceded that Virgil's treatment of Turnus presents a special difficulty. In his natural person Turnus rejects Allecto's temptation with contempt, and only through supernatural force is she able to overbear his mind; yet thereafter rage and violence seem to be settled and natural aspects of his character. This is quite different from the way that Allecto's action upon Amata and the countryfolk is described. Virgil's divine figures range from immortal people like Juno and Venus to personifications like Fama. Allecto occupies an ambiguous and perhaps shifting position somewhere in between; which in itself is unproblematic—indeed, rather fascinating. The puzzle in Turnus' case is that she seems, incompatibly, both to work upon his character and to represent the overcoming of that character by supernatural action from without. It is tempting to think that Virgil had himself not resolved the issue.

(D. C. Feeney, *The Gods in Epic* (Oxford, 1991), 168–71, is not troubled, but his careful discussion reveals the costs of supposing that Allecto overwhelms Turnus by a purely supernatural and external force. Virgil 'feels no compunction in jettisoning what might be necessary for us to establish a character for Turnus' (p. 171), and we are apparently to regard him as a victim, a madman possessed of bloodlust and not a moral agent, for the rest of the poem. That sounds more like Lucan than Virgil.)   [145] *Aen.* 7. 505 ff.

It is not that we should crudely blame the shepherds for the war; rather, Virgil suggests that their attractive simplicity is inseparable from a certain rough violence (somewhat, perhaps, as we see the innocence and cruelty of children to be two sides of a single coin). He describes the beginning of the brawl thus:[146]

> non iam certamine agresti
> stipitibus duris agitur sudibusve praeustis,
> sed ferro ancipiti decernunt atraque late
> horrescit strictis seges ensibus . . .

It was no longer a matter of a country brawl with hard clubs or scorched stakes, but they fight with the two-edged steel and a dark crop of drawn swords bristles all around . . .

'Non iam certamine agresti' is an equivocal phrase. The weapons of war are alien to the countrymen, and the metaphor in the last of these lines—a cornfield of drawn swords—is harshly ironical in this rural setting; yet in the very words with which Virgil tells us this, he tells us also that battles of a kind—with clubs and stakes—are a regular fact of rural life. The shepherds are reacting in their accustomed way; only this time they are out of their depth, and the consequences will be terrible. Thus we are made ready to see the Trojans as a beneficent as well as a destructive force. If there are alien habits to be purged out of the newcomers, so there is a violence to be chastened in the natives. It is important to realize that the Italians themselves ravage the land with a casual brutality far beyond anything that the Trojans do. In the next book Aeneas laments the devastation that he must wreak upon his adversaries: alas, what slaughter awaits the unhappy Laurentines; what a penalty must Turnus pay; how many brave bodies shall father Tiber whelm beneath his waters.[147] Rather different is the attitude of Turnus' own allies:[148]

> ductores primi Messapus et Ufens
> contemptorque deum Mezentius undique cogunt
> auxilia et latos vastant cultoribus agros.

Their chief leaders, Messapus and Ufens and Mezentius, scorner of the gods, levy their forces on all sides and strip the broad acres of their tillers.

These are notably brisk lines, from a terse, rapid paragraph in which every opportunity for emotional amplification is brusquely thrust aside. Virgil's empathy is at work again, matching form to content: the

---

[146] *Aen.* 7. 523–6.   [147] *Aen.* 8. 537–40.   [148] *Aen.* 8. 6–8.

harshness of the Italian leaders can be carelessly ridden over because to those leaders themselves the hurt that they may do, to men and to the land, is a routine matter, of slight importance. The fate of Tyrrhus' friends is lingered over, because to Aeneas, as to us, it is a matter for sorrow. That his destiny is a bleak one is in itself a sign of his fineness: the wounding of Italy matters to him, the Trojan, in a way that it does not matter to his Italian foes. And so by a profound paradox the sadness of what the Trojans must do, symbolically drawn out in the story of the stag, is a sign of progress; a new compassion is come into the land. By the end of the poem we learn that two good outcomes—the Italianizing of the Trojans and the civilizing of the Italians—will be be brought to pass through the providential working of fate; but the process cannot be painless. In the eighth book Evander will tell Aeneas how Saturn came to Italy and brought the blessings of order and civilization to a wild, lawless people;[149] Aeneas' own task is not altogether unlike. Virgil accepts —with what regret, yet firmly—the sufferings of men and the loss of charms and beauties as a price to be paid for the onward march of humanity.

Which may cast a new light on the 'sentimentality' of Silvia and the stag. The softness of the passage makes a foil to the scenes of impending war which precede and follow it. Virgil contrasts the grimness of warfare with the charms of rural peace, to be sure; but was he so entirely obvious? Perhaps the very prettiness of the scene has an excess of sweetness, and in the contrast of the little girl and her pet with the stern, larger world of action and conflict, the advantage is not all on one side. Aeneas' life is cast in a sphere which is harder and more austere than that of the shepherds, but also greater —one might perhaps say more adult. Such reflections do not obliterate the more obvious message implied by Virgil's contrast, but they make it more complex, and surely truer to the human condition.

Let us return to the names Silvia and Silvius. In the sixth book the poet lingers over the name, drawing attention to it: '*Silvius*, Albanum *nomen*'. And as he dwells upon the name, he explores its significance: '*Albanum* nomen, *tua* postuma proles'.[150] The two adjectives 'Albanus' and 'tuus' press against each other: Anchises stresses the curiousness of the fact that the son of Aeneas the Trojan will bear an Italian name. At the end of the sentence the same emphasis

---

[149] *Aen.* 8. 319 ff.   [150] *Aen.* 6. 763.

returns: 'unde genus Longa *nostrum* dominabitur *Alba*.'[151] And still the poet hovers over these proper nouns: the last in Anchises' list will fuse in his name both the Italian and the Trojan; appropriately he stands four-square in the middle of a sentence which has Aeneas on one side and Alba on the other:[152]

> . . . et qui *te* nomine reddet
> *Silvius Aeneas*, pariter pietate vel armis
> egregius, si umquam regnandam acceperit *Albam*.

. . . and he who shall revive you by his name, Aeneas Silvius, outstanding like you in virtue and in arms, if ever he shall attain the Alba that should be his to rule.

This is an example of Virgil's capacity to turn traditional matter into the stuff of his personal imagination. Aeneas Silvius was part of the legend; but no other poet could have grasped the name as he does and squeezed so much juice from it.

And so when the name returns, in the feminine form, as war is about to break out between Italians and Trojans, the reader may recall that its future history, as unfolded by Anchises, shows that the enemies will become friends, that their descendants will be one. Thus beyond the harsh blare of Allecto's trumpet we can hear faintly a more distant note of hope. That may seem a heavy weight of significance for one girl's name to carry. But Virgil is uniquely sensitive to the associative force of proper nouns; and the theme of reconciliation, of the ultimate union of apparent opposites, is recurrent in the poem to reach two superb climaxes in the eighth and twelfth books. Silvia's name alone would not amount to much as a signal of hope, but it is a small part of a general movement which runs wide and deep through the poem.

The narrative of the stag and the shepherds is less simple than some have supposed, but when all is said and done, it is not one of Virgil's supreme achievements. Though the softness of sentiment may be more subtly used than at first appears, the pathos may yet seem a little too easily won. It falls slightly too pat that Tyrrhus' eldest son is the first to die, that the best of the older men is among the earliest victims. More generally, the charms of this country society are not realized in the poetry to any great extent; we are told its virtues rather than made to feel them. But perhaps Virgil does as

---

[151] *Aen.* 6. 766. [152] *Aen.* 6. 768–70.

much as he needs to do. The treatment matches the subject: we do not discover very much about the herdsmen because there is not very much to them. A surface prettiness contrasts in one way with the rural but fuller charms of Evander's kingdom, reverberant with Homeric echoes and honourable lineage, as in another way with the deep solemnities of Latinus' city or the awesome darks beneath the crust of Italy by Amsanctus. In the next book Virgil and Aeneas will penetrate further.

CHAPTER 12

A Trojan in Italy: Evander's Kingdom

What seest thou else
In the dark backward and abysm of time?

(Shakespeare)

And indeed Rome is the natural home of those spirits with
which we just now claimed fellowship for Roderick—the spirits with a deep relish for the element of accumulation in the
human picture and for the infinite superpositions of history.

(Henry James)

The diversity of ancient Italy within the *Aeneid* could be sufficiently
accounted for in terms of Virgil's own experience of his country
and its history; none the less, it is in part inspired by the *Odyssey*.
Telemachus' travels take him to old Nestor at Pylos, then to
Helen and Menelaus at Sparta. The scenes at Pylos take place mostly
in the open air; the atmosphere is dignified, but not especially grand.
Menelaus' palace, by contrast, is wealthy and glamorous; in the eyes
of the young Telemachus it seems like the house of Zeus himself.[1]
Virgil takes up this contrast (indeed, Latinus' hall is in a new sense
like the house of Zeus, since it is a 'tectum augustum' and a temple,
foreshadowing the future temple of Capitoline Jupiter);[2] but he runs
it in the opposite direction, moving from Latinus' majestic setting
in the seventh book to the simpler life of Evander in the eighth.
This is one example, among many, of how Virgil's reading and his
response to the sights and sounds immediately around him are fused
together within his imaginative experience into a distinctive way of
seeing and interpreting the world.

Aeneas appears in the eighth book as the mature father of his people; still, he resembles the young, raw Telemachus from the third
book of the *Odyssey* at least in this, that he comes to a new place,

[1] *Od.* 4. 74.   [2] *Aen.* 7. 170 ff.

and learns from an old man. Evander, for his part, is modelled on two figures from Homer's poem, not only Nestor but Eumaeus also, the swineherd with whom Odysseus lodges upon his return to Ithaca. Now Eumaeus is a humble man, indeed a slave, but he receives Odysseus with such courtesy and hospitality as he might expect from a royal house; such as he has received in the land of the Phaeacians, at the court of King Alcinous; such as he will not receive from the suitors who have occupied his own palace. Symmetry, order and scale are the characteristics of the houses in which good kings live, and they characterize Eumaeus' homestead too. His swine live in a sort of pig palace, built of quarried stone, in a place commanding a wide view, and with the sows penned apart from the boars.[3] Moreover, he is of royal birth, but kidnapped by pirates as a child and sold into slavery.[4]

The narrative of Odysseus and Eumaeus in the swineherd's hut unfolds at a leisurely pace unique in the Homeric poems. Goethe understood its slow, gentle, domestic dignity when the *Odyssey* inspired him to write *Hermann and Dorothea*, that long and expansive epic idyll of German bourgeois life. And Virgil understood as he produced a mirror image of the Homeric idea. Whereas Eumaeus is a swineherd with something of the colour of a king, Evander is a king described at moments in terms which suggest a peasant. He is 'pauper', a man of modest means;[5] and as he bids Aeneas enter his house, he asks him not to despise its lowliness:[6]

> ut ventum ad sedes, 'haec' inquit 'limina victor
> Alcides subiit, haec illum regia cepit.
> aude, hospes, contemnere opes et te quoque dignum
> finge deo, rebusque veni non asper egenis.'
> dixit, et angusti subter fastigia tecti
> ingentem Aenean duxit . . .

When they reached his abode, Evander said, 'Victorious Hercules crossed this threshold, this royal house received him. My guest, dare to despise wealth and fashion yourself too to be worthy of godhead, and come not scornful to poverty.' So he spoke, and led big Aeneas beneath the roof of his narrow dwelling . . .

By these means Virgil alludes to the motif of theoxeny, the story in which a god or hero—Hercules, as Evander makes plain, was both—accepts the hospitality of the humble. Molorchus received Heracles, Hecale received Theseus (both stories had been told by

---

[3] *Od.* 14. 5 ff.   [4] *Od.* 15. 413 ff.   [5] *Aen.* 8. 360.   [6] *Aen.* 8. 362–7.

Callimachus); in Ovid's *Metamorphoses* Philemon and Baucis entertain Jupiter and Mercury unawares.[7]

Evander's correspondence to Nestor fills out the picture in
another way. Nestor, the wise and wordy counsellor of the Greek
army, a fund of unhurried reminiscence, is treated in the Homeric
poems with a genuine respect which none the less leaves a place for
irony. That irony is most elegant in the twenty-third book of the
Iliad, when the old man, in a speech of forty-four lines, tells his son
Antilochus how to conduct himself in the chariot race. Antilochus,
cool and shrewd, says not a word in reply, ignores his father's advice
altogether, and meets with conspicuous success. In Virgil's eighth
book the memory of Homer's Nestor readies us for an exploration
of ancient Italy in which, for all its seriousness, a quiet amusement
may not be out of place. The poet will allow himself touches of
humour, lightly sketched, not only in the description of some of
the sights that Aeneas sees, but even in the depiction of Evander
himself. The hint of a smile, for instance, may be glimpsed in the
phrase, 'talibus inter se dictis' (thus conversing one to another), coming after much talk from the old man, and none at all reported from
Aeneas (though we do hear that he asked questions).[8] We suspect
that the conversation was pretty one-sided. The next day Evander
makes for Aeneas' lodging 'sermonum memor et promissi muneris'
(mindful of (his) conversation and promised service).[9] On the surface the phrase 'sermonum memor' means 'remembering their previous conversation', but we may also catch a second meaning: Evander
recalls that he has a chance for more continuous utterance. And
indeed when he meets Aeneas, he gets in first: 'licito tandem ser-
mone fruuntur. | rex prior haec . . .'[10] We are told that it is a con-
versation, but the event proves otherwise: the old king speaks for
fifty lines, and Aeneas' response, we learn, is a silent meditation, or
would have been had not a portent intervened.[11]

Separately, the evocations of Nestor and Eumaeus each contribute
something to the tone; together they splendidly suit Virgil's prismatic method. The correspondence to Eumaeus alone suggests a
complex yet whole idea of royal simplicity, a vision which the merging of Nestor with the swineherd further enriches. Such exquisite
fusion of majesty and humility will not perhaps be found again until

---

[7] Cf. above, p. 142.   [8] *Aen* 8. 359 (Aeneas' questions, 312).   [9] *Aen*. 8. 464.
[10] *Aen*. 8. 468 f., '. . . At last they enjoy a free conversation. First the king said . . .'.
[11] *Aen*. 8. 520 ff.

Milton catches the note in *Paradise Lost*: Adam and Eve are gardeners, naked, ignorant of the world; but they are also the lords of nature, the king and queen of creation, and they address one another with an amorous ceremony worthy of the greatest court upon earth. Milton inverts Virgil, as Virgil had inverted Homer, for Adam and Eve are not literally monarchs but gardeners with the loveliness of kingship breathed upon them; and if Milton carries the conception to a pitch of beauty beyond even Virgil's treatment, Virgil was the man from whom he first took it.

The eighth Aeneid also continues Virgil's exploration of Italy. It is a sign of his fine discrimination that in this and the previous book he can describe two sets of country people and make them, though so similar, so distinct. And here again the memories of Homer, far from being the product of a literary imagination divorced from his Italian instincts, enhance the sense of Italy. Evander's people, the Arcadians, have a Greek ancestry behind them, Evander himself has a kind of country-gentlemanliness about him, and these qualities are evoked by the faint Homeric echoes in the verse which describes them. Tyrrhus and his friends have no Grecian culture behind them, no aristocratic or divine forebears, and correspondingly they lack a literary ancestry, beyond a hint or two of the colouring that Virgil himself had used in the *Eclogues*. The use of literary reminiscence, again, helps him to discriminate between the passages on Roman antiquities in these two books. The Italy of Evander is as much an ancestor of the poet's Italy as is the kingdom of Latinus, but Evander's Italy blends, evolves, and assimilates, as the Greekness of the Arcadians' origin reveals, while the world of Latinus is deeply, primevally Italic. Virgil's very success disguises how unpromising a subject for poetry was the prehistory of Roman institutions; it is an exceptional imagination that shapes from this dusty material a sense both of immemorial rootedness and of a developing complexity of traditions, tinged with Grecian civility, and makes each seem part of the true Italian inheritance.

The eighth is the most sunny and relaxed book of the *Aeneid*. There is only one moment of keen pathos, when Evander bids goodbye to Pallas, praying to the gods that his son may survive, but if not, that they should kill him first, while he still has the possibility of hope. He collapses, and his attendants carry him back to his home.[12]

---

[12] *Aen.* 8. 571–84.

Poetic drama has a tightness unlike the uncertainty of life: from this moment we know that Pallas will not return. But the book is so constructed that Evander's cry is felt as a single, sudden stab of high rhetoric in the middle of a book from which the note of anguish is otherwise kept out. Indeed, it may even accentuate, by force of contrast, the easy mood that elsewhere predominates.

The cheerful tone arises in part out of Aeneas' own experience: we shall find that this is a book in which things are going his way throughout. But the mood is created as much by the manner in which the story is told as by its content. In a small way, even the Homeric background helps the effect. We know that the *Aeneid* shadows successively the *Odyssey* and the *Iliad*, and we thought that we had left the *Odyssey* behind and moved into the *Iliad*'s harsher world. But suddenly we are allowed a 'holiday' in the *Odyssey*'s blithe atmosphere. If we recall that the scenes in Eumaeus' home are the most leisurely in Homeric poetry, the sense of liberty, for a space, from the grimness of warfare is all the greater. The generous quantity of aetiological antiquarianism, on the other hand, is not traditional to epic poetry at all: it suggests rather the concerns of Hellenistic verse, above all the *Aetia* of Callimachus. Part of our holiday is a departure from epic themes altogether; the echoes of a more modest genre match the modesty of Evander's little town.

The narrative, too, is expansive to a degree unparalleled elsewhere in the *Aeneid*. The book ends with a description of Aeneas' shield spread over more than a hundred lines, not much shorter than the account of Achilles' shield in the *Iliad*, though in general Virgil's design of squeezing the stories of both *Iliad* and *Odyssey* into a poem less than the length of either demands a formidable compression. This book is the more striking in that the book has already found space for Evander's tale of Hercules and Cacus, eighty lines long and a digression unlike anything else in the poem. That is not to say that it has no connection with the larger narrative. It is clear that there is a correspondence between Hercules and Aeneas, and some readers have believed themselves to detect a number of further correspondences with events elsewhere in the *Aeneid* or in Virgil's own day. But the number of such correspondences is less important than their nature, and it is this nature which gives the story its digressive character. For they are simply decorative. Suppose any number of parallels with Aeneas, with Turnus or Mezentius, with Augustus; they would still only be incidental to a tale elaborated for its own sake.

There are other set pieces within the *Aeneid* which do not advance the plot in a simple sense, including the description of the shield and even the visit to the underworld; but their relation to the poem as a whole is fundamentally important. Virgil uses the story of Cacus as a vehicle for bravura display; it is 'detachable' from the *Aeneid* in a sense that none of the poem's other set pieces is, and surely he designed it so: with an unobtrusive wit he gives this uniquely digressive tale to the Nestor of Italy.

His account of Venus and Vulcan is unique for this poem in another way: in its playful handling of the Olympians. Two Homeric models lie behind it: Thetis' appeal to Hephaestus to make a shield for her son Achilles, in the eighteenth book of the *Iliad*, and Hera's seduction of Zeus, in the fourteenth book. Perhaps Virgil also thought of Demodocus' story of the adultery of Ares and Aphrodite in the *Odyssey*. Each of these two latter episodes, as it happens, has a mood without exact parallel within the poem of which it forms a part: the deception of Zeus is a sensuous comedy of manners, in which the sexual act is celebrated as never again in the *Iliad*; and Demodocus' story treats adultery, elsewhere in Homer a sombre theme, as a joke. Virgil treats his gods here with a blend of the skittish, the voluptuous, and the picturesque not found elsewhere in the *Aeneid*.[13] Poor Aeneas was not allowed such language for his affair with Dido.

Nor are the notes of quaintness and humour absent. Venus seduces Vulcan, after all, so that he will make a shield for her son by another man. In the circumstances, the simile which likens the god to a woman who gets up in the dark to work and so keep her husband's bed chaste combines a light pathos with an irony not altogether solemn.[14] A woman, and a poor one at that—it is not a dignified comparison for the Olympian. The work of his factory is cheerfully anthropomorphized, with a pretended naïvety. The Cyclopes are busy on a chariot for Mars, an aegis for Pallas, a thunderbolt, forged but only half polished, for Jupiter; Vulcan tells them to drop everything for this special job.[15] Equally picturesque, in its way, is the famous line, a showpiece of metrical technique, whose hammerblow rhythm of heterodyne spondees mimics the Cyclopes' steady labour at the anvil: 'ílli ìn|tér sè|sé màg|ná vì | bracchia tollunt.'[16] Revealingly, the

[13] *Aen.* 8. 405 f.   [14] *Aen.* 8. 408 ff.
[15] *Aen.* 8. 426 ff.   [16] *Aen.* 8. 452 = *Geo.* 4. 174.

line is filched from the *Georgics*, where the comparison of giant Cyclopes to bees is plainly meant to entertain. But Virgil is a smooth performer, and the quaint or humorous notes are mostly quiet, covered by a floridly formal or heroic diction; we sense a subtle adjustment rather than a startling novelty of tone.

Taking together Venus, Hercules, the shield, we can see that the sense of ease and expansion is a matter not only of the book's individual sections but of the relations between them. This is an unusually episodic book, and Virgil is so careful and so masterly in his construction that this is surely not a chance or a miscalculation. The narrative itself rambles, just as Aeneas rambles with Evander over the site of Rome, for content and structure are matched. At Pallanteum even the walking and talking are conducted at a leisurely pace. A less urbane poet might have told us more bluntly that the old king was slow on his feet and generous of utterance; Virgil is blandly courteous:[17]

> ibat rex obsitus aevo,
> et comitem Aenean iuxta natumque tenebat
> ingrediens varioque viam sermone levabat.

The king went his way beset with age, keeping Aeneas and his son by him as company, and as he walked lightened the way with a wide range of conversation.

Moreover, Aeneas himself is curiously unhurried about getting his business done. By the time that night falls, at line 369, the hero has received a liberal quantity of tourist information, but he is no nearer to defeating his enemy, and the events of the next day suggest that his entire stay at Pallanteum has been largely purposeless. The god Tiberinus sent him forth on his journey to strike a treaty with the Arcadians and add them to his fighting forces;[18] arrived among them, he finds that their resources are scant. Despite the four hundred horse which they provide,[19] Virgil emphasizes, by deliberate choice, the Arcadians' inability to offer substantial help. Evander stresses his slight power, 'exiguae vires': instead, his service will be to tell of the Etruscans' revolt and their willingness to serve under a foreign commander.[20] These are the troops that will really matter in the imminent war, but Tiberinus has directed Aeneas to them by a remarkably roundabout route. And even now, the men who take

[17] *Aen.* 8. 307–9.   [18] *Aen.* 8. 56.
[19] *Aen.* 8. 518 f.   [20] *Aen.* 8. 473, 475 ff.

the ship back down river and bring the vital news to Ascanius are
in no hurry: they drift lazily with the stream:[21]

> pars cetera prona
> fertur aqua segnisque secundo defluit amni,
> nuntia ventura Ascanio rerumque patrisque.

The rest of them are borne by the water's current and drift idly down the
favouring stream, to come to Ascanius as messengers concerning his father
and the state of affairs.

And indeed the current of events is flowing their way.

In terms of plot the eighth book is important because it introduces Aeneas to Pallas, and under circumstances which kindle his
affection and sense of reponsibility for the young man. Structurally,
too, it is useful. A strength of the *Iliad*'s plot is that it keeps the greatest warrior away from the field of battle for much of the fighting;
it was harder for Virgil to find a way of delaying his climax, the
encounter of Aeneas and Turnus. The hero's journey up river assists
this end, and enables Virgil to add variety and tension by following the scenes in Pallanteum with a book, the only one in the poem,
from which Aeneas is entirely absent. Besides, the site of Rome is
obviously a theme of high intrinsic attraction. In view of all this, a
stern critic might conclude that the mechanism is unwieldy: that
the poet has wanted Aeneas on the site of Rome but has failed to
find a convincing reason for getting and keeping him there. However, Virgil seems to enjoy the improbability, and rather than conceal
the oddity of his hero's dalliance with a people who can give him
little help, he draws attention to it—and to good effect. The dry
rapidity of the book's first paragraph shows the speed at which Aeneas'
enemies are moving, and the lines that follow vividly describe his
anxiety;[22] it is therefore most striking that Tiberinus should, at this
of all moments, give him the assurance of certain success and send
him away for three days from the centre of action. Virgil invites us
to feel that the god knows what he is doing, for Aeneas is indeed
safe, he can afford to take his time, and perhaps the site of Rome,
like the show of heroes in Elysium, is something that Aeneas mysteriously ought to see, something which will obscurely modify his

---

[21] *Aen.* 8. 548–50. The irregular scansion of 549 (weak caesura in the third foot, with
no strong caesura following in the fourth) and 550 (no caesura at all until the fourth foot)
makes the lines strongly homodyne, creating an effect of continuous smooth flow.

[22] On the effect of these paragraphs, see above p. 329.

experience, even without his comprehending its significance. Certainly he finds much to brace him for the struggle ahead. He sees a foreign people that has become assimilated into Italy, and in Pallas the fine flower of a union between the newcomers and the native race; he learns of Italians who are not only willing but eager to serve under a leader from abroad; he meets his mother and receives his shield. He is refreshed and strengthened. When the others are alarmed at the vision of armour in the sky, he is confident:[23]

> tum memorat: 'ne vero, hospes, ne quaere profecto
> quem casum portenta ferant: ego poscor Olympo . . .'

Then he declares, 'Do not ask, my host, do not indeed, what event these portents foretell: it is I whom Olympus calls . . .'

We do not often hear him speak with this massive assurance.

The places where revelations come lie a little apart. Anchises unfolds to Aeneas the mysteries of nature and history 'in valle reducta'; it is 'in valle reducta' again that Venus displays to her son the shield with the Roman glories beaten upon it.[24] And the eighth book as a whole is set apart. The master of transition makes a complete break at the end of it. In every other case the narrative flows on from the end of one book to the start of the next; on this occasion it stops, goes back in time, and turns to what has been happening to others elsewhere. In the experience of Aeneas and in the structure of the *Aeneid*, the eighth book is marked off as a space of repose. In the concluding line, fusing metaphor and actuality, the hero, hoisting the shield, lifts the fame and fate of his descendants. He must pick up the burden of destiny again; the holiday is over.

These considerations suggest how inadequate it is to take any one aspect of the book on its own. The colour and atmosphere of Evander's world are like light mellowed by reflection and refraction off a multitude of textures and surfaces: structure, context, literary echoes all play their part; form, content, and allusion flow together into an expressive unity. The result is to bathe the Arcadians in a simple pleasantness. The Homeric parallels do not here have the tightness that awkwardly stiffens the narrative in (say) the third book; the ease and freedom with which they are applied may even enhance the freshness of the world which they evoke. Around Evander and Pallas glows the tender and affectionate nimbus of the sweet archaic world

---

[23] *Aen.* 8. 532 f.   [24] *Aen.* 6. 703; 8. 609, 'in a secluded valley'.

of the *Odyssey*. The nearest parallel to this elsewhere in the poem
is our first sight of Dido, surrounded through simile by the virginal
grace of Diana and the charm of Nausicaa.[25] There the irony was
cruel; Evander too is to have his happiness destroyed by his son's
death, but the emphasis is predominantly on the rural pleasures of
a settled life.

Evander's world, agreeable in itself, is also significant for the impression that it makes on Aeneas; so we must now turn to him. In the
seventh book, after the portent of the tables, he prays to the deities
of the land. Once again, Virgil has taken a motif already known in
epic poetry. Any hero, newly arrived upon an alien shore, will be
prudent to conciliate the local gods. Thus Apollonius' Jason, on first
reaching his goal, the land of Colchis:[26] 'The son of Aeson himself
poured into the river from a golden cup libations of honey and
unmixed wine to Earth and the gods dwelling in the country and
the souls of dead heroes . . .' But once again, Virgil has borrowed a
motif only to transform it. Jason is merely businesslike: Earth and
the gods who dwell in the land (*ennaetai theoi*) are simply the proper
deities for one in his situation to address. But Virgil will explore
their significance, and seek for their emotional force:[27]

> sic deinde effatus frondenti tempora ramo
> implicat et geniumque loci primamque deorum
> Tellurem Nymphasque et adhuc ignota precatur
> flumina, tum Noctem Noctisque orientia signa
> Idaeumque Iovem Phrygiamque ex ordine matrem
> invocat, et duplicis caeloque Ereboque parentis.

Having thus spoken, he then wreathes his temples with a leafy bough
and prays to the spirit of the place, Earth the first of gods, the Nymphs
and rivers as yet unknown; then he invokes Night and Night's stars now
rising, Jupiter of Ida and the Phrygian mother, each in due order, and
his two parents, in heaven and in Erebus.

Aeneas appeals to dark, ancient, intimate, female things: Night and
Earth—tellingly described as 'first of gods'—and the Earth's inhabitants, the Nymphs, and rivers and the indwelling spirit of the place.
We recognize the abiding themes of the seventh book, but the Trojan
has to address these things from the outside. 'This is your home,
your fatherland,' he has just told his men. He is factually correct,
but we are made to feel that the Trojans have a long way to go

---

[25] *Aen.* I. 494 ff.   [26] Ap. Rh. 2. 1271–4.   [27] *Aen.* 7. 135–40.

before they can know the land and its guardians to be their own, by instinct. The Jupiter invoked is the Jupiter of Trojan Ida, and associated with him is Cybele, identified by Virgil's favourite adjective for picking out an oriental element, 'Phrygius'; Aeneas does not even know the rivers to which he prays. The next day they explore Latium as an unknown land:[28]

> postera cum prima lustrabat lampade terras
> orta dies, urbem et finis et litora gentis
> diversi explorant: haec fontis stagna Numici,
> hunc Thybrim fluvium, hic fortis habitare Latinos.

When the next day, newly dawning, was visiting the earth, lifting her earliest light, by separate ways they search out the city, bounds and shores of the nation, learning that these are the pools of Numicus' spring, this is the river Thybris, here the brave Latins live.

Yet across those words and phrases that suggest the foreignness of the Trojans is woven another theme: the idea of process, that things will change. The adjective 'ignota' is qualified by 'adhuc': those streams will become familiar, in the course of time. 'Idaean Jupiter' is how Aeneas naturally regards the king of the gods; we know him to be also Capitoline Jupiter, the guardian of eternal Rome. And Aeneas has learnt from his father in the underworld that the image of oriental Cybele will one day return as the image of the goddess Roma herself.[29] Moreover, we realize, as Aeneas cannot, that the unknown Numicus is where he will die and be worshipped as 'indiges', a god of the land. The name comes again in the speech of Ilioneus to Latinus:[30]

> hinc Dardanus ortus,
> huc repetit iussisque ingentibus urget Apollo
> Tyrrhenum ad Thybrim et fontis vada sacra Numici.

Dardanus originated from this place, and Apollo seeks it out again, urging us with loud commands to Tuscan Tiber and the hallowed waters of Numicus' spring.

Here, lightly sketched, is that motif which Virgil will develop in the next book, the counterpart to his habit of empathy: we understand what the actors in the drama do not. Ilioneus is searching far back into the past; 'Numicus', in our ears, speaks of the future.

[28] *Aen.* 7. 148–51.   [29] *Aen.* 6. 784 ff.   [30] *Aen.* 7. 240–2.

For the time being, though, the principal stress is on the Trojans' alien character. Aeneas' prayer is followed by the arrival of his ambassadors at Latinus' city in 'unknown garb'; the description of the king makes him primordially Italian; Ilioneus' address associates the Trojans firmly with Jupiter, after Latinus has been linked to Saturn, and significantly calls the Trojan War a clash between Europe and Asia. Aeneas still feels a stranger in his destined home, and speaks like one; we await his next prayer with interest.

It follows the appearance of Tiberinus. This vision itself is approached through one of Virgil's finest transitions. As we have seen, there is a sharp contrast between the first paragraph—brisk, unemotional, with eight men named, and the action described covering half Italy—and the succeeding lines, with the hero pensive and alone.[31] But the contrast is also a connection: Aeneas' anxiety is the direct consequence of the events of the first paragraph, the rapid agitations of his thought are the mental reflection of the rapid actions of his foes. His troubles are described in a simile adapted from Apollonius. Here is the Greek poet's image:[32]

Her heart beat fast and passionate, as a sunbeam quivers in a house, reflected up out of water which has been freshly poured in a cauldron maybe or a bucket; it is shaken by the swift swirling, darting this way and that . . .

And this is Virgil's version:[33]

> sicut aquae tremulum labris ubi lumen aënis
> sole repercussum aut radiantis imagine lunae
> omnia pervolitat late loca, iamque sub auras
> erigitur summique ferit laquearia tecti.

as when a tremulous light flung off from water in brass bowls by the sun or the disc of the shining moon flits widely across every place, and now soars skyward and strikes the coffers of the lofty ceiling.

Apollonius' simile depicts the palpitations of the heart, Virgil's the agitation of the mind—that is the most obvious change. Medea feels simple fear, inspired by the imminence of one particular event; Aeneas is the prey of a wider, rootless anxiety. Apollonius' image is appropriately clear and precise, Virgil's vaguer. It may be day or night; there are high, wide spaces, undefined ('omnia . . . late loca', 'sub auras'); we are no longer among the pots and pans—the charming domesticity of the Greek simile suits a young girl—but in a great

---

[31] See above, p. 329.   [32] Ap. Rh. 3. 755–9.   [33] *Aen.* 8. 22–5.

grand chamber where the mote of light glances over the coffered ceiling high above.[34]

Superb as an image of restless anxiety, Virgil's simile yet has room for night, space, stillness, and a tremulous beauty—the lilting rhythm of 'radiantis imagine lunae' both troubles and delights.[35] The mood is shifting, and the tones of the image now become the tones of actuality. That is fitting in the account of a divine vision, for it is in such visions that dream and reality meet.[36]

> nox erat et terras animalia fessa per omnis
> alituum pecudumque genus sopor altus habebat,
> cum pater in ripa gelidique sub aetheris axe
> Aeneas, tristi turbatus pectora bello,
> procubuit seramque dedit per membra quietem.   30
> huic deus ipse loci fluvio Tiberinus amoeno
> populeas inter senior se attollere frondes
> visus (eum tenuis glauco velabat amictu
> carbasus, et crinis umbrosa tegebat harundo),
> tum sic adfari et curas his demere dictis . . .   35

It was night and throughout all lands deep sleep held the weary creatures, the tribes of birds and beasts alike, when father Aeneas, troubled in heart by grim war, lay down on the bank under the vault of the chilly sky, and let a tardy slumber overspread his limbs. He beheld the very god of the place, Tiberinus with pleasant stream, rise amid the poplar leaves; a thin lawn veiled him in green-grey raiment and shadowing reed covered his locks. Then he spoke and took away Aeneas' cares with these words . . .

The simile before diverged from Apollonius in offering us sun or moon; now it is unequivocally night, and again there is a sense of wide empty space, of big dimensions, solemn height and depth. Aeneas lies in the open air; sleep holds bird and beast, deep sleep; the high heaven, 'aether', is above him; it is cold. His weight of care is conveyed by the slow rhythm of line 29, but the slowness begins to soothe as well; the last word before the god appears is 'quies', rest.

---

[34] Virgil has 'laquearia' only here and in the description of Dido's palace (1. 726), where they are gilded. May we imagine the moon here striking a sudden glimmer of gold through the gloom?

[35] The dancing effect is produced by the combination of a dactylic third foot with the fourth-foot trochaic caesura. Virgil associates the same rhythm with the moon at 2. 255, 'tacitae per amica silentia lunae' (through the friendly silence of the mute moon)—an irrational, perhaps unconscious, but strangely evocative connection of a particular form to content. The context makes this earlier passage too ambiguous, both beautiful and sinister: the Greeks are advancing to sack Troy.   [36] Aen. 8. 26–35.

In his appearance landscape, religion, and sense of patriotic identity come together. Simply as visual description the lines are magnificent, not for clarity or precision, but as elsewhere in Virgil, for the
representation of dim light and things half seen. Significant are the
words that suggest concealment: 'velabat', 'umbrosa', 'tegebat'. The
greenish or bluish-grey lawn that veils the god's body is the colour
of river water, and at the same time it shades into the sedge around
his head; he merges into his background, rising out of the night,
out of poplar leaves (which are grey-green also, to be sure). It is a
marvellous evocation of a cold, glaucous, aqueous world; and the
sound of the lines matches the sense. The evocation is achieved, besides,
with economy of means. There is only one colour adjective, and
that applied to the Tiberinus' clothing, the tint of which would
otherwise be unknown: the reader is left to recall for himself the
hue of sedge and poplar leaf, to remember that it is dark, and to
find the shades of night echoed in the shadowy reeds around the
god's head. And thus the harmony of colour and texture is developed
largely by suggestion.

But all this visual beauty has also a religious and patriotic meaning.
The actual and the impalpable play against each other. Tiberinus is
old; his clothes and setting are grey. The correspondence between
these things is not spelled out, and the reader is again left to infer
the connection for himself, but he would be dull not to feel that
'senior' deepens the greyness of the landscape, that the greyness of
the landscape expresses its antiquity. That the god rises out of the
landscape and merges into the background is more than a visual effect,
more even than a further extension of Virgil's subtle sliding from
one scene to the next; it is a visible expression of the fact that Tiberinus
is a part of the landscape in a sense not far from literal. 'Deus ipse
loci'—that phrase is sharply actualized in the description that follows.
It has also an abstract appeal, reminding us that this is a particular,
an Italian landscape. And it is placed beside 'Tiberinus', the sacral
name of the river, evoking traditional religion and the institutions
of the future Roman state.[37]

However, this is Aeneas' vision, and counterpointing its effect
on us is its effect on him. Looking now from a Trojan angle, we
find the recurrence, and yet the transmutation, of old themes. We
have been reminded, at the beginning of the book, of Aeneas the

---

[37] For the effect of Virgil's various names for Tiber, see above, pp. 401 f.

foreigner. The name of Latium, together with a multitude of other Italian proper names, comes three times in the first paragraph, two of these in phrases which, in empathy with Aeneas' enemies, convey the shock of this alien presence in the homeland:[38]

> mittitur et magni Venulus Diomedis ad urbem
> qui petat auxilium, et *Latio* considere *Teucros*,
> advectum Aenean classi victosque penatis
> inferre et fatis regem se dicere posci
> edoceat, multasque viro se adiungere gentis
> *Dardanio* et late *Latio* increbescere nomen . . .

Venulus too is sent to the city of great Diomedes to ask for help and to inform him that Teucrians are settling in Latium, that Aeneas has arrived with his fleet, bringing his defeated gods, and is declaring that he is summoned by destiny as king, and that many peoples are joining the Dardanian hero and his name is being spread far abroad in Latium . . .

This motif, with the same play of proper nouns, persists as the scene shifts at the start of the next paragraph: 'talia per *Latium*. quae *Laomedontius* heros . . .'[39]

Tiberinus' first words seem to pick up the theme: they recall that Aeneas has come to Latium from another land, and once again use proper names to point up the contrast—'Troianam', 'Pergama', 'Laurenti', 'Latinis':[40]

> o sate gente deum, Troianam ex hostibus urbem
> qui revehis nobis aeternaque Pergama servas,
> exspectate solo Laurenti arvisque Latinis,
> hic tibi certa domus, certi (ne absiste) penates.

O seed of a divine race, who bring back to us the Trojan city rescued from the enemy and preserve eternal Pergamum, O long awaited by the soil of Laurentum and the fields of Latium, here are your sure home (do not shrink) and sure gods.

But the theme now has an entirely new emphasis, for the god sees not an opposition but the restoration to Italy of something that was once its own (once more Virgil exploits the idea that Dardanus was of Italian origin). 'Qui *revehis nobis*'—in the context of imminent war between Trojans and Italians these are dramatic words. But the

---

[38] *Aen.* 8. 9–14.
[39] *Aen.* 8. 18, 'Such were the events in Latium. The noble scion of Laomedon . . .'.
[40] *Aen.* 8. 36–9.

most suggestive and tantalizing phrase of all is in the next line, 'exspectate solo Laurenti arvisque Latinis'. So the earth of Italy does not merely receive Aeneas, it has been waiting for him; for how long? There opens up before us an abyss of undiscoverable time. We might perhaps compare the moment in the underworld when Charon is shown the golden bough and wonders at the venerable token 'longo post tempore visum'.[41] When has he seen it before? who bore it then? We do not know; the answers are buried in the darkness.

Moreover, it is the physical land of Latium that waits for Aeneas —the soil, the fields. The word 'solum' is almost a leitmotiv in this part of the book, returning twice more to keep one of Tiberinus' themes reverberating in the memory.[42] Not since the *Georgics* has Virgil brought us so close to the earth, the very dirt of Italy. The god is not the patron or guardian spirit of the river, but as he insists in a charming sentence, the river itself; and he gnaws at the soil of the land through which he passes:[43]

> ego sum pleno quem flumine cernis
> stringentem ripas et pinguia culta secantem,
> caeruleus Thybris, caelo gratissimus amnis.

I am he whom you see scraping the banks with full current and cutting through the rich tilth, blue Tiber, the stream most favoured of heaven.

It is not just an Italian god who welcomes Aeneas but the land of Italy itself.

Fittingly the god of the land emphasizes fixity: 'hic tibi *certa* domus, *certi* (ne absiste) penates.' The certitude expressed here is both physical and mental; it is closely linked both to the Latin earth and fields in the line before and to the confidence in victory that Aeneas is bidden to feel in the lines which follow. Tiberinus means both 'you may be sure that your home is here' and 'your home is firmly rooted here'. As Virgil recalled the emotional force that Lucretius had got out of the modest word 'certus', he will also have been aware of the difference in his own sensibility, for Lucretius had placed his certitude in knowledge rationally acquired, while Virgil places it in physical things, in earth and stone.[44] And so, after Tiberinus has prophesied, in a line weighted with an archaic majesty of alliteration, that Ascanius will found Alba, he adds, 'haud incerta cano'

---

[41] *Aen.* 6. 409, 'seen after long time'.   [42] *Aen.* 8. 45, 75.

[43] *Aen.* 8. 62–4.   [44] On 'certus' in Lucretius, see above, pp. 239 ff.

(What I foretell is not unsure).[45] For as in the second Georgic, Virgil's sense of Italy as a home firmly established embraces both the works of nature and the works of man. Thus Tiberinus ends his speech by describing his passage among lofty cities as well as fertile fields: 'hic mihi magna domus, celsis caput urbibus exit.'[46]

It is fitting, too, that the omen which confirms the apparition should be visually distinctive: Italy is to be not only felt but seen. This omen is described twice, first as foretelling, then as event:[47]

> iamque tibi, ne vana putes haec fingere somnum,
> litoreis ingens inventa sub ilicibus sus
> triginta capitum fetus enixa iacebit,
> alba solo recubans, albi circum ubera nati.
>
> .   .   .   .
>
> ecce autem subitum atque oculis mirabile monstrum,
> candida per silvam cum fetu concolor albo
> procubuit viridique in litore conspicitur sus; . . .

'And even now, lest you should think all this the empty imagining of sleep, you shall find a huge sow lying under the holm-oaks on the shore, having given birth to a litter of thirty; she will be reclining on the ground, white herself, with her white offspring at her teats.' . . . See, a sudden portent to amaze the eyes, a sow gleaming white through the wood, the same colour as her white litter, lay visible to them on the green shore . . .

In the first passage the colour contrast is implicit: the whiteness of sow and litter is described, indeed stressed, and so the reader may imagine for himself how they stand out against the background of the holm-oaks, trees of exceptionally dark foliage. The second time the contrast of colours is explicit, though it is now different, the green shore taking the place of the ilex trees. The monosyllabic 'sus' at the end of the line seems not far from humorous. It reflects the quaint, archaic character of the portent and, in the second passage at least, seems a verbal analogue to the visual picture, a small patch of white picked out against the green expanse behind.

The lines following Tiberinus' speech show Virgil's feeling for height and depth, light and dark, and their imaginative intertwining:[48]

---

[45] *Aen.* 8. 48, 49.

[46] *Aen.* 8. 65, 'Here is my mighty home, here my fountainhead flows forth amid lofty cities'.

[47] *Aen.* 8. 42–5, 81–3.   [48] *Aen.* 8. 66–70.

> dixit, deinde lacu fluvius se condidit alto
> ima petens; nox Aenean somnusque reliquit.
> surgit et aetherii spectans orientia solis
> lumina rite cavis undam de flumine palmis
> sustinet ac talis effundit ad aethera voces . . .

So spoke the river and then buried himself in his deep pool, seeking the lowest depths; night and sleep left Aeneas. He arises and looking towards the rising light of the sun in heaven in due form he takes water from the river in the hollow of his palms and pours forth these words to heaven . . .

The deeps are associated with night and sleep, the river *buries* himself in the *deep* lake, seeking the *deepest* part—'ima' reinforcing 'alto'—and at this moment day breaks and Aeneas awakes. His movements, in counterpoise to the god's, are all upwards: he rises, he looks up to the sun, he lifts the water in his hands; the repetition in 'aetherii . . . ad aethera' ('aether' is the higher air) adds to the joyful upward drive. The sound of line 69 is notably limpid, and the echo in 'lumina . . . flumine' makes light and water seem all of a piece. A little water in the palm succeeds to the glaucous depths of the nocturnal river. The mood is one of clarity and refreshment. Then Aeneas prays:[49]

> 'Nymphae, Laurentes Nymphae, genus amnibus unde est,
> tuque, o Thybri tuo genitor cum flumine sancto,
> accipite Aenean et tandem arcete periclis.
> quo te cumque lacus miserantem incommoda nostra
> fonte tenent, quocumque solo pulcherrimus exis,
> semper honore meo, semper celebrabere donis
> corniger Hesperidum fluvius regnator aquarum.
> adsis o tantum et propius tua numina firmes.'

'Nymphs, Laurentine Nymphs, company from whom rivers come, and you, O father Thybris with your hallowed stream, receive Aeneas and guard him at last from danger. In whatsoever spring your pools contain you, who pity our distresses, in whatsoever soil you rise in great beauty, always shall you be honoured by my veneration, always by my offerings, horned river, lord of the Hesperian waters. Only be with me, and confirm your will by your presence.'

There are similarities to the prayer in the seventh book, and differences. No longer is a Trojan god invoked, Cybele or Jupiter of Ida; instead the repetition and amplification in 'Nymphae, *Laurentes* Nymphae' shows Aeneas straining towards Italy. Before he had no

---

[49] *Aen.* 8. 71–8.

names: he could only pray to unknown rivers and the 'genius loci'. Now the 'deus loci' has appeared of his own accord; the river has named himself. There has been a development in Aeneas' experience, but it is a development still far from complete. One day he will be an 'indiges', belonging to the land like Tiberinus himself—the words 'exspectate solo Laurenti' looked forward to the future as well as back to the past—but for the present he still cannot feel 'at home' in Italy. If the words 'Laurentes Nymphae' express a striving towards Italy, it is hardly a phrase that a native would use. The Italian ground has been awaiting him, he has learnt, but he does not yet know from what ground Tiber arises. He invokes the river as father—'father Tiber, To whom the Romans pray'—but not by the title that a praying Roman would use. The Graecizing form 'Thybris' is a significant change in a line adapted from Ennius: 'teque pater *Tiberine* tuo cum flumine sancto.'[50] And Aeneas still sees the river, from the Trojan viewpoint, as lord of the rivers of the west, '*Hesperidum* fluvius regnator aquarum'.

The balancing of Aeneas' Trojan sensibility against his growing understanding of Italy is subtly done. It is interesting to note that in the vision of Tiberinus Virgil ignored tradition: according to Dionysius of Halicarnassus it was the 'family gods' who appeared to Aeneas after he reached Latium.[51] Virgil adapted this story for the vision of the Penates in the third book, but here he has wanted the hero, at this transitional point in his experience, to see a god who is both strange to him and yet able to welcome him 'home'.

The sense of certitude and fulfilment—the feeling that Aeneas has indeed 'arrived'—is strengthened in various ways. The line introducing Tiberinus' welcome has already been used twice before the utterance of a vision, first when Creusa bade farewell to Aeneas, and again when the Penates addressed him.[52] It speaks of the hero's cares being taken away, but in each of the two previous cases the element of consolation was balanced, as we saw, against a graver note. This time the removal of care is unqualified; indeed the river declares that the gods' wrath has wholly died away, a somewhat surprising statement in view of the continued importance of Juno's anger in the last books.[53] But Virgil has risked illogicality the better to convey a sense of optimism and completion. The three lines in which

[50] *Ann.* 26 Sk, 'And you, father Tiber, with your sacred stream . . .'.
[51] Dion. Hal. *Ant. Rom.* 1. 57.   [52] *Aen.* 8. 35 = 2. 775 = 3. 153.
[53] *Aen.* 8. 40 f.

Tiberinus describes the portent of the sow repeat verbatim part of
Helenus' speech in the third book. On that occasion the fulfilment
of the prophecy seemed indefinitely remote; now it follows almost
at once. The effect of double repetition, first by verbatim echo, then
by the quick succession of prediction and event, is untypical of Virgil,
though characteristic of Homeric narrative; it reinforces the sense
that Aeneas' long troubles are at last over, that events are moving
rapidly his way.[54] And now this feeling is to be yet further increased,
by a miracle:[55]

> Thybris ea fluvium, quam longa est, nocte tumentem
> leniit, et tacita refluens ita substitit unda,
> mitis ut in morem stagni placidaeque paludis
> sterneret aequor aquis, remo ut luctamen abesset.
> ergo iter inceptum celerant rumore secundo: 90
> labitur uncta vadis abies; mirantur et undae,
> miratur nemus | insue|tum fulgentia longe
> scuta virum fluvio pictasque innare carinas.
> olli remigio noctemque diemque fatigant
> et longos superant flexus, variisque teguntur   95
> arboribus, viridisque secant placido aequore silvas.
> sol medium caeli conscenderat igneus orbem
> cum muros arcemque procul ac rara domorum
> tecta vident, quae nunc Romana potentia caelo
> aequavit, tum res inopes Euandrus habebat.   100
> ocius advertunt proras urbique propinquant.

Throughout the length of that night Thybris calmed his swelling stream,
and flowing back with silent wave stood still so that like a gentle pool or
peaceful mere he should spread his waters into a smooth surface and there
should be no struggle for the oars. And so as the voyage is begun, they
speed it on with approving murmurs; the well-caulked fir-wood glides over
the waters; the waves too wonder, the wood, unused to such, wonders at
the far-gleaming shields of the men and the painted hulls floating on the
stream. The crew with their rowing give night and day no rest; they conquer the long bends and are covered by diverse trees and cut through the
green woods on the calm surface. The fiery sun had climbed to the mid
point of its circuit through the sky when they saw at a distance the walls
and citadel and scattered roofs of houses, a place which Roman might has
now lifted to the height of heaven but where then Evander had his poor
domain. Quickly they turn their prows and approach the city.

---

[54] *Aen.* 8. 43–5 = 3. 390–2. However, whether Virgil would have let the exact repetition stand is a moot point. Coming so soon after the half-line, 41, it raises a suspicion
that this part of Tiberinus' speech is unfinished.   [55] *Aen.* 8. 86–101.

This very beautiful passage indicates, not for the first time, how far some of Virgil's greatest evocations of landscape are from an accurate reproduction of the physical facts. It sounds as though the Trojans' journey up the Tiber lasts some thirty hours, but the distance from Ostia to Rome is too short to require so long a time. The alternative is to suppose that the Trojans set out before dawn and arrive a little after noon on the same day.[56] But even if this meaning can be tortured out of Virgil's account, it would do nothing to alter the impression given of endless travel, inspired not by explicit description but by a suggestiveness which goes beyond the literal signification. Through the language this short passage seems to become a voyage deep into the interior; 'noctemque diemque fatigant' does not state that the distance was great, but it appears to imply it, with even so small a detail as the repeated '-que . . . -que' adding to the effect of travellers pressing on and on. The Trojans are hastening on their mission, we remember (iter inceptum celerant); they 'wear out night and day'; and still they are travelling. Even as they arrive, the niceties of syntax continue to stretch out time and distance. 'The sun had reached its zenith when . . .'—as a factual indicator of time this does not differ from 'shortly after midday', but how great is the difference in emotional colour. The stretching of distance is most evocative of all in the phrase 'longos superant flexus', for here the feeling of length and the feeling of exploration are combined. We look through the Trojans' eyes: the rounding of each long bend is an achievement, a 'conquest', bringing them every time to a sight unseen before.[57]

In this sentence, indeed, we return to the jungly, Congo-like atmosphere suggested early in the seventh book.[58] Interpreters ponder over Virgil's meaning. Does 'varius' refer to the dappling of light and shade, or does the phrase mean only 'a variety of trees'? As the Trojans 'cut the green woods', does Virgil picture the ship slicing through the reflections in the water, as Servius thought, or is this is a metaphorical description of boats making their way between thickly wooded banks?[59]

---

[56] This is the suggestion of J. W. Mackail ('Notes on *Aeneid* VIII', *CR* 32 (1918), 103–6), who concluded from his memories of rowing downstream from Rome to the mouth that the journey in quiet water should take about five hours. Perhaps Scottish energy is superior to Trojan.

[57] Again, the modern traveller may wonder where these windings are between Ostia and Rome. [58] *Aen.* 7. 29 ff.

[59] We can reject another alternative: that the stilling of the current has made the Tiber flood, so that the Trojans can row between islanded clumps of trees. 'Longos superant flexus' rules out this interpretation, which in any case involves two misjudgements: the attempt to rationalize a miracle, and the literalist fallacy commonly identified by the phrase 'How many children had Lady Macbeth?' With regard to the second of these, it is enough

'Placido aequore' seems to support Servius' picturesque understanding of the line, with the other meaning possibly heard as an overtone.
In the case of 'varius' we may reasonably find both posited meanings
present. Like others of Virgil's ordinary adjectives, this one reaches
out in more than one direction, suggesting both a variety of foliage
and a speckled light (Latin 'varius' has to do duty for Greek *poikilos*).[60]
This sentence has something in common with the description of
towns and rivers in the *laus Italiae* of the second Georgic:[61] in the
midst of a passage which is exceptionally rich, as we shall shortly see,
in its appeal to the non-sensuous emotions, these are crystallized into
a visual picture of vivid sharpness.

If the more picturesque interpretations of line 95 are not accepted,
a good deal is lost, but it is remarkable how much remains. At first
blush it seems a little disturbing that Virgil's readers can agree in
admiring a descriptive passage without agreeing what it means; surprise becomes less as we appreciate the extent to which his greatest
evocations of the natural world are concerned with the emotions of
the spectator and the suggestive penumbra of words. Whatever the
exact meaning of 'varius' here, it will still seem to carry, as in the
previous book, a connotation of semi-exoticism; whatever 'cutting
the green woods' means, it will still, following upon the phrase 'they
are covered by trees', by force of suggestion thicken the forest and
close it in around the voyagers, evoking a penetration into the heart
of a dark unknown. The embowering woodland must surely create
a depth of shade; we should infer that from Virgil's description even
if he had not written of the 'opacum . . . nemus' in the next paragraph;[62] there is no need of a word for darkness (except to tell us
that part of the journey is by night). There is not a hint of fear;
instead, green woods and a still water whose stillness is matched by
the flat, paratactic construction of the sentence (in the lines describing
the voyage there is not one subordinate clause).[63] 'And . . . and . . .

to say that so unusual a feature of landscape cannot be present unless the poet has himself put it there, either explicitly or by implication; which he has not. As for the first, it
is of course true that if some agency dammed the Tiber at its mouth, much of the Campagna
would be flooded (and parts of Pallanteum would be under some feet of water, for that
matter); but naturally Virgil does not draw our attention to the fact. The miraculous stillness of the water resists rational explanation; one might as well enquire into the chemical
process involved in the transformation of the Trojan ships into nymphs.

[60] The effect of 'varius' here is influenced by its use in Lucretius and elsewhere in Virgil,
on which see above, pp. 256, 341 f.
   [61] *Geo.* 2. 155–7.   [62] *Aen.* 8. 107 f.
   [63] Lines 90–6 ('pictasque innare carinas' is a noun phrase, a second object for 'miratur').

and . . .'—like the ships themselves, the verse flows peacefully along the unresisting stream.

For richness of empathetic and prismatic effect this fluid and seemingly easy passage is probably the most complex that Virgil ever wrote. We are invited to see and feel the scene from at least four different viewpoints, and some of these viewpoints themselves afford a double, even a triple vision. First, there is the Trojans' view: we round the bends of the river with them; they catch sight of the walls and houses of Pallanteum. Theirs is the vision of a landscape previously unknown, and it is also the vision of a landscape changed by miracle. There are hardly any overt words about the Trojans' reaction to the miracle, but this is a matter to which we shall return.

Second, there is our own Italian view, or rather our multiplicity of views. We know this stream to be our Tiber, the river of Tuscany and Rome. But we are made to set this view of it against two others. The past turns this landscape into another country, and the populous area between Rome and Ostia, clustering round a waterway thick with traffic, disappears, to become one of the wild places of the earth. And there is another transformation, for this wild landscape is itself altered by miracle. The river was notoriously 'yellow Tiber', a violent current, thick with sandy silt. That is how the Trojans first see it, in the seventh book.[64] So the picture of still, glassy water is not just visually striking in itself, but also represents a dramatic metamorphosis of the river as every Roman knew it. Familiar Tiber is made strange in two separate ways, by past time, and by divine action.

Third, there is the Arcadians' view, revealed in the paragraph that follows:[65]

> ut celsas videre rates atque inter opacum
> adlabi nemus et tacitos incumbere remis,
> terrentur visu subito cunctique relictis
> consurgunt mensis. audax quos rumpere Pallas   110
> sacra vetat raptoque volat telo obvius ipse,
> et procul e tumulo: 'iuvenes, quae causa subegit
> ignotas temptare vias? quo tenditis?' inquit.
> 'qui genus? unde domo? pacemque huc fertis an arma?'
> tum pater Aeneas puppi sic fatur ab alta   115
> paciferaeque manu ramum praetendit olivae:
> 'Troiugenas ac tela vides inimica Latinis . . .'

---

[64] *Aen.* 7. 30–2. However, Tiber is unexpectedly 'caeruleus' at 8. 64, perhaps just a 'conventional' adjective, chosen for the word-play with 'caelum', perhaps an anticipation of the miracle to come.   [65] *Aen.* 8. 107–17.

When they saw the lofty ships and saw the Trojans silently gliding through the dark wood and bending to their oars, they are frightened by the sudden sight and leaving their tables rise up as one. Bold Pallas commands them not to break off the rite and snatching up a weapon flies to meet the arrivals, and from afar calls from a mound, 'Young warriors, what cause has driven you to try unknown paths? Where are you heading? What is your race? From what home do you come? Do you bring peace here or arms?' Then father Aeneas spoke thus from the high poop, holding out in his hand a branch of peace-bearing olive: 'You see men of Trojan stock and arms hostile to the Latins . . .'

Having seen the river-banks from the Trojan ships, we now see the Trojans from the land. Virgil's language conveys the Arcadians' amazement and terror: for the Trojans to glide up river is wondrous enough, but the syntax has them gliding through trees, a phrase which enhances the sense of the miraculous as well as echoing the ideas of the previous paragraph: the thickness of the trees, seeming to close around the vessels, the green obscurity even at midday. 'Adlabi', an echo of 'labitur' at line 91, and the silence in which the Trojans approach hint at a power higher than natural. And now Virgil's empathy focuses upon an individual. Pallas detaches himself from the group of Arcadians and rushes forward. The agitated rhythm of 111 expresses a feeling of alarm, but in Pallas' flood of questions there seems as much sheer boyish eagerness as bold confrontation of danger: 'procul' (he can hardly wait to speak); 'iuvenes,' he begins, youth calling to youth; two delicate touches. The questioning of a stranger is a Homeric motif ('Who and whence are you?' Telemachus asks the disguised Athena, 'where are your city and parents?'),[66] but as usual Virgil adapts as he borrows. Pallas' words are more staccato than any Homeric passage; they suggest young curiosity, even a fascination with the idea of exploration ('quae causa subegit | ignotas temptasse vias?'). They are then contrasted with the legato of the two measured lines prefacing Aeneas' reply: one line exactly to each clause and a succession of grave spondees softening into the more rippling rhythm of 116. Pallas' questions began in mid line; no word of saying preceded them, but an 'inquit' was slipped in at the end of the next line, a shape of construction that mimicked the way in which his words came bursting out. Aeneas' answer is introduced by the full epic panoply; the solemn 'fatur' replaces 'inquit', while

[66] *Od.* 1. 170.

the formular 'pater Aeneas' and the compound adjective 'pacifer' add further elements of the high style. His very first word is majestically archaic: 'Troiugenas'—like 'Dardania' three lines later a 'great name', by which Pallas, as we shall shortly hear, will be suitably amazed.

The passage has considerable charm. With tact and economy Virgil foreshadows, as much by the detail of rhythm and diction as by his content, the future relationship between the eager Pallas and the older, graver man. 'Pater' is an especially fine note in this place, a noun commonly linked to Aeneas but here acquiring a new poignancy, hinting at the fatherly part that he will play in the remaining fragment of Pallas' life. It has a further significance too. The Trojans have been seeing sights of high antiquity: we have felt them as newcomers in a primevally ancient realm. Now the prism turns and the light comes off another facet: 'obstipuit tanto percussus nomine Pallas';[67] through the eyes of inexperience, of a younger generation, these 'new' Trojans become the stablished names of heroic story, men such as are heard of in tales. In this light, Aeneas 'ages'; and 'father' becomes the appropriate word.

The Arcadian view of the Trojans thus shades into another view, that of youth. But we must return to the paragraph before, as we have yet to consider the most remarkable viewpoint of all, that of the landscape itself. The miracle is admirably described. The juxtaposition of 'labitur' and 'uncta'—greased keel slipping through supernaturally stilled water—is superbly slithery. The anaphora of 'mirantur . . . miratur' and the drift of line 92 across the third foot without caesura suspend action and glide through a long level calm. 'Wonder . . . wonder . . .' echoes through the verse; however, by a stroke of genius it is not men whom Virgil depicts as wondering but inanimate nature. The Trojans' emotions may be sufficiently inferred from the masterly skill with which the atmosphere of marvel is conjured up; when the whole landscape is flooded with wonder, it would be a prosaic superfluity to spell them out. Seldom has romanticism been expressed by such classical economy of means.

Though the miracle is extraordinary, it has in a sense been prepared. Nature has been 'alive' from early in the book: the soil and the fields have been waiting for Aeneas, the river itself has spoken. In a passage such as the one before us now, the phrase 'pathetic fallacy'

[67] *Aen.* 8. 121, 'Pallas stood amazed, struck by so great a name'.

may hinder rather than help understanding. This is not the kind of 'natural' pathetic fallacy that Ruskin discussed: the almost irresistible tendency to think of 'gloomy clouds' or 'savage mountains' and seldom to be more than half conscious that one is describing what is not in sober fact the case. On the contrary, Virgil stresses that what is happening is abnormal, 'unnatural': 'mirantur *et* undae', the very waves are amazed. Still less, of course, is this the consciously anti-natural trope familiar from the *Eclogues*: trees wilting at the death of the shepherd, and so on. Virgil's stress indicates a spirit such as we have met in Euripides' *Bacchae* and the thirteenth book of the *Iliad*;[68] brute nature, normally insensate, becomes instinct with emotion at the special epiphany of the divine. Virgil recovers this 'primitive' feeling, and yet combines it with the developed, picturesque sensibility of more recent times; it is a fusion perhaps without parallel in ancient poetry. Part of the genius in this is that the wondering of the waves and woods is itself part of the miracle: that they marvel makes the scene itself more marvellous, so that the amazement of the spectator and the amazement of the landscape reflect and magnify each other. This mutual amazement is realized visually. That the woods and water are picturesque to the spectator is obvious; now the prism turns and it is the Trojans who become exotically picturesque from the landscape's point of view, with the gleaming shields and painted hulls (crimson, surely, for we remember our Homer) bright and glittering against the sombre dark-green backdrop. These colours shine in the water:[69] the river reflects upon the marvellous sight and literally reflects it; natural and supernatural merge. Similarly, a glory of the picture in 95 f. (always supposing Servius' interpretation to be correct) is that it is not just a visual image (though it is beautiful enough as that) but a significant image, an identifiable Italian landscape which none the less only takes the form it has because of particular time and circumstance: the woods are so thick because we have gone back many centuries into the past, the waters so still because a god's action has stilled them. The scene may appear at first sight simply picturesque, but it is more than that; this is a landscape with a 'meaning'.

[68] See above, pp. 39, 25.
[69] As Gransden observes, ad loc., '*fluuio* is to be taken both with *fulgentia longe* (the shields "burn on the water" . . .) and with *innare* . . .'

This analysis has shown Virgil's empathy working multifariously, so that the Trojan journey is seen from four or five different aspects: the Trojans, the contemporary reader, the Arcadians (with young Pallas as a special instance) and the very scenery all have their distinctive view. Yet such an account still does not exhaust the complexity of the passage, for it separates strands that are in reality woven together. We have found already that the effect of the landscape's marvelling cannot be detached from the way that it is, seen from the outside, itself a marvel. Equally, Virgil's empathy with the Trojans is not separable from its opposite; though we see and feel with Aeneas, we are aware all the time of knowing much that he does not know, and like a theme in counterpoint, the simultaneity of this double consciousness is an essential part of the reader's experience. The combination of empathy and distance will run right through Aeneas' visit to the site of Rome; it is encapsulated in the rise and fall of the splendid parabola at 97–100: first the Trojans catch sight of Evander's settlement (it is hard to resist the image of a kraal in a clearing), then the verse soars up to a vision of modern Rome (the lifting is almost literal, as Roman might raises the city's buildings towards the heaven), then sinks back to the simplicity of Evander's day. 'Nunc' and 'tum' are set against each other at our first glimpse of Pallanteum, and that pairing will be implicit throughout.

After this shapely period comes 'ocius advertunt proras urbique propinquant', a brief sentence of one line, describing brisk action, to round off the paragraph like a cadence; Virgil's almost musical sense of paragraph structure makes that comparison seem appropriate. The grammarians' name for this figure is epiphonema; the next paragraph ends with a very similar pattern, the likeness extending even to the pair of main clauses divided by the fourth-foot caesura: 'progressi subeunt luco fluviumque relinquunt.'[70] The luminous simplicity of this line escapes critical attention, but it is the product of the most mature art. After all that has gone before, the simplest things have acquired such a weight of significance that plain words are best. 'They leave the river', 'they enter the wood'; woods and rivers now have such a fullness of emotional meaning that the mere facts of arrival and walking into a grove gain a quiet majesty. The sound is very subtle; *u* is the predominant vowel, favoured by Virgil in

---

[70] *Aen.* 8. 125, 'Advancing, they go into the grove and leave the river'.

contexts of mysterious import, but the euphony is as much a matter of variety as of repetition.

In *The Heart of Darkness* Conrad describes a journey up the Congo: 'On we went again into the silence, along empty reaches, round the still bends, between the high walls of our winding way . . . Trees, trees, millions of trees.' Earlier in the story Marlow looks out at the Thames and observes, 'This also has been one of the dark places of the earth . . . I was thinking of very old times, when the Romans first came here . . . darkness was here yesterday. Imagine the feelings of a commander of a fine—what d'ye call 'em—trireme . . . Imagine him here—the very end of the world . . .—and going up this river . . . Sand-banks, marshes, forests, savages . . . Here and there a military camp lost in a wilderness . . .' The comparison between these two very dissimilar writers is worth making to draw attention, once again, to the imaginative power which enabled Virgil to create so vivid a realization of *terra incognita* without having behind him the history of exploration that is so familiar to us. It is almost startling how many of Conrad's elements are present in Virgil: silence, still water, the bends, the forest, the darkness, the little settlement, the setting of the present against a distant past. But the contrast is perhaps even more revealing than the likenesses, for the ideas which in Conrad's story are separated by two or three dozen pages are in Virgil merged into one. Tiber is, as it were, both Congo and Thames: past and present, the alien and the known, are comprehended within a single multiplicity of vision. Expansion and concentration are the equal and opposite qualities of these great paragraphs; behind the apparently leisurely ease of Virgil's account is concealed a formidable compression.

His next paragraph, however, has occasioned some dismay; there are critics who have disliked the frigidity of Aeneas' genealogical diplomacy. That seems an unconsidered judgement. Virgil has given us a hundred lines of astonishing invention and beauty; the time has come for something less richly charged. 'Fluviumque relinquunt'—the lapidary finality of those words marks the end of an episode, emotionally as well as in narrative terms, and the poet rightly resumes in quite another key. The passage is effective in its own way, showing us a new aspect of Aeneas:[71]

---

[71] *Aen.* 8. 127, 129–42.

'optime Graiugenum . . .
non equidem extimui Danaum quod ductor et Arcas
quodque a stirpe fores geminis coniunctus Atridis;
sed mea me virtus et sancta oracula divum
cognatique patres, tua terris didita fama,
coniunxere tibi et fatis egere volentem.
Dardanus, Iliacae primus pater urbis et auctor,
Electra, ut Grai perhibent, Atlantide cretus,
advehitur Teucros; Electram maximus Atlas
edidit, aetherios umero qui sustinet orbis.
vobis Mercurius pater est, quem candida Maia
Cyllenae gelido conceptum vertice fudit;
at Maiam, auditis si quicquam credimus, Atlas,
idem Atlas generat caeli qui sidera tollit.
sic genus amborum scindit se sanguine ab uno . . .'

'Best of the sons of Greece . . . I indeed was not afraid because you were
a leader of Danaans and an Arcadian and joined by lineage to the twin
sons of Atreus; but my courage and the holy oracles of the gods, our fathers'
kinship, and your fame spread abroad through all lands, have joined me
to you and brought me here, under destiny but with my will. Dardanus,
first father and founder of Ilium's city, born, as the Greeks relate, of the
Atlantid Electra, came to the Teucrians; Electra was begotten by mighty
Atlas, who bears the round heavens on his shoulders. Your family's father
is Mercury, whom fair Maia conceived and bore on the chill peak of Cyllene;
while Maia, if we can at all believe what we have heard, was begotten by
Atlas, the same Atlas who holds aloft the stars of heaven. Thus the lineage of both divides from one blood . . .'

Aeneas speaks virtually the whole of the second and third books,
but his narration in that place is so unlike any other speech in the
poem that it may perhaps be excluded from any general assessment
of his talkativeness.[72] That exclusion made, he appears to say surprisingly little for an epic hero. This is in marked contrast to the
power and fluency with which Achilles expresses himself or the ease
and resourcefulness of Odysseus' invention, and surely Virgil means
us to notice the difference, for Aeneas is equally distinct from other
characters within the poem. He approaches both Dido and Latinus
through an ambassador, Ilioneus, who in each case delivers a speech

---

[72] He emphasizes the reluctance with which he utters: *Aen*. 2. 3 ff. On Aeneas as speaker,
see G. Highet, *The Speeches in Vergil's Aeneid* (Princeton, 1972), and D. C. Feeney, 'The
Taciturnity of Aeneas', *CQ* NS 33 (1983), 204–19, reprinted in Harrison, 167–90.

longer than any which Aeneas makes at any time (his narration apart).[73] Turnus is allowed an extended speech of passionate and articulate debate on the Homeric model;[74] Aeneas never. Jupiter, Venus, Sinon, Helenus, Achaemenides, Dido, the Sibyl, Anchises, Juno, Evander, Turnus, Venulus, Latinus, Drances, Diana all make longer speeches than any of Aeneas' (the narration always, of course, excepted). He is a man who must adjust painfully, with difficulty, to a new world; with the loss of the old Homeric certainties and clarities goes the Homeric ease of expression. It is perhaps fitting that his one enormous utterance should deal with his 'Homeric' past, the last battle of the Trojan War and an Odyssean wandering, during which Troy remains the chief focus of sentiment. He is a newly reflective man, a listener, a man under instruction—from Anchises, Evander, the Sibyl, the voices of dreams and oracles. When he meets his father in the underworld, he greets him with four lines only (half the length of Anchises' own greeting). He will speak only twice more in the book, each time to ask a question; it is hard to imagine Achilles or Odysseus playing so quietly the role of receptive pupil. When Achilles receives his armour, he rejoices: his eyes blaze, the wrath rises within him, and he tells his mother that he will arm forthwith. When Aeneas is shown his armour, he too rejoices, but in a different, a pensive fashion. He marvels, and he says not a word; an eloquent silence.[75]

His speeches have their eloquence too, if not of the conventional kind. His longest speech, in reply to Dido's attack, advertises its brevity: 'pro re pauca loquar,' he says, echoing the poet's own judgement, 'tandem pauca refert';[76] and we may indeed agree that for so supreme a crisis, his words are few. It is his only speech in the entire book, except for a few words of encouragement to his men. Dido's second great denunciation renders him literally speechless; she sweeps from his presence, leaving him hesitant and 'preparing to say many things'.[77] He longs to talk to her, but does not:[78]

> at pius Aeneas, quamquam lenire dolentem
> solando cupit et dictis avertere curas,
> multa gemens magnoque animum labefactus amore
> iussa tamen divum exsequitur classemque revisit.

---

[73] *Aen.* 1. 522–58, 7. 213–48.   [74] *Aen.* 11. 378–444.
[75] *Il.* 19. 15 ff.; *Aen.* 8. 617 ff., 729 ff.
[76] *Aen.* 4. 337, 333: 'I shall say a few words to meet the case', 'At last he says a few words'.
[77] *Aen.* 4. 390 f.   [78] *Aen.* 4. 393–6.

But loyal Aeneas, though he longs to soothe her grief with consoling speech and to turn aside her sorrow with his words, sighing much and shaken in spirit by a great love, nevertheless follows the gods' commands and returns to his fleet.

These lines do not mean that he thought of abandoning his duty and staying with her after all. The stress is upon speech ('solando', 'dictis'), not action. There is thus an oddity in the sentence, for the divine command, forbidding him to remain in Carthage, does not seem to forbid him to speak consolation. His failure is one of articulacy: he cannot find the words to offer. The inconsequence perhaps mirrors the confusion of his mind: the necessary harshness of his action ought not to require an austerity in his manner to her, but he cannot keep the two things separate: not only does he leave her, but he leaves without comfortable words. The speech which he does make once again presents a contrast: his angular defensiveness and evident difficulty in finding a fit language ('tandem') are dramatically unlike the torrent of Dido's magnificent rhetoric. But rightly understood, his stiff propriety, offended righteousness and emotional inadequacy in the face of this crisis are moving; it is the eloquence of awkwardness. Dido is superbly articulate, and he is not, but it is crude to suppose that we should therefore side with her against him. Their different manners of speaking are the expressions of two differently admirable if imperfect natures, as well as a tragic revelation of the gulf of incomprehension between them. This cannot be Aeneas' tragedy in the way that it is Dido's, but there is room for sympathy not only with a hero who is losing what he loves but with a dutiful man who finds himself caught in a position from which he cannot extract himself with style and dignity. Aeneas will have to endure the scorn of readers and critics, to be abused by Charles James Fox and T. E. Page; that, in a sense, is part of his misfortune.

It is a far cry from that famous scene to Aeneas at Pallanteum, but there is this in common between the two passages, that here too his awkward formality may be, in a modest way, a little moving. He could hardly hope to be victorious, we may think, in a battle of wits and passion such as that between Drances and Turnus in the eleventh book. A listener as alert and hostile as Dido would pounce on some of his last words: what grounds has he for saying that his enemies design to subject all Italy to their yoke?[79] Fortunately, things

[79] *Aen.* 8. 147–9.

are easy for him in this book, and he has a friendly audience. His address may not be brilliant, but it suffices.

It is effective within the poem's overall economy because we can recognize behind the mechanics of the genealogy ideas of emotional importance. Had it come early in the seventh book, it would have been less telling, but now it can echo themes which Virgil has by this time more deeply explored. One of these is the probing back into the furthest possible past. Dardanus reappears, as in the sixth book called 'auctor' of Troy,[80] but now the phrase is expanded and given new weight: 'Iliacae *primus pater* urbis *et* auctor'. 'Primus . . . auctor', indeed, resembles 'ultimus auctor' in the seventh book, describing Saturn's relationship to Latinus.[81] Yet despite this emphasis Dardanus is now to be only the beginning of a further thrust into the past: we are to be taken back to generations unnamed before, and again the journey is made stage by stage, from Dardanus to Electra, from Electra to Atlas. The Arcadians' ancestry is similarly presented: Aeneas begins with Mercury, like Dardanus made the parent of a race, as the plural 'vobis' shows, passes back from him to Maia, and from her to Atlas once more. The repetition of the proper names— 'Mercurius . . . Maia . . . at Maiam . . . Atlas, idem Atlas'—suggests the peeling away of layers of the past, one after another.

The genealogies completed, another Virgilian theme stands revealed: that different peoples, if their ancestries be traced back far enough, prove to have a shared experience, rather as parallel lines meet at infinity. We have already learnt that the Italians' adversaries, the Trojans, are Italian in their ultimate origin; now we hear that the Trojans and, of all people, a race of Greeks are children of the same primeval parent. 'Ut Grai perhibent' is a little clumsy in context—a Trojan telling a Greek what Greeks relate—but through it and the phrase a few lines later, 'auditis si quicquam credimus', we catch the echoes of that thought which Virgil has handled magically before, that the past is not something certainly known but filtered down to us through other men's words.[82]

A light irony plays over Evander's realm. The scattered township in the forest clearing is introduced to us, when the Trojans approach it, as 'urbs', and the word has a double meaning: the walls and citadel deserve the title as the seat of a kingdom, however modest, but behind

---

[80] *Aen.* 6. 650.   [81] *Aen* 7. 49.   [82] See esp. *Aen.* 7. 645 f.

that title we hear the knowledge, hidden from Aeneas and Evander, that the little town is Urbs, the City *par excellence*, whose supremacy among the cities of the world will indeed be asserted centuries after Virgil in the papal benediction 'Urbi et Orbi'. Pallanteum is 'urbs' also at 306, and again, with a more pronounced irony, at 554, where the oxymoron implicit anyway in the phrase 'parvam . . . urbem' is deepened by the fact that the 'little city' is none other than an earlier avatar of great Rome itself. 'Pauperque senatus' (humble senate) at 105 is likewise playful in tone. Virgil uses 'senatus' on one other occasion only: spying out the city of Carthage, the Trojans see its people appointing laws and magistrates and a 'holy senate' (sanctumque senatum).[83] In this earlier place also the word is pointed, but with a sombre, even tragic significance. Here is a splendid nation, young but maturely civilized, forming itself in a style that calls to mind the institutions of future Rome. It has every reason to be as happy and perdurable as the city of Romulus itself; but *dis aliter visum*. In the eighth book the allusion to Rome in the word 'senatus' is more obvious; the pointedness, however, is no longer painful but amused.

The humour is plainest a little later, when Virgil, deftly confusing two far different ages, describes cattle wandering around the elegant district of Carinae and the busy heart of Rome:[84]

> talibus inter se dictis ad tecta subibant
> pauperis Euandri, passimque armenta videbant
> Romanoque foro et lautis mugire Carinis.

Amid such mutual converse they came to humble Evander's house, and saw all around cattle lowing in the Roman Forum and smart Carinae.

The comedy is in itself simple—one might compare Beerbohm's Regency rake, Lord George Hell, escaping from London to an arcadian retreat in deepest Kensington[85]—but indeed the charm lies in its uncomplicated cheerfulness, combined with a sophisticated economy of expression. The wit appears in 'lautus', 'chic' or 'smart', a word that belongs to prose and the intercourse of everyday life; it is found nowhere in epic or lyric poetry except here.[86] As the poet makes his joke, so does his tone of voice change: the piquancy of the idea is matched by the piquantly incongruous diction of 'lautus', a

---

[83] *Aen.* 1. 426; 'sanctus' was a standard epithet for the Roman Senate.
[84] *Aen.* 8. 359–61.　　[85] *The Happy Hypocrite.*　　[86] Eden, ad loc.

note of worldly irony dropped momentarily into the epic idyll. In the next lines Evander urges Aeneas not to despise his humble home, but we need not suppose that Virgil is rebuking his contemporaries for abandoning the simplicities of the past. Modesty and splendour are alike qualities which he relishes (the 'golden Capitol' has been celebrated only a few lines earlier)[87] and it is the charm of the very contrast that attracts and entertains him.

We are in a realm where it comes naturally to dwell out of proportion upon thoughts of the morning. Aeneas prepares for his journey to Pallanteum by rising to pray to the deities of the landscape in the light of the rising sun.[88] The 'nourishing light' of a new day and the twittering of the morning birds beneath his eaves rouse Evander from his house. His Grecian sword and panther skin proclaim him king; yet at the same time he is a country squire. A nice awareness of canine psychology has his dogs pressing on ahead and yet holding back enough to accompany their elderly master.[89] His guest is also astir: 'nec minus Aeneas se matutinus agebat.'[90] 'Aeneas . . . matutinus' (morning Aeneas)—the attachment of the adjective to the man irradiates the weary hero with newness, freshness, and hope. Finally the themes of morning and youth are drawn together in a simile:[91]

> ipse agmine Pallas
> it medio chlamyde et pictis conspectus in armis,
> qualis ubi Oceani perfusus Lucifer unda,
> quem Venus ante alios astrorum diligit ignis,
> extulit os sacrum caelo tenebrasque resolvit.

Pallas himself rides in the middle of the column, conspicuous in cloak and emblazoned armour, like Lucifer, whom Venus loves above the other starry fires, when having bathed in Ocean's waters he lifts his sacred head in heaven and dissolves the darkness.

Venus' love for the star suggests Pallas' beauty, as well as linking him, by delicate implication, with Aeneas, another object of her care. The comparison and the thing compared flow in and out of each other, for it is indeed morning, and like Lucifer Pallas is restored by sleep. Bright new light and refreshing waters—the simile seems peculiarly apt in the setting of Evander's town.

---

[87] *Aen.* 8. 347 f.   [88] *Aen.* 8. 68 f.   [89] *Aen.* 8. 454–62.
[90] *Aen.* 8. 465, 'Aeneas was astir no less early'.   [91] *Aen.* 8. 587–91.

Youth and morning light, however, are only part of the mood in Pallanteum; Evander is as important in this book as his son. Sensitive to individuality and small distinctions, Virgil has made this king both like and unlike Latinus. The differences need no further description; the likeness emerges in the way that Evander too points us back towards a strange archaic past. Like Latinus he has a nymph for his mother, and one whose mighty prophecies strike awe into the heart. He has encountered monsters: he has seen Cacus and he has slain Erulus, whose mother, the Italian goddess Feronia, endowed him with three lives (it seems that we are supposed to think of him as having three bodies, like Geryon, upon whom Virgil presumably modelled him).[92] It is true that Aeneas meets monsters in the third book, a portion of the epic which, like the equivalent part of the *Odyssey*, is set at a discernibly different level of reality from the rest of the poem, but we can hardly imagine him finding such creatures in the Italy of his own time. As in the *Iliad* the more grotesque or bizarre fantasies of folk imagination are kept away from the battlefield; but Evander's experience reaches back to a world of a different kind.

Like Latinus again, he is very old to be the father of so young a child. Earlier legend placed Evander a good many years before the Trojan War and made Pallas his grandson;[93] in adapting the story to his own purposes Virgil has preserved some characteristics of the earlier myth. And though Evander is not genealogically connected, as Latinus is, with primordial Italy, his conversation points in that direction. He explains the memorials of men of yore; and while it is Latinus who is descended from Saturn, it is Evander who discourses of him. Even his ancestry has, in part, an irrationally Italian flavour. His mother, originally a Greek nymph, Themis or Nicostrata, had been identified with the native goddess Carmentis. Virgil adopts this latter name, so that although in his version of the story we must suppose her to be of Greek origin, she remains evocative of an aboriginally Italic past.

It is fitting that a young man and an old should alike be prominent in a book which looks both to past and future, which explores change and continuity, similarity and difference. The openings of Aeneas' diplomatic speech and the king's reply once more bring distinctions of race to our minds: 'optime Graiugenum', the Trojan begins,

---

[92] *Aen.* 8. 560 ff.
[93] Dion. Hal. *Ant. Rom.* 1. 31 f. Pallas is also the name of Evander's grandfather.

to which in due course Evander answers, 'fortissime Teucrum'.[94] Aeneas' speech delves into the past, as we have seen, and Evander's reply carries on the theme. As a greybeard, his memories will naturally be of time gone by—he recalls seeing Priam and the young Anchises—but that is not enough for Virgil: twice in five lines he has the king call Priam 'scion of Laomedon', using the immense and sonorous patronymic 'Laomedontiades'.[95] Behind the fathers an earlier father looms.

None the less, while the two men talk about the past, our own thoughts may already be turning towards the future. A passage in Aeneas' address reminds us of what is to come. The same foe confronts both Trojans and Arcadians, he observes; and these enemies believe that if they can succeed in driving the Trojans out, they will be able to bring beneath their yoke the whole of Hesperia, from sea to sea.[96] A dramatic irony hangs over these words. In the context they appear excessive, even untrue, for we have no reason to think that Turnus and the Rutulians have any such territorial ambitions; they merely want to be rid of the interlopers. We, however, know that the state founded by Aeneas' descendants will not only occupy the whole of Italy but conquer an empire stretching immeasurably further. In the short term Aeneas seems to exaggerate; in the long term the truth will surpass his wildest imaginings. Thus future Rome is put before our minds, and in a way that enhances our wonder at the scale of its achievement.

Virgil uses a similar technique later when Evander shows his guest a hill covered in scrubby woodland. A god dwells in this grove, he explains; which god is unsure; the Arcadians believe him to be Jupiter himself.[97] Their king seems unwilling on his own account to assert so much, but we know, once again, that the truth is far above any Arcadian's boldest fancy, for this is the great Capitol itself, the sacred heart of the world's central city, the abode of Jupiter Best and Greatest. Much earlier in his career, Virgil had augmented the splendour of Rome by seeing it through the eyes of Tityrus: the shepherd had

---

[94] *Aen.* 8. 127, 154: 'Best of the sons of Greece', 'most valiant of the Teucrians'.

[95] *Aen.* 8. 158, 162. These places apart, Virgil uses this seven-syllable form once only. He uses 'Laomedontius' twice in the *Aeneid* (on its effect at 8. 18 see above, p. 329). The heavier 'Laomedonteus' comes once in the *Aeneid* (4. 542) and once in the *Georgics* (1. 502), each time in allusion to the Trojan king's breach of faith. See above, pp. 382 f., on its force in the earlier poem.

[96] *Aen.* 8. 146–9.   [97] *Aen.* 8. 351–4.

ignorantly supposed it to be like his local town, and been overwhelmed by the reality.[98] With a similar subjectivity, the poet now looks at the future Capitol through the eyes of the Arcadians, and makes us aware how vastly its grandeur overtops their extremest speculation.

As the book unrolls, his double perspective becomes the plainer. Evander is something of an antiquarian, but it requires no great perception to see that while the old king is etymologizing the Argiletum or explaining how the ritual of the Salii originated, the poet is looking forward to the city that is yet to be. The theme of change and continuity is woven into the texture yet again, as in the very act of showing how different the Capitol was in Evander's time, Virgil insists that it has always been instinct with the numinous:[99]

> hinc ad Tarpeiam sedem et Capitolia ducit
> aurea *nunc, olim* silvestribus horrida dumis.
> *iam tum* religio pavidos terrebat agrestis
> dira loci, *iam tum* silvam saxumque tremebant.

From here he takes him to the Tarpeian abode and the Capitol, now golden, once bristling with woody scrub. Even then a dread awe of the place frightened the scared countryfolk, even then they trembled at the wood and the rock.

There is a play of adverbs: 'nunc' and 'olim', stressing change, are answered by 'iam tum . . . iam tum'. These latter words were used in the seventh book to bring out both the changes and the continuity in Italian history;[100] in their new context they stress the continuity and qualify the picture of transformation in the preceding lines.

The irony in Virgil's play with time emerges again just as Evander is about to make his furthest plunge back into the past with his disquisition on Saturn:[101]

> miratur facilisque oculos fert omnia circum
> Aeneas, capiturque locis et singula laetus
> exquiritque auditque virum monimenta priorum.
> tum rex Evandrus Romanae conditor arcis . . .

Aeneas wonders and turns his ready eyes on everything around; he is taken by the place and happily asks and hears about the memorials of the men of old, one by one. Then King Evander, founder of the Roman citadel, said . . .

---

[98] *Ecl.* 1. 19 ff. [99] *Aen.* 8. 347–50.
[100] *Aen.* 7. 643. [101] *Aen.* 8. 310–13.

Why does Aeneas wonder? why is he entranced and joyful? The
place is pleasant, to be sure, and the rest from struggle welcome,
but there seems little to capture his spirit, still less to stir amazement. We must suppose an experience mysteriously below the level
of consciousness—that he is moved by emotions stronger than the
circumstances seem to warrant because, without being aware of it,
he has his people's future shown to him through what he hears
and sees. His thoughts dwell on the past ('priorum' is emphatic at
the end of the sentence), but the fact that he is seeing his future is
brought out by the momentarily surprising description of Evander
as 'Romanae conditor arcis'. That Aeneas should meet another man
who can be described in any sense at all as a founder of Rome is
curious; yet the phrase is just. Aeneas, as we have known from the
beginning, is to found the Roman *gens*,[102] Evander has already
founded the Roman *arx*; neither will see Rome itself, but the passing hint of incongruity in the phrase holds our attention, shows us
that both men have their place in the prehistory of the destined city
and looks forward to the reconciliation of once hostile races as part
of the providential purpose. That too is a theme which other parts
of the book explore.

But now Evander presses back to earliest times:[103]

> 'haec nemora indigenae Fauni Nymphaeque tenebant
> gensque virum truncis et duro robore nata,   315
> quis neque mos nec cultus erat, nec iungere tauros
> aut componere opes norant aut parcere parto,
> sed rami atque asper victu venatus alebat.
> primus ab aetherio venit Saturnus Olympo
> arma Iovis fugiens et regnis exsul ademptis.   320
> is genus indocile ac dispersum montibus altis
> composuit legesque dedit, Latiumque vocari
> maluit, his quoniam latuisset tutus in oris.
> aurea quae perhibent illo sub rege fuere
> saecula: sic placida populos in pace regebat,   325
> deterior donec paulatim et decolor aetas
> et belli rabies et amor successit habendi.
> tum manus Ausonia et gentes venere Sicanae,
> saepius et nomen posuit Saturnia tellus;
> tum reges asperque immani corpore Thybris,   330
> a quo post Itali fluvium cognomine Thybrim
> diximus; amisit verum vetus Albula nomen . . .'

[102] *Aen.* 1. 33.   [103] *Aen.* 8. 314–32.

'These woods were once occupied by native Fauns and Nymphs and a race of men born from trunks of hard oak; they had no rule or art of life and did not know how to yoke oxen, store their resources or husband what they had gained, but branches and hunting's hard fare afforded them their food. First came Saturn from heavenly Olympus, an exile who had lost his kingdom. He ordered this unruly people, scattered over the high mountains, and gave them laws, and chose that the place be called Latium, because he had been safely hidden within its bounds. In his reign was the age which they call golden; thus he ruled the peoples in quiet peace, until gradually a worse and tarnished age succeeded, with frenzy for war and the love of possessions. Then came Ausonian bands and Sicanian peoples, and often Saturn's land laid down its existing name; then kings followed, among whom was harsh Thybris of huge bulk, from whom we Italians have since called the river by the name Thybris; old Albula has lost its true name . . .'

In the seventh book Saturn appeared as primordially ancient, but this account now pushes back earlier even than him. A sense of the extent of time and the complexity of the developments which it has wrought is also conveyed by Evander's explanation of subsequent history: one change after another (saepius), Ausonians, Sicans, then Thybris and those other kings. And this feeling for the multiplied layers of past time is associated with the importance of names. Often Saturn's land has changed its name: names shape and order history. Virgil expresses a sense of the power of names: there is such a thing as a 'true' name. This combines with a sense of the aboriginal: the true name is the old, the primal name, undiscovered by later incomers. 'Amisit' evokes a nostalgia, a vague sense of loss, and a sense of the hidden, as though the name could not be found, buried as it is in the darkness or dimness of the past.

The metaphorical idea that the Italians' identity and manliness have grown from the Italian land has been offered us before. Now in Evander's account it becomes actually true: the original, indigenous race were born out of trees. Virgil exploits the double meaning of 'robur', both timber and strength: the hardness of the wood and the hardness of the people are one and the same thing. These natives are like mankind in the *Georgics*, hard because their ancestors were formed from the stones flung by Deucalion's hand; like early man in Lucretius' anthropology, hard because literally generated out of the hard earth.[104]

---

[104] See above, pp. 260, 334.

The old king's first lines, then, contain a sense of the purely, primevally Italian which recalls the tone in early parts of the seventh book. But Virgil now puts this idea in a new context and bends it in a new direction. He sets the picture of a rooted, indigenous Italian-ness against the concept of becoming Italian through process: 'we Italians,' says Evander, born a Greek. And Virgil suggests that a pure Italian-ness, unaffected by any influence from outside, is imperfect after all, for he here introduces the method that he will develop in Numanus' speech.[105] The toughness of men in olden times, the strength and vigour of Italy, indigenousness, woodland, the Fauni— these things are the furniture of national and nostalgic sentiment. But as with Numanus' speech we are half denied the pleasure of an easy pride in our land. Evander's first two lines sound comfortably patriotic; it is a surprise when he continues, 'quis neque mos nec cultus erat.' The poet brings us up short, and guides us to a maturer judgement.

The savage aboriginals were tamed and civilized by Saturn, who came from abroad as a deliverer. That account gives him a resemblance to Hercules, a benefactor god who also came from afar and rid Italy of an evil thing. Now Hercules in turn has already been so depicted as to bring out the parallel between him and Aeneas. Parallels now multiply in Evander's speech. Saturn is 'regnis exsul ademptis', like Evander himself, and like Aeneas. There is by implication a modern comparison too: we have heard of the 'aurea saecula' once before in the *Aeneid*, in the sixth book; Saturn brought in the first golden age, Augustus will restore it again.[106] Here is one reason for Virgil's abandoning the notion of the golden age as an original paradise and making it a happy time achieved by the firm wisdom of a ruler: it makes the parallel between Saturn and Augustus possible.

Parallels are nothing in themselves and valuable only if a moral or emotional significance may be drawn from them. Here they evoke, once more, the majestic extent of time: as so often, just as Virgil is digging further down into the past than ever, he is simultaneously looking as far into the future as he possibly can. Saturn, Aeneas, Augustus stand immensely far apart, but all are godlike rulers, benefactors of Italy, and thus the actions of Aeneas, a single man, are set against the vast backdrop of history, spreading immeasurably in both directions.

[105] See above, pp. 414 ff.   [106] *Aen.* 6. 792–4.

We may be surprised, though, to find Saturn described as an exile, since he was as a matter of anthropological fact a native Italian god and indeed peculiarly felt as such: Italy was already 'Saturnia tellus' in the *Georgics*, 'Saturnia . . . arva' in the first book of the *Aeneid*;[107] and Evander is about to present 'Saturnia tellus' again as the fixed description of a land that has often changed its name. The effect is similar to Virgil's treatment of Carmentis: within his fiction we accept that Saturn came originally from Greece, but emotionally he retains an indigenous feel to him.

It is significant too that at this moment Evander should speak of himself and his people as Italians. Earlier in the book Virgil has stressed that his race is Greek; now we learn that this is not the whole story. We, as Italian readers of the poet's day, receive a double idea of our ancestry and identity. On the one hand, we have an ultimate origin that is fixedly indigenous, rooted in the Italian earth, and that literally. On the other, we see that Italian-ness may be a process of becoming. That Carmentis and even so quintessentially 'native' a god as Saturn can once have come from outside shows that there may also be a growing into the Italian land.

In a later speech Evander carries on the idea, telling of the city of Agylla upon its ancient rock, 'ubi Lydia quondam | gens, bello praeclara, iugis insedit Etruscis' (where a people once Lydian, famous in war, has settled on the Etruscan hills).[108] What could be more Italian than the Etruscans?—yet they too were once an Asian people. Once, but no more, 'quondam'—yet again a simple adverb speaks to us of process. Shortly after, Evander presents another kind of absorption, explaining that his son is of mixed blood: his mother was Sabellan, and he draws a part of his 'patria' from her.[109] Into this magnetic field of force Aeneas is himself being drawn. We have already seen that when he prays after the vision of Tiberinus he appears already less alien from his destined land. The suggestion of a development in his experience is made again in Evander's speech. The king opens it by calling his guest 'maxime Teucrorum ductor'. That echoes the form of address in his very first speech, 'fortissime Teucrum', and (with less purely verbal similarity) the vocative in his second speech, 'hospes Troiane'.[110] Nowhere, in fact, does Evander address Aeneas by his own name, or indeed use any vocative to him which

---

[107] *Geo.* 2. 173; *Aen.* 1. 569.   [108] *Aen.* 8. 479 f.   [109] *Aen.* 8. 510 f.

[110] *Aen.* 8. 470, 154, 188: 'Mightiest leader of the Teucrians'; 'most valiant of the Teucrians'; 'my Trojan guest'.

does not recall that he is a Trojan.[111] But as the present speech draws near its close, after Evander has spoken of the Etruscans' Lydian origin and his son's native blood, the address is significantly modified: 'o Teucrum *atque Italum* fortissime ductor.'[112] Aeneas, who began the speech as a Trojan leader, has by the end of it become an Italian leader too.

But none of this, it might be objected, actually makes Aeneas an Italian: he is merely learning more about the country and preparing to lead Italian forces. Indeed, the Etruscan rebels have held their hand precisely because their soothsayer has forbidden them to put themselves under an Italian commander; they must seek one from abroad.[113] No, Aeneas is not an Italian, or at least, not yet; but on the other hand his development is not complete even within the compass of the poem. It is time to look ahead to the last book. Not long before the end, as Aeneas is hunting down the doomed Turnus, he is likened to a hound in pursuit of a stag.[114] It is, one might suppose, a simile designed to engage our sympathies with the victim, and yet not exclusively so, for Virgil adds an odd detail: the hound is an Umbrian one. A man of Troy is hunting down a man of Italy, but it is the Trojan who is likened to an animal from the Italian heartland. Is it not curious?

Although this is only a small touch, it is the more noticeable after the striking simile preceding it by some fifty lines, in which Aeneas is compared to a mountain:[115]

> quantus Athos aut quantus Eryx aut ipse coruscis
> cum fremit ilicibus quantus gaudetque nivali
> vertice se attollens pater Appenninus ad auras.

Huge as Athos, huge as Eryx, or huge as father Appenninus himself, when he roars with shimmering holm-oaks and rejoices, rearing up to the high breezes with snowy peak.

The sequence of peaks follows the course of Aeneas' own journey, from the coast of Thrace not far from Troy to Sicily, and thence to

---

[111] The habits of epic courtesy and reticence may have something to do with this. Aeneas does not tell Evander his name, and Evander does not ask or use it, although he realizes that this is Anchises' son. (Much later, at 11. 170, he does refer to Aeneas, in his absence, by his name.) In the *Odyssey* Alcinous does not ask Odysseus' name, and Odysseus does not reveal it until the ninth book, so that Nausicaa has had to say goodbye to him without yet learning who he is.

[112] *Aen.* 8. 513, 'O most valiant leader of Teucrians and Italians'.

[113] *Aen.* 8. 502 f.   [114] *Aen.* 12. 749–57.   [115] *Aen.* 12. 701–3.

the core of Italy. Appenninus is the very backbone of the land, and the emotional 'pater' augments the patriotic note. It is impressively unexpected that a Trojan should be given this powerfully felt comparison, and at the moment that the Italian champion is going down to defeat. 'Non aliter Tros Aeneas et Daunius heros'—so Virgil not many lines later.[116] The epithets, as ever, are pointed, pitting not only man against man, but once more race against race. Yet it is Aeneas who has just received the Italian comparison, and there is a pathos in that: it adds to the bitterness of Turnus' defeat that his conqueror should take from him not only his bride and his life, but even the nobly patriotic simile which he seems so proudly to deserve. But there is a hopeful note also. Like the simile, Aeneas has moved from the east to Italy. 'At pater Aeneas'—the familiar formula is heard once more, and as it happens for the last time, at the start of the sentence in which the simile unfolds.[117] We have long known that he is a father to his Trojan people; by the end of the sentence we see him likened to an Italian father also. The simile belongs to that uncommon class which is rich in figurative language: while father Aeneas is compared to a mountain, the mountain is personified as a man, a parent who rejoices and lifts himself up. The boundary between man and landscape begins to blur.

Nor is it imagery alone that draws Aeneas into the Italian land. Very soon there follows the scene in which Turnus prays ineffectively to Faunus and Earth to hold fast Aeneas' spear in the remains of the god's sacred olive tree, which has been ignorantly torn up by the Trojans. It is a scene which should make us feel not only for Turnus but for the weakening of old and loved Italian things; it presents the Trojans in their alien aspect. The more striking, therefore, is the episode which follows. The scene moves to the heavens, where Jupiter addresses his wife:[118]

> 'quae iam finis erit, coniunx? quid denique restat?
> indigetem Aenean scis ipsa et scire fateris
> deberi caelo fatisque ad sidera tolli . . .'

'What shall the end now be, my wife? what finally remains? You know yourself and admit you know that Aeneas is owed to heaven as a god of the land and raised by destiny to the stars . . .'

---

[116] *Aen.* 12. 723, 'Not otherwise did Trojan Aeneas and the Daunian hero . . .'.
[117] *Aen.* 12. 697.   [118] *Aen.* 12. 793–5.

The identity of the *indigetes* and even the origin of their name are obscure, but for Virgil at least they have a strongly Italian flavour. They are among the national gods invoked to preserve Caesar in the first Georgic, along with Romulus and Vesta.[119] Now in sober historical fact Aeneas was worshipped as *indiges* by the river Numicus, and so the present passage also looks back to the seventh book, when he was a new arrival in Latium, not knowing the names of the local rivers and seeing Numicus for the first time.[120] As we think forward to the time when he will be an *indiges*, we find him completing the process previously completed by Saturn, seeing him at once as an exile in Italy and as a power embedded in the land. And there is a further complexity in Jupiter's speech following upon the invocation of Faunus: we feel a sense both of development and of the perennity of Italian institutions.

In the eighth book we observe process almost under our very eyes. The fact that things are flowing Aeneas' way (even, as we have seen, in a more or less literal sense) contributes to the vigour and relief that the book conveys. Trojans and Greeks, Trojans and Italians are starting to come together; Aeneas is beginning to learn more of the quality and nature of his new home. At the same time, the parallels to Aeneas in Saturn, Evander, Hercules, and by implication Augustus encourage us to feel that he too has good work to do. Four books of war and destruction await us, but before they begin we are allowed to see that there is something better beyond them. Aeneas too has the task of imposing laws upon a 'genus indocile'; to borrow a phrase from a more famous context, his task is 'paci . . . imponere morem'.[121] And as the sixth book has severely taught us, that is not a goal which can be achieved without force and the weapons of war.

The brief scene in which the hero meets his mother contributes to the mood of the book as a whole. The passage is quiet and understated: the encounter takes place away from the main scenes of action in a dark and private valley; Venus has only three lines to speak. Yet this is in a way a culminating moment. No doubt Virgil wanted to keep the episode cool and concise in part at least because he did not wish to steal the thunder from the great *ekphrasis* of the shield, but there is in any case an odd beauty in the simple brevity with which so significant a meeting is presented. A leitmotiv in the poem

[119] *Geo.* 1. 498.   [120] *Aen.* 7. 137 f., 150.   [121] *Aen.* 6. 852.

has been the meeting that is not fully a meeting, the encounter that is somehow frustrated or incomplete. In the first book Aeneas met his mother, but was not permitted to recognize her until the moment of her vanishing from sight. At the end of the second book he sought to embrace the wraith of Creusa, and found no substance to wrap his arms around. The three lines describing his baffled gestures of affection recurred in the sixth book, when he met his father; even in Elysium family love is denied its natural, physical expression. Father, mother, wife—three meetings, and every one of them unsatisfying.[122] So it is a great moment when Venus presents herself to Aeneas of her own accord; Virgil seldom concludes a sentence with an adverb, and 'ultro' at the end of 611 is quietly emphatic. Still happier is the moment when the goddess embraces her son; that embrace so long delayed is achieved at last, and on this occasion it is not Aeneas but the other who takes the initiative: 'amplexus nati Cytherea petivit.'[123] Virgil has been composing on a very grand scale: across eight books there have been preparations for this event. Often we have seen Aeneas alone, striving, bearing the weight of responsibility, and we shall see this again in the book's last line, when he lifts his descendants' future upon his shoulders. So there is a strong sense of tension and anxiety released when for once we see divine powers coming to aid and encourage him of their own motion, unbidden. The book's central action—Aeneas' sojourn at the site of Rome—is framed by two such visitations: Tiberinus at the beginning and Venus at the end. The river has much more to say than the goddess, and yet her coming must have an emotional importance for the hero that Tiberinus cannot rival. But indeed it is because the poem as a whole has taught us how much his mother's embrace must mean to Aeneas that Virgil can afford to be so understated, to leave so much unsaid.

Venus has come to bring Aeneas his shield, with the future events of Roman history beaten upon it, the Battle of Actium in the middle. It is notorious that the many accounts of Actium in Augustan poetry do follow a party line, and by omission and misrepresentation give a substantially distorted picture; divergences from the norm are therefore likely to be telling. Perhaps most distinctive in Virgil's version is his unique stress upon Italy. As a whole, the shield depicts a blend

---

[122] *Aen.* 1. 405 ff.; 2. 792–4; 6. 700–2.
[123] *Aen.* 8. 615, 'The goddess of Cythera sought her son's embrace'.

of Rome with Italy, its scenes representing 'res Italas Romanorumque triumphos'. That same fusion comes again towards the end of the *ekphrasis*, when Caesar, entering Rome's walls, sacrifices 'dis Italis', to the Italian gods. Most remarkable is the shield's central scene: 'hinc Augustus agens *Italos* in proelia Caesar . . .' (Here was Caesar Augustus leading Italians into battle).[124] This would have struck strangely on the ears of Virgil's first readers, for Rome was the name of their state, and it was the 'senatus populusque Romanus' that went to war.

This Italian stress must therefore have a strong significance, all the more since the description of the shield comes at the end of two books—three, one should perhaps say, since the underworld is not only rich in Roman import but lies below Cumae—which have been exploring the Italian land. There is an irony in the fact that as Aeneas, the Trojan, the easterner, prepares to go to war against Italians, he should be given a shield in which the chief event depicted is an Italian victory over the east. For the emphasis on the oriental character of Augustus' adversaries is heavy: they are peoples of the dawn, forces of the east, a barbarian army diversely accoutred, Bactrians, Egyptians, Indians, Arabs and Sabaeans; their gods of monstrous form, like yelping Anubis, are ranged against the Olympians, Neptune, Venus, and Minerva.[125] In part this irony is a painful one: Aeneas' triumph will bring about the end of things that he has held dear, as will become plainer in the last book, when Juno secures the obliteration of the Trojan name, customs and language.[126] The future history displayed on the shield shows the Trojan identity wiped out, the Italian identity as strong as ever. It is a poignancy of Aeneas' situation that his very victory should destroy what he has cherished; and it is fitting, correspondingly, that Virgil should find room within his picture of Actium for the pathos of the vanquished peoples. His treatment of the battle may be compared and contrasted with that in Horace's Cleopatra Ode, which also pays some tribute to the defeated, but in markedly different style. There is a grandiose compassion in Virgil's image of the mighty mourning figure of the Nile receiving the fugitives into his dark, concealing and capacious bosom, whereas Horace offers a carefully qualified praise of Cleopatra's boldness and serenity, a taut, tense balance of admiration and appalled amazement. Virgil's

[124] *Aen.* 8. 626, 'Italian deeds and the triumphs of the Romans', 714 f., 678.
[125] *Aen.* 8. 685 ff., 705 f., 698 ff.   [126] *Aen.* 12. 823 ff., 834 ff.

lines are richly, decoratively expansive, with a leisurely generosity of rhetoric:[127]

> contra autem magno maerentem corpore Nilum
> pandentemque sinus et tota veste vocantem
> caeruleum in gremium latebrosaque flumina victos.

opposite her the Nile mourning with massive body, opening his folds and with all his raiment summoning the defeated into his blue lap and hidden streams.

In Horace it is the terseness that counts, the hard, cool contemplation of Cleopatra as a 'monstrum', a portent, a thing, not like a woman; what impresses in this is the poet's refusal to go for an easy nobility, to be magnanimous without cost.[128] In Virgil the sentiment flows more freely; and we hear a compassionate note again, surely, in the midst of Caesar's triumph through the slow pained spondees—accent dragging against ictus—of 'incedunt victae longo ordine gentes'.[129] But this in turn is nothing so easy as a covert criticism of Augustus; rather, Virgil has the breadth of conception to comprise the misery within a picture of authentic glory.

The shield has its austerities, then; but it has much more besides. Much of its character lies in its divergences from its model, Homer's shield of Achilles. This portrays the whole world and the whole life of mankind within it: war, dancing, reaping, marrying, celebrating. Geographically the *Iliad* is extremely compressed: all the human action takes place in Troy or on the plain outside it, except for a short visit to an island off shore in the first book. There is thus a mighty sense of outward expansion in the description of a shield which represents all the activities of man. The siege of a city is depicted, for that is one kind of human business, but only one, so that warfare occupies no more than a small part of an object which mostly shows the works and recreations of peace. Virgil's shield is not expansive in this way: the *Aeneid* does not have the *Iliad*'s terrible concentration upon a single place and action, and there is not the same moral or aesthetic need to escape from wrath and battle to see the warfare in a larger perspective. Instead, the scenes on Aeneas' shield extend temporally. In a sense both poets show themselves historians, but of different types. Modern jargon distinguishes between diachronic and synchronic history, diachronic history being the narrative of events

---

[127] *Aen.* 8. 711–13.   [128] *Carm.* 1. 37. 21.
[129] *Aen.* 8. 722, 'the conquered races move in long column'.

in sequence, synchronic history being the study of things that usually change slowly if at all, such as the structures of society, economy,
culture and belief. In these terms, Homer offers synchronic history,
Virgil diachronic. Virgil dramatically narrows Homer's range of vision,
and in two ways. First, instead of escaping from warfare, he concentrates upon it: not only is the central scene a battle, but we are told
at the start that wars are the shield's theme.[130] Second, everything
is concerned with one city, Rome; other places, such as Actium,
are only present if they are important in the Roman story. At the
very end of the *ekphrasis* there is, briefly, one of those enormous
geographical expansions that Virgil already loved at the time of the
Georgics: the eye moves outward in all directions, eastwards to Asia
and the Euphrates, west to the Rhine, north-west to the Morini of
Gaul close to the English Channel (they are described as 'extremique
hominum', furthest of mankind, so that we feel the verse straining
at the limits of the world), north-east into Scythia, south to the Berber
tribes of Africa.[131] But all these immensely distant places are only so
many coordinates, as it were, geometrical points from which we locate
and fix the position of the world's central city, Rome itself. Or to
look at the passage another way, the sudden geographical expansion
(which is in fact a matter of names rather than actual depiction, for
these tribes and rivers are part of a triumphal procession in Rome)
brings out the more clearly, by force of contrast, the concentration
of all that has gone before.

The narrowing of the Homeric scheme energizes the diachronic
drive, the thrust that pushes chronologically through the whole of
Roman history and prehistory, from Ascanius to Augustus, in only
fifty lines, whereupon the speed with which scene has followed scene
gives way to the amply expansive account of Actium. This encap-
sulation of Roman history once more picks up the theme of change
and continuity. Now the impending loss of the Trojan name and
culture is a sorrow for Aeneas and his followers rather than for mankind as a whole; but in any case, as we have seen earlier, Augustus
carries into battle the very same household gods that Aeneas took
with him from his ravaged city, so that what is most sacred and
intimate of Troy does, strangely, survive in Italy after all, and thus
through the theme of continuity comes a message of consolation.

---

[130] *Aen.* 8. 629, 'pugnataque in ordine bella', 'the wars they fought, in their sequence'.
[131] *Aen.* 8. 724–8.

And besides, the irony of Aeneas carrying a representation of Italian glory into battle against Italians is more complex than we have yet said. Italian though these people be, they are none the less his own flesh and blood; it was the seed of Aeneas, as Virgil reminds us, who threw the Tarquins out of Rome and defied Porsenna: 'Aeneadae in ferrum pro libertate ruebant.'[132] Moreover, to say that Aeneas is preparing to fight against Italians is true but not the whole truth, for equally he is preparing to fight with them. In this respect too the vision of the Augustan future reveals both change and unchangingness in the operations of history. There is change in that whereas the Trojans and Italians are now at war with one another, the time is coming when their progeny will be united in war against external foes. There is continuity, because as Aeneas is about to lead Italians to battle for the first time, the shield presents the greatest of the Aeneadae doing the same; both heroes can claim the title bestowed on the Trojan by his host: 'Italum . . . ductor'.[133] The shield shows completed that unifying and assimilating process which is seen beginning in the earlier parts of the eighth book. Once more the operations of time bring about progress and convey a message of hope.

A new austerity enters, however, with the book's short but magnificent conclusion. The sentence is emotionally complex: Aeneas does delight in the images, but he does not understand them, and in that ignorance he resumes his burden and turns a symbolic truth actual, as he raises his shield, lifting the fame and fate of his descendants on his shoulders. But this final note of severity brings out, by contrast, the relaxed and expansive nature of the eighth book as a whole. The holiday is ended; the shadow falls; the horror is about to begin.

[132] *Aen.* 8. 648, 'Aeneas' descendants were rushing on the sword for freedom's sake'.
[133] *Aen.* 8. 513.

CHAPTER 13

A Trojan in Italy: The Later *Aeneid*

3. Norn: Hinab!
2. Norn: Zur Mutter!
1. Norn: Hinab!

(Wagner)

And I will give thee the treasures of darkness, and hidden riches
of secret places.

(Isaiah)

Within the *Aeneid* Virgil's exploration of time, nature, history, communal identity, and their relation to each other reaches its apogee
in the seventh and eighth books. Certain of these themes are continued and even enlarged in the last third of the poem; as we have
already seen, the idea of the Trojans as oriental is most fully treated in
the ninth book, and the idea of their being absorbed into Italy comes
to completion with the likening of Aeneas to father Appenninus in
the twelfth. But these passages carry on existing themes; by the end
of the eighth book Virgil has given us his idea of Italy virtually entire.

However, there is one place in the later books where he adds a
new colour or atmosphere to the evocation of his native land: in
the story of Camilla. She has been brought up by Metabus among
shepherds, on the lonely mountainsides amid rough scrub and the
lairs of beasts.[1] Such a life and landscape are pastoral in the most
general sense (and in the last line of the seventh book she carries,
symbolically, a spear of 'herdsmen's myrtle', 'pastoralem myrtum'),
but they are not soft or idyllic, and not like any of the pastoral
worlds of the *Eclogues* or the pretty rusticity of Silvia and her family.
Camilla's world is strange, fierce, and lovely;[2] she is clad in a tiger
skin, suckled by wild mares; her association with Diana takes her

---

[1] *Aen.* 11. 569 f.
[2] For the fierceness, observe the echo 'feritate . . . ferino' at 11. 568, 571.

away from cultivated country and into the wild wood.[3] A nimbus of mysterious romance is about her: the fleetness of her feet outstrips the winds; she might have flown across a field of corn without bruising the ears or sped over the sea without dipping her feet in the waters.[4] The breeze that she outruns seems her natural element, and breezes are caught up into the world of Diana in the words with which her father dedicates her as a baby to the goddess, tying her to a spear and throwing her across the river:[5]

> 'alma, tibi hanc, nemorum cultrix, Latonia virgo,
> ipse pater famulam voveo; tua prima per *auras*
> tela tenens supplex hostem fugit. accipe, testor,
> diva tuam, quae nunc dubiis committitur *auris.*'

'Gracious maiden, Latona's daughter, dweller in the woods, I her father dedicate this child to you as your servant; yours are the first weapons she holds as she flees the enemy through the breezes, your suppliant. Goddess, receive her as yours, I beseech you, as she is now committed to the uncertain breeze.'

Wondrously she combines maidenliness with a skill in battle surpassing a man's; the strangeness is brought out by a play of words: 'quotque emissa manu contorsit spicula *virgo*, | tot Phrygii cecidisse *viri.*'[6] A maiden and a killer—not two separate aspects of her being, but in the cult of Diana a singleness of spirit, a romantic fierce chastity:[7]

> sola contenta Diana
> aeternum telorum et virginitatis amorem
> intemerata colit.

Content with Diana alone, she cherishes a perpetual love of hunting and virginity, inviolate.

But this chastity is glamorous, and a sexual feeling surrounds her death: the nymph Opis calls her wound a violation; the spear clinging to her naked breast drinks her virgin blood; and as we have seen, Virgil's almost loving account of her dying seems coloured with an amatory languorousness.[8] What is more, nakedness marks her both literally and spiritually: one side of her body is bared for battle, a

---

[3] See esp. 843, 'nec tibi *desertae* in dumis coluisse Dianam | profuit' (Nor has it profited you to have worshipped Diana in solitude in the scrubland); but also 537, 557 ff., 582 ff., 652, 857. [4] *Aen.* 7. 808 ff.

[5] *Aen.* 11. 557–60. [6] *Aen.* 11. 676 f. [7] *Aen.* 11. 582–4.

[8] *Aen.* 11. 848, 803 f., 827–31 (see above, pp. 203 f.).

curious reversal of the usual epic theme of men putting on armour for the fight, and her very weaponry expresses her purity and simplicity: 'ense pedes *nudo pura*que interrita parma'.[9]

Now Camilla is a child of the Italian country in a special sense, and Turnus addresses her as 'o decus Italiae virgo'.[10] Part of the charm that she and her companions possess lies in their Italianness; yet this is given a Grecian, even a neoteric colour:[11]

> at circum lectae comites, Larinaque virgo
> Tullaque et aeratam quatiens Tarpeia securim,
> Italides, quas ipsa decus sibi dia Camilla
> delegit pacisque bonas bellique ministras:
> quales Threiciae cum flumina Thermodontis
> pulsant et pictis bellantur Amazones armis,
> seu circum Hippolyten seu cum se Martia curru
> Penthesilea refert, magnoque ululante tumultu
> feminea exsultant lunatis agmina peltis.

Around her were her chosen companions, the maiden Larina, Tulla, and Tarpeia shaking her brazen axe, Italy's children, whom bright Camilla herself had chosen to honour her, good helpers in peace and war: as when the Thracian Amazons make the river Thermodon echo and go to war with emblazoned armour, around Hippolyta, or when warlike Penthesilea rides back in her chariot, and the ranks of women with their crescent shields exult in a great howling mêlée.

Camilla's maidens are Larina, Tulla, Tarpeia; solidly Italian names, we say to ourselves, and Virgil seems to agree, for he sums them up in the word 'Italides'. But the diction of 657 is curious. The rare word 'Italis' here makes its first appearance in Latin literature, where we shall not find it again until the silver poetry of more than fifty years later.[12] The feminine termination in *-is*, *-idis* has a Greek flavour; here uniquely Virgil has chosen to give to Italy, of all names, a Hellenic tinge. Nor is this the only unusual word in the line: he employs the epithet 'dius', mysteriously evocative of radiance and sanctity, for the only time in all his works.[13] The lines that follow flood the

---

[9] *Aen.* 11. 649, 711 'on foot and fearless, with naked sword and shield pure from ornament'.

[10] *Aen.* 11. 508, 'Maiden, Italy's glory'.   [11] *Aen.* 11. 655–63.

[12] It is also rare in Greek, and this may be its earliest known occurrence in either language. The first Greek appearance is in an epigram by Antonius Thallus (*Anth. Pal.* 7. 373), who dates from the 1st cent. BC or AD.

[13] On 'dius' in Lucretius, see above, p. 280.

verse with Grecian names: 'Amazones' and 'Hippolyten' advertise
their exoticism by their Greek case endings, while 'Thermodontis'
imports that famous neoteric mannerism, the spondaic fifth foot.
The eerieness of 'magno ululante tumultu' in both sound and content adds a touch of the uncanny too.

That there is a Greek element in Italy Virgil has told us before: its
presence is demonstrated by Diomedes in Apulia and the Arcadians
on the site of Rome, and it is one of the strands woven into the
catalogue of Italian forces. An occasional phrase, in passing, may
gently remind us: 'in Euboico Baiarum litore', 'Aetolis . . . ab Arpis'.[14]
A little more elaborate is 'Alpheae ab origine Pisae, | urbs Etrusca
solo' (Pisa, whose origins are by the Alpheus, yet a city on Etruscan
soil), where the words 'origo' and 'solum', in formal terms indicating a distinction between the situation of the city and the race of
its inhabitants, none the less suggest a rootedness in both Italy and
Greece.[15] The novelty in the treatment of Camilla is that things purely
and aboriginally Italian are described in language of Hellenic colour:
it is not the substance here which is Greek but the tone and timbre.
We shall not easily find such a spirit abroad again until the advent
of that whimsy, so attractive to Edwardian and late Victorian taste,
which sought to evoke the very Englishness of England by discover-
ing nymphs on the Cotswolds and Apollo in the dales of Derbyshire.
Virgil, however, is not whimsical. He has coloured Camilla with a
high fantastical romanticism; her world is Italian, yet also wild, strange,
and remote. The elusive atmosphere is created in part through paradox; delicacy and ferocity, sweetness, and savagery are curiously inter-
mingled; and Virgil, with his sure feeling for the relation between
style and content, extends the paradox into the diction and metre,
which draw us towards the fanciful and the exotic even as the sense
of the words insists upon our own country. And so in yet one more
way Virgil irradiates a familiar land with a strange and enchanting
light, and shows us a mysteriousness that lies in things long and intimately known.

But novelty in the investigation of nature or patriotism is not primarily what we find in the last third of the *Aeneid*; rather the rever-
beration of ideas and emotions more elaborately realized in earlier
books. For it is important to the understanding of the poem's later

---

[14] *Aen.* 9. 710, 'on Baiae's Euboean shore'; 10. 28, 'from Aetolian Arpi'.
[15] *Aen.* 10. 179 f.

parts that we read them with the memory of what has gone before. This can be seen in quite small ways.

To take an example: Latinus contemplates building twenty ships of Italian oak, 'Italo . . . robore'.[16] Why does he trouble with the epithet? what other oak might they use? The phrase is not for Latinus' audience but for Virgil's: we think of the other meaning of 'robur' (strength); we recall (dimly perhaps, but atmosphere is more import-ant than exact reminiscence) the aboriginal Italians, born literally out of the trees of their land,[17] and multiple overtones sound around Latinus' simple plan. Our antennae should now be so sensitive to the complex vibrations that Virgil has stirred in simple words or simple things that even in seemingly unimportant phrases we may find a pressure of significance. Magus pleads for his life; all the mean-ing that he needs to convey to his conqueror is, 'I have enough wealth at home to pay a ransom'; but see how Virgil makes him say it:[18]

> est domus *alta*, iacent *penitus defossa* talenta
> caelati argenti, sunt auri *pondera* facti
> infectique mihi.

I have a high house, talents of embossed silver lie deep buried there; I have weight of gold wrought and unwrought.

The poet's feeling for the size and scale and substance of the world comes through in a scene of no great importance. Similarly, when Iris tells Turnus that Aeneas has entered Etruria, this is how she says it: '*extremas* Corythi *penetravit* ad urbes' (He has penetrated to the furthest towns of Corythus).[19] In so tiny a passage space and extent are felt and enjoyed.

Iris has found Turnus alone and at a distance from his army: 'luco tum forte parentis | Pilumni Turnus sacrata valle sedebat.'[20] Why is he in this place? No explanation is given; and in the *Iliad* no hero is seen away from the plain of Troy in a setting such as this, private, embowered, and reflective. The mood is characteristic of Virgil. We have come to know the valley, the place a little apart, as the scene of revelation or divine epiphany: in such a place Anchises unfolded the future to Aeneas and Venus brought him the shield. Add to this the wood, the ancestry, the sanctity and the sonorous Italian name, and we hear an obscure resonance around these unemphatic lines.

---

[16] *Aen.* 11. 326.   [17] *Aen.* 8. 315.   [18] *Aen.* 10. 526–8.   [19] *Aen.* 9. 10.
[20] *Aen.* 9. 3 f., 'It happened that Turnus was sitting in a hallowed valley, in the wood of his sire Pilumnus.'

The heroes of the *Iliad* act and speak with clarity and directness upon a stage of remarkably small extent: a plain, a camp, a city. Virgil has done away with all that. His heroes make their way through a resistant vastness (penetravit ad urbes), they move at measured pace through an atmosphere thick with religious and patriotic significances. Italy is very old; each place is solemnized by deity and heavy laden with memory. Camilla's lightness, light as a breeze, is the more charming, the more strange by contrast with the prevailing tone.

The place where Opis kills Arruns is given a slightly fuller description:[21]

> fuit *ingens* monte sub *alto*
> regis Dercenni terreno ex aggere bustum
> *antiqui* Laurentis *opaca*que ilice tectum; . . .

Beneath the high hill stood the mighty grave, built up from earth, of Dercennus, ancient Laurentine king, canopied by a dark holm-oak.

Nature and the ancient work of man, first brought together in the *laus Italiae* of the *Georgics*, are combined in this small picture; it is this mingling, the poet implies, that gives the scene a certain impressiveness. History, age, size, and darkness blend and interact. The 'opaca ilex' stirs memories—of that other 'opaca ilex' where grew the golden bough, of the elm, 'ulmus opaca, ingens' in the underworld, of the holm-oaks beneath which the white sow was found, more generally perhaps of the lofty woods near Cumae, or the thick forest around the Tiber, darkening the stream (fluvio . . . opaco).[22] It is not that Virgil means a specific allusion or that a 'message' is to be extracted from these parallelisms. It is rather that he has created a world in which trees have come to have what one may perhaps call an imaginative weight, not precisely explicable; he has made a poetry in which such ordinary adjectives as 'altus', 'ingens', 'antiquus', and 'opacus' are naturally found together, though the objects to which they are attached may vary, and in which their recurrence seems not banal or conventional but evocative. This is not a deep passage by any means, but it maintains the reverberations from earlier passages which were indeed profound. The dashes of emotional colour can be very light and brief. Rescuing Turnus for a short while from his fate, Juno lures him on board a boat and abducts him from the battlefield. Virgil rounds off the section with these concluding words: 'et patris antiquam

---

[21] *Aen.* 11. 849–51.   [22] *Aen.* 6. 208 f., 283; 8. 43; 6. 179 ff.; 7. 36.

Dauni defertur ad urbem' (And he is borne to the ancient city of his father Daunus).[23] 'Patris', 'antiqui'—the paragraph comes to rest with Turnus in safety, though not for long; and there is a momentary touch of pathos in the fact that his brief refuge should be the old, ancestral place.

Virgil's tone comes partly from historical geography and patriotism, partly from the time at which he writes. He portrays Italy thus because in his imagination it is thus: this is its distinctive character, to be so ancient, so charged with history and numen. But his cast of mind is also shaped by the fact that he is writing 'civilized poetry'. The Homeric freshness and rapidity were inimitable. A more sophisticated, learned society, with the experience of a great and varied literature, spread across many centuries, behind it, must produce poetry more reflective, associative, allusive, if it is to produce good poetry at all. It is evidence of the wholeness of his poetic personality that the way he apprehends the solid world about him—nature as a whole and the land of Italy in particular—and the way he apprehends human life—its seriousness, its responsibilities—are at one with an understanding of the problems and possibilities of poetry in an elaborately developed age.

His feeling for the soil too, both in its physical being and as a source of national sentiment, infuses these later books. For the death of Pallas he uses a motif drawn from Homer, but with an adaptation: 'et terram *hostilem* moriens petit ore cruento' (And as he dies he bites the enemy land with bloodied mouth).[24] This land, we are reminded, is the possession of one side, not of the other. Now the same is true, to be sure, of the plain of Troy in the *Iliad*; but Homer does not speak like this. Virgil's subjectivity modifies the epic tone. Pathetically Pallas, half Sabellan by parentage and wholly Italian by birth, dies in Italy but upon enemy ground. In itself the phrase 'terra hostilis' would amount to very little; it acquires its point from its context in the *Aeneid*, from the poem's distinctive vision. When Pallas is buried, Virgil likens him to a flower plucked by a maiden's hand, a soft violet or drooping hyacinth. It is one of those places where he allows a voluptuous decorative pathos, more characteristic of elegy or love poetry than epic, to suffuse the verse,[25] but the simile is none

---

[23] *Aen.* 10. 688.   [24] *Aen.* 10. 489.
[25] Compare the flower similes at Catullus 11. 22 ff., 62. 39 ff. Virgil doubtless remembered these passages.

the less peculiarly fitted to this poem. 'Non iam mater alit tellus virisque ministrat' (No more does mother earth nourish the flower and supply it with strength).[26] We may recall hearing before the catalogue of Italy's forces how its manpower has grown like a flower out of the nourishing Italian earth, 'terra alma'.[27] And suddenly the simile comes to seem not just ornamental or too easily pathetic but the expression of an essential truth.

We encounter the same feeling for the solidity of the earth, for the grasp of the soil, in a more animated passage, as Tarchon urges on his men:[28]

> 'nunc, o lecta manus, validis incumbite remis;
> tollite, ferte rates, inimicam findite rostris
> hanc terram, sulcumque sibi premat ipsa carina.
> frangere nec tali puppim statione recuso
> arrepta tellure semel.' quae talia postquam
> effatus Tarchon, socii consurgere tonsis
> spumantisque rates arvis inferre Latinis,
> donec rostra tenent siccum et sedere carinae
> omnes innocuae.

'Now, my chosen band, bend to your strong oars; lift and drive forward the ships, cleave with your beaks this enemy land, let the keel itself plough a furrow. I do not refuse to break my ship up on such a resting-place, once the land is seized.' After Tarchon had said this, his comrades rose to their oars and drove their foaming ships upon the fields of Latium, until their beaks held the dry land and all their keels came to rest unharmed.

The surface meaning of 'inimicus' is 'belonging to the enemy', but the word is used so often in the sense 'feeling enmity' that in this context an implication of pathetic fallacy is in the air. The adjective's emphatic position also suggests that Tarchon regards the shore as like an enemy ship that he wants to ram and cut apart with his beaked prows. At the same time he intensely feels the soil: he wants to cleave the land, to cut a furrow in it, to grasp it (arrepta tellure). The undercurrent of agricultural metaphor is continued in 'rates arvis inferre Latinis', which has the Etruscans driving their ships not merely upon the shore but upon Latium's very fields. Then the boats 'occupy' the dry land and 'settle' there. Through such language we feel the physical quality of the ground, the tilth; we feel also the emotional force in the idea of possession.

---

[26] *Aen.* 11. 71.   [27] *Aen.* 7. 643 f.   [28] *Aen.* 10. 294–302.

Some words of Latinus indicate another way in which the reminiscence of words earlier in the poem may suggest the intimate connection of man and his native soil:[29]

> est *antiquus* ager Tusco mihi proximus amni,
> longus in occasum, finis super usque Sicanos;
> Aurunci Rutulique serunt, et vomere *duros*
> exercent collis atque horum *asperrima* pascunt.

I have an ancient domain by the Tuscan river, stretching far west, as far as to cross the Sicans' borders. Auruncans and Rutulians sow it; they work the hard hillsides with the plough and graze the roughest parts.

As it happens, Virgil has used 'durus' and 'asper' together before: 'gens dura et aspera cultu | debellanda tibi Latio est' (In Latium you must subdue a people hard and rough in their way of life).[30] Setting the two passages side by side, we find a curious interplay. In the later passage the adjectives are all applied to the land; but 'antiquus' suggests the inhabitants, for the terrain is 'ancient' here only in the sense that it has been long either in cultivation or in the possession of one people; and 'durus' has the same effect, through its firm association with human and especially Italian hardihood. In the earlier passage 'durus' and 'asper' are used directly of the folk; on the other hand, 'cultus' is a metaphor taken from the tilling of the ground. Taking the two sentences together we learn that the Italians are as their land is; the men and their mountainsides seem to be of like substance. Probably the reader does not recall the exact phrase in the fifth book when he comes to the eleventh, but it is no great matter, for once we are steeped in Virgil's imagination we understand that such adjectives naturally bind humanity to the earth.

He allows his feeling for Italy to speak even through the mouth of Diomedes:[31]

> o fortunatae gentes, Saturnia regna,
> antiqui Ausonii, quae vos fortuna quietos
> sollicitat suadetque ignota lacessere bella?

O happy peoples, Saturn's realm, long stablished Ausonians, what chance troubles you in your calm and persuades you to agitate unfamiliar war?

The disturbing of a deep ancient quiet is conveyed by the metre: the slow spondees of the first line, the slightly greater speed of the

---

[29] *Aen.* 11. 316–19.   [30] *Aen.* 5. 730 f.   [31] *Aen.* 11. 252–4.

second, the agitated rhythm of the last.[32] The first words recall two passages from the second Georgic, his praise of country life, 'o fortunatos nimium', and the great invocation of the land, 'Saturnia tellus', at the end of the *laus Italiae*.[33] Virgil must surely have realized the supreme beauty that he had created in these two celebrations and appreciated that they would deepen the emotional appeal of Diomedes' language to anyone who knew them. Yet the *Aeneid* has woven its own nexus of associations, and even if we pretend not to know the *Georgics*, we may still claim to recognize from the present poem alone the proper connection of Italy with peace and antiquity and the half-felt presence of a vanished deity. What a memory of the *Georgics* may do is to enrich these feelings by linking them to agriculture and the land.

The effect of these lines is modified by a passage later in the same speech:[34]

> invidisse deos, *patriis* ut redditus *aris*
> coniugium optatum et *pulchram* Calydona viderem?

Have the gods begrudged me a return to my ancestral altars, to see the wife I long for and lovely Calydon?

Diomedes remains, unlike Evander, unshakeably a Greek: his feelings for the beauty of his landscape, for the emotional bonds of cult and ancestry, are still attached to his native land. In retrospect, therefore, the pathos of his opening words is tempered by Virgil's subjectivity. Diomedes is giving the ambassadors prudent advice: the Ausonians have enjoyed long peace; why should they get embroiled in war now? We though, through the associations that Virgil has wrapped around the idea of Italy, hear overtones of which the Greek himself is unaware (he has not read the *Georgics*). The way in which the poet's complex love of Italy breathes through the voice of a man who does not share it is curiously muted and evocative.

Diomedes is not the only one who is still looking back in these later books. Euryalus' mother laments, 'heu, terra *ignota* canibus data praeda *Latinis* | alitibusque iaces!' (Alas, you lie in a strange land, a prey given to the dogs and birds of Latium).[35] Here we recognize a

---

[32] 'Suadetque' momentarily suggests a trochaic caesura in the third foot, before the last syllable is cancelled by the elision; there is then a true trochaic caesura in the fourth foot. Though the third-foot caesura is technically 'strong', its force is weakened by the elision, and an effect of restlessness results.   [33] *Geo.* 2. 458, 173.

[34] *Aen.* 11. 269 f.   [35] *Aen.* 9. 485 f.

simple version of that subjectivity which was more elaborately woven around the death of Caieta.[36] 'Latinis' is emphatically placed, alien and unfriendly in the speaker's mouth, but with another resonance for ourselves. Antores, sent from Greece, had clung to Evander and settled in an Italian city (Itala consederat urbe); he perishes, 'et dulcis moriens reminiscitur Argos.'[37] Evander himself had said 'we Italians',[38] but Virgil now shows us the other side of that coin: a first home cannot be forgotten. Through so small a vignette as Antores' death, he can suggest to us that Aeneas in turn, though he will win the war and even become an Italian god, has suffered a loss which we must suppose can never be wholly made good.

An evident dweller in the past is the aged Aletes, who declares,[39]

> di patrii, quorum semper *sub numine Troia est*,
> non tamen omnino Teucros delere paratis . . .

Gods of our fathers, beneath whose protection Troy ever remains, you are not, after all, designing to blot out the Teucrians utterly . . .

We shall come to feel that he is at least half wrong. Troy itself is already destroyed and Aletes is like Helenus in trying to keep alive something that is past and can never return.[40] Aeneas no longer speaks in this fashion; he has had the strength to change. The Trojans will indeed survive and their descendants will go on to greater glories, but only at a cost of which the old man knows nothing, the obliteration of the Trojan name and language. Like Diomedes, Aletes says more than he knows, for he echoes Anchises amid the sack of Troy:[41]

> sequor et qua ducitis adsum,
> di patrii; servate domum, servate nepotem.
> vestrum hoc augurium, vestroque in numine Troia est.

I follow and where you lead, there am I, gods of our fathers; preserve my house, preserve my grandson. This omen is yours and Troy rests in your protection.

The 'semper' in the later speech suggests that Virgil intends the echo: the ancestral gods watched over Troy then, they watch over it still. But Anchises was looking to the future—'preserve my house, preserve my grandson'—and we think onward to the foundation of the

---

[36] *Aen.* 7. 1–4. [37] *Aen.* 10. 780, 782, 'and dying remembers his dear Argos'.
[38] *Aen.* 8. 331. [39] *Aen.* 9. 247.
[40] On Helenus see above, pp. 438–40. [41] *Aen.* 2. 701–3.

Julian line. 'Di patrii' has a rather Roman ring (it came, followed at once by seven proper names of Roman flavour, in the passionate patriotic cry at the end of the first Georgic).[42] The Roman overtone seems appropriate to the immediate context in the second book; perhaps also in the ninth? Does the poet hint, even as he shows us one of the Trojans clinging to the fantasy that Troy survives, that they have an embryonically Roman quality?

A phrase like 'di patrii' may seem little in itself, but in the course of the poem Virgil has created an atmosphere in which simple words become pregnant with significance; often he does not tell us what to think, but makes us alert to possibilities. For example, the adjective 'durus' seems so much the Italians' property that when the poet refers to 'Aeneadae duri' or Diomedes ruefully looks back to 'durae ... Troiae', we sense that a partial and prejudiced view is being adjusted.[43] When Mnestheus, the very man described in the fifth book as 'mox Italus', one who would become Italian in due course, calls out 'o cives' (fellow citizens) to his countrymen and bids them think of their fatherland and old gods (patriae veterumque deorum), he is referring to Troy and Trojan deities, but we may again ask: Is this not language of a Roman cast?[44] Now it might be objected that since the poem is in Latin, if any character of any nation is to speak about gods, country, and tradition he will tend to do so in terms that strike the modern reader as Roman; it might even be said that since Virgil is himself Roman, he is bound to give his poem a Roman tone, not merely from time to time as a designed effect but always and involuntarily. Such objections may warn us to be cautious, but they are not persuasive. The address 'citizens' is unusual in a mythological epic; its use is the poet's deliberate choice. And we have seen before how sparingly he uses the word 'senatus', and in contexts where its Roman connotations are pointed.[45] More generally, we should consider the method of the poem as a whole. Certainly, in a passage like Mnestheus' speech Virgil does not compel us to the conclusion that there are the makings of a Roman or Italian spirit in this foreign people, but it is not his purpose to compel; rather to persuade us, to coax us into his way of thought and feeling, to nurse a sensitivity to the nuances of words, so that we say not that it must but that it might be so.

---

[42] *Geo.* 1. 498.   [43] *Aen.* 9. 468, 'Aeneas' hardy folk'; 11. 288, 'stubborn Troy'.
[44] *Aen.* 9. 783, 786 ('mox Italus', 5. 117).   [45] Twice only; see above, p. 547.

For he sets up a kind of counterpoint, in which he looks to both past and future, both the eastern element in the Trojans and their embryonically Roman qualities. Sometimes he stresses the one aspect, sometimes the other, sometimes exposes both at the same time. Early in the ninth book Cybele plays a larger part than anywhere else in the poem. Her origins are oriental in any case, but lest we should forget, the proper names ('Phrygia in Ida', 'genetrix Berecyntia') keep our minds upon the east.[46] The very nature of the episode is in keeping with her exotic character: baroque and bizarre is the metamorphosis, through her intervention, of Aeneas' ships into sea nymphs; such an incident would be unthinkable in the *Iliad*, nor can we easily imagine an Italian god effecting such a result. And as Virgil goes back to the Trojans' Asian origins, so he also thrusts back into the past. Cybele is very old: she is 'deum . . . genetrix', mother of the gods, and she describes herself to very Jupiter, the father of gods and men, as 'tua cara parens'.[47] When Turnus, beholding the miracle, scornfully describes the invaders as 'Phryges' and with fine indignation declares it to be enough that the Trojans have so much as set foot upon Italy's fruitful fields, we may feel that on this occasion at least he has spoken tellingly:[48]

> sat fatis Venerique datum, tetigere quod arva
> fertilis Ausoniae Troes.

Enough has been granted to destiny and Venus, in that the Trojans have touched the fields of fruitful Ausonia.

'Troes' is placed next to the resonant name of Ausonia, and for further emphasis both words are delayed until the end of the sentence; what is more, the sudden stop in the middle of the fourth foot gives that last word an especially contemptuous inflection. Yet Virgil will soon show how incomplete is this picture of the Trojans: their warriors are called a legion, and more strikingly, they are represented as a people and their elders, 'populusque patresque', a phrase of unmistakably Roman cast.[49] Now it is not long since we saw Augustus at Actium, 'cum patribus populoque, penatibus et magnis dis'.[50] We found that the gods in this picture were both Trojan and Roman; we may now say that the 'people and elders' of the ninth book are

---

[46] *Aen.* 9. 80, 'on Phrygian Ida'; 82, 'the Berecynthian mother'.
[47] *Aen.* 9. 82, 84 'your loved mother'.
[48] *Aen.* 9. 134, 135 f.   [49] *Aen.* 9. 174, 192.
[50] *Aen.* 8. 679; (with the elders and the people, the penates and the great gods).

the same community, enduring through the centuries, that has since become the Roman state.

In the tenth book the nymphs reappear, dancing around Aeneas as he comes back by sea to the field of battle. Twice now have spirits of the waters revealed themselves to him: Tiberinus before he journeys to the interior, the nymphs on his return; first the native deity, grave and twilit, then goddesses made from Trojan ships and graced with such Grecian names as Cymodocea.[51] To match the change in national perspective are changes of style and allusion. The scene is rococo and fantastical, a far cry from the Italian solemnities of the Tiber. We may well recall the mannerism and preciosity of neoteric verse; more particularly the scene near the beginning of Catullus' *Peleus and Thetis* where the sea nymphs reveal themselves to the Argonauts.[52] This is Virgil's own thought: Cymodocea describes her company as pines from Ida's sacred peak, 'Idaeae sacro de vertice pinus', and we catch the echo of Catullus' first line, 'Peliaco quondam prognatae vertice pinus' (Pines once born on Pelion's peak).[53] Aeneas, as he marvels at the apparition, is identified as 'Tros Anchisiades' (the Trojan, Anchises' son), terms that thrust away from his present situation in both place and time, the adjective directing us away from Italy towards the east, the patronymic looking to the past.[54] He prays to Cybele, 'alma parens Idaea deum', and again the honorific has both a temporal and a geographical aspect, 'Idaea' placing her near the city of Troy, 'parens . . . deum' reminding us of her extreme antiquity.[55] He beseeches her to help the 'Phrygians';[56] yet only a few lines later the prism turns and we see him in a different light: he stands on the high poop ('stans celsa in puppi'), and behold:[57]

> ardet apex capiti cristisque a vertice flamma
> funditur et vastos umbo vomit aureus ignis . . .

The top of his head burns, flame pours from the crest on his helmet's peak and the golden boss spouts immense fire . . .

Indeed, he is like a comet or the star Sirius. Unmistakably this echoes Augustus at Actium,[58]

---

[51] Cymodocea is the only name given (10. 225); we infer that the others are like.

[52] Cat. 64. 12–18.

[53] *Aen.* 10. 230; Cat. 64. 1. The allusion is made not only by the repetition in the last two words but also by the use of a proper adjective ('Peliac peak', 'Idaean pines').

[54] *Aen.* 10. 250.

[55] *Aen.* 10. 252, 'goddess of Ida, nourishing mother of the gods' (literally, 'nourishing Idaean parent of the gods'). [56] *Aen.* 10. 255.

[57] *Aen.* 10. 261, 270 f. [58] *Aen.* 8. 680 f.

> stans celsa in puppi, geminas cui tempora flammas
> laeta vomunt patriumque aperitur vertice sidus.

standing on the lofty poop, while his glad temples spout twin flames and his father's star dawns on his brow.

A moment ago Aeneas was a son and a Phrygian; now he appears as the ancestor of Italy's chief.

In such passages as these we see first one aspect of the Trojans, then another. Sometimes the doubleness is almost simultaneous, as when Virgil presents a sequence of three warriors, each decorated with a tiny vignette:[59]

> te quoque magnanimae viderunt, Ismare, gentes
> vulnera derigere et calamos armare veneno,
> Maeonia generose domo, ubi pinguia culta
> exercentque viri Pactolusque inrigat auro.
> adfuit et Mnestheus, quem pulsi pristina Turni
> aggere murorum sublimem gloria tollit,
> et Capys: hinc nomen Campanae ducitur urbi.

You too, Ismarus, the noble-hearted peoples saw aiming wounds and arming your darts with poison, high-born to a Maeonian house, where men work the rich tilth and Pactolus irrigates them with gold. Mnestheus too was there, whom the fresh glory of driving Turnus from the walls' rampart lifts high, and Capys; from him the name of Campania's city is taken.

Though this trio are contemporaries, Virgil uses them to set forth past, present, and future in succession. Ismarus' name is taken from a mountain in Thrace, not very far from Troy;[60] his method of fighting is barbarian; he is seen, with a backward glance, in terms of his Lydian ancestry; the poetic extravagance which has Pactolus seemingly irrigating the land with gold imports a note of luxuriant exoticism. Mnestheus' feat of arms is a success of the present battle (the reader who recalls from the fifth book that he is to be 'soon an Italian' and ancestor of the Memmii may start to think about the future).[61] Capys, one day to give his name to Capua, invites us to look onward to the time when his Greek vowel will be transmuted into an Italian form. Here, then, is the movement through time and space from Troy to Italy in miniature; but sometimes the double vision is completely

---

[59] *Aen.* 10. 139–45.

[60] It is illuminating to compare Virgil's use of Ismarus in the *Georgics* (2. 37; see above, pp. 346 f.). The use at *Aen.* 12. 701 of Athos, a mountain in roughly the same part of the world, is also instructive (above, pp. 556 f.).   [61] *Aen.* 5. 117.

simultaneous. When Pallas prays to 'Thybri pater', we hear, along with the Greek form of the name, a foreshadowing of the Roman prayer to father Tiber, 'pater Tiberinus', and we are reminded that the Arcadians generally and Pallas especially, through his mixed parentage, are poised between Greece and Italy.[62]

The young are particularly fitting as objects of this double vision; Pallas, of course, but Ascanius too. The 'lusus Troiae' or 'Troy game', the display which he and his young companions put on at the games in the fifth book has a double implication almost inevitably, for the name looks one way, while the thing itself looks onward to the Roman custom which was to be so called. And Virgil reinforces that implication by his account of Ascanius' friend:[63]

> una acies iuvenum, ducit quam parvus ovantem
> nomen avi referens Priamus, tua clara, Polite,
> progenies, auctura Italos . . .
>
> .   .   .   .   .   .
>
> alter Atys, genus unde Atii duxere Latini,
> parvus Atys pueroque puer dilectus Iulo.
> extremus formaque ante omnis pulcher Iulus
> Sidonio est invectus equo . . .

One line of youths was led in its triumph by a small Priam, whose name revived his grandfather's, your noble offspring, Polites, destined to increase the Italian race . . . The second leader is Atys, from whom the Latin Atii have drawn their descent, little Atys, a boy loved by the boy Iulus. Last and handsomest of them all, Iulus rode on a Phoenician horse . . .

Priam, grandson of Priam, who will become an Italian ancestor —here are not only the gaze at once forward and back, but a pointed choice of proper noun, offering a hint of paradox in the thought that Italians should be sons of one who bears a name archetypally symbolic of Troy. No other name could have had quite the same force. The next names are repeated—'Atys . . . Atys . . . Iulo . . . Iulus . . .'—and we hear the poet's voice gently pressing them, his ear listening for their overtones. As with Capys, he has chosen a name whose sound advertises its Greek origin; the stress upon it brings out the contrast with 'Atii . . . Latini'. Yet at the same time he suggests continuity: Ascanius appears twice under the name which suggests the potentially Roman character of his race, and a graceful compliment is also paid to Augustus, whose mother was an Atia;

[62] *Aen.* 10. 421.   [63] *Aen.* 5. 563–5, 568–71.

we ponder the thought that the Caesares and the Atii were already bound by ties of friendship so long ago.

Ascanius is similarly treated when Apollo congratulates him for killing Numanus:[64]

> 'macte nova virtute, puer, sic itur ad astra,
> dis genite et geniture deos. iure omnia bella
> gente sub Assaraci fato ventura resident,
> nec te Troia capit.'

'A blessing on your young manhood, boy: such is the path to the stars, child of gods and future parent of gods. Beneath Assaracus' race shall all the wars that destiny brings rightly subside; nor does Troy contain you.'

The second of these lines incorporates all known time: 'dis genite' refers to Venus and Jupiter,[65] 'geniture deos' takes us all the way to Julius Caesar and Augustus. The pattern is repeated and developed in the next sentence. The man who stands as representative of the Trojan race is not Aeneas or Anchises or even Priam but Assaracus, that name evocative, like Tros and Dardanus, of high antiquity.[66] But he comes in the midst of a statement which points as far into the future as is possible, anticipating Augustus' closing of the gates of Janus as a symbol of universal peace.[67] The notion of the Romans as Assaracus' people looks back to Jupiter's unfolding of destiny in the first book, where it displayed the vast, slow reversals worked by history.[68] The mixing in of Assaracus here with Caesar's world empire suggests momentarily that impression of chronological paradox that we found more elaborately developed in the lament for Marcellus as an expression of Virgil's idea of continuity and transformation

---

[64] *Aen.* 9. 641–4.

[65] At the least. We can think of Jupiter as effectively the ultimate ancestor, the father of gods and men, or we can go beyond him to Saturn. Either way, Apollo's phrase takes us back to the beginning of things.   [66] See above, p. 385.

[67] Most commentators take the reference to be simply to Augustus (Page, Williams, Hardie); Conington thinks that the primary reference 'is to Ascanius putting down the wars that were to trouble Aeneas (if we suppose Virg. to follow this form of the legend . . .)', the reference to Augustus being secondary. Even if we take the latter view, the allusion to Augustus remains, and the language still appears so designed that it fits Ascanius less naturally than his descendant. But the first interpretation is preferable. Why should Apollo say 'gente sub Assaraci' if he means 'under you'? The phrase suggests a larger destiny (cf. 'domus Assaraci' of the Romans at 1. 284), as does the sentence as a whole. The ending of all the wars that destiny may bring is an idea that asks for some grander event than such modest success as Ascanius may be supposed to have had within the long history of conflict in Italy. The words 'geniture deos' lead Apollo to think on to the enormous glory of the race; then he turns back to Ascanius: 'nec *te* . . .'   [68] *Aen.* 1. 284.

combined.[69] The stronger emphasis here is on the future; Virgil insinuates into the god's words an essentially hopeful picture of human
progress. There is an air of freshness: a boy, new prowess.[70] Both in
their immediate context and within the poem's ethos as a whole
Apollo's last words seem just and satisfying. Yes, Troy is not enough,
and it is good news that Troy 'does not contain' the boy. Troy has
'contained' or 'captured' Helenus and Acestes, but we have felt in
them some failure of nerve or enterprise. The doom of Troy's name
and language, melancholy for the Trojans, is a healthy doom none
the less.

When Nisus and Euryalus come to Ascanius with their plan to
raid the enemy camp, his reply includes an adjuration, 'per magnos,
Nise, penatis | Assaracique larem et canae penetralia Vestae' (By the
great gods of the household, Nisus, by Assaracus' house god and
hoary Vesta's sanctum).[71] 'Assaraci' and 'canae' suggest an ancient past;
'Assaraci' also speaks of Troy, while 'penatis', 'larem', and above all
'Vestae' suggest Rome.[72] We sense Virgil's feeling for the layers of
the past: even a man of the heroic age is conscious of coming out
of a hoary, holy antiquity, and yet at the same time, through the
markedly Roman language that Ascanius unwittingly applies to Trojan
institutions, we look to the future and the changes it will bring.

The idea of progress implied in these lines subtly colours what
follows. We begin to notice that Ascanius sees the war, too baldly,
as a fight against a foreign foe. He speaks about the Trojan hope of
taking Italy, grasping the sceptre, sharing out the booty and having
Latinus' lands to distribute at pleasure.[73] Now both Ascanius and
Euryalus are very young, and there is some immaturity in each.
Euryalus' appetite for adventure is meant for our admiration, but his

---

[69] See above, p. 397.

[70] The tone of 641 perhaps eludes us. 'Macte' is unique in Virgil; in this context has it
an archaic glow? Cf. Hor. *Serm.* 1. 2. 31 f.: ' "macte | virtute esto," inquit sententia *dia*
Catonis' (' "A blessing on your virtue," was Cato's reverend saying').

[71] *Aen.* 9. 258 f.

[72] Compare the similar phrase at 5. 744: 'Pergameumque Larem et canae penetralia Vestae'
(by the house god of Pergamum and the sanctum of hoary Vesta). 'Pergameus' takes the
role of Assaracus in the later passage, paradoxical in connection with 'Lar' and 'Vesta'. For
the quintessentially Roman character of Vesta, see above all *Geo.* 1. 498 f., but also *Aen.*
1. 292 f. ('cana Fides et Vesta, Remo cum fratre Quirinus | iura dabunt', 'Hoary Faith
and Vesta, and Quirinus with his brother Remus shall bestow law').

[73] *Aen.* 9. 267 ff. It is important not to overstate this point. The ninth book sets up a
broad contrast between Euryalus, the young man who does not know where to set a limit
after his first success, and Ascanius, the young man who does.

delight in slaughter is surely not, and it carries its own punishment. We see Aeneas acting cruelly and under the extremity of passion, but never with a cheerful, uncomplicated blood-lust. With Ascanius' too simple picture of the war we may likewise contrast Aeneas' solemn sense of responsibility and the magnanimity with which he will ultimately use his victory. However, the contrast is not only with Aeneas but with another aspect of Ascanius' self, for he has sworn by the Trojan gods in terms which bring to our own minds the religion of Rome. He belongs to both sides without knowing it: he speaks of capturing Italy in the spirit of a conqueror come from abroad, yet we can hear in him an authentically Italian spirit. Thus the spirit of place and the nuances of language do not merely create a mood; by countless small touches they develop a moral vision, showing that through the miseries and confusions of the present time history is none the less shaping a meaning and purpose.

Such are Virgil's emotional subtlety and complexity that this vision can shine through passages of the darkest sorrow. Pallas, again, is one who can show us this, in life and in death:[74]

> hinc Pallas instat et urget,
> hinc contra Lausus, nec multum discrepat aetas,
> egregii forma, sed quis Fortuna negarat
> in patriam reditus.

Here Pallas presses and thrusts, here, against him, Lausus does the same. There is not much difference in age between them; both were outstanding in looks, but men to whom fortune had denied a return to their fatherland.

Every citizen from an Italian municipium, Cicero said, has two patriae,[75] and more or less the same may be said of Virgil's heroic age. In one sense (and this is the primary meaning) Lausus' patria is Tuscany, Pallas' Latium; in another sense the patria of each is Italy. The two young men are similar in age, looks and destiny; Virgil's careful parallelism invites us to discover a further likeness: both are fighting for what will ultimately prove to be the same nation, the same goal. Now there is division, but there will be reconciliation to come.

The glimmer of a happier futurity flickers again through the sombre scenes of lamentation for Pallas. An Ausonian spear has killed him, say the lines introducing Aeneas' threnody; but Aeneas ends

---

[74] *Aen.* 10. 433–6.   [75] *Leg.* 2. 3–5.

by weeping for the loss that both Ausonia and his own son have suffered by this death: 'ei mihi quantum | praesidium, Ausonia, et quantum tu perdis, Iule.'[76] Here is the great movement of history shown in miniature: Troy and Italy are now at war, but Pallas, had he survived would have become the bulwark of both. In these scenes of mourning three races are engaged, Greeks, Trojans and Italians; we see now two of them mingling and contrasting, now all three. Teucrians, Tyrrhenians, Arcadians all join in the funeral procession.[77] Yet the races remain distinctive in style. When the news reaches Evander's city, the Arcadians snatch torches in accordance with their ancient custom, 'de more vetusto'; the Trojans are seen separately ('contra turba Phrygum'), and a difference is implied.[78] So similarly Aeneas and his Etruscan ally Tarchon will conduct funerals for their men each in accordance with his ancestral custom, 'quisquis . . . more . . . patrum', a scene prophetic of the diversity in unity which will one day characterize Italy.[79] It shall be a consolation, Evander declares, that Pallas died leading Teucrians against Latium; what nobler death could one ask than that of which the mighty Phrygians and the Tyrrhenians deem Pallas worthy.[80] This passionate asseveration proclaims an alliance between peoples but also maintains an enmity between peoples; for indeed Virgil's is not a cosy picture. Amid the high due solemnities of Pallas' funeral is a glimpse of horror: the procession includes the prisoners whom Aeneas will sacrifice as an offering to the dead man's shade.[81] The passage is very brief—we do not witness the actual killings, and the poet offers no judgement on the act—but it recalls the place in the *Iliad* where Achilles slaughters Trojan captives in honour of the dead Patroclus, perhaps the most shocking moment in that poem.[82]

Virgil, then, shows us good things and bad mingled, encouraging in us a moral alertness but not supplying simple answers. We know why Achilles acts as he does: from the depth of his wrath and at the same time (for such is the appalling splendour of Homer's conception) touchingly, in a pathetic attempt to do some service to his friend, although it is plain that the deed is valueless to the man for whom it is done. But in what spirit and with what purpose does Aeneas kill his prisoners? The parallel with Achilles and the

[76] *Aen.* 11. 40 f., 57 f. 'Alas, how great a bulwark do you lose, Ausonia, and you also, Iulus.'   [77] *Aen.* 11. 92 f.
[78] *Aen.* 11. 142, 145.   [79] *Aen.* 11. 185 f.   [80] *Aen.* 11. 168, 171 f.
[81] *Aen.* 11. 81 f.   [82] *Il.* 23. 175 f.

uniqueness of the deed in the *Aeneid* as in the *Iliad* suggest that the hero has gone beyond the accepted bounds of heroic conduct; but if so, why is the passage so brief, and the act mentioned almost in passing? And how can he be 'good Aeneas' so full of pity for the Latins immediately afterwards?[83] Has he merely enacted a harsh ritual? or has he purged his bitterness by a private and personal cruelty? Is he better than Achilles in that his generosity of spirit is so soon restored? or worse in that he lacks the size and magnificence of passion that offer at least some degree of excuse for Achilles' wrath?

This is not the only time that Aeneas is blotted out from our vision when we are especially eager to know his mind. There is a genuine puzzle here. On the one hand it is in the nature of the *Aeneid* to replace Homer's lucidity with a veiledness: 'ad nos vix tenuis famae perlabitur aura.'[84] In the *Iliad* and *Odyssey* the god's motives may be hidden from the human actors in the drama, but they are perspicuous to Homer's audience; in the *Aeneid* they sometimes seem to baffle the poet himself. There is a kind of reticence or secretiveness or unclarity of perception in the poem which, for whatever purpose, is surely part of its design. While he is dallying with Dido Aeneas simply vanishes. Allecto's assault upon Amata and Turnus is so described that we cannot really tell how far she symbolizes their own passions and how far they are taken over by an external force. Here a doubt may creep in. Is this moral intelligence—a recognition of the complexity and indeterminacy of human motivation and responsibility—or is there some confusion or evasion? And with the immolation of the captives one may wonder again. After all, Virgil faced two testing problems in adapting the story of the *Iliad*. Aeneas is not, like Achilles, in a tragic situation: he does not fight under the shadow of death, nor do his passions and actions shape the plot. There was a danger that he would become the poet's dummy, confronting no hard choices, moving irresistibly and uninterestingly towards his destined victory. Second, Pallas is a problematic equivalent to Patroclus. Patroclus is the centre of Achilles' life: Pallas cannot be that to Aeneas, and could not have been even if we had heard nothing of Dido or Creusa. Virgil appears to be aware of the difficulty, and to recognize that grief would not in itself be a strong enough

---

[83] *Aen.* 11. 108–19 (his speech); 'bonus Aeneas', 11. 106.
[84] *Aen.* 7. 646 (to us there wafts barely a thin breeze of tale).

emotion for his hero. Accordingly, he seems to imply a sense in Aeneas of having pledged Evander to look after Pallas (the implication has to remain vague, because it is unreasonable: no one can be sent to war on condition that he is not hurt).[85] And Evander is also made to insist that Aeneas owes him Turnus' life.[86] Similarly, the killing of the prisoners seems designed to help with both the poet's difficulties. An Aeneas angry and troubled enough to act like Achilles might seem more interesting than a calmly successful one; and his cruelty might help to convince us that he feels intensely for the dead man. But one may doubt whether Virgil has brought off either trick. The truth is that he does not persuade us that Pallas' death is such a bitter wound to his hero, and the mechanisms that he uses to try and enforce conviction, like the human sacrifice and Evander's demand, do not improve matters. Nor, surely, has he made Aeneas live more in the reader's imagination. Homer shows us both the savagery and the generosity of Achilles, and through them the diversity of mood and behaviour that we know to exist in real people. Virgil presumably had the same intention, but he does not succeed. Aeneas' cruelty seems unnatural, unmotivated; we feel that it is not really fuelled by his experience but turned on and off at the poet's convenience.

What then shall we say about Aeneas' sudden switch from vengeance to magnanimity after Pallas' funeral? Maybe it is simply a lapse of judgement. Yet perhaps we may see the funeral as a catharsis for Aeneas, which makes possible his conciliatory reply to the Latin ambassadors who come asking for a suspension of hostilities so that they may bury their dead. Or perhaps he has felt a revulsion at his own act, since he expresses a reluctance to kill anyone at all. At all events, whatever local awkwardness there may be, Aeneas' clemency here is part of a counterpoint which reveals both the immediate harshness and the larger shape of history, holding them in balance. Between the darker notes in Pallas' funeral and Evander's speech is set the period of truce. Drances, Turnus' bitter enemy on the Latin side, speaks in favour of peace, ending,[87]

---

[85] *Aen.* 11. 45 ff. 'These were not the promises about you that I gave to your father Evander . . .' This need only mean (with bitter understatement), 'I certainly did not promise that you would be killed', but it might also be taken to mean, 'I promised something different.'

[86] *Aen.* 11. 178 f.   [87] *Aen.* 11. 130 f.

> quin et fatalis murorum attollere moles
> saxaque subvectare umeris Troiana iuvabit.

Why, it will even be our pleasure to raise the destined bulk of your walls
and to carry Trojan stones on our shoulders.

Drances is not a charming character; we are told just before this
speech of his envenomed nature,[88] and the poet's purpose, as so often,
is to make the speaker's words signify more than he realizes. Drances
addresses the immediate crisis, and hopes to damage Turnus, but
beyond these smaller purposes we hear a grander, calmer, larger tone.
'Fatalis' means much more to us than it can possibly mean to Drances:
he is observing that the Trojans are bound to win, but we know
that 'fatum' spreads an immense distance into the future, decreeing
that they, and Drances' people also, are to rule the world. 'Moles'
too signifies to the reader far more than the blocks of stone that
Drances has in mind: 'tantae molis erat Romanam condere gentem'[89]—
we ponder the enormous weight of future empire. And in the next
line, as the Latins lift the Trojans' stones upon their shoulders, we
should recall Aeneas at the end of the eighth book, lifting upon his
own shoulders the shield which is at once a solid weight of matter
and the burden of greatness to come. Through the surly Italian we
hear of the two races beginning to collaborate in a glorious work,
the culmination of which, as we know and he does not, is a thousand years away. The same idea continues, softened now, in the lines
that follow:[90]

> bis senos pepigere dies, et pace sequestra
> per silvas Teucri mixtique impune Latini
> erravere iugis.

They made a twelve days' truce, and in the time of peace that followed
the Trojans and Latins wandered together unharmed on the hills, through
the woodland.

Line 134 is especially relaxed, with its slow spondees and the predominance of the gentle *i* sound. 'Mixti' on the surface means simply
that the two sides accompany one another, but it also foreshadows
the future mingling of Trojans and Latins to form a single race. The

---

[88] *Aen.* 11. 122 f. Drances is elderly; we may observe, with some irony, that the delight
of carting rocks about is one which he will have to leave to others.
[89] *Aen.* 1. 33, 'Such was the weight of founding the Roman race'.
[90] *Aen.* 11. 133–5.

woodland and hillslope of Italy will be their home and their delight. The two peoples, wandering—a leisurely word—in this landscape, sound for a moment like Corydon, or Gallus in Arcadia; we catch an echo of pastoral dalliance in these evocative lines.

We are often conscious of knowing more than the human actors; in the scene on Olympus that opens the tenth book we may suspect ourselves wiser than some of the gods themselves. Earlier the Sibyl had declared to Aeneas the black prospect that history would repeat itself: more war must be fought, another Achilles awaits in Latium, the cause of conflict will again be the Trojan taking of a foreign wife from among those who have been their hosts.[91] Now Venus, pleading for her Trojans, takes up the theme, twice using the word which the Sibyl too had twice uttered with such grim import, 'iterum', 'a second time':[92]

> muris iterum imminet hostis
> nascentis Troiae nec non exercitus alter,
> atque iterum in Teucros Aetolis surgit ab Arpis
> Tydides.

A second time an enemy threatens the walls of rising Troy, a second army threatens; and a second time Tydeus' son rises against the Teucrians from Aetolian Arpi.

Yet history is not simply repeating itself, though such as Numanus Remulus and even Venus may suppose so. 'Nascentis Troiae' and the phrase which she uses later, 'recidivaque Pergama' (Pergamum reborn),[93] are expressions that distort the reality: the remnants of the Trojan people may endure but Troy itself shall never rise again, as we are to be forcefully reminded once more in the last scene on Olympus: the very name must be blotted out. The past cannot be recovered. As for the claim that Diomedes is preparing to engage the Trojans again, it is, we shall discover, mere falsehood: this time he desires only peace.

Looking back to the Sibyl's warning, we realize that she has offered this lesson already. For the second Trojan War, she has revealed, will in the end prove essentially different from the first. This time Aeneas will be victorious, and wonder of wonders, it is a Greek city that will help him to salvation. These differences may lead us to reflect further. The parallel between Aeneas and Paris is not close: in the one case, a treacherous and lustful act, in the other no lust

---

[91] *Aen.* 6. 86 ff.   [92] *Aen.* 10. 26–9 (the Sibyl: 6. 93 f.).   [93] *Aen.* 10. 58.

or treachery at all. Turnus and Amata may call Aeneas a Paris, but in so far as this is a moral judgement, it is false. And there is irony in the equivalence implied between Turnus and Achilles, for in the re-enactment of the *Iliad* which is to come, it is Aeneas who will play Achilles' part, while Turnus takes the role of Hector. Half consciously, Turnus comes to understand this himself: 'Even if he surpass great Achilles', he will say of his adversary, effectively granting him the very thing he means to deny him.[94] This is Virgil's prismatic method once more. Paris, Hector, Achilles, Augustus—these are at best but partial likenesses to Aeneas or Turnus or whomever. And by such means Virgil builds up his idea of history. These are patterns, but never simple recurrence: the cyclical and the linear conceptions are alike imperfect or incomplete ideas of historical process.

In the course of her speech Venus twice juxtaposes Trojan and Italian names.[95] These are just glancing touches, but they prepare the way for Juno's furious reply. This speech is an entertaining performance, in which the goddess sarcastically parrots Venus' words. There is wit, too, in the way by which Juno exploits as it were our own emotional relation to the idea of Italy. What is it that Aeneas has been encouraged to do? Juno can tell us: 'Tyrrhenamque fidem aut gentis agitare quietas' ([Did I encourage him] to assail Etruscan loyalty or stir up peaceful peoples?).[96] We feel the emotional pull of the association between peace, loyalty, and the old Italy, but we also know that Juno's implication is a lie: it is she who stirred up the present war, while the Etruscans were in rebellion against their king already. As with Numanus, Virgil both allows and withholds from us the pleasure of easy patriotic sentiment. The goddess warms to her theme:[97]

> indignum est Italos Troiam circumdare flammis
> nascentem et patria Turnum consistere terra,
> cui Pilumnus avus, cui diva Venilia mater:
> quid face Troianos atra vim ferre Latinis,
> arva aliena iugo premere atque avertere praedas?

So it is wrong for the Italians to gird this reborn Troy with flames and for Turnus to set foot on his ancestral land, whose grandfather is Pilumnus and mother the goddess Venilia! What of the fact that the Trojans are bringing force against the Latins with smoking torches, thrusting their yoke on fields foreign to them and carrying off spoils?

---

[94] *Aen.* 11. 438.   [95] *Aen.* 10. 31 f., 58.   [96] *Aen.* 10. 71.   [97] *Aen.* 10. 74–8.

Again that juxtaposition, 'Italos Troiam', but this time with a strong
sense of its impropriety: to think that Italy should be thus tainted
by the propinquity of the hated name. The same note of indignation is heard three lines later in the emphasis on 'Latinis' at the end
of the line. There is more jerking at the heartstrings in the names
and phrases that surround Turnus, 'patria . . . terra' and the good old
Italian names of Pilumnus and Venilia. The termination -umnus, characteristic of Umbria, is especially redolent of the Apennine heartland; one can compare Virgil's use of Clitumnus in a climactic passage
of the *Georgics*.[98] Here too is the sense of the soil. The theme adumbrated in 'terra' is picked up again three lines later: the last indig-
nity is that those foreign ploughs should cut into the very ground.
Next Juno rounds on the Trojans themselves: they are (of course)
Phrygians; the siege of Troy was a war between Europe and Asia.[99]
One more bitter sarcasm follows:[100]

> me duce Dardanius Spartam expugnavit adulter,
> aut ego tela dedi fovique Cupidine bella?

Was it by my direction that the Dardanian adulterer sacked Sparta, or was
it I who gave him weapons and through Cupid fostered war?

Juno refers to Paris abducting Helen, but expresses her meaning paradoxically. It is a shocking thought that a Trojan, and Paris at that,
the epitome of his race's languor and effeminacy, should 'take by
storm' that city which stands as a symbol of hard virility. Another
juxtaposition, 'Dardanius Spartam', stresses the outrage.

Juno's irony is heavy, overdone. Behind it the poet's own gentler
irony lurks, half concealed, for play with names and associations is
a game in which more than one can take part. It is a game in which
Virgil is at times deeply engaged, but his sophistication is such that
he can also observe it, upon occasion, with a certain wryness.

---

[98] *Geo.* 2. 146. Pilumnus' previous appearance, at 9. 4, is also instructive: Italian hero,
Italian landscape, sanctity and antiquity.
[99] *Aen.* 10. 88, 91.   [100] *Aen.* 10. 92 f.

PART SIX

After Virgil

CHAPTER 14

The Latin Experience:
Virgil and the Poets

'O degli altri poeti onore e lume . . .'
(Dante)

'Arma gravi numero violentaque bella' (Weapons and violent wars in heavy rhythm)—so Ovid begins his *Amores*, comically irrelevant from the start. Shorter poems almost always and even longer works quite often were known by their opening words: beginning 'Cynthia prima', Propertius had established that his first book should be called *Cynthia*—fittingly, since his love passion dominates it throughout. But no one could call Ovid's amatory collection 'Arma gravi numero' without absurdity; and besides, every reader will know that this is not the most famous Augustan work to take 'arma' for its beginning.[1]

A tease at Virgil's expense then? Not exactly, for mark how Ovid continues:

> Arma gravi numero violenta bella parabam
>   edere, materia conveniente modis.
> par erat inferior versus—risisse Cupido
>   dicitur atque unum surripuisse pedem.

I was preparing to set forth weapons and violent wars in heavy rhythm, the content fitting the metre. The second verse was equal to the first—Cupid is said to have laughed and filched one foot.

---

[1] We cannot absolutely prove that Virgil wrote the first line of the *Aeneid* before Ovid the first line of the *Amores*, but it is overwhelmingly probable. Though Virgil is said to have read from his work on various occasions (*Vita Verg.* 32 f.), Ovid never heard him (*Tr.* 4. 10. 51), but we may presume that parts of the *Aeneid* were circulated among the literati in the poet's lifetime (cf. E. J. Kenney in *CHCL II*, 10 ff., R. Starr, 'The Circulation of Literary Texts in the Roman World', *CQ* NS 37 (1987), 213–23).

Typically Ovidian, we might suppose, yet the motif is borrowed from the young Virgil, who had pretended that he was planning to write of kings and battles when Apollo interrupted and dissuaded him with a message drawn from Callimachus' *Aetia*.[2] Ovid replaces the Eclogue's somewhat chilly wit with a characteristically broader humour: Cupid is a gay substitute for Apollo, and the stealing of feet is cheerfully funny in a style quite different from Virgil's calculated balance of reticence and assertion. But the fact remains that the basic idea is Virgil's: in the very act of turning away from the older poet's theme of war, Ovid betrays his debt to the master, perhaps inadvertently, perhaps by design. In either case the moral holds: you could not mock Virgil; if you approached him at all, you could only hope to ally yourself with him, adding your own inflection of voice. The shadow of the Mantuan was inescapable.

The example of the *Aeneid* did not deter some minor figures from writing mythological poems,[3] but the bigger men saw that where epic was concerned, Virgil was a Bad King Wenceslas, in whose steps none might tread. Horace, Propertius, Tibullus all avoided the challenge of the long work: there is indeed no poem extant by any of Virgil's contemporaries, Ovid apart, which is as long as a single book of the *Georgics*. What of those longer poems that have perished? Varius' tragedy *Thyestes* was lavishly praised by some, but it has been observed that this work apart, we seldom hear him spoken of except in connection with Virgil or Horace; perhaps not a strongly individual talent. He it was who prepared the unfinished *Aeneid* for publication, and he did the job so well as to be invisible; a tribute to his tact and taste, but not an indication of irrepressible originality. And Rabirius? If he were good enough even to reach the front of the second rank, it might surprise us.[4]

Ovid stands as the exception, but even so, his longest poems date from almost a generation after Virgil's death. And paradoxically, he could dare to attempt the long poem because he had little taste, perhaps little talent, for composition on the large scale: the *Ars Amatoria* is carelessly thrown together (it matters little in so insouciant a piece), with myths and digressions tossed in casually from

---

[2] *Ecl.* 6. 3 ff.

[3] Ovid's list of poets in *Pont.* 4. 16 includes several writers of mythological pieces.

[4] Quintilian (10. 1. 98) reckons Varius' *Thyestes* equal to any Greek tragedy. Velleius names Rabirius as the outstanding poet of the age after Virgil (2. 36), but he also leaves out Horace and Propertius altogether.

time to time;[5] the *Fasti* and the *Metamorphoses* are congeries of small narratives. The *Metamorphoses* can rival and even surpass the *Aeneid* in size (it is the longest Augustan poem), but in other respects Ovid keeps his distance, at least until the poem's later books. Unity of theme was traditionally expected from the grandest works: Homer's epics, as Aristotle observed, each handle a single action, and Virgil followed the pattern as far as his theme allowed. Ovid shatters this unity into fragments, telling more than two hundred different stories. Homer's time schemes were short, the *Iliad* being limited to a single brief event in the tenth year of the Trojan War, while the *Odyssey* relates only the hero's homecoming, the years of his wanderings being told retrospectively by himself. Virgil conforms to this principle also, but Ovid, in outrageous contrast, announces that his song will proceed continuously from the beginning of the world to the present day.[6] Virgil composes in large blocks, with each book conceived as a distinct unit; Ovid declares that he will sing a 'perpetuum carmen', an unceasing song,[7] and his books tend to stop, like Scheherazade's narrations, in the middle of a story, so that the poem seems to flow on unendingly, and without pause. And yet for all this Virgil's shadow could not be eluded; indeed the very avoidance of comparison is a tribute to his effect.

In the *Metamorphoses* Ovid includes or at least makes allusion to a rainbow of literary types—he can do you Lucretian-cosmological, rural-idyllic, mythological-comical, neoteric-decadent, tragical-declamatory, tragical-melodramatic, epic-grotesque—but a kind of coherence is provided by a sense of irrepressible high spirits, which before too long will push a joke or epigram into even the more solemn or pathetic passages. The variety of genres comprised within the poem is a kind of anti-epic device, but despite that variety it is held together by a virtue, Ovid's inventive wit, and a limitation, the

---

[5] Some examples: the poem was originally planned to be in two books; Ovid then added a third, without even troubling to adjust the existing text to accord with the new plan (see e.g. 1. 771 f.). The excursus on the anticipated triumph of Gaius Caesar (1. 177–228) is a later addition, spatchcocked into the text with minimal effort to make it appear to fit (see M. Pohlenz, 'Die Abfassungszeit von Ovids *Metamorphosen*', *Hermes* 48 (1913), 1–13, at 3, Syme, *History in Ovid*, 13 f., Jenkyns, 'Virgil and the Euphrates', *AJP* 114 (1993), 117–21, at 120). The brilliant account of Bacchus and Ariadne (1. 525 ff.) begins without warning, and after forty lines Ovid returns to his proper theme with an absurd transition: his topic now is 'Bacchus', that is, drink. These things are part of the poem's ethos: Ovid could not care less, and shows it.

[6] *Met.* 1. 3 f.   [7] *Met.* 1. 4.

fact that his capacity for stylistic variation is actually not great, certainly far smaller than Virgil's. He puts a limit to his work in this also, that he is never genuinely tragic, epic, or philosophical. But the poem does not aspire to contain all genres; that would indeed be impossible, for a work is not properly tragic at all unless it is tragic *in toto*, and the same may be said of epic; these genres are by nature exclusive. Rather, Ovid's novelty is sometimes to present, sometimes to evoke or allude to genres in kaleidoscopic diversity, by indications of tone and colouring. Yet even this owes something to Virgil's example, for it was he who had thought to incorporate within the continuous elevation of style and matter required of high epic touches of pastoral idyll, neoteric romance, and Alexandrian aetiology. The large difference is that Virgil strangely succeeds, despite these variations of tone, in maintaining a high seriousness and grandeur of conception throughout, whereas Ovid is carefully careless, connecting story to story, tone to different tone, by links that are sometimes deliberately absurd.[8]

Late in the *Metamorphoses* Ovid does begin to square up to a direct comparison with Virgil. Aeneas journeys out of the Greek world—the eastern Mediterranean—towards Italy; curiously, Ovid's poem travels the same path. Ovid retells the Aeneas legend (once in Italy, he could hardly avoid it), mostly underplaying those parts of it more fully treated by Virgil, and enlarging upon those aspects which Virgil had passed by. He will even take an incident of Virgil's own devising, such as the encounter with Achaemenides, the companion of Ulysses accidentally left behind in the land of the Cyclopes, and recast it.[9] It is hard to fathom his purpose here. A later epic poet will make the anxiety of influence part of his theme: Statius ends the *Thebaid* by telling his poem not to challenge comparison with the divine *Aeneid*, but worshipfully to follow its footsteps.[10] The *Aeneid* itself, neither so open nor so deferential as Statius, nevertheless seems to be in a relationship of tension with its formidable models; the

---

[8] Quintilian is an odd mixture of the acute and the obtuse when he condemns a vogue in the rhetorical schools for ingeniously unexpected transitions, adding, 'ut Ovidius lascivire in Metamorphosesin solet, quem tamen excusare necessitas potest res diversissimas in speciem unius corporis colligentem' (Ovid likes to play about in this way in his *Metamorphoses*, but he can be excused by his need to gather the most diverse material into the semblance of a single whole, 4. 1. 77). 'Lascivire'—just so: the whole thing is a lark. But the notion that Ovid's behaviour needs excuse!—it is like faulting a nightclub for being short of respectability. The naughtiness is of the essence.

[9] *Aen.* 3. 588 ff.; *Met.* 14. 160 ff.   [10] *Theb.* 12. 816 f.

story was told that Virgil, accused of plagiarism, retorted that it was easier to steal the club from Hercules than to filch a line from Homer.[11] But perhaps Ovid nursed another hope. Seneca will tell Lucilius how pleased he is to hear that he is planning a poem about Etna, because the subject has been handled so often before; the poet's art, he suggests, lies in taking a well-worn theme and giving it a new twist.[12] But the attitude is an unwise one, though not perhaps untypical of the silver age. The idea that 'What oft was thought, but ne'er so well expressed' creates true wit is at best limited; the idea that it forms the matter for poetry of the first order is a large misjudgement. Seneca's conception is subtly different from that 'creative imitation' so important to Roman poetry in its greatest period. Those earlier poets knew that imitating the Greek masters could bring rich profits, and was in any case inevitable, but they also realized that where they took most, there most must be contributed; it would not be enough to rework Greek themes, with some new variation or extra touch. In the absence of real originality, the danger was of staleness and repetition: in Virgil's own words, 'cui non dictus Hylas puer . . .?'[13] But 'cui non dicta Aetna?' is what Seneca fails to say. It may be that Ovid attempts the anxious, difficult challenge to a great poetic monument, as Virgil had, as Statius will; more likely, he takes Seneca's line and regards the existing literary stock as his quarry. In either case, he has been drawn into Virgil's orbit, and we see the peril of that attraction, for we are bound to feel that he is not sufficiently different when handling Virgil's stories, and that Virgil has managed better.

Our particular concern, in considering Virgil's influence, must be with the effect of his conceptions of nature, landscape, history, and national identity. Of the major contemporary poets the one least affected was Virgil's own friend, Horace. But then Horace is in certain respects the most isolated of the Augustans. As a man he seems to have been sociable: he was friendly with Virgil and Varius, and close to Maecenas; Augustus hoped to secure him as a secretary; if the Albius to whom two of his poems are addressed is Tibullus, he was on good terms with him too.[14] But whereas the elegists are part of a common stream, Horace chose a lonely path when he chose to turn himself into a lyric poet. He was the first to bring

---

[11] *Vita Verg.* 46.   [12] *Epp.* 79. 5.
[13] *Geo.* 3. 6 (who has not told of the boy Hylas?).   [14] *Carm.* 1. 33; *Epist.* 1. 4.

Archilochus and Alcaeus to Rome, as he tells us himself;[15] and he lacked followers. When Quintilian looked for a second lyric poet in Latin, he came up only with Caesius Bassus, for whom enthusiasm could at best be moderate.[16]

Horace also appears to have been less popular than the elegists. In an early poem he had suggested that the poet should expect to be content to have only few readers; that was just as well.[17] In contrast, Propertius can exult in his success with the public: what wonder, he declares, that such a multitude of girls should adore his words; his songs are beloved of the reader.[18] And twisting the knife, he ends the poem by echoing a Horatian theme: his verse shall last longer than temples or pyramids; these fire or rain will destroy, but his fame will endure for ever.[19] The assertion of immortality Horace could indeed make; the claim to wide popularity he could not. 'I sing to youths and maidens,' he announced in one of his most vatic moments.[20] But were they listening?

Propertius clearly succeeded in irritating him, as a passage from a late epistle shows.[21] The impatience that he exhibits towards elegy generally may be aesthetic, moral, or social, or a combination of these things. Two of his odes, addressed to elegists, reproach them for the lachrymose self-indulgence of their verse.[22] He never mentions Gallus, who had meant so much to Virgil and whom we might have expected to find at least in the *Satires*. Ovid names him seven times; his verse, indeed, refers often to other poets. Famous names are given in a spirit of happy collaboration.[23] He adds himself to what evidently was already the canonical list of the great elegists.[24] He devotes a poem to lamenting Tibullus' death.[25] He speaks of the loftiest figure with appropriate deference: 'Vergilium vidi tantum' (Virgil I only saw).[26] He mentions Horace only once, to say that he had heard him recite. Though he sounds friendly enough, one might

[15] *Epist.* 1. 19. 23–5, 32 f. (cf. *Carm.* 3. 30. 13 f.). The *Epistles*, an original invention, also stand alone. The *Satires*, inspired by Lucilius, establish no continuous tradition (Persius, two or three generations later, is indeed deeply influenced; Juvenal's declamatory satire is quite different).
[16] Quint. 10. 1. 96. Statius' *Silvae* include one alcaic and one sapphic piece (4. 5, 7), and some of the lyrics in Seneca's tragedies adopt Horatian metres. Cf. also below, n. 27.
[17] *Serm.* 1. 10. 74.   [18] Prop. 3. 2. 9 f., 15.
[19] Prop. 3. 2. 19–26; cf. Hor. *Carm.* 3. 30. 1 ff.   [20] *Carm.* 3. 1. 4.
[21] *Epist.* 2. 2. 99–101; the reference to the sort of tiresome poet who can be gratified by being compared to Mimnermus and Callimachus is bound to bring Propertius to mind.
[22] *Carm.* 1. 33; 2. 9.   [23] e.g. *Am.* 1. 15.   [24] *Tr.* 4. 10. 51–4, 5. 1. 17–19.
[25] *Am.* 3. 9. Horace is silent.   [26] *Tr.* 4. 10. 51.

wonder if his words are tinged with irony, for Horace himself remarks that he did not care for reciting his work.[27] Perhaps he was not much good at it.

Late in life, Ovid pours out a cornucopia of obscure names too, and that is significant, for it suggests how ready Roman gentlemen with poetic ambitions were to follow in his footsteps.[28] Thus we see him, the supposedly dissident figure, in the heart of a literary milieu, in the mainstream. While Horace deplores the corruptions of his day, Ovid declares that the present age, with its cultivation, suits his style of life: 'haec aetas moribus apta meis.'[29] His later fate would taint these blithe words with a bitter irony, but from exile he would still defiantly assert his popularity: Augustus may play the part of an angry Jove, and take everything from him, but one thing he cannot take: that he is read.

Horace's boast is different: not that he has pleased the public but that he has pleased the great men of Rome.[30] Socially, he craved acceptance; poetically, his genius was proud and independent. Of course, he sometimes responded to Virgil's themes, from the time that the fourth Eclogue inspired or provoked him to write the sixteenth Epode,[31] but he seems comparatively little affected by the development in sensibility that Virgil had brought about. There are exceptions. The ode to the Bandusian spring combines a particularity in the description of a small fragment of landscape with a sense of the poet's distinctive identity; the point of the name Bandusia lies in its obscurity; the spot is significant because it happens to be Horace's local patch of water, where he will sacrifice his kid.[32] Concluding his collection of lyric poetry, he links his literary immortality not only to immortal Rome and its Capitol but also to little known Aufidus, the river of his childhood country.[33] In these places we catch echoes of the spirit in which Virgil had written about the Mincius. Somewhat similar is the lofty ode in which he mythologizes his childhood—the gods miraculously protected him, the birds dropped

[27] Ov. *Tr.* 4. 10. 49; Hor. *Serm.* 1. 4. 73 f.

[28] In *Pont.* 4. 16 he lists thirty poets (four of whom are not named). Some write mythological verse, some are explicitly said to be elegists. Only one appears to write lyric, Rufus, described significantly as unique player on the Pindaric lyre (27 f.).

[29] *Ars Am.* 3. 122.   [30] *Epist.* 1. 20. 23.

[31] The vexed question of the relationship between the fourth Eclogue and the sixteenth Epode is most recently discussed by Clausen in his commentary on the *Eclogues* (he concludes, however, that Horace has the priority).

[32] *Carm.* 3. 13.   [33] *Carm.* 3. 30.

leaves upon him to shelter his slumber in the woods—but sets this
cloudy fantasy against the obscure, particular names of his *Heimat*,
Acherontia, Bantia, and Forentum, and even the name of his nanny
Pullia.[34] The piquant, even poignant effect of modest place names
slipped into a grandiose setting is something that Virgil shows in
Anchises' great unfolding of the Roman future.[35] Pullia, humility
immortalized, might be likened to the momentary appearance of
Aeneas' old nurse Caieta.[36]

There is a particular aspect of Virgil's imagination that Horace
shares, in one place at least, as nobody else does. The herdsmen of
the *Eclogues* are found singing of love antiphonally, in competition
or collaboration; these loves may be fictions even within the fiction
of the poem; passion is felt, but by various devices kept at a distance. The elegists wrote no dialogues; we hear the voice of the
poet only, and if we are to suppose his interlocutor replying from
time to time, we must deduce the content of the reply for ourselves.
But just once, in a small and perfect poem, *Donec gratus eram*, Horace
did compose a dialogue.[37] It is set, like some of the Eclogues, in
a never-never land of half fantasy, populated by such figures as
Thracian Chloe and Calais from Thurium.[38] The speakers are a man
and woman; the composition is markedly symmetrical, each stanza
of the man's being matched by one from the woman, the correspondences extending to details of language or content, with a formal balance like that of music.[39] It emerges that the couple have once
been lovers, but each has now found a new partner; probing with
a defiant pride that modulates into regret, they begin to reveal that
they are still in love with one another; but it seems that nothing
can be done about it: the woman ends by confessing that for all
the man's faults, she *would* gladly live and die with him. Human

---

[34] *Carm.* 3. 4. 9–20.   [35] *Aen.* 6. 773 ff.   [36] *Aen.* 7. 1 ff.

[37] *Carm.* 3. 9. It is odd that the possibilities of dialogue did not attract poets more. In
a short epigram (*Anth. Pal.* 5. 46) Philodemus presents a quick-talk act: '"Good day."
"And to you too." "What might your name be?" "What's yours?"'—and so on. This is
utterly unlike Horace, but there is nothing closer in elegiacs.

[38] The poem is not a slice of Roman life. Chloe could conceivably be a freedwoman,
but for a gentleman from Thurium in the 20s BC to be called Calais is not on. (The name
Calais derives from Greek mythology. Apart from the present passage, the database of
the *Lexicon of Greek Personal Names* provides only one instance of it, in Iamblichus; there
are no epigraphical examples. It may be doubted whether it was ever the name of a real
person.)

[39] G. Williams's epithet 'Mozartian' seems well chosen (*The Third Book of Horace's Odes*
(Oxford, 1969), 76).

muddle and failure are presented with flawless, luminous control; the serene elegance of style makes all the more poignant the searing sense of irremediable loss, the anguished glimpse of a happiness that was missed.[40] In its balance of formality and feeling, its awareness that distance may actually become the vehicle of pathos, this comes nearer than anything to some parts of the *Eclogues*.[41]

Virgil's effect on the elegists was different but more extensive. When Propertius describes the *Eclogues*, he represents them as poems about love, telling of Corydon in pursuit of Alexis, or of how a gift of a kid or a few apples may win a girl's affections.[42] Now this, it may be said, is at best a partial account of what the *Eclogues* contain, and it is, besides, liberally inaccurate in detail. Propertius describes all of Virgil's works in the course of this poem, including the nascent *Aeneid*; it may suit him to distort so that he can represent at least part of the great man's poetry as occupying the same sphere as his own. None the less, his words may be worth our attention. Horace had already judged the character of the *Eclogues*

[40] One might compare the end of Browning's *Youth and Art*: 'And nobody calls you a dunce, | And people suppose me clever: | This could but have happened once, | And we missed it, lost it for ever.' He too conveys the pain of loss and needless failure while distancing it, in his case by a semi-comic manner (we feel that the woman is sardonically smiling so that she shall not weep). There is this resemblance also, that Browning too is like nothing else in his literature.

[41] It is strange to find critics saying that Horace treats love as an amusing or marginal experience in human life. A fair number of his amatory odes (indeed, not all) describe volcanic passions, and yet more present the speaker as at the mercy of a highly emotional and susceptible nature; one or two praise lifelong love as a supreme human blessing (e.g. *Carm.* 1. 13. 17–20; indirectly, the same implication is in 3. 9). Why the misconception? The reasons may be that readers have taken the humour in some of Horace's poems to extend to all of them; that they have not seen through the suavity of his manner to his content; that they are influenced by a preconception of him as an amiable, epicurean buffer; or that they expect proper love poetry to resemble elegy. The elegists present more or less naturalistic fictions, within which the speaker may be identified as Tibullus, Propertius, or Ovid (you may put inverted commas round those names, if you choose). In contrast, Horace subverts the stability of the first person: in some odes the 'I' must be Horace (maybe a partly fictionalized Horace), in some he seems likely to be Horace, in others he may be Horace, and on occasion he seems to be the single speaker in a dramatic monologue (*Carm.* 1. 13 is a case in point: Lydia and Telephus appear to inhabit a timeless Greek world). Horace also resembles the *Eclogues*, and diverges from the elegists' practice, in using the same name for differently imagined people: we can have no confidence that the Lydia of one poem is the Lydia of another. He teases us by moving along a spectrum towards and away from autobiography; *Donec gratus eram* lies beyond the spectrum's end. Dogmatic ideas about the nature of the first person in literature risk obliterating the distinction between Horace's method and the elegists'. The paradox of Horace is that although he genuinely tells us more about himself than any ancient poet (and this is true even of the *Odes*), he is also unusually elusive.   [42] Prop. 2. 34. 67–76.

as 'molle atque facetum',[43] and 'mollis' is the epithet peculiarly attached
to the life and literature of love.

In Propertius we find an indulgence in erotic enslavement and
enervation which extends at times to a play with the idea of death.
In his sixth poem he imagines a kind of protracted *Liebestod*, and
beyond the dying the state of being dead, covered by the earth, comfortably as it would seem:[44]

> multi longinquo periere in amore libenter,
> in quorum numero me quoque terra tegat.

Many have perished contentedly in a long love; among their number may
the earth cover me too.

Elsewhere he imagines the young coming to his tomb and saying,
'You the great poet of our passion lie here.'[45] It is as though the
poet—as in a child's fantasy—were listening and drinking in the com-
pliments paid to him. Where have we met before this refined egoism, contentedly languid, luxuriating in the fantasy of a slow erotic
death?—in the tenth Eclogue, where Gallus is seen perishing in a
lost lovely landscape. The tone is Propertius' own; yet it seems to
have drawn its first inspiration from Virgil's example.[46]

As for Tibullus, let none doubt that his elegies are the expression of a sincere and abiding love-affair—with the poetry of Virgil.
His praise of rural quietism combined with an enjoyment of the
traditional religious ceremonies of the countryside and the agreably
boorish merrymaking accompanying them is something a little more
than the common Roman nostalgia for the old Italy; it is the working of Tibullus' individual temper upon a reading of the *Georgics*.[47]
In his love poetry he is especially fond of the internal monologue
or soliloquy. His second elegy has him now before his mistress's
door, now wandering through the city, now addressing the girl herself. We would surely be wrong to imagine that any of the passages

---

[43] *Serm.* I. 10. 44, 'soft and neat'.   [44] Prop. I. 6. 27 f.

[45] Prop. I. 7. 23 f. (the couplet has been transposed, or suspected or having strayed into
the text from another poem). Compare Trimalchio having his shroud fetched and asking
his guests to pretend that he is dead and say something nice (Petr. *Sat.* 78).

[46] In these early poems Propertius revels in weakness, but eventually his sensuality and
his possession by death will lead him to one of Roman poetry's supreme moments, when
Cynthia's ghost tells him that other women may possess him now, for when he is dead they
will rub together once more, bone against bone (4. 7. 93 f.). These words draw some of
their force and pathos from a morbidity faced and yet transcended, the physical facts of love
and the earthy reality of death being both intensely felt.   [47] See Tib. I. 1; 2. 1.

supplied the poem's setting. 'More wine,' he begins; he is somewhere
—no need to specify the place—where drink is to be had, and the
rest, whether recollection or fantasy, is all in his mind. This technique reappears in other poems. In his eighth elegy he proffers advice
to Pholoe, then Marathus, then Pholoe again. It is best not to
suppose that boy and girl are together before the poet for admon-
ishment, like miscreants in the headmaster's study; rather, these thoughts
all revolve silently in the thinker's head. This method is employed
most elaborately and perhaps with most accomplishment in his ninth
elegy. Tibullus speaks first of Marathus in the third person, then
addresses him in the second, then assails the elderly rival who has
corrupted him in the second person, then briefly describes this
old man in the third person before returning to speak directly to
Marathus once more. These changes are matched by fluctuations of
mood. At first the poet is tearfully forgiving; then he reflects with
satisfaction that the boy will pay the penalty, when the dust and heat
of a long journey destroy his beauty ('pay *me* the penalty,' he says—
a psychologically revealing touch). When he turns to the elderly rival,
he hopes first for vengeance: may his wife make a cuckold of him.
Gradually the poet gains in confidence: the wife's sister is notorious for her depravity, and the wife herself is already unfaithful, her
husband being too stupid to notice. The mockery rises to a climax
with a bright new thought: the poor thing is not immoral; she simply has the good taste to shrink from her aged spouse's nasty, gouty
embrace. But this new twist is rapidly followed by another: the poet
relapses into despondency at the thought that this is the man with
whom his own beloved boy has lain. Quickly (rather too quickly
to carry conviction, we may fancy) he recovers himself: I shall soon
fall for another boy (he declares) and then you will be sorry. We
feel the pathetic childishness of this the more once we realize that
the youth is not even present to hear the unconvincing threat.

Where have we met this technique before?—in Virgil's second
Eclogue. There too we find the fluctuations of mood, the appeals and
reproaches to a boy who is absent and unable to hear them. There
are similarities of detail too. Corydon, like Tibullus, expects (or rather
implausibly claims) that he will find another boy to love; in both
cases the *donnée* is a homosexual triangle, with the speaker baffled
by a successful rival; both give a minor role to a woman who was
formerly the speaker's paramour. In theory it is again conceivable
that Gallus originated this kind of writing, but the *Eclogues*, where

not self-consciously drawing on Theocritus, have an air of such novelty, and Tibullus' dependence on Virgil in his ninth poem seems so direct that it is the most plausible as well as economical hypothesis to suppose that here, once more, Virgil was the inventor. Among the makers of Latin elegiac poetry was a man who wrote no elegy.

If Virgil influenced how the elegists treated even their especial theme of love, we should expect his effect to be the more forceful as they begin to turn away from amatory to other topics. And sure enough, the last books of both Tibullus and Propertius display evidence that the *Aeneid* has been weaving its spell. In the fifth elegy of Tibullus' second book appear elements of the amalgam that is found especially in the eighth *Aeneid*: the thrust back to the origins of Roman history in a time before even Romulus; twice the name of Roman household gods, Lares, in close association with both a Trojan and an Italian proper name (Rome and Ilion the first time, 'Troicus' and 'Laurens' the second), in each case as part of a description of how these foreign gods became our own; cows feeding in the smartest districts of Rome (Tibullus has Palatia in place of Virgil's Carinae); the contrast of lowly cottages with the Capitol, Jove's own citadel.[48] And there is a good deal more that suggests not just the Aeneas legend but Virgil specifically: Aeneas, Turnus, and Ascanius, the three crucial names in the struggle between Trojans and Rutulians; the memory of Saturn, king in Italy; the Sibyl; Aeneas worshipped as an Indiges beside the waters of Numicus. Tibullus might have come to one or two of these topics independently; the combination of them all must be owed to Virgil.[49]

Propertius drank deep from the same source. In his second book he announces that the *Aeneid* will be greater than the *Iliad*; in other words, the greatest poem of all time.[50] When all allowance has been made for a poet's licence it remains an astonishing statement to be made about a work not yet written. In a poem welcoming his friend

[48] Tib. 2. 5. 23 f., 20 ff., 40 ff., 25 (cf. *Aen.* 8. 361), 26.

[49] F. Cairns, *Tibullus: A Hellenistic Poet at Rome* (Cambridge, 1979), 68, toys with the possibility that Tibullus might have the priority. But Virgil is an original genius, who can be seen coming to this way of apprehending the Roman past through the long development of a deeply personal imagination. Tibullus comes to the theme late—the second, not the first book—and treats it dutifully but prosaically. That he was much affected by Virgil we know; that the Italian core of the *Aeneid* fed vitally upon one of the less successful pieces of a young elegist of the second rank is a hypothesis to make one boggle. (Tibullus' death was not much if at all later than Virgil's. Once more we may infer that parts of the *Aeneid* were heard or read in the poet's lifetime.)   [50] Prop. 2. 34. 66.

Tullus' return from service in the east he pays homage to the *laus Italiae* of the second Georgic.[51] He shows an appreciation of Virgil's vision in his contrast of Grecian lands and other exotic parts—Egypt, Colchis—with Italy, and by his play with proper names. Greek vowels and consonants are prominent in the first three lines—Cyzicus, Isthmos, Dindymis, Cybele—and there are many Greek declensions in the lines which follow: 'Helles', 'Athamantidos', 'Atlanta', 'Persea', 'Phorcidos', 'Ortygie' (Virgil's subtlety and economy are lost in this profusion). Then Propertius sets against this elaborated Grecianism the rivers, lakes, and places belonging to the old heart of Italy: Anio and Clitumnus, Lake Nemi and the Alban Lake, Tibur and Umbria. There are even waterworks in both poems: the great engineering works on the Bay of Naples in Virgil, the Marcian aqueduct in his imitator. Propertius has learnt from his model that man's labours form one of the splendours of the Italian scene: 'tot egregias urbes operumque laborem'; 'aeternum Marcius umor opus'.[52] Virgil had contrasted Italy both with the wonders of exotic lands and with the mythology of Greece; Propertius telescopes these two kinds of contrast, with slightly odd results. Though you see Atlas bearing the heavens, he tells Tullus (who has no prospect of seeing any such thing), and Geryon's stables and the Gorgon's head and the dances of the Hesperides; though you visit Ortygia, Cayster and the delta of the Nile; yet—[53]

> omnia Romanae cedent *miracula* terrae:
> *natura* hic posuit, quidquid ubique fuit.

All these wonders shall yield to the land of Rome: nature has placed here whatever is best anywhere.

Drawn from Virgil is the feeling that though Italy may not match the marvels of some other parts of the world, it is none the less the best place, and also the sense that set against myth-infested Greece it is the especially natural place. The phrase 'Romana terra' is a little curious, but Propertius has remembered Virgil's 'Romana per oppida'[54] and absorbed his more general message: Italy is Roman. This is a truth but not a truism; it is to be said in such a way that we feel the pressure of significance. Propertius will develop the theme in some of his last work.

---

[51] Prop. 3. 22.
[52] *Geo.* 2. 155; Prop. 3. 22. 24, 'That abiding work, the Marcian aqueduct'.
[53] Prop. 3. 22. 17 f.   [54] *Geo.* 2. 176 (see above, p. 369).

Like Tibullus, he turns to the early history of Italy in his final book. Now we have seen that a romantic antiquarianism and a fascination with the heart-warming simplicities of an honest, distant past were forms of escape from the pains of the present in the years of civil war. Those were among the experiences which acted upon Virgil's imagination; here were attitudes which in a way he shared, in a way transformed into the material of a personal and unique vision. But these are not the influences which direct the Augustan elegists to the theme of old Italy. In the springtime of their careers they are men of the moment; they write of love, they are popular, they could all have said, 'haec aetas moribus apta meis.' At this time it is the Augustan loyalists, Livy and Horace, who are viewing the present with a sombre eye. The elegists all turn to aetiology and antiquarianism as a new theme when the love poetry starts to fade; at last even Ovid, with the *Fasti*, six books of legend 'unearthed from annals of yore'.[55] For them the spur is not national disaster, still less the lucubrations of Varro; it is Virgil. This fact stands at the heart of Latin literary history. The modern enquirer is faced with an awkwardness of terminology: the label 'Augustan' may simply denote a period of history or it may indicate a connection with the beliefs and attitudes professed by Caesar Augustus himself. Yet in some degree this ambiguity is not so much an embarrassment as the revelation of a truth. Virgil's amalgam was so complete a fusion that its constituents could not again be separated. It was the achievement of Maecenas' work of patronage to bring about a condition in which the old sentimental–patriotic theme and the new imperial or Augustan theme could no longer be kept apart; if you wrote verse about Rome or Italy, if you celebrated the charm, quaintness, or splendour of the national past, you could hardly do so now without taking on something of the new ideology's tone. Such an outcome must surely have been beyond Caesar and his minister's boldest dreams; for indeed it was only the prestige and genius of Virgil that made it possible. Virgil finds an original way of seeing and feeling; though highly individual, it is a way that can be called Augustan in both senses, since not only did he accept and support the new order but his style of imagination colours the whole age; it affects almost everyone who counts, including, it may be, the master of the world himself. If we seem to detect signs of rebelliousness

[55] *Fasti* 1. 7 ('annalibus eruta priscis'). Virgil's influence is especially marked in the first book.

in the elegists from time to time, we may ask ourselves how they came in the end to reconcile themselves, more or less, to the Augustan dispensation. Maybe they settled into a recognition that Augustus was now as much one of the conditions under which human life was lived as sun and moon and seasons; with politics in the old style having ceased to exist and a universal realization spreading that no alternative to autocracy was possible or perhaps even desirable, they may have sensed that all people were now Augustans willy-nilly, even in the narrower signification of the word. Or was it that with amatory topics starting to stale and grow repetitious (and also perhaps, since their verse is not wholly separate from their lives, with a first stiffening of the joints warning them that the time to seek new material was at hand) the literary possibilities opened up by Virgil were too good to pass by? To look on the one hand to politics and society, on the other to literary developments is to put alternatives which may not have been evident to the poets themselves. That complex interweaving of influences which draws a man or a generation in a particular direction is not capable of being neatly unravelled into its constituent threads. Virgil is himself enmeshed in this complexity; often we can see other poets drawing on him directly, without mediation; but many times they are reflecting—perhaps shifting a little—the spirit of the age, and the question of how far Virgil formed that spirit does not admit an exact answer.

When he turns to Italian aetiology, in his last book, Propertius pronounces himself the Roman Callimachus.[56] In the sheer directness of that claim we may wonder if he does not protest too much; others had spoken of themselves as transferring into Latin poetry the themes or metres of a famous Greek, or implied this, but no one else claims to be 'the Roman So-and-so' in just those words. Perhaps Propertius wanted to establish some degree of independence from Virgil. It was not easily done: his claim to be Rome's Callimachus comes, as we shall see, in a curiously Virgilian context; and by a further irony, the very idea of applying Callimachean aetiology to romantic patriotism and the evocation of early Italy had been Virgil's originally: Propertius cannot even be Callimachus without incurring a debt to the eighth Aeneid. Indeed, the debt is not denied: the ninth poem retells the story of Hercules and Cacus. Naturally the elegist gives it a new slant: his story is quainter, his

<hr>

[56] Prop. 4. 1. 64.

Hercules more comic and undignified than Virgil could permit within an epic frame; but he follows the *Aeneid* in suppressing the grosser parts of the old tale, such as the hero's drunkenness and the violation of Evander's daughter. The picture of the mysterious shrine of the Bona Dea, the 'women's goddess', thick embowered in a deep and shadowed wood, where birds sing in the darkness of the foliage and incense burns within—evocations of a rich and strange femininity—bears a resemblance to Virgil's Circe.[57]

When Propertius told the tale of Tarpeia, he softened the wicked woman of Roman tradition into one of those heroines familiar from Alexandrian or neoteric poetry, torn between moral duty and sexual passion; lest we should miss the point, she obligingly explains that her situation resembles those of Scylla and Ariadne, women who betrayed family and country for love.[58] But the poet creates a novelty by mixing this tone with elements of epic colour:[59]

> *Tarpeium nemus et Tarpeiae turpe sepulcrum*
> fabor et antiqui limina capta Iovis.

I shall tell of Tarpeia's grove and Tarpeia's shameful grave and the capture of ancient Jupiter's threshold.

The gross alliterations of the first line suggest Ennius and early epic; the diction of 'fabor' is archaic and elevated; 'et' immediately before the caesura is a metrical quirk found a number of times in the *Aeneid*. In the lines that follow we meet what is by now a familiar blend of motifs: thick woodland and waters, the Italian forest god Silvanus, the juxtaposition of Rome and Italy, a consciousness of the changes wrought by time (Sabine lances stand in the Roman Forum, where laws are now given to a conquered world), a simple Rome—no walls, just her hills for defence—a spring from which horses drank in the place where the Senate House now stands. Virgil's influence is unmistakable.

It is still fuller in the first poem of the book, where Propertius seems to draw also on Tibullus' response to the *Aeneid*. He begins with a contrast

> Hoc quodcumque vides, hospes, qua maxima Roma est,
> ante Phrygem Aenean collis et herba fuit . . .

All that you see here, stranger, where mighty Rome now stands, before Phrygian Aeneas was hill and grass.

---

[57] Prop. 4. 9. 23–30 ('women's goddess', 25); cf. *Aen.* 7. 8 ff.
[58] Prop. 4. 4. 39–42.   [59] Prop. 4. 4. 1 f.

Virgilian in tone is the juxtaposition of proper names (Rome set against an Aeneas who appears in his most alien guise, as a Phrygian), especially in combination with two other ideas: the changes wrought by history visually demonstrated in the contrast between simple countryside and great city; and the pushing back to the most distant past, beyond earliest Rome to Aeneas, and to a period even before him. The Trojan story has indeed thrust the strictly Roman foundation myth into a subordinate role in the poem; such was the *Aeneid*'s magnetism. A problematic couplet seems to describe Virgil's work better than Propertius' own:[60]

> dicam: Troia, cades et Troica Roma resurges.
> et maris et terrae †longa sepulcra† canam.

I will declare, 'Troy, you shall fall and Trojan Rome, you shall rise again.' And I will sing of sway (?) over land and sea.

The contrast between Troy and Rome, the fact that Rome is none the less Trojan, hint at Virgil's idea of change and continuity. Another Virgilian motif, another Virgilian collocation of diversely associative proper names comes in the words, 'huc melius profugos misisti, Troia, Penates'.[61] That theme had appealed to Tibullus; and like Tibullus again, he cannot resist Virgil's cows:[62]

> atque ubi Navali stant sacra Palatia Phoebo,
> Euandri profugae procubuere boves.

And where the Palatine stands, hallowed to Apollo of the Ships, the cattle of Evander the exile lay.

As in the poem to Tullus he spelled out the implications of what Virgil had left magically unstated in the *laus Italiae*, so here he substitutes for Virgil's witty economy a more prosaic correctitude. Fusing past and present, Virgil has his kine lowing in the smart Carinae;[63] Propertius, with more exactness and at greater length, tells us that the cattle belonged to one period, the buildings of the Palatine to another. Other details of the *Aeneid* struck the elegist's fancy; and again we may observe, contrary perhaps to expectation, how neat, delicate and sparkling the epic poem appears in the comparison.

---

[60] Prop. 4. 1. 87 f. The couplet is out of place where it stands in the MSS (in Horos' reply to the poet). Various transpositions have been proposed; if placed after 52 (Mueller) or 54 (Baehrens) it becomes part of a prophecy spoken by Cassandra.

[61] Prop. 4. 1. 39, 'You did well, Troy, to send here your fugitive Penates'; cf. above, pp. 427 f.

[62] Prop. 4. 1. 3 f.   [63] *Aen.* 8. 361.

Propertius has noticed the piquancy of Virgil's 'parva urbs' and 'pauper senatus', and he duly expands the idea:[64]

> Curia, praetexto quae nunc nitet alta senatu,
>   pellitos habuit, rustica corda, Patres.
> bucina cogebat priscos ad verba Quiritis:
>   centum illi in prati saepe senatus erat
>
> .   .   .   .
>
> Vesta coronatis pauper gaudebat asellis,
>   ducebant macrae vilia sacra boves.

The Curia, now lofty and resplendent with senators in purple-bordered robes, then held Elders clad in skins, souls of a rustic stamp. A horn summoned those early citizens to debate: a hundred of them in the enclosure of a meadow formed a senate . . . Vesta was poor enough to take pleasure in garlanded mules, and skinny cattle brought a scant sacrifice.

The quaintness of that furry parliament and goddess of slender means is agreeable enough, but in comparison with the *Aeneid* the idea looks a little obvious, the writing a little slack; Virgil's brilliance and concision have gone.[65]

From Anchises' speech in the underworld Propertius has taken the contrast between the largeness with which places like Gabii and Fidenae once loomed and their present unimportance:[66]

> quippe suburbanae parva minus urbe Bovillae,
>   et, qui nunc nulli, maxima turba Gabi.
> et stetit Alba potens, albae suis omine nata,
>   tunc ubi Fidenas longa erat isse via.

The City being small, Bovillae was less a suburb, and Gabii, which is now nothing, was then a great multitude. Alba stood in might, born from the portent of the white pig, in the days when it was a long journey to go to Fidenae.

Propertius borrows two of his names from the *Aeneid*; beyond that, his lines are Virgilian in a more general sense: in combining a picture

---

[64] Prop. 4. 1. 11–14, 21 f.; cf. *Aen.* 8. 554, 105.

[65] The appositional phrase 'rustica corda' imitates a mannerism of the *Eclogues*, e.g. 'raucae, tua cura, palumbes' (the hoarse wood-doves, your delight, 1. 57), 'inter densas, umbrosa cacumina, fagos' (among the thick beeches, those shadowy heights, 2. 3). By stylistic allusion Propertius suggests an overtone of pastoral charm and *maniera*.

[66] Prop. 4. 1. 33–6 (cf. *Aen.* 6. 773 ff.). There are textual difficulties, but it seems reasonably clear that Propertius is expressing three main ideas: first, that the relative importance of places has changed over time (33); second, that once important places have declined in power and population absolutely (34 f.); third, that our horizons have widened, so that what once seemed a long distance now seems little.

of objective change—Rome has grown to greatness, while other towns have shrunk—with an interest in the subjectivity of experience: the distance from Rome to Fidenae has not altered, but once the journey between them was long, now it is short. Once more, these are pleasant lines; we should admire them more if we did not have the *Aeneid* to put beside them. But in the complexity of Virgil's conception—the awareness of history's many layers, the interplay of knowledge and ignorance, with Anchises knowing what Aeneas does not and ourselves aware of what is hidden from Anchises, a mood which blends the pleasures of patriotism with the humour of an affectionate condescension—there is a density and compression that were beyond Propertius' power.[67] Such comparisons indicate how difficult Virgil was to imitate, and also (a thing not often believed of the *Aeneid*) how light his touch could be; but however hard the challenge he presented, he had struck so rich a vein that others could not resist trying to extract more from the seam. Sometimes a poet draws a motif, theme or story directly from Virgil and tries to give it a new tone (as in Propertius' homage to the *laus Italiae* or his retelling of the tale of Cacus); sometimes it is rather the tone or the style of imagination, rather than the externals, that the imitating poet strives to catch; sometimes we find an intertwining of these two kinds of influence.

Consider this passage from the present poem:[68]

> moenia namque pio coner disponere versu:
>   ei mihi, quod nostro est parvus in ore sonus!
> sed tamen exiguo quodcumque e pectore rivi
>   fluxerit, hoc patriae serviet omne meae.   60
> Ennius hirsuta cingat sua dicta corona:
>   mi folia ex hedera porrige, Bacche, tua,
> ut nostris tumefacta superbiat Umbria libris,
>   Umbria Romani patria Callimachi!
> scandentis quisquis cernit de vallibus arces,   65
>   ingenio muros aestimet ille meo!
> Roma, fave, tibi surgit opus; date candida, cives,
>   omina et inceptis dextera cantet avis!

[67] Some have supposed that Propertius has a moral message, setting noble old simplicities against the degenerate grandeur of the present. They may be mistaken (line 37 seems moralistic taken on its own; taken in context, its significance is not at all clear). If they are right, we may contrast a somewhat banal moralism with the beautiful disengagement of the eighth Aeneid: Virgil just states, observes and leaves us to draw our own conclusions, with no facile exaltation or belittlement of one age or another.

[68] Prop. 4. 1. 57–68.

For I would strive to tell of these walls in reverent verse: ah me, how weak is the voice on my lips! But still, however thin the stream that flows from my narrow breast, it shall all be at my country's service. Let Ennius crown his verse with a ragged garland: to me, Bacchus, give leaves of your ivy, that Umbria may swell with pride at my books, Umbria, home of the Roman Callimachus! Let whoever sees the citadel rising up from the valley esteem its walls by my genius! Rome, favour me, for this work rises up for you; citizens, give me fair omens, and may a bird on the right sing good augury for my enterprise!

The first four lines suggest the Callimachean pose; line 59 in particular recalls the small stream of pure poetry which Callimachus contrasted with the broad muddy river of inferior verse.[69] But there is a difference in Propertius' version of the theme. In 'ei mihi' and 'quodcumque' there is a note of modesty or regret unlike the Greek poet's defiant pride. But as we know, it was not Propertius who originated this shift from the Callimachean tone but Virgil in the sixth Eclogue, mingling self-assertion with graceful self-deprecation. It is intriguing to note the Virgilian presence here in view of what follows. There is a stress upon the proper name in the repetition 'Umbria . . . Umbria', a stress which is continued through the emotional word 'patria'. In a context where the pull of local loyalty is so much felt, the juxtaposition of 'Umbria' and 'Romani' is pointed. Every word in the line is alert and working, playing against the other words; in such a setting Propertius' presentation of himself as both an Italian and a Roman becomes more than a statement of the obvious: it has the vividness of something newly experienced, the pressure of significance; it is quickened by just a hint of paradox. And with each word so alive, the third proper name of the line, Callimachus, will also be found reacting with the others. We have already noticed that Propertius differs from other Latin poets in directly entitling himself 'the Roman So-and-so'. One reason at least for this novelty is that in the context it is not a simple statement; it has the quality of surprise. As 'Romani' presses against 'Umbria', so does 'Callimachi' press against 'Romani'. The word 'Romani' is—well, Roman, while the neoterics' exploitation of Callimachus' reputation has associated him with all that is most ostentatiously Grecian. The prick of paradox is felt again: Propertius' language suggests that there is a curiousness in proclaiming oneself the Roman Callimachus which there

[69] *Hy.* 2. 108–12.

would not be in calling someone the Roman Alcaeus or Theocritus. The whole line tingles with little pressures and tensions.

The next four lines rework the theme of Rome and Italy in a more leisurely manner. The first of these couplets differs from the abstract nature of the rest of the passage in offering a picture of hill, valley and fortifications; then the poet addresses the City with an especial weight of emphasis: 'Roma, . . . tibi . . .' The significance of all this is made plain later (Propertius is no longer speaking in his own person but is being addressed by the astrologer Horos):[70]

> Umbria te notis antiqua Penatibus edit
>   (mentior? an patriae tangitur ora tuae?)
> qua nebulosa cavo rorat Mevania campo,
>   et lacus aestivis intepet Umber aquis,
> scandentisque Asis consurgit vertice murus,
>   murus ab ingenio notior ille tuo.

Ancient Umbria bore you to a distinguished household (do I lie? or do I touch the borders of your homeland?), where misty Mevania sheds dew on the hollow expanse of land and the Umbrian lake's waters grow warm in summer, and the wall mounts on the hill of climbing Assisi, a wall lent more distinction by your talent.

Once more Umbria is especially emphasized; Horos' questions in the second line, making fussily certain that here and nowhere else is the land of Propertius' origin, keep our attention fixed upon the name. The words 'antiquus' and 'Penates' bind local patriotism into a nexus which intertwines home, religion and the past—a blend familiar from the *Georgics* and the *Aeneid*. The first couplet invokes abstract emotions; the next two connect them with a series of pictures, distinctly visualized. And as with Virgil's pictures of the Mincius, Propertius puts before us the landscape of home in images which seek to capture the individual quality of a particular scene: not any line of mountainside, but a distinctive spot where the line of the hills draws back to cup round a combe where the mist gets caught; not a round deep volcanic pool, which is the most characteristic kind of lake in the Italian peninsula, but the marshy Umbrian mere, shallow enough for the waters to get warm in the summer months; not any hill-town either, it would seem: Assisi is distinctive to this

---

[70] Prop. 4. 1. 121–6. Probably Horos' address should be regarded as a separate poem (as in the third book the second poem answers the first).

day for the way in which it climbs the flank of its hill, rather than commanding the summit in the manner of most Apennine towns.[71]

No one had written like this until Virgil. As in the *laus Italiae* Propertius connects the abstract emotions of time and place, ancestry and local patriotism with the native landscape, sharply and individually realized; and as in the *laus Italiae* Propertius unites the work of man and the work of nature, hill-town and waters. Did he have the *Eclogues* and still more the *Georgics* consciously in mind as he wrote? In a place such as this he has absorbed the lesson of the master so completely that the question ceases to matter much: it would suffice to think of Virgil as the reagent by which a new way of seeing and feeling has been crystallized.

Propertius delighted in visual art.[72] Whimsically contemplating a voyage to Athens as an escape from the woes of love, he fancies himself cleansing his soul from error in Plato's Academy or the Garden of Epicurus; or perhaps he will study Demosthenes' eloquence or (here the seriousness of purpose begins to waver) Menander's wit. Then comes a gay dismissal of earnest literary or philosophical pursuits: at any rate, he will be taken by the feast for the eye:[73]

> aut certe tabulae capient mea lumina pictae,
> sive ebore exactae, seu magis aere, manus.

Or at least painted panels will take my eyes, and works of art wrought in ivory or, better, in bronze.

'Aut certe' is mischievous; the whole poem has the air of fantasy, but Propertius implies that even the pretence of planning to immerse himself in literary study is one that he cannot keep up for long. 'Ut pictura poesis' is a sentiment that he would seem to have absorbed before Horace uttered it. In one poem he reproaches Maecenas for pressing grander themes upon him: people have different talents and his are not suited to the big manner; and he illustrates the point by comparing eight artists—six sculptors, a painter, and a silversmith.[74]

---

[71] 'Vertice', strictly the summit of a hill, is surprising at 125, but the word can be used metonymically for a hill or mountain generally (as at Cat. 64. 1). Camps (ad loc.) proposes that 'a conical eminence is suggested, crowned by an *arx*, and with buildings "mounting" the hillside'. That is possible, but 'scandentis . . . de vallibus' at 65 suggests the distinctive picture that Propertius wants to evoke: a town on the flank of the hill, mounting it from comparatively low down, at a distance from the summit.

[72] J.-P. Boucher, *Études sur Properce* (2nd edn., Paris, 1980), ch. 2; M. Hubbard, *Propertius* (London, 1974), 164 ff.

[73] Prop. 3. 21. 29 f.   [74] Prop. 3. 9. 1–16.

In an earlier piece a painting of the Love God is his starting-point.[75] The praise of Caesar was a task not greatly congenial to him, but in one instance he found a solution by celebrating the statues on the great man's portico of Apollo.[76] The carven Phoebus seemed to him more beautiful than the god himself, his marble lips parted in silent song; the cattle of Myron, 'vivida signa', appeared as though alive. Some poets have explored the division between art and life; to seek for such an idea of separation in Propertius is occasionally appropriate, but often not, for he presents himself as an aesthete: Cynthia's lover is also the lover of painting and sculpture, and for creating a vivid picture of his life and milieu talk of art is as fitting as talk about sex. Thus some of the mythology in the poems should be seen as part of the poet's immediate response to experience. When the drunken Propertius breaks in upon Cynthia asleep, she looks to him like Ariadne, Andromeda, or an exhausted Maenad.[77] 'Talis visa mihi'—she *looked* so; the poet draws on his memories of pictures or statuary.[78] The effect is subtle: on the one hand there is a contrast between the world of high art and mythology, remote and romantic, and the poet's lurching irruption; on the other hand Cynthia's resemblance to these Grecian heroines is a genuine part of his tipsy amorousness.

Sight is the sense with which he is impassioned. In the most splendidly sensual of Latin poems, where he revels in the violent grapplings of lovers, he still insists upon the pre-eminence of the eye:[79]

> non iuvat in caeco Venerem corrumpere motu:
> si nescis, oculi sunt in amore duces.

I do not care to spoil love by unseeing movements: in case you do not know, the eyes are our guides in love.

There follows a paean in praise of nakedness, leading to the conclusion, 'dum nos fata sinunt, oculos satiemus amore' (While fate permits, let us gorge our eyes with love).[80] The tyranny of vision is a theme to which he recurs: among the women at the theatre it is his eyes that seek their own wound; though the fate of Thamyras

---

[75] Prop. 2. 12.   [76] Prop. 2. 31. 1–16.   [77] Prop. 1. 3. 1 ff.
[78] He begins with Ariadne, no doubt recalling that Catullus' Ariadne was herself not actual but a work of art, a figure upon a coverlet. 'Talis visa mihi' (7) does not mean 'thus she seemed to me (but I was in fact wrong)': the poem offers nothing to suggest that the speaker's belief in her beauty was mistaken, and indeed its tenderness depends on the drunken incursion into a scene of authentic loveliness.
[79] Prop. 2. 15. 11 f.   [80] Prop. 2. 15. 23.

come upon him, he will never be blind to pretty girls; his love for Cynthia grows by his constant gazing on her; the verdict of his eyes has made her proud.[81]

When he tells the story of Hylas in his first book, he is lushly descriptive:[82]

hic erat Arganthi Pege sub vertice montis
grata domus Nymphis umida Thyniasin,
quam supra nulli pendebant debita curae
roscida desertis poma sub arboribus,
et circum irriguo surgebant lilia prato
candida purpureis mixta papaveribus.
quae modo decerpens tenero pueriliter ungui
proposito florem praetulit officio,
et modo formosis incumbens nescius undis
errorem blandis tardat imaginibus.

Here beneath the peak of Mount Arganthus was the spring of Pege, a watery haunt dear to the Bithynian nymphs; above it from lonely trees hung dewy fruits which owed nothing to man's tending, and around in a water-meadow white lilies grew mingled with crimson poppies. Now picking these with delicate fingernail in boyish delight, he put the flowers before his assigned task, and now leaning in ignorance over the fair waters he lets the charming reflections prolong his truancy.

Propertius is here striving for a glossy, artificial surface: we observe the imitation of neoteric plangency and a profusion of Grecian names:[83]

iam Pandioniae cessit genus Orithyiae:
a dolor! ibat Hylas, ibat Hamadryasin.

Then the sons of Orithyia of Pandion's stock gave up. Ah woe, Hylas went on, went to the Hamadryads.

If there seems an excess of luxuriance, that is apt enough, for there is something consciously overripe in the telling of this erotically sinister myth. Propertius succeeds in his purpose, but it is a limited purpose: in this place we do not feel the working of a fresh visual imagination. He does not get much beyond a decorative prettiness in the manner of (say) Moschus, with more lushness added; the contrast of white and crimson blooms is conventional, the plucking of the flower is taken over from Catullus without preserving Catullus'

[81] Prop. 2. 22. 7, 20; 3. 21. 3; 3. 24. 2.   [82] Prop. 1. 20. 33–42.
[83] Prop. 1. 20. 31 f.

intensity of vision.[84] Later he seeks for a keener responsiveness to things seen. In his fourth book he offers a still life in the manner of the second Eclogue, depicting both flowers and fruits of the earth (the statue of the god Vertumnus is speaking):[85]

> caeruleus cucumis tumidoque cucurbita ventre
> me notat et iunco brassica vincta levi;
> nec flos ullus hiat pratis, quin ille decenter
> impositus fronti langueat ante meae.

The dark-green cucumber, the gourd with swollen belly and the cabbage bound with a flimsy reed mark me out; nor does any flower open in the meadows without drooping in comely style, placed on my brow.

Propertius does not match Virgil; still, he seems to be looking for the distinctive qualities of each vegetable, the shiny blue-green skin of the cucumber, the circularity of the gourd. And in the next couplet he appears to be after a contrast between the flower in the field, its petals open, and the flower withering on the god's forehead. In an earlier poem he had already adorned a representation of simple country life in olden days with a picture of fruits and blooms:[86]

> felix agrestum quondam pacata iuventus,
> divitiae quorum messis et arbor erant!
> illis munus erant decussa Cydonia ramo,
> et dare puniceis plena canistra rubis,
> nunc violas tondere manu, nunc mixta referre
> lilia vimineos lucida per calathos,
> et portare suis vestitas frondibus uvas
> aut variam plumae versicoloris avem.

Happy the country youth, then so peaceful, whose wealth was harvest and the tree! For them a gift meant to bring quinces shaken from the bough, or to offer baskets full of purple berries, sometimes to pluck violets, sometimes to bring a mingling of lilies shining through the wicker panniers, to carry grapes clothed in their own leaves or a bird speckled with dappled plumage.

Most of this is just a pretty catalogue once more, but in the third of these couplets he seizes on a curious and fascinating detail: the whiteness of the lilies shining through the loose wickerwork of the baskets. The author of the *Copa* recognized Propertius' affinity

---

[84] Cat. 62. 39 ff.; this passage gets detailed analysis in Jenkyns, *Three Classical Poets* (London, 1982), 50–3.
[85] Prop. 4. 2. 43–6 (cf. *Ecl.* 2. 45 ff.).   [86] Prop. 3. 13. 25–32.

with the second Eclogue: his catalogue joins the 'caeruleus cucumis' from Propertius' fourth book and the lilies in wicker baskets from the third to 'cerea pruna' and 'castaneasque nuces' pilfered from Virgil's poem.[87]

Perhaps Propertius' finest attempt at relating colours or textures comes, fittingly, in a celebration of female flesh.[88] How admirable is the Spartans' practice of sports and exercise, he declares—and we expect praise of toughness and vigour to follow. But we are being teased: what the poet likes about Sparta, we soon discover, is the chance to see girls without their clothes on. It is a comic twist, but he combines the comedy with a feeling for flesh and texture to create a light and stylish sensuality. We first see a girl, naked and singular, among a plurality of wrestling men; the contrast is piquant. We see the hoarfrost sprinkle her hair as she hunts on Mount Taygetus; but above all the poet is fascinated by the juxtapostion of flesh and weaponry. A girl ties the thongs of the cestus round her hands; she binds a sword to her snow-white flank; a brazen helmet curves round her maidenly head ('virgineumque cavo protegit aere caput' —'cavus', hard to translate, more 'enclosing' than 'hollow', draws our eye to the way feminine head and hard metal fit together).[89] The contrasts of girl and men, nudity and weaponry are brought together in this couplet:[90]

> inter quos Helene nudis capere arma papillis
> fertur nec fratres erubuisse deos.

Along with them [Castor and Pollux] Helen is said to have carried arms with breasts naked, and not to have blushed before her divine brothers.

The nicely judged blend of levity and lust creates a tone that is distinctive to Propertius; Ovid's mood is different.

At moments he can can make a picture that is both arresting in itself and instinct with a further significance:[91]

> tu modo, dum lucet, fructum ne desere vitae!
> omnia si dederis oscula, pauca dabis.
> ac veluti folia arentis liquere corollas,
> quae passim calathis strata natare vides,
> sic nobis, qui nunc magnum spiramus amantes,
> forsitan includet crastina fata dies.

---

[87] *Copa* 22, 16, 18 f. (cf. *Ecl.* 2. 52 f.).   [88] Prop. 3. 14.
[89] Prop. 3. 14. 12 'She shields her maiden head with hollowed bronze'.
[90] Prop. 3. 14. 19 f.   [91] Prop. 2. 15. 49–54; 4. 6. 85 f.

Only do you not, while there is light, abandon the rewards of life! If you give all your kisses, you will give few. And as the leaves have dropped from the withering garlands and you see them strewn about, floating in the cups, so for us, lovers who now breathe boldly, tomorrow's day will perhaps conclude our destinies.

> sic noctem patera, sic ducam carmine, donec
> iniciat radios in mea vina dies.

Thus I will spend the night with cup and song, until the day casts its rays into my wine.

Each of these passages rounds off a poem. The later ending is memorable enough, with its image of the dawn light striking through the opacity of the wine, but it pales beside the earlier lines. Who can forget the withered leaves floating on the surface of the cups? In this seizing of the odd, telling detail Propertius anticipates the method of a very different poet: Juvenal.[92] But what do we learn from the similitude? That men are as leaves, certainly, that the feast of life is transient; but is that all? For how do we look upon the remains of a really good party? Surely with a kind of satisfaction: it is over now, but ah, how it was sweet. These closing lines are a paean of praise to the 'fructus vitae', the goodness of life. The last line is sombre but it is fitting that the final word should be 'dies' (did he recall the gloomy conclusion of Catullus' *Peleus and Thetis*, which none the less ends with the words 'lumine claro'?).[93] This poem which has commemorated the glories of the night—'o nox mihi candida', 'O night that for me was bright', is the paradoxical cry of the first line—finishes with the coming of a new day, and there is a kind of vigour about that which the sombreness of the close cannot quite blot out. And the image of the leaves in the wine is part of this effect, a contrast of textures which is also expressive of mood: dryness and liquid, a deadness that floats upon the inspiriting fruit of the vine. This most exultant poem finally sweeps up even death into its exultation and displays it as the conclusion of a great celebration that has been seen through to the end.

And so Propertius' style of imagination emerges as partly personal, partly shaped by new ways of seeing and feeling developed in the

---

[92] A full history of visual perceptiveness in Latin poetry would need to give ample space to Juvenal, but he lies beyond the scope of the present book. How he uses the argument of the eye is studied in Jenkyns, *Three Classical Poets*, 173 ff.

[93] Cat. 64. 408, 'in the bright light'.

first century. His blending of erotic themes with a strong sense of the existence of the visible world—unlike Catullus, in whose love poetry the visual plays so small a part—marks him as decidedly an Augustan poet, in this sense at least, that Lucretius has already written, and been followed in his turn by Virgil.

Ovid begins his third book of *Amores* with a natural description:

> Stat vetus et multos incaedua silva per annos;
>   credibile est illo numen inesse loco.
> fons sacer in medio speluncaque pumice pendens,
>   et latere ex omni dulce queruntur aves.
> hic ego dum spatior tectus nemoralibus umbris,
>   quod mea, quaerebam, Musa moveret, opus;
> venit odoratos Elegia nexa capillos,
>   et, puto, pes illi longior alter erat.

There stands an old wood, uncut over many years; it is believable that there is a god in that place. There is a hallowed spring in the midst and a cave with pumice-stone overhanging, and on every side the birds sweetly complain. While I walked here, covered by the woodland shade, I was looking for a task that my Muse might undertake; Elegy came, with her scented hair bound up, and one of her feet, I think, was longer than the other.

Wood, water and cavern are the visible elements of the scene; the ideas of antiquity and the absence of man's hand add an emotional colour. Here are the the familiar ingredients for an *ekphrasis* such as one might find in (say) Virgil, but the solemnity proves to be a feint, as the goddess Elegy advances from the gloom—with a limp. But Ovid was not always content to dismiss such things with a joke: in the *Metamorphoses* virtually the same elements reappear in a place where there is no comedy:[94]

> silva vetus stabat nulla violata securi
> et specus in medio virgis ac vimine densus
> efficiens humilem lapidum compagibus arcum,
> uberibus fecundus aquis . . .

An ancient wood stood there, which no axe had violated, and in its midst, overgrown with twigs and branches, a cave whose framework of rocks formed a low arch and which abounded in bubbling waters . . .

---

[94] *Met.* 3. 28–31.

The context is interesting: like Aeneas in Italy, Cadmus has just arrived in a strange land, and like Aeneas, he makes a salutation to the unknown landscape (ignotos montes agrosque salutat) and prepares to pour a libation to Jupiter.[95] Ovid seems to be aiming for a blend of the beautiful, the strange and the sacral, but though he borrows Virgil's raw materials, he appears flat in comparison. His scene-setting feels, in Horace's terms, like a purple patch sewn on—an image which does not fit the best evocations of landscape in Augustan poetry but which does fit what could happen in default of a living imagination, or when the depiction of nature was not integrated into an entire way of apprehending the world.

Why does Ovid seem so inferior to Virgil in this area? The comparison between the two men suggests that to produce a sense either of natural beauty or of the numinous the standard stage properties are not enough. For one thing, Virgil's feeling for the mystery in landscape includes a sense of the individual quality of Italian belief and cult. Ovid has a traveller in Lycia coming upon an awe-inspiring spot where stands an ancient altar. To whom is it sacred? he enquires: to the Naiads, to Faunus, or to some native god?[96] In the *Aeneid*, by contrast, Faunus is primordially Italian, and it would be unthinkable for him to be present in Asia.[97] In another place Ovid presents Dryads on the hills of Latium, Naiads in the Italian rivers Albula, Numicus, and Anio.[98] But no special atmosphere comes from the mingling of Greek deities with Italian landscape; there is nothing of the elusive romance that irradiates Virgil's Camilla.[99] If Ovid designs a distinction between Greek and Italian here, it remains decorative merely, a matter of diction. He lists six Italian rivers, making up in quantity for Virgil's nice sense of individual quality, but he does not know how to draw the emotional resonance out of proper names. For him Albula is simply a synonym for the Tiber; for Virgil it was a doorway into the abyss of time.[100]

Ovid has little feeling for the wildness or apartness of nature—for example:[101]

[95] *Met.* 3. 25, 'he greets the unknown hills and fields'. Cf. *Aen.* 7. 133 (libation to Jupiter) and 136 ff. (prayers to the 'genius loci', to Earth and to 'adhuc ignota . . . flumina').

[96] *Met.* 6. 329 f.

[97] In the *Fasti* Ovid again treats Faunus as simply a Latin name for Pan; the god's bawdy escapades (2. 303–58) are in marked contrast to his formless obscurity in the *Aeneid*.

[98] *Met.* 14. 326 ff.

[99] On Greek and Italian elements in the presentation of Camilla, see above, pp. 566 f.

[100] See above, p. 402.   [101] *Met.* 3. 155–62.

vallis erat piceis et acuta densa cupressu,
nomine Gargaphie, succinctae sacra Dianae,
cuius in extremo antrum nemorale recessu
arte laboratum nulla: simulaverat artem
ingenio natura suo; nam pumice vivo
et levibus tofis nativum duxerat arcum.
fons sonat a dextra tenui perlucidus unda,
margine gramineo patulos succinctus hiatus . . .

There was a vale thick with pine and pointed cypress, Gargaphie by name, holy to girt Diana. In its furthest interior was a woody cave, wrought by no art: nature by her own genius had mimicked art; for she had carried across a natural arch of living pumice-stone and light tufa. On the right, its thin waters translucent, a spring plashes, girt with a grassy bank where the pool opened more widely.

This passage owes something to the African harbour in the first book of the *Aeneid*: here again are the hanging woods, the living rock and (as will be revealed in the lines following those quoted) the presence of the nymphs. Moreover, Ovid has sought to imitate Virgil's sense of recession, so that the spectator is drawn forwards, deep into the interior of the scene: 'cuius in *extremo* est antrum nemorale *recessu*' can be compared with Virgil's 'est in *secessu longo* locus' and 'inque sinus . . . *reductos*';[102] Ovid's 'recessus' combines memories of Virgil's 'secessus' and 'reductus'. Quite different, though, is Ovid's grotto, for he is intrigued by the very fact that it does not look natural: an artist's hand might have fashioned it. In Virgil such a thought might convey a feeling of magic or wonder; here we feel rather the predominance of decorative or pictorial values. That impression is strengthened by other passages, for example the cave of Thetis:[103]

myrtea silva subest bicoloribus obsita bacis.
est specus in medio, natura factus an arte,
ambiguum, magis arte tamen . . .

There is a myrtle wood nearby thick with berries of two colours. There is a cave in its midst; it is unclear whether it was made by nature or art, but one would rather suppose art . . .

It does not matter whether the cave is devised by art or not: nature is to be decorative rather than to be herself.

Whether by design or not, Ovid allows himself to lose touch with reality in a way that Virgil, for all his insouciance about botanical

---

[102] *Aen.* I. 159, 161.   [103] *Met.* II. 234–6.

probability, never quite does. Consider the fair field where Proserpine gathers flowers:[104]

> silva coronat aquas cingens latus omne suisque
> frondibus ut velo Phoebeos submovet ictus.
> frigora dant rami, Tyrios humus umida flores:
> perpetuum ver est. quo dum Proserpina luco
> ludit et aut violas aut candida lilia carpit,
> dumque puellari studio calathosque sinumque
> inplet et aequales certat superare legendo,
> paene simul visa est dilectaque raptaque Diti . . .

A wood crowns the waters, encircling every side, and keeps away Phoebus' rays with its leaves as with an awning. The branches afford coolness, the moist earth affords flowers of Tyrian hue; spring is everlasting. While Proserpina played in this grove and plucked violets or white lilies, and while with girlish eagerness she was filling her baskets and lap and striving to outdo her playmates in the gathering, in almost a single moment she was seen and loved and snatched by Dis . . .

'Perpetuum ver'—Ovid has created an unreal paradise, but meaninglessly, in a factitious attempt to make his *locus amoenus* seem the more beautiful. His scene sounds similar to the 'ver adsiduum' of Italy in the second Georgic, but the effect is very different, for Virgil subtly evokes the associations of the golden age without in fact depicting it.[105] Ovid's setting has the prettiness of a picture or embroidery: the flowers are of Tyrian purple, like the most expensive dyestuffs; and when we come to the violets and bright lilies, we may suspect him of having forgotten that he has removed the sunlight from the scene. While it might be pedantic to insist on botanical accuracy, it seems symptomatic that he ignores, if indeed he knows, the fact that though violets may like the shade, lilies do not, and would be unlikely to grow in the thickly shaded wood that he has imagined. And since spring is eternal in this place, we may doubt whether 'aut . . . aut' acknowledges that these flowers bloom at different seasons; Propertius had been more careful: '*nunc* violas tondere manu, *nunc* mixta referre | lilia . . .'[106]

Nor has Ovid that feeling for enchantment and the numinous without which the Virgilian elements could not be used or even adapted with full success. The pool in which Narcissus sees his own reflection well illustrates his capacities and limits:[107]

---

[104] *Met.* 5. 388–92.   [105] See above, p. 359.
[106] Prop. 3. 13. 29 f., quoted above.   [107] *Met.* 3. 407–12.

> fons erat inlimis, nitidis argenteus undis,
> quem neque pastores neque pastae monte capellae
> contigerant aliudve pecus, quem nulla volucris
> nec fera turbarat nec lapsus ab arbore ramus;
> gramen erat circa, quod proximus umor alebat,
> silvaque sole locum passura tepescere nullo.

There was a clear spring, its sparkling waters silvery, which neither herdsmen nor goats after feeding on the hill nor any other livestock had touched,
which no bird nor beast had stirred nor branch falling from a tree; there
was grass around, fed by the moisture near by, and a grove that would not
allow any sun to warm the spot.

The description is well fitted to its context: the beauty of the place
is apt in a story about a man who will be drawn to destruction by
his own beauty, seen reflected in this very pool. Furthermore, Ovid
has presented him in terms which bring him close to Hippolytus,
the one virgin hero in Greek mythology: he is a hunter, and a man
who has kept himself from the touch of male and female alike;[108]
his purity is reflected, metaphorically as well as literally, in the clarity of the pool and the inviolability of its setting. Yet it is over this
inviolability that doubts creep in. First, it is artificially magical, and
for no sufficient reason: no animal enters, no branch even falls from
a tree, a plain impossibility. Further, the absence of man and beast
has lost all sense of mystery and sanctity: it is either a routine feature of a set piece description or a rather flat symbol of Narcissus'
exclusiveness. It might be objected that Ovid should not be blamed
for failing to to do what he never intended; but there remains something unsatisfactory about the vulgarization of a motif which has
been so evocative in other hands.

   That feeling is confirmed by a later passage (Glaucus is speaking
to Scylla):[109]

> sunt viridi prato confinia litora, quorum
> altera pars undis, pars altera cingitur herbis,
> quas neque cornigerae morsu laesere iuvencae,
> nec placidae carpsistis oves hirtaeve capellae;
> non apis inde tulit conlectos sedula flores,
> non data sunt capiti genialia serta, neque umquam
> falciferae secuere manus. ego primus in illo
> caespite consedi . . .

---

[108] *Met.* 3. 355.   [109] *Met.* 13. 924–31.

There is a shore bordered by a green meadow, of which one side is bounded by the waves, the other by grass which the horned cattle have never disturbed by their grazing, nor have you placid sheep or shaggy goats ever cropped it; the busy bee has not gathered and taken the flower's honey nor any head been given festive wreaths from there, nor have hands holding scythes ever cut it. I am the first to have sat on that turf . . .

This scene bears a resemblance to the meadow in Euripides' *Hippolytus*,[110] but whereas that was an expression of the pure chastity of Artemis and her votary, here the inviolate nature of the place seems gratuitous, another purple patch stitched on. Besides, though the untouchedness of Euripides' meadow has a symbolic function, it is also actual within the fiction of the play: there is in Hippolytus' experience a real locality where flocks are kept out and the grass never cut, so that the sanctity of the spot is felt as real too, not perceptible by the senses but none the less inhering in the place. Ovid's loss of such feeling is shown by a revealing detail: only the bee flits about Euripides' meadow, no bee comes to his. Euripides keeps his eye upon reality: he knows that bees cannot be excluded from a field, and indeed he is able to use them as a symbol of purity. Ovid removes the bees as part of an idea of inviolability that has become mechanical. It might be said in his defence that Glaucus' meadow is indeed supernaturally affected—he chews the grass and is turned into a sea god—but after every allowance has been made for the difference in Ovid's purpose and poetry, one is left feeling that a motif once full of significance has been debased.

Ovid was happy to plunder Virgil's store. His description of the Tiber's mouth draws on the seventh Aeneid:[111]

> solvitur herboso religatus ab aggere funis,
> et procul insidias infamataeque relinquunt
> tecta deae lucosque petunt, ubi nubilus umbra
> in mare cum flava prorumpit Thybris harena;
> Faunigenaeque domo potitur nataque Latini,
> non sine Marte tamen . . .

The ropes are loosened from the grassy bank, and they leave far behind the wiles and halls of the ill-famed goddess and make for the woodland where Tiber, obscured in shade, bursts out into the sea with yellow silt. He [Aeneas] wins the home and daughter of Latinus, Faunus' son, not however without war.

---

[110] *Hipp.* 73 ff., quoted and discussed above, pp. 37 f.
[111] *Met.* 14. 445–50; cf. *Aen.* 7. 29–32, quoted above, p. 469.

Once again, comparison illustrates both the mesmeric effect of Virgil on his contemporaries and his abiding distinctiveness. Ovid borrows his language, but does not share his concerns: he has no interest, for example, in using the woodland to develop the mysterious complexity of Italy. The proper names do not have the importance that they had in the *Aeneid*: no significance springs from the closeness of the Greek form Thybris to the Italian Faunus. 'Nubilus umbra' is an appealing phrase, but the evocation of a river breaking out of thick jungle has been lost. Small touches helped Virgil to this effect: the phrase 'hunc inter', more forceful than Ovid's simple 'ubi', the dynamism implied in 'rapidis', the delaying of 'prorumpit' and then its abruptness before a full stop in mid line; indeed even Virgil's notoriously favourite adjective 'ingens' plays its part.

When Ovid tells the story of Polyphemus and Galatea, he draws on both Virgil and Theocritus.[112]

> sunt mihi, pars montis, vivo pendentia saxo
> antra, quibus nec sol medio sentitur in aestu
> nec sentitur hiems; sunt poma gravantia ramos;
> sunt auro similes longis in vitibus uvae,
> sunt et purpureae: tibi et has servamus et illas.
> ipsa tuis manibus silvestri nata sub umbra
> mollia fraga leges, ipsa autumnalia corna
> prunaque, non solum nigro liventia suco,
> verum etiam generosa novasque imitantia ceras;
> nec tibi castaneae me coniuge, nec tibi deerunt
> arbutei fetus: omnis tibi serviet arbor.

I have caves hanging with living rock, part of the mountain; neither is the sun felt there in midsummer heat nor is the winter felt. I have fruits that weigh down the branches, I have clusters of grapes like gold on trailing vines and purple ones too; I am keeping both this kind and that for you. With your own hands you shall gather the luscious strawberries that have grown in the woodland shade, and cherries in autumn, and plums, not only the ones that are purple, with dark juice, but also the large ones that mimic fresh wax. Nor shall you lack chestnuts nor arbutus fruits with me as your husband: every tree shall be at your service.

The 'vivo pendentia saxo antra' are derived from the harbour in the first Aeneid,[113] and once more Virgil's complex evocativeness is lost

---

[112] *Met.* 13. 810–20.
[113] 'Scopulis pendentibus antrum . . . vivoque sedilia saxo', *Aen.* 1. 166 f. (see above, p. 63).

in the imitation; but the chief inspiration has been the *Eclogues*.[114] The 'still life' is less compact than that in the second Eclogue: though Virgil's list of flowers is quite leisurely, his fruits occupy a mere three lines, and Ovid seems a little rambling in comparison. Once again, lucidity replaces Virgil's suggestiveness. Instead of the compression of the Eclogue's 'cerea pruna' Ovid spells things out: 'novasque imitantia ceras'. Virgil does not so much describe as imply a contrast of textures; Ovid wants us to know just what to see: some golden grapes, others purple; some plums purple-black, others presumably yellow (for the context suggests that the likeness to wax is primarily a matter of colour contrast with the dark fruits of the preceding line).

Ovid is indeed interested in the exploration of colour. In this he is to an extent the child of his time: it is hard to imagine anyone investigating this matter quite as he does before the first century BC (and we may compare Lucretius searching for new colour words).[115] But this concern is also plainly the product of his individual imagination. His clarity and straightforwardness impose limits upon him, but they can also help him to a precision of observation which Virgil does not exhibit. Virgil's feeling for quality, distinctiveness, particularity is incomparable; but one would not be incredulous if told that he was either short-sighted or colour-blind. When Ovid writes about his mistress's hair, we feel an exploratory pressing forward: no, not dark, not golden—neither and yet a mixture of both:[116]

> nec tamen ater erat neque erat tamen aureus ille
>   sed, quamvis neuter, mixtus uterque color,
> qualem clivosae madidis in vallibus Idae
>   ardua derepto cortice cedrus habet.

However, its colour was not black, nor yet was it golden, but though it was neither, it was a mixture of both, just the colour that the lofty cedar has in the valleys of dewy Ida when its bark has been stripped.

And when he arrives at his solution, we say, Ah yes, that is right. The feeling of investigation persists: the bark is stripped from the tree, and see, there at last is the answer. The vales of dewy Ida add a romantic tone, yet at the same time there is an accuracy of perception: if we think of the colour of cedarwood, and search our

---

[114] Nor has Ovid wished to conceal his debt: 'ipsa tuis manibus . . . leges'; cf. *Ecl.* 2. 51, 'ipse ego . . . legam'. Two of the three fruits in *Ecl.* 2, the chestnuts and the waxy plums, reappear here.

[115] See above, p. 276.   [116] *Am.* I. 14. 9–12.

own experience, we shall know exactly the tint of hair that he has in mind.

In the *Metamorphoses* the almost decadent voluptuousness of the story of Salmacis and Hermaphroditus is appropriately accompanied by a lushness of description, but the poet's eye is keen nevertheless. The youth blushes:[117]

> hic color aprica pendentibus arbore pomis
> aut ebori tincto est aut sub candore rubenti,
> cum frustra resonant aera auxiliaria, lunae.

This is the colour of apples hanging from a sunny tree or of stained ivory or of the eclipsed moon reddening beneath brightness, when bronze objects clash in vain to aid her.

In these similitudes Ovid studies the effect when one colour seems to glow through another laid on top of it. The boy bathes in a pool:[118]

> in liquidis translucet aquis, ut eburnea siquis
> signa tegat claro vel candida lilia vitro.

He shines through in the clear waters, as though someone were to encase ivory statues or bright lilies in transparent glass.

The water nymph Salmacis will pour herself around him until the two bodies flow into one, and so these lines are prophetic of metamorphosis, but they are also alert to the effects of colour and light, to a translucence which seems to preserve colour and yet change it.

Ovid's nicety of observation can be seen again as he introduces aerodynamics into poetry, watching the careful craftsmanship with which Daedalus *slightly* curves the edge of his artificial wings:[119]

> tum lino medias et ceris adligat imas,
> atque ita conpositas *parvo* curvamine flectit,
> ut *veras* imitetur aves.

Then he fastens the feathers in the middle with thread and at the bottom with wax, and he bends them, thus arranged, with a slight curve, to mimic real birds.

The same book gives us Meleager, fated to live only so long as a certain billet of wood survives; the wood is burnt and he perishes:[120]

---

[117] *Met.* 4. 331–3. [118] *Met.* 4. 354 f.
[119] *Met.* 8. 193–5. [120] *Met.* 8. 522–5.

> crescunt ignisque dolorque,
> languescuntque iterum: simul est exstinctus uterque,
> inque leves abiit *paulatim* spiritus auras
> *paulatim* cana prunam velante favilla . . .

The fire and the pain grow and sink down again; each is extinguished together, and his spirit gradually departed into the light breeze, as the hoar ash gradually veiled the glowing coal.

The beautifully veiled sonority of the last two lines matches their content, and the descriptive skill is superb. How does a red-hot coal look as it goes out? Ovid has found the perfect words for the way in which the grey gradually overspreads the glow.

'Paulatim . . . paulatim . . .'—Ovid shares with Virgil (and Lucretius) a fascination with process;[121] in his case, though, the interest is not in the immense and invisible movements of history but with those changes that are observable by the eye. And after all, the subject of his longest poem is alteration. Naturally he treats his innumerable metamorphoses in differing ways; in some he is especially concerned with the actual business of transformation. Perhaps the best of these studies is the story of Pygmalion, which in its present form is first found in his poem. Earlier, Pygmalion had been a king who slept with a statue, one of many myths of sexual perversion; it may well have been Ovid himself who first transmuted the tale into a delicate parable about the relation between a creator and his creation. 'Tempto' is a recurrent word in his account:[122] touch and test are at the heart of the story. This is the moment of metamorphosis:[123]

> ut rediit, simulacra suae petit ille puellae
> incumbensque toro dedit oscula: visa *tepere* est;
> admovet os iterum, manibus quoque pectora *temptat*:
> *temptatum mollescit* ebur positoque rigore
> subsidit digitis ceditque, ut Hymettia sole
> cera *remollescit tractataque pollice* multas
> flectitur in facies ipsoque fit utilis usu.
> dum stupet et medio gaudet fallique veretur,
> *rursus* amans *rursusque* manu sua vota *retractat*;
> corpus erat: saliunt *temptatae pollice* venae.

On returning he makes for the image of his girl, and leaning over the bed, kisses her. She seemed to be warm. He brings his lips to her a second time,

---

[121] Cf. above, pp. 202 f., 242.   [122] *Met.* 10. 254, 282, 283, 289.
[123] *Met.* 10. 280–9.

and with his hands tries her breast as well. The ivory softens as he tries it, and losing its hardness, yields to his fingers and gives, as Hymettian wax softens in the sun, and moulded by the thumb, is fashioned into many forms and becomes usable by use itself. As he stands amazed and at once rejoices and fears that he may be mistaken, he lovingly tries again and again with his hand what he had prayed for. It was a body: the veins throb as his thumb tries them.

Change and development are conveyed by the mutation and expansion of words—the sequences 'tep- . . . tempt-', 'temptat: temptatum', 'rursus . . . rursusque', 'tract- . . . retract-', 'mollescit . . . remollescit'. The inceptive endings and the repeated 'pollice' (thumb) express the tentative, the exploratory.

Virgil, as it happens, had briefly shown the sculptors of Greece putting breath in their bronzes and drawing living faces from the marble.[124] Perhaps we may suppose Ovid pondering the implications of that famous passage; or maybe we should rather think of the two poets, each in his own way, exhibiting a mode of perception that had become part of their age's spirit. A study of Ovid, so unlike Virgil in temper, exemplifies the unmistakable impress of Virgil's genius on his contemporaries, with effects both liberating and inhibitory. It is not merely a case of Virgil's words and motifs being imitated by others; he also offered a fresh style of imagining. We can see his mastery as imperious, stamping its mark on all the poets of the age; but we can also see him as a catalyst, helping to form in others qualities that are not his own, like Ovid's occasional exactness of observation and his painterly sense. A feeling for nature, landscape, and things seen acutely yet imaginatively persists in Latin literature; the full story would take us to Juvenal, to Apuleius, and beyond. Virgil is one of the makers of this sensibility.

[124] *Aen.* 6. 847 f.

CHAPTER 15

A Roman Experience:
Virgil, Augustus, and the Future

Caesar. Now he is come out of Campania
I doubt not, he hath finished all his *Aeneids* . . .

(Jonson, *Poetaster*, v. i)

Caesar. Where are thy famous *Aeneids*?

(Ibid. v. ii)

Lust—tiefer noch als Herzeleid!

(Nietzsche)

We have been studying Virgil's vision of nature, history, and process, and finding it bound up with his idea of what it is to be an
Italian and a Roman. Such a conception is, in modern terms, an
ideology; indeed it is in the large sense a political ideology, since it
concerns the individual's relation to his society, affirms the emotional
as well as practical importance of the city and its institutions, and
explores the character of nationhood. This raises the question of its
relationship to politics in the more obvious sense—that is, to the
figure of Augustus and, perhaps more interestingly, to his constitutional settlement and to the moral and social outlook associated with
his name. It has often been asked how far Virgil was a genuine admirer
of Augustus and a believer in his cause. In looking for an answer,
we should also ask how far Virgil was creating his own ideology,
and inviting Augustus to follow that, if he should so choose.

All writers have conscious intentions, but they are also concerned
to express the fullness of themselves, and thus their work may often
embody their thoughts and attitudes in ways which, though not contrary to intention, may not be deliberately designed. It is illuminating to look at Virgil's use of value terms, both those that he favours

and those that he neglects, and here the border between intended and unselfconscious expression may be unclear. No one doubts that the weight laid upon 'pietas' in the *Aeneid* is calculated and significant, but in other places we may infer something of his outlook upon Rome's situation not because he is putting across a message but in the same way that we pick up a notion of the attitudes of the people we meet from their conversation: we listen to them, and inevitably we learn.

Cicero's goals were 'dignitas', 'otium', 'libertas'. Augustus claimed to have restored the republic; as we read Virgil, we may be interested to see what use he has for these republican watchwords. The noun 'dignitas' is impossible in the hexameter; the adjective 'dignus' occurs seven times in the *Eclogues*, but only twenty in the *Aeneid*, and it is doubtful whether any of the occurrences in the *Aeneid* could be described as political even in a loose sense. 'Dignus' is a very common word, which any Latin writer will want to use from time to time, and so the imbalance in frequency between the *Eclogues* and the *Aeneid*, though large, may be mostly a matter of chance. But it does indicate, negatively, how unconcerned Virgil is in his epic to put any weight on the word, and that is telling. 'Dignitas' is an individualistic and aristocratic value, the assertion of personal distinction, a more everyday equivalent to the *time* or honour pursued by the heroes of Greek epic. Half the story of the *Iliad* is generated by Achilles' passion to uphold his *time*, but Aeneas, an epic hero and the founder of the Roman race, lacks the concern with self-assertion displayed by his poetic ancestors and his Roman descendants. And thus Virgil's intertextuality—the distance he puts between his idea of the hero and Homer's—carries also, in the broad sense, a political force: it turns away from the values of the republican oligarchy. As it happens, two of the three occurrences of 'dignus' in the *Georgics* come in contexts which are political in a broad sense: the farmer is warned to get his equipment ready well before he will need it, 'si te digna manet divini gloria ruris'; and because of civil war, the plough is not getting its due honour, 'non ullus aratro | dignus honos'.[1] 'Gloria' and 'honos' are words that belong to the public sphere, to rank, public office, or success in war; with deliberate paradox, Virgil brings them to the modest world of the farmer, ennobling the ordinary. And so we are led to feel the reserves of emotional force held

---

[1] *Geo.* 1. 168 (translated and discussed above, p. 319); 1. 506 f.

within the simple word 'dignus' also. It is the more notable, then, that he does not choose to draw upon them in his epic poem.

'Libertas' comes twice in the first Eclogue, with heavy emphasis.[2] Though it refers here to manumission from slavery, not to the political freedom of the citizen, the reader might be led to suppose from this prominent and early stress that liberty in its various aspects would become an important theme for this poet. If so, he would be in for a surprise: the word does not recur in the *Eclogues*, is absent from the *Georgics*, and comes thrice only in the *Aeneid*. The adjective 'liber' comes four times in the *Aeneid*, twice in the *Georgics*, and not at all in the *Eclogues*, and it has no moral or political import in any of these places. One of the occurrences of the noun in the *Aeneid* is insignificant;[3] the other two refer to the expulsion of the Tarquins from Rome: in the sixth book Lucius Brutus sacrifices the lives of his sons for fair freedom, 'pulchra pro libertate', and in the eighth it is again for freedom, 'pro libertate', that Aeneas' descendants rush to battle.[4] These phrases may sound forthright, but in fact they stir no controversy. All Romans, of whatever political persuasion, were agreed that the expulsion of the kings was an act of heroic liberation. What is more, it was seen very largely as a struggle against a foreign enemy: that is explicit in the eighth book, where Virgil names the Etruscan king Porsenna, and implicit in the sixth, where Lucius Brutus' sons are plotting to bring about a new war. True, more combative people might apply the story to the internal affairs of Rome: Cicero imagines Marcus Brutus roused to free his country from Julius Caesar by the daily sight of his ancestor's bust, and when Tacitus opens his *Annals* with the tersely suggestive statement that the city of Rome had kings, until Lucius Brutus brought in liberty and the consulate, he implies that the principate took liberty away again.[5] But in itself the legend of the Tarquins was a shared possession, as safely patriotic as (say) the story of William Tell and the apple. Virgil mentions 'libertas' in the *Aeneid* only in such a way that it causes no trouble.

As it happens, he gives himself a golden opportunity to treat the theme of political liberty, and declines it. The uprising of Etruria against Mezentius offered ample scope for reflection on the use and abuse of power, the responsibilities of rulers, the virtues of resistance

---

[2] *Ecl.* 1. 27, 32.   [3] *Aen.* 11. 346.   [4] *Aen.* 6. 821; 8. 648.
[5] Cic. *Phil.* 2. 26; Tac. *Ann.* 1. 1.

to autocracy. Instead, Virgil turns Mezentius into a monster of depraved cruelty, and the Etruscan rebellion becomes an act of necessary desperation; the portrayal is so extreme that the more testing political questions do not arise. His treatment is the odder in that it creates a feeling of inconsistency. The Mezentius who meets his death in the tenth book with an unrepentant, coarse-grained courage could have been a brutal and callous ruler, but hardly the fiend of motiveless malignancy depicted earlier.[6] Equally, while we can believe that the amiable Lausus might love the later Mezentius, to feel affection for the Mezentius of the eighth book would seem well-nigh impossible in a decent man. But on the other hand, the less odious Mezentius became, the harder it might be to distinguish him from a triumvir.

Virgil, then, leaves the topic of political liberty aside. That might be because he dared not do otherwise. But there is another possibility: that he was not interested. For Cicero liberty meant the freedom to influence public action and the chance to compete for real power. Virgil was too young to have known a republic that was not under the shadow of the dynasts; had he been older, he would have been effectively debarred by his geographical and perhaps also his social origins from the hope of playing a significant part in public affairs, even if he had nursed such an ambition. To judge this matter we shall need to enquire further into his political attitudes.

The word 'otium' may be especially illuminating, because it is so hard to translate, and because it extends across a range of meanings: peace, leisure, safety, personal independence. It comes twice in the *Eclogues*: 'deus nobis haec otia fecit' (A god has brought me this peace); 'amat bonus otia Daphnis' (Good Daphnis loves peace).[7] In each case the context shows that the word connotes not only peace but also security or freedom from interference; but as we expect, it represents the herdsmen's life at its most agreeable, and no shadow falls over it. 'Otium' comes three times in the *Georgics*, where the account of country life lays more stress upon steady labour. Accordingly, 'otium' is absent from the first book, in which the theme of toil predominates, but 'latis otia fundis' are among rural blessings in the second: 'otium' still seems to Virgil, as it had seemed to Lucretius, part of the country's delightfulness.[8] Such a conception of 'otium'

---

[6] We hear of Mezentius' tyranny from Evander. Virgil's subjective method would certainly have allowed him, had he wished, to represent the old man as a credulous believer in exaggerated stories of atrocities. But it seems pretty clear that such is not his intention.

[7] *Ecl.* 1. 6; 5. 61.   [8] *Geo.* 2. 468; cf. Lucr. 5. 1387.

had indeed been known to Cicero, but now the idea of escape from
the harshness of modern life is more strongly felt; it is significant that
the phrase comes in that part of the poem where town and country
are contrasted and Virgil comes closest to anti-urban sentiment. In
the *Georgics'* closing lines we detect an equivocation in the word
for the first time, as the poet sets great Caesar, energetically victorious in the east, against himself, 'studiis florentem ignobilis oti'.[9]
Whereas for Cicero 'otium cum dignitate' was a goal for the man
of public action, for Virgil 'otium' has become a quietist ideal, and
is contrasted with the life of action. And his view of the life of leisure
is now tinged with what we may perhaps call an 'Augustan' feeling: however delightful, it is 'ignobilis', and elsewhere there is work
to be done. Of course, Virgil's critical adjective is not to be taken
too simply: the lines are suffused with a pride which modifies the
apparent self-deprecation, and the reader reflects that an 'otium' which
has produced the *Georgics* is neither slothful nor lightly to be despised. Naturally Virgil does not say this openly; he does not need
to: *lector, si monumentum requiris . . .* But it is apt that as he seals the
Georgics and prepares to move on to his sterner, more fully Augustan
poem, the idea of 'otium' should be found in a transitional state,
no longer purely favourable as before, but not yet as suspect as it
will become in the *Aeneid*.

The two uses of 'otium' in the *Aeneid* are indeed strikingly different. First: 'quid struis? aut qua spe Libycis teris otia terris?' (What
are you planning? with what hope do you idly spend your time
in the land of Libya?)[10] This is Mercury castigating Aeneas for his
dalliance in Carthage: on his lips 'otium' is merely a term of abuse,
and he will go on to contrast it with the 'gloria' of great deeds which
should be the hero's ambition.[11] We may want to protest that Aeneas
is not being idle in any natural sense: Mercury has found him actively
engaged in directing the construction of Carthage. The passage excites
a complex reaction. On the one hand, we may feel some meanness
of spirit in the god's speech,[12] and think that in his pejorative use

---

[9] *Geo.* 4. 564 (blossoming in the pursuits of inglorious ease). 'Otium' at *Geo.* 3. 377
has no especial significance (the Scythians in the winter spending their leisure time
underground).

[10] *Aen.* 4. 271.   [11] *Aen.* 4. 272.

[12] In particular, when Mercury scorns Aeneas for being 'uxorius' (4. 266), we may want
to retort that this is a virtuous fault, especially since the god comes as the messenger of
Jupiter, who, we have recently been told, has been pleased to gratify his lust by ravishing
an African nymph (4. 198).

of 'otium' there is a falsity. On the other hand, we may find a truth, for Mercury's point is really that Aeneas is doing what he wants, not what he should; though he is acting as a public man, he is not acting according to duty. Vigorous, glamorous, richly dressed, busy with the governance of a foreign city, he is behaving in the style that a dynast of the late republic would approve, mingling public energy with culture and opulence. Yet this happy splendour, admirable though it may be, is somehow no longer enough.[13] The Homeric hero's fight to excel others must give way to an obedience to the demands of the national destiny; the republican dynast's struggle for individual glory is replaced by Caesar Augustus' sterner attention to the common good. To the severe ideology of the new order the old, aristocratic idea of 'otium cum dignitate' becomes suspect.

In the sixth book 'otium' returns in a curious passage:[14]

> cui deinde subibit
> otia qui rumpet patriae residesque movebit
> Tullus in arma viros et iam desueta triumphis
> agmina.

He shall be succeeded by Tullus, the man who will break his country's peace and rouse to arms again men become slothful and ranks grown unused to triumphs.

Virgil is counting the cost of Rome's military destiny, and to that extent 'otium' here is a favourable word: for a career of conquest the loss of 'otium' is a price that must be paid, but with regret. Yet 'otium' here is not a blessing without qualification. To be sure, Tullus Hostilius was a sombre figure, an exemplar of warlike mettle, but still he was traditionally regarded as one of the heroes of the Roman story, a judgement loudly endorsed at the end of the sentence, which insists through the emotive word 'triumphus' that Tullus' bellicosity, harsh though it may seem to the lover of peace, has recalled Rome back to its proper course. Virgil so constructs the sentence as to surprise us. Suppose that we break it off in the middle: 'cui deinde subibit | otia qui rumpet patriae . . .' At this point we might expect that one of the villains of Roman history is about to step on to the

---

[13] But as we have seen (Ch. 2, n. 116), we should not attribute to Virgil the sour asceticism which would condemn Aeneas' jewelled sword and purple raiment. A ruler is properly vigorous and opulent, and Aeneas' case is the more touching because what is naturally good must be denied him, and his instinct, though directed to the wrong place, is so virtuous.

[14] *Aen.* 6. 812–15.

stage, and we should receive a small stab of shock when the word 'resides' follows and then the emphatic positioning of 'Tullus' makes that austerely heroic name ring out. The two parallel clauses 'otia cui rumpet patriae' and 'residesque movebit | Tullus in arma viros . . .' form an example of that Virgilian trick of composition that has been called 'theme and variation', a term that may usefully remind us that variation can sometimes be transformation also. The second clause is not merely a graceful echo of the first but shifts the moral perspective. There is no dying fall to the sentence; instead it gathers in strength and sternness. Livy's account is similar and yet different: 'cum aetas viresque tum avita quoque gloria animum stimulabat. senescere igitur civitatem otio ratus undique materiam excitandi belli quaerebat' (Youth and vigour and also the glory of his grandfather spurred his spirit. So thinking that peace was causing the nation to decline, he looked everywhere for a pretext for stirring up warfare).[15] Here 'otium' passes by without emphasis, whereas Virgil seems to explore the word, shaping the sentence so that we first think to approve of 'otium' and then put it aside. And in that putting aside there is a splendid hardness. A rather similar pattern of thought recurs a few lines later, and with an increase of emotional intensity:[16]

> consulis imperium hic primus saevasque securis
> accipiet, natosque pater nova bella moventis
> ad poenam pulchra pro libertate vocabit,
> infelix, utcumque ferent ea facta minores:
> vincet amor patriae laudumque immensa cupido.

He shall be the first to receive a consul's authority and the fierce axes, and when his sons stir civil war, he, their father, shall summon them to execution for the sake of fair liberty—unhappy man, however posterity shall regard these deeds; but love of country will prevail and a limitless appetite for glory.

No one will doubt that Virgil is here counting the full and bitter cost. Still, the final note is again resolute, and the last line monumental. Victory, glory, vast desire—like the form of the sentence, the words themselves, expressive of huge appetite, gather to a greatness and fiercely affirm.

Curiously enough, the two references to 'otium' in the *Eclogues* come in what could in a sense be called political contexts. Daphnis

---

[15] Livy 1. 22. 2.   [16] *Aen.* 6. 819–23.

the lover of 'otium' is a figure who in some respects seems to put us in mind of Julius Caesar; he is certainly a figure who has power over the life of the pastoral world. The 'god' of the first Eclogue is a young man who wields power from Rome. The significance of 'otium' here is not that it belongs to a political vocabulary but rather the contrary: that the word has lost the political edge which it had for Cicero. 'Otium' is no longer the product and proof of a man's independence but something that is bestowed from outside, from above, by figures invested with a quasi-divine aura. The world was becoming ready for monarchy; Cicero's body was barely cold when Virgil began his *Eclogues*, but the young poet would hardly have remembered a time before there were first triumvirs. He was born in the year that Pompey held his first consulship despite being six years below the legal age and not having held any of the lesser magistracies, as the law required. Pompey and Crassus had waited with their armies outside Rome in the confident hope that a grateful senate and people would reward their services; the consular elections were duly held, and the choice fell upon Pompey and Crassus. This incident, more than the blatantly unconstitutional dominations of Sulla or Cinna, foreshadowed the style of the Augustan principate: forms and proprieties for the most part soberly observed, while the reality of power lies elsewhere. We may recall the coin which shows Augustus giving freedom to a kneeling *respublica*.[17] When a national emergency appears to call for decision in one particular direction, the boundaries between choice and compulsion can become unclear. The decision for Pompey was probably welcome to many—as indeed was the rule of Augustus. Tacitus, not excessively lenient in his view of the principate, allowed as much: Augustus, he agreed, had allured everybody by the charms of 'otium'.[18] Like the troubled shepherds of the *Eclogues*, a war-weary generation was glad enough to have peace imposed, with god-like authority, from above. Tacitus, however, did not confound popular autocracy with liberty, and nor did Cicero: what mattered to both was where the ultimate sources of power lay. But both had been senators and consuls, and Cicero had lived in a state that he considered free; to Virgil, from the viewpoint of Mantua or Campania, the battles in the Roman senate, in the forum and even in the Roman streets may have seemed hazy with distance or antlike in their insignificance.

[17] See above, p. 114.   [18] *Ann.* I. 2.

So Cicero's political values seem to be absent from Virgil. Conversely, 'pietas' is not prominent in Cicero's political vocabulary. When Augustus restored the republic in 27 BC, the senate voted him a golden shield on which his merits were inscribed: 'virtus clementia iustitia pietas'.[19] We have no means of determining certainly whether Virgil had yet decided to make Aeneas 'pius', though it seems probable that he had. Perhaps it does not matter very much, and it may be sufficient to say that the conceptions of Virgil and Caesar Augustus were conformable to each other. After all, Caesar did not sit down after the Battle of Actium and invent the Augustan ideology; we must suppose more of an evolutionary process. The ruler's personality was indeed one of the forces influencing that evolution, and the poets were another, Virgil especially; indeed in some respects he was an Augustan before Augustus himself was: back in the 30s, when he was working on the *Georgics*.[20] But both men were, like everyone else, people within the flow of history. The concept of 'pietas' itself was evolving. It had been a familial virtue: when Livy spoke of the 'pietas' of Appius Claudius' uncle, battling to maintain the dignity of the gens Claudia despite his nephew's crime, he was thinking of loyalty purely to one's name and kin, as indeed were those who maintained that it was out of 'pietas' that Caesar Octavian had taken up arms.[21] Later 'pietas' would become the subject's duty of homage to the emperor, and disloyalty to him might be indicted as 'impietas'.[22] We might say that Virgil catches 'pietas' at the right moment in its evolution (if that is not to underestimate the effect of his own imagination in enlarging the idea). The 'pietas' of Aeneas is no longer an entirely familial virtue: it combines the personal and the public, loyalty to one's descendants and loyalty to Rome. Not until a later generation would it degenerate into a collectivist or monarchical value: loyalty to Rome embodied in the person of the emperor.

Virgil was shrewd enough about political realities: he is early in accepting the 'royal' character of the new order. When Augustus' nephew Marcellus died, there can have been no compulsion to include a lament for him in the *Aeneid*. Propertius' poem on the dead youth

---

[19] Aug. *Res Gest.* 34; there were copies of the words inscribed, e.g. *ILS* 82.

[20] In L. P. Wilkinson's *The Georgics of Virgil* (Cambridge, 1969) the chapter on 'Political and Social Ideas' includes a section entitled 'Augustanism'.

[21] Livy 3. 58. 5. Tacitus imagines some people at Augustus' funeral attributing his taking up of arms to 'pietas', while others thought the avenging of Julius Caesar was an empty pretext (*Ann.* 1. 9 f.). [22] Tac. *Ann.* 6. 47.

is a rather slight piece, not aspiring to be impassioned or greatly impress-ive;[23] the loyal Horace does not commemorate him at all. This is not very surprising: if Augustus had died in the 20s—a prospect that must have been in people's minds, since his health was frail at the time—this untested boy could not have stepped into his shoes; the succession must have fallen to Agrippa. If Marcellus has occupied a large place in the thoughts of some modern historians, that is due to Virgil. Augustus married his daughter Julia to Agrippa, and he must have hoped that she would produce a son who might even-tually succeed; Marcellus' death did not ruin his plans, as did the later deaths of his grandsons Gaius and Lucius. Marcellus earns his place in the *Aeneid* simply as a member of the imperial house, as a kinsman of the princeps; in other words, Virgil recognizes that there is, in effect, a royal family. Had he honoured an heir presumptive from among Augustus' kin, that would be striking enough at so early a date; but Marcellus was not even that.

When Virgil praises Nisus and Euryalus, he declares that if his verse has any power, their names will abide as long as the house of Aeneas occupies the rock of the Capitol and the Roman father main-tains his sway.[24] The language is interestingly imprecise. The house of Aeneas, 'domus Aeneae', would naturally be taken to mean the family of Aeneas, that is, the gens Iulia, an implication which can-not be resisted, yet its signification can hardly be restricted to that family alone: it is not the Caesares who dwell on the Capitol, but the Roman race. There is thus a doubleness in the phrase, and Virgil's habit of theme and variation encourages us to find a similar double-ness in 'pater Romanus', the Roman father, also. It looks as though this expression appeared as vague in its reference to Virgil's first readers as it does to us. We think perhaps of Jupiter Capitolinus, of the senate (the 'patres'), of each and every Roman paterfamilias, of the father of the state—Augustus and his successors, whoever they might be. The effect is to fuse celebration of the dynast with celebration of the state. By implication, Augustus is installed as emblematic representative of the nation, and the continuance of the Caesares is conflated with the continuance of Rome. This is not something that Virgil could have stated directly, nor is Virgil's fusion something that Augustus could himself have commanded or con-ceived. It is the product of a poetic imagination—an imagination that has taken the reality of monarchy into itself.

[23] Prop. 3. 18.   [24] *Aen.* 9. 446–9.

But if Virgil in some respects gave Augustus more than he could have hoped for, in others he fell short. He gives the impression of one who can afford to let his mind play freely over the national situation, confident enough to choose what he will include or leave out. The *Aeneid* is markedly cool in its treatment of Julius Caesar: he is never mentioned by name, and appears only once, in the pageant of heroes, where Anchises in effect attributes to him the greater blame for the civil war.[25] It has been supposed that in this Virgil is obedient to official policy: that Augustus, who had begun his career by exploiting his adoptive father's name, later glossed over his connection with a man whom he now associated with unconstitutional dictatorship. That can hardly be so: Augustus continued to call himself Caesar, encouraging a process that was to turn the family name into a synonym for emperor; he began his *Res Gestae* by asserting that he restored liberty and avenged the killers of his father; he built temples dedicated to Julius the God and Mars the Avenger; and the iconography of his forum affirmed his descent from the Julian family. The conclusion must be that Virgil makes his own judgement: he is independent of Augustus when he casts upon Julius the shadow of reproach.[26]

He is also selective in those aspects of the great man's work that he chooses to celebrate. His praise concentrates on two things: peace at home and conquest abroad. The highest form of glory was military glory—even Cicero concedes that—and the hope of conquest was a theme that an encomiast of the ruler could scarcely avoid. It is hard to know how seriously Virgil took it. He grossly exaggerates the extent of what Augustus had already achieved, and as Horace does, he looks for the future not to the places where war might probably take place but to romantic and wildly remote peoples, Garamantes, Indians and the like, though we have seen that his cloudy vagueness commits him to rather little that is specific. Still, perhaps

---

[25] *Aen.* 6. 826–35. In one other place Julius is vestigially present: at 6. 792 Augustus is 'divi genus', 'a god's son'.

[26] Syme consistently argued that Augustus treated Julius Caesar as an embarrassment once he had set up the principate. This view is criticized by P. White, 'Julius Caesar in Augustan Rome', *Phoenix* 42 (1988), 334–56, but supported by G. de Ste Croix, *The Class Struggle in the Ancient Greek World* (London, 1981), 623, and defended by G. Herbert-Brown, *Ovid and the Fasti* (Oxford, 1994), 109 ff. Syme was sometimes guarded: for example, '[Augustus] exploited the divinity of his parent and paraded the titulature of "Divi filius". For all else, Caesar the proconsul and dictator was better forgotten' ('A Roman Post-Mortem', *Roman Papers I* (Oxford, 1979), 205–17, at 214). Those terms are defensible; but a judicious silence about parts of Julius's career—if such there was—is a long way from the undisguised reproach in the *Aeneid*.

the flamboyance of his predictions represents a conscious turning away from reality to courtly fantasy;[27] perhaps he was being merely conventional. With this exception, however, he may be reckoned politically serious and acute. He stands at a certain distance from the other Augustan loyalists: he does not, as Livy and Horace do, suppose that the war against moral degeneracy is one of the great man's principal tasks.[28] He saw which parts of the new order mattered, and which did not. Like his admirer Tacitus, he focuses on peace and authority when he writes about Augustus;[29] the scheme of the *Aeneid* gave him ample chances to expand on the recovery of liberty, the re-establishment of the republic, the drive for moral purity, the rebuilding of temples and the buttressing of religious institutions; he passes them by. In the speeches of Jupiter in the first book and Anchises in the sixth we should be struck by how much they do not say. Horace says all the right things, Virgil only some of them. The poet who had written so emphatically about freedom in the first Eclogue now lets the theme drop; he was not deceived. But we should not conclude that he was unimpressed by Augustus if he recognized that parts of the programme were unimportant, perhaps even bogus. A subtler analysis will see Virgil as a man comfortable enough with the present order to be able to treat it easily, without looking over his shoulder, and possessed of the sympathetic understanding to discover where Augustus' genius truly lay (for he was a genius, as hostile historians have acknowledged, from Tacitus to Syme).[30]

However, the myth of Actium was one part of the Augustan image which formed early and which surely did come down from the Palatine

[27] One might compare the proem to the *Georgics*, where the stars withdraw to make space for Caesar as a thirteenth sign of the zodiac—Hellenistic rococo, obviously not to be taken too gravely. The extravagances of Elizabethan poets on the subject of their queen are similar: the rules of the fantasy game are understood by all the players. In the sixth book of the *Aeneid* Virgil puts the encomium of his leader at a comparatively early point in Anchises' speech, carefully separating it from the social and moral earnestness of the close; there is a baroque ebullience in the picture of Augustus extending the empire to a land that lies beyond the stars, where Atlas turns the sphere of heaven upon his shoulders (795 ff.), which differs in tone from the deep Roman seriousness of Anchises' climax. These tonal variations are controlled with consummate mastery; even so, the high solemnity of Virgil's epic perhaps makes his flatteries uncomfortable within the *Aeneid* in a way that they are not in his earlier poem.

[28] Propertius, too, from his own opposed point of view, grants importance to this theme.

[29] Tac. *Ann.* 1. 9.

[30] Compare the verdict of the Marxist de Ste Croix, *The Class Struggle*, 360: 'a political genius . . . one of the ablest political figures known to human history'.

itself. We know of at least six poetic treatments of the battle dating from Augustus' lifetime.[31] There is pretty general agreement among them, as far as we can judge: Actium is presented as an enormous conflict, in which the enemy was effectively wiped out; it was a fight against a foreign foe (Cleopatra dominates the opposition, though she is never named in these poems, or indeed anywhere in Augustan verse); and Augustus is the central figure who brings about the victory. But the poets agree in falsehood. Actium was of course part of a civil war; none of these accounts mentions that two consuls for the year and more than two hundred senators were on Antony's side. There may not have been very much fighting. The war had been effectively decided in an earlier sea-battle by Agrippa's defeat of Antony's lieutenant Sosius. Some of Antony's fleet refused to engage; he himself broke through and got away. Such credit as is deserved for the victory at Actium should probably be given again to Agrippa, in view of Augustus' proven incapacity as a military commander.[32]

In other words, Actium seems hopelessly unfitted to be the centre-piece of Augustus' glory; yet it is immensely stressed by the poets. The explanation must be that Augustus, as a great dynast, required glory in war, and he had no choice. All his propaganda could not conceal the fact that he had not been present at the Battle of Philippi (he was said to have been ill), and he had suffered subsequent military setbacks, which had needed to be retrieved by his lieutenants. It says much for his political mastery that he could defeat Antony despite lacking ability as a commander in the field; but for a lord of the world, a Roman Alexander, political skill was not splendour enough. And so the great lie about Actium had to be created: this was the only grand victory to which he could lay claim. Accordingly, it must be represented as a battle against Egypt, a battle on an enormous scale, and a battle won by the supreme mastery of Augustus himself.

[31] Hor. *Epod.* 9 (and cf. *Epod.* 1, anticipating the battle), *Carm.* 1. 37; Virg. *Aen.* 8. 675 ff.; Prop. 4. 6; the lost poem by Rabirius; the anonymous *Carmen de bello Actiaco*; an anonymous Greek epigram (*Select Papyri*, iii (London and Cambridge, Mass., 1941), ed. D. L. Page, 113).

[32] See R. Syme, *The Roman Revolution* (Oxford, 1939), 295 ff. He suggests the possibility of treachery, and that Antony's legions may have been able to bargain for terms before surrendering some days after the battle. His conclusion (297): 'There may have been little fighting and comparatively few casualties . . . Actium was a shabby affair.' A less acid analysis is offered by C. B. R. Pelling in his commentary on Plutarch, *Life of Antony* (Cambridge, 1988), 278–80 (with further bibliography).

So Virgil's picture of the event, like those of the other poets, was fraudulent, and probably he knew it. Yet, within limits, he appears less tied to the party line than the rest. He alone, in the surviving accounts, finds a place for Agrippa; he alone names Antony, and allows that Cleopatra was subordinate to him. These divergences are not, of course, covertly subversive; rather they suggest a mind confident enough to expand as it will, not needing to check narrowly with the Palatine or Esquiline. The fact is that the fabricated Actium story appealed strongly to Virgil's imagination. Of the three grand encomiums of Augustus in the *Aeneid*, we might expect that in the eighth book to be the most constrained, since Actium is the area where the regime would be likeliest to press the poets for what they were not disposed to give. Instead, it is that appearance of Augustus which is best integrated into the poem as a whole: we have seen how firmly Virgil binds his vision of Actium into his sense of Italian identity evolved through the centuries and his feeling for the changes and continuities of history. If he knew that Actium was a myth, it was a myth which he found powerfully engaging. At the end of the eighth book one kind of 'politics' in poetry—praise of the ruler—is fused with political ideology of a wider and deeper kind—the sense of nationhood achieved through historical process and shared experience.

Virgil presented his patron's leader as the central figure in the history of the world, and there is an awkwardness about that which all his skill cannot quite overcome.[33] If he had written in such terms about Tiberius, Claudius, or Nero (we may reflect), he would now be judged more severely. But assessment here is a nice matter. Maybe he was just lucky: he was not to know that posterity would look upon Augustus as the founder of a monarchy that would last for centuries, as the first and probably greatest of the Roman emperors. Besides, in the 20s, when Augustus' health was uncertain, it could not have been predicted that he would enjoy what would prove to be the longest reign of all the western emperors, establishing his governance as an unquestioned fact, since at his death most Romans could not remember a time when he had not been master of their world;

---

[33] Censure is easy, perhaps too easy. Auden's poem *Secondary Epic* adds something more by alluding to the fact that the name of the last emperor in the west, Romulus Augustulus, carries echoes of both the founder and the refounder of the city. If Anchises had really been able to see into the future, Auden implies, he could hardly have overlooked this irony.

this was the pure gift of fortune. But another judgement is possible. We should perhaps allow that Virgil made his own reckoning, calculating that Augustus was big enough, more or less, to sustain the weight of grandeur that the *Aeneid* would lay upon him. At all events, his treatment of the man is political in a sense that ordinary encomium is not. The sixth book somehow brings together the idea of Augustus and the idea of empire in such a way that the two ideas are not easily separated, and such a fusion must have been carefully meditated.[34] The Hellenistic kingdoms had not combined monarchy with a sense of 'patria'. Such a combining of ideas is not obvious, and if it seems obvious to us, it is largely because Virgil has done it so well as to make it appear natural. Part of his originality in panegyric, whether he is praising Italy in the *Georgics* or his ruler in the *Aeneid*, is that he draws it into an ideology.

In the proem to the third Georgic he claims that he plans a future work on the glory of Caesar. Possibly this is a literary game, and the scheme is a simple fiction, as imaginary as the epic which he pretends to have been planning in the sixth Eclogue,[35] but more probably we should regard it as an essentially genuine glimpse of his creative processes. A first reason for this lies in the difference between what he says here and in the Eclogue: it is one thing to pretend to have contemplated a work which has now been abandoned and another to claim to have a future work in mind; in the former case the poet slips from his patron's grasp, while in the latter the patron is offered a promissory note which he may later try to cash. The second reason for believing Virgil is that we do seem to be witnessing a stage in the evolution of what would become the *Aeneid*. The Georgic describes a poem about Caesar which will glance back to a very distant past, relating the origins of Troy; the poem actually written deals with the very distant past, with glances forward to Caesar. It appears, therefore, that we are watching Virgil pondering the problem of how to handle the praise of his master in an aesthetically tolerable way. He has reached the idea of moving between the present and the past, but not yet found the solution of setting the poem as a whole in the past, with Caesar being directly treated in only a very few grandiose passages.

---

[34] Modern discussions commonly treat Virgil's attitude to empire and his attitude to Caesar Augustus as a single issue. That is to be bamboozled by the poet's sleight of hand.
[35] *Ecl.* 6. 3.

The putative work foreshadowed in the *Georgics* is indeed not easy to imagine. Panegyric alone would not suffice; narrative would be needed. To be sure, the great man's history was extraordinary. When the young Octavius heard the news of his great-uncle's assassination, he faced a multitude of difficulties. There were strong and experienced men ready to assume power: Antony, Julius Caesar's right-hand man, and the tyrannicides themselves. Octavius was not even in Italy at the time, but at Apollonia in Illyria, far from the centre of events. He had held no political office. Time would reveal the further weakness of his military ineffectiveness on both land and sea. Against these formidable obstacles he could set one advantage: the dead man's will made him his heir, and henceforth he could bear the talismanic name of C. Iulius Caesar. He was 18 years old, the cards were stacked against him, and he decided to take over the world. And he succeeded.

It was an astonishing story, but it could not be told. To defeat Antony needed exceptional qualities: patience, resilience, a nerve of iron, and supreme political skill. It also required less amiable characteristics: ruthlessness, deceit, the readiness to break alliances when the time was ripe. Much would have to be distorted, or passed over in silence: an encomiast would not wish, like the inconvenient Propertius, to reawaken memories of the Perusine War. Conceivably it might have been possible within the framework of panegyric to tell something of the strange adventure that was this Caesar's life: the poet could have contemplated a hero guided by destiny and the austere duty of vengeance, bearing the burden of responsibility for the future of his people, with patience and virtue overcoming long trials, and triumphing, in sorrow and glory, over the machinations of his foes. Virgil was indeed to create such a hero, but he would be a figure from the mythical past. No doubt that was just as well: dynasts did not care to be represented as fearful, dispirited, or in danger; they preferred to be seen as serenely victorious, prevailing with godlike ease.[36]

We might ask what use Augustus got from the poets. The organization of opinion is a theme inviting treatment in aphoristic prose, sardonic and abrupt. Doubts obtrude.[37] Whose opinions were being

---

[36] It would be interesting to know what filled the three books of Cicero's *Consulatus Suus* and what he expected to find in the Greek poem on his success that he hoped Archias would write for him.

[37] The refined analysis which Syme gives in the last chapter of *The Augustan Aristocracy* (Oxford, 1986) is subtler than his account in *The Roman Revolution*, almost fifty years before. He may be taken as conceding a partial change of view, obliquely offered, *more suo*.

organized? Virgil and Horace did not write even for the greater part of the literate minority, but for a highly educated audience. Such people could not be deceived; they knew. There was indeed propaganda in the triumviral period—squibs and invectives, representing Antony as intoxicated or sexually enslaved, and irritant enough to goad him into an unwise self-defence, 'On His Drunkenness'. But the poets' work cannot be called propaganda in any ordinary sense. We know that Maecenas had acquired Horace by 36 BC, Virgil and Varius a little earlier.[38] His patience was extraordinary. Virgil was allowed to finish the *Eclogues* at leisure, and it would be roughly a decade before he completed his first work for his patron, two thousand lines about farming. Horace (whose entire œuvre was to be remarkably small) spent the 30s mostly on some satires and a handful of epodes —not much for Caesar there; his collection of odes would not be ready for the bookseller until 23 BC. Fifteen years are a long time in revolutionary politics: as propagandists the poets were useless.

Poets might be simply part of the apparatus of magnificence. For great men splendour was a duty, and their ostentation decorated the life of the community. Poetry belonged with other outward manifestations of glory: verses, like statuary and inscriptions, games, triumphal arches, slaves, jewels and diadems, ranked among the trappings of public eminence. Dynasts, if they chose, might deck themselves in poetry as they decked themselves in purple; in such cases display was the essence, rather than persuasion. The surviving works of Messalla's poets may stand as an example: all they really tell us about him is how very grand he is. Even the persons of the poets might serve the purpose of display. When Octavian met Antony at Tarentum, Varius, Virgil, and Horace were summoned to attend him there;[39] it is hard to see what function they were to perform beyond swelling the entourage with which a grandee expected to be surrounded.

Poets could bestow immortality. This was an old theme, revived by Horace in one of his late odes: brave men lived before Agamemnon, but their names have passed into oblivion.[40] A story told that Alexander had visited the tomb of Achilles and lamented not for the dead hero but for himself, since Achilles had had the best of all poets to proclaim his greatness; the Macedonian would have to make

---

[38] The evidence is in Hor. *Serm.* 1. 5 and 6.
[39] As we learn from Hor. *Serm.* 1. 5. Horace tells us that he himself got only as far as Brundisium; we do not know about the other two.   [40] Hor. *Carm.* 4. 9. esp. 25 ff.

do with Choerilus of Iasus, not a genius.[41] Historians and panegyrists had the power to transmit the glory of a name to future generations, if they were good enough, and posterity was surely the audience with whom Augustus was principally concerned. Horace in what is perhaps the most political of his odes—much of his verse on larger themes might better be labelled public than political—makes the point: if you wish 'Father of Cities' to be inscribed beneath the leader's statues, let him have the courage to repress immorality; the task will not be popular, but later ages will praise him.[42] Many years later, when the leader himself wrote the account of his deeds which no poet had composed, he echoed the idea: 'ipse multarum rerum exempla imitanda posteris tradidi' (I handed down exemplary practices in many matters for posterity to follow).[43] That is put in moral terms, but it scarcely bothers to disguise the essential message: 'I offer myself for posterity to admire.'

Yet Achilles and Agamemnon enjoyed undying fame not because Homer had named them but because he had told of their deeds. We may still enquire, therefore, why the subsidized poets were free to write so little, and why so small a proportion of that little was directly about Augustus himself. Maecenas' limitless patience suggests a deeper purpose. His genius was to see that it hardly mattered what the poets wrote, or how much; their freedom was the best prospect of success. If Augustus was to be regarded by future ages as the central figure in a culminating epoch of the world's history, a necessary condition was an efflorescence of literary talent. If the brilliance was there, if the poets were gathered together by a patronage that implied some community of outlook, and if the glory of Augustus was loudly asserted in their verse somewhere, it would be enough, and they could otherwise do much as they chose: Horace could descant on the pleasures of idleness and infidelity; Propertius could even utter some impertinences about the new order. The sheer greatness of Virgil could not have been predicted, and here Maecenas had a stroke of luck; but a part of genius is to spot one's luck and exploit it.

The project succeeded. The Augustan age has indeed been commonly regarded as a climactic era, the adjective 'Augustan' itself coming to signify a consummated civility, and it is a fact of history that

[41] Cic. Arch. 24; on Choerilus, Hor. Epist. 2. 1. 232 ff., cf. Ars Poet. 357 f.
[42] Carm. 3. 24. 25–32.   [43] Res Gest. 8.

this has been due not to the achievements of Augustus himself, however remarkable, but to the literature of the time. In this respect poets
have indeed been, after all, the unacknowledged legislators of mankind; Virgil and Horace were cheap at the price. Augustus is said
to have discouraged literature about himself unless it was serious and
written by the best authors.[44] That seems to show a shrewd assessment of how to appear magnificent to posterity, and not ridiculous,
but the evidence suggests that his touch was not as sure as the story
implies. As Maecenas slips from the scene, the mood changes. In
his first lyric collection Horace can allude to his unfortunate error
in fighting on the wrong side at Philippi with a suavity which com-
pliments the princeps by implicitly attributing to him humour and
worldly understanding,[45] but in the last book of odes he celebrates
the imperial house with a stiff correctness, and in the Epistle to
Augustus there is a new tone of apologetic subservience, almost of
fear: the approach to the man must be gingerly.[46] Maecenas had
recognized, we may suppose, that a little harmless disaffection from
Propertius was of no account—a useful safety-valve perhaps—but
Augustus would eventually use Ovid's verses as a pretext for wreck-
ing his life. Of course, that was many years later, in the crabbed
bitterness of his old age, but it represents the final stage of a development that had begun long before.[47] Among the reasons for the
change we should not forget a very simple one: the habit of abso-
lutism is a poison in the bloodstream, and autocrats become greedy
for adulation. Modern example confirms this truth.[48]

[44] Suet. *Aug.* 89. 3.   [45] See *Carm.* 2. 7. 9 ff. and 3. 14. 27 f.

[46] *Epist.* 2. 1. 1 ff. The fact that earlier Augustan verse was not directly addressed to
Augustus did not change the reality but nevertheless helped to avoid the impression of
obvious servility.

[47] Historians usually reckon that Ovid's verse was not the principal reason for his exile,
and they are almost certainly right, but the significant thing is that that Augustus was prepared to make it one of the charges against him; that tells us much about the emperor's
judgement in his last years. Ovid sometimes hints in his exile-works at what he will not
quite say openly: that as a poet he has the power to make Caesar look a fool.

[48] Among recent cases that of Brezhnev is especially instructive (those of obvious monsters and megalomaniacs—Amin, Bokassa, Saddam—are less so): a man astute enough to
remain leader of a superpower makes himself absurd by having vacuous honours constantly
paid to him. 'Fontenelle has ridiculed the impudence of the modest Virgil. But the same
Fontenelle places his king above the divine Augustus; and the sage Boileau has not blushed
to say, "Le destin à ses yeux n'oseroit balancer." Yet neither Augustus nor Louis XIV
were fools' (Gibbon, *Decline and Fall*, ch. 44). Perhaps it was like taking a hot bath: one
knows that the warm water entertains no sincere feelings towards one, but the sensation
is still pleasant.

Early in his reign, too, Augustus was not perfectly assured in his style of presenting himself, but here he may have learnt a lesson that endured. The autobiography in thirteen books which he wrote in the 20s included polemic and apologia, carping at the senate, defensive about his private life.[49] Far different is the *Res Gestae*: here is no narrative or self-justification but a dazzle of splendour, as Augustus proclaims his achievements one after another; it does not describe, it declares. Many things had happened between the time that he wrote his first memoir and the completion of the *Res Gestae*; among them was the *Aeneid*. Virgil is the first to treat Augustus at length in words without description or narrative but simply in a blaze of almost superhuman glory; in the eighth book, indeed, Augustus at Actium is not a living human being but a figure on a shield, so that he may be caught and held at one moment of supreme magnificence. This was better than telling the story of Caesar, and the man himself surely knew it; no poet would be paid to write a *De Augusto* or *Sebasteid*, and his own final self-summation would be lapidary, like panels of sculpted relief.

We do not naturally think of the *Res Gestae* as poetic, yet at moments we may see him responding to the stimulus of the literary imagination. Horace had anticipated conquests in Britain and Persia, far-flung and exotic nations, where action could not have been seriously contemplated.[50] Augustus was unable to gratify so wild a hope, but like his poets, he puts less emphasis on the striking achievements of his reign nearer to home—in Spain, for example—than on more indecisive and rather pointless activities in vastly distant lands. He submits to the romance of geographical remoteness, and follows Virgil's practice, displayed in some climactic passages, of pressing to the edges of the known world at different points of the compass simultaneously. His fleet (he declares) had sailed to the far north, to German regions where no Roman had gone before; his armies had penetrated in Ethiopia as far as Nabata and advanced in Arabia to the bounds of the Sabaeans and the town of Mariba. Charydes and Semnones sent embassies; envoys came from kings of India, never before seen in the camp of any Roman general, and friendship was sought by Scyths and Bastarnae and kings of the Sarmatians who live by the river Don.[51]

---

[49] The surviving evidence is collected in E. Malcovati (ed.), *Imperatoris Augusti operum fragmenta* (4th edn., Turin, 1947), 84–97; cf. F. Blumenthal, 'Die Autobiographie des Augustus', *WS* 35 (1913), 267–88, esp. 270.   [50] *Carm.* 3. 5. 3 f.

[51] *Res Gest.* 26 (where army action in Spain, Gaul and Germany is briefly recorded), 31.

Poets and sculptors shaped the image of Augustus, literally in figures, figuratively in letters. 'Image' had not been a concern of the early rulers of Greece: they were keen to project their fame to posterity but show no particular interest in preserving the impress of their individuality. The first 'image' perhaps belongs not to a ruler but an intellectual: Socrates. We all know what Socrates was like, physically and mentally, or at least we believe we do, and it is that belief which is significant. The literary portraits—by Plato, Xenophon, and Aristophanes—are each different, and one is satirical, but they share the sense that he was not only a thinker but a personality. The early Plato's idea was that Socrates' teaching should emerge as the product of a distinctive character.

Alexander was the first to link individuality of character and physical appearance to the arts of command; he is also the first clean-shaven man in Europe. These two phenomena are connected. He took with him historians and literati to record his acts and behaviour; around him cluster *legomena*, sayings and anecdotes. If these were often invented, it would be of no great account: the important thing was that he should be the sort of man about whom legend and reminiscence should gather. Not only his great deeds were to be recalled but his particular personality: the world should be shown an image. Part of that image was his *pothos*, longing or desire, a pining after new worlds and new experience, and this idea enters his visual image too. The sculptors conform to a pattern: those long romantic locks, the head inclined slightly to one side, the eyes staring yearningly into an unknown distance—and the beardless face, suggesting that the conqueror sustains through manhood a youth's passion for adventure.[52] Even in the midst of battle on the Issus mosaic, a Campanian copy of a Greek painting, he keeps the romantic melancholy, the great wide eyes, the long careless hair. Was the picture true? who can say? But as an image it was unforgettable.

The Roman dynasts were haunted by Alexander: this was the man against whom they measured themselves. Pompey modelled his career on Alexander's from the start; even the sobriquet Magnus, 'the Great', acknowledges the influence. Flatterers assured him that his piggy features resembled Alexander's, and sculpture showing him with a hairstyle apparently imitating the Macedonian's suggest that he hoped to believe this implausible claim. Julius Caesar wept

[52] Cf. A. Stewart, *Faces of Power: Alexander's Image and Hellenistic Politics* (Berkeley and Los Angeles, 1993). On Alexander's *pothos*: V. Ehrenberg, *Alexander and the Greeks* (Oxford, 1938), ch. 2 (52–61).

when he saw Alexander's statue in a Spanish temple, lamenting how little he had himself achieved; Trajan was to boast that he had outdone Alexander in the places to which he had carried his armies; Augustus had Alexander's portrait on his signet ring, and made a show of visiting his tomb when he came to Egypt.[53] But Augustus was the Roman Alexander as Propertius was the Roman Callimachus— that is, with a difference. The poets' treatment of their Greek models does indeed form an instructive parallel. Aeneas is an Achilles and an Odysseus, and yet also is not, for he bears a new kind of responsibility for his city, people, and descendants. Horace 'Romanizes' Alcaeus in the Cleopatra Ode. The Greek had begun, 'Now we should get drunk', and exulted at the death of a tyrant who had been a private enemy. Horace changes this to 'Now let us drink' (Nunc est bibendum); the celebration will be a sacred feast of the Saliares, a national priesthood, the wine will be a noble Caecuban from 'ancestral cellars', and the dead tyrant Cleopatra is declared to have threatened Rome itself. Alcaeus' personal feud is solemnized by being given a public and patriotic dimension.[54]

We may see Augustus' image in a similar light. His statues, like Alexander's, all have the same face. We all know what he looks like, or at least we think we do (he was actually small, spotty, and weak in the leg, with bad teeth and hair that could not quite be called fair).[55] Like Mao Tse-Tung's, his face does not alter with the years: he is godlike in his immutability, superbly monarchical, aloof. As with Alexander, the pose and features vary little, and yet there is a difference. In place of those flowing tresses, the hair is close to the head, the lips drawn narrowly together, the brow severe and tightened by something that might be care. It is not, like Alexander's, an adolescent face, but suggests a kind of timeless late youth or early middle age. Alexander (so the images tell us) is wrapped up in his private romance; Augustus bears the weight of public responsibility, for the Roman race and empire. The image is regal, yet not exactly serene; majestic but austere.

Austerity, even sombreness, is an authentic part of the early-Augustan tone. We meet it in Livy's preface, where he reflects that

---

[53] Pompey: Sall. *Hist.* 3. 88 M; Plut. *Pomp.* 2; hairstyle: P. Zanker, *Augustus und die Macht der Bilder* (Munich, 1987), 20. Julius Caesar: Suet. *Jul.* 7. 1 (cf. P. Green, 'Caesar and Alexander: Aemulatio, Imitatio, Conparatio', *AJAH* 3 (1978), 1–26). Trajan: Dio 68. 29. 1.

[54] Alc. fr. 332 LP; Hor. *Carm.* 1. 37. 1 ff.   [55] Suet. *Aug.* 79 f.

his generation can bear neither their own vices nor the remedies needed to combat them; we meet it in Horace, who ends his grandest sequence of patriotic odes with contemplation of the black fear that the Roman race may slide into an ever deeper degeneracy.[56] We do not find this kind of pessimism in Virgil, who is more hopeful about society and its morals than the other loyalists; however, where his hero's lot seems bleak and joyless, we should regard him as entirely consonant with the official tone, and not at odds with it. Augustus' image is both refulgent and severe; and yet even this is not the whole truth, for he has two images. Roman dynasts, such as Lucullus, Pompey, and Antony, had long presented different faces at home and abroad; in Greece and the east they were monarchs, accepting the quasi-divine honours paid to Hellenistic kings, while at Rome they preserved the semblance of republican forms and manners. Where Augustus is new is in presenting both faces in the same place. On the one hand, he restores republican forms, calls himself 'princeps', 'first citizen', lives in a modest house, and wears homespun clothes, requiring the ladies of the imperial family to toil over their wool so that the ruler of the world may appear unassuming.[57] On the other, the monuments of monarchic magnificence are already under construction in the 20s: the sacral title Augustus, the colossal, overbearing tomb rising by the Tiber—and the *Aeneid*.

We might say that one image is for his contemporaries, the other for posterity; but in a sense the two images are not incompatible, as we may learn from the more recent case of Chairman Mao, the boiler-suited god. We may also contemplate the twists of human psychology: it is vanity that leads autocrats to stress their modesty. The significance of Augustus' simplicity may be seen from the example of his two principal ministers, both of whom, in their very different styles, fit the pattern, Agrippa by his show of a rough, uncultivated manner, Maecenas by refusing to assume the rank of a senator. Others might struggle for the outward marks of distinction: the man with real power could afford to pass them by. When Petronius has Trimalchio boast on his self-epitaph that he could have held office in Rome but chose otherwise, fiction follows life: the actions of Maecenas and Sejanus had silently declared the same.[58] Any shows of splendour that Augustus declines are as eloquent of his authority

---

[56] Livy *praef.* 9; Hor. *Carm.* 3. 6. esp. 45 ff. (cf. the tone of *Carm.* 3. 24. 25 ff.).
[57] Suet. *Aug.* 73. But grand clothes were kept for special occasions.
[58] Petr. *Sat.* 71.

as the grandest titles and the broadest purple stripes. Yet he seems to have been in a fashion sincere: much in his career attests to a genuine wish to restore the sober decencies of the past. Whereas so many of his policies were designed to secure public favour, he pushed forward his moral programme despite its unpopularity.

The Augustus of the *Aeneid* conforms to the godlike image, radiant and remote; yet the epic also embodies a portrait of the dogged, dutiful leader who sustains the burden of his people's manifest destiny in the person of Aeneas himself. A poem directly on the subject of Caesar might have shown him wrestling manfully with the problems that beset him; the poem which Virgil wrote leaves the great man free to blaze brilliantly in a few dazzling tableaux, while honouring him by associating him with an ideal of devoted leadership which it represents by other means. Aeneas can sometimes be awkward, hesitant, uneasy or cruel, as Augustus in a praise poem could not have been, and yet still exemplify a serious and well-founded conception of the good ruler. And thus the *Aeneid* does more for Augustus than a poem *De Caesare* could ever have done, for it can both glitter on the surface and give depth to the Augustan idea of governance.

But Virgil's service to his master's reputation has in the event proved to go deeper still. Augustus' luck was to find his name linked to a profoundly evocative conception of man, society, nature, and history, one which was shaped by the *Georgics* as well as the *Aeneid*. The Altar of Peace, dedicated by Augustus in 13 BC, effectively acknowledges as much. One side depicts Aeneas and the portent of the sow, described in Virgil's eighth book. The hero is a grave presence, no longer young; the style in which his torso is carved imitates fifth-century Greece; his beard displays him as an archaic figure, from a distant past; but his head veiled for the sacrifice is prophetic of the customs of future Rome. The sobriety, the echoes of classical Greece, the sense of a present that has evolved out of a long history recall the *Aeneid*. The spirit of the *Georgics* is felt in another part of the altar's iconography: a female figure probably representing Earth, but possibly Peace, Venus, or Italy, with fruits in her lap and around her corn and flowers, a sheep and an ox, signifying the produce of a bounteous land.

The ideology into which Augustus found himself drawn possesses richness and complexity. It is a serious ideology: Virgil has a better understanding of social and political reality than Cicero. It is more alien to us than Cicero in its indifference to representative institutions and forms of government; this is partly because Virgil is a poet, not a philosopher, but also because he seems content with an unchecked autocracy. It presents a vision of man's relationship to his community, state, and nation; it has an organic conception of society as drawing coherence and pleasure in itself from prizing the land which it inhabits and from shared experience over long time. It is conservative in the sense that it affirms the value of custom and tradition, progressive in its evolutionary idea of the nation as an entity which undergoes change—change in its physical boundaries, change in the peoples from which it is comprised. It is progressive too in viewing the processes of history as essentially beneficent and ameliorative: it is not pessimistic or despondent, but has the flexibility to enjoy the charms of the past while recognizing much in earlier ages which needed to be chastened or reformed. It is poetic, but also realistic and psychologically acute, in appreciating the importance of sentiment and imagination in the making of a good society. Its feeling for the interpenetration of nature and culture in human experience is loving; and it offers an intimation of how men might be happy.

This book, by virtue of its subject, has indeed been drawn towards some of the more heartening elements of Virgil's imagination; but it has not denied his sadder and darker side. That more sombre aspect is not, however, in danger of neglect, for throughout this century there has endured, through many changes of fashion, what remains in essence the late nineteenth-century view of Virgil as himself a Victorian poet *avant la lettre*, a Tennysonian aesthete, languidly and compassionately melancholic, shedding warm soft tears as he contemplates the perennial sorrows of humanity. Such an interpretation, while missing his toughness and vigour, contains a solid measure of truth; it becomes misleading, though, when sadness and melancholy are confounded with rooted disillusionment or despair.[59] When Virgil laments, it does not mean that he thinks the world contains nothing but misery; he is more mature, various, and flexible—and simply more interesting—than that.

---

[59] A considered view of life need not be—is not likely to be—straightforwardly positive or negative: the case of 'Christian pessimism' is instructive. Though in some sense Christianity, for obvious reasons, must be 'optimistic', there has been Christian thought of sombre cast, stressing the ineradicability of sin and the unlikelihood of social improvement (and in some ages expecting the eternal damnation of most of mankind). A philosophy which believes that the ultimate reality is good may often be grave, and may even be bleak.

We may also reflect that the pessimist interpretation of Virgil is at odds with the view of him that has predominated for most of the two thousand years since he wrote. Augustine and Dante, Milton and Dryden surely did not underestimate the grief and compassion in his poetry, but they also saw him as a confident proclaimer of the imperial order.[60] We should at least pause to listen to earlier generations, for there is a certain provincialism—a provincialism not of place but of time—in the assumption, so commonly and casually made, that the academic culture of our own age has achieved an understanding of literature denied to the great minds of the past. We may also suspect that there are forces extraneous to Virgil's poetry which could tempt the modern reader to hear him as a pessimistic voice.

One of these is political. Augustus has been seen as a forerunner of the twentieth-century dictators, a classical Mussolini, and some of the poet's admirers have been eager to detach him from such a monster, an aim achieved by depicting him as in some degree a critic of the Augustan idea. More broadly, many people today tend to assume that the ideologies of monarchy and imperialism are necessarily shallow or dishonest. But there are also academic influences at work. Modern criticism has been fruitfully concerned with ambiguity and ambivalence, terms which have been freely used in this book. But like all good things, these terms can be overdone, and their charms have lured some critics into being unable to find in any texts any tones that are not equivocal, subversive, or unsettling. At worst this leads to an impoverished sense of literature's possibilities.

A further influence is the prestige attached to tragedy, and here moral and literary fashions are both in operation. On the moral side the 'tragic view of life' is accorded more reverence than it deserves.[61] On the aesthetic side, tragedy is commonly regarded as the highest

---

[60]   Tennyson himself in his poem *To Virgil* depicts a Virgil less Tennysonian than is often supposed.

[61]   Thus J. Griffin, *Homer* (Oxford, 1980), 46: 'The tragic view of life is, alas, more deeply true than the view which sees straightforward poetic justice in the working-out of events, and that in part is why the *Odyssey* cannot equal the insights of the *Iliad* . . .' Actually, poetic justice is found in most great works of tragedy, including the *Iliad*, and real life is full of happy endings. That apart, there is a huge leap from recognizing that much is wrong in the world to adopting a 'tragic view' of life as a whole. The phrase was made current by Unamuno's *Del sentimiento trágico de la vida en los hombres y en los pueblos* (1913), but the roots of the sentiment lie in late 19th-cent. agnosticism. It offers profundity at a cheap rate ('more *deeply* true . . .') and lends the denial of redemption an appearance of manly maturity. Thomas Hardy makes a good example, and Orwell's retort—that his philosophy was not tragic but querulous—is just. It is a quirk of human nature that ease and prosperity

form of art. That is perhaps too lightly assumed. Maybe there is nothing in literature better than the *Iliad* or *King Lear*, but there are also very great works which are not tragic in any degree at all—*De Rerum Natura*, the *Georgics*, *The Marriage of Figaro*, *The Mastersingers*—and others which, while containing tragedy, are not tragic in their totality: *The Divine Comedy*, the *Oresteia*, indeed, if we view it entire, Beethoven's Fifth and Ninth Symphonies, *Parsifal*.[62] Even if tragedy is the highest form of art, it is at the least clear that literature which is not tragic can reach such heights that we should feel no need to force those works which we most admire into the tragic genre.

As a literary form, tragedy stands quite separate from the tragic view of life. It is a means of presenting and interpreting the suffering which all of us, whatever our moral and religious beliefs, know to be part of the human lot. As Aristotle knew, tragedy is different from horror. Those things which in our everyday discourse we readily call tragic—earthquake and famine, the torture and murder of innocents—are not, within literature, the matter of tragedy at all: they are too ghastly. Tragedy requires a kind of greatness, and that greatness resides not merely in the literary form, nor in the quantity of suffering depicted, but in its quality; tragedy is concerned not with the most pain that can be imagined but with the manner in which it is experienced and understood.[63] Further, the greatness of tragedy distinguishes it not only from sheer horror but from pathos.[64] Pathos is not necessarily less affecting than tragedy: we have seen indeed that Creusa's farewell is supremely moving in part for the very reason that she avoids the tragic note.

---

breed indulgence in the 'tragic view'. Orwell again: 'What is less obvious is just *why* the leading writers of the twenties were predominantly pessimistic . . . Was it not, after all, *because* these people were writing in an exceptionally comfortable epoch? It is just in such times that "cosmic despair" can flourish. People with empty bellies never despair of the universe . . .' ('Inside the Whale').

[62] The musical examples are included for the sake of the observation that music critics do not seem to be embarrassed, as their literary counterparts often are, by the expression of confidence, serenity or joy. Nor are art critics anxious to underplay the joyousness in some works of (say) Titian or Tiepolo. There is a certain parochialism in those literary scholars who search for the half light upon all occasions.

[63] Compare A. J. A. Waldock's remarks on Sophocles: 'Antigone is of tragic stature: Creon does not approach within hail of it . . . his talent for suffering is not vast' (*Sophocles the Dramatist* (Cambridge, 1951), 123, 125).

[64] The distinction is nicely brought out by Tovey's observation that contemporaries objected to the titles of Brahms's *Tragic Overture* and Tchaikovsky's *Symphonie Pathétique* but that in either case the composer knew best (*Essays in Musical Analysis* (London, 1935), ii. 151).

Tragedy is not intrinsically truer than other forms of artistic expression, but in any case it is not clear that literature should be a vehicle of 'truth' in the ordinary sense of the term; truth in some sense, maybe, but one which resists simple definition and which perhaps we do not yet well comprehend. This consideration takes us to what is plainly for some readers a further incentive to find Virgil discontent with his world: the amiable wish that a great poet should be true in his moral outlook—that is, that he should think more or less as we do. But the purpose of reading is not self-congratulation: what we should seek in literature is not our own ideas but a great idea, and indeed one reason for studying great literature is to enlarge our understanding of the human heart and mind by entering into views of the world alien, even repugnant, to those that we cherish ourselves. The morality of the *Iliad* is one which we should condemn, were anyone to espouse it today. What matters, though, is not that Homer's idea should be 'true', at least in the ordinary sense, but that it should be deep; and this his readers understand well enough. Dante's conception of power and authority—Shakespeare's too, indeed—is unattractive to our notions, and this too their readers understand. But we pay the Augustans the backhanded compliment of expecting them to know better. We seem still to be prisoners of the perceptive half-truth popularized by Matthew Arnold: that certain periods of ancient history—the fifth century in Athens, for example, or the first century in Rome—were peculiarly 'modern' epochs.[65] This idea is not false, but it can be misleading. If we seek in Virgil, or in any ancient Roman, the sort of humanely liberal enlightenment that we find so pleasing as we contemplate it in ourselves, we are destined for disappointment.

Virgil himself articulates his conception of man, nature, and history partly through comparison and contrast with poets whose outlook is far different from his own—Hesiod, for example, and above all Homer. In measuring his epic against the *Iliad* and *Odyssey*, he was not concerned only with local effect but with clarifying his distinctive vision of the world. Sometimes, of course, the comparison shows us the Homeric sparkle quenched in darkness, as in Dido's story; but with an epic as austere and solemn as the *Aeneid* the abiding comparison, if we take the work as a whole, must be with the *Iliad*. That poem is indeed tragic to the core, but there is an enormous buoyancy and vitality about it none the less. And the buoyancy

---

[65] Arnold, 'On the Modern Element in Literature'.

and the tragedy, strange though it may at first sight seem, are part and parcel of each other. Consider the famous simile of the leaves, inserted into a warrior's speech rather inorganically, as though the poet intended a significance beyond the immediate context:[66]

As is the generation of leaves, so is that of men also. The wind scatters the leaves on the ground, but the forest burgeons and puts forth more, and the season of spring comes round. Even so one generation of men puts forth and another ceases.

Leaves die; but (and herein lies the idea's profundity) the spring will come again and other leaves grow in abundance: growth and freshness are the themes with which the simile comes to its close. When Mimnermus took up the likening of man to leaf, he spoke of spring and fall, but not of the coming of another spring; the languor of a pessimistic hedonism replaces the Homeric energy. Virgil in the *Aeneid*, Dante in his *Inferno*, carry the theme on with similes describing the fall of the leaf; Milton describes the leaves already fallen.[67] Homer alone looks onward to nature's everlasting power of renewal. Life, the *Iliad* declares, is charged with vigour and glory; this is wonderful and yet terrible, for there is nothing, at least nothing worthy desire, once life is done. Vigour and energy are everything and death is the negation of vigour and energy. Worse still, life can only be lived at its fullest height at the risk of being cut brutally short, for the finest thing in life, the supreme expression of human greatness, is war. Battle is *kudianeira*, glorious, but it is also cruel, miserable, and humiliating. Therefore the hero's condition is both immensely desirable and immensely grievous and the poem itself radically tragic.[68] And this is the terrible vision against which the *Aeneid* of set purpose measures itself.[69]

[66] *Il.* 6. 146–9.

[67] Mimn. fr. 2; Virg. *Aen.* 6. 309 f.; Dante *Inf.* 3. 112 ff.; Milton *Paradise Lost* 1. 302 ff. On the leaf simile in these and other classical poets see Jenkyns, 'Unconscious Classical Sources of the *Divine Comedy*', forthcoming in *IJCT* 1998.

[68] Everyone knows that the *Iliad* is tragic; for an argument that it is still more radically tragic than the dominant strand of modern interpretation has allowed, see Jenkyns, *Classical Epic: Homer and Virgil* (London, 1992), 19–31.

[69] The *Iliad* may well come nearer than any other great poem to justifying us in talking about a 'tragic view of life', but even here the term does not seem entirely apt. The poem does indeed find tragedy embedded in the nature of things, in the indissoluble bonds that tie death and wretchedness to the highest human possibility. The hero's situation is fundamentally tragic; but most people have no chance of being heroes in the Homeric sense. And even among this exclusive group, some will survive to prosper: Diomedes, for instance, and Odysseus.

What should be stressed, at all events, is that the view that life is flat, stale, depressing, empty, or meaningless is not a 'tragic' view, however qualified. This at least is the antithesis of the *Iliad*'s idea.

Let us then cast a Homeric light upon what have been seen as some striking expressions of Virgil's pessimism. In his very first paragraph he reveals that his theme will be a man of outstanding virtue pursued by Juno's unforgetting anger, and he concludes with the question, 'tantaene animis caelestibus irae?' (Do heavenly spirits feel such rage?).[70] There is no answer, only silence before he resumes, after the pause, in quite another tone.

It sounds despairing, but it is not. Against the bleakness of that cry he sets Jupiter's assurance, some two hundred and fifty lines later, that Juno will change and come to cherish the Roman race.[71] Though many will suffer greatly before she can be induced to relent, ultimately her purpose can be altered. In the *Iliad*, however, we learn that Hera and Athena will remain implacable until Troy's utter destruction. We have only to carry Virgil's question across to the *Iliad* to realize that Homer could not have asked it or thought of asking it. The answer is too obvious: of course the gods bear such resentments, and resentments still worse. We may recall the ghastly coolness of the scene in which Hera asks Zeus for Troy's ruin. She offers a concession. Three cities are dearest to her, she says, Argos, Sparta, and Mycenae. Zeus may destroy them whenever he chooses; she will not begrudge them to him.[72] That is how Hera treats even her favourites; Virgil's Juno is mild in comparison. His protest may be baffled and sorrowful, but it is something that he can protest at all, expressing shock and an appalled wonderment at what the *Iliad* takes for granted.

At the other end of the poem he utters another unanswered question:[73]

> tanton placuit concurrere motu,
> Iuppiter, aeterna gentis in pace futuras?

Was it your will, Jupiter, that peoples who would live in everlasting peace should clash in so great a shock?

The lines are characteristic in fusing the notes of triumph and melancholy into a single phrase: so much waste of life and passion, futile to all appearances; and yet so noble a future. The pathos is joined with the expectation of better things, and that good expectation dominates in the end, as the sentence reaches its climax with the words asserting the everlasting peace that is to come. In view of the

---

[70] *Aen.* I. II.   [71] *Aen.* I. 279–82.   [72] *Il.* 4. 51 ff.   [73] *Aen.* 12. 503 f.

centuries of conflict between Rome and her Italian neighbours, we may feel that there is some *suggestio falsi* here; when we consider how different a picture of the future Virgil could have painted, we may hear how deliberately the sadness is balanced by a strongly affirmative note.

Even in these impassioned lines he finds a place for the prospect of political progress, a theme which we have observed quietly pervading much of the poem. In anachronistic terms: Homer is a tory, Virgil a whig.[74] But there is always a risk that whiggishness may become priggishness, the picture of moral and social advance too bland, and Virgil shows signs of recognizing the danger. Jupiter's majestic prophecy, a paean to future Roman glory culminating in Caesar Augustus, ends with eager savagery, as Furor is displayed bound with a hundred brazen chains, howling and dribbling blood.[75] This symbolizes peace and order triumphant, and like medieval pictures of St Michael and the serpent, it does so with a lusty ferocity. Jupiter's peroration could easily sound complacent (as perhaps it is); Virgil shrewdly gives a harsh edge to the trumpets' blare.

This passage shows that harshness need imply no questioning note; but in other places the poet's message is indeed severe, as when Pallas, about to face Turnus and knowing himself outmatched, prays to Hercules for aid.[76] The god hears him, but can only groan and weep. Jupiter consoles Hercules 'with kindly words' (dictis . . . amicis), but the consolation is austere:[77]

> 'stat sua cuique dies, breve et inreparabile tempus
> omnibus est vitae; sed famam extendere factis,
> hoc virtutis opus.'

Each man's appointed day stands firm, and the span of life is short and irrecoverable for all; but to spread one's fame by one's deeds—that is valour's task.

Many sons of gods fell before Troy, Jupiter continues, his own child Sarpedon among them; Turnus too will shortly meet his end. The god turns his eyes away from the battlefield, and Pallas is soon dead.

By making Jupiter recall Sarpedon's lot, Virgil draws attention to his model in the *Iliad* with an explicitness that goes beyond his usual

---

[74] Separately, these judgements have been made before. 'I am . . . a violent Tory of the old school;—Walter Scott's school, that is to say, and Homer's' (Ruskin, *Praeterita* 1. 1); 'The *Aeneid* is a whig poem' (J. W. Burrow, *A Liberal Descent* (Cambridge, 1981), 197.
[75] *Aen.* 1. 294–6.   [76] *Aen.* 10. 457 ff.   [77] *Aen.* 10. 466, 467–9.

practice and thus invites us to contemplate the Homeric scene with some care. Zeus, seeing that Sarpedon will fall to Patroclus, reflects whether he should save him. Hera charges him not to, adding the placatory suggestion that he bid Sleep and Death carry the body back to its home in Lycia. Zeus complies, shedding tears of blood upon the ground to honour his dear son.

Sombre though Virgil's scene is, it is not as comfortless as Homer's. Zeus weeps, to no avail; Jupiter does not weep, but rather answers Hercules' tears with stoical consolation. His tone is not far from the hard bare realism of Horace's lament for Quinctilius: 'durum; sed . . .' (It is hard; but . . .).[78] Life is brief and irrecoverable, there is no dodging that bitter fact; but—'sed' again—the brave man has a task to do. The sentence is shaped so that it too moves towards an affirmative conclusion. Posthumous glory, Jupiter asserts, is indeed a goal worth striving for. Though the heroes of the *Iliad* do exhibit a concern with their future fame, no Homeric god or hero strikes quite this note of exhortation and moral uplift. In the *Iliad* it is indeed Sarpedon who most plainly sets out the heroic condition, and this may be why Virgil introduces his name. He reminds Glaucus that the two of them are honoured above other men by the Lycians, who look upon them as gods and give them seats of honour, more wine, the best of the meat, and so on. Therefore they must fight in the front line of battle, so that the Lycians may say that their rulers are not without fame.[79] Sarpedon is not speaking about duty or loyalty to others, and indeed he goes on to say that if they could be ageless and immortal, he would not fight among the foremost himself nor urge Glaucus into glorious battle. It is not, then, for the Lycians that he is fighting: his part in the warfare is, in an ordinary sense, quite useless, and the tragic paradox of the hero's lot is that it is his very mortality which compels him to engage in battle, without the prospect of doing any good to himself and his people. It is a conception of extreme bleakness. Jupiter's praise of stoical valour, stern but bracingly moral, is consoling in comparison.

Perhaps we should remember, too, that the scene among the gods before Sarpedon's death is of the first importance in the poetical economy of the *Iliad* because it foreshadows the moment before the death of Hector himself. Once more Zeus ponders whether to save a man dear to him; this time it is Athena who answers, repeating

---

[78] *Carm.* 1. 24. 19.   [79] *Il.* 12. 310–28.

three lines from Hera's speech, but omitting her placatory addition.[80] The echo of the earlier scene brings out the hopelessness of Hector's situation, a hopelessness deepened by the terrifying lightness of Zeus' brief reply: cheer up, he tells the goddess: he was not talking seriously. So casually can the supreme god handle a man he likes. The gods treat men not as wanton boys treat flies, but rather as they treat their toys: they love them, play with them, abandon them according to their pleasure. And Hector achieves nothing by his end: he faces the humiliation of panic and death, but gains no advantage for his people thereby; instead, as Priam rightly tells him, his killing will ensure the destruction of his family and city.[81] Once again, it is a situation of starkest tragedy; once again, when we consider how much Aeneas finally achieves for his people, his descendants and even himself, we can see how much less stark is Virgil's picture.

Whereas the *Iliad* typically pushes towards an extreme, the *Aeneid* commonly brings out a tension between opposing forces. We have already contemplated the Sibyl's rebuke to Aeneas when he wishes to spend longer with Deiphobus: 'We squander the hours in weeping' (nos flendo ducimus horas).[82] Compassion pulls in one direction, resolution in another. A little earlier Aeneas has met the spirit of Palinurus, unable to cross the river, though innocent, because he lies unburied; such is the divine ordinance. The Sibyl's voice is stern: 'desine fata deum flecti sperare precando' (Cease to hope that the gods' decrees may be turned by prayer).[83] But then she offers some comfort: '*sed* cape dicta memor, *duri* solacia casus' (But take and remember these words, a solace in your hard lot).[84] Here again are the two words that we met in Horace's lament for Quinctilius. The ode is impressive in its reticence: 'durum; sed levius fit patientia | quidquid corrigere est nefas' (It is hard; but patience makes lighter what it is not lawful to amend).[85] 'Levius' is all the indication we are allowed: there will be some alleviation, but we do not know if it will be great or little, swift or slow. To ask whether Horace is optimistic or pessimistic seems an irrelevance: he simply states the nature of things, barely.

Virgil's lyric pathos is more expansive than the ode, but he resembles Horace in the opposition between hardness and a comfort of uncertain scope. The juxtaposition of 'duri' and 'solacia' is

[80] *Il.* 22. 166–87.   [81] *Il.* 22. 38–76, esp. 56 f. and 60–5.
[82] *Aen.* 6. 539; see above, p. 190.   [83] *Aen.* 6. 376.
[84] *Aen.* 6. 377.   [85] *Carm.* 1. 24. 19 f.

terse and strong. Then the Sibyl speaks four more lines in which she promises Palinurus high honours: the peoples of the territory where he met his death will raise a mound in his memory and make yearly offerings; the place will bear his name forever. Then we hear the spirit's response:[86]

> his dictis curae emotae pulsusque parumper
> corde dolor tristi; gaudet cognomine terra.

At these words his distress was taken away and the pain driven from his sad heart for a while; he rejoices in the land that will bear his name.

There is a continual fluctuation of feeling in these two lines. First we hear that Palinurus' sorrows are removed, in the vigorous rhythm of 'his curae emotae'; but then comes the pathetic qualification, moving in its economy, of 'parumper', a word which Virgil uses here only. The progress of the sentence draws us back into the dead man's grief (dolor tristi . . .), but then—following another strong juxtaposition, 'tristi gaudet'—his joy is once more asserted, and that is the note on which we leave him.

Virgil brings a tension between divergent impulses even to the patriotic culmination of Anchises' show of heroes:[87]

> excudent alii spirantia mollius aera
> (credo equidem), vivos ducent de marmore vultus,
> orabunt causas melius, caelique meatus
> describent radio et surgentia sidera dicent:
> tu regere imperio populos, Romane, memento
> (hae tibi erunt artes), pacique imponere morem,
> parcere subiectis et debellare superbos.

Others, I do not doubt, will beat out bronzes that breathe more softly, will draw living faces from marble, will plead cases better, will trace with their rod the courses of the sky and tell the rising of the stars: do you remember, Roman, to rule the nations by your authority (these shall be your arts), to build custom upon peace, to spare the humbled, and in war put down the proud.

We shall feel the pang in the first part of this sentence the more if we hear the Roman cliché that lies behind them.[88] Of course

---

[86] *Aen.* 6. 382 f.   [87] *Aen.* 6. 847–53.

[88] e.g. Cic. *Flacc.* 9: 'However, I say this about the Greeks in general: I grant them literature, I allow them skill in many arts, I do not deny their charm of speech, keenness of intellect and richness of utterance' etc.; but they lack 'religio' and 'fides'. (The double way in which they were regarded is developed at 61 ff.: the 'true, unimpaired Greece' of the past is contrasted with the degenerate present, and there is warm praise of the beauty and glories of Athens: the city's fame still sustains the nation's broken reputation.)

the Greeks were first rate at art and philosophy and that sort of thing; it was fine for a young man to spend some time in Athens acquiring a polite culture; but as far as the manly virtues were concerned, the life of action and ambition, of politics and war—well, the Greeks were poor creatures enough. With a modesty born of condescension, one might allow, *de haut en bas*, that captive Greece had taken her rude conqueror captive,[89] but only because one was sure, deep down, that Rome was best at the things that mattered most.

These were plump, comfortable sentiments, but by Virgil they are sharpened to poignancy. He implies a close connection between the Roman supremacy in arms and their inferiority to the Greeks in the things of the mind. 'Non omnia possumus omnes,' he had written in an early poem:[90] no one people can be the champions in every field, and the shape that the Romans' character had taken, fitting them for empire, must always deny them the highest mastery elsewhere; their destiny had exacted its cost.[91] Gone is Cicero's sanguine belief that the Romans could match the Greek achievement by converting it into Latin and making it their own. Others will be better orators (how Cicero would have hated that); there is no qualification, no prospect that this state of affairs can ever change.

Not only must the Roman pay a price for his glory but that price is heavy. Here too Virgil departs from the mass of his countrymen: he will not blandly assume that the business of sculpture, astronomy, or whatever is manifestly a lesser splendour than the work of empire. How seductive he makes that statuary appear: the writing has been vigorous in the previous lines, culminating in a quotation from Ennius, the thumping monosyllable of its last word archaically robust.[92] Now the language turns softly mysterious as in curious phrases he calls forth the beauty of art. The Greeks become magicians almost, miracle workers: the bronzes breathe, the marble lives beneath their hands; to anticipate Ovid's myth, they turn into a race of Pygmalions, warming a multitude of statues into life. Indeed with

---

[89] Hor. *Epist.* 2. 1. 156 f.   [90] *Ecl.* 8. 63.

[91] The cost is that of taking second place to the Greeks: the contrast between them and the Romans is in terms of glory. Virgil does not say—and his language is incompatible with his saying—that the Romans must renounce art and culture; see above, Ch. 7, n. 35.

[92] *Aen.* 6. 846 (= Enn. *Ann.* 363 Sk, with one word changed and one letter altered in another word): 'unus qui nobis cunctando restituis rem' ([you] who singly restore the state by delaying).

the word 'ducent' we watch the actual process of metamorphosis, the gradual transformation of brute stone into humanity. 'Mollius', 'ducent'—it is all so delicate, so strange.[93]

Who now shall say that the cost of empire has been cheap? And yet Virgil does not leave the matter there, in a soft, wistful ambivalence. In such a place as this we may see how like the poet of the *Aeneid* is to the poet of the *Eclogues*; and how unlike. The greatness of the passage is that the softness and wistfulness remain, and yet are caught up and carried along by a rhetorical momentum of fierceness and power. Its full effect cannot be felt in isolation: we need to look both forward and back.

In the early part of his enormous speech Anchises is thoughtful of Aeneas: 'Look,' he says; 'Do you see?' 'This is the man promised you.'[94] But later the father seems to forget his son. The sight of Pompey and Julius Caesar overcomes him, and he cries out to them to hold back from civil war.[95] The two dynasts are left unnamed: Aeneas can have no idea of what the old man is talking about. 'Who could pass you by in silence, great Cato, or you, Cossus?' Anchises asks a few lines on.[96] 'Why not?' his son might reasonably reply. He must be bemused by all this: what's Cossus to him or he to Cossus? This is no inadvertence on the poet's part, as we can see from the similar effect at the end of the eighth book, where Aeneas gazes upon the shield depicting his descendants' history, with pleasure but 'rerum ignarus', not knowing what he sees.[97] Here likewise it is Virgil's deliberate purpose that Anchises should eventually leave Aeneas far behind, as we can see also from his last vocative, 'Romane'. For whom is he addressing? Not his son, who is not a Roman and never will be: Virgil has made it clear that centuries will elapse between

[93] Tentatively one might suggest another conclusion. Anchises says nothing about poetry; perhaps Virgil wanted concision here, or perhaps he refused to acknowledge another people's superiority in this field. But we may wonder whether he would have wished, even on behalf of Lucretius and himself, to dispute the crowns of Homer and Aeschylus. May it not rather be that in the very silence about poetry there is another stab? Anchises cannot bring himself to identify the Greeks by name—'others', he says; and likewise perhaps the thought that in poetry too, even in poetry, the Greeks will forever stand supreme is too unkind for utterance.

For a judicious assessment of this and other interpretations see H. Hine, 'Aeneas and the Arts', in M. Whitby, P. Hardie, and M. Whitby (eds.), *Homo Viator* (Bristol and Oak Park, 1987), 173–83, at 178 ff.

[94] *Aen.* 6. 771, 779, 791 ('aspice', 'viden', 'hic vir, hic est, tibi quem promitti saepius audis'). [95] *Aen.* 6. 832–5.

[96] *Aen.* 6. 841. [97] *Aen.* 8. 730.

Aeneas' death and Rome's foundation.[98] The speech begins coolly; the excitement and agitation grow as it proceeds; at last under the immense rhetorical pressure that has been forced into the verse the contextual framework breaks open and Anchises projects himself out of his proper position in time and space to exhort the distant future.[99] Out of the past, out of the dead, across a thousand years and from another species of existence, he calls to each and every Roman; here, now, in the empire of Caesar Augustus. Rightly understood, that 'Romane' is the most dramatic word in Latin literature.

Aeneas' visit to the underworld ends on a dying fall, with the lament for Marcellus, a passage which is aesthetically incoherent unless the poem fully accepts the worth of the Roman destiny. You cannot make a long diminuendo unless you begin forte; you cannot turn your mood to melancholy if you are melancholy already. It is because Virgil has reached a towering height of emphatic assertion that he makes Anchises pause at this point and gives him another five lines to make the transition towards Marcellus. Here we can admire his consummate mastery of transition for the last time: it was a right instinct that led him to drop gradually to the elegiac note. Yet we do not need Marcellus to show us the strength of affirmation at the end of Anchises' speech: form and content are married in it, and the moral meaning is shaped by the aesthetics of climax. It would be poetically meaningless to impose on Anchises the mighty illogicality of addressing the present day if all he is going to say is, 'Well, Roman, your destiny will be a second-best, and an equivocal one at that.' He has worked himself up across nearly a hundred lines into a vast enthusiasm: whatever he says now must be charged with power. If we look at that final sentence alone, the same moral emerges. Its first limb concerns the Greeks, its second the Romans; the second part answers the first, and indeed outsoars it in the monumentality of the last line and a half, reaching its climax in the heavy, sonorous syllables of 'debellare superbos'.

These final words fall with a massive weight. If anyone doubts this, let him make an experiment. Let him read the sentence, giving a melancholy or dubious inflection to its last clauses. It can hardly be done without discomfort. Now let those concluding lines be read with an eager, emphatic hardness; at once the rhetoric falls into place.

---

[98] With especial emphasis at *Aen.* 1. 272–7. Nor will Aeneas ever have the task of governing an empire.

[99] For the singular 'Romane' in solemn public exhortation compare Hor. *Carm.* 3. 6. 2.

The last line begins by recommending clemency to the conquered, and it would be wrong to deny the importance of mercy in Virgil's scheme, but it is no less wrong to quote the words 'parcere subiectis' on their own, without completing the sentence: that is to shirk the severity and complexity of his idea. Anchises looks to the future, but Virgil is describing Roman history as it has actually been. He knew what 'debellare superbos' meant: devastation, slaughter, and enslavement; captives dragged in chains through the Roman streets and strangled in a dungeon.[100] In the fierceness of this ending, as in the seductiveness with which the Greek achievement is evoked, he shows that he knows the price to be paid. The entrancements of the sentence's beginning do not suck the force from its conclusion, for loss and gain are in equilibrium, and everything in these lines is charged with an exceptional intensity: the price is great, the reward is great, and the almost musical balance between the two limbs of the sentence enforces the message that the greater the price, the greater the reward will be. The strength of the passage is due to this: that Virgil counts the cost and counts it fully; and yet he accepts.

Let us consider an analogy. Imagine a back-bencher sitting in the House of Commons in 1940. He is not only a politician but a literary critic, and unfortunately he is a bad literary critic. As he hears the new Prime Minister declare that he has nothing to offer but blood, toil, tears, and sweat, he says to himself, 'Notice the ambivalence, the doubt and the questioning; the sensitive listener can tell that Churchill's heart is not wholly in the struggle', and he quits the chamber in a state of cultivated despondency.

Now plainly this story is absurd: nobody responded to Churchill's oratory in that fashion. Instinctively everyone knew that in counting the cost he made his sentiments stronger and fiercer, the determination keener, the ultimate triumph more glorious. A similar moral can be drawn from a purely literary analogy. Dante records the words inscribed over the gates of Hell.[101] They occupy three stanzas exactly.

---

[100] According to Tacitus, the virtuous Germanicus declared that the peoples between the Rhine and the Elbe had been 'debellati'; he had insisted on massacre: there was no use in prisoners, only the extermination of the race would put an end to the war (*Ann.* 2. 21. 3 and 22. 1). Nothing is sweeter than victory, says Cicero, and the surest evidence of victory is to watch one's enemies being led in chains to their execution (*Verr.* 2. 5. 66). Compare too the toughness in the Roman idea of 'pax' (see above, p. 494). It should be unnecessary to observe that no Roman could have taken 'parcere subiectis' to mean that every opponent should be forgiven the moment he has laid down his arms.

[101] Dante, *Inf.* 3. 1-9.

The first of these proclaims the pain and ruin that lie beyond, the third the eternity of the punishment. In between comes perhaps the most terrible sentence in all the *Divine Comedy*: justice moved God to create Hell, the inscription declares; divine power made it, supreme wisdom, and primal love. Love created all this torment; the paradox is appalling to contemplate.

Passing across Acheron, Dante meets the inhabitants of Hell's first circle; the eternal air trembles with their sighs. Who are these sorrowing multitudes? the lustful? the cruel? Not at all: these are the virtuous pagans, who did not sin, but are punished only because, being born before Christ's coming, they could not worship God aright. 'For no other fault are we damned,' Virgil explains, concluding, 'Without hope we live in desire.' Great grief seizes upon Dante at these words.[102]

There is one interpretation of this passage which nobody (one supposes) has yet put forward. It goes like this. 'Dante cannot have swallowed the medieval church's harsh dogmatism whole; it would be crude to suppose so. Instead we have something more complex and ambivalent. The inscription on the gate makes the sensitive reader aware of this, for anyone can see that however great a man's sins, eternal suffering must of necessity be a punishment greater than the crime. Through the words about primal love the poet's doubts about God's goodness are still more clearly heard. The undercurrent of protest and subversion is even plainer in what follows: the first of the damned are good men; Virgil trembles and grows pale when he thinks upon the anguish of Hell's denizens; Dante weeps with pity for Francesca. There is a tension between the poet's public voice, loudly asserting God's love and justice, and a private voice, tremulous with doubt and sorrow. That tension is far richer and subtler than a rigid triumphalism could be. To represent Dante as an uncritical propagandist for this God is to degrade him.'

Since this argument is similar to claims commonly advanced about Virgil (with Augustus and the Roman empire taking the place of Dante's God), it is worth asking why we so immediately reject it. Partly we do so because of external evidence derived from Dante's life and other works, but a more interesting reason lies within the poem itself. The terror and beauty of his paradox depend upon its being accepted literally and without flinching. If we try to resolve

---

[102] Dante, *Inf.* 4. 25–45.

the paradox into an irony, the glory and tragedy disappear, and an easy sneer at the Deity takes their place. So too with the just pagans, or the doomed lovers Paolo and Francesca. The wonder and horror inspired by their fates come from a recognition of God's love and justice; they are tragic, and not merely melodramatic, because they are so sympathetic and yet so rightly condemned. In purely aesthetic terms Dante's conception, with its moral and intellectual rigour, proves better than hesitations, doubts, and questionings.

To be sure, Virgil does not have Dante's adamantine framework of theological doctrine, but the analogy may at least cause us to ponder whether we do him a service if we suppose him to be at all times elusive and unsure. The *Eclogues* are indeed masterly in their delicate ambivalence, but at their close the poet hints at his awareness that their exquisite equivocations could take him only so far.[103] His next poem was written in emulation of Lucretius, the expounder of a dogmatic system. Sometimes Lucretius sets out the views that he is to reject with superb eloquence, only to ride over them by calmly affirming the truths of Epicureanism. He describes the worship of Cybele or the laments of those who dread extinction in terms that make us for a while enthralled by the goddess or assured that death is an evil; and then he corrects us.[104] It is a rhetorical technique of great power, in which giving the other point of view is not the enemy of dogmatic assertion but subsumed into the larger argument: the more eloquently falsehood is allowed to speak, the more impressive is the capacity of philosophy to confute it. Virgil learnt from Lucretius: whereas he tends to leave ambivalences in the *Eclogues* unresolved, in the *Georgics* he catches them up into the affirmation of confidence, love, and pride. He approaches his paean to the glories of his country by way of describing the wonders which other lands possess and Italy lacks; then he declares that Italy surpasses even such marvels as these. This pattern of thought, worked out in the *Georgics* across sixty lines or more, is at the end of Anchises' speech compressed into a mere seven. We might put the case like this: ambivalence does not disappear from Virgil's later poetry—on the contrary, it develops into still subtler or richer forms—but in the process it is incorporated into a larger whole in which strength of assertion finds its place along with complexity and refinement of sensibility.

[103] See above, pp. 190 f.
[104] Lucr. 2. 600–60, 3. 894–930. On the latter passage, see above, p. 276, and for a fuller analysis of this technique in Lucretius Jenkyns, *Three Classical Poets*, 130.

Here is one more way in which his career curiously combined change and continuity: just as his Alexandrianism stayed with him throughout his strange metamorphosis from neoteric virtuoso to epic bard, so too he remained the master of ambivalence all the while that he was transforming himself from the conjuror of faint, fleeting beauties to the hierophant of imperial power.

Nowhere is the interplay of confidence and questioning in the *Aeneid* more complex and searching than at its close.[105] Virgil's finale is a unique combination of density and rapidity: probably no other long poem whistles through so much narrative incident in its last lines;[106] none surely introduces so much new turbulence, moral and emotional, so near to the end. It is harsh and abrupt, yet complete. Meanwhile, the comparison with Homer, which might be thought to have outlived its usefulness, offers in the concluding scenes fresh insight into the poem's vision of history and providence. Let us look closer.

Priam and Achilles come together in the last book of the *Iliad*, but there is no reconciliation between the human actors in the last book of the *Aeneid*. Some readers, struck by this contrast, have deduced that Virgil's mood is harder or more bitter than Homer's. But this is to take a superficial view, to undervalue both the tragedy in Homer's conception and Virgil's imaginative understanding of it. For the ending of the *Iliad* is a resolution which is no resolution. On one level it appears that the last book is full of wrongs put right, of wounds bound up. Achilles displays a generosity which seems unique to himself: no other hero, we feel, would have chosen, unbidden, to return a part of the ransom to the man who had paid it. The rhythms of life, disrupted by the hero's wrath, are restored. Achilles, who has not eaten, now eats and compassionately urges Priam to eat; Achilles, who has refrained from sexual contact, is last seen lying with Briseis; Hector, who has been denied his funeral rites, now receives them in abundance: the women keen over him one after another, the body is burned, the tomb raised, and the poem ends, almost like a fairy tale, with a glorious banquet in the halls of Priam.

---

[105] Virgil has to kill Turnus (any other outcome would feel sanctimoniously high-minded, as well as being poetically flat); it does not follow that Aeneas must. The present discussion will not address the much debated question of the morality of Aeneas' last actions (except for one detail): it is concerned with the relation of the poem's ending to its broader scheme.

[106] But one might compare Tovey's observation on Beethoven's Ninth Symphony: 'The orchestra rushes headlong to the end. Even here there is no waste of energy . . . The very last bars are a final uprush of melody which happens to be quite new and might easily have been an important theme' (*Essays in Musical Analysis* (London, 1935), ii. 45).

But upon a deeper consideration there is no comfort, nothing soothing, in these closing scenes. Think of Priam's final words to Achilles: for nine days let us mourn Hector, he says, on the tenth day let us bury him, on the eleventh day let us raise a mound; and on the twelfth day we shall fight, 'if so it must be'—*ei per ananke*.[107] There is despair in this: 'if', says Priam, and we know that the wish is hopeless. Must it be?—yes, it must. Nine days, ten, eleven, twelve: we hear time moving remorselessly on. The *Iliad* ends with feasting; the *Iliad* ends poised on the brink of hell. In structural terms the conclusion is slow, ample, and complete; in immediate personal terms the encounter of Priam and Achilles does honour to human nature; the contrast between these things and the horror to come is incomparably tragic.

Virgil understood this very well, for is it not clear that he has inverted Homer's scheme? In the *Aeneid* there is in the actual narrative no reconciliation between the hero and his adversaries, no funeral of Turnus, no marriage with Lavinia, but we know that these things are to come. Virgil faced a difficult technical problem: how was he to end the story after Aeneas' victory? Noble speeches of forgiveness would seem flat and tedious, and the poetry would be likely to feel self-satisfied in its consciousness of virtuous magnanimity.[108] Besides, Aeneas and Lavinia have never met and mean nothing to each other, while her mother has killed herself sooner than see them betrothed: their encounter is rich in possibilities of embarrassment. But Virgil has turned his difficulty to advantage: promising reconciliation in advance, he leaves himself free to compose an ending without parallel for speed, density and excitement. Even within this final scene there is a comparison with Homer's story not to Aeneas' disadvantage. At intervals throughout the *Iliad* there are scenes of supplication on the battlefield, growing in emotional force and culminating in Hector's plea to Achilles that his body be returned for burial and not defiled by the Achaeans' dogs.[109] Every one of these appeals is denied; the only human supplication granted in the poem is Priam's to Achilles in the last book. Turnus supplicates Aeneas, as Hector supplicated Achilles; but there are also significant differences.

---

[107] *Il.* 24. 664–7.
[108] The 'thirteenth book of the *Aeneid*', composed by the Italian humanist Vegius and printed in many early editions of Virgil, is eloquently uninteresting. Some have worried about Aeneas' wedding night. They could have spared themselves anxiety: he spends it in antiquarian discussion with his new father-in-law.   [109] *Il.* 22. 338–43.

Turnus declares that he has deserved to die and does not beg for life (Hector had said neither of these things); he then asks Aeneas to pity his father Daunus, to return the body to his people, to prolong hatreds no further.[110] Virgil is moving with such rapidity that he does not pause to tell us if this supplication is granted, but he does not need to, for we are sure that it is. In the midst of passion and violence, he can admit a glimmer of better things.

More importantly, the whole of the last scene among men lies under the shadow of the last scene among the gods, which reconciles Jupiter and Juno. And what a reconciliation that is. The old pattern is to be broken and a new order to begin: a new race is to be formed; a great goddess is to change and come to the support of her former enemies.[111] There is to be reconciliation among men,

---

[110] *Aen.* 12. 931–8. He does indirectly suggest to Aeneas the possibility of mercy (12. 935 f.): 'et me, seu corpus spoliatum lumine mavis, | redde meis' (Return me or, if you prefer, my body stripped of life, to my people). Compactly, but also with great care, Virgil sets out three data significant to the moral economy of this last scene: Turnus, on his own account, has deserved to die; he wants to be spared; he does not directly ask to be spared.

[111] It is debated how fully and immediately Juno commits herself to Rome: some take Virgil to imply that she will not be completely on the Roman side until after the Punic Wars (see D. C. Feeney, 'The Reconciliations of Juno', *CQ* NS 34 (1984), 179–94, and E. L. Harrison, 'The *Aeneid* and Carthage', in T. Woodman and D. West (eds.), *Poetry and Politics in the Age of Augustus* (Cambridge, 1984), 95–115). But the 'inconcinnity' which Harrison finds in Virgil's picture can be accounted for by the illogicality of syncretic polytheism: it is a fact of history that Juno was both a great Roman goddess and (being identified with Tanit) the presiding deity of Carthage. Another possibility is that in this as in some other cases different parts of the *Aeneid* are imperfectly consistent, either because Virgil tolerated some inconsistency for literary effect or because the poem is unrevised. But whether the transformation of Juno's attitude be reckoned fast or slow, it cannot be denied that transformation there is, or that the reconciliation between men is permanent and complete.

However, it seems best to suppose that Juno, while maintaining her hostility to the Trojan name and culture, now commits herself fully to Latium and Rome. We may note her joy at the news that she will be honoured by the Romans above all other people; (840 f.) honour is what gods demand above all things from mankind, and no god can respond to such a prospect except by reaching for it with open arms. Line 827 is also vital: 'sit Romana potens Itala virtute propago' (Let the Roman stock be mighty through Italian valour). It is strained to fancy this spoken in a grudging tone; rather it marks a rhetorical climax. The crucial (and unexpected) words are 'Itala virtute'. Juno goes far beyond what she needs to say; her imagination grasps the poet's own conception of Rome and Italy intertwined. Virgil is psychologically true in this best of his divine scenes: he does not let Juno go soft, and her thought leaps back to the detested Trojans, with whom her speech ends. Her zest for Roman power and her hatred of Troy are both felt with the passionate intensity of her nature. This gives the poet's own patriotism a fierce lustiness and a keen edge. (Feeney, *The Gods in Epic*, 147 n., objects that 'It will not do to quote the first two of these three lines [826–8] only, and present them as some kind of celebration by Juno, as does Jenkyns . . .'; he quite misses Virgil's complexity.)

as among gods; not a brief evening's encounter, as in the *Iliad*, but an alliance 'in everlasting peace'.[112] The *Iliad* ends with ritual and feasting, but deep down nothing has changed. The *Aeneid* ends with an act of violence, but deep down everything has changed. Which of the two endings, in the larger view, offers the kinder prospect? Which is the more essentially tragic? The answers are plain. Nowhere perhaps did Virgil use the Homeric comparison more finely than at his poem's close. The contrast offered by the stark tragedy of the *Iliad* and the dramatic harshness of the final lines together enable him to blend ferocity with the brighter gleam beyond, and through that blend to present a view of man and history which is serious and realist, neither complacent nor glibly pessimistic.

The *Aeneid* brims full with the deaths of fine and lovely youth: Dido, Marcellus, Nisus and Euryalus, Lausus, Pallas, Camilla, Turnus —such waste, such grief. Yet most of these figures are treated with an elegiac pathos rather than with truly tragic effect. Marcellus, Lausus, and Pallas are not like Homer's Achilles and Hector, or Sophocles' Oedipus, or Hamlet or Lear: they have charm and beauty, not greatness; they are not torn by internal struggles; they face no lacerating dilemmas. Their deaths are not necessary or inevitable—Euryalus especially is a pitiable fool, who brings about the destruction of his lover and himself—but sad side-effects of the advance of the Roman destiny. Further, though these fair young men die, they die to some purpose. There will be progress: Trojans and Italians are alike imperfect, and from the merging of the two races a new and better people is to be formed. We have this from the highest authority, Jupiter himself:[113]

> hinc genus Ausonio mixtum quod sanguine surget,
> supra homines, supra ire deos pietate videbis, . . .

You shall see the race which springs from them, blended with Ausonian blood, rise above men, above the gods, in devotion . . .

To this great end the war proves to have been essential. The *Aeneid* is not on the whole outstandingly skilful in its plotting, but the plot twist here is one of the finest in all literature. We had supposed that Juno's malignancy was merely an impediment to the providential purpose, but it is now suddenly revealed as the means of effecting the mixed outcome that we ourselves most desire: victory for Trojan

---

[112] *Aen.* 12. 504.   [113] *Aen.* 12. 838 f.

arms and Italian institutions. Troy's success is the cause of Juno's change of heart, and it is through the concessions granted to her in return for that change that Italy can triumph in defeat, retaining its language and customs and advancing towards a more excellent future. Dante saw the truth when he imagined a coming saviour for his land:[114]

> Di quell'umile Italia fia salute,
>   per cui morì la vergine Cammilla,
>   Eurialo, e Turno, e Niso di ferute . . .

He shall be the salvation of that lowly Italy, for which died the maiden Camilla, Euryalus, Turnus, and Nisus of their wounds.

Both sides are intertwined in this list of names: not only Turnus and Camilla, but two Trojans also. They all died for Italy, Dante says; and he is right.

Dido is without question a tragic figure; it is not certain that there is a second such. What of Aeneas himself?[115] Let us reckon up the balance. He loses Creusa and Dido, gaining only Lavinia, who is nothing to him.[116] He loses Troy. He gains a kingdom, which according to the first book he will enjoy for only three years, though the sixth book may imply a longer reign.[117] He is left with a son, with victory, with the assurance of lasting fame; and he will become an *indiges* after his death, a deity of the Italian nation.[118] Does this amount to a tragic lot?—'bleak' might be a better word, though in the light of his future apotheosis even this may seem too strong. On the other hand, a darker thought suggests itself; perhaps Aeneas' last misfortune is that after all he has endured, he is not permitted to be a tragic figure; that final splendour is denied him. Such a paradox would be worthy of Virgil's subtlety. At all events, he does not find tragedy embedded in the heroic condition as such. In another generation Aeneas might have been happy and glorious in Troy; that is one

---

[114] Dante, *Inf.* 1. 106–8.

[115] And what of Turnus? One supposes that Virgil wanted him to provide the tragic element in the poem's second half, as Dido in the first, but if so, his execution did not match his intention. Turnus is not quite interesting enough to be properly tragic, and we hardly ever see beneath his surface. A particular obstacle is the difficulty of understanding whether he is driven by natural impulse or controlled by supernatural agency.

[116] Ovid saw the mischievous possibilities: Lavinia, jealous of Dido's memory, would surely be quick to suspect her husband of an affair with Dido's sister, now arrived in Latium (*Fasti* 3. 629 ff.).

[117] *Aen.* 1. 265 f., 6. 764.   [118] *Aen.* 12. 794.

reason why the loss of his city is such a sorrow to him. Even as it is, his sufferings are the product of his peculiar destiny, not of a hero's common lot; but for the unique burden laid on him, 'to stablish the Roman race',[119] he might have been comfortably resettled, like Acestes in Sicily, or Helenus and Andromache in Epirus, or with a loving wife in Carthage. But Achilles and Hector and Sarpedon are tragic of necessity: in the *Iliad* tragedy is the very stuff and significance of the hero's being.

In terms of literary tradition and national history alike Virgil both looks back to the past and reaches forward to distant eras that are yet to be: he sees himself and his land within the great continuum of time. In the *Georgics* he imagines unborn generations, aeons on, reading his praise of Caesar, and a distant posterity gazing in bemused wonder on the Roman dead of the civil wars.[120] He raises the question of how a remote futurity will regard his work and his epoch; and we have the power to answer him. Dante has already spoken; it shall now be Milton's turn. Though Tennyson has often been called the most Virgilian of English poets, that is true, if at all, only of surface; deep down, there is nothing more Virgilian in our literature than the end of *Paradise Lost*. Adam and Eve are cast out of Eden:[121]

> They, looking back, all the eastern side beheld
> Of Paradise, so late their happy seat,
> Waved over by that flaming brand, the gate
> With dreadful faces thronged and fiery arms.
> Some natural tears they shed, *but* wiped them soon:
> *The world was all before them*, where to *choose*
> Their place of rest, and *Providence their guide* . . .

Amid ferocity and desolation comes a kinder note, quiet but firm. Milton had in mind the account of Jupiter's purpose in the *Georgics*.[122] He has shown us the loss of paradise, and yet he sees, as Virgil had seen, that despite that loss—indeed because of it—a whole new world of action, choice and discovery lies before the human race. He invites comparison with the *Aeneid* also. Of course there are large differences. Milton has been handling the supreme, indeed the only tragedy of mankind, to which all the woes that have afflicted humanity since are but a corollary; the sufferings in the *Aeneid*, great

---

[119] *Aen.* 1. 33.   [120] *Geo.* 3. 47 f., 1. 493–7.
[121] *Paradise Lost* 12. 641–7.   [122] *Geo.* 1. 121 ff.

though they be, are incidental to the hero's final victory. Milton describes failure softened by a good providence, Virgil success shadowed by sorrow. And yet:

> supra homines, supra ire deos pietate videbis . . .

> The world was all before them . . .

For all their unlikenesses of theme, temper and belief, they have this in common, that they are yea-sayers, they affirm: beyond the ruck and reel of immediate and painful circumstance, the further vision is of hope.

APPENDIX

Labor Improbus

The paragraph in the first Georgic, running from lines 118 to 159, which describes the loss of the golden age and man's subsequent history, has been much debated and diversely understood;[1] this appendix therefore offers a more detailed argument for the interpretation given on pages 335–40. One sentence has been especially controversial:[2]

labor omnia vicit
improbus et duris urgens in rebus egestas.

Three lines of interpretation seem worth consideration:

A. The words mean that toil and the pinch of need drove men on, with the result that they succeeded in defeating the obstacles before them. A laboured translation might be, 'Tiresome toil and the pressure of need amid hard circumstances conquered all.' On this account the sentence continues and sums up the account of progress in the preceding ten lines: man discovered agriculture, fire, astronomy, carpentry, metal-working, then the various arts—in short, through effort, impelled by the goad of need, he got on top of his circumstances. This was the standard interpretation in earlier generations; among recent scholars, R. D. Williams, Huxley, and Wilkinson adopt it.[3] Let us call it the progressive interpretation. (It is better not to label it 'optimist', since it is compatible with a pretty dour view of man's lot.)

B. The meaning is that trouble and neediness came to dominate man's life: to borrow Thomas's (partial) translation, 'Insatiable toil occupied all areas of existence.' On this account the sentence looks back to a point rather earlier in the paragraph, where Virgil describes how Jupiter destroyed the golden life of old. This is the interpretation adopted by Altevogt, in the fullest examination of the question,[4] and it is accepted by most recent commentators: Richter, Thomas, and (probably) Mynors.[5] Possibly we should

---

[1] It is misleading to call the passage 'Virgil's Theodicy', not only because this implies a Christian concern to justify the ways of God to men that Virgil does not have, but also because the divine motivation plays only a small part in the passage, which is centred upon the consequences for humanity. [2] *Geo.* 1. 145 f.

[3] L. P. Wilkinson, *The Georgics of Virgil* (Cambridge, 1969), 141.

[4] H. Altevogt, *Labor improbus, eine Vergilstudie* (Münster, 1952).

[5] Mynors's commentary is delphic; in his lectures he was plainly of the pessimist school.

reckon it the orthodox view at the present time. Let us call it the pessimist interpretation.

C. In principle at least, we might consider some combination of A and
B. Klingner's account could perhaps be put under this heading, though it
seems better to regard it as a modified form of A.[6]

Let us now examine the arguments put forward in favour of B:

1. This is the argument on which Thomas relies. He maintains that A
is wrong because '(a) in this poem (as in life) toil does *not* overcome all
difficulties . . . (b) the realities of *labor* and its susceptibility to failure provide the major theme of the poem . . .'

To this it can be answered that (a) the *Georgics* contains plenty of statements which are not easily reconciled to a strict logic, and a few which,
at least on the face of it, are flatly incompatible; and (b) the argument rests
on a view of the poem as a whole which will seem to many misguided,
or at least one-sided. As a rule, it is seldom satisfactory to try to solve the
problems of a particular passage by reference to very general considerations.
But the decisive answer to this argument is (c): that there is nothing in
the progressive interpretation incompatible with the rest of the poem. The
sentence (on this view) does not imply that hard work has removed every
awkwardness and made life comfortable: it refers back to the invention
of arts and crafts in the distant past, and maintains that these gave man
mastery over all his various areas of endeavour. Did he need food? He
invented farming, trapping, hunting, and fishing. Did he need to travel?
He invented boats and the science of navigation. Did he need tools? He
devised metal-working—and so on. There is nothing in this to deny that
man may have to labour constantly and face painful setbacks and disasters,
and thus nothing incompatible with the *Georgics* as a whole. We may conclude that there is no substance in this argument.

2. 'Labor omnia vicit' is to be compared with 'omnia vincit amor; et
nos cedamus amori' at *Ecl.* 10. 69 ('Love conquers all; let us too yield to
love'). Just as love has man in its power in the Eclogue, compelling his
submission, so do 'labor' and 'egestas' in the *Georgics*.

At first sight this seems a strong argument; upon further reflection it looks
less good. Let us presume that 'vinco' can be translated 'conquer' or 'defeat'.
'Love conquers all' in the Eclogue presents no problem. In another context the meaning might be that lovers' wills are so strong that they can
overcome every obstacle to their desires' fulfilment, but in this place the
meaning is plain: no one can resist the power of love over himself. Now
consider the context in the *Georgics*. We have ten lines describing one human
discovery after another, culminating in the statement 'Toil conquered all'
or 'toil defeated all'. What would this mean to an English-speaker? Surely

---

[6] Klingner, 203–5.

that toil overcame the difficulties in man's way. Could he understand 'toil conquered (*or* defeated) all' to mean 'toil ruined men's lives'? It is well-nigh impossible. We may notice that the pessimist school has to resort to paraphrase to convey what it supposes to be the significance of the words, whereas the translations given here and under A above, though stilted, stick close to the Latin. Now it is open to the pessimist interpreters to argue that the range of meaning covered by 'vinco' is sufficiently different from English 'conquer' or 'defeat' for these translations to mislead, but the burden of proof is plainly on them, and it is pretty clear that such an argument could not be sustained. So the parallel does not work in the way that the pessimist interpreters believe; it may even be an argument in favour of A. Virgil may well have had the parallel consciously in mind, in which case it is between forces which dominate man's mental experience and determine his behaviour: in the *Eclogues* that force is, characteristically, love; in the *Georgics*, no less characteristically, the sterner *labor*-and-*egestas*. It might be noted, more subjectively, that the context in the *Eclogues* is by no means disagreeable: the surrender to all-powerful love has a voluptuousness about it. In other words, a reader of the *Georgics*, recalling the phrase in the *Eclogues*, is not going to say at once, 'Oh no, here's *another* ghastly thing coming along'; rather, 'Ah, here's another driving-force for mankind; I expect the mood will be tougher than in the *Eclogues*.'

3. (*a*) 'egestas' is necessarily a pejorative word. (*b*) 'labor' is not necessarily pejorative, but in association with 'egestas' it becomes so: Egestas and Labos (an archaic variant of 'labor') are among the dread forms that Aeneas meets in the underworld.[7]

(*a*) is certainly correct; Servius auctus comments that 'egestas' is worse than 'paupertas', since 'paupertas' can be honourable, whereas 'egestas' is shameful.[8] (*b*) should perhaps be qualified, as we shall see, but it may at least be allowed that 'egestas' (like 'improbus', which we shall consider shortly) reminds us of the unpleasant connotations of labor. It is also true that Virgil can use 'labor' to mean something like 'woe'—compare English 'toil' in such usages as the 'toil and trouble' of Shakespeare's witches—and this must be roughly the meaning at *Aen.* 6. 277.[9] Not too much should be made of these lines, though: some of the personified abstractions in

---

[7] *Aen.* 6. 276 f.

[8] 'peior est egestas, quam paupertas: paupertas enim honesta esse potest, egestas enim turpis est.'

[9] This sense of 'labor' may perhaps help us with one of the most perplexing passages in Virgil: Jupiter's speech at *Aen* 10. 104–13. 'sua cuique exorsa laborem fortunamque ferent' (111 f.) is commonly taken to mean 'let each man's efforts bring him his task and allotted outcome'. More probably 'labor' and 'fortuna' are in disjunction to each other: 'woe' and 'success'. One might translate, 'Let each man's efforts bring him ill fortune or good.' A consequence of this would be that 'fortunam' in 112 carries a meaning very different from that of 'fata' in 113; some take them as near synonyms.

it, like Sleep, are made grim only by the context; Labos here seems sure to have a meaning somewhat different from that which it bears in the passage which we are investigating; and 'labor' and 'egestas' are not an obvious pair. It may be that a memory, conscious or unconscious, of the *Georgics* led Virgil once more to put the words in close proximity, and this in turn confirms what 'improbus' has in any case made certain: that Virgil wants us to feel some disagreeable connotations to the idea of 'labor'.

In sum, the advocates of B are right to find pejorative language in the sentence. But this is not necessarily an argument against A. 'Egestas' is not, after all, unqualified: 'duris urgens in rebus egestas' is very much a single concept, conveying the idea of the pressure of need. The idea that some-thing in itself unpleasant may have good consequences is not a difficult one (compare the English saw, 'Necessity is the mother of invention', though 'egestas' is sharper than 'necessity' in modern usage), and though needi-ness in itself may be a bad thing, the driving force produced by neediness can be seen as good. So 'egestas' cannot of itself be used to refute A.

4. Altevogt has demonstrated that 'improbus' must be a pejorative word: it cannot be translated (for example) 'unflinching' or 'unremitting', but must carry the idea of blame.[10] It might fairly be argued that the case here is different from that of 'egestas' on two grounds. (*a*) 'egestas' is basically a descriptive word. To make a comparison: 'hunger and 'thirst' are pejorative words—they denote states which we know to be unpleasant—but they are descriptive none the less: it is not a matter of opinion that a man in the Sahara without water is thirsty. (They can also be said to have pleasant consequences: 'He enjoyed the drink immensely because of his great thirst.') 'Improbus', by contrast, is purely evaluative, and without descriptive con-tent: to say that something is 'improbus' is precisely to find fault with it. And the word is emphatically placed. (*b*) It is common ground between A and B that the whole sentence refers back to the distant past. But B supposes the beginnings of a state of affairs that has persisted ever since: toil and misery overspread everything in consequence of Jupiter's acts, and mankind is toilsome and miserable to this day. The progressive interpreta-tion, however, refers 'egestas' to a situation that is over and done with. Virgil has been developing a version of the hard-primitivist myth: the life of early man was poor and needy, and that drove him to strive for the discovery of arts and crafts which would improve his lot. In other words 'egestas' was a pressure that led to discoveries which removed, or at least mitigated, 'egestas'. But the same cannot be said of 'labor'. Virgil has in fact coalesced two ideas in the preceding lines: the 'labor' needed for the invention of crafts and the 'labor' needed to practise them after they have

---

[10] Contrary to Servius, and to *TLL*. Huxley translates 'unremitting drudgery'—fairly, since the blame is conveyed by the noun. But 'unremitting labour' or even 'unremitting toil' would not do.

been invented. So the 'labor' which (according to A) overcame difficulties remains a permanent part of the human condition. In any case, since 'labor' is such a central theme of the poem as a whole, we are bound to refer the word here to the world that we know. And it is this which is labelled, emphatically, as 'improbus'.

All of this seems true, and indeed important, but not to counteract the case for A. In considering the effect of 'improbus' here, we may begin with a general consideration: a pejorative word may be used in a favourable sense, and for the very reason that it is pejorative. That may sound paradoxical, but it is true to common experience. The word 'naughty' in 'naughty knickers' or 'naughty but nice' is a case in point: something is being recommended for the very reason that it is indecent or improper or self-indulgent. 'Tough' is used in the school playground in this way; or compare the Glaswegian usage, 'hard man'. Anyone who supposed that the adjectives in these cases were synonyms for 'strong' or 'brave' would miss the point entirely: the pejorative flavour in the words is an essential part of the praise. Virgil's use of 'durus' is a subtilization of this phenomenon, which is less a curiosity of language than a curiosity of human nature. Clearly words that are very strongly pejorative—like 'vile' or 'detestable' —cannot be so used, except by a pervert; the issue is whether 'improbus' belongs to the milder range of adjectives in which the pejorative element can be qualified by some other nuance or overtone. The examples given on pp. 337 f. show clearly that it does: it can express light or humorous annoyance without connoting serious moral blame.

One of these examples is 'improbus anser', the 'rascally' or 'wretched' goose, at line 119. It is surely no accident that the same adjective comes twice in so short a space: Virgil wants a tone that links his meditations on the human condition to the farmer's practical problems. Now the sentence about 'labor improbus' comes, as we have seen, at the climax of twelve lines devoted to human progress and invention; thus far the progressive interpretation seems irresistible, and the tone of these two words therefore needs to be, as suggested on p. 339, something like 'bloody hard work'—the adjective being pejorative but not without some dour pride. The fact that 'labor' is forced upon mankind and the fact that it is disagreeable indicate a certain austerity in the poet's thought, but they do not require it to be pessimistic.

We must also consider the order of the words and the way that they are placed in the line: 'labor omnia vicit | improbus'. The sentence seems complete at 'vicit', and the line-ending encourages the voice to make a pause. 'Improbus' is thus both unexpected and emphatic; its effect must be surprising, it must give the tone a new twist. The cheerful picture of the previous dozen lines is given a jolt; and 'egestas' follows to reinforce the sterner note. Virgil's technique of construction also demands that 'improbus', by its position, should be interesting; a general expression of disapprobation will hardly be enough. The word needs something more to justify its prominence—the nuance of wryness, the tough grimace. Line 146 shifts the tone, but it cannot utterly change the meaning: if 'labor omnia vicit' supports the progressive idea, as it must, 'labor omnia vicit improbus' must do the same, if in more acid voice. The meaning of lines 133–45 requires the progressive interpretation, as does the construction of 145–6; for unless the mood is confident to begin with, there is nothing worth giving a twist to.

But we have yet to examine the bleakness in the lines which follow, surprisingly neglected by the pessimist school, since here their case may seem strongest. After Ceres has taught men arable farming, they face yet more toil and trouble: mildew and weeds. Has the paragraph now turned firmly in a gloomy direction? Two considerations may deter us from a simple pessimism.

(*a*) Out of 147–59 one can extract these propositions: (i) Ceres taught men agriculture; (ii) they have to struggle against weeds and mildew; (iii) if you (the arable farmer) do not work hard, you will go hungry; (iv) meanwhile the good farmer piles up a big heap of grain. Put together, these propositions tell us that toil is necessary, but it brings success; in sum, they seem consistent with the rest of the paragraph and book.

(*b*) We might be tempted to think of lines 145–6 as a pivot: before, progress; after, pessimism. That is not exactly the case. At line 147 the account of progress continues to surge forward, with Ceres teaching man to plough: the picture of a god guiding men to new discoveries recalls the work's proem. This is the context in which the weeds and blight appear. The technique is polyphonal: at line 146 the account of progress is given a twist of austerity; it presses on, but then is twisted again, and the gloomier note starts to predominate as the theme descends once more to the practical problems of farming. As Klingner observes, the sentence at 146–7 marks a boundary: before, the theme is man's invention; after, his exertion.[11] The second theme is naturally a tougher one, particularly since it is to lead us back to the topic of practical nuisances which began the paragraph. At its end the lazy farmer's troubles are more prominent than the good farmer's success, but the good farmer's success is nevertheless there for those who have ears to hear. The tone at the end is ironic, and asks to be taken with a pinch of humour, for the reasons given on p. 340.

In brief conclusion: the pessimist interpretation cannot stand. The progressive interpretation is broadly right, provided that it recognizes the twist at 146–7 and does not try to draw the sting from 148 ff. It does not, of

---

[11] Klingner, 204.

course, deny the sternness of Jupiter's purpose or the need for unremitting hard work. For the purposes of argument in a controversial case, Virgil's paragraph as a whole and lines 146–7 in particular have here been treated as a problem to be tackled; the discussion in Chapter 7 tries to show that the passage ought not to be intrinsically hard or puzzling but that the things which have been felt as difficulties are explicable (and enjoyable) as elements of a complex, flexible rhetoric, subtly various in tone.

Index of Passages Cited

Index of Greek and Latin Words

General Index

Virgil, Works of (*cont.*):
   Eclogues 56, 134, 143–208, 279, 280, 284,
      289, 299, 322 f., 503 f., 600–4, 670 f.
     closure in 180 ff., 299
   Georgics 20, 32, 57, 134, 199, 236, 249, 273,
      274 f., 277, 282, 284 f., 289, 291,
      297–386, 417, 573, 654, 670
     Aristaeus epyllion 302–8, 315
     bees 310–13
     structure 299 ff., 307 f., 369
     truth and invention 308 ff., 321, 359
Volusius 100

Wagner, Richard 4, 33, 134, 186, 314, 463,
   564, 657
Wolf, Hugo 5, 186
wonder 278, 311 f., 343 f., 347, 356 f., 358,
   366, 537–41
   see also familiar as wonderful
woods 29 f., 63, 69 f., 185, 191 f., 450 f., 459,
   470 f., 480–4, 486 f., 503, 531, 535 f.,
   538, 541 f., 565, 568 f., 587, 608, 620, 622
Wordsworth, William 96, 350–2, 501

Xenophon 651